Read this book online today:

With SAP PRESS BooksOnline we offer you online access to knowledge from the leading SAP experts. Whether you use it as a beneficial supplement or as an alternative to the printed book, with SAP PRESS BooksOnline you can:

- Access your book anywhere, at any time. All you need is an Internet connection.
- Perform full text searches on your book and on the entire SAP PRESS library.
- Build your own personalized SAP library.

The SAP PRESS customer advantage:

Register this book today at *www.sap-press.com* and obtain exclusive free trial access to its online version. If you like it (and we think you will), you can choose to purchase permanent, unrestricted access to the online edition at a very special price!

Here's how to get started:

1. Visit *www.sap-press.com*.
2. Click on the link for SAP PRESS BooksOnline and login (or create an account).
3. Enter your free trial license key, shown below in the corner of the page.
4. Try out your online book with full, unrestricted access for a limited time!

Your personal free trial **license key** for this online book is:

wsxf-pmuq-2dbk-zj4a

**Warehouse Management with SAP® ERP:
Functionality and Technical Configuration**

SAP PRESS is a joint initiative of SAP and Galileo Press. The know-how offered by SAP specialists combined with the expertise of the Galileo Press publishing house offers the reader expert books in the field. SAP PRESS features first-hand information and expert advice, and provides useful skills for professional decision-making.

SAP PRESS offers a variety of books on technical and business related topics for the SAP user. For further information, please visit our website: *www.sap-press.com*.

Martin Murray
Materials Management in SAP ERP: Functionality and
Technical Configuration, 3rd Edition
2011, 666 pp., hardcover
978-1-59229-358-2

Brian Carter et. al.
SAP Extended Warehouse Management: Processes, Functionality, and Configuration
2010, 847 pp., hardcover
978-1-59229-304-9

Martin Murray
Maximize Your Warehouse Management Operations with SAP ERP
2010, 300 pp., hardcover
978-1-59229-309-4

Othmar Gau
Transportation Management with SAP LES
2008, 574 pp., hardcover
978-1-59229-169-4

Martin Murray

Warehouse Management with SAP® ERP: Functionality and Technical Configuration

Bonn • Boston

Galileo Press is named after the Italian physicist, mathematician and philosopher Galileo Galilei (1564–1642). He is known as one of the founders of modern science and an advocate of our contemporary, heliocentric worldview. His words *Eppur si muove* (And yet it moves) have become legendary. The Galileo Press logo depicts Jupiter orbited by the four Galilean moons, which were discovered by Galileo in 1610.

Editor Meg Dunkerley
Copyeditor Ruth Saavedra
Cover Design Graham Geary
Photo Credit iStockphoto.com/tuchkovo
Layout Design Vera Brauner
Production Graham Geary
Typesetting SatzPro, Krefeld (Germany)
Printed and bound in the United States of America

ISBN 978-1-59229-409-1

© 2012 by Galileo Press Inc., Boston (MA)
2nd edition 2012

Library of Congress Cataloging-in-Publication Data
Murray, Martin, 1964-
Warehouse management with SAP ERP : functionality and Technical configuration / Martin Murray. -- 2nd ed.
  p. cm.
Includes bibliographical references.
ISBN 978-1-59229-409-1 -- ISBN 1-59229-409-X
1. Inventory control--Computer programs. 2. Business logistics--Computer programs. 3. Material accountability-Computer programs. 4. SAP ERP. I. Title.
TS161.M85 2012
658.7'87--dc23
2011045055

All rights reserved. Neither this publication nor any part of it may be copied or reproduced in any form or by any means or translated into another language, without the prior consent of Galileo Press, Rheinwerkallee 4, 53227 Bonn, Germany.

Galileo Press makes no warranties or representations with respect to the content hereof and specifically disclaims any implied warranties of merchantability or fitness for any particular purpose. Galileo Press assumes no responsibility for any errors that may appear in this publication.

"Galileo Press" and the Galileo Press logo are registered trademarks of Galileo Press GmbH, Bonn, Germany. SAP PRESS is an imprint of Galileo Press.

All of the screenshots and graphics reproduced in this book are subject to copyright © SAP AG, Dietmar-Hopp-Allee 16, 69190 Walldorf, Germany.

SAP, the SAP logo, mySAP, mySAP.com, mySAP Business Suite, SAP NetWeaver, SAP R/3, SAP R/2, SAP B2B, SAPtronic, SAPscript, SAP BW, SAP CRM, SAP EarlyWatch, SAP ArchiveLink, SAP GUI, SAP Business Workflow, SAP Business Engineer, SAP Business Navigator, SAP Business Framework, SAP Business Information Warehouse, SAP inter-enterprise solutions, SAP APO, AcceleratedSAP, InterSAP, SAPoffice, SAPfind, SAPfile, SAPtime, SAPmail, SAP-access, SAP-EDI, R/3 Retail, Accelerated HR, Accelerated HiTech, Accelerated Consumer Products, ABAP, ABAP/4, ALE/WEB, Alloy, BAPI, Business Framework, BW Explorer, Duet, Enjoy-SAP, mySAP.com e-business platform, mySAP Enterprise Portals, RIVA, SAPPHIRE, TeamSAP, Webflow and SAP PRESS are registered or unregistered trademarks of SAP AG, Walldorf, Germany.

All other products mentioned in this book are registered or unregistered trademarks of their respective companies.

Contents at a Glance

1 Introduction to Warehouse Management 27
2 Basic Warehouse Functions 37
3 Stock Management 81
4 Warehouse Movements 125
5 Goods Receipts 179
6 Goods Issues 205
7 Stock Replenishment 249
8 Picking Strategies 281
9 Putaway Strategies 315
10 Inventory Procedures 343
11 Storage Unit Management 385
12 Hazardous Materials Management 413
13 Electronic Data Interchange (EDI) 435
14 Mobile Data Entry 443
15 Radio Frequency Identification Technology 467
16 Cross-Docking 481
17 Yard Management 499
18 Developments in Warehouse Management 519
19 SAP Extended Warehouse Management 547
20 Conclusion 555

Dear Reader,

If you currently use Warehouse Management in SAP ERP or need to get up to speed on it, this is your updated and comprehensive guide. In this second edition of one of our best-selling books, Martin Murray will help you master warehouse management techniques, everything from stock replenishment to picking and putaway strategies to storage unit management. Each chapter provides practical explanations, business processes, useful screenshots, and practical tips to help you understand and master warehouse management.

Working with Martin on this project was a pleasure, as usual. Martin's sense of humor and ability to make me sweat the deadlines are like no other author I've worked with before. Yet, as always, I'm honored to witness such expertise and proficiency, and I'm confident that you will find this new edition with SAP PRESS up to the same high standard as his previous books.

We appreciate your business, and welcome your feedback. Your comments and suggestions are the most useful tools to help us improve our books for you, the reader. We encourage you to visit our website at *www.sap-press.com* and share your feedback about this work.

Thank you for purchasing a book from SAP PRESS!

Meg Dunkerley
Editor, SAP PRESS

Galileo Press
Boston, MA

meg.dunkerley@galileo-press.com
www.sap-press.com

Contents

Preface 21

1 Introduction to Warehouse Management 27

1.1 Introduction to Warehousing 27
    1.1.1 Earliest Examples of Warehousing 27
    1.1.2 Tobacco Warehouses in the United States 28
    1.1.3 Bonded Warehouses 28
    1.1.4 20th Century Port Warehousing 29
    1.1.5 Warehousing as Part of Physical Distribution 30
    1.1.6 Warehousing and Distribution Centers 31
    1.1.7 Public Warehousing 32
1.2 History of Warehouse Management Systems (WMSs) 33
    1.2.1 Early Warehouse Management Systems 33
    1.2.2 The Rise of Enterprise Resource Planning (ERP) 34
1.3 Summary 35

2 Basic Warehouse Functions 37

2.1 Warehouse Structure 37
    2.1.1 Configuring a Warehouse 38
    2.1.2 Assignment of the Warehouse 40
    2.1.3 Warehouse Control Parameters 41
2.2 Storage Type 46
    2.2.1 Warehouse Layout 46
    2.2.2 Configuration of a Storage Type 48
    2.2.3 Data Entry for a Storage Type 49
2.3 Storage Sections 56
2.4 Storage Bins 58
    2.4.1 Storage Bin Types 58
    2.4.2 Define Storage Bin Structure 59
    2.4.3 Creating a Storage Bin Manually 65
    2.4.4 Creating a Storage Bin Automatically 66
    2.4.5 Block Storage Bins 67
    2.4.6 Creating Blocking Reasons 69

Contents

	2.4.7	List of Empty Storage Bins	70
	2.4.8	Bin Status Report	71
2.5	Quants		73
	2.5.1	Quant Record	74
	2.5.2	Display a Quant	74
2.6	Business Examples—Basic Warehouse Functions		75
	2.6.1	Warehouse Structure	75
	2.6.2	Storage Types	76
	2.6.3	Storage Bins	78
	2.6.4	Quants	79
2.7	Summary		80

3 Stock Management 81

3.1	Warehouse Management Data in the Material Master	81
	3.1.1 Creating the Material Master	82
	3.1.2 Entering Data into WM Screens	87
3.2	Types of Warehouse Stock	94
	3.2.1 Stock Categories	94
	3.2.2 Status of Warehouse Stock	98
	3.2.3 Special Stock	100
3.3	Batch Management in Warehouse Management	104
	3.3.1 Batch Definition	105
	3.3.2 Batch Level	105
	3.3.3 Batch Number Assignment	106
	3.3.4 Creating a Batch Record	107
	3.3.5 Batch Determination	109
3.4	Shelf Life Functionality	116
	3.4.1 Shelf Life and the Material Master	116
	3.4.2 Production Date Entry	118
	3.4.3 SLED Control List	119
3.5	Business Examples—Stock Management	121
	3.5.1 Types of Warehouse Stock	121
	3.5.2 Batch Management	122
	3.5.3 Shelf Life Functionality	122
3.6	Summary	123

4 Warehouse Movements 125

- 4.1 WM Movement Types 125
  - 4.1.1 Movement Types in IM 126
  - 4.1.2 WM Reference Movement Types 127
  - 4.1.3 Creating WM Movement Types 128
  - 4.1.4 Assigning Warehouse Management Movement Types 138
- 4.2 Transfer Requirements 141
  - 4.2.1 Automatic Transfer Requirements 142
  - 4.2.2 Create a Manual Transfer Requirement 143
  - 4.2.3 Create a Transfer Requirement for Replenishment of a Fixed Bin 145
  - 4.2.4 Display a Transfer Requirement for a Material 149
  - 4.2.5 Display a Transfer Requirement for a Single Item 152
  - 4.2.6 Display a Transfer Requirement for a Storage Type ... 152
  - 4.2.7 Deleting a Transfer Requirement 154
- 4.3 Transfer Orders 156
  - 4.3.1 Creating a Transfer Order with Reference to a Transfer Requirement 157
  - 4.3.2 Creating a Transfer Order Without a Reference 162
  - 4.3.3 Cancel a Transfer Order 164
  - 4.3.4 Confirm a Transfer Order 166
  - 4.3.5 Print a Transfer Order 171
- 4.4 Business Examples—Warehouse Movements 174
  - 4.4.1 Warehouse Movements 174
  - 4.4.2 Transfer Requirements 175
  - 4.4.3 Transfer Orders 176
- 4.5 Summary 178

5 Goods Receipts 179

- 5.1 Goods Receipt with Inbound Delivery 179
  - 5.1.1 Inbound Delivery Overview 180
  - 5.1.2 Creating an Inbound Delivery 180
  - 5.1.3 Creating a Transfer Order for an Inbound Delivery 182
  - 5.1.4 Using the Inbound Delivery Monitor 183
- 5.2 Goods Receipt Without an Inbound Delivery 187
  - 5.2.1 Goods Receipt in IM 187
  - 5.2.2 Reviewing the Material Documents 188

		5.2.3	Reviewing Stock Levels after Goods Receipt	190
		5.2.4	Displaying the Transfer Requirement	191
		5.2.5	Displaying the Transfer Order	194
	5.3	Goods Receipt Without Inventory Management		196
		5.3.1	Creating the Transfer Order for the Goods Receipt	196
		5.3.2	Displaying Transfer Order for the Goods Receipt	198
		5.3.3	Displaying the Stock Levels	198
	5.4	Business Examples—Goods Receipts		201
		5.4.1	Goods Receipt with Inbound Delivery	201
		5.4.2	Goods Receipt Without an Inbound Delivery	202
		5.4.3	Goods Receipt Without Inventory Management	203
	5.5	Summary		204

6 Goods Issues ... 205

	6.1	Goods Issue with Outbound Delivery		205
		6.1.1	Displaying the Sales Order	206
		6.1.2	Creating the Outbound Delivery	207
		6.1.3	Outbound Delivery Status	209
		6.1.4	Creating the Transfer Order	213
		6.1.5	Confirming the Transfer Order	219
		6.1.6	Posting the Goods Issue for Outbound Delivery	220
		6.1.7	Reviewing Material Documents	221
	6.2	Goods Issue Without an Outbound Delivery		222
		6.2.1	Goods Issue in IM	222
		6.2.2	Negative Balance in the Warehouse	224
		6.2.3	Creating a Transfer Order	225
	6.3	Multiple Processing Using Groups		228
		6.3.1	Definition of a Group	228
		6.3.2	Creating a Group for Transfer Requirements	229
		6.3.3	Creating Transfer Orders for a Group of Transfer Requirements	231
		6.3.4	Definition of a Wave Pick	233
		6.3.5	Creating a Group for Outbound Deliveries	233
		6.3.6	Creating the Wave from the Outbound Delivery Monitor	233
		6.3.7	Using the Wave Monitor	234
		6.3.8	Results of the Pick Wave Monitor	238
	6.4	Picking and Packing		241
		6.4.1	Picking Schemes	241

		6.4.2	Packing	243
	6.5	Business Examples—Goods Issue		244
		6.5.1	Goods Issue with Outbound Delivery	244
		6.5.2	Goods Issue Without an Outbound Delivery	245
		6.5.3	Picking and Packing	245
	6.6	Summary		247

7 Stock Replenishment 249

	7.1	Internal Stock Transfers		249
		7.1.1	Keeping the Warehouse Running	249
		7.1.2	Checking Empty Bins	250
		7.1.3	Moving Material Between Storage Bins	252
		7.1.4	Confirming the Stock Transfer	255
		7.1.5	Configuring the Difference Indicator	256
	7.2	Fixed Bin Replenishment		258
		7.2.1	Replenishment and the Material Master	258
		7.2.2	Configuration for Replenishment	260
		7.2.3	Creating the Replenishment	260
		7.2.4	Displaying the Transfer Requirement	262
		7.2.5	Creating the Transfer Order	263
		7.2.6	Confirming the Transfer Order	264
		7.2.7	Reviewing the Stock Overview	266
	7.3	Posting Changes		267
		7.3.1	Posting Change for a Release from Quality Inspection Stock	267
		7.3.2	Posting Change from Material Number to Material Number	272
		7.3.3	Dividing Batches Among Other Batches	275
	7.4	Business Examples—Stock Replenishment		277
		7.4.1	Internal Stock Transfers	277
		7.4.2	Fixed Bin Replenishment	278
		7.4.3	Posting Changes	278
	7.5	Summary		279

8 Picking Strategies 281

	8.1	Storage Type Indicator	282

Contents

- 8.2 Storage Type Search 284
  - 8.2.1 Configuring the Storage Type Search 284
  - 8.2.2 Configuring Storage Section Search 286
- 8.3 FIFO (First In, First Out) 287
  - 8.3.1 Configuring the FIFO Picking Strategy 288
  - 8.3.2 Stock Removal Control Indicators 288
  - 8.3.3 Example of FIFO Picking Strategy 289
- 8.4 LIFO (Last In, First Out) 292
  - 8.4.1 Configuring the LIFO Picking Strategy 292
  - 8.4.2 Example of LIFO Picking Strategy 293
- 8.5 Fixed Storage Bin 294
  - 8.5.1 Fixed Storage Bin in Material Master 294
  - 8.5.2 Configuring the Fixed Bin Picking Strategy 296
  - 8.5.3 Example of Fixed Bin Picking Strategy 297
- 8.6 Shelf Life Expiration 299
  - 8.6.1 SLED Picking and the Material Master 299
  - 8.6.2 Configuring Shelf Life Expiration Picking Strategy 300
  - 8.6.3 Displaying SLED Stock 301
  - 8.6.4 Example of Shelf Life Expiration Picking Strategy 303
- 8.7 Partial Quantities 304
  - 8.7.1 Configuring Partial Quantities Picking Strategy 304
  - 8.7.2 Using the Partial Quantities Picking Strategy 305
- 8.8 Quantity-Relevant Picking 306
  - 8.8.1 Configuring the Quantity Relevant Picking Strategy 306
  - 8.8.2 Quantity-Relevant Picking and the Material Master Record 308
- 8.9 Business Examples—Picking Strategies 309
  - 8.9.1 Storage Type Search 309
  - 8.9.2 First In, First Out (FIFO) 310
  - 8.9.3 Fixed Bin 311
  - 8.9.4 Shelf Life Expiration Date (SLED) 312
- 8.10 Summary 312

9 Putaway Strategies 315

- 9.1 Fixed Bin Storage 316
  - 9.1.1 Fixed Storage Bin in the Material Master 316
  - 9.1.2 Configuring the Fixed Bin Storage Putaway Strategy 317

	9.1.3	Stock Placement Control Indicators	317
	9.1.4	Example of Fixed Bin Storage Putaway Strategy	320
9.2	Open Storage		322
	9.2.1	Configuring the Open Storage Putaway Strategy	322
	9.2.2	Example of Open Storage Putaway Strategy	323
9.3	Next Empty Bin		326
	9.3.1	Configuring the Next Empty Bin Putaway Strategy	326
	9.3.2	Displaying Empty Bins	327
	9.3.3	Example of Next Empty Bin Putaway Strategy	328
	9.3.4	Cross-Line Stock Putaway	330
9.4	Bulk Storage		332
9.5	Near Picking Bin		334
	9.5.1	Storage Type Control Definition	336
	9.5.2	Search per Level Definition	337
9.6	Business Examples—Putaway Strategies		338
	9.6.1	Fixed Bin Storage	338
	9.6.2	Open Storage	339
	9.6.3	Next Empty Bin	340
9.7	Summary		340

10 Inventory Procedures ... 343

10.1	Annual Physical Inventory		343
	10.1.1	Before the Count	343
	10.1.2	Configuring Annual Inventory	344
	10.1.3	Processing Open Transfer Orders	348
	10.1.4	Blocking the Storage Type	350
	10.1.5	Creating Annual Inventory Documents	350
	10.1.6	Displaying the Count Documents	353
	10.1.7	Entering the Inventory Count	354
	10.1.8	Count Differences	356
	10.1.9	Entering a Recount	357
	10.1.10	Clearing Differences	358
10.2	Continuous Inventory		360
	10.2.1	Configuring Continuous Inventory	360
	10.2.2	Creating a Continuous Inventory Count Document	361
	10.2.3	Printing a Continuous Inventory Count Document	363
	10.2.4	Entering the Count Results	364

10.3 Cycle Counting 366
  10.3.1 Benefits of Cycle Counting 366
  10.3.2 Materials Management Configuration Steps with
         Cycle Counting 366
  10.3.3 Using the ABC Analysis 367
  10.3.4 ABC Indicator and Material Master 369
  10.3.5 Cycle Counting Configuration for Storage Type 369
  10.3.6 Creating a Cycle Count Document 370
  10.3.7 Printing the Cycle Count Document 372
  10.3.8 Entering the Cycle Count 372
10.4 Zero Stock Check 373
  10.4.1 Configuring Zero Stock Check 374
  10.4.2 Performing an Automatic Zero Stock Check 375
  10.4.3 Performing a Manual Zero Stock Check 378
10.5 Business Examples—Inventory Procedures 380
  10.5.1 Annual Physical Inventory 380
  10.5.2 Continuous Inventory 381
  10.5.3 Cycle Counting 382
10.6 Summary 383

11 Storage Unit Management 385

11.1 Introduction to Storage Unit Management 386
  11.1.1 Activating Storage Unit Management 386
  11.1.2 Defining Storage Unit Number Ranges 387
  11.1.3 Defining Storage Type Control 388
  11.1.4 Defining the Storage Unit Type 389
11.2 Storage Unit Record 390
  11.2.1 Creating a Storage Unit Record by Transfer Order 390
  11.2.2 Displaying a Storage Unit 393
11.3 Planning Storage Units 393
  11.3.1 Planning Storage Units by Transfer Order 394
  11.3.2 Receiving Planned Storage Units 396
  11.3.3 Recording Differences in Planned Storage Units 397
11.4 Storage Unit Documentation 398
  11.4.1 Transfer Order Document 398
  11.4.2 Storage Unit Contents Document 400
  11.4.3 Storage Unit Document 400
  11.4.4 Storage Unit Transfer Order Document 401

11.5	Putaway with Storage Unit Management		402
	11.5.1	Creating a Storage Unit	402
	11.5.2	Storage Unit — Single Material	402
	11.5.3	Storage Unit — Multiple Materials	404
	11.5.4	Storage Unit — Add to Existing Stock	405
11.6	Picking with Storage Unit Management		407
	11.6.1	Complete Stock Pick	407
	11.6.2	Partial Stock Pick	408
	11.6.3	Complete Stock Pick with Return to Same Bin	408
	11.6.4	Partial Stock Removal Using a Pick Point	409
11.7	Business Examples — Storage Unit Management		410
	11.7.1	Planning Storage Units	410
	11.7.2	Putaway with Storage Units	411
	11.7.3	Picking with Storage Units	411
11.8	Summary		412

12 Hazardous Materials Management — 413

12.1	Introduction to Hazardous Materials		414
	12.1.1	Classification of Hazardous Materials	414
	12.1.2	Master Data Configuration for Hazardous Materials	415
	12.1.3	Configuring Hazardous Material Management	420
12.2	Hazardous Material Record		425
	12.2.1	Creating a Hazardous Material Record	425
	12.2.2	Assigning the Hazardous Material to a Material Master Record	426
12.3	Hazardous Material Functionality		427
	12.3.1	List of Hazardous Materials	427
	12.3.2	Fire Department Inventory List	428
	12.3.3	Check Goods Storage	429
	12.3.4	Hazardous Substance List	431
12.4	Business Examples — Hazardous Materials Management		431
	12.4.1	Storing Hazardous Material	432
	12.4.2	Hazardous Material Functionality	432
12.5	Summary		433

13 Electronic Data Interchange (EDI) 435

13.1 Introduction to EDI 435
    13.1.1 Advantages of Using EDI 435
    13.1.2 Types of EDI 436
    13.1.3 EDI and IDOCS 438
13.2 Using EDI in Warehouse Management 440
    13.2.1 Inbound Processing 440
    13.2.2 Outbound Processing 441
13.3 Business Examples—EDI 441
13.4 Summary 442

14 Mobile Data Entry 443

14.1 Introduction to RF Devices 444
    14.1.1 Graphical User Interface Devices 444
    14.1.2 Character-Based Devices 445
    14.1.3 SAPConsole 445
    14.1.4 Functionality Available with SAPConsole 446
14.2 Bar Code Functionality 446
    14.2.1 UPC Bar Code Format 447
    14.2.2 UPC and EAN 448
    14.2.3 Bar Code Structure 448
    14.2.4 Bar Code Readers 449
    14.2.5 Bar Code Reader Technologies 450
    14.2.6 Bar Code Support in SAP Systems 451
    14.2.7 Configuration for Bar Codes 452
14.3 Radio Frequency—Supported Processes in SAP WM 456
    14.3.1 Defining the Radio Frequency Queue 456
    14.3.2 Adding a User for Mobile Data Entry 457
    14.3.3 Logging on for Mobile Data Entry 458
    14.3.4 RF Menus and WM Processes 459
14.4 Radio Frequency Monitor 462
    14.4.1 Accessing the RF Monitor 462
    14.4.2 Using the Radio Frequency Monitor 463
14.5 Business Examples—Mobile Data Entry 463
    14.5.1 Bar Code Functionality 463
    14.5.2 RF Functionality 464
14.6 Summary 465

15 Radio Frequency Identification Technology ... 467

- 15.1 Introduction to Radio Frequency Identification ... 468
  - 15.1.1 Mechanism of RFID ... 468
  - 15.1.2 Electronic Product Code ... 468
  - 15.1.3 The Wal-Mart RFID Mandate ... 469
  - 15.1.4 RFID Benefits ... 470
  - 15.1.5 RFID vs. Bar Codes ... 470
- 15.2 Types of RFID Tags ... 472
  - 15.2.1 Tag Classes ... 472
  - 15.2.2 Active and Passive Tags ... 473
- 15.3 Current Uses of RFID ... 474
  - 15.3.1 Electronic Payments ... 474
  - 15.3.2 Retail Stores ... 474
  - 15.3.3 Individual Product Tagging ... 475
  - 15.3.4 Parts Tracking ... 475
- 15.4 RFID and SAP ... 476
  - 15.4.1 Supported Functions in SAP AII ... 476
  - 15.4.2 Outbound Processing (Slap and Ship) ... 476
  - 15.4.3 Flexible Delivery Processing ... 477
  - 15.4.4 Generation of Pedigree Notifications ... 477
  - 15.4.5 Returnable Transport Item Processing ... 478
- 15.5 Business Examples—RFID ... 479
- 15.6 Summary ... 480

16 Cross-Docking ... 481

- 16.1 Planned Cross-Docking ... 482
  - 16.1.1 Types of Cross-Docking ... 482
  - 16.1.2 Types of Material Suitable for Cross-Docking ... 483
  - 16.1.3 Planned Cross-Docking in SAP ... 483
  - 16.1.4 Configuration for Cross-Docking ... 484
  - 16.1.5 Cross-Docking Decisions ... 486
- 16.2 Cross-Docking Movements ... 486
  - 16.2.1 One-Step Cross-Docking ... 486
  - 16.2.2 Two-Step Cross-Docking ... 489
- 16.3 Cross-Docking Monitor ... 492
  - 16.3.1 Accessing the Cross-Docking Monitor ... 493
  - 16.3.2 Cross-Docking Alert Monitor ... 494

	16.4	Business Examples—Cross-Docking	496
		16.4.1 Planned Cross-Docking	496
		16.4.2 Cross-Docking Movements	497
	16.5	Summary	498

17 Yard Management ... 499

	17.1	Introduction to YM	499
		17.1.1 Yard Management Configuration	499
		17.1.2 Yard Management Structure	507
	17.2	Yard Management Processes	510
	17.3	Business Examples—Yard Management	517
	17.4	Summary	518

18 Developments in Warehouse Management ... 519

	18.1	Task and Resource Management	520
		18.1.1 Definitions in Task and Resource Management	520
		18.1.2 Resource Management	529
		18.1.3 Request Management	533
		18.1.4 Task Management	533
		18.1.5 Route Management	534
		18.1.6 Bin Management	536
		18.1.7 TRM Monitor	537
	18.2	Value-Added Services	538
		18.2.1 Configuring VAS	538
		18.2.2 Creating the VAS Template	542
		18.2.3 Creating a VAS Order	543
		18.2.4 VAS Monitor	545
		18.2.5 VAS Alert Monitor	545
		18.2.6 VAS and TRM	546
	18.3	Summary	546

19 SAP Extended Warehouse Management ... 547

	19.1	Introduction to SAP Extended Warehouse Management	547
		19.1.1 History of EWM	547
		19.1.2 Integrating SAP EWM and WM	548
	19.2	Organizational Structure	548
		19.2.1 Activity Areas	548

		19.2.2	Product Master	548
		19.2.3	Transportation Data	548
		19.2.4	Resources	549
	19.3	Documents in SAP EWM		550
		19.3.1	Warehouse Tasks	550
		19.3.2	Warehouse Orders	550
		19.3.3	Inbound Delivery Notification	550
		19.3.4	Outbound Delivery Request	550
	19.4	Processes in SAP EWM		551
		19.4.1	Inbound Processing	551
		19.4.2	Outbound Processing	551
		19.4.3	Internal Warehouse Movements	552
	19.5	Summary		553

20 Conclusion 555

20.1	Lessons Learned	555
20.2	Future Directions	557

Appendices 559

A	Bibliography	561
B	Glossary	563
C	The Author	569

Index 571

Preface

This book is a comprehensive review of the warehouse management functionality in SAP ERP (which we'll refer to as SAP WM or simply WM) as it functions in the latest version of SAP ERP, which at the time of writing is SAP ERP Central Component 6.0 (SAP ECC 6.0). We will also discuss warehouse functionality outside of SAP ECC 6.0, which can be found in SAP Supply Chain Management (SCM), currently in release SAP SCM 5.0.

Who This Book Is For

The subject matter in this book is not of interest just to those who work directly with SAP WM, but also for those who work in related application areas such as materials management (MM), production planning (PP), and sales and distribution (SD). The subject matter should also interest warehouse managers and distribution managers who want to understand more of the functionality that they have implemented and functionality they may be considering, such as task and resource management and storage unit management.

For those involved in SAP MM, this book will help them understand more of the functions that occur when material has been moved to a storage location where WM is active. A general knowledge of warehouse functionality with regard to the way material is stored and moved in the warehouse is of great benefit.

Those working with SAP SD will benefit from a greater understanding of the outbound side of warehouse management, how material is picked for customer sales orders, and the movement of the material for outbound deliveries.

SAP PP staff will benefit from gaining familiarity with the way material is received from production and the picking of material for production orders.

Staff working with other SAP functionalities such as quality management (QM) and plant maintenance (PM) will gain from a greater understanding of the general topics addressed in WM.

How This Book Is Organized

This book is structured to serve the purposes of the various individuals that work in the SAP WM environment, be they SAP configuration experts or users who have been tasked to use SAP WM as part of their everyday work and want to gain more understanding of the functionality.

Each chapter focuses on a specific SAP WM function, exploring the different facets of the function and providing examples. The book starts by examining the SAP WM functionality: from the basic key elements through standard SAP WM functions such as stock placement and stock removal, to more advanced technology such as RFID, and the more recent developments in warehouse management, such as Value Added Services and Extended Warehouse Management. We briefly describe each chapter now:

- **Chapter 1**
  Chapter 1 provides a brief history of warehousing and the development of warehouse management systems (WMS) over time. It helps set modern warehouse management in context with its past.

- **Chapter 2**
  Chapter 2 describes some of the basic warehouse functionalities in SAP WM. These provide the basis for setting up a warehouse in an SAP system and are key to understanding the makeup of a warehouse, a storage type, a storage section, a storage bin, and a quant. The chapter will take you though these key elements, showing key configuration and examples.

- **Chapter 3**
  The content in Chapter 3 will be familiar to readers who have SAP MM backgrounds. The chapter builds on the key elements described in Chapter 2 and explores the warehouse data required in the material master, batch management, and the important functionality concerning shelf-life expiration.

- **Chapter 4**
  Chapter 4 uses the data that is part of the material master to describe the basic movements inside the warehouse using the transfer requirement and the transfer order. These drive all movements in the warehouse, and it is important to understand how these functions are processed.

- **Chapter 5**
  Chapter 5 takes the transfer requirement and transfer order further to describe how they are used in the goods receipt process. This chapter will be of interest

to those involved in SAP MM, because it examines the integration of SAP WM with SAP MM for inbound deliveries.

▶ **Chapter 6**
Chapter 6 describes the goods issue process and outbound delivery. Those with SAP SD backgrounds will find the examination of the integration of SAP WM and SAP SD of great benefit.

▶ **Chapter 7**
Chapter 7 explores the functions of the transfer requirement and transfer order and describes how these are used in replenishment of stock to areas within the warehouse, focusing on fixed bin replenishment.

▶ **Chapter 8**
Chapter 8 takes the elements examined in previous chapters and uses them to describe the stock removal or picking function in the warehouse. The chapter describes the various picking strategies that warehouse management can adopt for a variety of materials and situations. It is useful to understand why these strategies are in place and why they are used for certain materials.

▶ **Chapter 9**
Chapter 9 looks at the other side of the picking functionality and describes the stock placement of putaway functions in the warehouse. The development of the putaway strategies is a key to making warehouses more efficient.

▶ **Chapter 10**
Chapter 10 examines the methods used to count the material in the warehouse once it is fully stocked. This is of particular interest to those with financial experience, as it is an important part of a company's financial health. This chapter introduces the importance of accurate and regular counts.

The functionality examined in the first 10 chapters involves basic warehouse management, which is implemented in almost all SAP WM implementations.

Chapter 11 and the subsequent chapters focus on functionality that is available for warehouse management implementations but is not mandatory. It is up to the individual warehouse manager or supply chain management to investigate and then make a decision on implementation. Readers can learn about the functionality and use that knowledge to advise the warehouse owner about what is available and how it can be successfully used.

Preface

- **Chapter 11**
  Chapter 11 focuses on Storage Unit Management (SUM), which can be used in warehouses that move material in the warehouse by a container that they wish to track. SUM was originally designed for warehouse management before the idea was expanded for SAP MM, where it is called Handling Unit (HU) Management. The functionality is similar but not identical. This chapter highlights some of the differences.

- **Chapter 12**
  Chapter 12 examines the warehouse functionality of hazardous materials. Every warehouse has some kind of hazardous material, and many warehouses have to use the hazardous material functions to document and manage the dangerous materials stored. This will be of interest to anyone familiar with the SAP Environmental Health and Safety functions.

- **Chapter 13**
  Chapter 13 examines the use of Electronic Data Interchange (EDI) in the warehouse. EDI offers cost-saving benefits as well as greater efficiencies across the enterprise. This chapter describes several EDI transactions that are used in WM for both inbound and outbound processes that assist in creating a more efficient warehouse.

- **Chapter 14**
  Chapter 14 examines one aspect of the technological advances that have been adopted in the warehouse. The mobile data entry functionality in SAP WM harnesses the advantages of bar codes and radio frequency readers to provide accurate and efficient data entry from the warehouse floor. The chapter also introduces the RF Monitor, which is the key function to managing mobile data entry in the warehouse.

- **Chapter 15**
  Chapter 15 moves forward with the latest technological advances in data entry in the warehouse and gives the reader an examination of radio frequency identification (RFID) functionality in the warehouse. The chapter discusses the RFID technology and the SAP solution that integrates RFID into the standard warehouse functionality.

- **Chapter 16**
  Chapter 16 discusses the function of cross-docking. Not all industries and warehouses are suitable for cross-docking, but it is a key element in making retail and grocery warehousing more efficient and cost effective. The scope of

cross-docking implementation may be limited, but some industries can adopt the functionality to improve delivery times for certain materials. Understanding the principles and mechanism of cross-docking will help readers give knowledgeable advice to their warehouse management.

▶ **Chapter 17**
Chapter 17 describes the functionality found in yard management. The functionality is useful for some companies that need to efficiently deal with a large number of vehicles moving into and out of the yard before they reach the warehouse. This chapter describes the processes involved in yard management and how it interfaces with WM.

▶ **Chapter 18**
Chapter 18 briefly introduces readers to some of the new developments in warehouse management. Task and Resource Management (TRM) is the software that takes the warehouse and warehouse resources to a new level, where the efficiency of the warehouse is constantly improved by managing the resources and the tasks. The chapter is only an introduction to this powerful tool.

▶ **Chapter 19**
Chapter 19 introduces the Extended Warehouse Management (EWM) function provides warehouse functionality. EWM can be implemented without SAP WM, and can be used as a standalone operation interfaced with SAP ECC 6.0. The discussion of EWM is focused enough for the reader to become aware the basic functionality of EWM.

▶ **Chapter 20**
We conclude the book with a final chapter that briefly recaps the book, while sharing lessons learned, and gives you some direction for the future. This should help you keep track of what you've discovered in this book.

Summary

Please use this preface as a guide. Now that you have an idea of what this book is about and what it covers, you can either jump ahead to specific chapters or proceed to read it chapter by chapter.

We hope that after reading this book, you will find that it has met its objectives of delivering a comprehensive review of SAP WM and exploring topics that will reinforce your current knowledge or help you develop your skills in unfamiliar areas. We hope you find yourself using this book as a key reference in your current and future SAP WM experiences. Now let's proceed to Chapter 1, in which we introduce you to SAP WM.

Warehousing has evolved from early man's need to store food in a safe environment for future use to become an integral part of the supply chain of almost every company on the planet.

1 Introduction to Warehouse Management

Warehouses have been around ever since humans decided to store excess food from their harvests. Today, the warehouse is a key component of the supply chain. Technological advances in computerized warehouse management systems have meant that the warehouse can operate at maximum efficiency, thus reducing delivery times to the customer, minimizing the cost of the warehouse operation, and maximizing company profits.

1.1 Introduction to Warehousing

The history of warehouses goes back thousands of years. The earliest evidence of warehouses was found in areas where some cultures' cities used buildings to store food for their inhabitants to use.

1.1.1 Earliest Examples of Warehousing

In 1955, an archaeological study was performed in the current day Indian state of Gujarat. In that area, the study found the city of Lothal, which was part of the Indus valley civilization dating back to around 2400 BC. As part of the study, archaeologists found the earliest known example of a dock. It was discovered that the dock was used to load and unload vessels traveling from the Arabian Sea, as Lothal became a major trade center in West Asia and Africa.

The dock was connected to a warehouse by a direct ramp to facilitate loading. The warehouse was central to the prosperity of the city and was originally built on a 3.5-meter-high (11.5 ft) mud-brick podium. The pedestal was high enough to provide maximum protection from floodwaters.

> **Example**
>
> We can see many other examples of early warehouses based on trade between different cultures. In the Henan Province of China, many examples have been found of warehouses of the Eastern Han Dynasty (15–100 AD), where warehouses of 180 by 30 meters (600 by 100 ft) in size have been found. These are situated in areas along the "Silk Road," a route that developed from Chang'an through Xianjiang and Central Asia to the Mediterranean. Trading between the Eastern Han Dynasty and other empires such as the Roman and the Kushan Empire in India has been documented.

1.1.2 Tobacco Warehouses in the United States

Many examples of warehouses in the United States and Europe have been found that stem from the introduction of tobacco into European society. In 1580, cultivation of tobacco started in Cuba, along with the storing of tobacco before its shipment to Spain, which led to building of the first tobacco warehouses. In 1612, John Rolfe grew the first commercial tobacco crop in Virginia that led to the trade between Virginia and England.

As the number of tobacco farmers grew in Virginia, warehouses were created where farmers could store their tobacco crop before shipment to England. In 1730, *tobacco notes* became legal tender in Virginia. Tobacco notes attested to the quality and quantity of a farmer's tobacco kept in public warehouses. Soon after, inspection warehouses were created to verify weight and kind of tobacco to prevent the export of *trash tobacco:* shipments diluted with leaves and household sweepings, which were debasing the value of Virginia tobacco.

Examples of the early Virginia tobacco warehouses, such as the 1788 Mecklenburg Tobacco Warehouse in Shepherdstown, West Virginia, can still be found in much of the eastern United States.

1.1.3 Bonded Warehouses

In 1733 in England, Sir Robert Walpole, considered the first prime minister of Great Britain, proposed a warehouse *excise scheme* for items that required a duty to be paid on them, such as tobacco and wine.

At the time of Walpole's suggestion, the payment of duties on imported goods had to be made at the time of their arrival at the port, or a bond with security had to be issued for future payment of the duty. There were a number of issues with the duty system at that time, as it was not always possible for the importer to find the money for the duty, and it was often necessary to make an immediate sale of the goods to raise the duty. Walpole saw the hindrance this was causing to commerce and proposed the bonded warehouse. Using an act of Parliament, Walpole created a law that required imported goods to be placed in warehouses approved by the customs authorities, and importers were to give bonds for payment of duties when the goods were removed. This is where these warehouses received the name of *bonded* or *bonding*.

The system of bonded warehousing was of great advantage to the importers and purchasers of goods because the payment of the duty was deferred until the goods were required, and the title-deeds, or warrants, were transferable by endorsement.

The bonded warehouse system is still in operation today. In many countries, companies can provide added services or operations to the material in a bonded warehouse. While the goods are in the warehouse, the owner can rack, vat, mix, and bottle wines and spirits; roast coffee and manufacture certain kinds of tobacco. Certain specific allowances are made for waste or byproducts resulting from such processes.

1.1.4 20th Century Port Warehousing

In the early 20th century, warehouses were often large, mostly bonded, and found at big ports. In 1901 in England, the world's largest brick warehouse was built in Liverpool. The Stanley Dock Tobacco Warehouse was built to accommodate the increasing ocean traffic into Liverpool and the barges from the Leeds and Liverpool Canal.

In Los Angeles, the port's only bonded warehouse was built in 1917. It still exists today and still is used for its original function in spite of the revolution of cargo containerization. From the time of its completion in 1917, Warehouse No. 1 at the Port of Los Angeles was the critical site for the growth of Los Angeles as a commercial center. It allowed train access directly to the warehouse, ensuring the least possible time between ship and final destination. The warehouse is six stories high, with a capacity of a half-million square feet. In the early 20th century, it housed the majority of nonpetroleum goods shipped into and out of the Southern California markets.

The port warehouses of that time operated a break-bulk cargo system. This required a series of labor- and space-intensive operations. Cargo loading was labor-intensive and extremely time-consuming. Longshoremen had to load and unload the cargo, such as drums, boxes, bags, and crates, as individual pieces. This was known as break-bulk, and material was brought to the ports by train and unloaded into warehouses or buildings that lined the wharf, called transit sheds. Cargo was stored in warehouses until a ship was ready to receive it. When a ship was ready, cargo was transported to the transit sheds, where it was sorted and organized for loading. The cargo was stowed by longshoremen.

Break-bulk cargo workers operated in three areas on a ship. First, the deck men drove the winches. Hold men stowed and unstowed the cargo hold of the ship, and the front men affixed and released the sling loads on the deck. In addition to the ship gangs, dock men physically transferred the cargo to and from the ships. Warehousemen moved the cargo into and out of the warehouse building on carts known as *4-wheelers*.

For the Port of Los Angeles and many other ports with large warehouses, factors in the commerce of the early 1900s created a need for long-term warehousing. First, the shipping schedules of the day were erratic, and distributors would want their goods at the port ready for shipment when a ship bound for the desired destination arrived. It was therefore more economical to store their goods at a warehouse at the port than at their own site.

Second, distributors would accumulate goods at the port warehouses as they were available or produced and then arrange for shipment when enough goods had accumulated to make shipping economically worthwhile. This allowed for the most economical use of cargo space on the outbound ship or inbound train.

1.1.5 Warehousing as Part of Physical Distribution

Prior to World War II, commerce in the industrialized nations was primarily concerned with the production and sales of goods, with the accounting function joining the two and directing the future of the business.

However, the wartime period focused many industrialists on how goods needed to be stored and distributed to arrive at their final destination as soon as possible. Military logistics functions organized the distribution and transportation of military hardware separate from its production. This helped business understand that physical distribution was a separate function that could provide significant leverage if successfully implemented.

In postwar America, the increase in consumer purchasing combined with increasingly efficient production systems and improved advertising techniques gave companies an opportunity to serve greater geographic areas. The downside of this expansion was that the physical distribution methods had not kept up.

U.S. businesses that wanted to become national brands had different distribution issues than companies in Europe. For example, a business that was a national brand in England had a much smaller geographic area to distribute to than a company in the United States.

The idea of regional warehouse and distribution centers was one that large corporations could afford to implement. A successful local family company did not often have the funds to compete in areas outside of their hometown or state.

As companies sold their products nationally, they created regional distribution centers with large warehouses that stored the companies' products to be sold within the area serviced by that distribution center. The warehouses were sourced from the company's domestic and overseas manufacturing plants.

As national companies became international companies, the distribution centers spread across the world to service the local markets in their respective areas.

1.1.6 Warehousing and Distribution Centers

In today's business environment, distribution centers are associated specifically with retailing.

The warehouse of a retail distribution center can contain tens of thousands of items from thousands of vendors. Each vendor supplies the distribution center, which in turn distributes to many retail outlets.

In the United States, a large retail company like Wal-Mart has more than 3,800 retail operations with more than 300 regional distribution centers. In the United States alone, Wal-Mart has 61,000 vendors.

In Oldham, England, the national distribution center of the Littlewoods home-shopping catalog is Europe's largest warehouse distribution center, covering 23 acres and containing 1 million square feet of products. The one site has a workforce of close to 700. Goods are received from thousands of vendors, stored, and packed and sent to customers within the same storage facility.

These vast warehouse and distribution centers rely wholly on state-of-the-art computer warehouse management systems (WMSs) to operate at maximum efficiency. Before the advent of the computer-based WMS, the operation of the warehouse was a manual paper-based system that was prone to errors and relied upon the knowledge of warehouse staff for the warehouse to operate successfully.

1.1.7 Public Warehousing

A public warehouse is a warehouse that performs warehouse services for many companies. In a public warehouse, the company running the warehouse does not own the goods but performs goods receiving, storing, shipping, and other warehouse functions. The company owning the warehouse charges companies a fee for using the warehouse and the facilities.

There are many reasons why a company would use a public warehouse instead of or in addition to, its own warehouse facilities. Let's take a look at these.

Cost of Warehousing

A company may decide to use a public warehouse if it does not have the space or the capital to invest in building a purpose-built warehouse and the staff to run the facility. A public warehouse has trained staff and is able to perform the warehouse functions immediately.

Seasonal Warehousing Requirements

If a company has warehousing requirements that are seasonal and would not provide the need for year-round warehousing, a public warehouse is an ideal solution.

Overflow Warehousing

Some companies may have seasonal requirements that their warehouse facilities cannot cope with. For example, in the beverage industry, seasonal fluctuations of consumer purchasing and sales drives may require a company to use public warehousing for stock that has been produced and cannot be stored in the company's warehouse because of lack of space.

1.2 History of Warehouse Management Systems (WMSs)

The warehouse of today no longer runs on a paper-based system. The advances of computer-based WMSs, computer-enabled warehouse equipment, radio frequency (RF), and radio frequency identification (RFID) have transformed the warehouse into a technological entity.

Not all warehouses require a WMS. As we will discuss later, there are often decisions to be made about whether in an SAP environment, a warehouse should run the warehouse management functionality in SAP ERP (which we'll refer to moving forward SAP WM or simply WM) or run as a storage location in SAP Materials Management (SAP MM). Some warehouses have operations that are simple and require limited data collection. In these cases, it would be unwise to implement a system that would hinder the operation of the warehouse.

1.2.1 Early Warehouse Management Systems

The first warehouse management systems carried out simple warehouse tasks. The systems were designed to control the movement and storage of items within the warehouse. These systems operated on algorithms that used information on the item, location, quantity, unit of measure, and order data to determine where to place and pick items and the particular sequence required to correctly perform the operations.

In the 1960s, many of the systems implemented in company warehouses were nothing more than data-processing programs. The terminals in the warehouse were connected to card-punch machines or magnetic-tape writers. Data was entered into the terminals from paper documents relating to the inbound and outbound shipments.

The cards or tape would be run on a leased or company mainframe computer, where the data-processing systems were stored. The implemented systems in the warehouse were controlled mostly by the accounting departments and provided data on inventory levels for accounting purposes. These systems did not help the warehouse staff run the warehouse more efficiently, and in fact they caused more work and increased warehouse costs. This downside was overshadowed by the accounting accuracies the systems provided.

In the 1970s, warehouse systems were often custom-built software efforts that companies decided to develop themselves rather than implement partial-fit systems offered by large computer companies.

In the 1980s, with the advent of the IBM PC, software companies developed software packages that ran standalone from other company systems. These PC-based systems were often as simple as locator programs but did allow more control on the warehouse floor.

1.2.2 The Rise of Enterprise Resource Planning (ERP)

In the late 1980s, when the mainframe version of SAP ERP (SAP R/2) was becoming popular in Europe, many companies decided to implement systems that were fully integrated; that is, ERP systems.

For the first time, businesses had all of their main functionality on a single platform under a single suite of programs. Companies implementing SAP R/2 implemented the core functionality of their business: accounting, production, sales, and materials management. In many cases these companies kept their existing systems for human resources, plant maintenance, and warehouse management. Often, these legacy systems were interfaced into the R/2 system to provide batch or real-time updates.

When the client/server version of SAP ERP (SAP R/3) was introduced in 1992, the software became a phenomenal success in Europe and in the United States. With the ability to use SAP on a growing number of platforms, including Microsoft NT, the number of integrated WMS offerings also grew. Even with the presence of SAP R/3 Warehouse Management (SAP WM), companies could also use external WMSs that offered more specialized functionality than the early versions of SAP WM.

In the 1990s, specialized WMS software companies, such as Manhattan Associates, EXE Technologies, and Catalyst International, developed WMS software that contained much of the core functionality of the SAP WM software with extended transportation and distribution capabilities. Many companies bought and implemented these standalone systems prior to implementing of SAP R/3. Quite often, the WMS remained as the legacy system until the businesses decided it was economically favorable to move from the legacy WMS packages to native SAP WM.

As SAP released new versions of R/3, the functionality of SAP WM grew to become more effective than many standalone packages. By the release of SAP R/3 4.6, many companies included the conversion to SAP WM as part of their upgrade strategies. The functionality of SAP WM has expanded further as part of the latest version, SAP ECC 6.0.

Many of the WMS software companies have diversified their portfolios to include the wider SCM functionality, SAP WM data interfacing, and SAP WM consulting and specialist functions such as RFID.

1.3 Summary

In this chapter, we have shown that warehousing is something that mankind has used for thousands of years. Although the primitive warehouses of the Indus Valley civilization and the tobacco warehouses of 18th century America cannot be compared to the technological spectacles of warehouses in the 21st century, the underlying principles remain. Goods are received, stored, picked, and removed from the warehouse. Today's technology allows that to occur in the most efficient and cost-effective manner.

In Chapter 2, we discuss some of the basic warehouse functionality in SAP WM with regard to the components that make up a warehouse.

In the warehouse management functionality in SAP ERP, the warehouse is divided into several components. The storage type, storage section, and storage bin together describe a unique space where a material has been stored, and these coordinates allow that material to be located.

2   Basic Warehouse Functions

Before any implementation of the warehouse management functionality in SAP ERP (which we'll refer to as SAP WM or simply WM) at a company, the physical warehouse layout normally exists; that is, the warehouse is operating and contains materials. Therefore, defining the warehouse in terms of warehouse management components is an exercise in transposing the physical warehouse into the terms defined by SAP. In some instances, simple warehouses can be defined as storage locations within the inventory management functionality of SAP ERP (SAP IM or simply IM). However, storage locations do not offer any of the functionality required to operate a modern warehouse.

It is important to realize that the warehouse management functionality allows us to replicate the warehouse within the SAP system and provides the necessary management of materials.

2.1   Warehouse Structure

The warehouse we define by configuring SAP WM relates directly to the storage location or locations in the materials management functionality of SAP ERP (SAP MM or MM). We can create a warehouse during configuration, but no physical address is attached to the warehouse when configuration takes place. The warehouse only relates to a physical entity when it is assigned to a storage location.

2.1.1 Configuring a Warehouse

In the SAP Customizing Implementation Guide (IMG), the WM configuration is part of the Logistics Execution area in SAP, which incorporates other functions such as shipping, transportation, and direct store deliveries.

The warehouse is defined in the IMG. You can find the transaction for creating a warehouse via the menu path IMG • ENTERPRISE STRUCTURE • DEFINITION • LOGISTICS EXECUTION • DEFINE, COPY, DELETE, CHECK WAREHOUSE NUMBER.

You can use this transaction to create a warehouse number from scratch or to create a warehouse number by copying the information from another warehouse, as shown in Figure 2.1. The option to create a warehouse by copying is particularly useful when you need to create many warehouses with the same name.

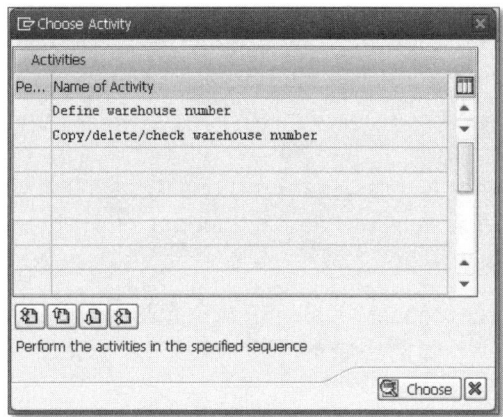

Figure 2.1 Define Warehouse Transaction: Initial Selection Screen

Selecting the DEFINE WAREHOUSE NUMBER option, as shown in Figure 2.1, displays a list of existing warehouses, as shown in Figure 2.2.

To enter the information to create a new warehouse, click the NEW ENTRIES button, as shown in Figure 2.2.

The NEW ENTRIES screen can be accessed in two other ways, either by pressing the [F5] function key or by selecting EDIT • NEW ENTRIES from the header menu.

The warehouse number to be added can only be three characters in length, as shown in Figure 2.3. The number can be alphanumeric, and the numbering scheme often depends on existing warehouse numbering or on recommendations from a data governance (DG) group at your client. The DG group administers the overall management of the availability, usability, integrity, and security of the data used in an enterprise, which includes an SAP implementation. The DG program often includes a governing body or council, an agreed-upon set of procedures, and a plan to execute those procedures.

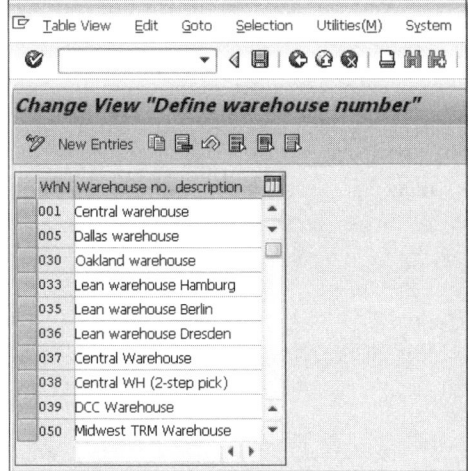

Figure 2.2 Existing Warehouses Displayed When Defining a New Warehouse Number

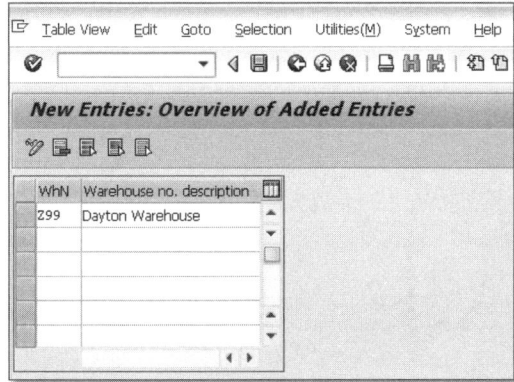

Figure 2.3 New Warehouse Details Added to "New Entries" Screen

The description for the new warehouse can be up to 25 characters in length. You can use a standard description template, so check the existing description or check with the DG group.

After you save the warehouse number and description, the next stage is to assign the warehouse to a plant and storage location. The warehouse needs to be linked to a storage location so that the interaction between SAP IM and SAP WM can be applied. For example, when a goods receipt is posted to a storage location in SAP IM, the goods will be received at the warehouse if that warehouse is assigned to the storage location.

2.1.2 Assignment of the Warehouse

A warehouse has to be assigned to a physical location in SAP MM. This includes one or more storage locations. The warehouse configuration often refers to just one storage location, but—depending on how the storage locations have been defined in MM—the warehouse may have to be assigned to more than one storage location.

You can find the transaction for assigning a warehouse to a plant/storage location combination by following the menu path IMG • ENTERPRISE STRUCTURE • ASSIGNMENT • LOGISTICS EXECUTION • ASSIGN WAREHOUSE NUMBER TO PLANT/STORAGE LOCATION.

The warehouse can be assigned to a plant/storage location combination or to several plant/storage location combinations. Figure 2.4 shows several warehouses assigned to more than one storage location within a plant.

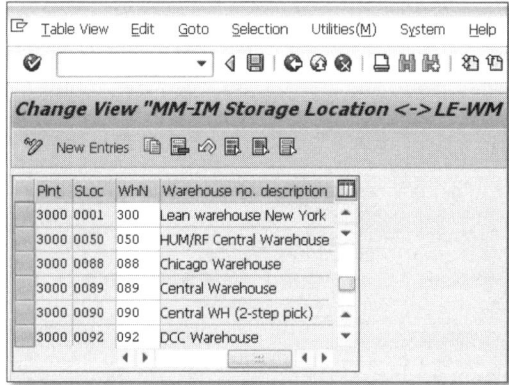

Figure 2.4 View of the Transaction Assigning a Warehouse to a Plant/Storage Location Combination

To enter the information to create a new warehouse, click the NEW ENTRIES button, as shown in Figure 2.4. You can access the NEW ENTRIES screen either by pressing the [F5] function key or by selecting EDIT • NEW ENTRIES from the header menu.

Figure 2.5 shows just one plant/storage location combination for the warehouse, but more assignments can be made on this same screen. When assignments are completed, the data can be saved.

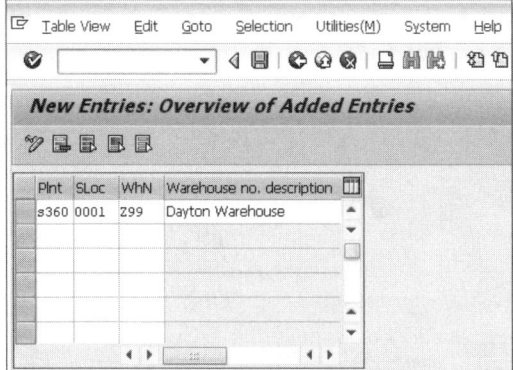

Figure 2.5 Adding Warehouse Assignment Details for the Warehouse and Plant/Storage Location to the "New Entries" Screen

2.1.3 Warehouse Control Parameters

After defining and assigning the warehouse, you can configure the control parameters, which are required for the warehouse to operate within certain constraints. If the warehouse uses kilograms instead of pounds for the unit of measure of weight, you need to configure this parameter. To find the transaction for configuring the control parameters for the warehouse, follow the menu path IMG • LOGISTICS EXECUTION • WAREHOUSE MANAGEMENT • MASTER DATA • DEFINE CONTROL PARAMETERS FOR WAREHOUSE NUMBER.

The initial screen, displayed in Figure 2.6, shows all the warehouses that have been defined in the configuration. If, as in our example above, you have created a warehouse, a blank control record is written in table T3000, and you can modify the control parameters of that record with this transaction.

2 | Basic Warehouse Functions

To change the parameters of the warehouse, the relevant warehouse must be selected, as shown in Figure 2.6. To reach the detail screen, select the DETAILS icon or press the function keys [Ctrl]+[Shift]+[F2], can be used. The method used in Figure 2.6 is to use header menu: GOTO • DETAILS.

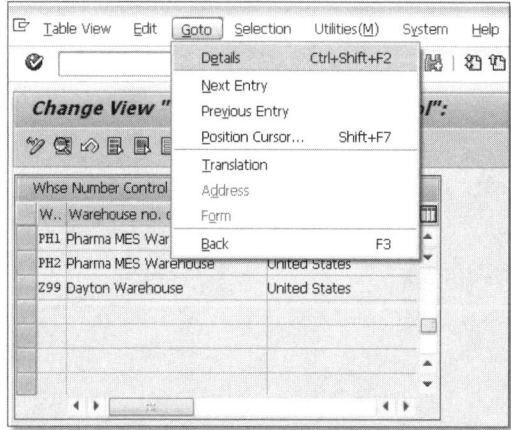

Figure 2.6 Control Parameters for "Warehouse: Initial" Screen

The detail screen, seen in Figure 2.7, shows the parameters relevant for the warehouse that can be entered.

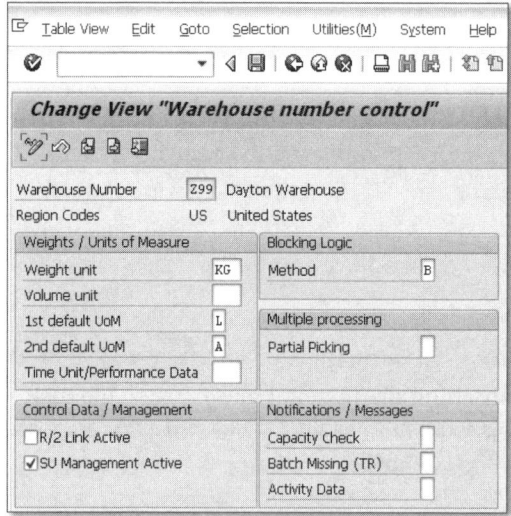

Figure 2.7 Configuration of Control Parameters for "Warehouse: Detail" Screen

Weight Unit

If a weight unit such as kilograms or pounds is entered in this field, then all units of weight, both gross and net, will be in this defined unit. Depending on the unit of weight given, errors—including mathematical rounding errors—can occur if the unit is too small or too large. A weight unit must be entered before you can create any storage bins.

Volume Unit

Similar to the weight unit, the volume unit defined the unit of volume for the warehouse (for example, cubic meters or cubic yards).

First Default Unit of Measure

The material master record can contain several units of measures for different functions such as sales, purchasing, Materials Requirements Planning (MRP), and so on. If the material master record does not contain a unit of measure for warehousing, this parameter can be used as a default. However, this default can only be used if the material is defined in the unit of measure for another function.

For example, if there is no warehouse unit of measure for material XYZ, the system will select the first default unit of measure defined. If that unit of measure is kilograms, the system will check the material master to find if the material had been defined in any other unit of measure than kilograms. If the system finds that the unit of measure for purchasing is kilograms, then the first default unit of measure will be used.

Second Default Unit of Measure

If the first default unit of measure has not been defined on the material master for any other function, the system performs the same check for the second default unit of measure defined in the warehouse control parameter screen. If this unit of measure has been used on the material master, it will be used as a default. If the second unit of measure has not been used on the material master, then the material's unit of measure will be used as the warehouse unit of measure.

Time Unit/Performance Data

On this screen, you can define the unit of measure for time for the warehouse. This time unit, if defined, will be used in any time information and for any processing time and performance data.

Blocking Logic — Method

This is a particularly important parameter because it determines the level of users' simultaneous access to materials in the warehouse. For normal warehouse operations, the blocking logic is set to ensure that when a user is creating a transfer order, the material numbers being processed are blocked for the entire warehouse and the storage bins in the transfer order are temporarily blocked. The field is left blank for this level of blocking.

For blocking that allows more than one user to access the same material, but not the same bin, the parameter should be set to A. Warehouses where there are few material numbers — such as a manufacturer that makes one or two products — can use this blocking logic. When the blocking logic is set to B, more than one user can access the same bin.

Multiple Processing — Partial Picking

In multiple processing, several transfer requirements (TRs) are grouped together. However, if there is a shortage of material, this parameter defines how the system deals with the shortage. The parameter selection has four options:

- **1**
  Partial picking for multiple processing for delivery is allowed.
- **2**
  Partial picking for multiple processing for TR is allowed.
- **3**
  Partial picking for multiple processing for TR and delivery is allowed.
- **Blank**
  Partial picking for multiple processing for TR and delivery is not allowed.

Notifications and Messages—Capacity Check

This field controls the type of message displayed for the warehouse when a capacity check cannot be completed because of missing data on the material master records. Warehouse management can choose no message, warning message, or error message.

Notifications and Messages—Batch Missing (Transfer Requirement)

If the material on the transfer requirement is a batch-managed material, the user creating the TR should enter a batch number. However, this parameter allows the configuration to display an error message, warning message, or no message when a batch number is expected but not entered.

Notifications and Messages—Activity Data

The activity data describes the planned times for activities on the transfer order. If there is an error in this data, the message display can be defined as an error message, warning message, or no message.

R/2 Link Active

This checkbox is selected if the warehouse in the SAP WM system is being used as a decentralized warehouse management system with SAP R/2.

Storage Unit Management Active

This checkbox should be selected if you are implementing the storage unit management functionality (SUM) at the warehouse. More information on storage unit management can be found in Chapter 11.

After you enter the relevant parameters for the warehouse, save by clicking the SAVE icon, pressing [Ctrl]+[S], or using the header menu and selecting TABLE VIEW • SAVE. Now we can proceed to learning about storage types in a warehouse.

2.2 Storage Type

Several areas can be defined within the warehouse. The defined areas of storage in SAP are called storage types. When a warehouse is initially designed, its layout is analyzed based on a number of objectives, including the following:

- Provide the most efficient handling of the stored material
- Provide the maximum flexibility to meet any changes in warehousing that the company may require
- Use the space inside the warehouse to a maximum
- Provide the most economic warehousing procedures based on layout

The layout of the warehouse is divided into storage types, and these defined areas relate directly to the requirements of the materials to be stored in the warehouse.

2.2.1 Warehouse Layout

Storage types need to be defined because of the nature of the material being stored or the environment a material must be stored in. Let's explore this idea further.

Fast-Moving Materials

A company will have a number of materials that are defined as fast-moving; that is, they are shipped quickly once they are received at the warehouse. Therefore, these materials need to be stored in a manner that allows for optimum handling.

In a normal warehouse, this area for the fast-moving materials should be situated along the quickest path from goods receiving to shipping. That location depends on how that material is shipped. If the material is received in large amounts but shipped in small amounts, the fast-moving materials storage type should be placed close to the shipping area. This reduces the duration of each trip between storage type and shipping. If the material is received in small amounts and shipped in large quantities, then the storage type needs to be close to goods receiving to reduce the length of the frequent trips from goods receiving to storage type.

Rack Storage

There are a number of reasons a material should use the rack storage type. Sometimes the material is not shaped in a manner suitable for any other storage. Other materials are fragile and cannot be stacked. Some rack storage is used close to shipping to allow picking of materials that are small; a limited supply is located in the order-picking racks and replenished from bulk storage.

Bulk Pallet Storage

The majority of bulk products are stored on pallets, and the pallets are stacked. This is a good use of space in the warehouse and reduces the need for and cost of racking. Some materials can only be stacked a limited number of pallets high.

Slow-Moving Materials

Although every company tries to reduce, if not eliminate, materials that are sold infrequently, slow-moving materials are a feature of a company's inventory. Many companies use the theory that in general, the slowest-moving 80% of materials represent only 20% of sales volume.

Slow-moving materials make up inventory that has had some movement but less than one and a half turns a year. Slow-moving items are similar to dead stock items, but they have experienced some customer demand during the past 12 months. These items may be suitable for being discontinued.

However, if the item falls into one of the following categories it may not be suitable for being discontinued and will need to be stored in the warehouse:

- If it is expected that demand for this material will continue or increase during the next twelve months
- If customers expect to always have the material available for immediate delivery
- If the material is inexpensive and does not require a costly investment in inventory

Slow-moving material is often stored at the furthest location from the shipping area, as it is not accessed often.

Special Storage

Some companies have special needs for the storage of their materials. These may involve hazardous materials, which are discussed in Chapter 12.

Refrigeration and climate control are some other special needs for storage. Many retail companies need to have part of the warehouse refrigerated for perishable materials. Other companies may need to define certain warm areas for chemicals that need to be stored at a certain temperature. All of these can be defined as storage types within a warehouse.

2.2.2 Configuration of a Storage Type

You can find the transaction for creating a storage type by following the menu path IMG • LOGISTICS EXECUTION • WAREHOUSE MANAGEMENT • MASTER DATA • DEFINE STORAGE TYPE.

The transaction shows the storage types that have been previously created for warehouses, as shown in Figure 2.8. To create the new storage type, click the NEW ENTRIES button.

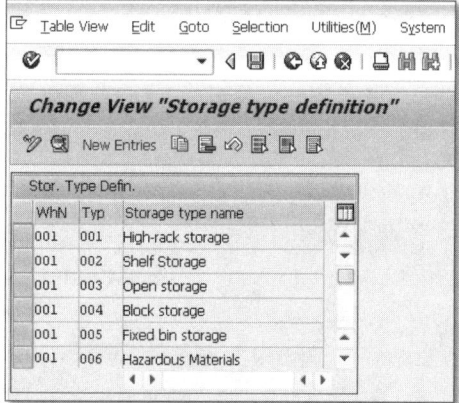

Figure 2.8 Create Storage Type, Showing Existing Storage Types

Figure 2.9 shows the data entry screen for the storage type. This screen requires decisions about the content of several fields. The parameters for the storage type relate to stock placement and stock removal. This content of the fields determines how material is placed and removed from this particular storage type.

2.2 Storage Type

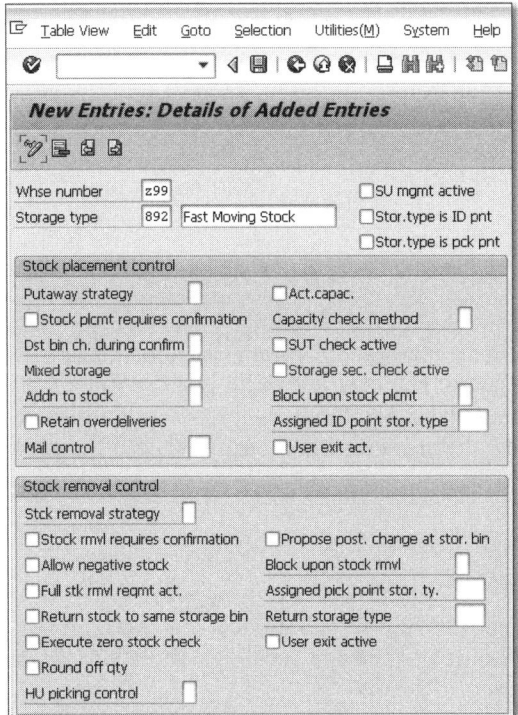

Figure 2.9 Create Storage Type Transaction: Initial Data Entry Screen

In the following subsections, we will describe the fields on the storage type data entry screen.

2.2.3 Data Entry for a Storage Type

Let's explore in detail the fields shown in Figure 2.9.

Storage Unit Management Active

This checkbox, SU MGMT ACTIVE, is selected if the storage type allows the management of storage unit management (SUM). A storage unit (SU) is a group of one or more amounts of material that can be managed in the warehouse as a distinct unit. If the checkbox is set for the storage type, you can assume that all material in the storage type is part of a storage unit.

Storage Type Is an ID Point

If the STOR.TYPE IS ID PNT checkbox is selected, the storage type is an identification point for goods movements. An identification point is a location in an automated warehouse where the incoming goods are identified. You can configure identification points in the IMG via the menu path IMG • LOGISTICS EXECUTION • WAREHOUSE MANAGEMENT • STORAGE UNITS • ACTIVITIES • DefineID POINT TRANSACTIONS.

Storage Type Is a Picking Point

If the STOR.TYPE IS PCK PNT checkbox is selected, the storage type is a picking point for another storage type. For example, if there is a packaging storage type in the warehouse, material for the packaging storage type may be picked from a storage type called fast-moving goods. The STOR.TYPE IS PCK PNT checkbox would be set on the fast-moving goods storage type.

Putaway Strategy

The stock putaway strategy is a procedure that can be defined for each storage type. It operates during stock placement of material in which the SAP system automatically searches within a storage type for a suitable storage bin for the material to be placed into storage. This strategy will be discussed in more detail in Chapter 9.

Stock Placement Requires Confirmation

Selecting this checkbox requires that all stock placements into bins within this storage type be confirmed. This means that before any material is available, all the relevant transfer orders must be confirmed.

Destination Storage Bin Changed During Confirmation

The DST BIN CH. DURING CONFIRMATION field can be set to allow the destination storage bin to be changed on a transfer order when the transfer order is being confirmed for this storage type. The field must be set to 1 to allow this. If the field remains blank, you cannot change the destination storage bin on a transfer order for this storage type.

Mixed Storage

This field determines how different materials are stored in this storage type. If the field is left blank, the storage type does not allow any mixed storage. Mixed storage refers to different materials or different batches of material being located in one storage bin.

However, if the storage type does allow for mixed storage, you can set several parameters to reflect how mixed storage can be used, as shown in Figure 2.10.

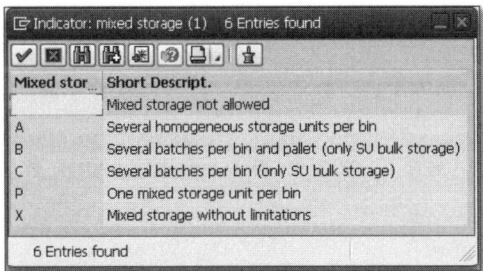

Figure 2.10 Display of Mixed Storage Parameters that Can Be Selected

Addition to Stock

This field can be configured to allow a quant of a material with a certain batch number to be added to a storage bin with the same material and the same batch as the material being added.

> **Note**
> A quant is a uniquely defined object in SAP systems. It is a quantity of material with the same material number and the same batch number—if the material is batch managed—in a single storage bin. A quant has a quant number to identify it.

If the field is left blank, then the addition to stock is not allowed. If the field is marked with an X, then the addition to stock is allowed.

Mail Control

This field is only used for the production planning material staging functionality of SAP ERP (SAP PP or PP). If any of the background processes for automatic creation of transfer orders for PP material staging fail, this field defines which user is to be informed of the error. The user for the mail notification can be found in table T333M.

Capacity Check Method

This checkbox can be configured to check if one of the six SAP WM capacity checks can be carried out for the storage bins in this storage type. Figure 2.11 shows the six types of capacity checks that are available to be configured for the storage type.

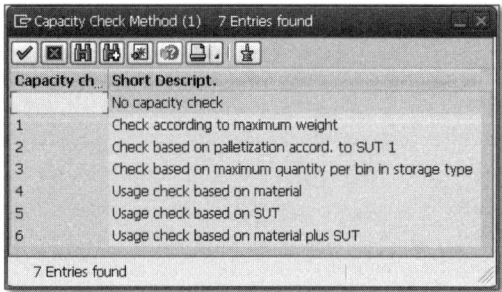

Figure 2.11 WM Capacity Checks Available for Storage Type

Active Capacity Check

If this checkbox is selected, an active capacity check is executed when goods are placed into stock. The check ensures that a capacity check is made when material is moved into a storage bin. If the capacity of the bin is exceeded, the material cannot be moved into the bin.

Storage Unit Management Check Active

This checkbox is selected if the storage unit type check for stock placement is active. If this checkbox is selected, the storage unit type needs to be specified for stock placements.

Storage Section Check Active

When this checkbox is selected, the SAP system searches for storage bins in storage areas defined in the storage area check table.

Block Upon Stock Placement

With this checkbox selected, the quant and the storage bin can be blocked during stock placement. The following two options are available in configuration:

- Block the storage bin during stock placement
- Block only the quant during stock placement

ID Point for a Storage Type

This field, ASSIGNED ID POINT STOR. TYPE, allows the configuration of the identification (ID) point for the storage type. Any goods movement that does not have a specific storage bin in this storage type as its destination is initially directed to the ID point.

User Exit Active

Select this checkbox if a stock placement strategy for this storage type will be accessed via a user exit. The checkbox informs the system that instead of using a stock placement strategy defined in configuration, the system must use the user-defined placement strategy that has been coded outside of the SAP system and access it via a user exit.

Stock Removal Strategy

The stock removal or picking strategy is a procedure that can be defined for each storage type. This procedure operates during stock removal of material so that the SAP system automatically searches within a storage type for a suitable storage bin for the material to be removed.

A more detailed discussion of picking strategies can be found in Chapter 8. Figure 2.12 shows the standard picking strategies that are available for assignment in the storage type configuration.

Stock Removal Requires Confirmation

This checkbox must be selected if there is a requirement for the confirmation of a stock removal. This requires a transfer to be confirmed for every stock removal that takes place with relation to the storage type.

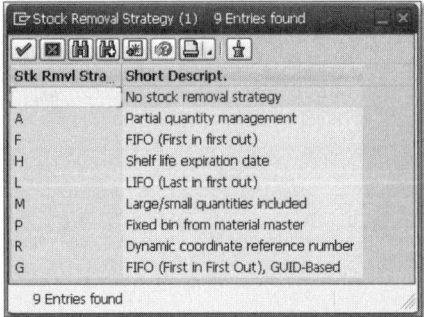

Figure 2.12 Stock Removal or Picking Strategies Defined in Standard SAP Systems

Allow Negative Stock

If this checkbox is selected, a negative figure can exist for quants in the storage type. This is not commonly configured for storage types that are not interim storage types. SAP defines interim storage types as storage types that are used for posting goods receipts, goods issues, and differences that may occur. Interim storage types are defined with numbers between 900 and 999.

Full Stock Removal Required

This checkbox can be selected if the warehouse needs to ensure that all quants are removed if a complete stock removal is required. A complete stock removal is a component of SUT and requires all storage units to be removed, but quants that are not part of an SU can remain. If this checkbox is selected, then all quants are removed.

Execute Zero Stock Check

If this checkbox is selected, a zero stock check must be carried out if a storage bin becomes empty after a stock removal.

Round off Quantity

You can select the checkbox to round off a requested quantity for stock removal when rounding is required for transfer-order items. This checkbox sets rounding for the total storage type. It may be more appropriate to set the rounding quantity in the material master record at the storage-type level.

Rounding is useful in picking when the picking is easier in certain amounts, for example, in pallets or boxes. Rounding the quantity to those values can save time in filling orders.

Handling Unit Picking Control

This field is the control for the handling unit (HU), or storage unit picking. We will prove more information about storage units in Chapter 11. Figure 2.13 shows the options that are available for this field

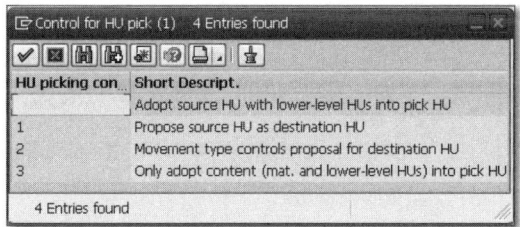

Figure 2.13 Options for Control of Handling Unit During Picking

Propose Posting Change at Storage Bin

You can select this checkbox to ensure that if a posting change is made for a material, the transaction is posted and the materials are left in the same storage bin. If the checkbox is not selected, then the material can be moved to a different storage bin as part of the posting change.

Block Upon Stock Removal

This checkbox makes it possible for the quant and the storage bin to be blocked during stock removal. The following two options are available in configuration:

- Block the storage bin during stock removal
- Block only the quant during stock removal

Assigned Pick Point for Storage Type

In SUT, if complete removal of storage units is required and the FULL STK RMVL REQMT ACT checkbox is not selected, the quants that are not removed should be taken to a pick point. The pick point is a storage type and is configured in this field.

Return Storage Type

Similar to the pick point, this field can be configured to set the storage type where material is returned after events such as a stock removal or over-delivery.

User Exit Active

This field is similar to the field in stock placement. If this field is selected, a stock removal strategy for this storage type will be accessed via a user exit.

This section has explained the characteristics of storage types. The next section looks at the division of the storage type into storage sections.

2.3 Storage Sections

The storage type can be divided into several areas, which are called storage sections. A storage section contains the storage bins where the material is stored. Many storage types have only one storage section because there is no requirement to break the storage type into further distinct areas. At least one storage section must be defined for each storage type. In some warehouses, storage sections are important in the stock removal process.

> **Example**
> The storage type for high racking can be divided into several storage sections. The storage sections could refer to the levels of racks in the storage type. The first rack level could be one storage section, the second level another storage section, and so on.

You can find the transaction for creating a storage section by following the menu path IMG • LOGISTICS EXECUTION • WAREHOUSE MANAGEMENT • MASTER DATA • DEFINE STORAGE SECTIONS.

The initial screen for the configuration of the storage sections shows the storage sections already created, as shown in Figure 2.14. To create a new storage section, click the NEW ENTRIES button. You can also reach the configuration screen by selecting EDIT • NEW ENTRIES from the header menu or by pressing the [F5] function key.

Figure 2.14 Initial Screen for Configuration of a Storage Section

The new storage section must be assigned to both a warehouse number and a storage type. Figure 2.15 shows the warehouse and storage type created in this chapter. Three storage sections are assigned to storage type 892. The storage section is a three-character field and normally is configured as 001 if only one storage section is to be used.

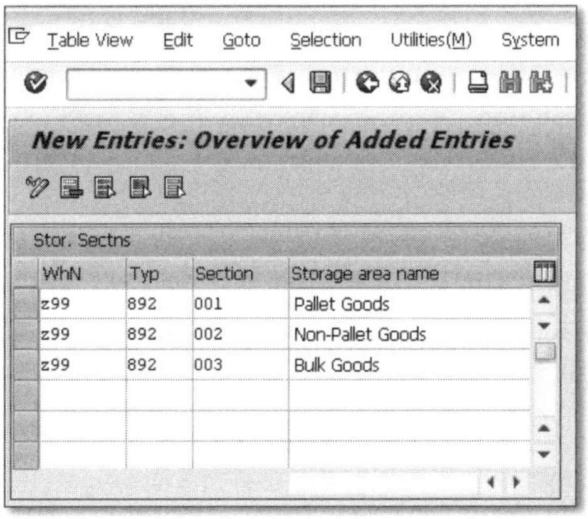

Figure 2.15 Configuration Screen for Creating New Storage Sections

The storage section name field is 25 characters in length and should describe the use of the storage section. For example, if a storage section is for unboxed items on a single rack, the name may be "Level One—Unboxed." After the storage section is configured, the storage bins can be created.

2.4 Storage Bins

The storage bin is the smallest unit of storage in the warehouse. There is no set size for a storage bin, and its size can vary between companies, warehouses, and even within the same storage type.

A storage bin can be a location on a shelf, a location on a carousel, or a plastic tub in a rack. A storage bin can have many physical appearances, but as defined logically in SAP WM it is the location where a quant of material is stored.

Several steps need to be completed in the IMG before storage bins can be created. These steps are described in more detail in the following subsections.

2.4.1 Storage Bin Types

The storage bin type is a grouping that can be assigned to storage bins of a similar nature. For example, a storage bin type could be created called Bin Height One Meter. This grouping could then be assigned to bins in the warehouse that are one meter in height.

You can configure the storage bin type in the IMG. The transaction for creating a storage bin type can be found by following the menu path IMG • LOGISTICS EXECUTION • WAREHOUSE MANAGEMENT • MASTER DATA • STORAGE BINS • DEFINE STORAGE BIN TYPES.

Figure 2.16 shows the initial screen for the configuration of storage bin types, with the existing configuration shown. Click the NEW ENTRIES button to create a new storage bin type. You can also reach the configuration screen by selecting EDIT • NEW ENTRIES in the header menu or by pressing the [F5] function key.

Figure 2.17 shows the addition of a storage bin type for the warehouse in our previous examples. The storage bin type field is limited to two characters. The description of the storage bin type is 20 characters.

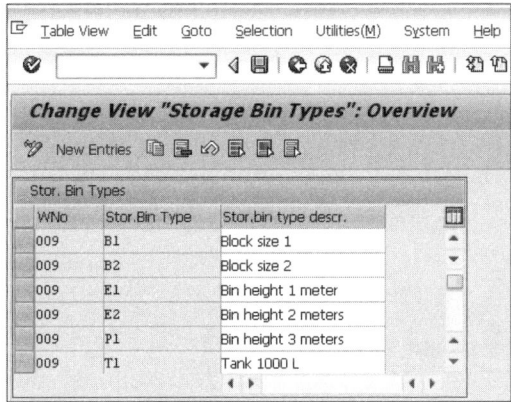

Figure 2.16 Initial Screen for Configuration of Storage Bin Types

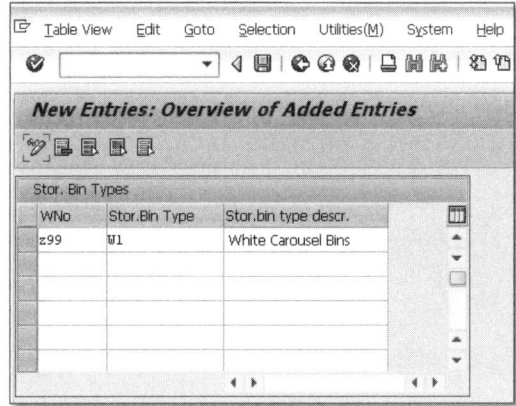

Figure 2.17 Configuration Screen for Creating New Storage Bin Types

2.4.2 Define Storage Bin Structure

Assigning the storage bin structure is a transaction that can be configured to contain the templates and structures of the storage bin numbering schema activated when automatic storage bin creation is triggered.

The transaction to define the storage bin structure is Transaction LS10. This can be found in two areas. In the IMG, follow the menu path IMG • LOGISTICS EXECUTION • WAREHOUSE MANAGEMENT • MASTER DATA • STORAGE BINS • DEFINE STORAGE BIN STRUCTURES.

You can also find Transaction LS10 in the application area, by following the menu path SAP • LOGISTICS • LOGISTICS EXECUTION • MASTER DATA • WAREHOUSE • STORAGE BIN • CREATE • AUTOMATICALLY.

Figure 2.18 shows the various structures for automatic creation of storage bins. The structure is defined for each warehouse/storage type combination. The third field on this screen, SQN, is the sequence number that will be followed in the creation of storage bins for the warehouse/storage type combination.

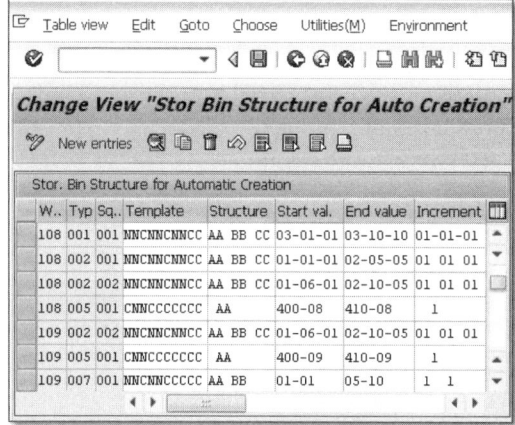

Figure 2.18 Storage Bin Structure Configuration Screen: Transaction LS10

Template

In Figure 2.18, the template is shown as a field with 10 characters. These characters represent numeric and alphabetical character ranges. This template determines the structure of the storage bin when it is created automatically.

- **N**

  This represents a numeric character between zero and nine.

- **A**

  This represents an alphabetical character.

- **C**

  This represents a character that is common across the bins.

Structure

This field defines the structure of the storage bin number. Figure 2.18 shows the structure field as AA or AA BB CC. This structure defines how the number appears, as we can easily understand by using Figure 2.18 as an example.

Review the second line of the figure, Warehouse 108, Storage Type 002, and Sequence Number 001. The template for this entry is Number, Number, Common Character, Number, Number, Common Character, Number, Number, Common Character, and finally another Common Character.

The structure defined for that record is AA BB CC. Therefore, using the structure with the template, the storage bin number could be 11 – 03 – 05, assuming the common character between the numbers is a dash and the last two common characters are spaces. The definition of the common characters is shown in the next fields.

Start Value

This field is the storage bin starting value for the particular warehouse/storage bin/sequence number combination. This value is the starting value for the automatic creation of storage bins. The value entered has to adhere to the template and structure defined for the combination. Taking the example above, the starting value of 03 – 01 – 01 follows both the template and structure and now includes the common characters of a dash between the numbers and spaces after the last set of numbers.

End Value

The entry for the particular warehouse/storage bin/sequence number combination is the end value for the automatic creation of storage bins for that sequence. The end value must follow the same format as the starting value.

Increment

This figure determines the addition to the numbering and is calculated during the automatic generation of storage bins. In our continuing example, the increment for the automatic generation of storage bins has been entered as 01 – 01 – 01, which implies that each set of numbers will increase by one until the end value has been reached. In this example, the start value was 03 – 01 – 01 and the end value was 03 – 10 – 10; therefore, during the automatic creation of bins, the increment only refers to the second and third sets of numbers because the first set of numbers is always 03 and does not change.

During the automatic storage bin creation in this example, the starting bin location would be 03 – 01 – 01, the next bin to be automatically generated would be 03 – 01 – 02, the next 03 – 01 – 03, and so on. The last storage bin created for this location would be 03 – 10 – 10.

Enter a New Bin Structure

To enter a new storage bin structure, click the NEW ENTRIES button, shown in Figure 2.18. You can also reach the entry screen by going to the header menu and selecting EDIT • NEW ENTRIES or by pressing the [F5] function key.

The configuration screen, shown in Figure 2.19, requires the entry of the template, structure, start and end values, and increment. Additional data fields can be entered for the storage bin structure.

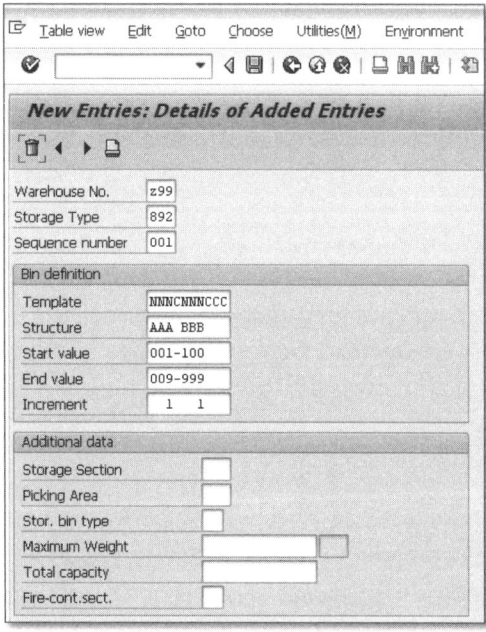

Figure 2.19 Configuration Screen for Entering New Storage Bin Structure: Transaction LS10

Storage Section

If the bin structure is only relevant for a certain storage section, that section should be entered on this screen, shown in Figure 2.19. This may be the case if the template that is being configured is only relevant for a certain storage section, for example, for high-racking or open storage. The start and end values for the bin number range may only relate to a single storage section.

Picking Area

A picking area is similar to a storage section in that it groups a certain number of storage bins. The difference between a storage section and a picking area is that the group of bins for a picking area relates to the picking process and removal strategies. For example, a picking area may include storage bins from several storage sections—that is, different sizes—because they all contain material that is relevant for a certain removal strategy.

You can configure a picking area in the IMG by following the menu path IMG • LOGISTICS EXECUTION • WAREHOUSE MANAGEMENT • MASTER DATA • DEFINE PICKING AREAS.

Figure 2.20 shows the data entry required to configure a picking area. The PICKING AREA field allows you to enter a three-character alphanumeric ID. The picking area name can have a maximum of 25 characters. Once the name is entered, the picking area can be added to the storage bin information.

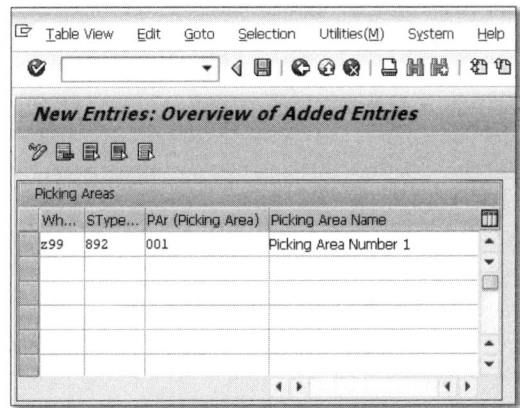

Figure 2.20 Configuration Screen for Creating a New Picking Area

Storage Bin Type

A storage bin type can be added to the entry of the bin structure that will be a default for the bins created. This is useful if the bins are all of the same kind. The storage bin type is a way to identify different types of storage bins; for example, one type of storage bin may be one meter high, while another type represents tank containers for fluids.

Maximum Weight

You can fill in this field if you know the maximum weight of the material that can be stored in the bin. This weight value is used during any capacity check that may be activated. If the weight of the material to be added into the storage bin will cause the weight of material in that bin to exceed the maximum weight allowed, then the system will not permit the placement.

Total Capacity

You can fill in this field if you know the total capacity of the storage bins to be created. This is important if the material to be stored in some bins can easily exceed the capacity of the bin. This is especially useful in warehouses with large or heavy materials.

Fire-Containment Section

You can fill in this field if the fire-containment section needs to be added for the storage bins to be created. The fire-containment sections are defined as part of the hazardous materials configuration for warehouse management. More information on hazardous materials can be found in Chapter 12.

You configure the fire-containment section in the IMG via the menu path IMG • LOGISTICS EXECUTION • WAREHOUSE MANAGEMENT • HAZARDOUS MATERIALS • MASTER DATA • DEFINE FIRE-CONTAINMENT SECTIONS.

The new fire-containment sections can be added to a warehouse in the IMG, as shown in Figure 2.21. The fire-containment field can be two characters in length, whereas the name of the fire-containment section can be up to 20 characters long. Once the fire-containment section is configured, it can be entered into the storage bin structure.

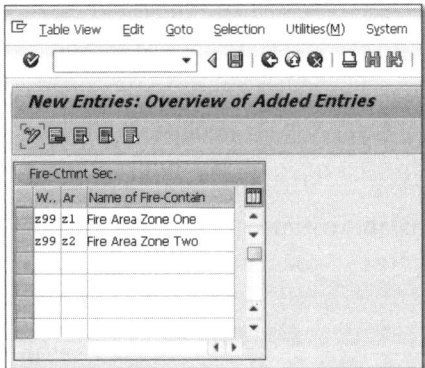

Figure 2.21 Configuration Entry Screen to Create Fire-Containment Sections in IMG Hazardous Material Area

2.4.3 Creating a Storage Bin Manually

You can manually create a storage bin using Transaction LS01N. This can be found by following the menu path SAP • LOGISTICS • LOGISTICS EXECUTION • WAREHOUSE MANAGEMENT • MASTER DATA • STORAGE BIN • CREATE • MANUALLY.

To create the storage bin, enter the warehouse number, storage type, and the storage bin number, as shown in Figure 2.22. Once these fields are filled in, you have to enter a storage section number to create the storage bin. The other fields on the entry screen, such as PICKING AREA and FIRE-CONT. SECT, are optional.

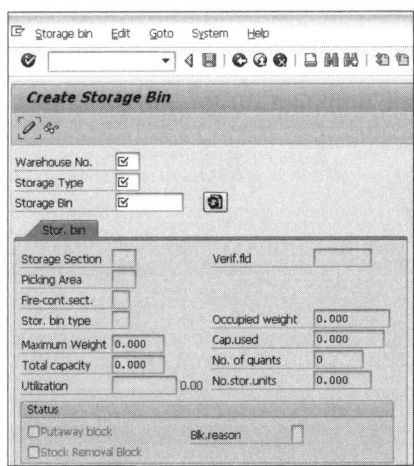

Figure 2.22 Data-Entry Screen for Creating a Storage Bin: Transaction LS01N

2.4.4 Creating a Storage Bin Automatically

Storage bins can be created automatically using the storage bin structure transaction we previously discussed previously: Transaction LS10. Once the template, structure, start and end values, and intervals are entered into the transaction, the storage bins can be created automatically.

You can find Transaction LS10 by following the menu path SAP • LOGISTICS • LOGISTICS EXECUTION • MASTER DATA • WAREHOUSE • STORAGE BIN • CREATE • AUTOMATICALLY.

After you select the relevant warehouse, storage type, and sequence number, the bins can be automatically created. From the header menu select ENVIRONMENT • CREATE BINS, as shown in Figure 2.23. The process then calculates the number of bins to be created and returns the information to the screen, as shown in Figure 2.24.

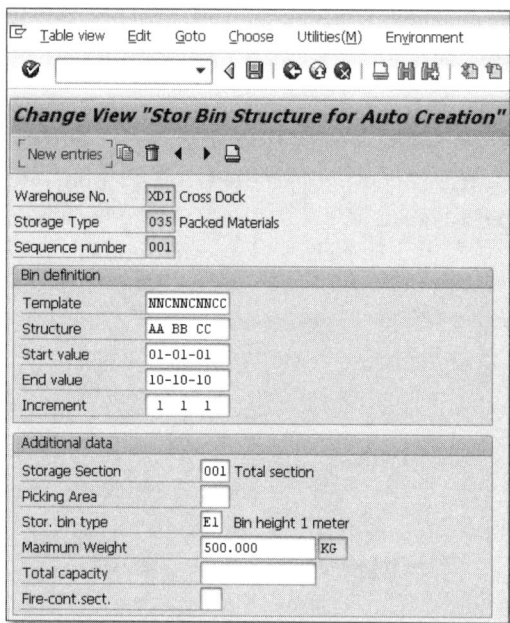

Figure 2.23 Automatically Creating Storage Bins—Transaction LS10

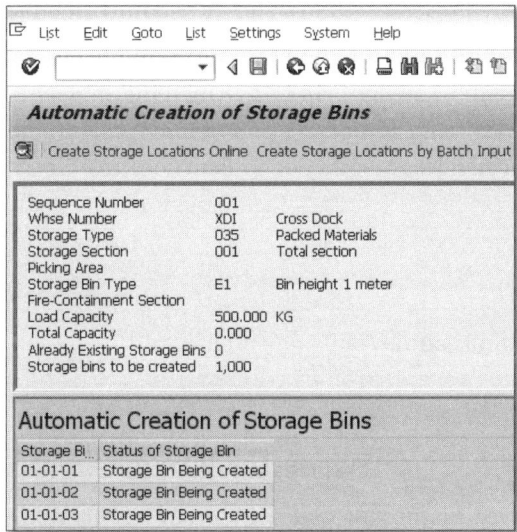

Figure 2.24 Information Screen During Automatic Creation of Storage Bins: Transaction LS10

2.4.5 Block Storage Bins

During normal warehouse operations, you may need to block storage bins or a range of storage bins. This may occur because of damage to the bins or normal warehouse maintenance, which can include cleaning bins and racks, as well as replacing racking shelves. It is possible to block a single storage bin or a range of storage bins.

The transaction to perform this is Transaction LS08, which you can find by following the menu path SAP • LOGISTICS • LOGISTICS EXECUTION • MASTER DATA • WAREHOUSE • STORAGE BIN • BLOCK • RANGE OF BINS.

To block a range of bins, the initial screen, shown in Figure 2.25, requires the entry of the warehouse number and the storage type. At this point, you can enter a range of storage bins, if required. If no selection is made, then all of the valid storage bins for the particular warehouse/storage type combination will be selected for blocking.

The selection screen, shown in Figure 2.26, shows the number of bins that can be selected for blocking. In this example, the bins can be blocked. However, you have the option of unblocking them. The screen shows clearly that none of the bins are blocked for putaway and none are blocked for stock removal.

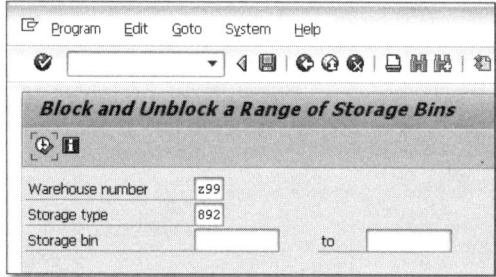

Figure 2.25 Initial Entry Screen to Block a Range of Storage Bins: Transaction LS08

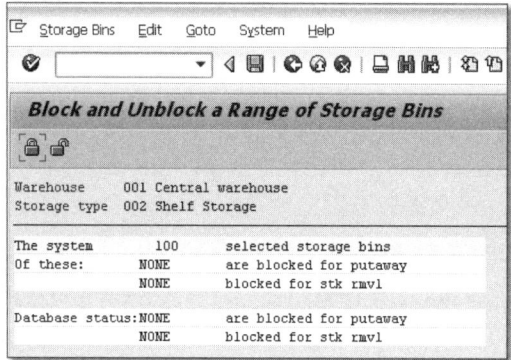

Figure 2.26 Selection of Storage Bins that Can Be Blocked: Transaction LS08

To block the bins, select the locked padlock icon. You can also press the [F5] function key or select EDIT • BLOCK from the header menu to block the storage bins.

When blocking the storage bins, you need to choose the type of block assigned to the bins. Figure 2.27 shows the choices: a block to be made for putaway or for stock removal. In addition, you can add a blocking reason if any have been configured. The configuration steps to create blocking reasons are described in the next section.

When the block for putaway is selected, the bins are blocked for any stock placement transactions, but stock removal can still take place. The resulting situation is shown in Figure 2.28.

Figure 2.27 Option to Select Type of Block Allocated to Selected Bins: Transaction LS08

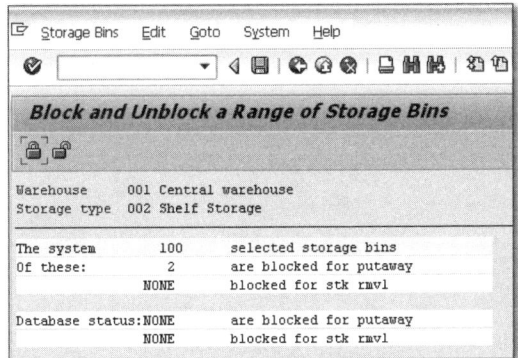

Figure 2.28 Screen Showing Number of Bins Blocked for Putaway: Transaction LS08

2.4.6 Creating Blocking Reasons

The reasons for blocking storage bins can also be applied to storage units, quants, and storage types. The blocking reasons are created at the warehouse level. To configure blocking reasons, in the IMG, follow the menu path IMG • LOGISTICS EXECUTION • WAREHOUSE MANAGEMENT • MASTER DATA • STORAGE BINS • DEFINE BLOCKING REASONS.

You can add the blocking reasons at the warehouse level. In the entry screen, shown in Figure 2.29, it is possible to add several blocking reasons at once. The blocking reason is a single character, but some non-alphanumeric characters, for example, # and @, can be selected to increase the number of blocking reasons for each warehouse.

You should add a description of the blocking reason. This is limited to 20 characters in length.

2 | Basic Warehouse Functions

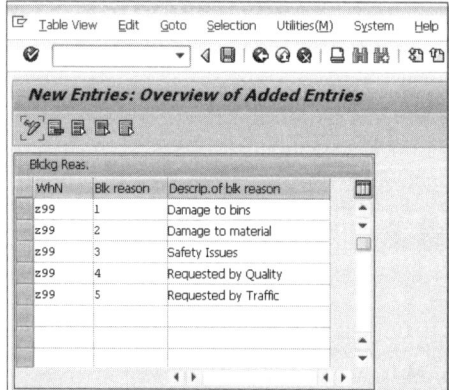

Figure 2.29 Configuration Screen for Creating Blocking Reasons at the Warehouse Level

2.4.7 List of Empty Storage Bins

This list is a key report used by warehouse managers, as it is informs them immediately what empty bins are available. When the warehouse is short of space and has to unload trailers, having a list of empty bins is critical.

The transaction for this report is Transaction LX01, which you can find via the menu path SAP • LOGISTICS • LOGISTICS EXECUTION • MASTER DATA • WAREHOUSE • STORAGE BIN • EVALUATIONS • LIST OF EMPTY STORAGE BINS.

You can add several parameters to reduce the scope of the search for empty bins. As Figure 2.30 shows, you can choose to show the empty bins at the warehouse level or by a selecting the storage type or range of bins.

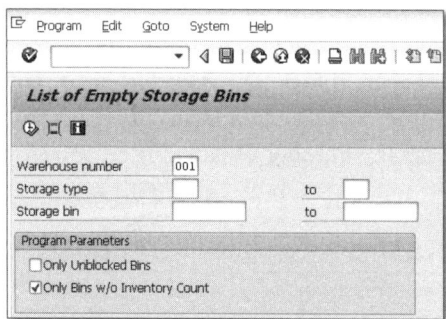

Figure 2.30 Initial Screen to Enter Parameters for List of Empty Storage Bins: Transaction LX01

You also can choose to show empty bins that are unblocked and those with no inventory count. This is important, as it is often necessary to find empty bins that can be used, especially if warehouse space is short. The resulting report, shown in Figure 2.31, shows the list of empty bins for the parameters entered in Figure 2.30.

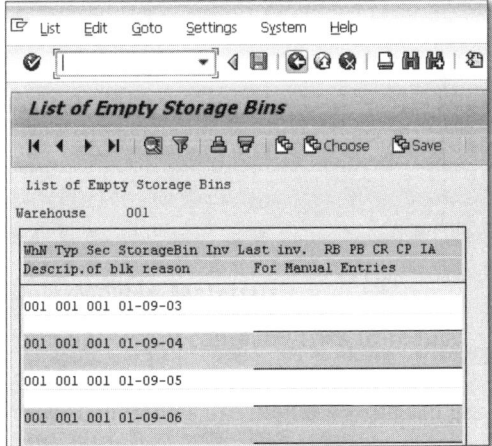

Figure 2.31 List of Empty Storage Bins Created by Transaction LX01

2.4.8 Bin Status Report

The bin status report is crucial to a successful warehouse operation. This report shows the contents of storage bins for a specified search. The transaction for this report is Transaction LX03, which you can find by following the menu path SAP • LOGISTICS • LOGISTICS EXECUTION • MASTER DATA • WAREHOUSE • STORAGE BIN • EVALUATIONS • BIN STATUS REPORT.

The report can be made to specify a certain warehouse, range of storage types, or range of bins, as shown in Figure 2.32. In addition, there are several parameters that can be entered to return specific bins.

Inventory Method

You can restrict the results of the bin status report to materials that have been counted by a certain inventory method. The inventory methods can be entered into this screen.

2 | Basic Warehouse Functions

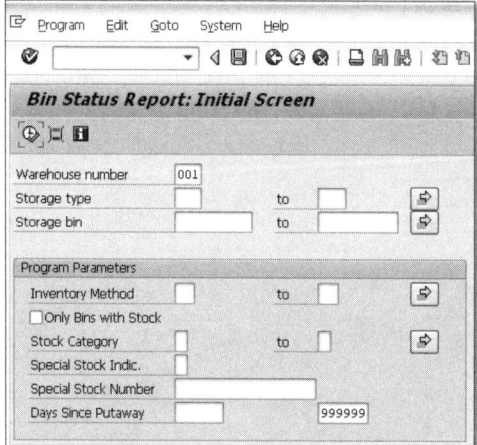

Figure 2.32 Initial Screen for Bin Status Report: Transaction LX03

Stock Category

The stock category restricts the bin status. The stock categories include the following:

- **Q**
  Stock in quality control
- **R**
  Return stock
- **S**
  Blocked stock
- **Blank**
  All available stock

Special Stock Checkbox

The special stock checkbox identifies special materials that need to be managed separately. Examples include project stock and return packaging.

Special Stock Number

This number is assigned to a quantity of material that is flagged by a special stock checkbox. The special stock checkboxes include Q for project stock and E for sales order stock. To identify a specific quantity of special stock, a special stock number is allocated to that unique quantity.

Days Since Putaway

You can restrict the bin status search to materials that have been in stock for a certain number of days since the putaway date.

The results screen for the bin status report is shown in Figure 2.33. The screen shows the results for the warehouse. It identifies the storage type, storage bin, material in the bin, plant, and the length of days in the bin (TiL).

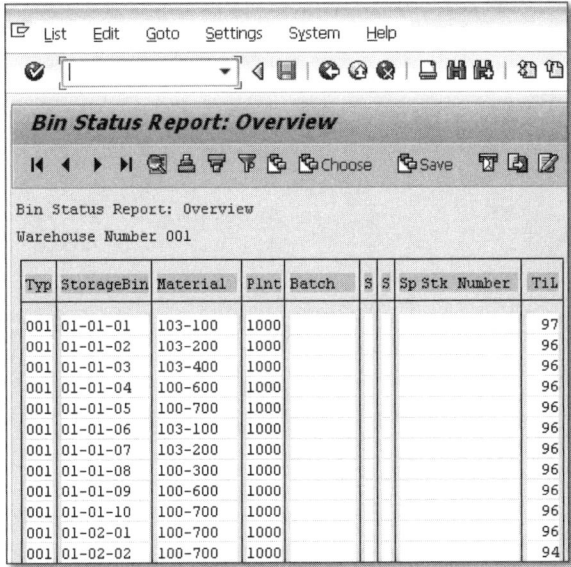

Figure 2.33 Results Screen for Bin Status Report: Transaction LX03

The storage bin is the smallest location in the warehouse, but now we will look at the units of material contained in the storage bin, which are the quants.

2.5 Quants

A quant is a quantity of material with the same material number and the same batch number (if the material is batch managed) in a single storage bin. The total quantity of material in a quant can be increased or decreased through the addition or removal of material for the storage bin. The quant can only change in quantity through a goods movement.

2.5.1 Quant Record

The SAP system automatically creates a quant when the same material of the same batch is placed in a storage bin that does not contain material of the same number or batch. The SAP system assigns a quant number to the material. When all of the quant is removed from the storage bin, the system automatically deletes the quant. The record created for the quant includes the following data:

- Quant identification
- Plant
- Material number
- Batch number
- Stock category
- Special stock checkbox and number

2.5.2 Display a Quant

One method of displaying a quant is to view the details of a storage bin. One report that displays information on the contents of a storage bin is the bin status report (Transaction LX03) discussed earlier in this chapter.

Figure 2.33 shows the details of material in the storage bins in a warehouse. Clicking on the line required and then selecting the magnifying glass icon displays the details of the storage bin/material combination, which triggers Transaction LS23. The function keys — Ctrl + Shift + F3 — can also be used to display the details. If the quant number is known, then Transaction LS23 can be used directly.

Figure 2.34 shows that the information on the quant is not just related to the quantity and location, but includes data on the goods receipt (GR NUMBER), last movement date, and the document number.

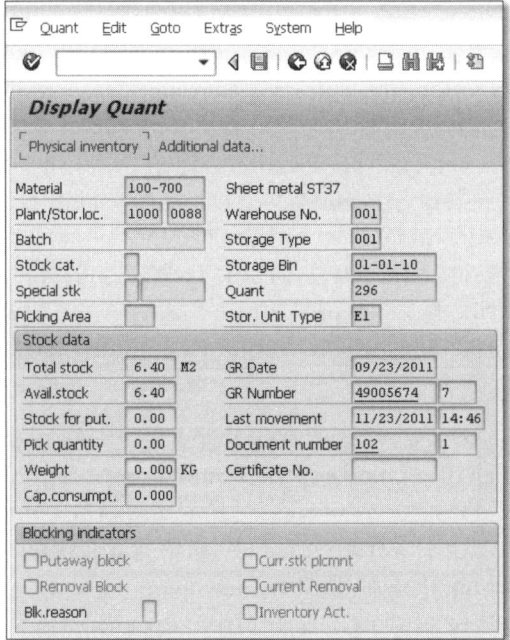

Figure 2.34 Details of a Quant in a Storage Bin: Transaction LS23

2.6 Business Examples—Basic Warehouse Functions

This chapter describes the basic structure of a warehouse as it is configured in WM. The implementation of the WM is not always required, and many SAP customers operate very successfully using only the functions of IM. However, if SAP WM is to be implemented, it is important that the customer understand how their warehouse operations need to be configured in the system.

2.6.1 Warehouse Structure

The warehouse is the highest level of the warehouse management structure and relates directly to storage location or storage locations in SAP MM. The warehouse only relates to a physical entity when it is assigned to a storage location. It is important for customers to understand that a warehouse can be assigned to one or more storage locations.

Example

A manufacturer of small hand tools in Bangor, Maine, had implemented SAP ERP five years before they purchased the tool business from a Vermont-based company that had declared Chapter 11 bankruptcy. The existing Bangor location used SAP IM to operate the warehouse at several storage locations. The new business line in Vermont had been using their parent company's SAP ECC 6.0 system, and they had implemented the SAP WM functionality to run the warehouse facility. When the company made plans to bring the new Vermont facility onto their existing SAP system, they were undecided as to continue using WM for the new facility, or to just use IM to run both the Bangor and Vermont warehouse facilities.

The company hired a consulting firm to review how each warehouse operated, including warehouse size, the number of employees, the number and types of materials stored, and the number of transactions processed each day. The company was surprised to find that though the Vermont facility they had just purchased was smaller than their existing Bangor facility, operated with fewer employers, and stored a similar number of materials, it processed almost 40% more transactions per day. Upon reviewing the data, the company concluded that they should implement SAP WM at both locations, not only to ensure that the same processes would be used across the company, but also to take advantage of the benefits that were evident in the new warehouse.

The implementation to bring the Vermont warehouse onto the existing SAP system and introduce SAP WM to the existing Bangor warehouse took the company less than four months. Several issues occurred during the project, including creating the data for the existing materials in the existing warehouse and training the Bangor employees to use the new SAP WM functionality.

2.6.2 Storage Types

Different areas can be defined within a warehouse, and these are referred to as storage types. Each company defines their warehouse slightly differently. Warehouses can contain racking, open areas, refrigerated rooms, hot rooms, and so on. Each of these can be defined as storage types within the warehouse.

Example

After 11 years of using an SAP system, a British automotive parts manufacturer lost its contract with a major automotive parts store. To replace the loss of the majority of its sales, the company bid for and won several smaller contracts with customers operating automotive parts stores in Europe, Russia, and South America.

The manufacturer had been producing only 60 parts for their major customer, so warehouse operations had been relatively simple, with four racks for finished goods and a single rack for raw materials, each of which was designated as a storage type. Because of the small number of finished goods that they stored and shipped, warehouse staff knew where the parts were located, so inventory accuracy was very high and the warehouse processed outbound deliveries with minimum delays.

Once the manufacturer started work on the new contracts, the number of finished goods they produced exceeded 500. Correspondingly, the raw materials required increased, and warehouse supervisors informed management that the area designated for the raw materials was exhausted and that warehouse operators had to store finished goods outside of the racking area due to size limitations.

A review of the warehouse layout was quickly performed, and it was found that the existing racking systems were not sufficient to handle the increase in raw materials and finished goods. The review also proposed changes to the way the warehouse was described in SAP WM, including increasing the number of storage types to reflect the changes in the warehouse.

Based on the review, the manufacturer changed the racking system to accommodate larger items, increased the size of the raw material area, and rented a smaller warehouse facility close to the airport so that deliveries ready to ship were not taking up room in the main warehouse. The warehouse structure in the SAP system was changed so that there were different storage types for categories of parts they were manufacturing. The changes to the warehouse layout brought inventory accuracy back to an acceptable level; with the changes to storage types and the corresponding removal strategies, delays in processing deliveries were reduced.

2.6.3 Storage Bins

The storage bin is the smallest unit of storage in the warehouse. There is no set size for a storage bin, and its size can vary between companies, warehouses, and even within the same storage type. A storage bin can be a location on a shelf, a location on a carousel, or a plastic tub on a rack.

Example

Due to the economic downturn in the United States, a Canadian distributor of electrical components purchased the inventory of several failed companies in the United States, Canada, and Mexico. As the inventory was shipped to the company's main facility in Windsor, Ontario, the items were identified, material master records created in the SAP system, labels produced, and the items stored in the warehouse.

The warehouse staff had not been given detailed instructions about where to store the incoming items, and they were told to just store them where there was space, make a note of where they had stored them, and then give the information to the warehouse clerk. The information was then supposed to be entered into the SAP system so that the items could be available for deliveries. Since the warehouse operated three shifts, the staff on the third shift performed most of the putaway of the new items in the warehouse. The information was not entered into the system SAP immediately because a warehouse clerk was on site only during the first and second shifts. When the clerks arrived, there were often dozens of pieces of paper with incomplete information about the items and their locations.

After a monthly physical inventory, the warehouse was found to have below 70% accuracy. The company immediately halted the putaway of incoming items until the problem was fixed. The inventory count indicated that some storage bins closest to the area where the incoming inventory was stored contained over 50 different materials, some of which had no inventory entered into the SAP system.

The company reviewed their warehouse layout and found that many storage bins were too large, storing more items than expected. The existing bins had been used to allow large quantities of the same part to be stored in one location. The company changed the size of bins, creating almost a third more storage bins, and transferred items from congested bin locations to new bins. Another inventory count was performed after the new bins were created, and inventory accuracy had improved to over 90%. In addition, the company introduced a more stringent process of placing new stock into the warehouse to avoid the situation occurring again.

2.6.4 Quants

A quant is a quantity of material with the same material number and the same batch number (if the material is batch managed) located in a single storage bin. The total quantity of material in a quant can be increased or decreased through the addition or removal of material from the storage bin.

Example

A German manufacturer and distributor of electronic components had been an SAP customer for almost 15 years and was operating an ECC 6.0 system using WM. The warehouse in its Hamburg location primarily contained parts used in consumer products such as laptop computers, MP3 players, and smartphones. As well as manufacturing custom electronic components, the company imported items from manufacturers in Japan, South Korea, China, and Malaysia. The company would purchase an item from vendors in more than one country, and these were stored in the warehouse in the same storage bin. When a sales order was picked, the warehouse staff would take parts from the storage bin without knowing the origin of the item.

This process had been in place for many years; often the item did not indicate where it had been manufactured. Unfortunately, the company began to receive requests from its customers to indicate where the items were manufactured, and in many cases, the customers would not accept materials made in certain countries.

This trend caused the manufacturer to change its processes for imported materials. The first change was to ensure that its vendors label each part with their batch number and the country of manufacture and to check that the country of manufacture was consistent for the items they were sending. The next step was to manage all materials in the warehouse batch and, as a delivery arrives from a vendor, create a batch record using the vendor's batch number. The batch record was updated with the region or country of origin. After putaway, it was then possible to identify the country of manufacturer for each quant so that when staff picked material for a delivery, the correct quant would be pulled.

2.7 Summary

In this chapter, we have discussed the overall warehouse structure with regard to the physical layout of the warehouse. Configuration of the warehouse, its assignment to a storage location, and storage type setup are all parts of the initial warehouse design.

The importance of this initial design work cannot be stressed enough. The physical warehouse has to be represented in the SAP system, and it is the job of the WM consultant to understand the needs of the warehouse staff and day-to-day warehouse operations. Observation is the key to acquiring this knowledge.

Forcing the warehouse to fit into a theoretical design in the SAP system that does not reflect the operations of the existing warehouse can cause significant problems for shipping and receiving. If the warehouse cannot ship products, or production cannot manufacture products because stock is not available in the warehouse, the company loses money.

In Chapter 3, we will discuss the stock management aspects of WM and its integration with the material master.

Stock management is an important aspect of warehouse management. This chapter takes into account not just the SAP WM material master data, but also how stock is categorized in the warehouse, including batch and shelf life expiration functionality.

3 Stock Management

In this chapter, we will discuss the stock management aspects of material stored in warehouse management locations. Material that is stored in SAP WM–managed locations requires additional data entry to exploit the functionality of the warehouse. A material that is stored only in a storage location and not in a warehouse does not require information on the material master other than that relating to the storage location.

A material that is stored in a warehouse needs the material master to be extended for the specific warehouses and storage types in which it is stored. You may need to enter hazardous material information in the warehouse section of the material master if the material can be hazardous.

This chapter covers stock management in detail, as it relates to SAP WM.

3.1 Warehouse Management Data in the Material Master

Each material that is stored in a warehouse-managed storage location needs to have that information entered in the warehouse management area of the material master. Without that data, the material cannot be stored in a storage bin in the warehouse.

> **Note**
> The material master screens and fields we are about to discuss relate to SAP ECC 6.0. Please be aware that other versions of SAP ECC may have a different number of screens for WM, and different fields may be displayed.

Let's now take an in-depth look at the material master, starting with its creation.

3.1.1 Creating the Material Master

You create a material is created in an SAP system using Transaction MM01 or via the menu path SAP • LOGISTICS • LOGISTICS EXECUTION • WAREHOUSE MANAGEMENT • MASTER DATA • MATERIAL • CREATE.

You can create the material with the SAP system automatically, assigning the next available material number based on the internal number ranges configured in the IMG: Transaction MMNR. The material can also be created with the material number provided for data entry. The data governance (DG) team maintains external numbering.

Figure 3.1 shows that the initial screen for entering a material master requires the entry of an industry sector and a material type.

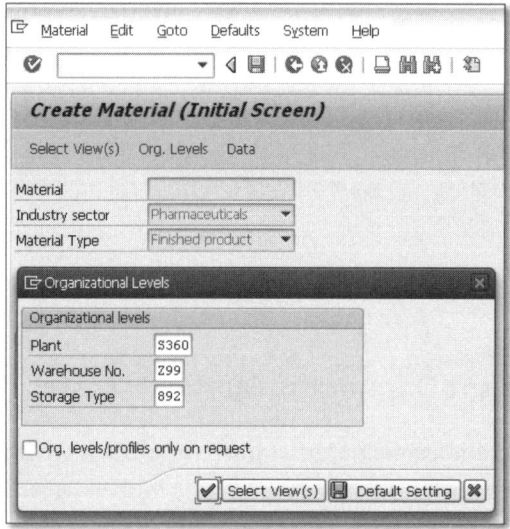

Figure 3.1 Create Material Master for Warehouse-Relevant Material: Transaction MM01

Industry Sector

You must assign the industry sector for each material master record added. In general, SAP customers use just one industry sector for all their material master records, but this is not mandatory.

To configure the industry sectors, use Transaction OMS3 or the menu path IMG • LOGISTICS — GENERAL • MATERIAL MASTER • FIELD SELECTION • DEFINE INDUSTRY SECTORS AND INDUSTRY SECTOR-SPECIFIC SCREEN SELECTION.

The SAP ECC 6.0 system has several predefined industry sectors, including:

- Pharmaceutical industry
- Chemical industry
- Mechanical engineering
- Automotive industry

Defining a new industry sector requires the choice of a single character for the industry sector and a description. The new industry sector must be linked to a field reference. You define this field reference in Transaction OMS9 or via the menu path IMG • LOGISTICS — GENERAL • MATERIAL MASTER • FIELD SELECTION • MAINTAIN FIELD SELECTION FOR DATA SCREENS

The field reference comprises a list of material master fields and determines whether the individual field is hidden, displayed, optional entry, or required entry. You should consider carefully when configuring a new field reference.

> **Note**
> If materials that are pharmaceuticals are entered into the material master, it may be necessary for those materials to have the EAN (European Article Numbering) category entered. In the configuration, you need to make the field mandatory for pharmaceuticals but not for other industries.

Material Type

A material type is a group of materials with similar attributes. The material type enables management of different materials in a uniform manner. SAP is delivered with several standard material types:

- **CONT—kanban container**
  SAP delivers this material type for creating kanban containers. These materials only have the basic data view.
- **DIEN—services**
  Services are either internally supplied or externally supplied by a vendor. Service

material master records do not have storage information. The services can involve activities such as consulting, garbage collection, and legal services.

- **ERSA — spare parts**
  Spare parts are materials used for equipment maintenance in the plant. The material is purchased and stored like any other purchased item, but a spare part is not sold and therefore does not contain sales information. If a maintenance item is sold, this should use a different material type, such as a trading good.

- **FERT — finished good**
  A finished good is a material that has been manufactured by some form of production from items such as raw materials. The finished good is not purchased, so it does not contain any purchasing information.

- **FHMI — production resources/tools (PRTs)**
  PRTs are purchased and used by the plant maintenance department. This material type is assigned to items used in the maintenance of plant equipment, such as test machines, drill bits, and calibrating tools. The material type for PRTs does not contain sales information, because the PRTs are not purchased to sell. In addition, PRTs are only managed on a quantity basis.

- **HALB — semi-finished goods**
  Semi-finished products are often purchased and then completed and sold as finished goods. The semi-finished products can come from another part of the company or from a vendor. The semi-finished material type allows for purchasing and work scheduling, but not for sales.

- **HAWA — trading goods**
  Trading goods are generally materials purchased from vendors and sold. This type of material type only allows purchasing and sales information, as no internal operations are carried out on these materials.

- **HERS — manufacturer parts**
  Manufacturer parts are materials that can be supplied by different vendors who use different part numbers to identify the material.

- **HIBE — operating supplies**
  Operating supplies are vendor-purchased and used in the production process. This HIBE material type can contain purchasing data but not sales information. This type of product includes lubricants, compressed air, and solder.

- **IBAU — maintenance assembly**
  Maintenance assembly is not an individual object but a set of logical elements to separate technical objects into clearly defined units for plant maintenance. For example, a car can be a technical object; the engine, transmission, axles, and other components are the maintenance assemblies. An IBAU material type contains basic data and classification data.

- **KMAT — configurable material**
  Configurable materials form the basis for variant configuration. The KMAT material type is used for all variant configuration materials. A material of this type can have variables that the user determines during the sales process. For example, automotive equipment may have variable attributes that each car manufacturer needs to be different for each car, such as length of chain or height of belt.

- **LEER — empties**
  Empties are materials consisting of returnable transport packaging and can be subject to a nominal deposit fee paid to the owner of the pallet by the company renting them. Empties are usually sent to a company by their vendors. Empties can be made from several materials, grouped together in a bill of material assigned to a finished material. An example of an empty is a crate, drum, bottle, or pallet.

- **LEIH — returnable packaging**
  Reusable packaging material is used to pack finished goods to send to the customer. When the finished good is unpacked, the customer is obliged to return the returnable packaging material to the vendor. This material type is used in the sales process, where the material type for empties (LEER) usually refers to the packaging your company gets from its vendors.

- **NLAG — nonstock material**
  The nonstock material type is used for materials that are not held in stock and not inventoried. These materials can be called consumables and include maintenance gloves, safety glasses, and grease. Items like these are purchased when needed.

- **PIPE — pipeline material**
  The pipeline material type is assigned to materials that are brought into the production facility by pipeline. Materials like this are not planned for because they are always at hand. This material type is used, for example, for oil, water, electricity, or natural gas.

- **ROH—raw materials**
  Raw material is purchased material that is fed into the production process and may result in a finished good. There is no sales data for a raw material, as it is not sold. If the company wants to classify a material that would normally be treated as a raw material, then it should be classified as a trading good.

- **UNBW—non-valuated material**
  The non-valuated material type is similar to the NLAG (non-stock material) type, except that the non-valuated material is held by quantity and not by value. This is often seen in plant maintenance, where there are materials that are extremely important to the plant equipment but of little or no other value. Therefore, the plant maintenance department monitors inventory to allow for planned purchases.

- **VERP—packaging material**
  Unlike LEER (empties), the packaging material type applies to materials that are packaging but are free of charge to the customer in the delivery process. This does not mean that the packaging material has no value; often, the packaging material has a value, and a physical inventory is recorded.

- **WETT—competitive products**
  The sales department uses this material type to monitor competitors' goods. The material type is used to identify these types of products. Only basic data is held for these materials.

If one of the standard material types is not appropriate for the SAP client, then a new material type can be configured in Transaction OMS2 using the menu path IMG • LOGISTICS — GENERAL • MATERIAL MASTER • BASIC SETTINGS • MATERIAL TYPES • DEFINE ATTRIBUTES FOR MATERIAL TYPE.

You create a new material type by selecting an existing material type and copying to a new one. Copying from an existing material type reduces the amount of configuration required. The four-character material type should always start with a Z for a user-defined material type.

Organizational Levels

Any material that is to be used in the warehouse must have the correct organizational level data entered. For warehouse materials, these are plant, warehouse number, and storage type. Once this data is entered, the material master record can be created and the correct level of data expected.

3.1.2 Entering Data into WM Screens

In SAP ECC 6.0, there are two WM data entry screens for the material master. In other versions, there may only be one. Please use this section as a guide.

> **Note**
> You may not see all the data fields in this section in your version of SAP ECC.

Other data is entered into the SAP system before data is entered into the WM screens. Basic data such as material description, unit of measure, purchasing information, and so on will have been entered.

In Figure 3.2, the system has assigned the material a number, and a description and base unit of measure have been added for the new material. Other data relevant for warehouse management can be added to this screen.

Figure 3.2 First WM Screens for Entering WM Data into the Material Master: Transaction MM01

WM Unit of Measure

Like the other units of measure, this WM unit is the unit of measure defined for the material as it moves through the warehouse. For example, a material such as a can of soda may be sold in single units, but in the warehouse the material is moved in crates of 24 cans for ease of movement.

Unit of Issue

This UNIT OF ISSUE field allows the warehouse department to define a different unit of measure for items issued from the warehouse, as an alternative to the base unit of measure.

Proposed Unit of Measure from Material

This field defines how the warehouse unit of measure was derived. The options for this field are to allow the unit of measure to be the base unit of measure for the material, where this field is left blank. The other options are as follows:

- **A**
  WM unit of measure to be the same as the issue unit of measure
- **B**
  WM unit of measure to be the same as the ordering unit of measure

WM Unit of Measure Used in the Warehouse Picking Storage Type

The picking storage type is used by planning as the storage type that will contain material used in rough-cut planning. For example, in the production planning procedure, the high level of planning—called rough-cut planning—uses the material levels from this defined storage type for creating production plans.

Batch Management

The BATCH MANAGEMENT checkbox configures the material to allow batches to be created for the material. This checkbox is found in several other screens on the material master—such as purchasing, plant/storage, and MRP—and might already be activated. If other staff members are authorized to enter material master information, the batch management checkbox may be selected and will appear on the warehouse screen as already highlighted.

Hazardous Material Number

A hazardous material number can be assigned to the material at the client level. This links the material number with the hazardous material information defined for that hazardous material number, such as water pollutant, hazardous storage class, or warnings. The hazardous material is defined not in configuration, but in the logistics execution functionality. You can create a hazardous material with Transaction VM01 or via the menu path SAP MENU • LOGISTICS • LOGISTICS EXECUTION • MASTER DATA • HAZARDOUS MATERIAL • CREATE.

Gross Weight

The gross weight of one unit of the material should be added to this screen, with the correct unit of measure for the weight, to ensure that any limitation on bin storage is calculated correctly.

Volume

The VOLUME and volume unit of measure of the material also are critical to ensuring that the material is correctly stored in the warehouse. Any incorrect data entry on the material master can cause problems during putaway.

Stock Removal Field

The STOCK REMOVAL field enables users to enter the storage type checkbox that defines the sequence in which storage types are searched in order to pick the material in the warehouse. The storage type checkbox can be defined in Transaction OMLY. The menu navigation is IMG • LOGISTICS EXECUTION • WAREHOUSE MANAGEMENT • STRATEGIES • ACTIVATE STORAGE TYPE SEARCH.

Storage Section Checkbox

The storage section search is a more specific strategy for stock placement, as it defines one level below the storage type search for stock placement. The storage section checkbox (STORAGE SECTION IND.) must be defined for each warehouse and storage type. The strategy allows up to 10 storage sections to be defined in sequence for the placement strategy. The configuration can be found in Transaction OMLZ or the menu path IMG • LOGISTICS EXECUTION • WAREHOUSE MANAGEMENT • STRATEGIES • ACTIVATE STORAGE SECTION SEARCH.

Special Movement Checkbox

The SPECIAL MOVEMENT checkbox allows the material to be identified as requiring a special goods movement. The checkbox is configured in SAP WM to allow special processing for a group of materials. You can find the configuration by following the menu path IMG • LOGISTICS EXECUTION • WAREHOUSE MANAGEMENT • MASTER DATA • MATERIAL • DEFINE SPECIAL MOVEMENT INDICATORS.

Once the special movement checkbox has been defined, it can be used in the LE-WM interface to inventory management, where the configuration determines the warehouse management movement type. The special movement checkbox can allow certain materials assigned with that checkbox to behave differently during goods movements. You can access the configuration for the warehouse goods movements via the menu path IMG • LOGISTICS EXECUTION • WAREHOUSE MANAGEMENT • INTERFACES • INVENTORY MANAGEMENT • DEFINE MOVEMENT TYPES.

Two-Step Picking

In WM, you can choose between one-step and two-step picking for materials. If the materials are large and bulky, one-step removal is optimal. However, if the materials to be picked are small and numerous, then one-step picking may not be an efficient use of warehouse resources.

Therefore, two-step picking is used to minimize workload. The two-step process defines an interim storage type (normally 200) to which items are picked and transferred; from there, the final pick takes place. The menu path for the configuration for two-step picking is IMG • LOGISTICS EXECUTION • WAREHOUSE MANAGEMENT • INTERFACES • SHIPPING • DEFINE 2-STEP PICKING.

Stock Placement Field

The STOCK PLACEMENT field acts in a manner similar to the stock removal field, except that the strategy defined in the storage type search is for a placement strategy rather than a removal strategy.

Bulk Storage Checkbox

Within the placement strategies, it is possible to define how bulk materials should be placed in stock. You can use the BULK STORAGE checkbox if the bulk storage placement strategy has been activated in WM. The bulk storage checkbox can indicate the height or width of a particular storage type. Use Transaction OMM4 for this configuration or follow the menu path IMG • LOGISTICS EXECUTION • WAREHOUSE MANAGEMENT • STRATEGIES • PUTAWAY STRATEGIES • DEFINE STRATEGY FOR BULK STORAGE.

Message to Inventory Management

The MESSAGE TO IM field is used if the warehouse management system is decentralized. If the checkbox is selected, it allows the warehouse management information for this material to be sent to IM immediately.

> **Tip**
>
> If your company uses Extended Warehouse Management (EWM) on a separate server, then the communication between the regular SAP system and EWM may require that this checkbox be selected.

Allow Addition to Stock

Selecting the ALLOW ADDN TO STOCK checkbox allows the system to add material to the existing stock of the same material in the same storage bin. This is only true if the characteristics of the two quantities of material are the same. If the storage type table does not allow additions to existing stock for this storage type, the checkbox is redundant.

Figure 3.3 shows the second screen for WM data entry for a material. The organizational level for this screen is the storage type level. The data on this screen relates to the storage type displayed.

Palletization Data

Palletization is used in storage unit handling within WM. The palletization process uses pallets to store and move material in the warehouse. The palletization data determines how the material should be entered into stock. It may be possible to place the material into storage in different ways depending on what storage unit type is being used.

3 | Stock Management

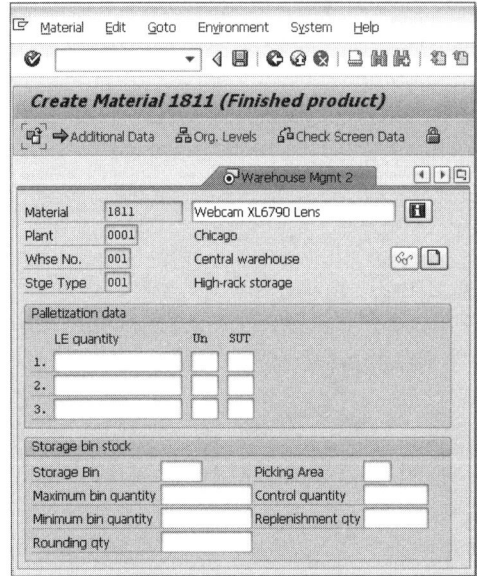

Figure 3.3 Second WM Screen for Entering WM Data into the Material Master: Transaction MM01

Loading Equipment Quantity

The loading equipment quantity (LE QUANTITY) entered here is the amount of material to be placed on the storage unit type. For example, if the quantity is to be loaded on a standard pallet—which is a storage unit type—the quantity may be 24.

Unit of Measure

The UN field is the unit of measure for the loading equipment quantity, entered in the previous field. For example, the quantity may be 24, and the unit of measure can be EA, for each.

Storage Unit Type

The storage unit type (SUT) describes how the material is stored in the storage bin. For instance, some bins may not accommodate a full pallet due to height restrictions, but a half pallet may fit. Therefore, the warehouse can define a storage unit type that defines a half pallet and the quantity of the material that can fit on that half pallet.

Suppose that 30 boxes of a material are equivalent to one half pallet. The storage unit type is configured in the IMG and has to be activated in each warehouse before it can be used. The storage unit type for each plant is defined. You can make the configuration by following the menu path IMG • LOGISTICS EXECUTION • WAREHOUSE MANAGEMENT • MASTER DATA • MATERIAL • DEFINE STORAGE UNIT TYPES.

Storage Bin

The storage bin is the lowest level of storage defined in the warehouse. This field allows the warehouse user to enter a storage bin that this material will be added to for the plant/storage type combination. Pressing the [F4] function key makes it possible to display the empty storage bins.

Maximum Bin Quantity

This value defines the maximum quantity of a material that can be entered into any storage bin defined in the storage type. The quantity is defined in the base unit of measure, not the WM unit of measure. For example, the bin quantity may be 300 units of material, but this may be equivalent to a partial quantity in WM units—for example, 7.45—so the base unit of measure is used for capacity calculations.

Minimum Bin Quantity

This field allows the warehouse users to define a minimum quantity that can be stored in the bin locations for this storage type. This results in efficient use of storage bins. For example, if the material is small, the maximum bin quantity is high, and no minimum quantity is set. As a result, there could be many bins containing small amounts of stock. Entering a minimum bin quantity allows the bin to be used efficiently and minimizes picking. Like the other quantities, the minimum bin quantity is recorded in the base quantity unit.

Rounding Quantity

This quantity is used if the material is subject to the quantity-dependent picking strategy. The rounding quantity is the figure that the picking quantities are rounded down to for this material/storage type combination. This quantity is also defined in the base unit of measure.

Picking Area

A picking area is a group of warehouse management storage bins that are used for picking. The picking area is similar to the definition of storage section. You can configure the picking area by following the menu path IMG • LOGISTICS EXECUTION • WAREHOUSE MANAGEMENT • MASTER DATA • DEFINE PICKING AREAS.

Control Quantity

The control quantity defines for a particular storage type the amount of material that reaches the level where stock removal can take place. Similar to the maximum bin quantity, the control quantity is in the material base unit of measure.

Replenishment Quantity

The replenishment quantity defines the quantity that should be placed in the storage bin. Similar to other quantities, the replenishment quantity is recorded in the base quantity unit of measure.

This section has discussed the warehouse management data found in the material master record for a material. In the next section, we will discuss the types of stock that are found in the warehouse.

3.2 Types of Warehouse Stock

The warehouse contains different types of stock: available, unavailable, and so on. There are also special stocks, such as project stock and consignment stock, which need to be managed separately from other stock. In this section, we will discuss the different types of stock found in the warehouse.

3.2.1 Stock Categories

Although the warehouse staff can physically see the stock in the storage bins, the WM system determines that the stock has a particular category that determines what can happen to it.

Available Stock

This is unrestricted stock. It is not subject to any restrictions on its use. The material can be picked, put away, and transferred between bins. Figure 3.4 displays a detail screen from the warehouse stock overview (Transaction LS26) and shows the available stock for a material in a warehouse. You can find Transaction LS26 by following the menu path SAP MENU • LOGISTICS • LOGISTICS EXECUTION • MASTER DATA • MATERIAL • STOCK • STOCK OVERVIEW.

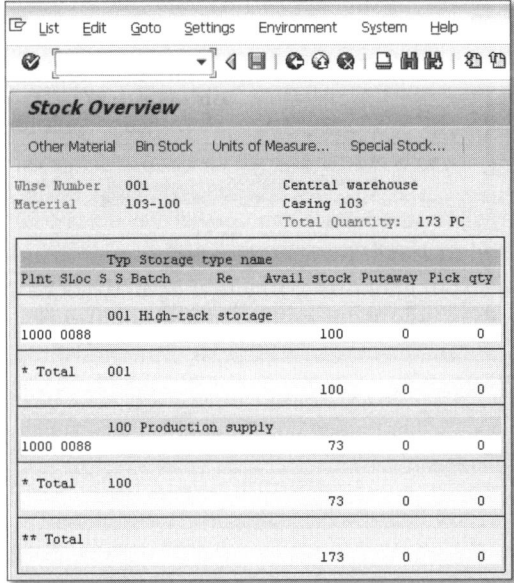

Figure 3.4 Detail Screen from the Warehouse Stock Overview: Transaction LS26

The material illustrated in Figure 3.4 is in two storage types:

- High-rack storage
- Shelf storage

All the material is in available stock.

Inspection Stock

This stock carries the stock category Q to indicate that it is undergoing quality inspection. Stock in quality inspection has been valuated but does not count as unrestricted use stock.

3 Stock Management

The inspection data in the Quality Management (QM) view of the material master determines whether a percentage of stock is to be designated as inspection stock when it is received in the warehouse. After the stock has been inspected and a usage decision has been made, the warehouse user can make a transfer posting in IM and a subsequent posting change in WM to remove the category Q to convert it back to available stock.

In Figure 3.5, you can see there has been a goods receipt of material into the storage location and it has been moved to the shelf storage, storage type 022. Some of the material has been put on a quality inspection hold and some has not. Figure 3.5 displays the stock overview screen of Transaction LS26, which shows that the material in quality inspection has a Q checkbox on the detail line. Those materials not in quality inspection do not have this checkbox.

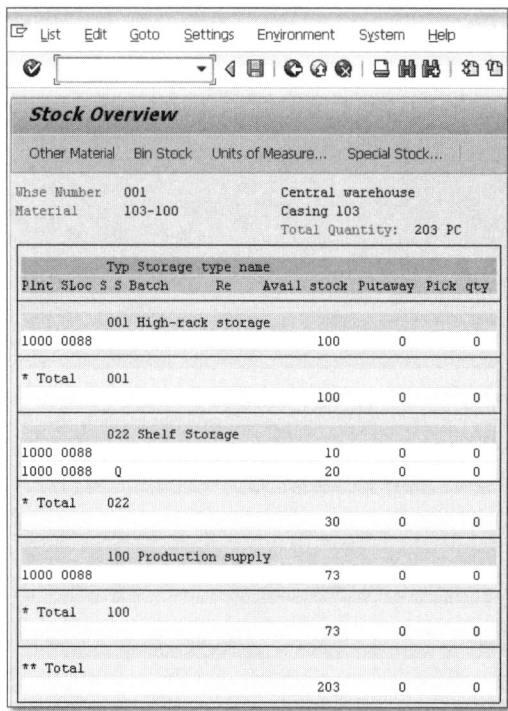

Figure 3.5 Detail Screen from Warehouse Stock Overview: Transaction LS26

Blocked Stock

When goods arrive damaged or unusable at the loading dock, IM provides a function that allows the goods receipt of material to be treated as blocked stock. This stock is displayed in WM with a stock category of S. This stock is processed in exactly the same manner as inspection stock.

The screen displayed in Figure 3.6 shows that there has been a goods receipt of material into the storage location and it has been moved to the shelf storage, storage type 022. This material has been moved into blocked stock. Figure 3.6 displays the stock overview screen of Transaction LS26, which shows that the blocked material has the S checkbox on the detail line.

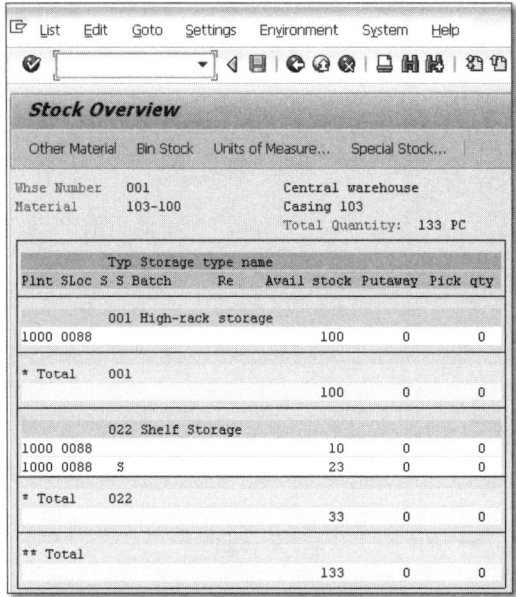

Figure 3.6 Detail Screen from Warehouse Stock Overview: Transaction LS26 (Material Designated as Blocked Stock)

Blocked Stock Returns

When goods are returned from the customer to the warehouse, they are received using the IM movement type 451. In the warehouse management stock overview report LS26, the stock is shown with a stock category of R. This stock is not valuated, and it should not be considered to be available stock. Therefore, it is very important to ensure that this material is kept separate from the available material. Many companies maintain a special area for customer returns or ensure that returns are labeled clearly to prevent the stock from being used.

In Figure 3.7, you can see that there has been a goods receipt for a customer return of material into the storage location, and it has been automatically assigned to storage type 904 for returns. Figure 3.7 displays the stock overview screen of report LS26, which shows that the material in returns has the R checkbox on the detail line.

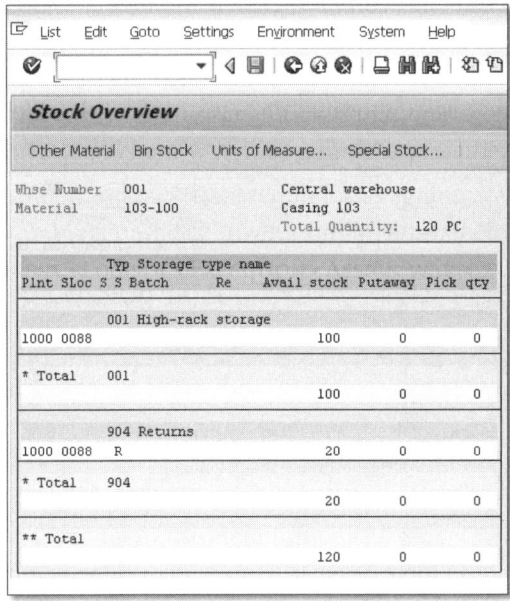

Figure 3.7 Detail Screen from Warehouse Stock Overview: Transaction LS26

3.2.2 Status of Warehouse Stock

As goods arrive at the warehouse, they are moved from the arriving trailers on the loading dock or from the production area to an area where they are officially received. This is usually called the goods receipt area (GR area) and is either near the receiving dock or close to the end of the production line. Once the material has arrived and is received, it is transferred using a transfer order to another storage area within the warehouse.

When the transfer orders are created, they can be confirmed or not confirmed. If they are not confirmed, a period of time elapses between the creation of transfer orders and the movement of material to the final storage bin. The stock that has not been moved thus has two availability statuses: material to be picked and material to be placed. Using the warehouse stock overview Transaction LS26, the system displays the following three headers.

Available Stock

This header defines the total quantity of material quants stored in the warehouse, not including quantities for planned putaway or picks. The display of materials in a bin also shows the total quantity in each storage bin.

Stock for Putaway

This header defines the total material intended for putaway that currently is in nonconfirmed transfer orders, for example, transfer of material from the goods receipt area to available stock. Figure 3.8 shows the amount for storage type 022.

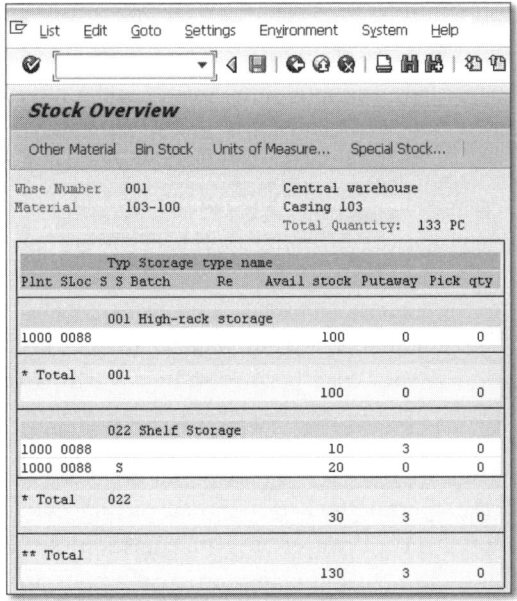

Figure 3.8 Detail Screen from Warehouse Stock Overview: Transaction LS26 (Material in Stock for Putaway Column)

Pick Quantity

The PICK QTY field defines the total material for picking that is currently in non-confirmed transfer orders, for example, transfer of material from the available stock area to the shipping area. Figure 3.9 shows the pick quantity amount for storage type 001.

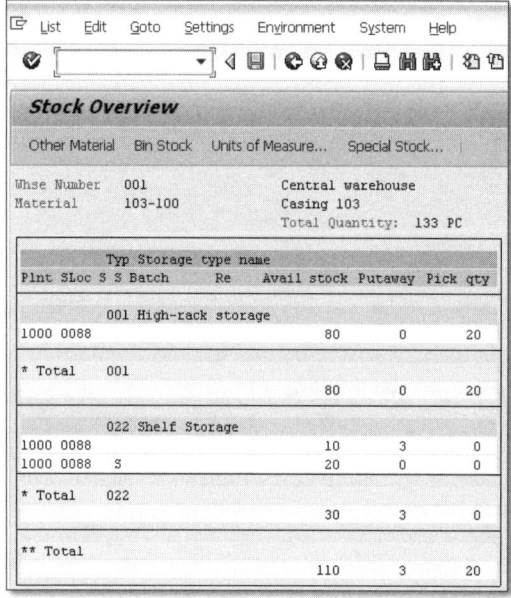

Figure 3.9 Detail Screen from Warehouse Stock Overview: Transaction LS26 (Material in Pick Quantity Column)

3.2.3 Special Stock

Special stock is material that is managed separately from regular stock. These materials are processed differently because they may be owned by a third party or be project stock.

Each category of special stock has its own checkbox, which allows it to be identified on warehouse stock reports. If the special stock is assigned during goods movement transactions, these are shown on the warehouse management stock screens—for example, Transaction LX03—and used in warehouse movement processing.

Sales Order Stock

Individual customer stock is managed with a special stock number and the special stock indicator E. The special stock number is 16 characters long and is a combination of the sales order number, which has 10 characters, and the sales order item, which has 6 characters.

When the system makes inventory movement to goods-receipt a material into a storage location that has a special stock indicator (E), the material is subsequently goods-receipted into an interim storage type in the warehouse. From there, the material is moved via a transfer order to a storage location in the warehouse. Transaction LX03—bin status report—shows the quant in a storage bin with the special stock indicator and the special stock number.

You can find Transaction LX03 by following the menu path SAP MENU • LOGISTICS • LOGISTICS EXECUTION • MASTER DATA • STORAGE BIN • EVALUATIONS • BIN STATUS REPORT.

Figure 3.10 shows the initial selection screen for Transaction LX03. Users can select the warehouse number, storage type, and storage bin combination. They also can use the inventory method, special stock indicator, and other criteria to narrow the selection.

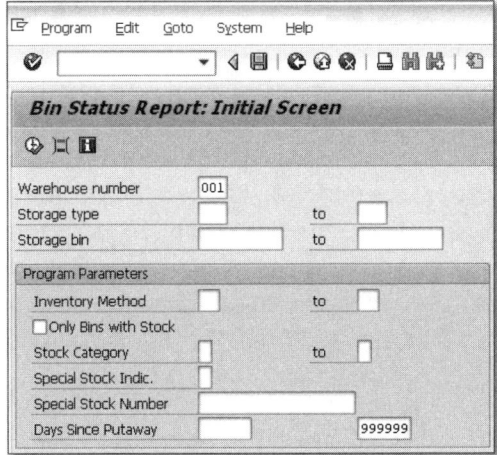

Figure 3.10 Initial Screen for Bin Status Report: Transaction LX03

Figure 3.11 shows the sales order stock with checkbox E and the special stock number, derived from the sales order number and the sales order item number.

3 | Stock Management

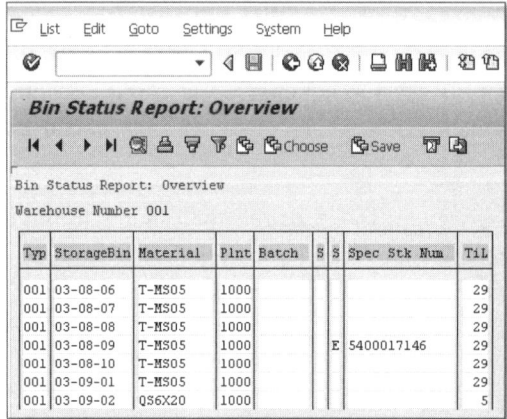

Figure 3.11 Results Screen for Bin Status Report: Transaction LX03 (Sales Order Stock with Checkbox E)

Consignment Stock

Consignment stock is material owned by a vendor but stored at a customer's premises. It is used by the customer in production orders or transferred to the customer's stock, at which time ownership of the material transfers from the vendor to the customer.

The system identifies consignment material in the customer's warehouse by using a special stock indicator, K. This can be seen in the bin status report (Transaction LX03). The special stock number for the vendor's consignment stock is the same as the vendor number.

The vendor's consignment stock is goods-receipted into the warehouse using inventory management transactions for goods receipt; for example, Transaction MB1C. Figure 3.12 shows the vendor consignment stock in storage bin PROD-1320. The system used vendor number 1000 for the special stock number.

Project Stock

Project stock is material that is being stored in the warehouse for a project per a work breakdown structure (WBS) element, defined in the Project Systems module (SAP PS). The material is moved into a storage location by an inventory management transaction, such as MB1C. It can be seen in the bin status report, identified by the special stock indicator Q.

Types of Warehouse Stock | 3.2

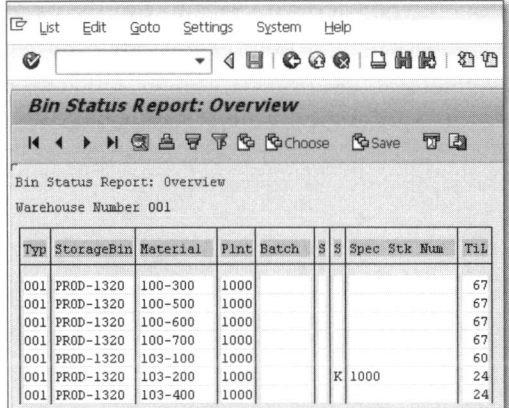

Figure 3.12 Results Screen for Bin Status Report: Transaction LX03 (Vendor Consignment Stock with Checkbox K)

Figure 3.13 shows the project stock in storage bin 05 – 02 – 01. The special stock number for the project stock is the same as the WBS element that was entered in the inventory movement transaction for the goods receipt.

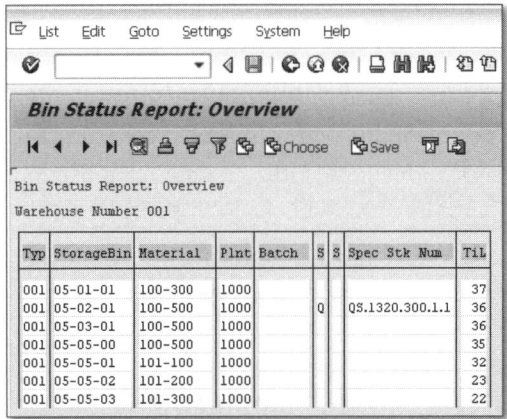

Figure 3.13 Results Screen for Bin Status Report: Transaction LX03 (Project Stock with Checkbox Q)

Returnable Transport Packaging

With returnable transport packaging (RTF), materials may be delivered to the warehouse on, or in, returnable transport packaging, such as pallets or containers. The delivered materials can be removed from the packaging or remain with the packaging in the warehouse. If the returnable packaging is not immediately returned to the vendor, it can be stored in the warehouse. The returnable materials are the property of the vendor and do not become part of the customer's valuated stock.

The returnable transport packaging is identified in the customer's warehouse by using a special stock indicator, M. This can be seen in the bin status report (Transaction LX03). Figure 3.14 shows the project stock in storage bin 05 – 05 – 01. The special stock number for the returnable transport packaging stock is the same as the number of the vendor that supplied the packaging material.

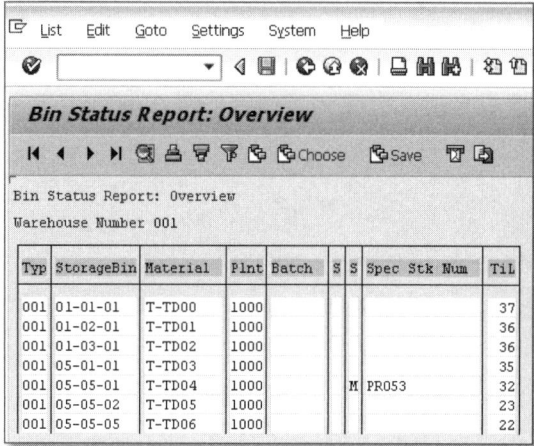

Figure 3.14 Results Screen for the Bin Status Report: Transaction LX03 (Returnable Transport Packaging with Checkbox M)

This section described the types of stock that can be found in the warehouse. Next, we will discuss the role of batch management in the warehouse.

3.3 Batch Management in Warehouse Management

SAP WM users can configure created materials to be batch managed. This requires that for each movement or processing of the material, the quantity of material associated with that movement or process be identified by one or many unique batch numbers.

3.3.1 Batch Definition

A batch is a quantity of material grouped for various reasons. The materials often have the same characteristics and values. For instance, in the chemical industry a certain number of containers of a certain product may be considered a batch because they were produced at the same time and have the same physical and chemical characteristics. These characteristics may differ from those of another batch of material produced on the same day.

> **Note**
>
> The pharmaceutical industry is one sector where material batches are extremely important. Each batch of material is recorded throughout the product and distribution process. In case of a product recall, the batch number stamped on the pack or bottle of material provides the needed identification.

To understand how important batch recording has become, consider the regulations in the European Union (EU). The EU requires that each batch of pharmaceutical material imported into the EU must be accompanied by a batch certificate. This must specify the testing specifications of the product, analytical methods and test results, and statements that indicate that it conforms to current Good Manufacturing Procedures (cGMP) and has been signed off by a company official.

3.3.2 Batch Level

The batch number can be determined at different levels. You need to make this determination early in any implementation project. Batches can be determined at the client level, plant level, and material level.

Client Level

If the batch level is configured at the client level, the batch number can only be assigned once throughout the SAP client. One batch number exists for one batch regardless of material or location. This poses no problem when batches are moved from plant to plant, as the batch number does not exist in the receiving plant. This is a level where, in some countries, batch numbers are unique to a company and not to a material.

Plant Level

Batch level at the plant level is the SAP default. This means the batch is unique to a plant and material but is not applicable across the company. Therefore, a batch of material at a different plant within the company can have the same batch number as another batch with different characteristics. When batch material is transferred from one plant to another, the batch information is not transferred, and the batch information needs to be re-entered at the receiving plant.

Material Level

Batch level at the material level means the batch number is unique to a material across all plants. Therefore, if a batch of material is transferred to another plant, the batch information will be adopted in the new plant without re-entering the batch information. This is because that batch number cannot have been duplicated for that material in the receiving plant.

3.3.3 Batch Number Assignment

The batch number range is predefined in SAP systems. The predefined range 01 is defined as 0000000001 to 9999999999. The number range object for this is BATCH_CLT. You can change this in configuration with Transaction OMAD or via the menu path IMG • LOGISTICS — GENERAL • BATCH MANAGEMENT • BATCH NUMBER ASSIGNMENT • MAINTAIN INTERNAL BATCH NUMBER ASSIGNMENT RANGE.

Two configuration steps can be carried out if the customer requires batch number assignment:

1. Assign the batch number internally using the internal number range. To configure this use Transaction OMCZ or follow the menu path IMG • LOGISTICS — GENERAL • BATCH MANAGEMENT • BATCH NUMBER ASSIGNMENT • ACTIVATE INTERNAL BATCH NUMBER ASSIGNMENT • ACTIVATE BATCH NUMBER ASSIGNMENT.

2. Configure the system to allow the automatic numbering of batches on a goods receipt with account assignment. Follow the menu path IMG • LOGISTICS — GENERAL • BATCH MANAGEMENT • BATCH NUMBER ASSIGNMENT • ACTIVATE INTERNAL BATCH NUMBER ASSIGNMENT • INTERNAL BATCH NUMBER ASSIGNMENT FOR ASSIGNED GOODS RECEIPT.

3.3.4 Creating a Batch Record

The batch record can be created manually through the SAP menu with Transaction MSC1N. The menu path is SAP MENU • LOGISTICS • MATERIALS MANAGEMENT • MATERIAL MASTER • BATCH • CREATE.

To create a batch number for a material, you may need to fill in several key fields such as material number, plant number, and storage location. Other information can be used to describe the batch, such as production date, vendor batch number, last goods receipt date, and so on, as shown in Figure 3.15. The batch number assignment can be configured in the number range transactions in the IMG, as described in Section 3.3.3.

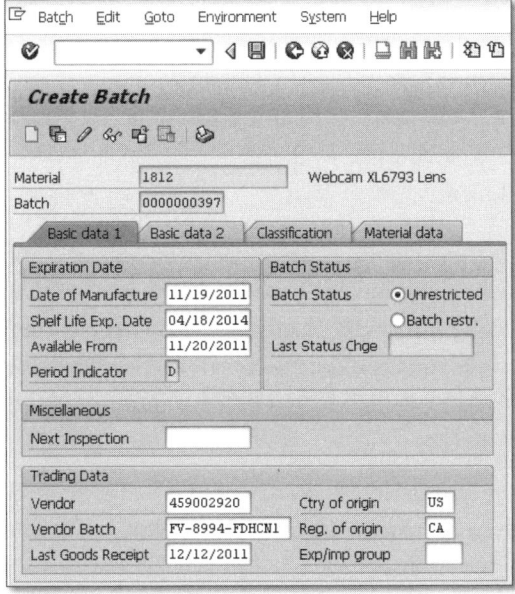

Figure 3.15 Initial Entry Screen for Batch Record Creation: Transaction MSC1N

Production Date

The WM user can enter the date when the batch was produced in this field. In some industries, this field is also used as the date the material was tested or retested. If a material is found to be still useable after the shelf life date has expired, the material can be retested, and the date of the retest is entered in this field, in addition to a new shelf life expiration date. Check with your clients to see how they need to use this field.

Shelf Life Expiration Date

This shelf life expiration date (SLED) is the date on which the shelf life of a batch expires. The shelf life of a product can vary between plants. The expiration date can be used in the sales process, when customers have set a requirement on the number of days of shelf life remaining for a batch to be acceptable. Some companies use this field to indicate the date on which a batch needs to be retested.

Available From

This field indicates when the batch will be available. For example, if a material needs to remain in the quality inspection process for a certain number of days after testing, then the quality assurance department can enter a date to inform other departments when to expect the batch to be available.

Batch Status

The batch status checkbox allows the batch to be classified as having restricted or unrestricted use. If the unrestricted radio button is selected, then no restriction is placed on the batch's use. If the BATCH RESTR. radio button is selected, the batch is treated like blocked stock in planning, but can be selected by batch determination if the search includes restricted use batches.

The batch status can be changed from unrestricted to restricted by changing the checkbox in the batch record. The system posts a material document that shows the movement of stock between the two statuses.

Next Inspection

This date field enables the quality assurance department to enter the date of the next quality inspection of the batch, if applicable to this material.

Vendor Batch

If the material is purchased, then you can add the batch number assigned by the vendor to the batch record. Notation of the vendor batch number is important to any product recall procedure. The vendor batch number field allows a 15-character string to be entered.

3.3.5 Batch Determination

Batch determination in SAP WM uses strategy types, search strategies, and search procedures for identifying a batch in the WM transaction.

The batch determination process uses the same type of selection protocol as found in purchasing pricing conditions; that is, it uses condition tables and access sequences.

Condition Tables

The batch determination condition table consists of fields that are selected and records that are created to assign values to those fields. The WM condition tables can be created in Transaction OMK4, which you can find by following the menu path IMG • LOGISTICS — GENERAL • BATCH MANAGEMENT • BATCH DETERMINATION AND BATCH CHECK • CONDITION TABLES • DEFINE WAREHOUSE MANAGEMENT CONDITION TABLES.

Figure 3.16 shows the field where you enter a new condition table. You also can create a new table by copying the conditions from an existing condition table. In the figure, the search for condition tables has returned five tables that can be copied.

If the condition table is not copied from an existing table, you can assign the fields to the condition table from the field catalog. Figure 3.17 shows that for the new WM condition table, three fields have been selected. Once the condition table is complete, it should then be generated by selecting CONDITION • GENERATE from the menu or by pressing the [Shift]+[F4] function key combination.

Access Sequence

For each batch strategy type, there is a batch determination access sequence. This allows the batch strategy type to access the condition tables in the correct sequence. We will describe the strategy type in the next section. Before configuring the access sequences, note that these access sequences are cross-client. Any changes in one client will affect all clients.

109

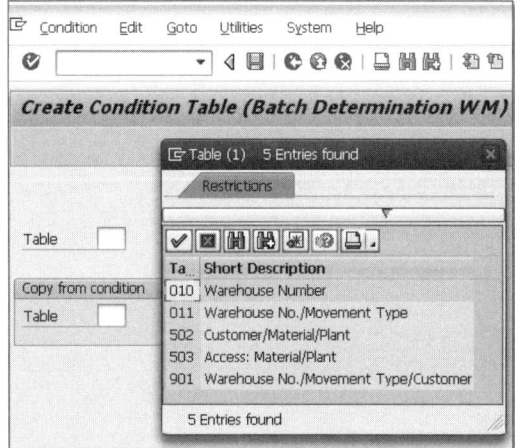

Figure 3.16 Create Warehouse Management Condition Tables for Batch Determination: Transaction OMK4

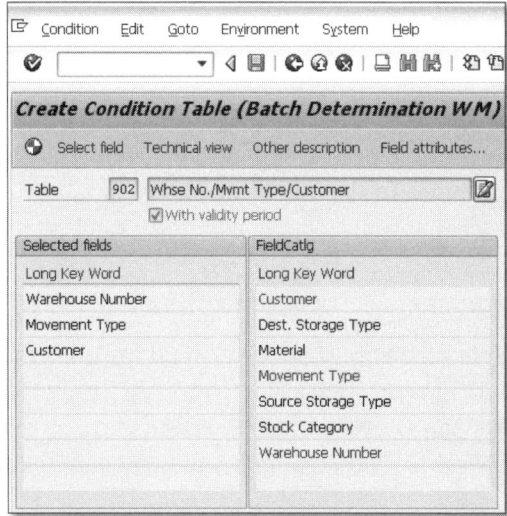

Figure 3.17 Assign Selected Fields for New Warehouse Management Condition Table: Transaction OMK4

You can complete the configuration by following the menu path IMG • LOGISTICS — GENERAL • BATCH MANAGEMENT • BATCH DETERMINATION AND BATCH CHECK • ACCESS SEQUENCES • DEFINE WAREHOUSE MANAGEMENT ACCESS SEQUENCES.

Figure 3.18 shows the access sequence WM02. The access sequence uses condition table 11, and the sequence of the access is defined by the two condition fields. If a new access sequence needs to be created, it should begin with the letter Z to indicate a customer-defined access sequence.

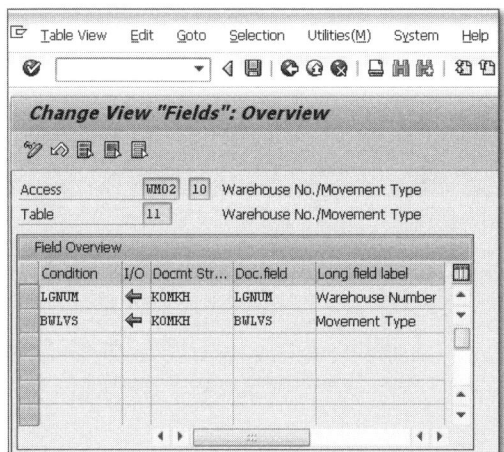

Figure 3.18 Create Access Sequence for Batch Determination

Batch Strategy Type

The batch strategy type is the specification that tells the system what type of criteria to use during the batch determination process. You can configure the batch strategy type by following the menu path IMG • LOGISTICS – GENERAL • BATCH MANAGEMENT • BATCH DETERMINATION AND BATCH CHECK • STRATEGY TYPES • DEFINE WAREHOUSE MANAGEMENT STRATEGY TYPES.

Figure 3.19 shows the strategy type for WM02. The strategy type is defined by a class and its relevant characteristics that define how the strategy works. We define a strategy type so that different scenarios can be used when finding batches. In Figure 3.19, the strategy type is configured with a class, SHELF_LIFE_SEL, which searches for batches in the warehouse that have a certain shelf life. Figure 3.20 shows the class and the characteristics that are defined.

Other strategy types may include a strategy to find batches with a certain shelf life date in the warehouse or a strategy to find batches with a certain production date. The classification data, class, and characteristics can be defined for the required strategy.

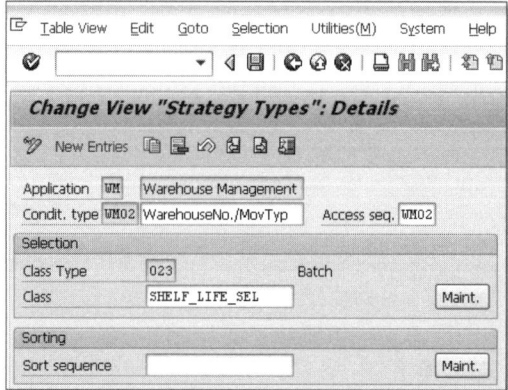

Figure 3.19 Create a Strategy Type for Batch Determination

The selection class function of the strategy type lets you define how batches are sorted when they are located. For example, if the strategy type is to locate certain batches by goods-receipt date, then the class can define how these are displayed. They can be shown either ascending or descending, based on the characteristic criteria in the sort rule.

You can define the selection class in the IMG by using Transaction CU71 or following the menu path IMG • LOGISTICS – GENERAL • BATCH MANAGEMENT • BATCH DETERMINATION AND BATCH CHECK • DEFINE SELECTION CLASSES.

In Figure 3.20, the classification data, class, and characteristics that are defined for the batch strategy type show that there are three characteristics. Therefore, the strategy for selecting batches in the warehouse can be defined accurately based on three criteria, which are shown in Figure 3.20:

- Remaining shelf life for batch
- Batch determined delivery date
- Expiration date, shelf life

The characteristics can be given values so that the selection of the batch falls into the range defined by these three characteristics. Batch strategy types can have classes with more or fewer characteristics, to increase or decrease the specificity of the search for batches.

Batch Management in Warehouse Management | 3.3

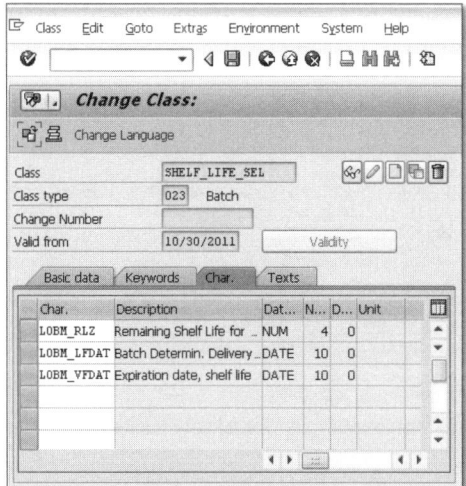

Figure 3.20 Classification Data for Strategy Type for Batch Determination

Batch Search Procedure

You define the batch search procedure to allow the combination of a single or a group of batch strategy types. The procedure is allocated to a warehouse or material movement, where it is used to determine the correct batches for the selection.

To configure the batch search procedure, use Transaction OMKV or follow the menu path IMG • LOGISTICS — GENERAL • BATCH MANAGEMENT • BATCH DETERMINATION AND BATCH CHECK • BATCH SEARCH PROCEDURE DEFINITION • DEFINE WAREHOUSE MANAGEMENT SEARCH PROCEDURE.

Figure 3.21 shows the batch search procedure ZWM001, which uses the three batch strategy types (CTYP), ZWM1, ZW03, and ZWM2, to find relevant batches based upon the criteria within those strategy types. Several search procedures may be required, depending on the batches you need to locate within the warehouse.

> **Example**
>
> When material is removed from a warehouse that has racks, the search procedure may require the shelf life to be the determining factor, whereas determining batches for outside warehouses may require that the batch be determined by the goods-receipt date. The search procedure can be assigned to various warehouses or warehouse/movement type combinations, based on the needs of the supply chain.

113

3 | Stock Management

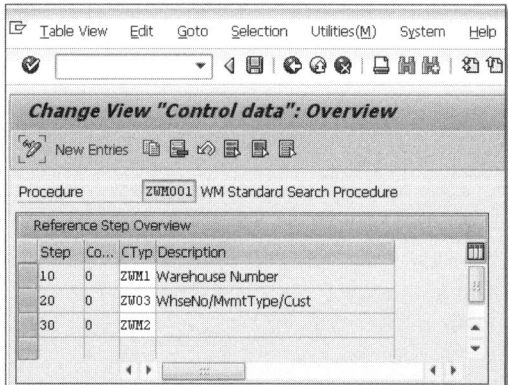

Figure 3.21 Batch Search Procedure with Associated Strategy Types: Transaction OMKV

Batch Search Procedure Assignment

After creating the warehouse search procedures, you can assign them for batch determination based on the warehouse or the warehouse/movement type combination.

You can configure the batch search procedure assignment with Transaction OMK1 or by following the menu path IMG • LOGISTICS — GENERAL • BATCH MANAGEMENT • BATCH DETERMINATION AND BATCH CHECK • BATCH SEARCH PROCEDURE ALLOCATION AND CHECK ACTIVATION • ASSIGN WM SEARCH PROCEDURE.

The transaction allows assignment of the batch search procedure to either a warehouse or a warehouse/movement type combination. Figure 3.22 shows the assignment for a warehouse.

The batch search procedure can be assigned to a warehouse, as shown in Figure 3.22. The procedure determines how batches are determined for the warehouse.

Select the BATCHES IN BULK STGE checkbox if you plan to ignore search strategy for the bulk area storage. In bulk area storage, the batches are mixed and the strategy will not pick out individual batches. Selecting this checkbox ensures that the total stock is included in the batch determination, even though it is batch-neutral.

Figure 3.23 shows the assignment of the batch search procedure to the warehouse/movement type combination. With this part of the transaction, the specific movement type that is used at the warehouse is given a batch search procedure.

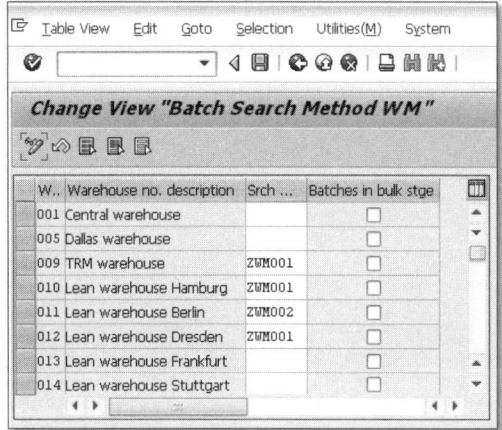

Figure 3.22 Batch Search Procedure Assigned to Warehouse: Transaction OMK1

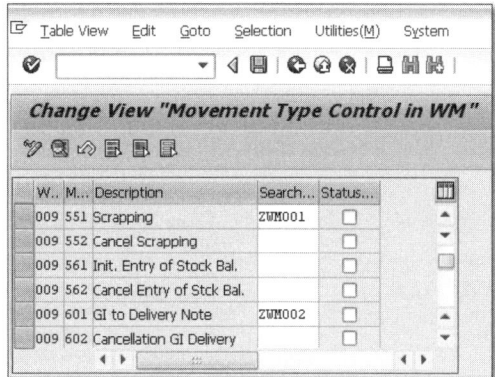

Figure 3.23 Batch Search Procedure Assigned to Warehouse/Movement Type Combination: Transaction OMK1

Select the checkbox shown in Figure 3.23, STATUS "RESTRICTED" AI., if the batches defined as blocked need to be included in the batch determination in the warehouse. Normally, restricted batches are not included in batch determination.

Figure 3.24 shows more details of the assignment of the batch search procedure assigned to the warehouse/movement type combination. To access this screen, select GOTO • DETAILS or press [Ctrl]+[Shift]+[F2].

3 | Stock Management

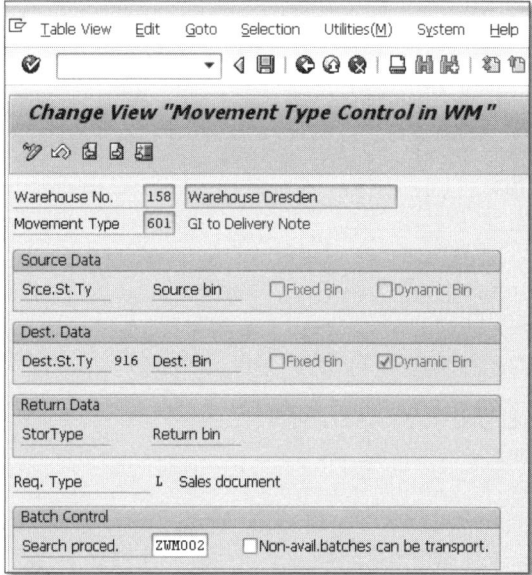

Figure 3.24 Detail Screen of Batch Search Procedure Assigned to Warehouse/Movement Type Combination: Transaction OMK1

This section described the functionality of the batch and functionality such as batch search procedures in the warehouse. Next, we will discuss the important topic of shelf life functionality.

3.4 Shelf Life Functionality

In many industries, such as the grocery and pharmaceutical industries, the shelf life of materials is a very important characteristic, both for sales and for production. It is important that the warehouse management review the shelf life expiration date (SLED) to ensure that material does not expire and have to be scrapped.

3.4.1 Shelf Life and the Material Master

When material is created using the material master record transaction, MM01, you can enter information regarding the shelf life characteristics on the plant storage view.

Figure 3.25 shows the shelf life data that can be added to the material. This data is used in calculating the shelf life expiration date in batch determination. Let's take a quick look at the fields in this figure.

Figure 3.25 Shelf Life Expiration Data Entry on Material Master Record Plant Data Screen

Max Storage Period

This field is for information only and does not have any functionality. Users can define the maximum storage period for a material before it expires. This field can be used for reporting.

Time Unit

This is the unit of measure of the maximum storage period in days, months, and years.

Minimum Remaining Shelf Life

The minimum remaining shelf life field determines whether a material can be received via goods receipt based on the remaining shelf life of the material. If this field has the value 100 days, and the material to be goods-receipted has only 80 days of shelf life left, then the system will not accept the goods receipt. The minimum remaining shelf life field works at the client level and is the same for the material across all plants.

Total Shelf Life

The total shelf life figure is at the client level and does not vary by plant. The total shelf life is the amount of time the materials will be kept, from the production date to the shelf life expiration date. The shelf life is only checked if the expiration date check has been activated. The activation is configured at plant level or movement type level in Transaction OMJ5 or via the menu path IMG • LOGISTICS — GENERAL • BATCH MANAGEMENT • SHELF LIFE EXPIRATION DATE (SLED) • SET EXPIRATION DATE CHECK.

Period Checkbox for Shelf Life Expiration Date

This period field is defined for the shelf life expiration date (SLED) fields used in this material master screen. The period can be defined as months, days, and so on. You can configure the period checkbox in Transaction O02K or via the menu path IMG • LOGISTICS — GENERAL • BATCH MANAGEMENT • SHELF LIFE EXPIRATION DATE (SLED) • MAINTAIN PERIOD INDICATOR.

Rounding Rule SLED

The rounding rule allows the SLED to be rounded up to the nearest unit of the time defined in the period checkbox. For example, if the period checkbox is set to months, then the rounding rule is either the first day of the month or the last day of the month, or there is no change if there is no rounding rule. The rounding rule is for calculated dates rather than dates entered into the record.

3.4.2 Production Date Entry

To ensure that the shelf life expiration date functionality produces the correct results, it is important that the manufacturing date for a batch is entered at the time of goods receipt.

Figure 3.26 shows the goods receipt of a batch of material. The goods receipt requires that a manufacturing date of the batch be entered. This date is used to determine the start date for the calculation of shelf life.

3.4 Shelf Life Functionality

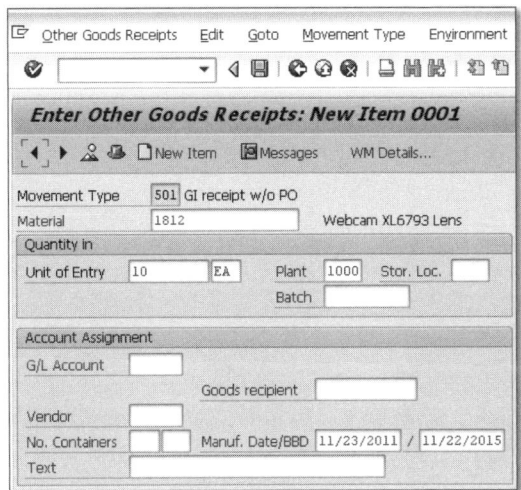

Figure 3.26 Goods Receipt Entry with Batch Production and Best-Before Dates

3.4.3 SLED Control List

The shelf life expiration date control list shows batches in the warehouse that are actively monitored for shelf life. To run the SLED control list, use Transaction LX27 or follow the menu path SAP • LOGISTICS • LOGISTICS EXECUTION • WAREHOUSE MANAGEMENT • MASTER DATA • MATERIAL • EVALUATIONS • SLED CONTROL LIST.

Remaining Shelf Life

The remaining shelf life field (REMSL) restricts the results of the report. This field is the upper limit for the remaining shelf lives of all materials that are to be selected. It can be used in the shelf life calculation in two ways depending on what checkbox is selected. It can refer to either the total remaining shelf life or the remaining shelf life in the warehouse.

Figure 3.27 shows the selection criteria that can be entered for the shelf life expiration date control list. The report shows the batches of product in the warehouse that is active for SLED, which is shown in Figure 3.28.

The report shows whether the batch is in exception; that is, if the shelf life is below the minimum stated on the material master. The remaining shelf life is shown in column REMSL, as well as the expiration date, storage location, storage type, and amount of stock in the bin.

Figure 3.27 Initial Date Entry Screen for Shelf Life Expiration Date Control List: Transaction LX27

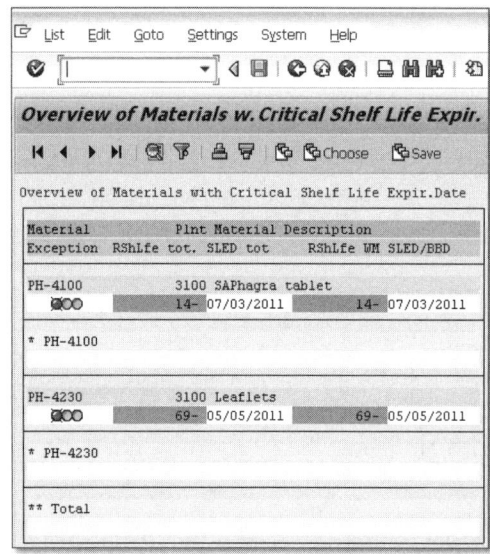

Figure 3.28 Results Screen for Shelf Life Expiration Date Control List: Transaction LX27

This report is provided to ensure that the warehouse management knows the stock that is soon to expire and to inform sales management if action needs to be taken to discount the expiring stock for sale. Having expired stock in the warehouse is not a desirable situation. Because that stock takes up warehouse space with material that cannot be sold, it incurs a financial loss to the company and may create an additional cost for disposing of the expired material or reworking it.

3.5 Business Examples—Stock Management

Each material that is stored in a warehouse managed storage location needs to have warehouse information entered in the warehouse management area of the material master. Without that data, the material cannot be stored in a storage bin in the warehouse.

3.5.1 Types of Warehouse Stock

A warehouse can contain types of stock that are identified in different ways. Items that are free to be used are referred to as unrestricted, whereas other stock can be waiting for inspection by the quality control department and cannot be used. Other types of stock that need to be identified in the warehouse include consignment stock, which belongs to a vendor but is stored in the warehouse, and project stock that is available only for a specific project.

Example

A manufacturer of paint additives in Alabama had used the same raw materials purchased from the same local vendor for over a decade. The vendor delivered the materials to the warehouse on the day (or the day before) they were to be used in production. A Chinese company purchased the local vendor, and some of the product lines used in the production of the additives were no longer made in the United States. The paint additives company was then forced to find other vendors to supply several the raw materials they needed. Fortunately other local vendors could supply three of the four critical raw materials, but one item was only available from a vendor in Ohio. The first several purchase orders with the Ohio vendor were delivered on time to the facility in Alabama, but the next few deliveries were late, forcing changes in the production schedule.

Even after another search, the company could not find a suitable vendor who could provide the material on the schedule they required, so they negotiated with the Ohio vendor to keep product in the warehouse on consignment and purchase the raw material when they required it. The company assigned an area in their warehouse for the consigned raw material, and the material was transferred from consignment stock to the production order when it was required.

3.5.2 Batch Management

Items in the warehouse can be batch managed, but it is not mandatory. A batch is a quantity of material that is grouped for one or more reasons. The items often have the same characteristics and values. The batch is identified with a batch number.

Example

A beverage manufacturer based in Spain was operating a number of disparate systems for its manufacturing and warehouse functions. The company printed a lot number on each bottle and can that was produced, but their warehouse management system could not manage inventory by batch. To keep items with the same batch number together, pallets were stored together in the warehouse and the batch number was attached. The issue was that the number of pallets varied for each batch and the warehouse could not have any fixed sized areas. The company decided to implement an SAP system but decided against using WM. The system went live with the company managing the warehouse with IM and interfacing to their existing warehouse management system.

After three months of operating the warehouse with the existing system interfacing with the SAP system, the company decided to decommission the old warehouse management system and implement SAP WM. The warehouse layout was reconfigured to allow the introduction of racking systems for pallets to replace the open storage area. The batch number of the product coming off the production line was entered into the SAP system at goods receipt, and the pallets were stored in the warehouse based on the configured stock placement strategy. Because batches no longer had to be stored together, the change in the warehouse layout meant the capacity of the warehouse increased by over 120%.

3.5.3 Shelf Life Functionality

The shelf life of a material is an important characteristic. In a production facility it is vital to know that raw materials going into making a finished item have not passed their shelf life. Equally, for sales functions, customers require the materials they purchase to be in date, so it is important to know which batches in the warehouse are within their shelf life tolerance and how many days of shelf life they have before their shelf life expiration date (SLED).

Example

A Mexican manufacturer of metal cans and drums had been using the same process since the 1970s. The company provided aluminum cans to the beverage industry and tin-plated steel cans for food products. Items in the warehouse were supposed to be sold on a first-in first-out (FIFO) basis, but often warehouse staff would select items closest to the shipping dock. This left pallets of materials remaining in the warehouse longer than expected.

When customers received cans that were older than normal, some of those customers rejected the whole delivery if the cans had any blemishes or signs of corrosion. After several customer returns the company decided to identify the date on which the cans were manufactured. In the SAP system the date of manufacture was entered into the relevant batch number. The stock removal strategy was then changed so that the quants selected for outbound deliveries were chosen by the number of days of shelf life remaining.

The company also gave their customers the option to ask for cans based on shelf life. Several manufacturers of premium beverages required that the newest cans be selected for their deliveries, whereas other customers did not have that requirement.

3.6 Summary

In this chapter, we discussed the stock management aspects of warehouse management. You need to understand several subjects before entering warehouse information in the material master. It is important that the correct information be entered at the time of material creation. It is often difficult to add or change data in the material master once it released and in use. Stock categories and stock types are primarily issues for materials management, but the warehouse consultant must understand how and why stock is categorized.

Batch management and shelf life expiration dates (SLED) are important for the warehouse. Batch management plays an important role in many industries, as does SLED. Incorrect identification of batches can be costly for the client in monetary terms and in customer confidence. More and more products are being labeled with expiration dates, so this is becoming a more important aspect of warehouse management.

In Chapter 4, we will discuss the movements that can occur in the warehouse, including transfer requirements and transfer orders.

Movements inside the warehouse determine where material goes, how it gets there, how it is stored, and how it is retrieved. The transfer requirement and the transfer order are the processes that move the material, and it is important to know how these processes work.

4   Warehouse Movements

In this chapter, we will discuss the movements that occur in the warehouse. Material moves into the warehouse, around the warehouse, and ultimately out of the warehouse. We will identify and review the mechanism of material movements and what triggers these movements. Two types of movements are relevant for the warehouse:

- Warehouse movements triggered by another SAP functionality, such as IM and shipping, that result in picking, packing, and warehouse-to-warehouse transfer.

- Warehouse movements internal to the warehouse, such as bin-to-bin transfers or posting changes. The goods movements inside the warehouse do not affect the total stock position, and no information is passed to the IM function.

Let's now venture deeper into this chapter, starting with movement types.

4.1   WM Movement Types

Within the WM functionality, there are goods movements that are movements inside a plant that can change stock levels in the storage locations designated to that plant. The movement of stock is either inbound from a vendor, outbound to a customer, a stock transfer between plants, or an internal transfer within a plant.

4.1.1 Movement Types in IM

A movement type is a three-character field used to describe the type of material movement that needs to be performed. The movement type is used for all type of movements: receipts, issues, transfers, and reversals.

The SAP system is delivered with predefined movement types between 100 and 899, for example, movement type 201, for moving warehouse material to a cost center. Movement types 900 and beyond can be used for customized movement types.

> **Note**
> You may need to change some standard movement types to accommodate warehouse processes. The standard movement type can be copied to a new movement type in the 900 range to be modified.

To create a movement type, use Transaction OMJJ or follow the menu path IMG • MATERIALS MANAGEMENT • INVENTORY MANAGEMENT AND PHYSICAL INVENTORY • MOVEMENT TYPES • COPY, CHANGE MOVEMENT TYPES.

Figure 4.1 shows the initial screen of Transaction OMJJ. The dialog structure in Figure 4.1 shows several configuration steps for each movement type.

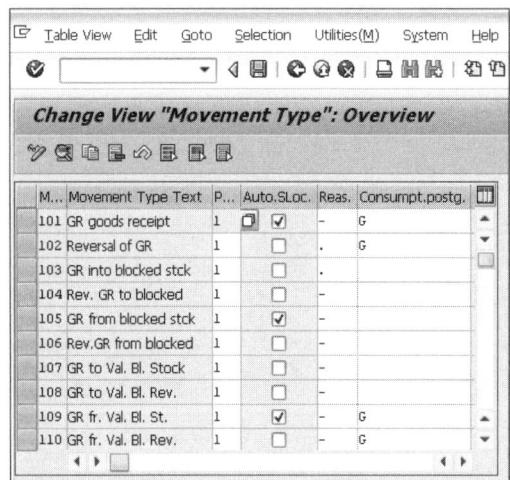

Figure 4.1 Initial Screen for Configuring Inventory Management Movement Types: Transaction OMJJ

The movement type is a key to the inventory management process because it controls the updating of the quantity of the stock, determines what fields are displayed and required for entry, and can update the account information.

When a movement type is used in IM goods movement with respect to a storage location that is warehouse managed, a corresponding movement in the warehouse is driven by a WM movement type. In the following subsections we will explain the connection between the IM movement types and the movement types in the warehouse.

4.1.2 WM Reference Movement Types

The IM movement type is linked to a warehouse movement type. The linkage is not direct but is made through a reference movement type, which is a key that can be assigned to an IM movement type. One reference movement type can be associated with several IM movement types.

You can assign the reference movement type to the IM movement type via the menu path IMG • LOGISTICS EXECUTION • WAREHOUSE MANAGEMENT • INTERFACES • INVENTORY MANAGEMENT • DEFINE MOVEMENT TYPES.

Figure 4.2 shows the following three configuration steps that are defined for this transaction:

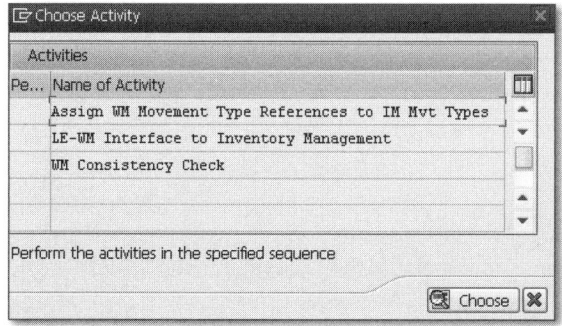

Figure 4.2 Initial Screen for WM Movement Type Definition

1. Add the reference movement type to the IM movement type.
2. Configure the links between WM and IM.
3. Check the consistency of the configuration.

Figure 4.3 shows several IM movement types that have been assigned a reference movement type. The screen shows the IM movement type field, Mvt, and the WM reference movement type field, Reference.

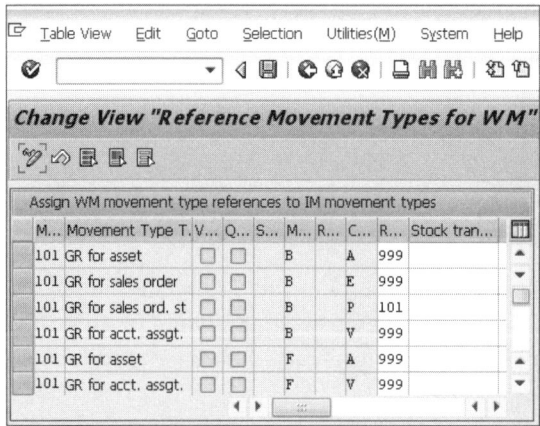

Figure 4.3 Assign Reference WM Movement Type to IM Movement Type

Each IM movement type is unique and depends on the movement checkbox, special stock indicator, and special movement checkbox. Each of the combinations is assigned a reference movement type.

In Figure 4.3, only two reference movement types are noted: 101 and 999. Reference movement type 999 indicates that for that particular IM movement type there is no corresponding WM movement type, and the IM movement has no effect on the warehouse. Reference movement type 101 is a valid reference movement type and will be linked to a WM movement type.

4.1.3 Creating WM Movement Types

The WM movement type contains information the system needs to determine stock placement and removal. The system is delivered with several predefined WM movement types. The movement type—such as 801, which represents goods receipt from production to the warehouse—contains information about what interim storage type is used, the coordinates for the interim storage bin, and control checkboxes for confirmations.

A WM movement type can be created via the menu path IMG • LOGISTICS EXECUTION • WAREHOUSE MANAGEMENT • ACTIVITIES • TRANSFERS • DEFINE MOVEMENT TYPES.

Figure 4.4 shows the initial screen for creating the WM movement types. The transaction requires that a movement type be associated with a particular warehouse. A movement type may have to function differently in different warehouses.

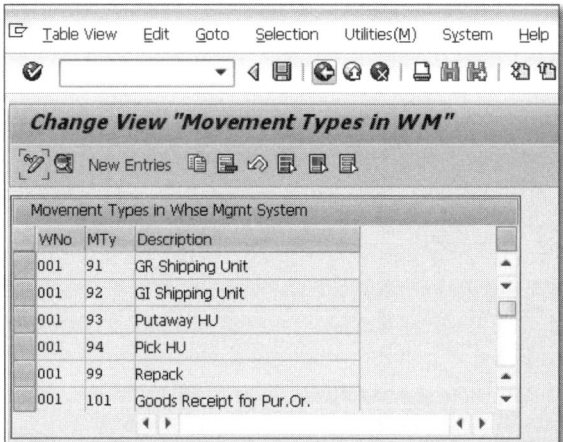

Figure 4.4 Initial Screen for WM Movement Types

You can find detailed information about the warehouse/movement type combination by selecting GOTO • DETAILS. The detail screen can also be accessed by pressing Ctrl+Shift+F2.

Figure 4.5 illustrates the detailed information available concerning the WM movement type. In configuring the source, destination, and return data, you should consider several scenarios:

▶ If no storage type or storage bin has been specified for either the source, destination, or return fields, then the system tries to determine the storage type and bin to assist in creating a transfer order.

▶ If the storage type is defined, the system searches for a storage bin for that storage type.

▶ If the storage type and bin are entered for a movement type, then the data is transposed into the transfer order and cannot be changed in the created transfer order.

4 Warehouse Movements

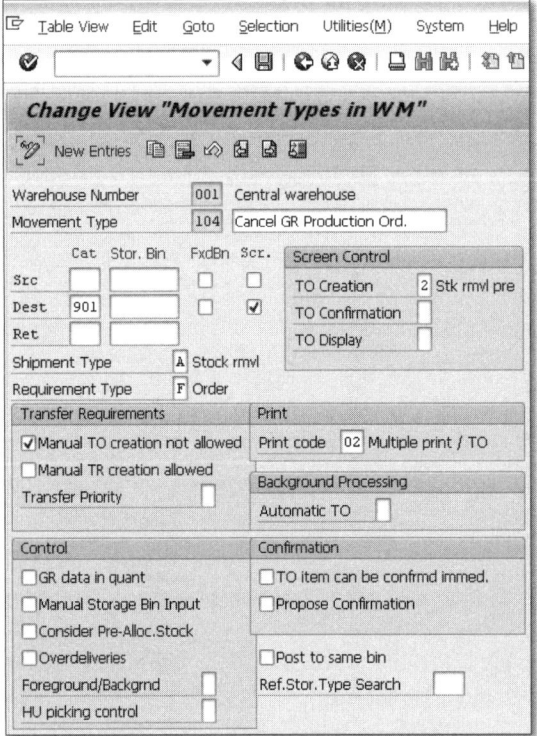

Figure 4.5 Detail Screen for WM Movement Type

The fields shown in Figure 4.5 are described in the following subsections.

Source Storage Type

This field (SCR — CAT) is the source storage type. This storage type is the location from which the material is sourced for stock removal. For example, when this movement type is used for the transfer order, the transfer order processing uses this storage type as the location where the material is sourced.

Source Storage Bin

This field (SCR — STOR. BIN) is the source storage bin for the source-storage type entered. So when this movement type is used, the transfer order uses this storage bin, located in the configured storage type, to indicate where the material will be sourced.

Source Fixed Bin Checkbox

This checkbox (Scr — FxdBn) identifies that a fixed storage bin is used as the interim storage bin for the relevant storage type. The fixed bin is assigned to a material for that particular storage type. It is where material is located and is used mostly in the picking process. If this checkbox is selected, then the source storage bin must be left blank.

Source Dynamic Storage Bin Checkbox

This field (Scr — Scr) is the dynamic storage bin checkbox, which when selected indicates that the source storage bin is created dynamically. In a movement type where the interim bin is flagged as having a dynamic location, this signals that the bin will have the reference from the document corresponding with the movement, that is, a cost center or a purchase order number.

Destination Storage Type

This field (Dest — Cat) is the destination storage type. This storage type is the location where the material will undergo putaway. For example, when this movement type is used for the transfer order, the transfer order processing uses this storage type as the location where the material will be moved.

Destination Storage Bin

This field (Dest — Stor. Bn) is the storage bin where the material is placed for the destination storage type entered. For example, when this movement type is used for the transfer order, the transfer order processing uses this storage bin, located in the configured storage type, to indicate where the material will be moved.

Destination Fixed Bin Checkbox

This field (Dest — FxdBn) indicates that a fixed storage bin is used as the interim storage bin for the relevant storage type. The fixed bin is assigned to a material for that particular storage type. If this checkbox is selected, then the destination storage bin must be left blank.

Destination Dynamic Storage Bin Checkbox

If this field (DEST-SCR) is selected, then the destination storage bin is determined dynamically. In a movement type where the interim bin is flagged as having a dynamic location, this indicates that the bin has the reference from the document corresponding with the movement, that is, a cost center or a purchase order number.

Return Storage Type

This field (RET-CAT) is the return storage type used when a quantity is left over from a complete stock removal. This is performed when the complete quantity is removed from the bin whether or not the total amount is needed. Therefore, there is a remainder quantity that has to be returned to stock.

Return Storage Bin

This field (RET — STOR. BN) is the return storage bin where the remaining quantity is moved if the warehouse needs a complete stock removal from the storage bin. This occurs when a quantity of material is removed from the source storage bin and sent to the destination bin, but not all the quantity is required. When this field is not configured, the remaining material goes back to the source storage bin. When this is configured, the remainder material goes to this return storage bin. This function is used when the warehouse cannot return the material to the source storage bin because of material specifications.

Screen Control—Transfer Order Creation

This field can be configured to determine whether to create transfer orders using a dialog screen. There are three options:

- 1
  Preparation screen for material putaway. This allows the amount of material to be put away to be divided between multiple storage bins.

- 2
  Preparation screen for material picking. This allows the total amount of the material to be picked to be searched for in the warehouse.

- 3

  Preparation screen for each individual line item for material putaway and material picking

Screen Control—Transfer Order Confirmation

This field can be set either to display the amount to be confirmed for the putaway or picking or to display a screen with no input values. The options are:

- 1

  Produces a screen with no input values

- 2

  Produces a screen with putaway values for input

- 3

  Produces a screen with picking values for input

Screen Control—Transfer Order Display

This field dictates which of the standard views is displayed in the foreground. There are three options:

- **1: Source Data View**

  For this view, the source data and the transfer order items appear in the foreground. The source data includes the quantity to be removed from the bin and any relevant batch numbers.

- **2: Destination View**

  For this view, the destination data is for the transfer order.

- **3: General View**

  For this view, the system displays data about the transfer order that does not appear in other views. This includes special stock type, stock category, goods-receipt date, and confirmation date.

Shipment Type

The shipment type classifies the movement types in the warehouse. The options that can be chosen include:

- **A**
  Stock removal
- **E**
  Stock placement
- **U**
  Posting change

Requirement Type

The requirement type refers to the origin type, for example, a goods receipt for a purchase order. The requirements number that can be entered at the same time is the originating document, which can be an item such as a purchase order. Options that can be selected include:

- **A**
  Asset
- **B**
  Purchase order
- **D**
  Storage bin
- **K**
  Cost center
- **L**
  Sales document
- **V**
  Sales order

Transfer Requirements — Manual Transfer Order Creation Not Allowed

If the MANUAL TO CREATION NOT ALLOWED checkbox is selected, then the transfer orders for this movement type cannot be created manually, but must be created with reference to another relevant document such as a transfer requirement.

Transfer Requirements — Manual Transfer Requirement Creation Allowed

If the MANUAL TR CREATION ALLOWED checkbox is selected, then a transfer requirement can be created manually when this movement type is used. For example, if movement type 801 — goods receipt from production — must be used, then a transfer requirement can be manually created for the movement type, providing this checkbox is selected.

Transfer Requirements — Transfer Priority

The transfer priority entered in the movement type determines which transfer requirements are to be processed. The smaller the transfer priority value, the higher the priority will be.

Control — Goods Receipt Data in Quant

Selecting the GR DATA IN QUANT checkbox ensures that the goods receipt date and number will be reset and automatically assigned in the quant as part of the transaction using this movement type.

Control — Manual Storage Bin Input

Select the MANUAL STORAGE BIN INPUT checkbox if you need to manually enter the storage bins when this movement type is used. The checkbox tells the system to ignore any strategy to automatically find a storage bin, so the storage bin can be entered manually.

Control — Consider Preallocation Stock

If the CONSIDER PRE-ALLOC. STOCK checkbox is select, the system checks to see if the material is preallocated. This check occurs during the stock putaway procedure. If the stock is preallocated, the system displays a message informing the user of the preallocation.

Control — Overdeliveries

Selecting the OVERDELIVERIES checkbox forces the system to assign complete quants to be removed during picking. If the checkbox is selected and whole quants are removed, overdeliveries may occur even if the storage type does not require removal of all stock from the bin.

Control—Foreground/Background

The FOREGROUND/BACKGROUND field determines whether the system controls the transaction in the background or foreground. If the checkbox is left blank, then the system has control of the transaction. The other options include D for background processing and H for foreground processing.

Control—Handling Unit Picking Control

The HU PICKING CONTROL field defines what happens in the system during the confirmation of a complete stock removal of the handling unit. You have three options:

- **1**
  On the confirmation screen, the issuing-handling unit is proposed as the destination storage unit during confirmation of the transfer order item and the handling-unit copy checkbox is selected.

- **3**
  On the confirmation screen, the first pick handling unit assigned to the transfer order is proposed as the destination storage unit. The HU COPY checkbox is not selected.

- **Blank**
  On the confirmation screen, the first pick handling unit assigned to the transfer order is proposed as the destination storage unit, and the HU COPY checkbox is selected.

Print Code

The PRINT CODE field defines the print format of the transfer order, the sort sequence, and the printer to be used. Each movement type can use a different print code.

To define the print code, use Transaction OMLV or follow the menu path IMG • LOGISTICS EXECUTION • ACTIVITIES • DEFINE PRINT CONTROL • PRINT CODE.

Automatic Transfer Order

The AUTOMATIC TO field controls whether the system automatically creates a transfer order in the background for a transfer requirement or a posting change notice.

Settings for this field are automatically proposed when a transfer requirement or a posting change notice is created from the movement type. The transfer orders are created by batch input using report RLAUTA10 for transfer requirements and report RLAUTA11 for posting change notices.

To configure this field, use Transaction OMKZ or follow the menu path IMG • LOGISTICS EXECUTION • ACTIVITIES • SET UP AUTOMATIC TO CREATION FOR TRs/POSTING CHANGE NOTICES.

Transfer Order Can Be Confirmed Immediately

The TO ITEM CAN BE CONFIMD IMMED. checkbox allows the transfer order to be confirmed immediately during the transfer order creation process. The transfer order is normally confirmed when the material is moved to the destination storage bin. However, if the material is moved and the transfer order is created afterward, this checkbox allows the transfer order to be completed immediately during the creation process for this movement type.

Propose Confirmation

Select the PROPOSE CONFIRMATION checkbox when the confirmation is to be allowed during the creation of the transfer order item. For example, when a transfer order is being created, you can propose the confirmation; that is, enter the confirmation information, but not actually confirm the transfer order.

Post to Same Bin

When the POST TO SAME BIN checkbox is selected for the movement type, the posting change does not result in a transfer; instead, the material is relabeled in the storage bin. Therefore, if the material is assigned as special stock—such as consignment stock—a posting change can convert that material to unrestricted stock. Instead of moving the material out of the bin and to a storage type for posting changes, this checkbox allows the posting change to occur in the storage bin where the material is located.

Reference Storage Type Search

The REF. STOR. TYPE SEARCH field refers to the movement type during the storage type search. The movement type can influence the storage type search. For each movement type you can set up certain storage types to be proposed. The necessary reference movement types must be set up for the movement types concerned. You must take these reference movement types into account in the storage type search function.

4.1.4 Assigning Warehouse Management Movement Types

After each IM movement type has been assigned, you can establish a WM reference movement type, the link between the IM reference movement type and the WM movement type.

A WM reference movement type doesn't directly correlate with a WM movement type. The limiting factor is the warehouse in which the movement takes place. The combination of the warehouse number and the WM reference movement type determines what WM movement type is assigned.

Therefore, WM reference movement type 101 may refer to WM movement type 101 in warehouse 100 but refer to WM movement type 103 in warehouse 200.

Figure 4.6 shows the warehouse number and reference movement type and the corresponding warehouse movement type. For example, reference movement type 503 in warehouse 104 corresponds to WM movement type 505 in Figure 4.6. The other fields on this screen are explained next.

- **Warehouse number**
  This field (WNo) is the number of the warehouse where the reference movement type is relevant. Entering "***" in this column indicates that the reference movement type is valid for all warehouses.

- **Reference movement type**
  This field (REF) is the reference movement type that links the IM movement type to the WM movement type.

- **Special stock**
  This field (SPSTL) is the special stock indicator that allows the goods movement transaction to process differently from normal stock. In this instance, it is referenced from the IM movement type to aid in the identification of the correct WM movement type.

WM Movement Types | 4.1

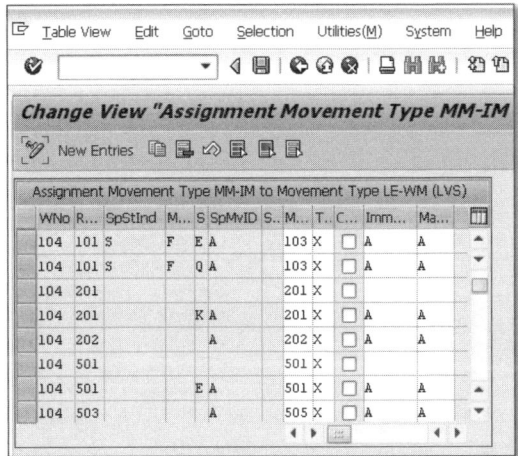

Figure 4.6 Assign WM Movement Type Based on Warehouse Number and WM Reference Movement Type

- **Movement**

  This field (Mov) specifies what type of document is the basis for the IM goods movement.

- **Special stock type**

  This field (Sp) identifies what type of stock is being moved, for example, project stock or consignment stock.

- **Special movement**

  This field (SpM) separates special posting procedures for the Materials Management (MM) documents for the standard processing method. The system uses this information to determine the WM movement type. Different movement types in the warehouse can be assigned to one IM movement type.

- **Storage location reference**

  Depending on the storage location, this field (Stor) influences the storage type search within the transfer order as well as the interim storage type search in the IM posting.

  The storage location reference indicator is created in configuration via the menu path IMG • LOGISTICS EXECUTION • WAREHOUSE MANAGEMENT • INTERFACES • INVENTORY MANAGEMENT • DEFINE STORAGE LOCATION CONTROL.

Figure 4.7 shows the storage location reference indicator being created for the Z99 warehouse. The storage location reference field is two characters long.

4 | Warehouse Movements

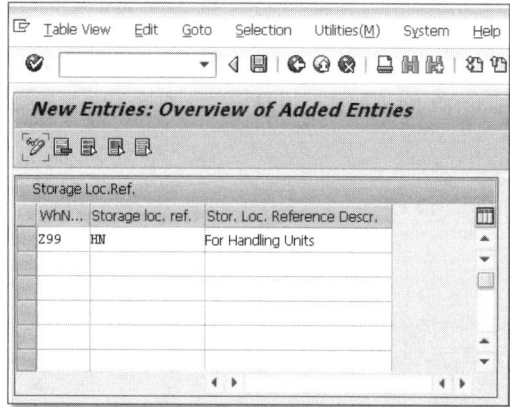

Figure 4.7 Creation of Storage Location Reference Indicator for Warehouse Z99

Continuing with the description of the fields in Figure 4.6, the next field after Stor is the movement type.

- **Movement type**
  Each movement that occurs in the warehouse requires a WM movement type, which affects the creation of the transfer order.

- **Creation and cancellation of transfer requirement**
  You use the TF indicator to create or cancel a transfer requirement.

  - **X**
    This entry means a transfer requirement will be created for the material document item.

  - **1**
    With this entry, the system will try to cancel any existing transfer requirement.

- **Creation of posting change notice**
  This field (Cre) specifies the creation of a posting change notice (PCN). A PCN is created for each material document item.

- **Create transfer order immediately**
  This field (Imm. TO) triggers the creation of a transfer order immediately when the IM movement is processed. Two indicators can be used.

  - **A**
    The system creates a transfer order automatically when a material document is posted in IM.

- **X**
  The system calls up the Create Transfer Order transaction when you post an IM material document.
- **Mail control**
  Created in the background, this field (MAIL) controls who should be contacted in case of errors.
- **Delivery type**
  Depending on the delivery type (specified in the DEL.TYPE field), the system determines which screens to display and which data has to be entered.

To configure the delivery type, follow the menu path IMG • LOGISTICS EXECUTION • SHIPPING • DELIVERIES • DEFINE DELIVERY TYPES.

This concludes our discussion of the movement types used in WM. Now we'll focus on transfer requirements.

4.2 Transfer Requirements

The WM movement type, described in Section 4.1, determines the movement of the material into the warehouse. Once the material is in the warehouse, it can be moved for a pick, putaway, or transfer. The movement consists of two elements:

- Transfer requirement
- Transfer order

The transfer requirement is the phase of planning to move material from one warehouse location to another, and a transfer order is used to perform the move and confirm the move when it is completed.

For WM movement types, the transfer requirement is used to translate the information from the IM goods movement to a planned movement in the warehouse, based on the configuration of the WM movement type. The transfer requirement is automatically created so that the material can be moved into the warehouse.

The transfer requirement comprises header information and several item lines of material for the transfer requirement. The item line includes information such as:

- The material to be moved within the warehouse
- The quantity of material to be moved

4 | Warehouse Movements

- The date when the material should be moved
- The transfer type that is the basis of the goods movement such as a putaway, pick, or transfer
- A reason why the material has to be moved; for example, it is needed to fill a production order or a purchase order

4.2.1 Automatic Transfer Requirements

An automatic transfer requirement is created when a transaction for a goods movement is executed and the warehouse movement type is configured for automatic creation of a transfer requirement.

You can configure the automatic creation of a transfer requirement via the menu path IMG • LOGISTICS EXECUTION • WAREHOUSE MANAGEMENT • INTERFACES • INVENTORY MANAGEMENT • DEFINE MOVEMENT TYPES.

Figure 4.8 shows the configuration screen for the WM movement types. When defining the movement types, you can decide to configure the movement to automatically create a transfer requirement for the movement or to leave the creation as a manual process.

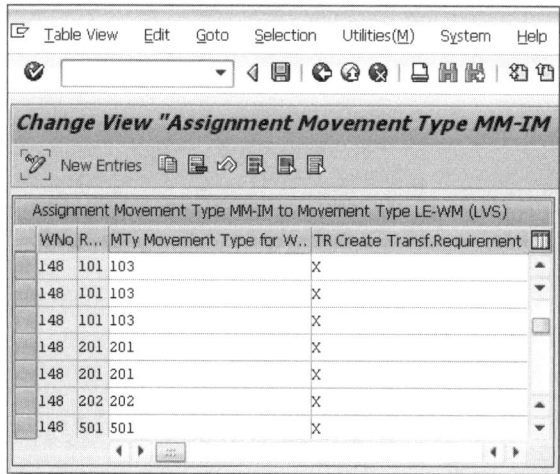

Figure 4.8 Configuration of Manual Transfer Requirements in WM Movement Type Screen

4.2.2 Create a Manual Transfer Requirement

You may need to create a transfer requirement manually for a variety of reasons. The most common include the need to perform a goods issue to a cost center—often done when issuing materials to a salesman for samples—and for replenishment of material in the fixed bins.

A manual transfer requirement can be created using Transaction LB01, which you can access via the menu path SAP • LOGISTICS • LOGISTICS EXECUTION • WAREHOUSE MANAGEMENT • TRANSFER REQUIREMENT • CREATE • WITHOUT REFERENCE.

Figure 4.9 shows the initial data entry screen for creating a transfer requirement. The warehouse number and the movement type must be entered. However, if the movement type does not allow manual entry of a transfer requirement, the system will display an error message at the bottom of the screen, stating that a manual transfer requirement is not allowed and the creation of the transfer requirement cannot proceed.

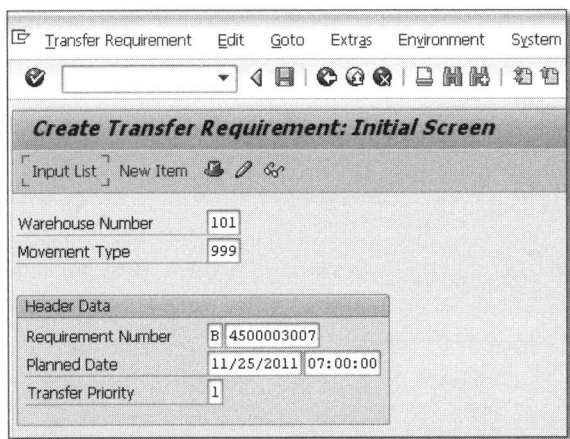

Figure 4.9 Initial Screen for Creating Manual Transfer Requirement

You can enter the transfer requirement header data on this screen. The header data consists of the requirement type, requirement number, planned date, and transfer priority.

Figure 4.10 shows the detail screen for the creation of a transfer requirement. This screen shows the information that may have been entered on the header screen.

4 | Warehouse Movements

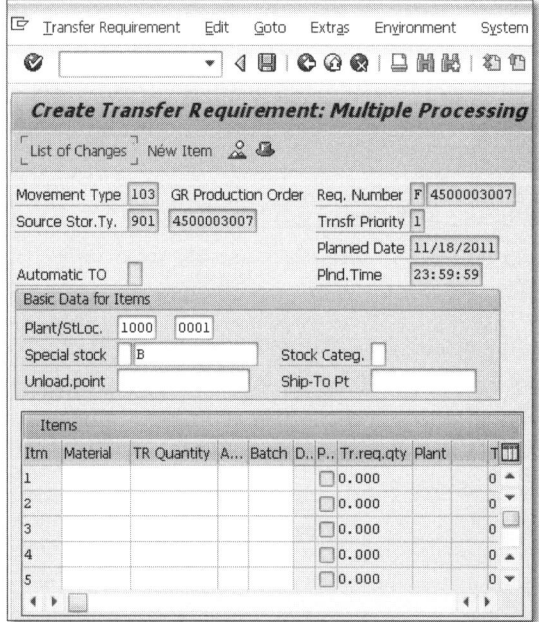

Figure 4.10 Multiple-Processing Screen for Creating Transfer Requirement

Let's take a closer look at what's involved in the creation of transfer requirements.

- **Automatic transfer order**
  In addition to the header information, you can select the AUTOMATIC TO checkbox to allow an automatic transfer order. If this is selected, transfer orders are created by batch input using report RLAUTA10.

- **Special stock**
  The SPECIAL STOCK field determines what type of stock is being moved, for example, project stock or consignment stock. The second of the two special stock fields is for the special stock number. This identifies the material. If the material is a consignment stock, then the consignment vendor number is used as the special stock number. If a special stock number is entered, then a special stock indicator must be entered also.

- **Unloading point**
  You can manually enter the unloading point in the UNLOAD POINT field. This can be a dock or a location within the warehouse where the material is unloaded. This field accepts a value up to 25 characters long.

- **Stock category**
  Use the warehouse stock category field (STOCK CATEG.) if the stock is returned or blocked. Enter "Q" if the stock is in quality control, "R" if the stock has been returned, or "S" if it is blocked stock.

- **Ship-to point**
  Enter a ship-to point to indicate the person or location to which the material ultimately will be shipped. The SHIP-TO PT field accepts a value up to 12 characters long.

- **Items**
  The line item in the transfer requirement requires the material number, quantity, unit of measure, and batch number if applicable. You can add several lines to the transfer requirement. When finished, the document can be posted, and the system will display the transfer requirement number assigned.

4.2.3 Create a Transfer Requirement for Replenishment of a Fixed Bin

You can use a transfer requirement to add material to the stock in fixed storage bins. The system can automatically create transfer requirements for the required quantities. However, this process can be done manually using Transaction LP21.

Instead of the system calculating the quantity necessary for replenishment, the warehouse staff can manually determine the level required and create a transfer requirement for this amount.

To ensure that a manual transfer requirement can be created to replenish the fixed bins, the storage type must be configured with the correct movement type.

The transaction to configure the movement type for the storage type is located in the IMG. Follow the menu path IMG • LOGISTICS EXECUTION • WAREHOUSE MANAGEMENT • ACTIVITIES • TRANSFERS • DEFINE STOCK TRANSFERS AND REPLENISHMENT CONTROL.

Figure 4.11 shows the configuration required to allow replenishment by entering the relevant movement type against the required warehouse/storage type combination. In this case, storage type 100 is defined as production supply bins that contain material used in production orders. Movement type 319 is defined for replenishment for production and needs to be assigned to areas, which means storage type 100, which requires ongoing replenishment.

4 | Warehouse Movements

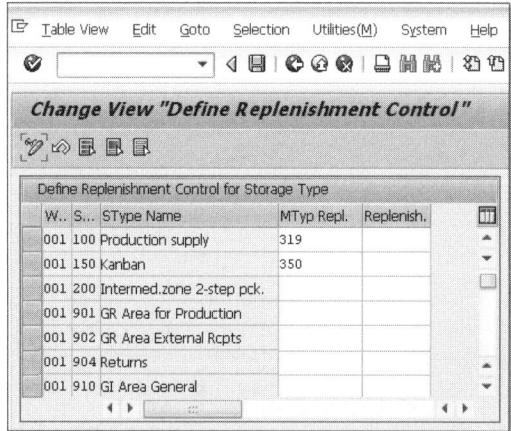

Figure 4.11 Configuration of Replenishment Control for Storage Types

You can create a manual transfer requirement with Transaction LP21 to replenish the bins in the storage type for production material. You can also follow the menu path SAP • LOGISTICS • LOGISTICS EXECUTION • WAREHOUSE MANAGEMENT • TRANSFER REQUIREMENT • CREATE • REPLENISHMENT FOR FIXED BINS.

To create the transfer requirement, the warehouse user must enter the plant, storage location, warehouse number, and storage type. Figure 4.12 shows these fields filled in as well as fields such as the requirement type and requirement number, transfer priority, and planned date and time. The planned date should always be in the future. The unloading point was added in this example but is an optional field.

The transaction references the material master records of those materials in the storage type, unless specific storage bins or materials are entered. The material information for replenishment is reviewed against the stock in the storage bins of the storage type. If the stock levels are below the minimum stated in the material master, then the system displays this information in the results screen.

The material master record can contain the replenishment data for the material at the storage type level. Figure 4.13 shows the replenishment data in the material master.

Transfer Requirements | 4.2

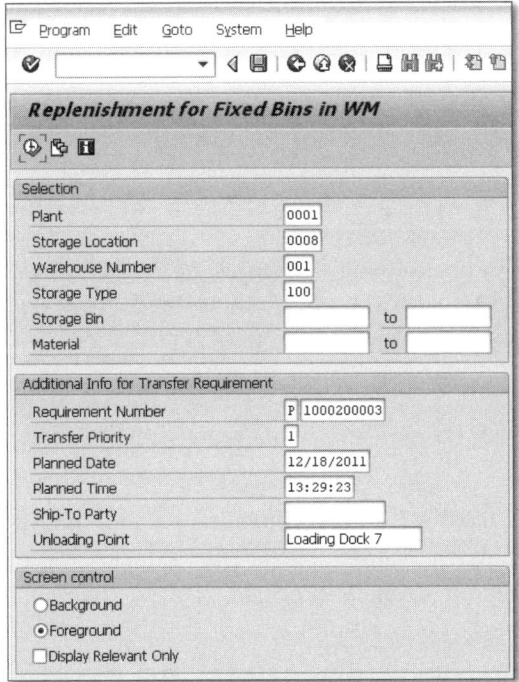

Figure 4.12 Selection Screen for Creating Transfer Requirement for Fixed Bin Replenishment: Transaction LP21

Figure 4.13 Replenishment Data in Warehouse Screen of Material Master Record

Minimum Bin Quantity

The MINIMUM BIN QUANTITY field specifies the minimum quantity that can be stored in the bin location of this storage type. This field is used for calculating the replenishment of material.

Replenishment Quantity

The REPLENISHMENT QTY field specifies the quantity of material to be replenished in the storage bin. This replenishment quantity applies only to the storage type for which it is entered. This value can be seen when the transfer requirement is created for the material.

After you complete the selection screen for Transaction LP21, you can executed it by pressing the [F8] function key.

Figure 4.14 shows the results for the fixed-bin replenishment for the storage type 100 production supply. The material shown, R-F101, shows a zero stock level and a requirement quantity of 300. To see the detailed information on the fixed bin, select EDIT • CHOOSE DETAIL or press the [F2] function key.

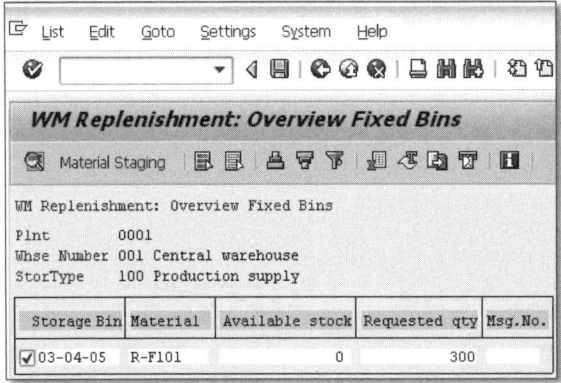

Figure 4.14 Results Screen for Fixed Bin Replenishment: Transaction LP21

Figure 4.15 shows details of the material in the storage bin for which the replenishment transfer requirement has been created. The detailed information shows the data from the material master record, as shown earlier in Figure 4.13. For this storage type, the maximum material in a bin is 344, the minimum quantity allowed is 1, and the replenishment quantity is 50.

Transfer Requirements | **4.2**

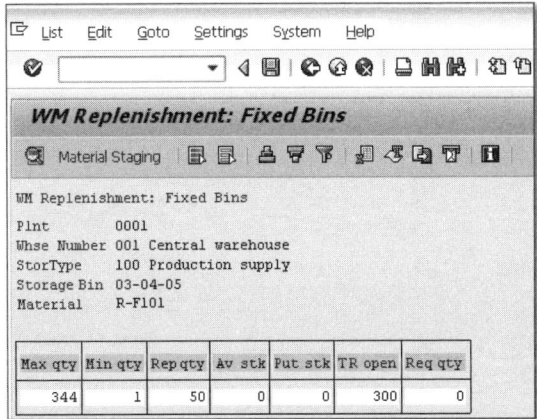

Figure 4.15 Detailed Information on Fixed Bin Selected for Replenishment

4.2.4 Display a Transfer Requirement for a Material

Several transactions can be used to display a transfer requirement. The open transfer requirement shown in Figure 4.15 is for material R-F101. You can find this transfer requirement by using the system to display a transfer requirement for a material via Transaction LB11 or the menu path SAP • LOGISTICS • LOGISTICS EXECUTION • WAREHOUSE MANAGEMENT • TRANSFER REQUIREMENT • DISPLAY • FOR MATERIAL.

Figure 4.16 shows the selection screen for Transaction LB11. The material and the warehouse number are required, but the other fields are optional. Most of the options on this screen have been described previously in this chapter.

Shipment Type

The shipment type is the type of movement required in the transfer requirement. The movement can be stock placement, stock removal, posting change, or warehouse supervision.

Processing Complete

If the PROCESSING COMPLETE field is filled in, then the list that is produced will include transfer requirements that have been completed. If the checkbox is left blank, completed transfer requirements will not be included.

4 | Warehouse Movements

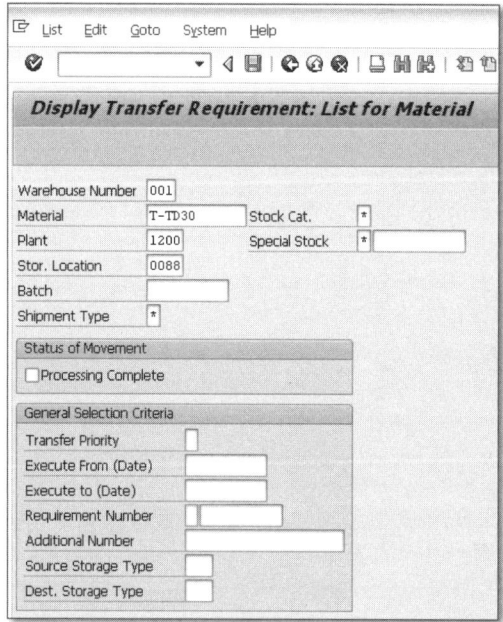

Figure 4.16 Initial Screen for Displaying Transfer Requirement for Material: Transaction LB11

Choosing to see all of the transfer requirements for a material enables the system to give a complete picture of material requirements.

Figure 4.17 shows that for the material and warehouse entered there is only one relevant transfer requirement. This is the transfer requirement that was created as an example earlier in this chapter for the replenishment of a fixed bin.

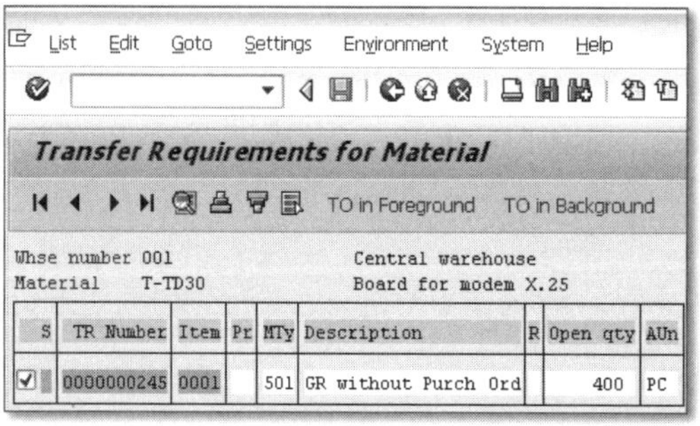

Figure 4.17 Results Screen Displaying Transfer Requirements for Material: Transaction LB11

You can view the transfer requirement by double-clicking the item line you want to review. The system processes through to Transaction LB03 to display the transfer requirement.

Figure 4.18 shows the transfer requirement for the fixed bin replenishment. The transfer requirement shows that the checkboxes PROCESSED and DELETION FLAG are both blank, so the transfer requirement has not been completely processed, and the line item has not been deleted.

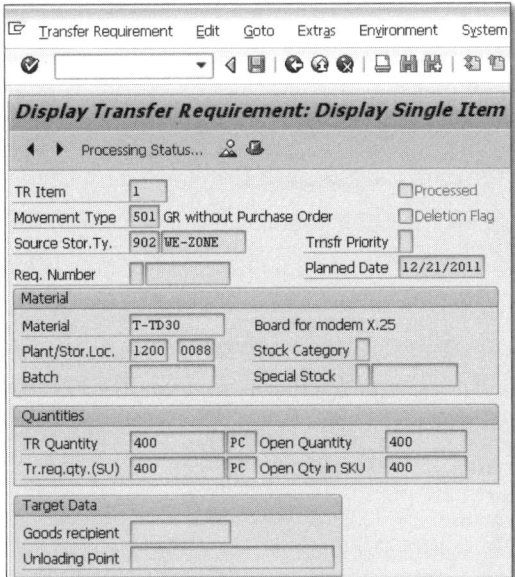

Figure 4.18 Display of Transfer Requirement for Line Item: Transaction LB03

You can display the processing status of the transfer requirement by clicking the PROCESSING STATUS button, pressing [Shift]+[F5], or selecting GOTO • PROCESSING STATUS.

Figure 4.19 shows the processing status of the transfer requirement. The processing status screen shows that a transfer order has not been created for the transfer requirement. This is clear because the TO QUANTITY field is zero and the NUMBER OF TO ITEMS field is also zero.

4 | Warehouse Movements

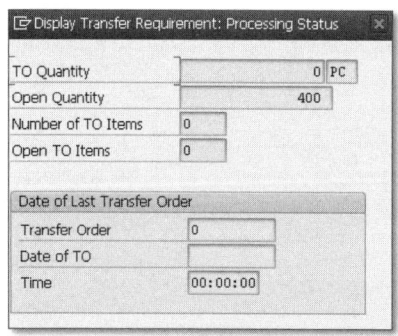

Figure 4.19 Processing Status of a Transfer Requirement in Display Transfer Requirement: Transaction LB03

4.2.5 Display a Transfer Requirement for a Single Item

Transaction LB03 can be used to display a transfer requirement for a single line item. Alternatively, follow the menu path SAP • LOGISTICS • LOGISTICS EXECUTION • WAREHOUSE MANAGEMENT • TRANSFER REQUIREMENT • DISPLAY • SINGLE.

Figure 4.20 shows the initial screen for Transaction LB03. The warehouse number and transfer requirement number must be entered. The system proposes the transfer requirement number if it is not entered. The detail screen for LB03 was shown earlier in Figure 4.18.

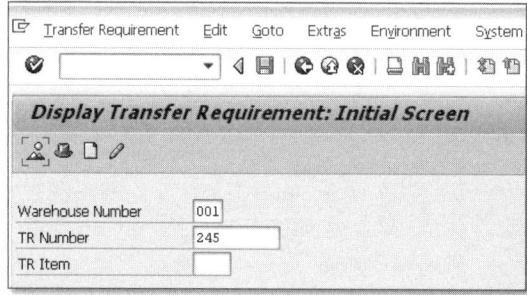

Figure 4.20 Initial Screen for Displaying a Transfer Requirement: Transaction LB03

4.2.6 Display a Transfer Requirement for a Storage Type

You can use Transaction LB10 to display a transfer requirement for a storage type, or follow the menu path SAP • LOGISTICS • LOGISTICS EXECUTION • WAREHOUSE MANAGEMENT • TRANSFER REQUIREMENT • DISPLAY • FOR STORAGE TYPE.

Figure 4.21 shows the initial screen for the display of transfer requirements for storage types. You can choose to show the transfer requirements for the source or destination storage types. In Figure 4.21, the destination storage type has been entered (DEST. STORAGE TYPE), and the resulting transfer requirements will only be relevant for that storage type.

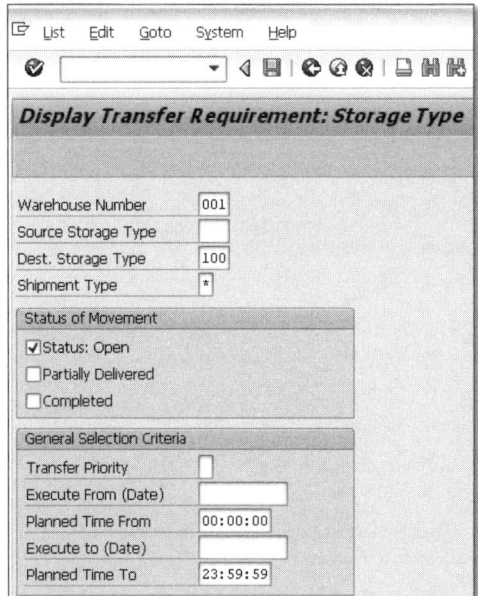

Figure 4.21 Initial Screen for Displaying Transfer Requirements by Storage Type: Transaction LB10

The status of movement section in Figure 4.21 indicates that the selection can be made for combinations of open, partially delivered, or completed transfer requirements.

Figure 4.22 shows the following transfer requirements that have been found for the destination storage type selected in Figure 4.21:

- **HS: Header status of transfer requirement**
  This is automatically derived from the system and refers to the amount of the transfer requirement already processed by transfer orders.
- **PR: Transfer priority**
  The lower the number, the higher the priority. The transfer requirements are processed by this priority list.

153

▶ **S: Shipment type**
This classifies the movement types in the warehouse. The options are A for stock removal, U for posting change, and E for stock placement.

▶ **R: Requirement type**
This refers to the origin type, for example, a goods receipt for a purchase order. The options include A for an asset, B for a purchase order, D for a storage bin, K for a cost center, L for a sales document, and V for a sales order.

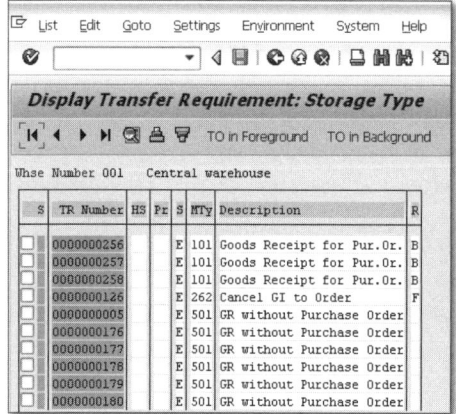

Figure 4.22 Display of Transfer Requirements for Selected Storage Type: Transaction LB10

From this report, a transfer requirement can be selected and processed to create a transfer order. This report can perform this process either in the background or in the foreground.

To create a transfer order from the selected transfer requirement in the foreground, click the checkbox on the line you require, and select ENVIRONMENT • TO IN FOREGROUND, or press Ctrl + Shift + F8.

Depending on processing time and the size of the transfer requirement, you can create a transfer order from the transfer requirement in the background by clicking the button on the screen, selecting ENVIRONMENT • TO IN BACKGROUND, or pressing Ctrl + Shift + F9.

4.2.7 Deleting a Transfer Requirement

You may find that the transfer requirement was created unnecessarily or with an error in the entry of the storage type. If the transfer requirement is not needed and you need to delete it, use Transaction LB02, which you can find by following the menu path SAP • LOGISTICS • LOGISTICS EXECUTION • WAREHOUSE MANAGEMENT • TRANSFER REQUIREMENT • CHANGE.

The data required to change a transfer requirement is the warehouse, transfer requirement number, and item number, as shown in Figure 4.23.

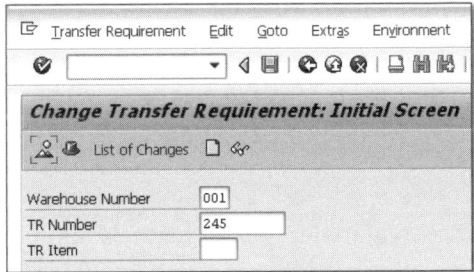

Figure 4.23 Initial Screen for Changing a Transfer Requirement: Transaction LB02

Figure 4.24 shows the line item for the transfer requirement with the deletion flag selected. This signals that the line item will be deleted when this transfer requirement transaction has been saved.

Figure 4.24 Transfer Requirement Line Item with Deletion Flag Selected: Transaction LB02

Now that we have discussed the processes surrounding transfer requirements, the next section will follow up with a discussion of transfer order functionality.

4.3 Transfer Orders

As we mentioned in Section 4.2 when describing a transfer requirement, a transfer order is used to perform a move and confirm a move when it is completed. A transfer order can be created with reference to a source document either from warehouse management or from another SAP functionality, such as MM. A source document can be a transfer requirement, delivery document, material document, or a posting change notice (PCN).

The transfer order contains the information required to move materials into the warehouse, out of the warehouse, or from one storage bin to another within the warehouse.

The transfer order can also perform logical movements in the warehouse. This includes movements from a blocked status to an unrestricted status or from quality control status to blocked. These movements are considered to be posting changes and are executed with a transfer order.

The transfer order comprises a header and several item lines. The header contains the transfer order number and the dates of creation and confirmation. If the transfer order has been created with reference to a transfer requirement, then the transfer requirement number is shown in the header. If the transfer order is created with reference to a delivery, then the delivery number is shown on the header.

A transfer order can have a single or multiple line items. The transfer order is a document that tells where the material is coming from and where it is going. Therefore, each line item is an individual movement of a certain quantity of material from a source storage bin to a destination storage bin. The number of line items depends on how many destination storage bins are required for the total quantity of material.

4.3.1 Creating a Transfer Order with Reference to a Transfer Requirement

Many of the transfer orders created in the warehouse result from transfer requirements. The transfer requirement is created as a plan of what needs to be moved and when. Transfer requirements can be converted into transfer orders for the movement of the material to be completed.

The transaction to create a transfer order from a transfer requirement is Transaction LT04, which you access via the menu path SAP • LOGISTICS • LOGISTICS EXECUTION • WAREHOUSE MANAGEMENT • TRANSFER ORDER • CREATE • FOR TRANSFER REQUIREMENT.

Figure 4.25 shows the initial screen of Transaction LT04, where the transfer requirement number and the item number are entered as the reference document for creating a new transfer order.

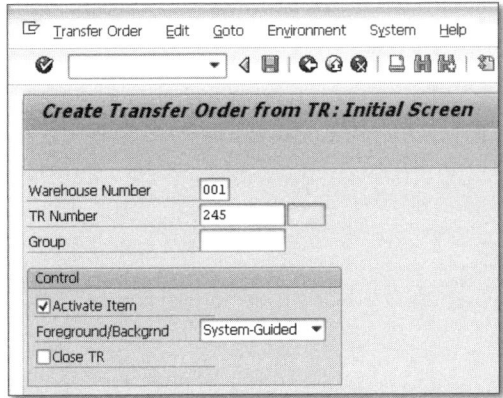

Figure 4.25 Initial Screen for Creating a Transfer Order with Reference to a Transfer Requirement: Transaction LT04

The GROUP field in Figure 4.25 refers to a user-defined group number that can be used to label certain related WM documents for easy retrieval at a later date. For example, if the documents all relate to a certain sales order, the sales order number of customer number may be used as a group number for the warehouse documents so they are easy to retrieve.

Select the ACTIVATE ITEM checkbox when it is necessary to select the line items in the transfer order and enter them into the active work list. If the checkbox is not selected, the items are not activated.

The FOREGROUND/BACKGROUND field specifies which type of processing is used for transfer order creation. The process can be either in the foreground, where the processing can be seen, in the background, where it processes like a batch job, or driven by the system.

The CLOSE TR checkbox determines the processing that should occur with the transfer requirement referenced in Transaction LT04 to create the transfer order. If the checkbox is selected, the transfer requirement is closed when the transfer order is processed. However, if the checkbox is not selected, the transfer requirement is not closed if the transfer order did not totally complete the transfer specified by the transfer requirement.

> **Example**
>
> If the transfer requirement shows a quantity of 10, and the transfer order is processed with a quantity of 8, then the remaining quantity of 2 will remain open on the transfer requirement, and a manual process will be required to complete the transfer requirement. This will not occur if the CLOSE TR checkbox is selected, because the transfer requirement will be closed.

After the transfer requirement details are entered into the initial screen, the detail screen is displayed as shown in Figure 4.26. This screen shows the item information for the material to be moved.

Figure 4.26 shows the details transferred from the transfer requirement, such as the movement type, plant, storage location, and destination storage type and storage bin.

The storage type search shows the storage types that will be used to find material to supply the production fixed bin, PROD-1320, for this transfer requirement. Initially, the line items are blank. When the system searches the storage types listed in the storage type search, the material from the source bins are noted on the line items with the quantity they are supplying for the transfer requirement.

To create the line items for the movement of a quantity defined in the transfer requirement, the transaction reviews the bins in the storage type search and proposes several line items for the total quantity defined by the transfer requirement.

Transfer Orders | 4.3

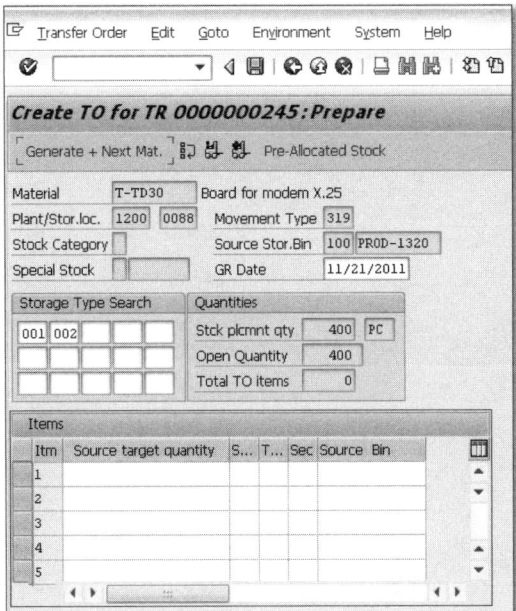

Figure 4.26 Detail Screen for Creating a Transfer Order from a Transfer Requirement: Transaction LT04

You can choose to have this performed in either the foreground or background. The reason to perform this in the background is that it allows the user to continue with other work. If the transfer requirement has a large quantity, the process to create the number of line items on the transfer order may take some time.

To perform the process in the foreground, select EDIT • REMOVE FROM STOCK • FOREGROUND or press the F5 function key.

Figure 4.27 shows the first proposed movement of material from the source storage bin to the destination storage bin. This is based on the storage type search of storage types 001 and 002, which was proposed in Figure 4.26.

In this screen the requested quantity is copied from the transfer requirement, along with the material number, plant, storage location, and storage unit type.

The certificate number can refer to a document that relates specifically to the quant whose movement is being proposed. This document can be a certificate of origin or an identification document, for example.

4 | Warehouse Movements

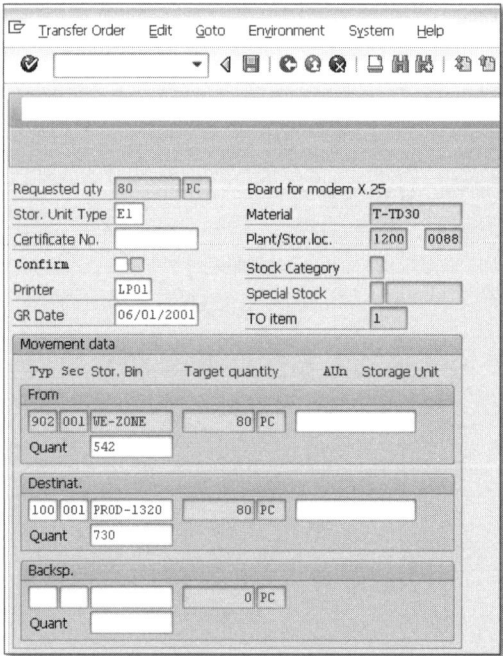

Figure 4.27 Generating Line Items for a Transfer Order with Reference to a Transfer Requirement: Transaction LT04

The CONFIRM checkbox allows the line item to be confirmed as soon as it is created. If the checkbox is selected, then the confirmation will occur immediately. This may occur if the transfer order is being created after the movement has taken place.

The PRINTER field is used if the transfer order line item is to be printed as used as a picking slip. The printer number should reflect the printer used for printing warehouse documents such as picking slips.

The GR DATE field shows the goods receipt date of the movement of material. This defaults to the current date but can be amended if the movement has already occurred when the transfer order is created. The TO ITEM field is for the line item numbering for the transfer order.

The movement data section shown in Figure 4.27 shows the source and destination storage information. The data shows the storage type, storage section, storage bin, quantity of the quant, unit of measure, storage unit (if applicable), and quant number.

In addition to entering information for the source and destination locations, you can use another section to enter information for the return of any materials. If any surplus material cannot be returned to the original storage bin, then it can be returned to this storage destination, as defined in the BACKSP fields.

You fill in the GOODS RECIPIENT field if you know the person or area that is receiving the material. The GROSS WEIGHT field shows the gross weight of the material for this specific line item of the transfer order. This is important for warehouse staff because the weight of the quant may require special equipment or exceed the recommended load of a forklift or storage bin.

Figure 4.28 shows the transfer order with five line items from the total quantity in the transfer requirement that have been proposed for movement from the source locations to the single destination fixed bin.

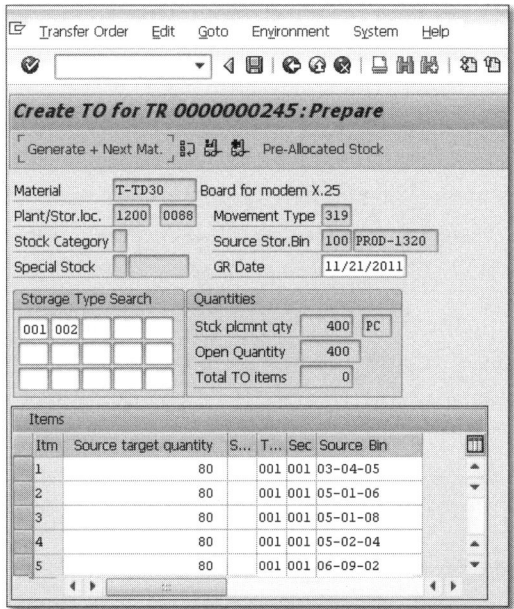

Figure 4.28 Display of Transfer Order Line Items Showing Source Storage Type and Storage Bins

The total amount of source quantity from the line items equals the required amount from the transfer requirement. After the line items have been reviewed, posting the transaction creates the transfer order. The warehouse user can achieve this by selecting TRANSFER ORDER • POSTING or pressing Ctrl+S. After the posting has been completed, the system displays the transfer order number on the screen.

4.3.2 Creating a Transfer Order Without a Reference

The warehouse staff can create a transfer order manually without reference to a transfer request, delivery, and so on. This may be required if an error has been made or if the warehouse needs to move inventory quickly. The movement type that is used must be configured to allow creation of a manual transfer order.

The configuration to allow a manual transfer order is on the movement type configuration for a particular warehouse. Therefore, a manual transfer order for a movement type may not be allowed in other warehouses.

To access the configuration, follow the menu path IMG • LOGISTICS EXECUTION • WAREHOUSE MANAGEMENT • ACTIVITIES • TRANSFERS • DEFINE MOVEMENT TYPES.

Select the warehouse/movement type combination that is required, and then select GOTO • DETAILS, or press Ctrl + Shift + F2.

In Figure 4.29, in the TRANSFER REQUIREMENTS area, the configuration for movement type 309 in warehouse 001 shows that manual transfer orders are not allowed. Transfer orders can only be created with reference if this checkbox is not set.

If the checkbox is not checked and a manual transfer order can be created, you can use Transaction LT01, which you can find by following the menu path SAP • LOGISTICS • LOGISTICS EXECUTION • WAREHOUSE MANAGEMENT • TRANSFER ORDER • CREATE • WITHOUT REFERENCE.

Figure 4.30 shows the initial screen for creating a manual transfer order. The warehouse number, movement type, material number, plant, storage location, and quantity of material to be moved should be entered.

You can include other information, such as stock category if the stock to be moved is blocked, or use a special stock indicator if the material is project stock or consignment.

You can enter a batch number for the stock to be moved if the material is batch managed and if a certain batch has been identified for movement. The control option can allow foreground, background, or system-controlled processing.

Transfer Orders | **4.3**

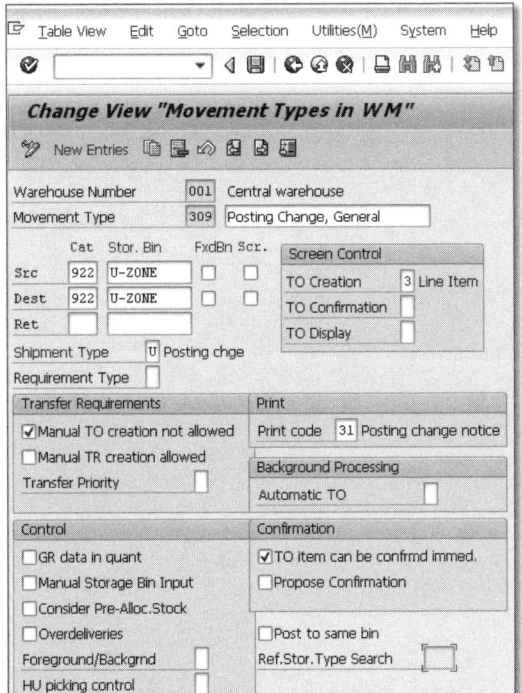

Figure 4.29 Configuration for Manual Transfer Orders per Warehouse/Movement Type Combination

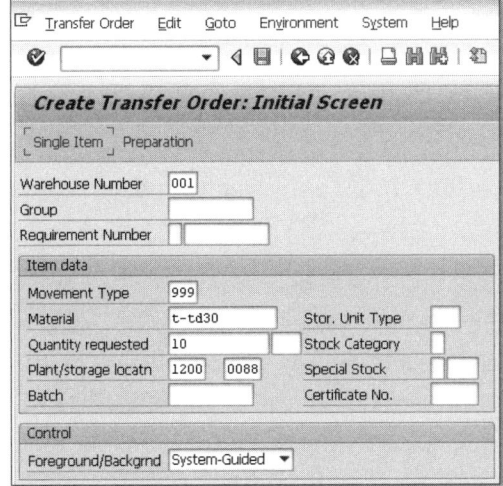

Figure 4.30 Initial Screen to Create Transfer Order Without Reference: Transaction LT01

Figure 4.31 shows the source storage type, storage section, and storage bin. When these are entered, the system automatically assigns the quant. The same is true when the destination location is entered. The system also calculates the gross weight of the material to be moved.

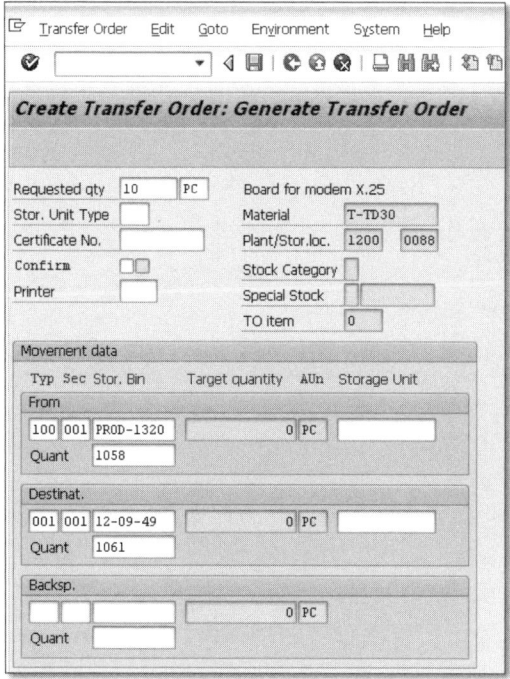

Figure 4.31 Entry Screen for Data to Create a Manual Transfer Order: Transaction LT01

When the items are complete, you can save the transfer order. After the posting has been completed, the system displays the transfer order number on the screen.

4.3.3 Cancel a Transfer Order

After a transfer order has been created, you might need to cancel it if the material is not to be moved or is to be moved via a different movement type. You can cancel a transfer order by using Transaction LT15 or via the menu path SAP • LOGISTICS • LOGISTICS EXECUTION • WAREHOUSE MANAGEMENT • TRANSFER ORDER • CANCEL • TRANSFER ORDER.

Figure 4.32 shows the initial screen for canceling a transfer order. It requires entry of the warehouse number and the transfer order number/item number. The screen also allows the entry of a delivery number if applicable.

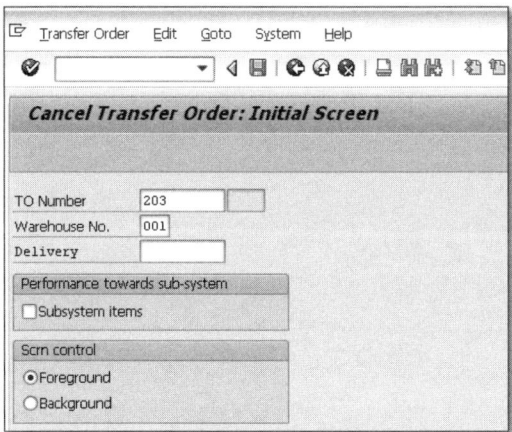

Figure 4.32 Initial Screen for Cancelling a Transfer Order: Transaction LT15

Figure 4.33 shows the line item of the transfer order to be cancelled. The transfer order is cancelled when the transaction is posted. When the processing is complete, the system returns a message confirming cancellation.

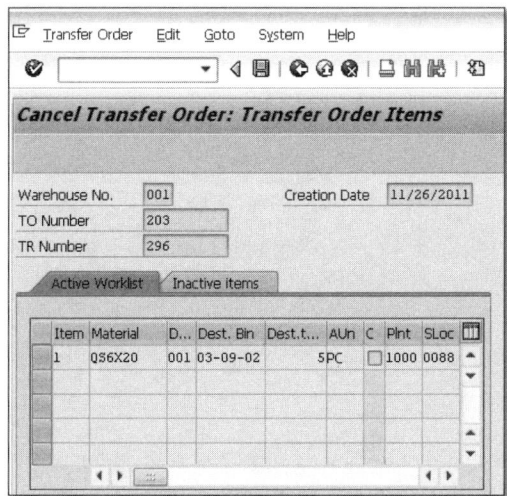

Figure 4.33 Detail Screen Showing Line Items to be Cancelled: Transaction LT15

4.3.4 Confirm a Transfer Order

When a transfer order is created, the system can confirm when the movement of the material has been completed. However, a transfer order can be confirmed at any time, allowing the material to be picked even though the material has not been physically moved. This is useful for warehouse operations when a material has arrived from a vendor in response to a purchase order and needs to be used in production before putaway in the warehouse. You can use three transactions to confirm a transfer order:

- **LT11**
  Confirm a single item on a transfer order
- **LT12**
  Confirm the transfer order
- **LT13**
  Confirm by storage unit

Now we will review the confirmation of the complete transfer order using Transaction LT12, which you can find by following the menu path SAP • LOGISTICS • LOGISTICS EXECUTION • WAREHOUSE MANAGEMENT • TRANSFER ORDER • CONFIRM • TRANSFER ORDER.

Figure 4.34 shows the selection screen for transfer order confirmation. The selection for the transaction can include more than the just the warehouse number and transfer order.

Open TO Items

Selecting this checkbox allows only open transfer order line items to be displayed; that is, line items that are not confirmed. This is useful when a transfer order has many line items. If all line items are to be displayed whether they are open or confirmed, then the checkbox should be unselected.

Subsystem Items

This checkbox refers to any external warehouse management system that is processing some element of the warehouse process. For example, the transfer order may be passed to an external system that controls a warehouse carousel system outside the SAP system.

Transfer Orders | 4.3

Figure 4.34 Initial Screen for Confirming a Transfer Order: Transaction LT12

If this checkbox is selected, then the display will show transfer orders that have been passed to the external system, and these can be reprocessed. Normally, when items are passed to an external system they are not processed further in the SAP system. However, this depends on the interfaces between the SAP system and the external system. Check with your data integrity team to confirm this.

Adopt Pick Quantity

This field determines the link between the picked quantity and the quantity posted. Five options are available:

- 1

    Include picking quantity in delivery

- 2

    Include picking quantity in delivery and post goods issue

- 3

    Do not include picking quantity in delivery

167

- **4**
  Do not take pick quantity as the delivery quantity but post goods receipt
- **Blank**
  Allow control through the movement type

The relationship between the pick quantity and the delivery quantity is more relevant in options 1 and 2. If the pick quantity is lower than the delivery quantity, the pick quantity overwrites the delivery quantity, and it is the pick quantity that gets posted.

Adopt Putaway Quantity

This field functions like the ADOPT PICK QUANTITY field, except that this field relates to the putaway quantity and not the pick quantity. There are five options for this field as well:

- **1**
  Stock placement quantity adopted into delivery as delivery quantity
- **2**
  Copy stock placement quantity as delivery quantity and post goods issue
- **3**
  Stock placement quantity is not adopted into delivery as delivery quantity
- **4**
  Do not take putaway quantity as delivery quantity but post goods receipt
- **Blank**
  Allow control through the movement type.

This field is used for the inbound delivery of material. Use option 1 or 2 if the delivery for the transfer order is complete, even if the quantity for putaway is less than the delivery expected. If more deliveries are expected for the transfer order, then the fourth option is most relevant.

Pick and Transfer

Select this radio button if the confirmation is required in one step for withdrawal of the material from the source storage bin and arrival of the material at the destination storage bin.

Pick

Select this radio button if you only need to confirm withdrawal of the material from the source storage bin for the transfer order items. When the material arrives at the destination storage bin, a second confirmation step will be required.

Transfer

Select this radio button if you only need to confirm the arrival of the material at the destination storage bin for the transfer order items.

Figure 4.35 shows the line item detail for the transfer order to be confirmed. The option to pick before confirmation is applicable when storage units are used for the material. This will be described in Chapter 11.

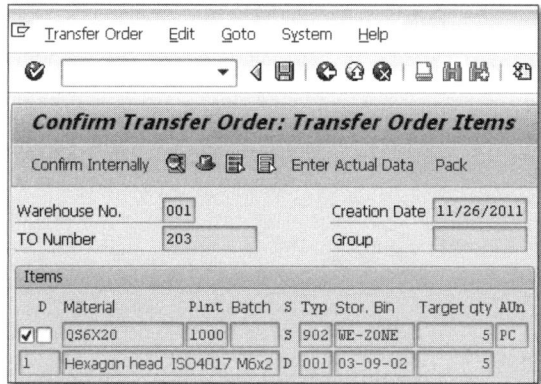

Figure 4.35 Detail Line Item Screen for Transfer Order Confirmation: Transaction LT12

Enter Actual Data

Instead of accepting the values proposed by the transfer order, you can enter the actual values, and a difference in quantities may arise. For example, the amount of material in the source storage bin may be less than the amount documented on the transfer order, or the amount counted into the destination bin may be more than expected.

To enter the actual quantities, click the INPUT LIST button shown in Figure 4.34. This displays a list of the actual data to be entered.

169

Figure 4.36 shows that the quantities for line items 1 and 2 have been entered as actual quantities that have produced a difference between the actual quantity and the quantity in the transfer order. The transfer order states that for item 1, the quantity to be received in the destination storage bin is 3, but an actual quantity of 4 has been entered.

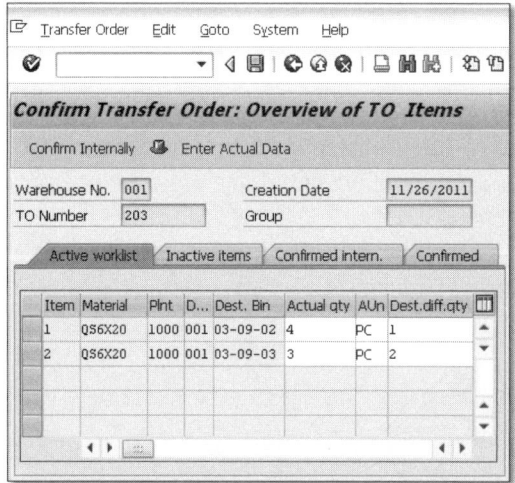

Figure 4.36 Active Worklist Allowing Actual Quantities for Transfer Order Confirmation: Transaction LT12

This has caused the destination difference quantity field (DEST. DIFF. QTY) to show a quantity of 1, which is the amount of the overage. Similarly, line item 2 was expected to show a quantity of 1, and a quantity of 3 was placed in the destination storage bin, causing a difference of 2. Posting the confirmation of the transfer order with actual data will cause a difference to be entered.

Figure 4.37 shows every difference between the transfer order quantity and the actual quantity entered into the transfer order confirmation screen. For each line item where there is a difference in quantities, a dialog box is displayed so that the user confirming the transfer order can confirm each stock difference. The differences are logically stored in storage type 999, and the storage bin is named the same as the transfer order where the differences occurred.

Once all the differences are confirmed, the transfer order is completed, and a message is displayed with the information that the transfer order is confirmed.

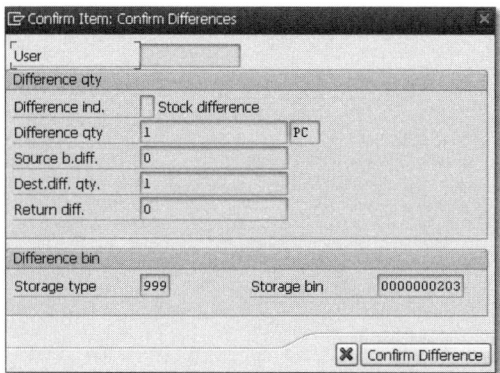

Figure 4.37 Confirmation of Quantity Differences Between Transfer Order Quantity and Actual Entered Quantity: Transaction LT12

4.3.5 Print a Transfer Order

The transfer order can be printed and used as a picking or putaway document for the warehouse staff. The transfer order is often printed so that each line item is a separate document, making it easier to manage.

The transfer order can be printed using Transaction LT31 and can be accessed via the menu path SAP • LOGISTICS • LOGISTICS EXECUTION • WAREHOUSE MANAGEMENT • TRANSFER ORDER • PRINT • TRANSFER ORDER.

Figure 4.38 shows the initial selection screen for the transfer order print transaction. The screen allows a single line item to be entered so the document contains just one movement.

Print Code

The print code is a two-character field that determines the printed layout of the transfer order. The print code is configured so that it is determined by warehouse. Therefore, a print code may be assigned for one warehouse only. One practical reason for this is that each warehouse needs different information printed out, such as instructions, addresses, or language.

The print code can be configured in Transaction OMLV and accessed through the menu path IMG • LOGISTICS EXECUTION • WAREHOUSE MANAGEMENT • ACTIVITIES • DEFINE PRINT CONTROL.

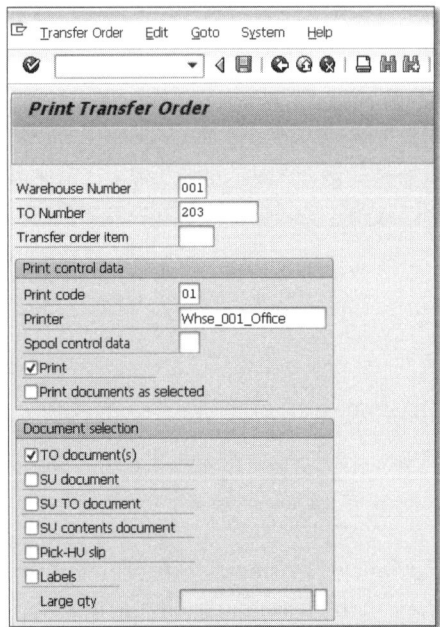

Figure 4.38 Selection Screen for Transfer Order Printing: Transaction LT31

Figure 4.39 shows the configuration of the print codes for the warehouse. The print code relates to a form layout that is assigned to a warehouse. If a custom layout for a form is designed, this transaction is where you assign the form to a warehouse with a new print code. The print code can then be used in the transfer order print transaction.

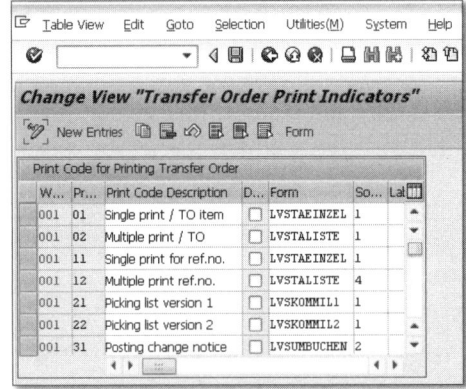

Figure 4.39 Configuration of Print Control for Transfer Order Printing: Transaction OMLV

Printer

Figure 4.38 shows the printer designation that has been entered as the location where the transfer order should be printed. The technical department should help if you have any issues with the locations of printers in the warehouse.

Spool Control Data

The spool code is defined in the same transaction as the print code: Transaction OMLV. It is a code that defines several parameters involved in printing documents. This print code is defined for each warehouse, and the configuration includes the number of copies, the delete after print checkbox, the print immediately checkbox, the new spool request checkbox, and so on.

Figure 4.40 shows the spool code configuration for each warehouse. Each spool code defines a set of parameters, which determine how the transfer order is printed along with the parameters in the print code.

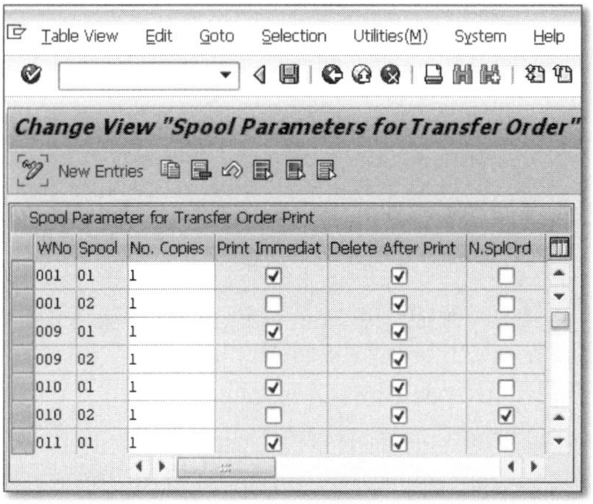

WNo	Spool	No. Copies	Print Immediat	Delete After Print	N.SplOrd
001	01	1	☑	☑	☐
001	02	1	☐	☑	☐
009	01	1	☑	☑	☐
009	02	1	☐	☑	☐
010	01	1	☑	☑	☐
010	02	1	☐	☑	☑
011	01	1	☑	☑	☐

Figure 4.40 Configuration of Spool Control for Transfer Order Printing: Transaction OMLV

Document Selection

You can select the document to be printed from the options on the initial screen: transfer order, storage unit documents, labels, and so on. To print the document, select Transfer Order • Print or press Ctrl+P.

Now that we have examined the transfer order functionality, we'll summarize the information contained in this chapter.

4.4 Business Examples—Warehouse Movements

Material is moved into the warehouse, around the warehouse, and ultimately out of the warehouse. Two different types of movements are relevant for the warehouse. These are warehouse movements triggered by other SAP functionalities, such as IM, and warehouse movements internal to the warehouse, such as bin-to-bin transfers or posting changes.

4.4.1 Warehouse Movements

In the warehouse there are movements of materials that relate either to a movement in the IM system, for example, a goods receipt or a goods issue, or to an internal warehouse movement that has no corresponding movement in IM. All of the movements that affect the warehouse need to be defined to ensure efficient warehouse operation.

Example

Some SAP customers use the IM functionality but interface to their existing warehouse management system (WMS). For whatever reason they choose to implement this method there are sometimes issues with the two systems getting out of sync. A manufacturer of generic pharmaceutical products implemented an SAP system across its enterprise but kept a highly customized legacy WMS in several of its locations. The WMS had provided the company with significant gains in productivity and was deemed to be too valuable to be replaced. The interface between the SAP system and the WMS was not complex but did not offer real-time processing. The interface was designed so that the WMS received information from the SAP system about the material and quality to be picked for an outbound delivery and similar information for an inbound movement into the warehouse. Because the SAP system did not have any information about the structure of the warehouse, the WMS did not receive any information about where to place or pick inventory.

The WMS independently created the movements in the warehouse based on the information that was received from the SAP system. This meant that the WMS processed individual movements in isolation, so that the warehouse staff would complete one movement and then return to the office to pick up the information about their next movement.

The management soon saw that this disconnect between the two systems was significantly reducing efficiencies in the warehouse. Before the SAP system was implemented, the warehouse completed over 100 movements per hour, but since the implementation, the number of movements had fallen to below 40.

The management decided to perform a pilot SAP WM project in one warehouse to gauge whether a full SAP WM implementation was required. After a month of developing the warehouse functionality in the SAP system, the trial began. Immediately, the warehouse started to outperform the legacy warehouses, as the warehouse staff had the ability to review the movements required in the warehouse and allocate them to operators, so travel time was reduced. After six weeks of the pilot project, the warehouse that was using SAP WM was operating at over 150 movements per hour, in spite of the steep learning curve for warehouse managers and operators. The pilot project ran for three months, and at the end of that period, warehouse movements exceeded more than 200 per hour. Over the next year the legacy WMS was replaced in the remaining warehouses.

4.4.2 Transfer Requirements

The transfer requirement is the phase of planning to move material from one warehouse location to another. When an IM movement is performed for an item located in a warehouse, a transfer requirement is generated to inform the warehouse that a corresponding movement is required in the warehouse.

Example

Occasionally, an SAP customer believes that SAP WM will be difficult to implement and that they need to automate the processes as much as possible to make it simple for users. One chemical company in Alabama believed that to have a successful, and fast, implementation they needed to ensure that every inventory movement would automatically generate a transfer requirement, automatically generate a transfer order, and then immediately confirm that transfer order. They assumed that by doing this the warehouse could organize itself based on the confirmed transfer order.

Ignoring advice from its consulting partner, the company implemented the process so that each inbound goods receipt would automatically generate a transfer requirement, then a transfer order, and then confirm the transfer order. The material would immediately show as confirmed in a storage bin, even though the product was likely still sitting on the receiving dock waiting for a warehouse operator to move it.

As the warehouse staff was used to a legacy warehouse system that was inaccurate, they were used to spending time looking for product that was not in the location suggested by the computer. After the SAP implementation, nothing much changed for the warehouse staff; they spent much of the shift finding and moving items that were confirmed in the SAP system but still located elsewhere. Often the warehouse operators would find that the storage bin where they were trying to place stock was already occupied by material waiting to be moved, as it was confirmed elsewhere. The warehouse manager spent more time moving material in the SAP system to empty bins, because movements were being performed out of sequence.

The issue came to a head after the first month end after the SAP implementation when a physical count of the warehouse found that accuracy had fallen below 60%, compared with 71% with the old system.

The company realized that it had made some rash decisions about how the warehouse processes should have been developed, and they asked their consulting partner for assistance. This time the processes were developed so that each movement was reviewed to see if a transfer order should be automatically created or whether the transfer requirement should be reviewed by warehouse staff and then a transfer order manually created. After each movement was analyzed and reconfigured, a reimplementation of the warehouse was performed. After a few weeks, some adjustments were made to the processes and configuration to make the warehouse operations more efficient.

4.4.3 Transfer Orders

A transfer order can be created with reference to a source document such as a transfer requirement, delivery document, material document, or posting change

Business Examples—Warehouse Movements | 4.4

notice (PCN). The transfer order contains the information required to perform the movement of materials into the warehouse, out of the warehouse, or from one storage bin to another storage bin within the warehouse.

Example

A manufacturer of automotive spare parts in Canada had acquired a smaller company in Detroit that was producing parts solely for a foreign car manufacturer who had several production sites in North America. The acquired company had a small warehouse facility, as most of its product was shipped out soon after being produced. The Canadian company had been using a leased warehouse in Michigan for parts that were shipped to customers in the United States but decided to move their stored parts to the warehouse of the company they had just purchased in Detroit.

The Canadian company rolled out their SAP system to the new company, and this included WM functionality. At the same time, the contract with leased warehouse expired, and the parts began arriving at the Detroit warehouse.

The Detroit warehouse was operating without major issues when the parts from the leased warehouse started arriving. Almost immediately the warehouse staff found that the parts that were arriving often would not fit in the bins that were noted on the transfer order. The operator would then take the items to an overflow storage area, note this on the paperwork, and return it to the warehouse office. The data entry clerk would change the storage bin on the transfer order and hand the amended document back to the operator. The item was picked up from the overflow area and moved to the new storage bin.

The issue arose because the bins were designed for the parts manufactured at the site, and the new company had parts that were significantly larger and would not fit in the existing bins. The result was that almost 40% of the transfer orders needed to be amended. When the warehouse was busy, the operators would place the items close to the bin noted on the transfer order and then confirm it. Additional transfer orders were then required to move the material to a suitable storage bin.

After almost a month of drowning in transfer orders, the company redesigned one area of the warehouse so that larger items could be accommodated. The number of transfer orders that could not be confirmed on putaway fell to almost zero.

However, another warehouse layout change was required six weeks later when the last of the items arrived from the leased warehouse.

4.5 Summary

Movements of material in the warehouse are of the utmost importance in making the warehouse work efficiently. IM passes information to the WM system about the movements of material in and out of the warehouse and how those movements should be addressed in WM.

Movements inside the warehouse determine where that material goes, how it gets there, how it is stored, and how it is retrieved. The transfer requirement and the transfer order are the two documents that move material inside the warehouse. Therefore, you need to know how the processes of each work individually and in combination.

This chapter explained the basic functionality of the transfer requirement and transfer order. The best way to learn more about how these processes work and how they are used in your particular industry is to practice in your sandbox development space with test data. Develop test plans and go through different scenarios with different materials to understand more about these important processes.

In Chapter 5, we will discuss the goods receipt process in more detail and show you how these movements are dealt with in the warehouse.

The warehouse receives material, and most of the material is received into SAP IM, which creates a transfer requirement and then a transfer order in SAP WM. It is important to ensure that the material is moved into the warehouse stock correctly.

5   Goods Receipts

In warehouse management, a goods receipt is the movement of material into the warehouse from an external source, which could be a production system, a vendor, and so on. The warehouse management functionality checks the goods receipt for accuracy and then processes it, moving the material into the warehouse and increasing the stock levels of the material received. A goods receipt into the warehouse is triggered by one of two documents, which can be either:

- A transfer requirement from inventory management or production
- An inbound delivery if handling unit management or an external system is used

Now that we have introduced the concept of goods receipts, we can go on to discuss the goods receipt process with inbound deliveries in detail.

5.1   Goods Receipt with Inbound Delivery

An inbound delivery is a document containing all the data required for creating and completing the inbound delivery process. This process starts on receipt of the material at the receiving dock and ends with the putaway of the material in a storage bin in the warehouse.

This section will review goods receipts with inbound deliveries, so we will start with an overview of the process.

5.1.1 Inbound Delivery Overview

An inbound delivery can be created with reference to several processes:

- Purchase order
- Stock transport order
- Customer return

There are many reasons to create inbound deliveries. The most useful one is that you can perform some processes in the SAP system before the material arrives and a goods receipt is posted. The vendor can send information about the inbound delivery, which informs the warehouse of the items being sent, the information they contain, and the precise date and time of delivery.

5.1.2 Creating an Inbound Delivery

You can create an inbound delivery using the information from a vendor regarding a single purchase order for which it is supplying the material. The transaction to create a manual inbound delivery is Transaction VL31N, which you can find by following the menu path SAP • LOGISTICS • LOGISTICS EXECUTION • INBOUND DELIVERY • INBOUND DELIVERY • CREATE • SINGLE DOCUMENTS.

Figure 5.1 shows the initial screen for creating a manual inbound delivery. The vendor number and the purchase order number are required fields. Let's discuss them here:

- **Delivery date**
  The delivery date is the date the vendor has given for delivery of the material. This is not necessarily the date stipulated in the purchase order to the vendor.

- **External ID**
  This is the identification that the vendor has assigned to this delivery. It may be the vendor's outbound delivery number or any identification that it requires. This field can be up to 35 characters long.

- **Means of Trans.**
  The means of transport is the packaging material type. It can be configured using Transaction VHAR or by following the menu path IMG • LOGISTICS EXECUTION • SHIPPING • PACKING • DEFINE PACKAGING MATERIAL TYPE. The packaging material type defines how the materials are shipped.

▶ **Means of transport ID**
The field to the right of the MEANS OF TRANS. field is the identification field, where you can enter a reference. For example, if the means of transport is a truck, then the means of transport ID may be the license plate of the truck or the trailer number or the vehicle VIN number. Up to 20 characters can be entered into this field.

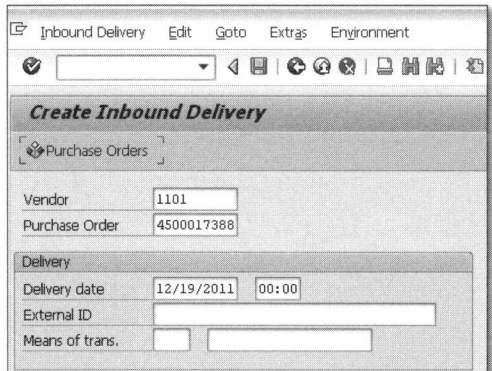

Figure 5.1 Initial Screen for Manually Creating an Inbound Delivery: Transaction VL31N

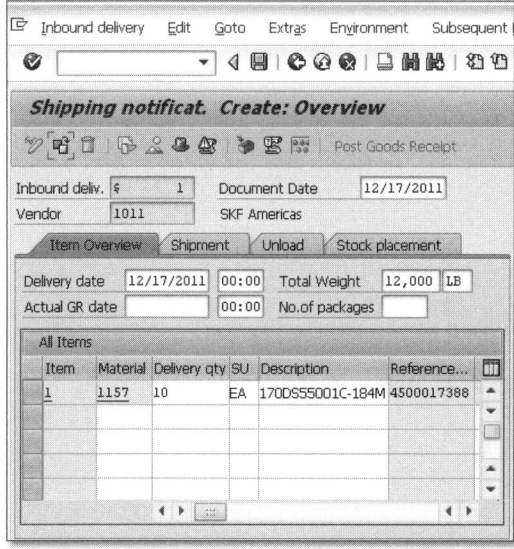

Figure 5.2 Item Overview Screen for Creating an Inbound Delivery: Transaction VL31N

Figure 5.2 shows the item overview for the inbound delivery being created. The delivery quantity and the item number have been entered, with the purchase order entered in the reference document field. The delivery item category field has been filled with ELN, which is used for inbound deliveries. The system proposes this value, but you can change it. The value determines how the line item is processed.

From this screen, the inbound delivery can be processed and an inbound delivery number is returned to the screen after posting.

5.1.3 Creating a Transfer Order for an Inbound Delivery

Once the inbound delivery has been created, the transfer order is created with reference to the inbound delivery document. Use Transaction LT0F to create a transfer order for an inbound delivery. You can find the transaction by following the menu path SAP • LOGISTICS • LOGISTICS EXECUTION • INBOUND PROCESS • GOODS RECEIPT FOR INBOUND DELIVERY • PUTAWAY • CREATE TRANSFER ORDER • FOR INBOUND DELIVERY.

Figure 5.3 Initial Screen for Creating a Transfer Order for Inbound Delivery: Transaction LT0F

Figure 5.3 shows the initial screen of Transaction LT0F, which shows the selections you can make to aid the creation of a transfer order. You must have the warehouse number and the inbound delivery when creating the transfer order. The other selection fields shown in Figure 5.3 are optional.

5.1.4 Using the Inbound Delivery Monitor

If you do not know the inbound delivery when using Transaction LT0F, you can use the Inbound Delivery Monitor to display open and completed deliveries. You also can use the monitor to process inbound and outbound deliveries.

Figure 5.3 also shows that you can access the Inbound Delivery Monitor through Transaction LT0F by clicking the DELIVERY MONITOR INB. DELIVERIES button on the initial screen. Otherwise, execute the Inbound Delivery Monitor via Transaction VL06I or by following the menu path SAP • LOGISTICS • LOGISTICS EXECUTION • INFORMATION SYSTEM • GOODS RECEIPT • INBOUND DELIVERY LISTS • INBOUND DELIVERY MONITOR.

In Figure 5.4, the monitor offers several options. In this section, we are creating transfer orders based on goods receipts. Therefore, you should select FOR GOODS RECEIPT on the monitor.

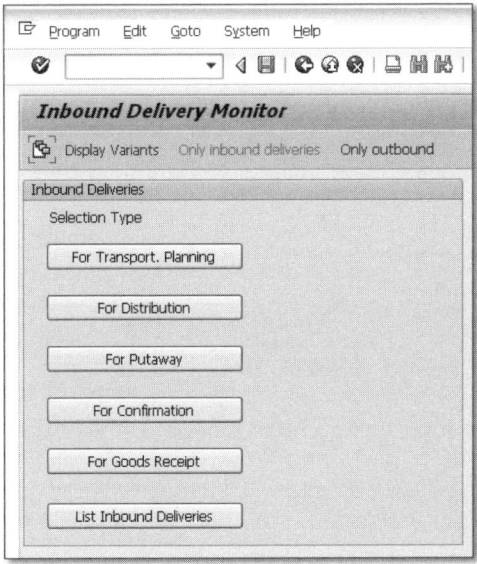

Figure 5.4 Initial Selection Screen for Inbound Delivery Monitor: Transaction VL06I

Figure 5.5 shows the selection fields that can be filled in to search for particular inbound deliveries based on the following search criteria. These are:

- **PO Data**
  A range for the purchase order and purchase order item
- **Time Data**
  The delivery date entered into the inbound delivery document
- **Putaway Data**
  The storage location and warehouse number

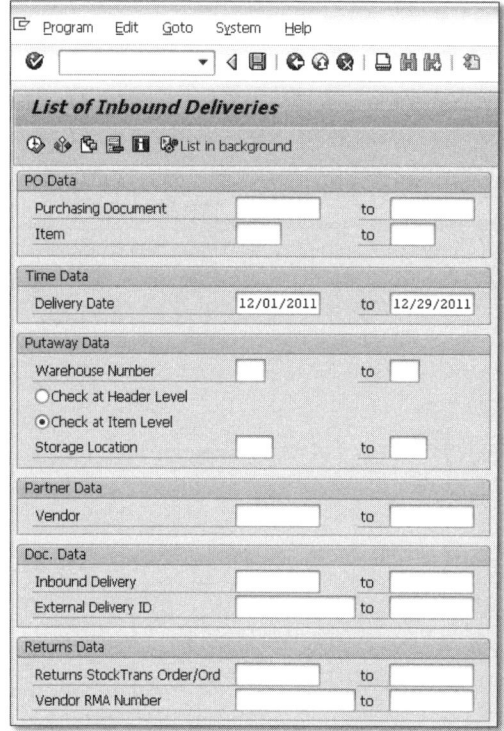

Figure 5.5 Inbound Delivery Monitor for Goods Receipts Selection Screen

The other two radio buttons in this area refer to warehouse checks at the header or item level.

If the CHECK AT HEADER LEVEL radio button is selected, then the system will only find inbound deliveries that have warehouse numbers in the header that meet the selection criteria.

If the CHECK AT ITEM LEVEL radio button is selected, then all deliveries that include at least one item that meets the warehouse number criteria are selected. Let's take a look at these criteria:

- **Partner Data**
  The vendor number or a range of vendor numbers of the required inbound deliveries
- **Doc. Data**
  The inbound delivery number and the external delivery number
- **Material Data**
  The UPC code or the vendor material number, if these are known

Once all the search criteria have been entered into the search, you can execute the transaction by choosing PROGRAM • EXECUTE or by pressing the [F8] function key.

After the data is entered into the selection criteria, the resulting inbound deliveries, shown in Figure 5.6, are found to have met those criteria. You can create a transfer order from a chosen inbound delivery by selecting SUBSEQUENT FUNCTIONS • CREATE TRANSFER ORDER.

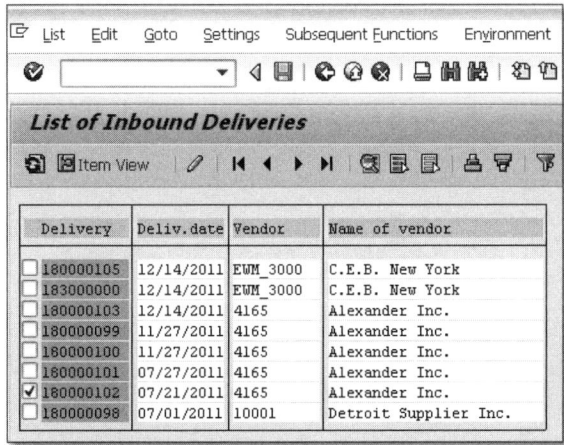

Figure 5.6 Search Results for Goods Receipt for Inbound Deliveries from Inbound Delivery Monitor

In Figure 5.7 a dialog box appears that requires you to enter parameters to create the transfer order from the inbound delivery. In the ADOPT PUTAWAY QTY field enter one of the options shown in Figure 5.7.

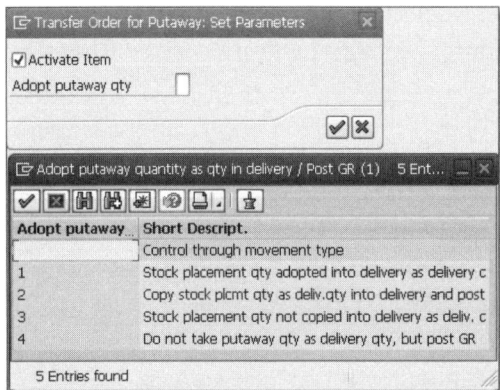

Figure 5.7 Creating a Transfer Order from Inbound Delivery 180000102: Adopting Putaway Quantity

Once you have selected a parameter, the process of creating a transfer order is performed in the background. If the transfer order is created, the system will generate a message saying the transfer order has or has not been created successfully.

If the transfer order has been created, you can see the document flow for the inbound delivery by selecting the inbound delivery from Figure 5.6 and choosing ENVIRONMENT • DOCUMENT FLOW.

Figure 5.8 shows the original inbound delivery and the handling unit associated with it. The transfer order has been created for the inbound delivery and is shown as an element of the document flow.

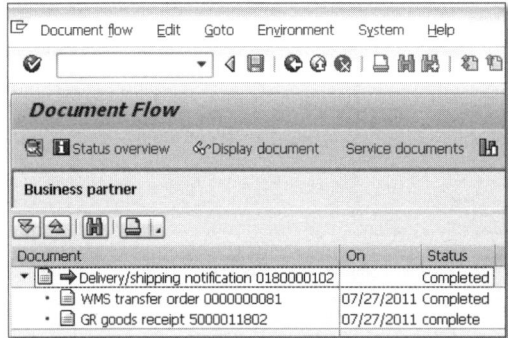

Figure 5.8 Document Flow for Inbound Delivery 180000102 Showing Created Transfer Order Number 81

Transaction LT21 enables the display of the transfer order, noted in the document flow for the inbound delivery.

Figure 5.9 shows the transfer order created for the inbound delivery. The system sets the confirmation flag because the transfer order was confirmed when it was created in the Inbound Delivery Monitor.

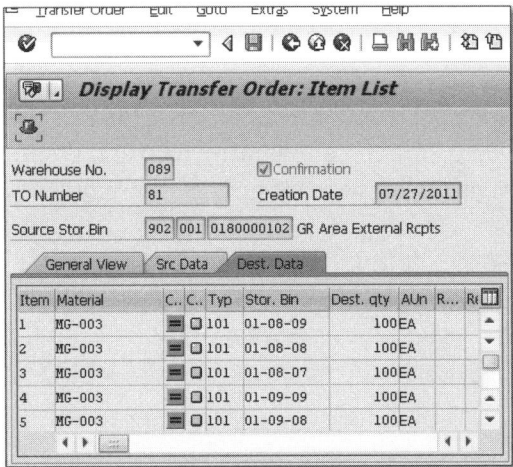

Figure 5.9 Display of Transfer Order Created for Inbound Delivery: Transaction LT21

Now that we have examined the goods receipt process with inbound deliveries, let's look at what happens when goods receipts are made without inbound deliveries.

5.2 Goods Receipt Without an Inbound Delivery

A goods receipt without an inbound delivery can occur when material arrives at the receiving dock without reference to an inbound delivery. The goods receipt occurs in IM, and a transfer requirement is created for the movement of the material into the warehouse.

5.2.1 Goods Receipt in IM

Goods receipts relevant to a warehouse management system can be produced by the arrival of material at the plant from a purchase order with a vendor. A goods receipt can be defined as a company's formal acceptance that materials were received from a vendor against a purchase order. Once the material is received and the transaction completed, the value of the material is posted to the general ledger.

The goods receipt transaction is Transaction MIGO, which you can access via the menu path SAP MENU • LOGISTICS • MATERIALS MANAGEMENT • INVENTORY MANAGEMENT • GOODS MOVEMENT • GOODS RECEIPT • FOR PURCHASE ORDER • GR FOR PURCHASE ORDER.

Figure 5.10 shows the goods receipt for a purchase order of material 1157. It also shows the quantity of material that will be receipted into plant 1000 and the GR goods receipt type 101, which represents a goods receipt for a purchase order.

Figure 5.10 Goods Receipt for Purchase Order in IM: Transaction MIGO

5.2.2 Reviewing the Material Documents

After all the relevant details such as storage location, batch number, and so on, have been added to the goods receipt transaction, the goods receipt can be posted. If the goods receipt does not return any error messages, the transaction will post and display the number of the material document for the movement of the material.

To view the material document, use Transaction MB03, which you can find by following the menu path SAP MENU • LOGISTICS • MATERIALS MANAGEMENT • INVENTORY MANAGEMENT • MATERIAL DOCUMENT • DISPLAY. On the initial screen, enter the material document number displayed after the goods receipt posted and the year, as shown in Figure 5.11.

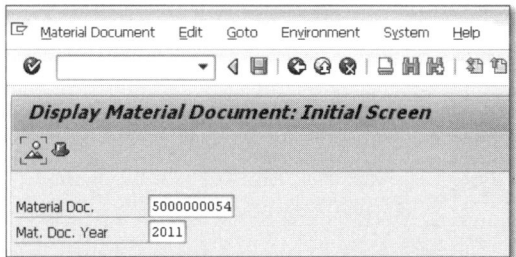

Figure 5.11 Initial Screen for Displaying a Material Document: Transaction MB03

After the material document number and the fiscal year have been entered, the material document can be displayed.

Figure 5.12 shows the material document that was created during the processing of the goods receipt for a purchase order. The material document shows the material, the plant, the storage location where the material will be stored, the purchase order number, the batch number of the material being receipted, and the movement type of the goods receipt that produced the material document.

In addition, the material document contains an option to show the accounting documents created because the material was received at the plant and moved into stock. The company therefore assumes financial liability for the material.

Figure 5.13 shows the accounting document relevant to the goods receipt of the material from the purchase order. The two lines of the accounting document show the financial liability moving from account 191100 (goods receipt account) to account 790000, which is the finished goods inventory account.

5 | Goods Receipts

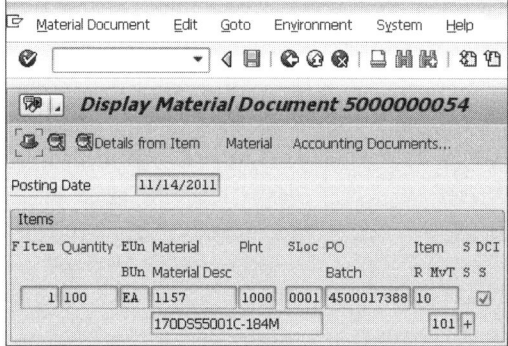

Figure 5.12 Display of Material Document Created by Goods Receipt for Purchase Order

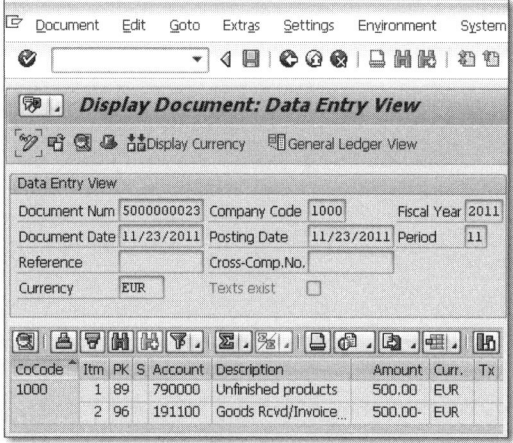

Figure 5.13 Display of Accounting Document Created as Part of Goods Receipt of Purchase Order

5.2.3 Reviewing Stock Levels after Goods Receipt

Once the goods receipt of the purchase order into inventory is complete, you can perform a stock overview to show the material in stock. To execute the stock overview, use Transaction MMBE, which you can access via the menu path SAP Menu • Logistics • Materials Management • Inventory Management • Environment • Stock • Stock Overview.

The stock overview screen shows the material that has been posted as a result of the goods receipt. The information regarding material 1157 is shown on the stock overview, shown in Figure 5.14. It matches the information in the material document, shown in Figure 5.12.

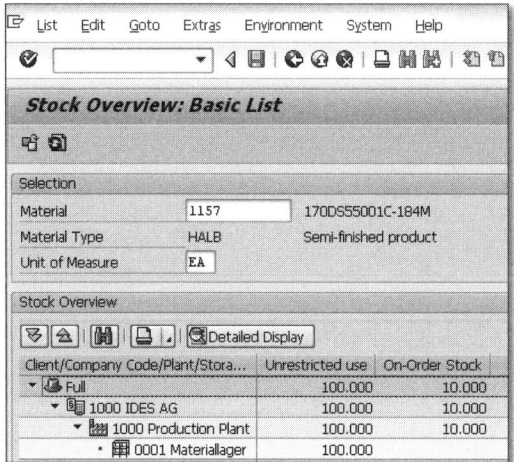

Figure 5.14 Stock Overview of Material 1157 in All Stock Locations: Transaction MMBE

5.2.4 Displaying the Transfer Requirement

The goods receipt of the material from the purchase order has been receipted into stock, as shown by the material documents and the stock overview program. This information reflects the movement into the stock location relevant to IM, but not the movement relevant to WM.

When the movement into the storage location was made, a transfer requirement was created, as the storage location is warehouse managed. You can find the transfer requirement by using Transaction LB11, which allows for a search of the transfer requirements by material number. To find this transaction, follow the menu path SAP MENU • LOGISTICS • LOGISTICS EXECUTION • INTERNAL WAREHOUSE PROCESSES • TRANSFER REQUIREMENT • DISPLAY • FOR MATERIAL.

Figure 5.15 shows the initial screen of Transaction LB11. To find all the transfer requirements for the material that has been goods receipted, enter the material number, warehouse number, and plant. You can also enter other information such as shipment type. In this example, shipment type E has been entered, restricting the transfer requirement search to stock placements.

5 | Goods Receipts

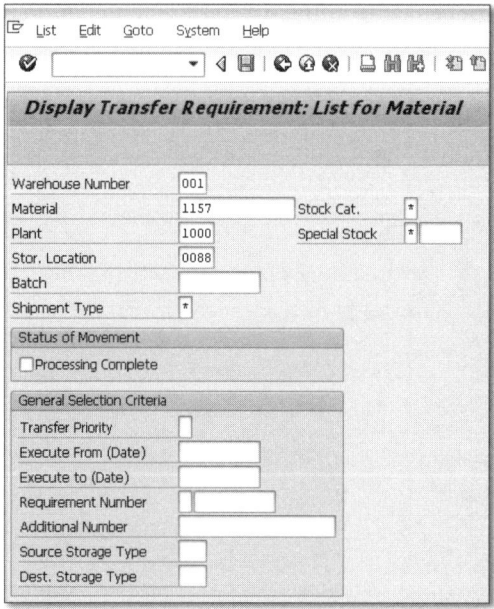

Figure 5.15 Display of Transfer Requirements for Single Material: Transaction LB11

Figure 5.16 shows the transfer requirement found using the search criteria entered in Figure 5.15. The transfer requirement has been created as a result of the goods receipt for the purchase order. The line item shows the transfer requirement number, movement type, and description that created the transfer requirement, the purchase order number that has been receipted into stock, and the quantity on the transfer requirement.

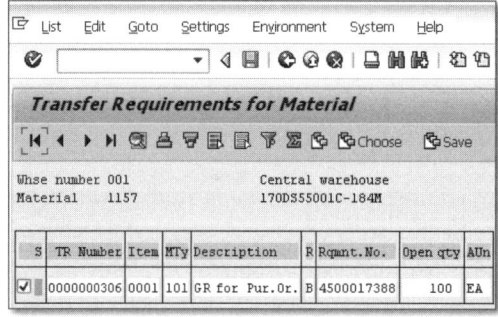

Figure 5.16 Display of Transfer Requirement Resulting from Search Criteria: Transaction LB11

Now that we have identified the transfer requirement, we can convert it to a transfer order. As Figure 5.16 shows, there are two ways to do this. You can create a transfer order in the foreground or the background.

To convert to a transfer order in the foreground, click the TO IN FOREGROUND button or press [Ctrl]+[Shift]+[F8]. You can also create the transfer order by selecting ENVIRONMENT • TO IN FOREGROUND.

Figure 5.17 shows the first screen displayed after you click the TO IN FOREGROUND button. You can review and change the information if necessary and then click the GENERATE + NEXT MAT button to complete the line item.

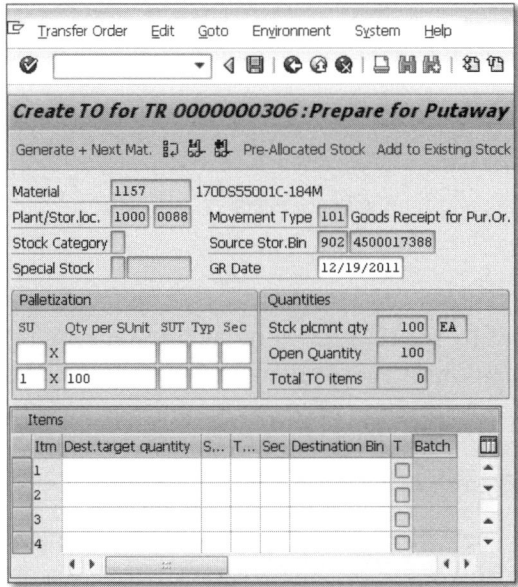

Figure 5.17 Conversion of Transfer Requirement to Transfer Order: Transaction LB11

Figure 5.18 shows the transfer order that has been created from the information shown in Figure 5.17. You can post the transfer order by selecting TRANSFER ORDER • POSTING or pressing [Ctrl]+[S].

Once the transfer order has been posted, the system returns to the display of transfer requirements, as shown in Figure 5.16, and the transfer order number is displayed at the bottom of the screen.

5 | Goods Receipts

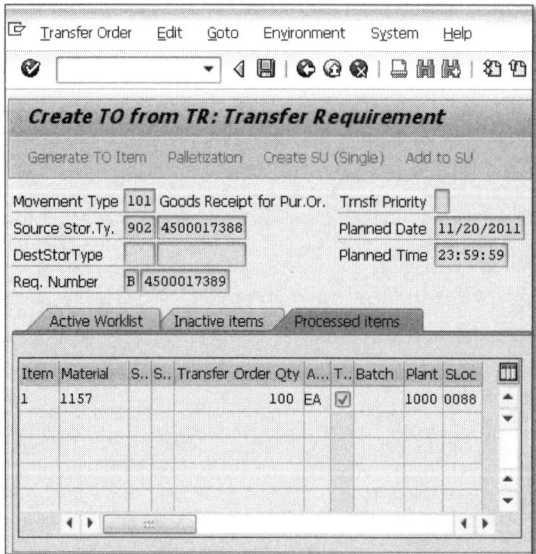

Figure 5.18 Display of Transfer Order Created from Transfer Requirement

5.2.5 Displaying the Transfer Order

You can see the transfer order created by the conversion of the transfer requirement to a transfer order with Transaction LT21 if you know the transfer order number. If just know the material, use Transaction LT24 or follow the menu path SAP MENU • LOGISTICS • LOGISTICS EXECUTION • INTERNAL WAREHOUSE PROCESSES • STOCK TRANSFER • DISPLAY TRANSFER ORDER • FOR MATERIAL.

Figure 5.19 shows the initial selection criteria screen for displaying transfer orders. All the transfer orders can be displayed for a material in a warehouse. In this example, the transfer order created for the goods receipt of material 1157 is being searched for, and the selection criteria reflect this.

Figure 5.20 shows the transfer order that has been created for purchase order 4500017388 that was receipted into the plant. A transfer requirement has been created to start the putaway in the warehouse. The conversion of the transfer requirement to the transfer order and the confirmation of the transfer order have moved the 100 units of material 1157 into warehouse storage bin 01 – 01 – 01 in storage type 001.

5.2 Goods Receipt Without an Inbound Delivery

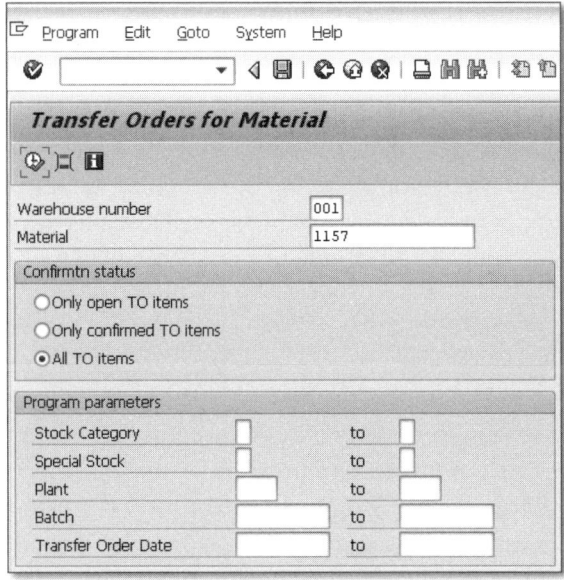

Figure 5.19 Initial Screen for Displaying a Transfer Order by Material Number: Transaction LT24

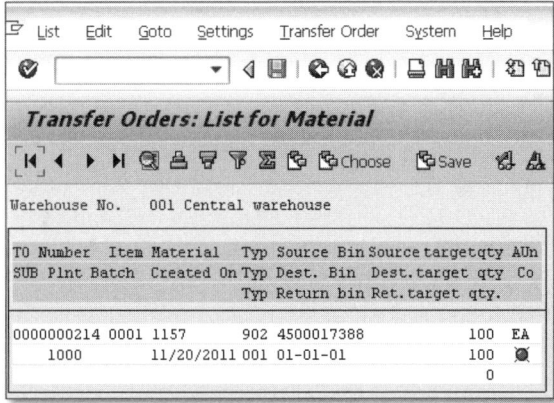

Figure 5.20 Display of Transfer Orders Available from Selection Criteria: Transaction LT24

In the last two sections, we described goods receipts with and without inbound deliveries. Now we will examine goods receipts that do not involve inventory management.

5.3 Goods Receipt Without Inventory Management

At first glance, this process may appear somewhat uncharacteristic. Normally, materials are receipted into a storage location, and that triggers a transfer requirement and a transfer order in WM. However, there are materials in the warehouse that sometimes do not require a goods receipt in IM but are required for warehouse operations. An example of this is packaging materials, such as pallets and crates. These are used for material storage and shipment but do not have to be goods receipted into IM.

5.3.1 Creating the Transfer Order for the Goods Receipt

You can create the transfer order without reference to a goods receipt from IM or a transfer requirement in WM. You can create a transfer order in Transaction LT01 or via the menu path SAP MENU • LOGISTICS • LOGISTICS EXECUTION • INTERNAL WAREHOUSE PROCESSES • STOCK TRANSFER • CREATE TRANSFER ORDER • NO SOURCE OBJECT.

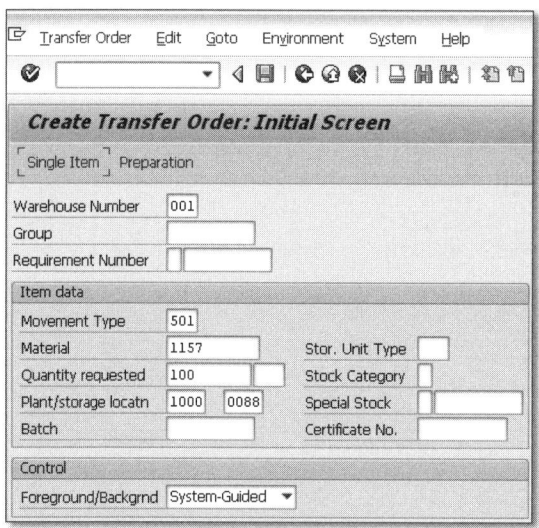

Figure 5.21 Initial Screen for Creating a Transfer Order Without IM: Transaction LT01

Figure 5.21 shows the initial screen for creating the transfer order using Transaction LT01. Goods movement number 501 is used here refer to a receipt without a purchase order. In this scenario, a vendor may have dropped off a shipment of 100 pallets to be used in the shipment of parts. Many industries use pallets that they lease at a very small charge per day; for example, GKN pallets.

> **Note**
>
> A GKN pallet is a series of blue wooden strips and blocks crafted into a square shape, about 1.2 square meters. It is manufactured by CHEP, a division of GKN, and is rented to companies for less than a dollar per day.

Figure 5.22 shows the detail screen for Transaction LT01. The screen shows that the material putaway will come from source storage type 902, which is the goods receipt area. The system will generate the destination storage type and storage bin. To create the transfer order, press [Ctrl]+[S] or select TRANSFER ORDER • POSTING. Once posting is complete, the system returns to the initial screen and displays the transfer order number it has created.

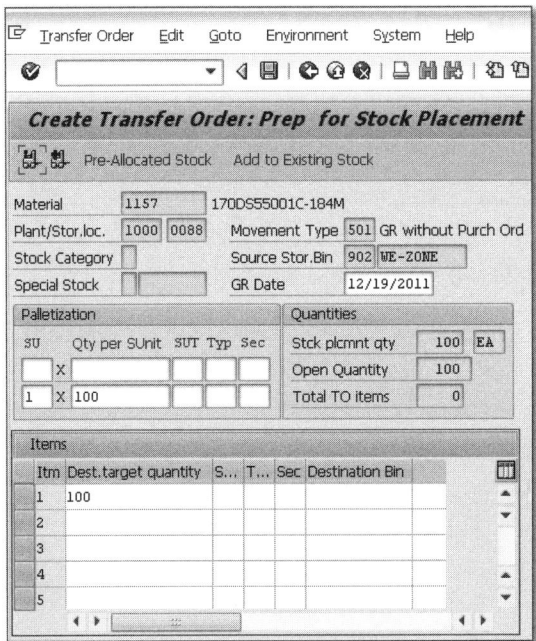

Figure 5.22 Detail Screen for Creating a Transfer Order for Material Receipt Without IM: Transaction LT01

5.3.2 Displaying Transfer Order for the Goods Receipt

You can review the information in the transfer order by using Transaction LT21 to display the contents of the transfer order or following the menu path SAP Menu • Logistics • Logistics Execution • Internal Warehouse Processes • Stock Transfer • Display Transfer Order • Single Document. The transaction requires that the just the warehouse number and the transfer order number be entered to display the transfer order details.

Figure 5.23 shows the details of the line item in the transfer order created for the goods receipt. The material has been moved from storage type 902, storage section 001, and storage bin WE-ZONE to storage type 001, storage section 001, and storage bin 01 – 09 – 03. Note that the quantity of 100 has not been confirmed because the system has not selected the confirmation checkbox next to the warehouse number.

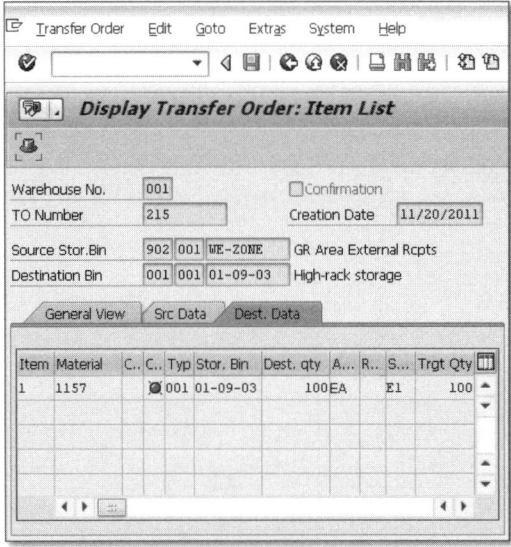

Figure 5.23 Display of Transfer Order Created for Material Goods Receipt Without IM: Transaction LT21

5.3.3 Displaying the Stock Levels

Prior to the posting of the transfer order and the receipt of the material into the warehouse stock, you can review the stock levels for the material in the warehouse. To do this, use Transaction LS24 or follow the menu path SAP MENU • LOGISTICS • LOGISTICS EXECUTION • INTERNAL WAREHOUSE PROCESSES • BINS AND STOCK • DISPLAY • BIN STOCK PER MATERIAL.

Figure 5.24 shows initial screen for Transaction LS24, which allows selections to be made to report on the stock levels for the material required. In this example, the display for stock levels of material 1157 is limited to warehouse number 001, but for all storage types.

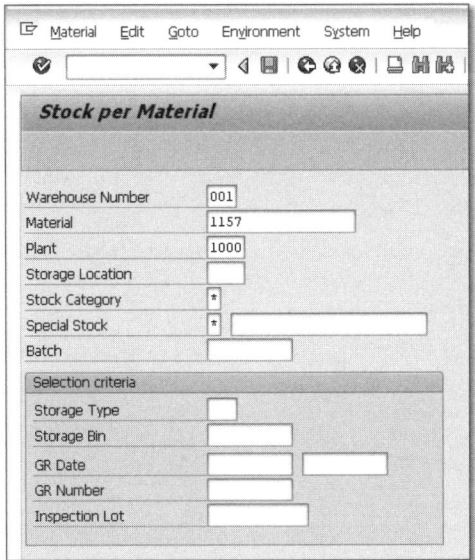

Figure 5.24 Initial Screen to Display a Transfer Order by Material: Transaction LS24

Figure 5.25 shows the stock levels for material 1157. It shows that the material is located in the 902 receiving area that is not yet moved to storage type 001 and placed in bin 01 – 01 – 01. Therefore, the transfer order should be confirmed using Transaction LT12 or by following the menu path SAP MENU • LOGISTICS • LOGISTICS EXECUTION • INTERNAL WAREHOUSE PROCESSES • STOCK TRANSFER • CONFIRM TRANSFER ORDER • SINGLE DOCUMENT • IN ONE STEP.

Figure 5.26 shows the information required to confirm the transfer order and move the material from the goods receipt area to storage bin 01 – 01 – 01 in storage type 001.

5 | Goods Receipts

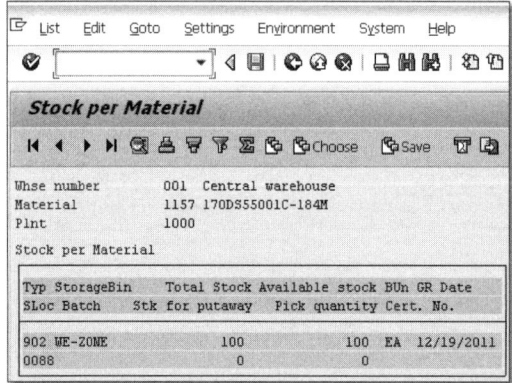

Figure 5.25 Display of Stock Levels for Material 1157 in Warehouse 001: Transaction LS24

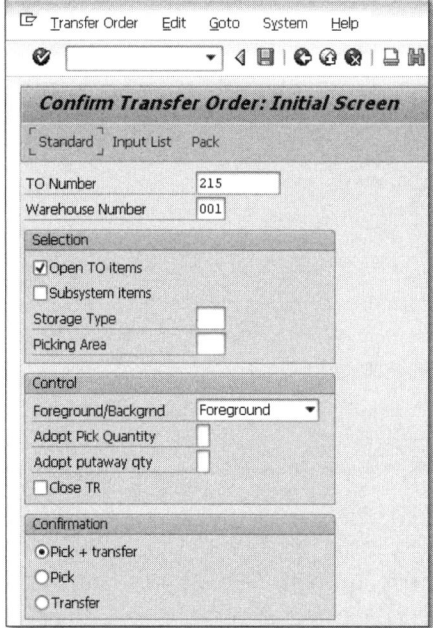

Figure 5.26 Initial Screen to Confirm Transfer Order: Transaction LT12

You can confirm the movement by checking the bin stock using Transaction LS24. Enter the same information in the initial screen as in Figure 5.24. The resulting screen after confirmation of the transfer order shows the material posted into the correct storage bin. Figure 5.27 shows the final placement of the material in the warehouse.

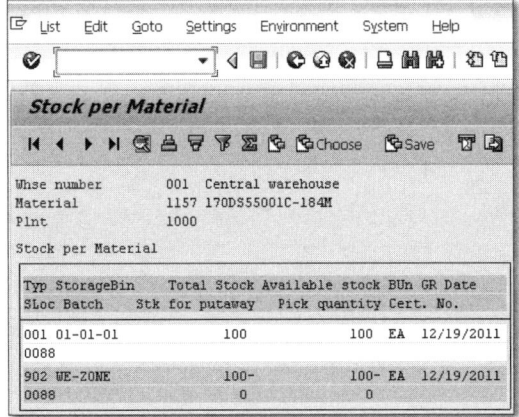

Figure 5.27 Stock per Material Report Showing Movement from WE-ZONE to Storage Bin 01 – 01 – 01

5.4 Business Examples—Goods Receipts

A goods receipt into the warehouse is a movement of material into the warehouse from an external source, which could be a production system, a vendor, and so on. The functionality checks the goods receipt for accuracy and then processes it, moving the material into the warehouse and increasing the stock levels of the material received.

5.4.1 Goods Receipt with Inbound Delivery

You can create an inbound delivery with reference to several processes, such as a purchase order, stock transport order, or customer return. Inbound deliveries are useful, as it is possible to perform some processes in the SAP system before the material arrives and a goods receipt is posted.

Example

A manufacturer of elevator parts developed a goods receipt procedure for receiving raw materials used in their manufacturing process. Because the parts they manufactured had to pass strict quality control standards the company had a goods receiving procedure that was equally as stringent. Each delivery of raw material was visually examined by the receiving staff for damages to the packaging, and if they believed the item was damaged, it was rejected before any other tests were made. If the packaging was found to be satisfactory, the raw material was received into a blocked stock area where physical and chemical tests were performed. If the quality department approved the items, then the goods receipt was processed and received into the warehouse.

The process ensured that only materials meeting the specifications were received into the warehouse, but it was a lengthy process that only verified the results given to them by the vendor. The length of the process was a problem on occasion due to material being needed for production orders that were about to commence. The production department became concerned that time and money was being wasted verifying the data supplied by vendors who they had been working with for many years.

The supply chain management team reviewed the concerns of the production department as well as the purchasing and quality teams who were equally apprehensive that items could be received that were not of sufficient quality.

The management worked with the most trusted vendors and proposed a revised procedure. Some vendors would allow testing of the parts at their facilities on a regular basis, and if the material was passed, inbound deliveries were created to expedite the goods receipt into the warehouse. The creation of an inbound delivery meant that the warehouse and quality departments spent less time and resources on receiving material that had already been tested.

5.4.2 Goods Receipt Without an Inbound Delivery

A goods receipt for a delivery that is not an inbound delivery can occur when the material is not packed, such as when material arrives at the receiving dock from the vendor without any containers or pallets. The goods receipt occurs in IM, and a transfer requirement is created for the movement of the material into the warehouse.

Example

A beverage company based in Austria purchased a small Polish regional beverage company. The Polish company operated with a variety of custom systems that were interfaced using overnight batch processes. The disparate systems were often out of sync, and it was possible for items to arrive at the receiving dock without a purchase order, and sometimes the material file was still waiting for an update. The staff was aware of these issues, and items were received into the warehouse due to a lack of space to hold these incoming deliveries without valid paperwork.

After the migration to their parent company's SAP system, the warehouse staff in Poland was informed that they should always have an inbound delivery available due to the real-time nature of the data. Nevertheless, the staff would still on occasion receive deliveries directly into stock without an inbound delivery. This practice was immediately halted when it was found that one vendor frequently sent deliveries with quantities greater the order quantity, with a shorter shelf life and no order documents.

After this situation was found, the company instituted a zero-tolerance policy, where no delivery was accepted without an inbound delivery.

5.4.3 Goods Receipt Without Inventory Management

Sometimes there are materials in the warehouse that do not require a goods receipt in IM but are required for warehouse operations. An example of this is packaging materials, such as pallets and crates. These are used for material storage and shipment but do not have to be goods-receipted into IM.

Example

A manufacturer of specialty parts for small aircraft had been supplying parts to customers with basic packaging when they were shipped by a local freight company. Several years ago the freight company implemented increased restrictions on shipping parts that contained fluids, such as batteries. The company was informed that fluids would have to be placed within a leak-proof plastic container supplied by the freight company.

Because the customer returns the damaged or worn part and the container to the manufacturer, the container is not sold and is nonvaluated. The containers are sent out with the part, and there is a period of time before the container is returned. At any one time there were over a hundred containers at customer sites or in transit. The company required a stock of containers delivered to them at regular periods to cover this shortfall and to replace damaged containers.

Because the containers were not purchased, the shipping company delivered them to the manufacturer when they were required. The company did not receive the containers using a purchase order but created a transfer order for the items so they could be stored in the warehouse.

5.5 Summary

Material is receipted into stock using purchase orders or production orders. The material can easily be goods-receipted using inventory management, but several steps are needed to move and store the material in SAP WM. This chapter explained the procedures required when material is brought into the warehouse, either as a normal receipt or as a receipt that involves handling units.

Chapter 6 will examine the opposite of goods receipt: goods issue. Moving the material from the warehouse involves a variety of procedures that you should understand clearly.

The outbound delivery process can be complex and labor-intensive. You should understand the goods issue function clearly to use more complex strategies such as wave picking to implement a successful outbound process in the warehouse.

6   Goods Issues

In warehouse management, a goods issue is the movement of material from the warehouse to an external source, which could be a production order or a customer. The warehouse also can use goods issue as the process for consuming material and assigning the costs of the material consumed to a cost center.

A goods issue from the warehouse is triggered by one of two documents: a transfer requirement from inventory management or production, or an outbound delivery if one has been created for a customer sales order.

This chapter will examine the goods issue functionality that includes outbound deliveries, groups, and wave picks. Now let's proceed to the next section, which will examine the goods issue process with outbound deliveries.

6.1   Goods Issue with Outbound Delivery

An outbound delivery involves picking materials in the warehouse, reducing the material level in the warehouse, and shipping the materials to the customer. The goods issue is important to the customer because it creates a link between the manufacturer and the customer. If the goods issue process does not run at optimum efficiency, delays in delivery can cause the customer financial problems and create customer dissatisfaction.

The outbound delivery is created from a sales order that specifies an amount of material to be delivered to a customer. The sales order is usually created by the sales clerks or received in electronic format.

6 | Goods Issues

6.1.1 Displaying the Sales Order

When the sales order has been created, the customer is given a delivery date by which they can expect the material to arrive at their location. The sales order contains this information as well as the material details, quantity, and pricing.

If the sales order number is known, SAP WM users can view the sales order using Transaction VA03 or by following the menu path SAP • LOGISTICS • SALES AND DISTRIBUTION • SALES • ORDER • DISPLAY.

The sales order displayed in Figure 6.1 is used to create an outbound delivery. The sales order shows that the customer's purchase order was placed on 11/10/2011 and the delivery date for the material is 11/11/2011. The sales order shows the item details, such as the material number and the quantity ordered.

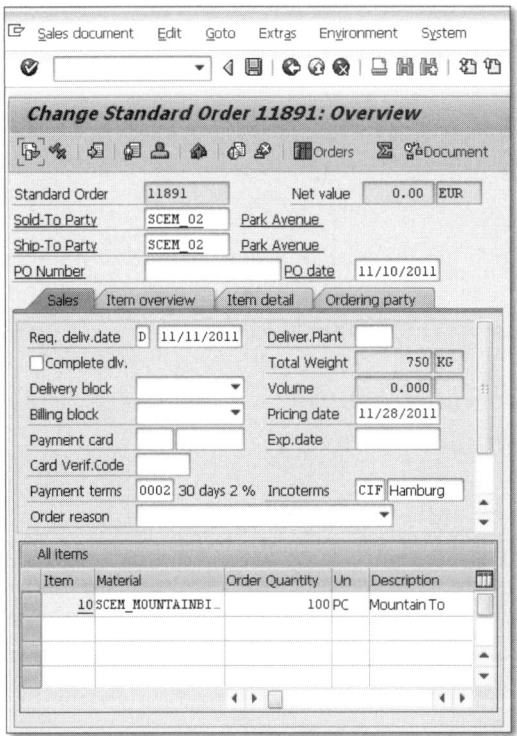

Figure 6.1 Detailed Display of Sales Order: Transaction VA03

6.1.2 Creating the Outbound Delivery

When the sales order has been placed, you can create the outbound delivery, which can occur at a specific time before the material needs to be picked. The specific procedure from which outbound deliveries are created varies from company to company.

> **Tip**
>
> Ask your sales or warehouse staff when the outbound delivery needs to be done.

To create the outbound delivery, use Transaction VL01N or follow the menu path SAP • LOGISTICS • SALES AND DISTRIBUTION • SALES • ORDER • SUBSEQUENT FUNCTIONS • OUTBOUND DELIVERY.

When you create outbound deliveries, the initial screen of Transaction VL01N (shown in Figure 6.2) requires you to enter the shipping point. The shipping point is a location from which items are shipped and is configured in the Logistics Execution section of the IMG. The menu path is IMG • ENTERPRISE STRUCTURE • DEFINITION • LOGISTICS EXECUTION • DEFINE, COPY, DELETE, CHECK SHIPPING POINT.

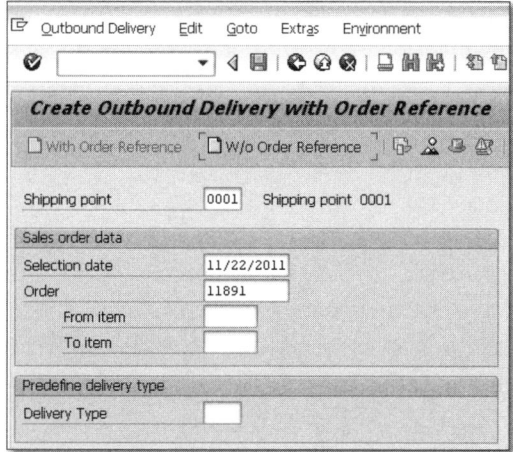

Figure 6.2 Initial Screen for Creating an Outbound Delivery with Reference to a Sales Order: Transaction VL01N

The shipping point can be assigned to several plants. In large distribution or retail operations, the loading area for vehicles may be a separate location that supports several locations on the company's campus. A shipping point can be further divided into loading points.

Figure 6.3 shows the detail screen for a shipping point. The information required for a shipping point includes the factory calendar and country location.

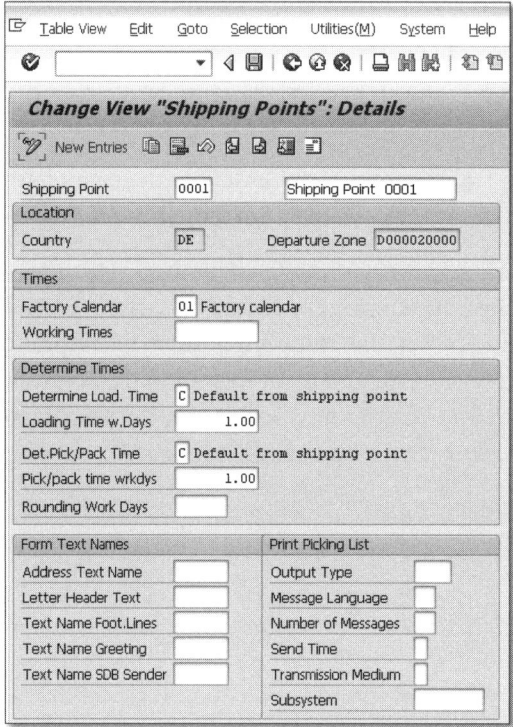

Figure 6.3 Configuration Details for a Shipping Point

After entering the shipping point into the initial screen of Transaction VL01N (Figure 6.2), you can also enter the sales data, which includes the delivery date and the sales order number. If no other data is required, you can enter information such as the delivery date and sales order document number, and the detail screen will be displayed.

Figure 6.4 shows the detail screen for delivery creation based on a sales order. The information from the sales order has been entered, such as the material number, the quantity to be delivered, the date for staging the material for delivery, and the planned goods issue date.

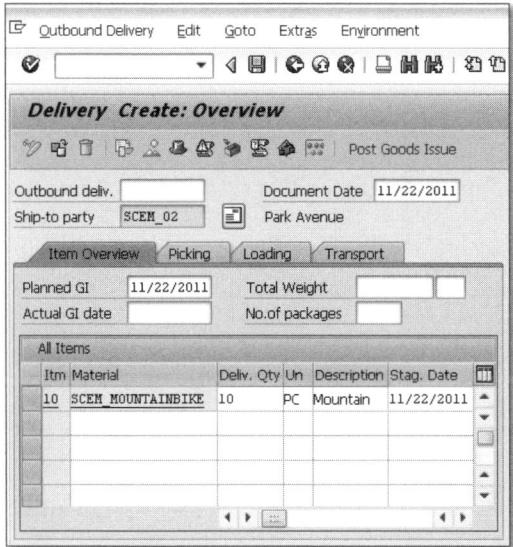

Figure 6.4 Detail Screen for Delivery Creation: Transaction VL01N

If this information is correct and does not require any changes, then you can create the outbound delivery by selecting OUTBOUND DELIVERY • SAVE or by pressing [Ctrl]+[S]. Once processing is complete, the system returns you to the initial screen for outbound delivery creation and displays the outbound delivery number on the screen.

6.1.3 Outbound Delivery Status

We can analyze the status of the elements of the outbound delivery by displaying the status overview. Executing Transaction VL03N to display the outbound delivery displays of the status overview information. The navigation path for this transaction is SAP • LOGISTICS • SALES AND DISTRIBUTION • SHIPPING AND TRANSPORTATION • OUTBOUND DELIVERY • DISPLAY.

Figure 6.5 shows the status overview for the outbound delivery. The overview reports two elements: the delivery shown in the overall status and the material shown in the line item status. Each element has several items for which a status is given.

6 | Goods Issues

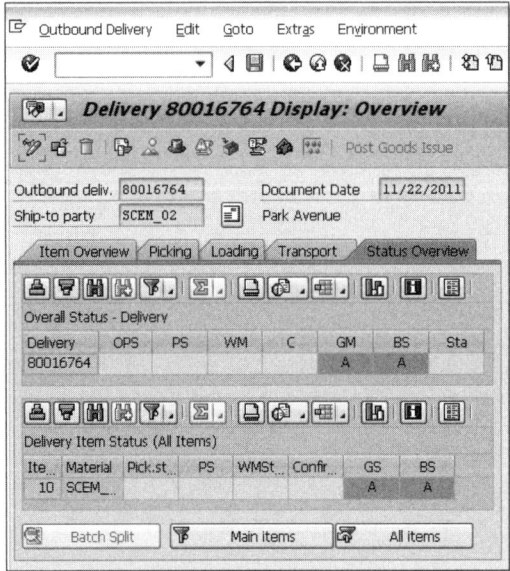

Figure 6.5 Status Overview Information from Outbound Delivery Display: Transaction VL03N

Overall Status

This overall status line refers to the status of the delivery. Several indicators provide details of the status:

- **OPS**

    This status field shows the overall status for picking the delivery. It tells whether the delivery has been completely picked (option C), is in the process of being picked (option B), or has not yet been processed (option A).

- **PS**

    This field contains the packing status, which indicates whether there are items that are relevant for packing. Status A is allocated when the packing has not been processed, status B when the delivery is partially packed, and status C when it is completely packed.

- **WM**

    This field shows the overall status of warehouse management activities. The status indicates whether a transfer order for SAP WM is required and, if required, whether it is confirmed or still open for processing.

- **C**

    This field shows the status of picking confirmation. This confirmation status indicates whether picking must be explicitly confirmed for the delivery or whether picking already has been confirmed. The confirmation status is only relevant if transfer orders are not for picking.

- **GM**

    This field shows the total goods movement status. It informs you whether the delivery has left the warehouse or is still being processed and whether processing has begun.

- **BS**

    This indicator shows the billing status of the sales or delivery document. The status describes if the document is completely billed, partly billed, or not relevant for billing.

- **Sta**

    This field shows the status for intercompany billing.

- **TS**

    This field indicates the transportation planning status and is set on the basis of the leg indicator (preliminary, subsequent, direct, return) in the headers of the shipment documents to which delivery has been assigned. The status can be:

    - **A**

        Not yet planned

    - **B**

        Partially planned

    - **C**

        Completely planned

- **OvCS**

    This indicator is relevant for the overall status of credit checks.

- **POD Status**

    This indicator is the proof of delivery (POD) status for the entire delivery. The status informs whether the customer reported a POD for this delivery. The values can be:

    - **A**

        Relevant for the POD process.

- B

  Differences were reported.

- C

  Quantities were verified and confirmed.

Delivery Item Status

In Figure 6.5, the delivery item status line refers to item 10. Several indicators report on the item status:

- **Pick St**

  The status message indicates whether the item is relevant for delivery. The status indicates whether picking has not yet processed (A), is partially processed (B), or is completely processed (C). Some items are not relevant for picking and show no indicator. These can include text or service materials.

- **PS**

  This field refers to the packing status for the line item.

- **WM Stat**

  This field shows the SAP WM status of the delivery item. If the delivery processing uses the WM functionality, then the status for each item in a delivery is updated by the system.

- **Confir.**

  This field shows the pick confirmation status for each delivery item. When a delivery item is subject to pick confirmation, the item is assigned the status A to indicate that the line is subject to confirmation but not yet confirmed. Once the pick is confirmed, the system assigns either status B for partially confirmed or status C if the line item is fully pick-confirmed.

- **GS**

  This field is for the goods movement status. For outbound deliveries, the status shows whether the item has left the warehouse or company premises or is still being processed.

- **BS**

  This is the billing status of delivery-related billing documents. The status line tells you if the item is not yet billed, partly billed, completely billed, or not relevant for billing.

- **IBS**
  This indicator shows the status for the intercompany billing.
- **POD status**
  This indicator is for the proof of delivery status of each item. The status value informs the user whether the customer reported a proof of delivery for this item. This status can have the following values:
  - **Blank**
    Not relevant for the POD process.
  - **A**
    Relevant for the POD process.
  - **B**
    Differences were reported.
  - **C**
    Quantities were verified and confirmed.

6.1.4 Creating the Transfer Order

The transfer order needs to be created for the material to be removed from its storage bin in the warehouse and moved to the area where materials are staged for delivery.

The transfer order is created with reference to the outbound delivery document that has been created. You can have more than one transfer order per delivery, but only if the configuration parameters for transfer order split have been entered for the relevant warehouse.

Transfer Order Split Configuration

Multiple transfer orders can be created for an outbound delivery to ensure that a single transfer order does not exceed certain limitations. Creating multiple transfer orders distributes the workload more evenly. The configuration entered determines at what point multiple transfer orders are created.

You can find the configuration for the transfer order split by following the menu path IMG • LOGISTICS EXECUTION • WAREHOUSE MANAGEMENT • ACTIVITIES • TRANSFERS • PROCESSING PERFORMANCE DATA/TO SPLIT • DEFINE PROFILES.

Figure 6.6 shows the configuration to create the profiles used in the relevant warehouses. Configuring the profile's parameters at certain levels can cause transfer order splits.

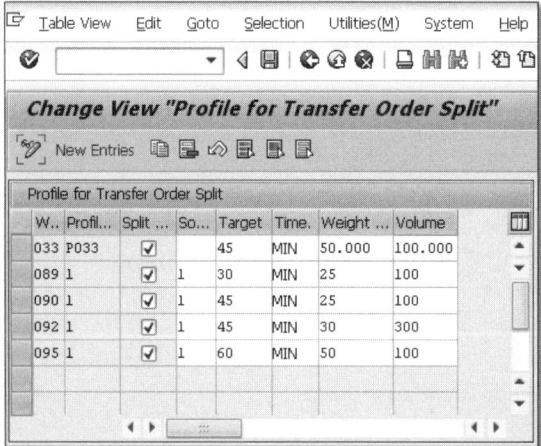

Figure 6.6 Configuration for Allowing Transfer Order Splits in Outbound Delivery

For each warehouse, a series of indicators can be set to define the profile for the transfer order split that occurs in that warehouse. The indicators are described as follows:

- **Split picking**
  Various criteria control the way a transfer order is split. When this checkbox is selected, the transfer order will be split; that is, a new transfer order is created when the picking area is changed.

- **Sort**
  This field determines the sort profile for the transfer order. The sort profile is used to maximize warehouse efficiency in picking transfer orders. In the sorting fields, you can enter sort criteria such as storage bin, material weight, and so on, that are saved in the sorting profile.

- **Time (Limit)**
  You can configure this field with the value that indicates the maximum limit of processing time for a transfer order. For example, a value of 60 will be the total processing time for a single transfer. If the processing time exceeds this value, a new transfer order will be created. If this field is blank, there is no limit for

processing time for a transfer order. A limit is used to ensure that the workload is evenly spread in the warehouse.

- **Weight (Limit)**
  Similar to the time limit, this field allows entry of a weight limit to control transfer order splitting. If the weight of the transfer order exceeds the value in this field, this triggers a new transfer order. For example, if a value of 200 is entered into this field and a transfer order is entered with a total weight of 670, then four transfer orders will be created. A blank field indicates that there is no weight limit to a transfer order.

- **Volume (Limit)**
  Similar to the weight and time limit fields, this field allows you to enter a volume that will trigger a new transfer order when it is exceeded.

Outbound Delivery Monitor

The Outbound Delivery Monitor is a comprehensive tool that enables the shipping department of the warehouse to view deliveries that need to be picked, based on a variety of criteria entered into the transaction. You can use the outbound delivery monitor to create the transfer order for the delivery.

You can access the Outbound Delivery Monitor using Transaction VL06P. The navigation path to this transaction is SAP • LOGISTICS • SALES AND DISTRIBUTION • SHIPPING AND TRANSPORTATION • PICKING • CREATE TRANSFER ORDER • VIA OUTBOUND DELIVERY MONITOR.

Figure 6.7 shows the selection criteria that can be entered into the Outbound Delivery Monitor to select specific deliveries. In this example, the criteria have been entered to select all applicable deliveries that are due to be shipped from shipping point 1200 and to be picked using warehouse management between 11/02/2011 and 11/10/2011.

To execute the transaction, press the [F8] function key or select PROGRAM • EXECUTE.

Figure 6.8 shows the deliveries that fall within the criteria entered into the Outbound Delivery Monitor selection screen. These deliveries are all warehouse management-relevant, to be picked between 11/02/2011 and 11/10/2011, and all are to be shipped from shipping point 1200.

6 | Goods Issues

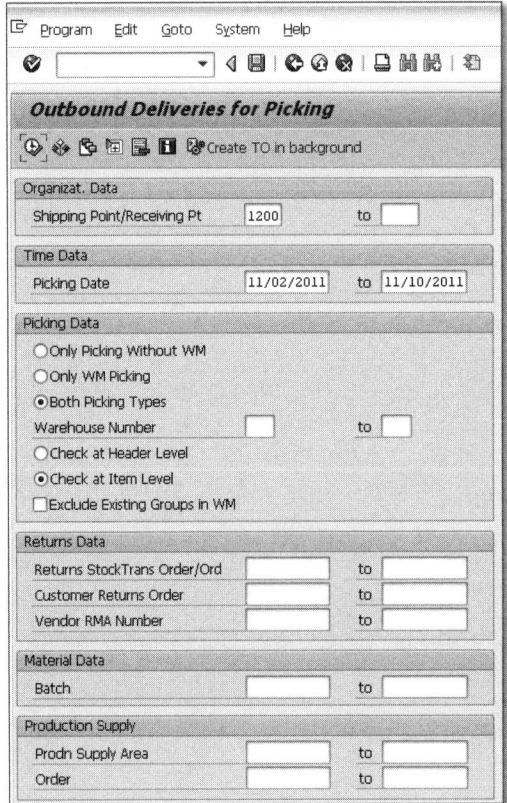

Figure 6.7 Selection Screen for Outbound Delivery Monitor

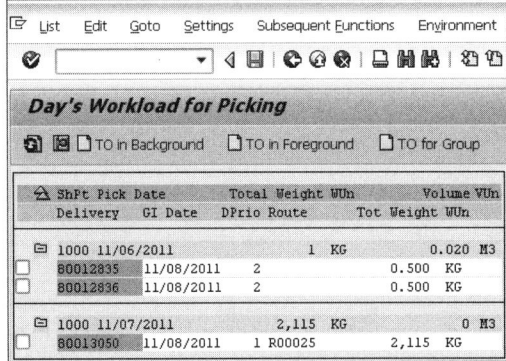

Figure 6.8 List of Deliveries Based on Selection Criteria Entered in Outbound Delivery Monitor

You can create the SAP WM transfer order from this screen. In Figure 6.8, you can see buttons for allowing a transfer order to be created either in the foreground or the background. You also can create a foreground transfer order by pressing the F8 function key and a background transfer order by pressing F7.

After you select a delivery and start the process of creating a transfer order from the delivery note, the Outbound Delivery Monitor transaction passes the parameters to Transaction LT03. Figure 6.9 shows the initial screen of that transaction. At this point, you have the option of creating the transfer order in the foreground or in the background.

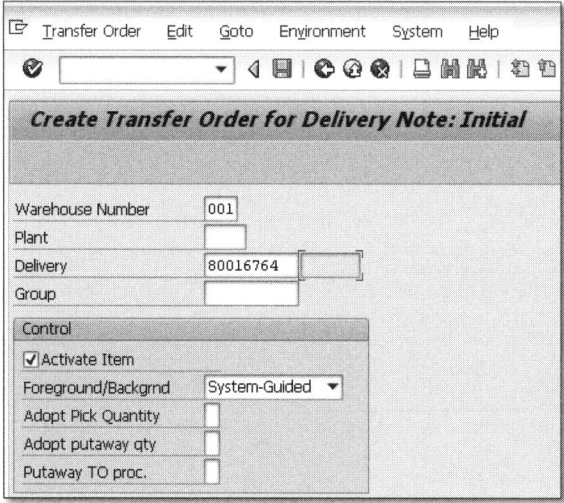

Figure 6.9 Creating a Transfer Order from the Outbound Delivery Monitor

Figure 6.10 shows the work list of delivery line items to be converted to a transfer order. The line item shows the outbound delivery number, material, plant, storage location, and picking quantity.

You can create the transfer order by clicking the GENERATE TO ITEM button or selecting SUBSEQUENT FUNCTIONS • GENERATE TO ITEM. The transaction processes the work list information, generates a list of processed items that can be saved, and creates a transfer order.

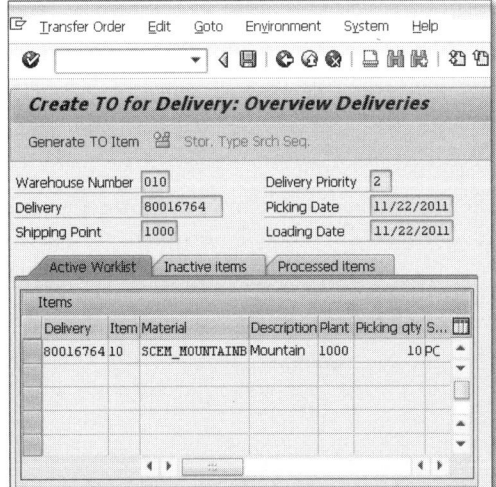

Figure 6.10 Display of Delivery Line Item Used to Create a Transfer Order

Figure 6.11 shows the item that has been processed from the work list and will be the line item in the transfer order. To complete this transaction, you must post it by pressing `Ctrl`+`S` or selecting TRANSFER ORDER • POSTING. The transaction will return to the results for the Outbound Delivery Monitor, and the transfer order number will be displayed.

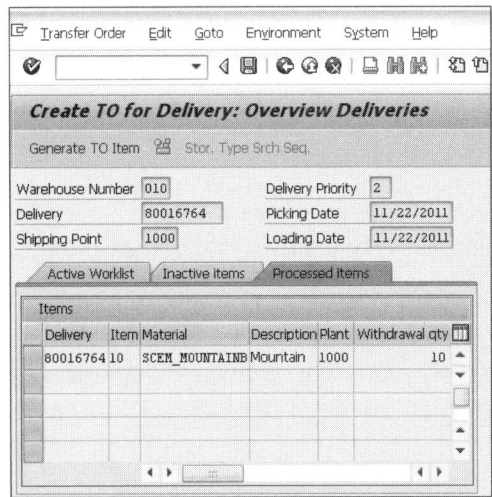

Figure 6.11 Display of Items Processed when Creating a Transfer Order from Outbound Delivery

6.1.5 Confirming the Transfer Order

Once the transfer order has been created, the material can be picked and moved to the packing area or loading area, depending on the processes that need to be carried out on the material before it leaves the warehouse. Many materials that are shipped on pallets are shrink-wrapped in plastic before they leave the warehouse to prevent damage in transit.

You can confirm the transfer order using Transaction LT12 or via the menu path SAP • LOGISTICS • LOGISTICS EXECUTION • OUTBOUND PROCESS • GOODS ISSUE FOR OUTBOUND DELIVERY • PICKING • CONFIRM TRANSFER ORDER • SINGLE DOCUMENT • IN ONE STEP.

Figure 6.12 shows the initial screen for confirming the transfer order for the outbound delivery. The confirmation is performed in one step that combines a pick and a transfer of the materials. If the pick and the transfer are to be separate processes, the confirmation radio buttons at the bottom of the screen can be changed to reflect that.

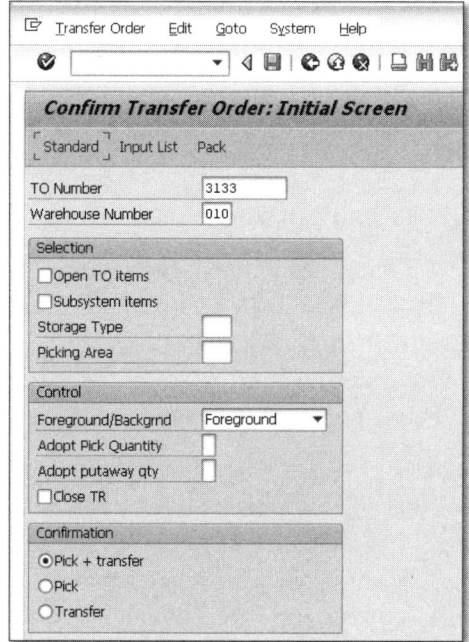

Figure 6.12 Confirmation of Transfer Order: Transaction LT12

Figure 6.13 shows that the material to be picked and moved is located in storage type 005. The destination storage location is 916, which is the interim storage type used as the shipping area.

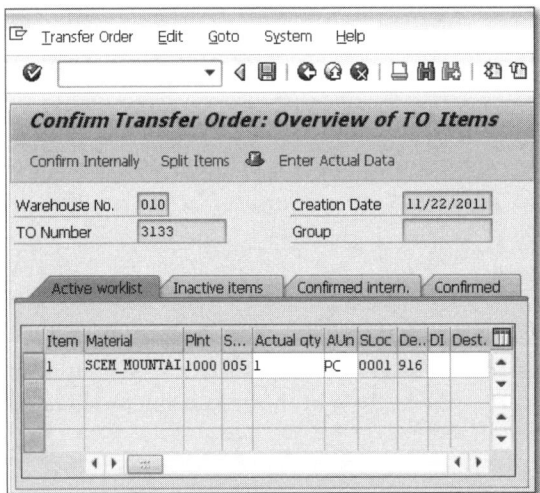

Figure 6.13 Confirmation of Transfer Order: Transaction LT12

You can confirm the transfer order internally by clicking the button on the screen, pressing the [F5] function key, or selecting EDIT • CONFIRM INTERNALLY.

6.1.6 Posting the Goods Issue for Outbound Delivery

After the transfer order has been confirmed and is completed, the material is ready for delivery. The material is sitting in the delivery area, awaiting loading onto a delivery vehicle or delivery by a third party such as UPS or FedEx. The outbound delivery document is ready to be closed, and the movement of the material out of the warehouse is completed in the system by posting the goods issue.

Figure 6.14 shows the goods movement data for the inventory management side of the delivery. The IM movement type is 601 for a goods issue for a delivery. You can click the POST GOODS ISSUE button in the toolbar to post a goods issue. If for any reason the delivery cannot be posted, an error log will be displayed to identify the problems that are preventing goods issue for the line items on the document. Posting the goods issue moves the material from the warehouse, and the inventory value is removed from the plant.

6.1 Goods Issue with Outbound Delivery

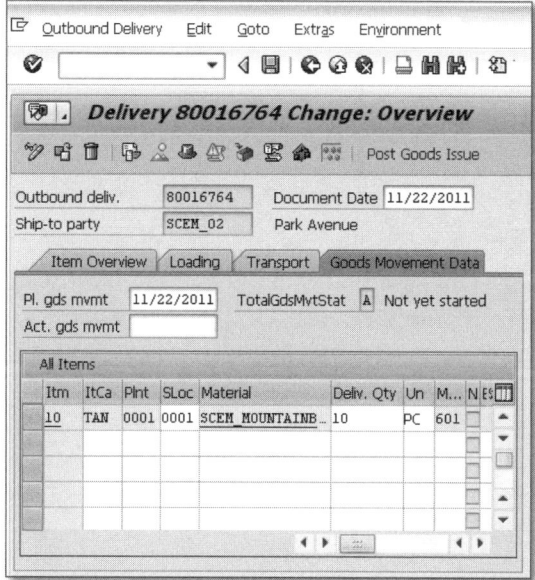

Figure 6.14 Outbound Delivery Ready for Posting of Goods Issue

6.1.7 Reviewing Material Documents

To review the movement of the outbound delivery, you can use two transactions for reviewing the material documents, MB51 and MB03. Transaction MB51 can be used to show all the movements of the material, either inbound or outbound. You can find this transaction by following the menu path SAP • LOGISTICS • MATERIALS MANAGEMENT • INVENTORY MANAGEMENT • ENVIRONMENT • LIST DISPLAY • MATERIAL DOCUMENTS.

Figure 6.15 shows the material documents created for the outbound delivery. The material document can be viewed in detail using Transaction MB03, which can be found using the navigation path: SAP • LOGISTICS • MATERIALS MANAGEMENT • INVENTORY MANAGEMENT • MATERIAL DOCUMENT • DISPLAY.

Figure 6.16 shows the material document that was produced by posting the goods issue for the outbound delivery. The outbound delivery number is shown in the material document as the material slip number.

Now that we have examined the goods issue process supported by outbound delivery, we'll review the goods issue process without outbound deliveries.

6 | Goods Issues

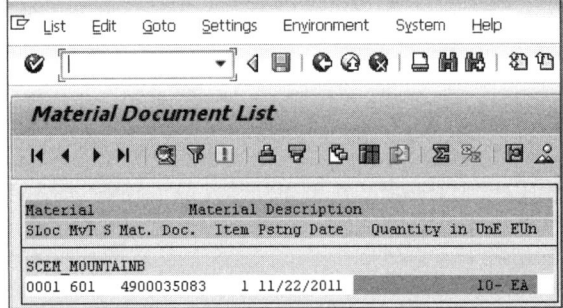

Figure 6.15 Material Documents for a Single Material: Transaction MB51

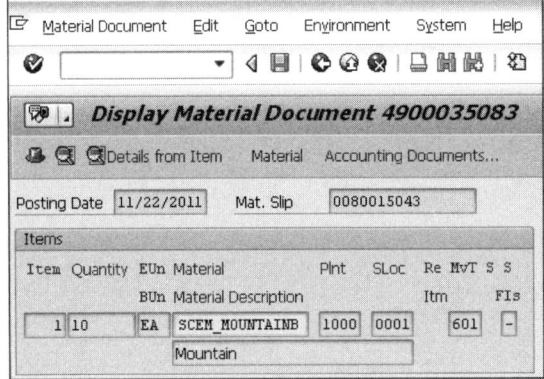

Figure 6.16 Material Document for Outbound Delivery: Transaction MB03

6.2 Goods Issue Without an Outbound Delivery

The goods issue created without an outbound delivery starts with a goods issue that is created in SAP IM. This may be a goods issue to a cost center, a goods issue to a project, or several different scenarios.

6.2.1 Goods Issue in IM

The goods issue to a cost center does not require an outbound delivery and can be performed in inventory management. This transaction is made prior to the movement of the material in the warehouse. Therefore, the accounting movement is performed before the actual movement of the material.

6.2 Goods Issue Without an Outbound Delivery

You perform the goods issue with Transaction MB1A, which you can find by following the menu path SAP • LOGISTICS • LOGISTICS EXECUTION • OUTBOUND PROCESS • GOODS ISSUE FOR OTHER TRANSACTIONS • ENTER GOODS ISSUE.

Figure 6.17 displays the initial screen for Transaction MB1A and shows the movement type for the goods issue as 201, which refers to a goods issue to a cost center. There are many reasons for issuing a material to a cost center. The issue to a cost center consumes the material, and the value of the material is moved from the inventory account to the cost center. In this case, the material will be issued to the plant maintenance cost center for use in a repair project.

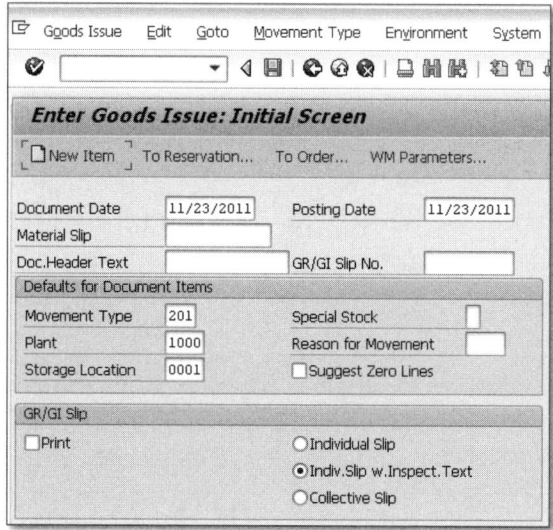

Figure 6.17 Initial Screen for Goods Issue to a Cost Center: Transaction MB1A

Figure 6.18 shows that the cost center has been added to the detail screen. The cost center relates to plant maintenance, and the value of the material will be passed to the cost center.

The material and quantity are added to the detail screen, and the goods issue is then posted. This creates a material and accounting document for the goods issue.

6 | Goods Issues

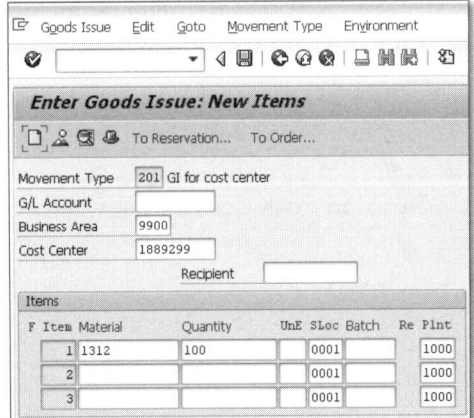

Figure 6.18 Detail Screen for Goods Issue: Transaction MB1A

6.2.2 Negative Balance in the Warehouse

Since the material in question is governed by SAP WM, the goods issue creates the need for a movement to occur in the warehouse. To initiate a transfer order to move the material, the goods issue creates a negative balance in the goods issue interim storage area in the relevant warehouse.

To see the negative balance for the material referred to in the goods issue, you can use Transaction LS24 by following the menu path SAP • LOGISTICS • LOGISTICS EXECUTION • INTERNAL WAREHOUSE PROCESSES • BINS AND STOCKS • DISPLAY • BIN STOCK PER MATERIAL.

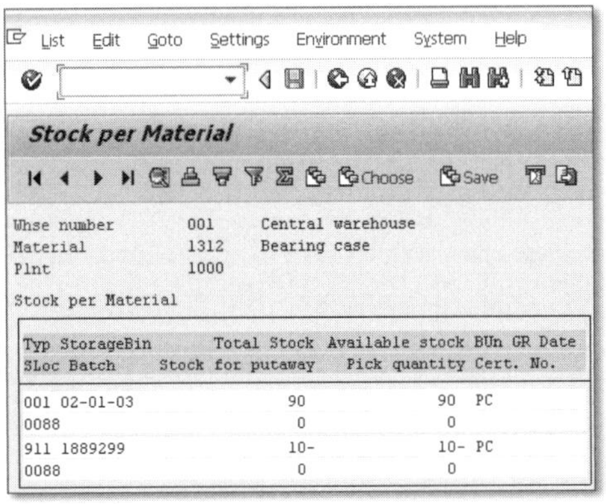

Figure 6.19 Display of Stock in Warehouse for a Specific Material: Transaction LS24

Figure 6.19 shows that the goods issue created in SAP IM has created a negative balance in interim storage type 911. The storage bin has been named the same as the cost center where the material is to be consumed.

6.2.3 Creating a Transfer Order

The transfer order is created from the material document produced from the goods issue. Normally, once the goods issue is posted, the processing automatically passes through to Transaction LT06. You can find this transaction by following the menu path SAP • LOGISTICS • LOGISTICS EXECUTION • OUTBOUND PROCESS • GOODS ISSUE FOR OTHER TRANSACTIONS • PICKING • CREATE TRANSFER ORDER • FOR MATERIAL DOCUMENT.

Figure 6.20 shows the initial screen for creating the transfer order based on the material document for the goods issue. The system needs to create the transfer order to move the material from the warehouse to balance the negative value in the goods issue interim storage area.

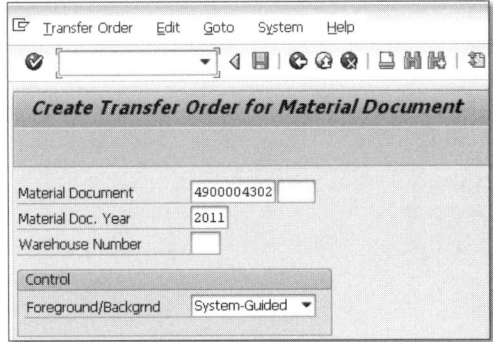

Figure 6.20 Creating a Transfer Order from a Goods Issue Material Document: Transaction LT06

Figure 6.21 shows the requirement passed through to the transfer order from the material document. The storage type search shows that the transfer order will fulfill the requirement from either storage type 001 or 002. The transfer order item information is generated from this screen.

Figure 6.22 shows the item details for the transfer order. The material quantity shown is to be removed from a source storage type and transferred to the goods issue interim storage area to offset the negative value caused by the goods issue.

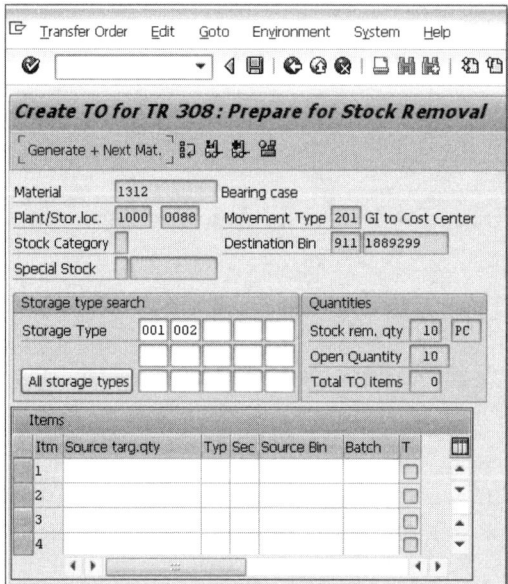

Figure 6.21 Item Information from a Goods Issue Material Document: Transaction LT06

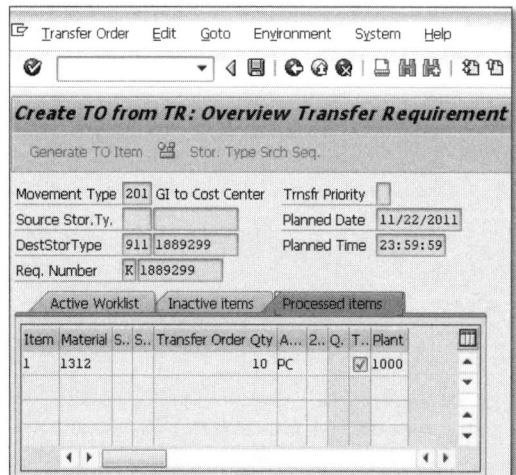

Figure 6.22 Transfer Order Creation from a Goods Issue Material Document: Transaction LT06

After the transfer order has been created in Transaction LT06, it must be confirmed. You should do this after the material has physically been moved from the source storage bin to the goods issue area to ensure that the correct materials are moved and there is no damage or loss.

> **Tip**
>
> In many warehouses, an automatic confirmation is assumed, and the confirmation may take place as soon as the transfer order is created. Check with the warehouse staff to see how this is performed in their organization.

Complete the transfer order by using Transaction LT12 or by following the menu path SAP • LOGISTICS • LOGISTICS EXECUTION • INTERNAL WAREHOUSE PROCESSES • STOCK TRANSFER • CONFIRM TRANSFER ORDER • SINGLE DOCUMENT • IN ONE STEP.

Transaction LT12 requires that the transfer order number and the warehouse be entered for the confirmation. After the transfer order number and warehouse have been entered, the detail screen for the confirmation is displayed as shown in Figure 6.23.

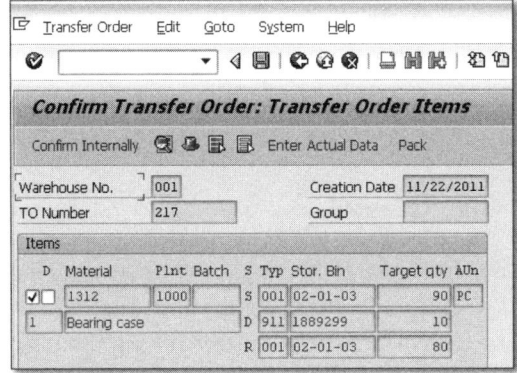

Figure 6.23 Confirmation of Transfer Order: Transaction LT12

The screen shows that material 1312 has a quantity of 90 in storage bin 02 – 01 – 03 and that a quantity of 10 is required to offset the negative quant in the goods issue storage type. The remainder of the material, a quantity of 80, is stored back in storage bin 02 – 01 – 03. Confirm the transfer order by clicking the CONFIRM INTERNALLY button.

To see the resulting stock balance in the warehouse again, use Transaction LS24.

Figure 6.24 shows that all of the warehouse processes are now complete. The quantity of the material, 1312, is now 80. This has been reduced because negative quant in storage type 911, as shown in Figure 6.19, has been offset by the quantity transferred from storage type 001.

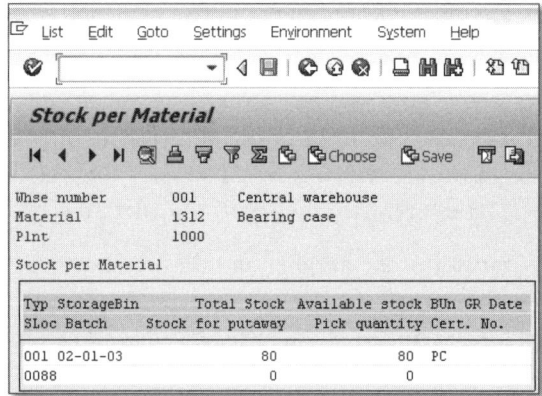

Figure 6.24 Display of Stock in Warehouse for a Specific Material: Transaction LS24

In this section, we examined the goods issue process without outbound deliveries. The next section will review multiple processing using groups.

6.3 Multiple Processing Using Groups

Multiple processing allows the SAP WM user to group transfer requirements or outbound deliveries and process the group together. Processing a group of requirements or deliveries, rather than converting each transfer requirement or each outbound delivery into a transfer order, can reduce the amount of administration time taken on these tasks.

6.3.1 Definition of a Group

A group is defined as a work package containing several transfer requirements or outbound deliveries. This work package is used for optimizing picking operations. Grouping transfer requirements together for the same movement type or the same storage type can increase the productivity of the warehouse operation.

6.3.2 Creating a Group for Transfer Requirements

Groups are often created for transfer requirements when many material movements in the warehouse are triggered by transfer requirements. In a distribution warehouse, many movements are required to satisfy the deliveries to satellite warehouses or retail establishments. If these movements are based on transfer requirements, the use of a group enables the warehouse to reduce the number of transfer order conversions to one per group.

Use Transaction LT41 to create a group for transfer requirements. You can find the transaction by following the menu path SAP • LOGISTICS • LOGISTICS EXECUTION • OUTBOUND PROCESS • GOODS ISSUE FOR OTHER TRANSACTIONS • PICKING • GROUP OF TRANSFER REQUIREMENTS • CREATE.

Figure 6.25 shows the initial screen to search for transfer requirements that will be combined into a single group. The shipment type shown in the screen is A, which indicates stock removal. Other options include E for putaway and U for posting change transfer requirements. The requirement type relates to the process of the transfer requirement.

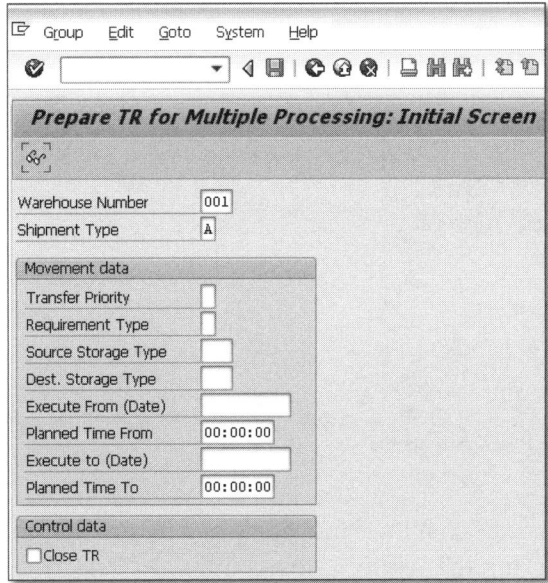

Figure 6.25 Initial Screen for Creating a Group for Transfer Requirements: Transaction LT41

> **Example**
>
> You can enter a "B" for a purchase order, "K" for cost centers, "V" for sales orders, and so on.

The CLOSE TR checkbox at the bottom of the screen indicates whether the transfer requirement should be closed. If this checkbox is selected, then once the transfer order is confirmed the transfer requirement will be considered complete and will be closed.

Figure 6.26 shows that for the selection criteria entered in the previous screen, four open transfer requirements for warehouse 001 refer to stock removal. Figure 6.26 shows that there are three open transfer requirements (OPEN TR) for movement type 201 and one open transfer requirement for movement type 231.

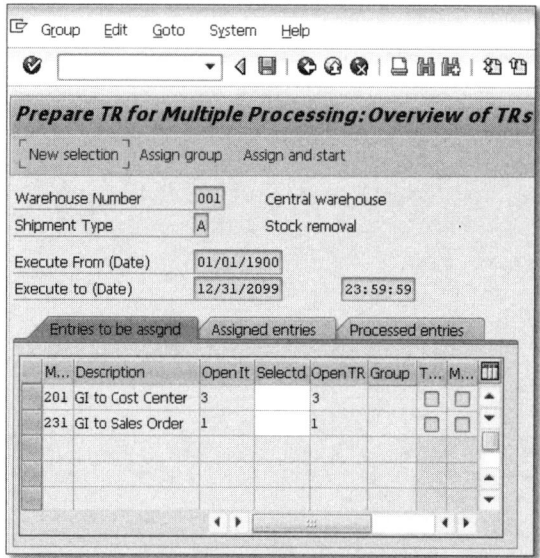

Figure 6.26 Creating a Group of Transfer Requirements for Movement Types 201 and 231

These four transfer requirements can be combined into one group for processing. To create the group, start by clicking the ASSIGN GROUP button. A dialog box appears, as shown in Figure 6.27. This dialog box requires a description for the group and a group name. The group is created once the information is entered into the dialog box.

6.3 Multiple Processing Using Groups

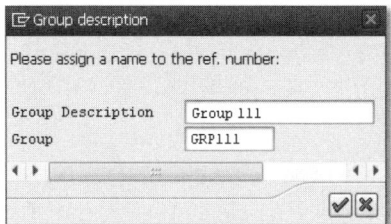

Figure 6.27 Entering the Group Description and Group Name: Transaction LT41

6.3.3 Creating Transfer Orders for a Group of Transfer Requirements

After the group has been created, transfer orders for the items in the group can be created when that group of transfer requirements is ready to be converted. Use Transaction LT42 to create transfer orders for a group. You can access this transaction by following the menu path SAP • LOGISTICS • LOGISTICS EXECUTION • OUTBOUND PROCESS • GOODS ISSUE FOR OTHER TRANSACTIONS • PICKING • CREATE TRANSFER ORDER • FOR GROUP.

Figure 6.28 shows the entry fields for the conversion of the transfer requirements inside the group to transfer orders. The REFERENCE DOC CAT field can be set to B for a group of transfer requirements or L for a group of deliveries.

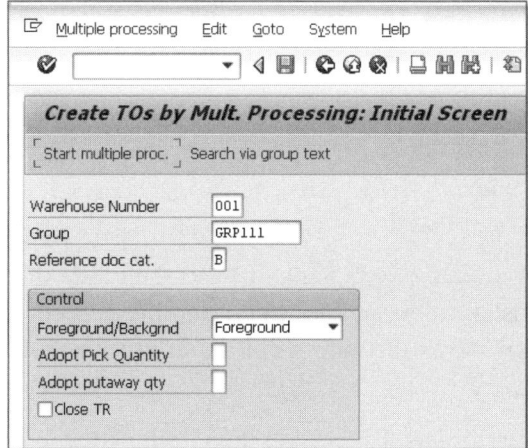

Figure 6.28 Creating Transfer Orders from a Group of Transfer Requirements: Transaction LT42

231

The FOREGROUND control has been selected in Figure 6.28, but this is only advisable if there are a small number of transfer requirements in the group. If the group contains a vast number of transfer requirements, then the BACKGROUND control is more appropriate.

After entering the necessary data, you can start the process by clicking the START MULTIPLE PROC button. When the FOREGROUND control is selected, each transfer creation appears, and the process can be monitored.

If the material is missing from a storage bin or a storage bin cannot be found, changes can be made during processing to ensure that transfer orders are created. This cannot be done in background processing. Once the processing has been completed for the group, the resulting screen will be displayed as shown in Figure 6.29.

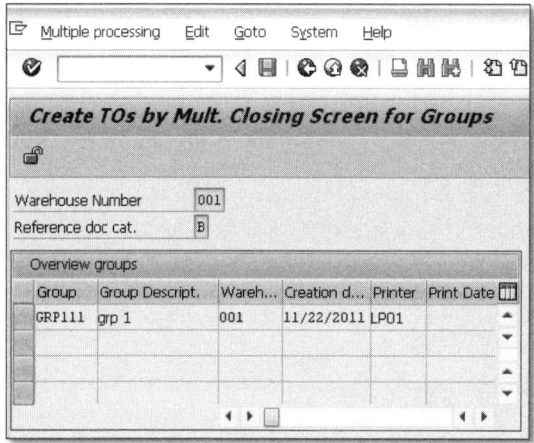

Figure 6.29 Transfer Orders Created for a Group of Transfer Requirements: Transaction LT42

The closing screen for the group, shown in Figure 6.29, displays the group that was entered and the number of transfer orders and transfer order line items that were created. In addition, the screen shows the number of the printer that will output the transfer orders.

You can release and print the transfer orders by pressing the [F5] function key, clicking the padlock icon on the screen, or selecting GOTO • RELEASE/PRINT.

6.3.4 Definition of a Wave Pick

When groups are used with outbound deliveries, we normally refer to them as waves. A wave pick is defined as a work package, like a group, but it contains several outbound deliveries. This wave pick is created using the Wave Monitor. The advantage of using a wave pick is that it is possible to select the outbound delivery according to time slots.

> **Example**
>
> If a warehouse has 2,000 outbound deliveries per shift, the wave pick can group these deliveries for each time slot. If the shift starts at 6 a.m. and ends at 3 p.m., a wave pick can be run for each time slot, which can be hourly, and the deliveries can be processed in that manner.

6.3.5 Creating a Group for Outbound Deliveries

A warehouse creates a wave for outbound deliveries when many transfer orders must be created for deliveries outside the warehouse. The outbound deliveries are for sales orders that have been received and need to be fulfilled by the material in the warehouse.

6.3.6 Creating the Wave from the Outbound Delivery Monitor

You can create a wave pick using the Outbound Delivery Monitor (Transaction VL06P). Enter selection criteria to display deliveries from a specific shipping point on a certain date so that deliveries can be selected and combined in a wave pick group.

Figure 6.30 shows the shipping point and date criteria entered to obtain all deliveries due to be shipped, so that selection can be made for a specific wave pick group.

Figure 6.31 shows deliveries relevant for the criteria entered into the Outbound Delivery Monitor. You can highlight the deliveries and create the wave by selecting SUBSEQUENT FUNCTIONS • GROUP • WAVE PICK. The processing returns to the Outbound Delivery Monitor, and the wave number is displayed at the bottom of the screen.

6 | Goods Issues

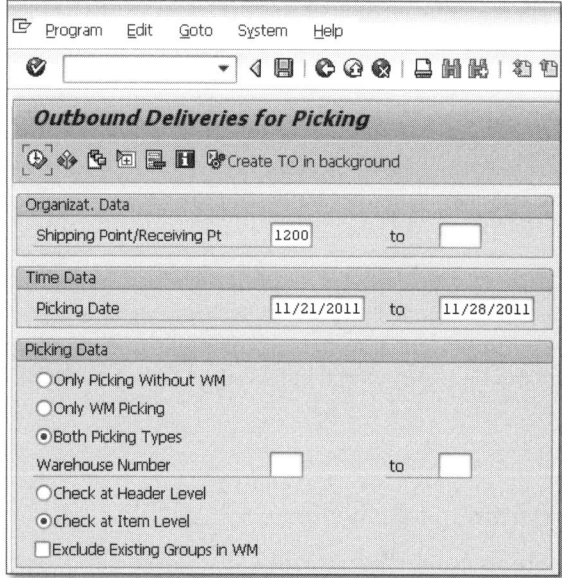

Figure 6.30 Outbound Delivery Monitor Selection Screen for Wave Creation

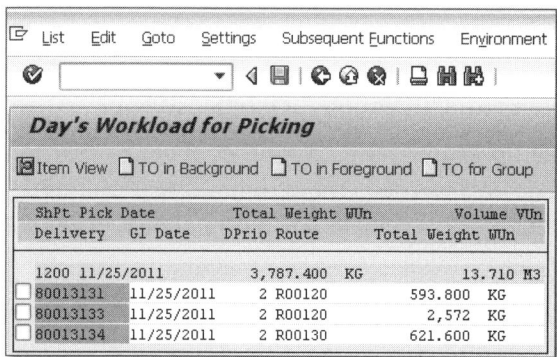

Figure 6.31 Picking Workload Results from the Outbound Delivery Monitor

6.3.7 Using the Wave Monitor

The Wave Monitor allows the selection of waves for certain outbound deliveries. You execute it via Transaction VL37 or the menu path SAP • LOGISTICS • LOGISTICS EXECUTION • OUTBOUND PROCESS • GOODS ISSUE FOR OUTBOUND DELIVERY • PICKING • WAVE PICKS • MONITOR.

Figure 6.32 shows the initial selection criteria screen where you can make entries to view waves from the outbound deliveries fitting the selection. The date and time selection allows the use of either a time slot or a time-slot group. Let's take a look at these now.

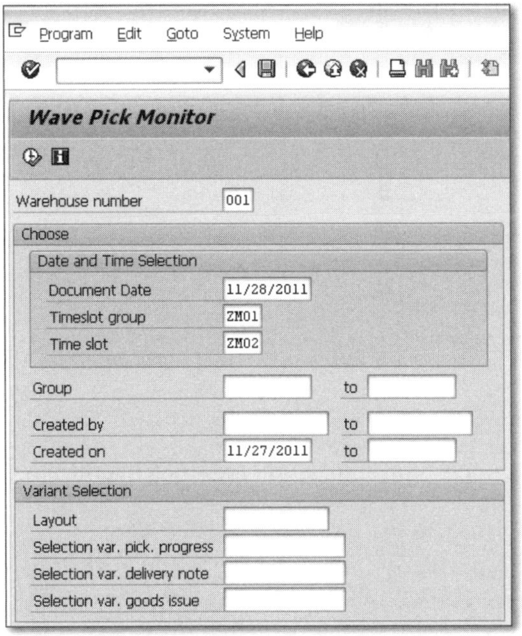

Figure 6.32 Wave Pick Monitor Selection Screen: Transaction VL37

Time Slot

A time slot is defined as a period of time that can be configured in the IMG. The time slot can be defined for the warehouse where it is to be used. In many cases, a time slot can be a one-hour time period in a warehouse shift or a whole shift. You can configure the time slot via the menu path IMG • LOGISTICS EXECUTION • SHIPPING • PICKING • WAVE PICKS • MAINTAIN TIME SLOTS.

Figure 6.33 shows the configuration for a time slot. Each time slot is created with a description and a start and finish time. The other field you must fill to configure the time slot is the picking wave profile, which is also defined in the system configuration and sets the limits for the wave.

6 | Goods Issues

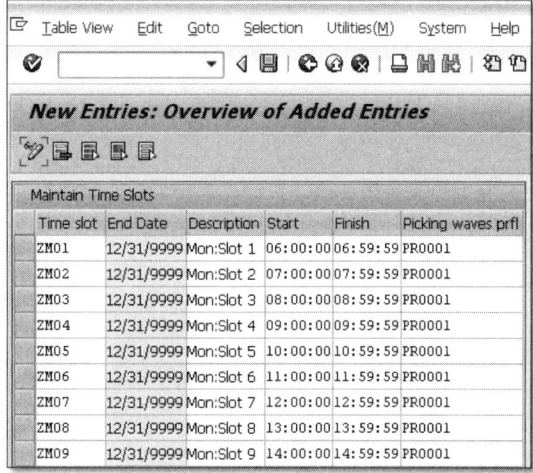

Figure 6.33 Configuration of Time Slots for Wave Picking

Picking Wave Profile

The picking wave profile allows you to set limits on certain criteria when reacting to waves during wave picking.

You can configure the picking wave profile by following the menu path IMG • LOGISTICS EXECUTION • SHIPPING • PICKING • WAVE PICKS • MAINTAIN WAVE PICKS PROFILE.

Figure 6.34 shows the configuration for the picking wave profile used in time-slot configuration. The picking wave profile is defined for each warehouse, and capacity limits can be configured for each time slot.

You can limit the number of items to be picked, the number of picking activities, the maximum number of packaging materials, the maximum weight and volume, and the maximum number of available hours for the pick wave.

Time Slot Group

In Figure 6.32 on the previous page, the other date and time selection field is the TIMESLOT GROUP. The time-slot group is configured from several time slots. For example, a time-slot group can contain all the time slots for a particular shift or a particular working day.

6.3 Multiple Processing Using Groups

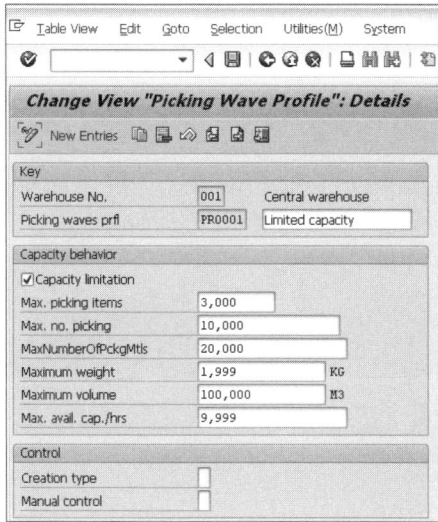

Figure 6.34 Configuration for a Picking Wave Profile

You can configure the time-slot group in the IMG by following the menu path IMG • LOGISTICS EXECUTION • SHIPPING • PICKING • WAVE PICKS • MAINTAIN TIME-SLOT GROUP FOR WAVE PICK.

Figure 6.35 shows the time-slot group ZM01 created from the nine individual time slots, which reflect each hour of the first warehouse shift on a Monday. Each time slot is assigned a sequence number for the time-slot group. The start and finish times of the time slots cannot overlap.

Slot grp	Timesl no	Description	Timeslot day	Start	Finish
ZM01	1	Monday - Friday	ZM01	06:00:00	06:59:59
ZM01	2	Monday - Friday	ZM02	07:00:00	07:59:59
ZM01	3	Monday - Friday	ZM03	08:00:00	08:59:59
ZM01	4	Monday - Friday	ZM04	09:00:00	09:59:59
ZM01	5	Monday - Friday	ZM05	10:00:00	10:59:59
ZM01	6	Monday - Friday	ZM06	11:00:00	11:59:59
ZM01	7	Monday - Friday	ZM07	12:00:00	12:59:59
ZM01	8	Monday - Friday	ZM08	13:00:00	13:59:59
ZM01	9	Monday - Friday	ZM09	14:00:00	14:59:59

Figure 6.35 Creating Time-Slot Groups from Individual Time Slots

6.3.8 Results of the Pick Wave Monitor

After you have entered the selection criteria, execute the transaction by pressing the [F8] function key. The Wave Monitor displays all waves for the relevant time slot that was entered for the specific warehouse.

Figure 6.36 shows the wave and the deliveries within that wave for the selected time slot. The wave shown here can be highlighted and the transfer orders created for the deliveries that make up the wave pick.

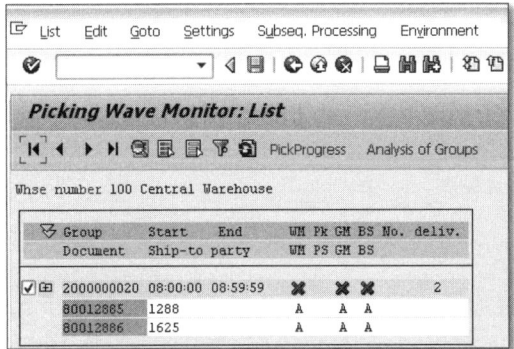

Figure 6.36 Wave Monitor Results Screen: Transaction VL37

Create the transfer order by selecting SUBSEQUENT PROCESSING • TRANSFER ORDER or by pressing [Shift]+[F4].

Figure 6.37 shows the transfer order creation screen for wave pick group 2000000020. The reference document category is defaulted to L, which indicates outbound deliveries. This can also be found using transaction LT42.

You can create the transfer orders by clicking the START MULTIPLE PROC button or pressing the [F5] function key. Once the transfer orders have been created, they need to be released and printed for the material to be pulled. Release and print the wave by selecting SUBSEQUENT PROCESSING • RELEASE/PRINT or by pressing [Shift]+[F5].

Figure 6.38 shows that the wave group has been released and printed. The transfer orders are printed at the printer in the warehouse and are given to the staff so they can pick the materials. Once the materials are picked, you can confirm the transfer orders for the wave by using the Wave Monitor and selecting SUBSEQUENT PROCESSING • CONFIRM or by pressing [Shift]+[F7].

Multiple Processing Using Groups | 6.3

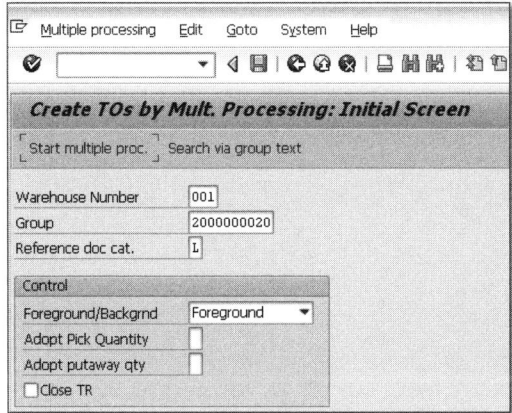

Figure 6.37 Creating Transfer Orders for Deliveries in a Wave Pick

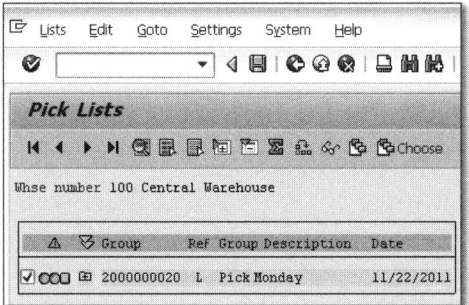

Figure 6.38 Pick List for Wave Group 2000000020

The transaction displays the selection screen for the transfer order confirmation, as shown in Figure 6.39. The transfer orders that have been produced for the wave pick can be confirmed after they are printed and the movement of the material has been completed. The confirmation screen, as shown in Figure 6.39, allows the selection of certain transfer orders in the wave by storage type or picking area, depending on what movements have been completed in the warehouse. If all transfer orders are ready for completion, these fields will be blank.

From the selection used in Figure 6.39, the relevant transfer orders are displayed and ready for confirmation, as shown in Figure 6.40. You can confirm them by selecting TRANSFER ORDER • CONFIRM IN FOREGROUND or by pressing the [F5] function key.

Figure 6.39 Initial Screen for Confirming Transfer Orders for a Wave Group

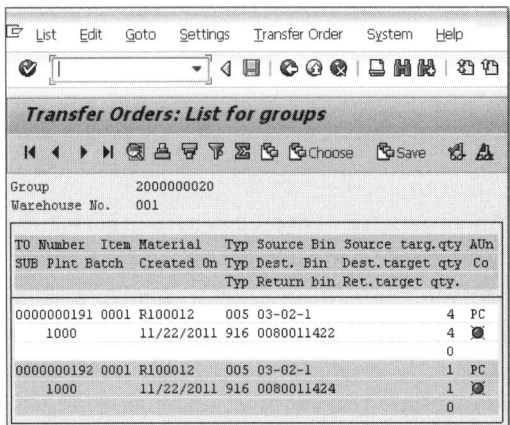

Figure 6.40 Transfer Orders Selected for Confirmation from the Wave Group

This section has examined multiple processing using groups. Now we'll discuss the processes of picking and packing in goods issue.

6.4 Picking and Packing

Sections 6.1.3 and 6.1.5 touched on the picking process has been touched on. The transfer orders created to remove material from the warehouse can be used as the picking instructions. As a part of the picking process, several optional steps can be carried out with the material.

These steps can include pricing the material with price stickers. This may involve repricing if the material was priced at the end of the manufacturing process or inbound delivery process and the price has since changed. In addition to the pricing process, a packing process can occur after picking and before the materials leave the warehouse.

Picking within the warehouse can be the most costly part of the warehouse operation, with estimates suggesting that order picking can be over 50% of the total warehouse operating expense. Order picking is the most labor-intensive operation within the warehouse and usually employs the majority of the staff. In addition, picking errors, and therefore delivery errors, are a major source of customer dissatisfaction.

Warehouse designers try to reduce or combine several human functions in the picking process, including:

- Removing items from the storage bin
- Traveling between the storage bins and the picking station
- Searching for the storage bins
- Sorting items for transfer orders
- Confirming the line item picking, using the SAP system or noting in paperwork

6.4.1 Picking Schemes

Warehouses can adopt several picking schemes to reduce the time and effort spent by the warehouse staff picking material. Not all of these schemes are relevant for all companies. In the following subsection, we will briefly describe some of those currently found in warehouse operations.

Single-Order Picking

In this picking scheme, the picking staff completes one order at a time. This takes a lot of time and effort but results in the most accurate picking. This method is used in the majority of warehouses.

Batch Picking

The batch picking method is similar to the single-order method, except that the picker picks a batch of orders at one time, rather than a single order. Picking errors creep in when line items are missed, and additional time is required to sort the items for each order when the items are returned to the picking station. The efficiencies of this type of picking are limited and are negligible for more than five orders in a batch pick.

Zone Picking

In this scheme, a picking operator is assigned to one zone, which can be an aisle, a partial aisle, a carousel, and so on. For this scheme, the picker is only responsible for picking items in his zone and not responsible for all the items in the transfer order. The advantages of this method are that the picker's travel time is reduced because of the smaller area of operation. Pickers also become familiar with the items they pick every day and errors are reduced. The disadvantage with this method is that it can cause bottlenecks if pickers work at different speeds; slower zone operators can minimize the benefits of this method.

Progressive Assembly

In the progressive assembly method, the contents of the transfer order to be picked are moved from one zone to the next. This is also called the "pick and pass" system. The line items of the transfer order can be moved from zone to zone in a tote container on a conveyor belt or some other transport method.

Downstream Sortation

This method uses some aspects of progressive assembly but is used for wave picking. In a wave, many transfer orders are grouped. Downstream sortation allows the picker to deposit all the materials listed on all transfer orders of the wave into the tote on the conveyor. This means a significant level of sorting takes place after the material leaves the picking zone. This method can only be used where downstream sorting has been perfected; otherwise, shipping delays will most likely occur.

6.4.2 Packing

We will discuss Storage Unit Management and the way packing is performed with storage units in Chapter 11. In the warehouse, the material that has been picked is usually packed before it is loaded onto vehicles or sent via a shipping company, such as UPS or FedEx.

The packing area contains the packaging material used for packing the materials to be shipped. These packaging materials can be as simple as cardboard boxes, shipping pallets, and tape. However, there may be specialized packaging materials that are used only for a specific item. For example, a fragile item may be stored in one container while it is in the warehouse, but for shipping it may require custom polystyrene packaging for a specific size of container.

Whichever materials are needed in the packaging area, they must be available to the packing staff. In the same way that a production line comes to a halt if material is missing for the production order, the packaging of materials will stop if the packaging material is missing from the packing area.

> **Note**
> Some companies spend some of their labor resources in preassembling packaging items. If the same person has to locate a flat cardboard box, assemble it, pack it with pellets, place the item inside, seal it, label it, and move it to the next location, this can be time-consuming and not the best use of labor. Preassembling boxes and filling them with pellets can make the packing area more efficient.

Another labor-saving method used in warehouses is to standardize the packing materials and packing process. Reducing the number of sizes of the materials and formalizing a packing process that all employees follow are important ways to save time getting product from the packing area into shipment.

This section has examined aspects of picking and packing in the goods issue process. Now we'll look at some business examples of some of the processes discussed in this chapter.

6 | Goods Issues

6.5 Business Examples—Goods Issue

A goods issue is the movement of material from the warehouse to an external source, which could be a production order or a customer. The warehouse can use a goods issue as the process of consuming material and assigning the costs of the material consumed to a cost center.

6.5.1 Goods Issue with Outbound Delivery

An outbound delivery is made up of three components; picking, packing, and goods issue. The material for the outbound delivery is picked using transfer orders in SAP WM. If the outbound delivery process in the warehouse does not run at optimum efficiency, delays in delivery can cause the customer financial problems and create customer dissatisfaction.

Example

For many years a medium-sized beverage manufacturer in Austria did not use outbound deliveries, as they manufactured only three products that were in great demand. The finished goods were taken directly from the production line to waiting trailers, where they were sent to third-party distributors who delivered products to supermarket distribution centers across Europe. The sales orders were rarely delivered on time due to the lack of manufacturing capacity at the company's single facility. Because of this, the company rarely used the warehouse facility they had except for storing empty cans and promotional materials they used on occasion.

Three years ago the company was purchased by a private investment company that began modernizing the manufacturing equipment and increasing capacity. In addition, new products were introduced and more promotions were launched, requiring different cans and special packaging.

The production process was radically improved, and the company was now producing the items for the promotional cans in advance of the promotion starting. This change led to items being made to stock, rather than made specifically for an order. The warehouse was now a vital part of the new strategy, and the company realized that the warehouse was filling up and staff had to find finished goods in the warehouse based on the promotions and shelf life date. This change required the introduction of the outbound delivery process so that the warehouse managers could prioritize picking in the warehouse for orders that needed to be filled first and ensure that the right quants were selected for the correct delivery.

6.5.2 Goods Issue Without an Outbound Delivery

The goods issue created without an outbound delivery starts with a goods issue that is created in SAP IM. This may be a goods issue to a cost center, a goods issue to a project, or other similar scenarios.

Example

A small manufacturer of electrical components implemented an SAP system for human resources, finance, and materials management. The company was using their legacy sales system, as they believed that the customization they had performed could not be replicated in the SAP system. However, they were proceeding with an implementation of WM, as their existing WMS system was running on hardware that was no longer supported.

After the implementation of WM, the company decided to move to SAP Sales and Distribution due to the increase in maintenance costs for their legacy systems as well as an aging and increasingly unreliable hardware platform.

Before the SD project could be implemented, the legacy sales system failed, and the company was unwilling to lease new hardware for a system that would be replaced in a matter of weeks.

The company decided to use their SAP systems to record the sales to their customers in spite of no sales orders being placed on the SAP system. The company used a PC program to enter sales but needed to reflect the movement of stock to the customer fulfilling the sales order on the SAP system. The process they derived was to allocate a cost center for each of their customers with an order, and the warehouse could then post a goods issue to the customer cost center when the product was processed for shipment. This way, the stock was reduced, and a correct financial posting would be made.

6.5.3 Picking and Packing

Transfer orders can be used as picking instructions for warehouse staff. While picking takes place, other steps can be carried out with the material. These can include pricing the material with price stickers or other labeling for the customer. Order picking is the most labor-intensive operation within the warehouse and usually employs the majority of the staff.

Example

Some companies have very simple picking requirements and few picks per hour. However, in a complex warehouse the picking operation can make or break a company. A small distribution center for an automotive parts company operated a warehouse in the south of Spain that contained fewer than two thousand parts and mostly fulfilled online orders. The number of picks per hour was low, and most of the warehouse staff knew what area parts were stored in, making picking straightforward.

After some company reorganization several warehouses in Portugal and the south of France were closed, so that the warehouse in southern Spain was now expected to carry around 7000 parts and process orders for companies throughout southern Europe. The warehouse was expanded and the parts were delivered from the warehouses being shuttered. When the warehouse operations began to ramp up, it was clear that the previous method of single-order picking was not efficient enough for the growing number of picks that would be required per hour.

The warehouse manager decided to try other methods of picking as the warehouse became busier to see which method suited the company. Orders that needed to be fulfilled could be from an auto parts store that required up to 100 items, from customers online who would normally order one part, or from a distribution center that would order several hundred parts. Based on analysis the company performed, the majority of the orders were single-item orders, and based on this, the company decided to implement a zone picking strategy. This meant an operator would be responsible for a section of the warehouse and be given pick tickets for that area. Picks would be performed quickly, and operators would not be travelling all over the warehouse to get items. Several warehouse operators were assigned solely to multiline orders so they could be assembled quickly and shipped without delay.

6.6 Summary

Goods issue is a labor-intensive process that has been refined to minimize waste in picking and maximize the output of the warehouse. A company has to ship product to make a profit, and the outbound process of the warehouse is key to successful shipping. In this chapter, we have discussed how goods issues can be created with outbound deliveries and without them.

We have also discussed some of the more complex scenarios for outbound shipping, for example, the use of wave picks in a busy warehouse. It is important to realize that the outbound delivery process is twofold. First, the configuration and the processes used by the warehouse must be suited to the warehouse operations, because an overly complex solution will stop products from being shipped. Second, because the outbound process is labor-intensive, training staff on the warehouse solution is very important. Once these two factors have been balanced, significant productivity should flow from the SAP WM outbound process.

In Chapter 7, we'll discuss the stock replenishment that takes place in the warehouse. Keep in mind that a warehouse is not just a place where material is stored. Material constantly moves in the warehouse, and replenishment of fixed bins for picking and for production supports some of this movement.

Stock replenishment and internal movements are daily activities that support efficient warehouse operations. Posting changes occur less frequently but must be carefully processed to ensure synergy between the warehouse and SAP IM stock balances.

7 Stock Replenishment

Material is moved from one location to another as a part of everyday warehouse operations. Some movements are initiated within the inventory management process, for example, plant to plant or storage location to storage location. If the storage location is warehouse managed, then this triggers the movement of the material in the warehouse.

Replenishment of storage bins in the warehouse requires moving material from one location to another. With this overview of stock replenishment in mind, we'll now discuss internal stock transfers.

7.1 Internal Stock Transfers

The internal stock transfer can only be triggered by a requirement to move a material from one part of the warehouse to another, storage bin to storage bin.

There are many reasons for moving material in the warehouse, but every time a quant is moved, a cost is incurred. Sometimes the labor cost of moving material outweighs the need to move the material.

7.1.1 Keeping the Warehouse Running

Many warehouses have come to a complete standstill when there was no more space in the warehouse to unload trailers at the goods receiving dock. In the worst situation, warehouses become grid-locked because material that needs to be shipped is sitting in trailers outside the warehouse, unable to be unloaded into the warehouse.

Warehouses need a certain amount of empty space where material can be unloaded and stored. Without a working reserve of empty bins, the warehouse can become congested, and customer orders won't be fulfilled on time.

To keep a reserve of empty bins, a warehouse needs regular analysis of the material in the storage bins to see where combining quants can free up a bin or ensure that the picking areas are fully supplied. The optimum amount of empty bin space in the warehouse depends on the materials and industry involved but is usually somewhere between 10% and 20%.

To move this material in the warehouse, a requirement must be created in SAP WM to move the stock.

7.1.2 Checking Empty Bins

You can analyze the empty bin situation by using Transaction LS04, which displays the empty bins for a specific warehouse and storage type.

You can find the transaction by following the menu path SAP • LOGISTICS • LOGISTICS EXECUTION • INTERNAL WHSE PROCESSES • BINS AND STOCK • DISPLAY • EMPTY STORAGE BINS.

Figure 7.1 shows the initial screen for the list of empty bins. You must fill in the warehouse number and storage type fields, but use of the storage section is optional. You can enter additional selection criteria such as the storage bin—if only one storage bin has to be reviewed—or the storage bin type, tank, bin height, and so on. The number of storage bins reflects the number of bins required on the report.

> **Note**
>
> If the warehouse staff only wants to see if there are a few empty bins in a specific storage type, they may only want to see the first 10 and not all of the empty bins. Entering a figure in this field stops the report after the specified number of bins has been retrieved.

You can select the blocked bins and sectioned bins checkboxes if the report should only show empty storage bins that are blocked or sectioned, rather than all empty bins.

Internal Stock Transfers | **7.1**

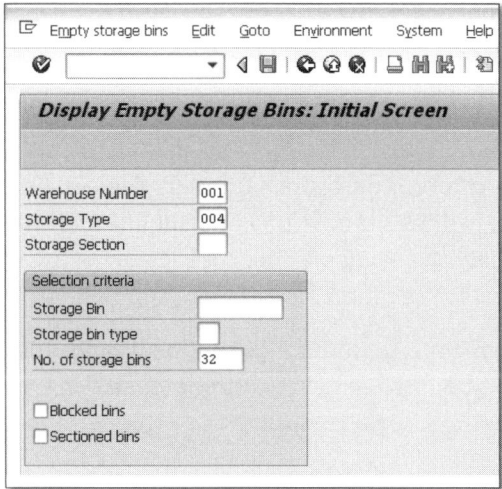

Figure 7.1 Initial Selection Screen for List of Empty Bins: Transaction LS04

Figure 7.2 shows the empty storage bins that were requested by the selection criteria in Figure 7.1. The display shows the storage bin, bin type, blocking indicator for stock removal, blocking indicator for putaway, current block for removal, current block for putaway, current block due to physical inventory count, maximum weight, and total capacity.

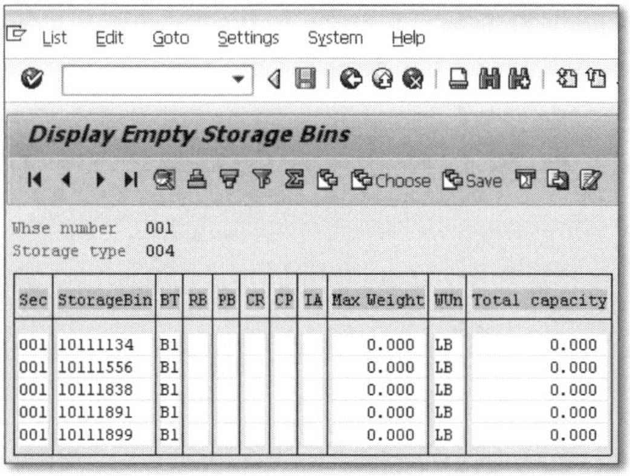

Figure 7.2 Display of Empty Storage Bins: Transaction LS04.

The display is useful to the warehouse staff because they can see at a glance where the empty bins are for stock putaway.

251

7.1.3 Moving Material Between Storage Bins

Movement of material between storage bins is triggered by creation of a transfer order. If material needs to be moved from one storage bin to another storage bin, a transfer order is required.

Transaction LT10 can produce a transfer order for a stock transfer. You can find this transaction by following the menu path SAP • LOGISTICS • LOGISTICS EXECUTION • INTERNAL WHSE PROCESSES • STOCK TRANSFER • CREATE TRANSFER ORDER • FROM STOCK LIST.

Figure 7.3 shows the selection screen for Transaction LT10. The WAREHOUSE NUMBER and STORAGE TYPE fields must be filled in, as must the MOVEMENT TYPE field in the PROGRAM CONTROL section.

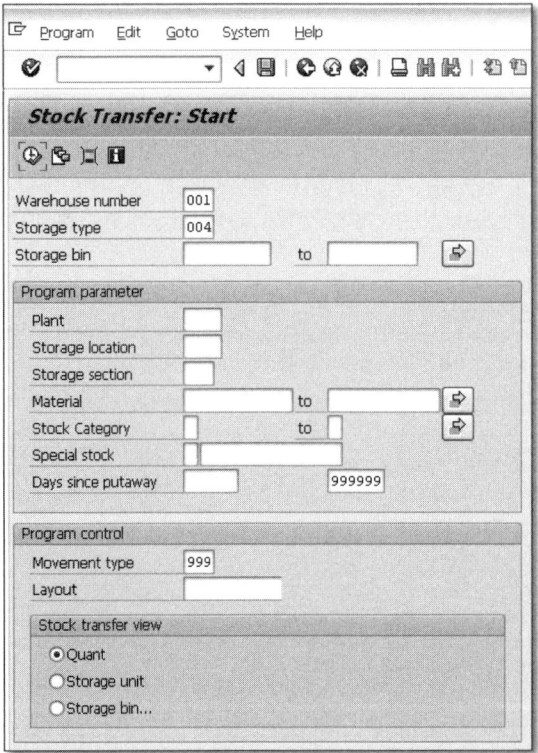

Figure 7.3 Initial Screen for Creating a Stock Transfer: Transaction LT10

The user must enter a warehouse management movement type in the MOVEMENT TYPE field. This entry controls the type of internal stock transfer that will take place.

The STOCK TRANSFER VIEW section allows the resulting data to be shown either in a quant format, by storage unit, or by storage bin. The default is for the results to be shown by quant. Execute the transaction by pressing the F8 function key.

Figure 7.4 shows the material that is available for stock transfer. The available quants are identified with a blank box in the SL (Selection) field. If the quant is not available, then the field will contain a lock.

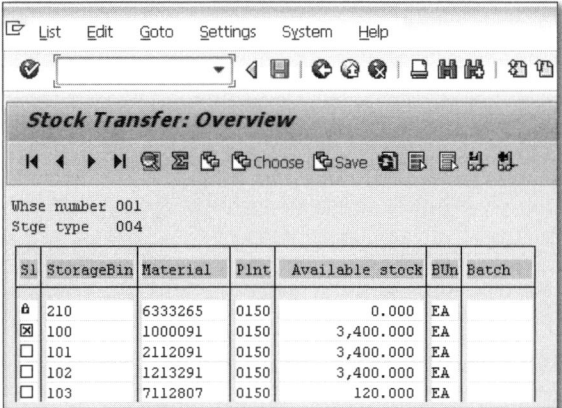

Figure 7.4 Display of Quants Available for Stock Transfer

To select a line item for a stock transfer, check the box. The line item is then available for a stock transfer. You can create the stock transfer in the foreground by pressing Ctrl + Shift + F12.

Figure 7.5 shows the dialog box that is displayed when the stock transfer is created in the foreground. You must enter destination data for the stock transfer. You can enter a print code and printer number or select the DO NOT PRINT checkbox so that the stock transfer is not printed.

After you enter the required data, the transaction uses the information to create a transfer order. Then the results screen is redisplayed.

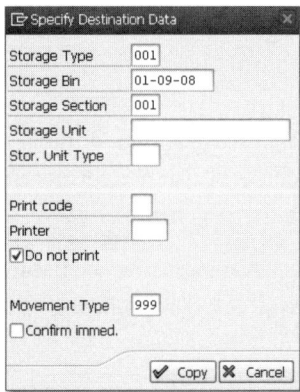

Figure 7.5 Destination Data Entry Dialog Box for a Stock Transfer

Use Transaction LT21 to view the transfer order created by Transaction LT10. If the transfer order number is not known, use Transaction LT24 to find the relevant transfer order using the material number matchcode. You can find Transaction LT24 by following the menu path SAP • LOGISTICS • LOGISTICS EXECUTION • INTERNAL WHSE PROCESSES • STOCK TRANSFER • DISPLAY TRANSFER ORDER • FOR MATERIAL.

Figure 7.6 shows the information that should be selected to find the transfer order via the material involved in the stock transfer. The warehouse and material entries are mandatory. This selection also includes the date of transfer order creation to narrow down the potential list.

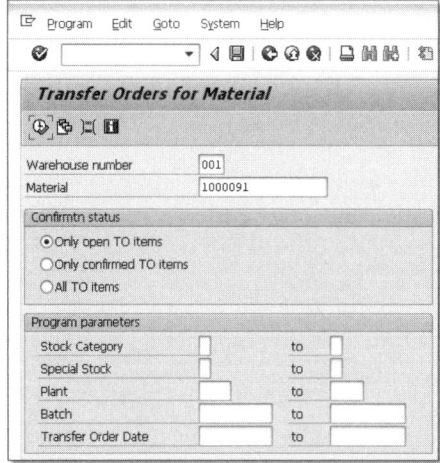

Figure 7.6 Selection Screen to Display Transfer Orders by Material: Transaction LT24

Execute the transaction by pressing the [F8] function key or by selecting PROGRAM • EXECUTE. The display of the resulting transfer order (see Figure 7.7) shows the information that was entered in Transaction LT10.

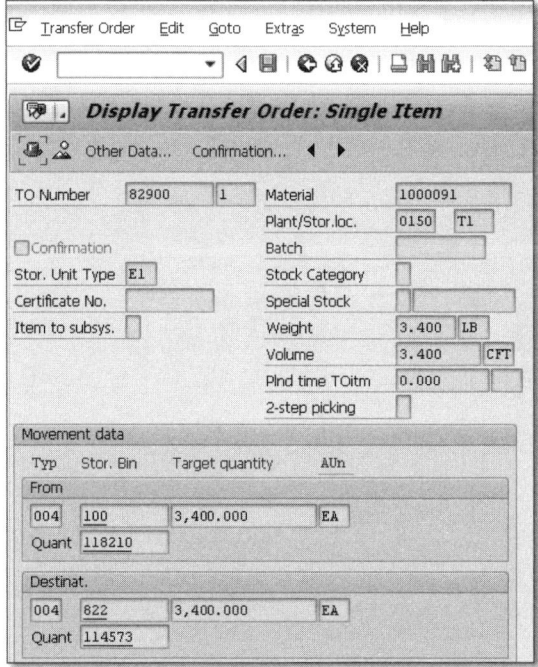

Figure 7.7 Detailed Display of Transfer Order Created by Stock Transfer

7.1.4 Confirming the Stock Transfer

The movement information shows the material that needs to be moved from storage bin 100 to 822 within the storage type 004. You can confirm the stock transfer in this screen by selecting TRANSFER ORDER • CONFIRM IN FOREGROUND or by pressing the [F8] function key.

Figure 7.8 shows the confirmation screen for the transfer order created for the stock transfer. In the MOVEMENT DATA section of this screen, the destination information in the DESTINAT. area must be entered for the quantity of the material to be transferred.

Often, when material is transferred, the quantity of material received into the destination storage bin is not equal to the quantity removed from the storage bin.

7 | Stock Replenishment

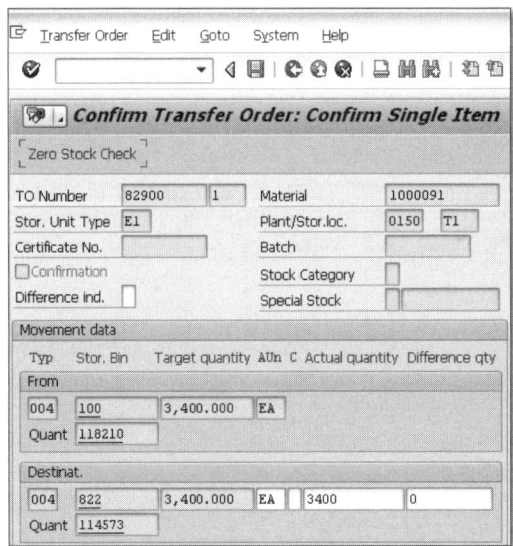

Figure 7.8 Confirmation Screen for Transfer Order to Move Stock from Storage Bin to Storage Bin

In these instances, it is important to enter the correct quantity in the receiving storage bin as well as a reason for this discrepancy. Four options are available for the confirmation checkbox:

- **X**
  Target quantity is equal to the actual quantity.
- **U**
  Actual quantity is the balance between the target and difference quantity.
- **S**
  Difference quantity is the difference between actual and target quantity.
- **Blank**
  Allows the actual and difference quantities to be entered manually.

In Figure 7.8 an X has been entered for the confirmation checkbox, which means the target and actual quantities are equal and there are no differences.

7.1.5 Configuring the Difference Indicator

The other field on this screen you should pay attention to is DIFFERENCE IND. This field controls how the difference is managed. The field is configured via Transaction OMLX in the IMG. You can find the transaction by following the menu path IMG • Logistics Execution • Warehouse Management • Activities • Confirmation.

The configuration of the confirmation screen, shown in Figure 7.9, defines how the confirmation transaction deals with the difference between the source and destination storage bins. Let's look closely at the fields shown in Figure 7.9:

▶ **Ty**
This field specifies the storage type to which any differences in the source and target quantities are posted.

▶ **Diff. Bin**
This should be configured if a specific storage bin must contain the stock differences.

▶ **TO**
If this checkbox is selected, the system creates a dynamic storage location, which is named the same as the transfer order number, and the difference is posted to this bin.

▶ **Srce Bin**
If this checkbox is selected, the quantity difference is posted to the source storage bin.

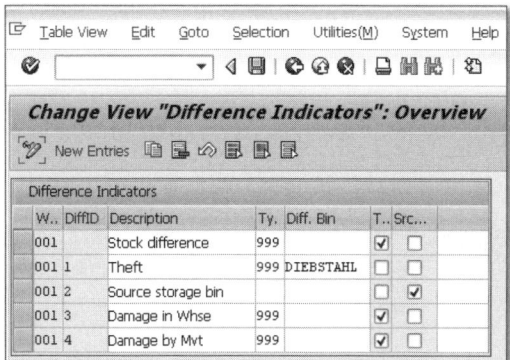

Figure 7.9 Configuration of the Difference Indicator: Transaction OMLX

This section has described the functionality of internal stock transfers. Now we'll examine the process of fixed bin replenishment.

7.2 Fixed Bin Replenishment

A fixed storage bin is a storage bin in which a specific material is stored. This material is always stored in this bin. This may be because it is a bin that has been specifically created for the material. In many cases, it is a storage bin in the picking area, where storage bins do not need different material constantly moved in and out.

In fixed storage bin replenishment, the storage bin in the picking area needs to be replenished so that the outbound deliveries remain at maximum efficiency.

> **Example**
> In a warehouse that ships vacuum cleaners, each vacuum may have to be packed with the attachments. The attachments should be stored in the picking area and in sufficient quantity that the shipping process does not slow down due to a lack of attachments. Fixed bin replenishment is a process that helps keep this from happening

7.2.1 Replenishment and the Material Master

The basis for the replenishment process is defined in the material master record for the items that need to be replenished. Replenishment details for a material in a specific fixed bin can be entered using the material master change Transaction MM02 if the material has already been created. You can find this transaction by following the menu path SAP • LOGISTICS • MATERIALS MANAGEMENT • MATERIAL MASTER • MATERIAL • CHANGE • IMMEDIATELY.

You should select the WM views, although this may vary depending on the version of the SAP system.

> **Note**
> As noted in Chapter 1, this screen layout refers to SAP ECC 6.0.

The information that must be entered is located in the WAREHOUSE MANAGEMENT 2 screen shown in Figure 7.10. To access this screen, you must enter the plant, warehouse number, and storage type for the fixed bin location.

7.2 Fixed Bin Replenishment

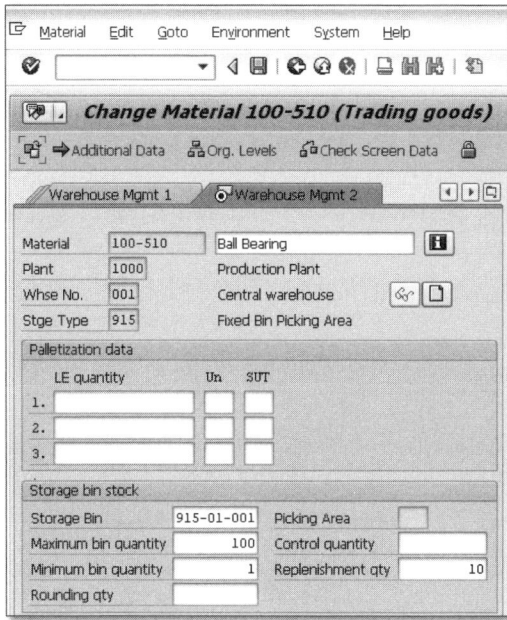

Figure 7.10 Replenishment Data in the Material Master Record

The information stored in the material master record for the storage bin defines how replenishment is processed. Figure 7.10 shows the data in the storage bin stock section in the second WM screen.

We'll now describe the fields displayed in the STORAGE BIN STOCK section, shown in Figure 7.10:

- **Storage bin**
  The specific bin of storage type 915 where the material is stored.

- **Maximum bin quantity**
  The largest quantity that can be stored in this storage bin. This figure is used for checking the capacity of the storage bin.

- **Minimum bin quantity**
  The minimum quantity that can be stored in the storage bin. This figure is used in calculating the bin replenishment

- **Replenishment quantity**
  The quantity of material to be replenished in the storage bin.

In addition to the information in the material master file, you need to complete several configuration steps, which we'll describe in the next section.

7.2.2 Configuration for Replenishment

You need to complete the warehouse management movement type configuration for replenishment before transfer orders can be created for replenishing fixed bins. A replenishment movement type needs to be assigned to the storage type so that any transfer orders are created correctly.

You can access the transaction for this configuration by following the menu path IMG • LOGISTICS EXECUTION • WAREHOUSE MANAGEMENT • ACTIVITIES • TRANSFERS • DEFINE STOCK TRANSFERS AND REPLENISHMENT CONTROL.

Figure 7.11 shows the configuration for the replenishment control for storage type 915, the fixed bin picking area. A movement type has been entered that is appropriate for fixed bin replenishment. This is normally movement type 320, but it can be copied to a user-defined movement type that can be used for the configuration. Replenishment of the production supply bins uses movement type 319.

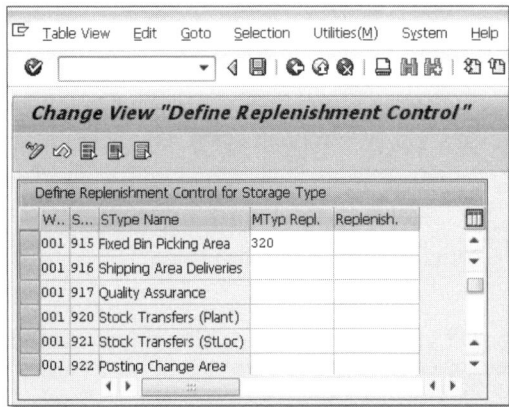

Figure 7.11 Configuration for Fixed Storage Bin Replenishment

7.2.3 Creating the Replenishment

To create the transfer orders for replenishing the fixed bins, use Transaction LP21, which you can find by following the menu path SAP • LOGISTICS • LOGISTICS

7.2 Fixed Bin Replenishment

EXECUTION • INTERNAL WHSE PROCESSES • STOCK TRANSFER • PLANNING FOR REPLENISH-
MENTS • ACCORDING TO BIN SITUATION.

Figure 7.12 shows the selection screen for stock replenishment. The plant, storage location, warehouse number, and storage type have been entered. Because the movement type is set for replenishing fixed bins, the requirement number is needed.

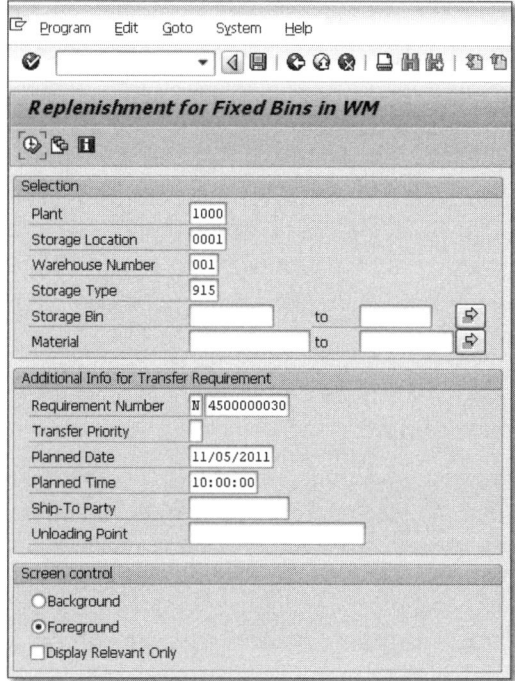

Figure 7.12 Initial Selection Screen for Replenishment of Fixed Bins: Transaction LP21

The requirement number is prefixed by a one-character requirement type, in this case N, representing the replenishment for fixed bins. The requirement number entered is usually the purchase order number or sales order number. You execute the selection screen by pressing the [F8] function key or by selecting PROGRAM • EXECUTE.

Figure 7.13 shows the storage bin selected for replenishment based on the selection criteria entered. Storage bin 915 – 01 – 001 is the storage bin entered into the material master record for material 100-510, as shown in Figure 7.10, previously.

261

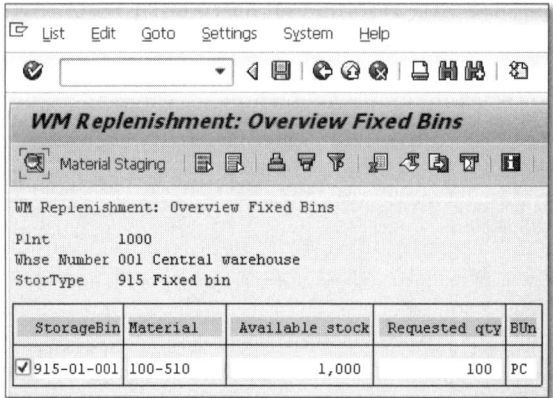

Figure 7.13 Overview of Fixed Bins Subject to Replenishment

To produce the picking documents for the highlighted line on the report, save the transaction by pressing [Ctrl]+[S]. When the transaction has been executed, the processing returns to the initial screen of Transaction LP21 as shown back in Figure 7.12.

7.2.4 Displaying the Transfer Requirement

The replenishment Transaction, LP21, created a transfer requirement that you can display with Transaction LB11 or by following the menu path SAP • LOGISTICS • LOGISTICS EXECUTION • INTERNAL WHSE PROCESSES • TRANSFER REQUIREMENT • DISPLAY • FOR MATERIAL.

Figure 7.14 shows the selection screen for displaying transfer requirements for a specific material. You must enter the warehouse number and the material number fields. If there are many transfer requirements for the material, you should enter other selection criteria to filter the results.

Figure 7.15 shows the transfer requirements that match the criteria entered. The transfer requirement, shown by the TR NUMBER field in Figure 7.15, is the result of the fixed bin replenishment. To complete the replenishment, you must convert and then confirm the transfer requirement into a transfer order.

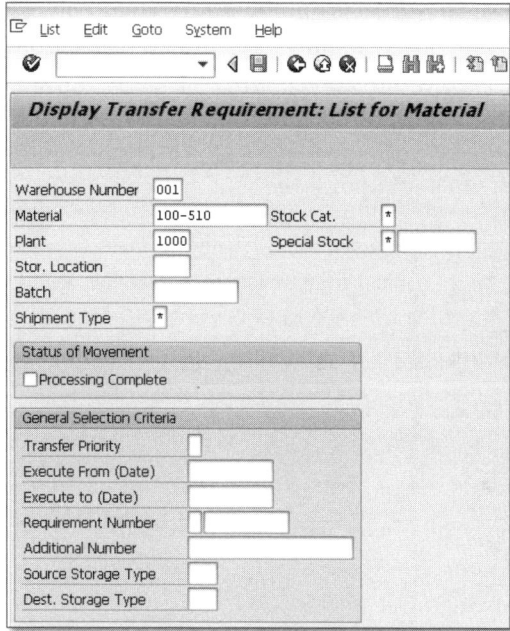

Figure 7.14 Selection Screen to Display a Transfer Requirement

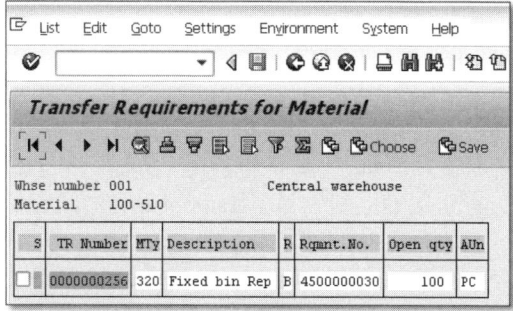

Figure 7.15 Display of Transfer Requirements for Criteria Entered in the Selection Screen

7.2.5 Creating the Transfer Order

To convert the transfer requirement to a transfer order, select the correct transfer requirement and click the button from the application toolbar to convert in either the background or foreground, as shown in Figure 7.15.

Figure 7.16 shows the creation of a transfer order from the information entered in the transfer requirement. The movement data shows the source storage bin and the destination storage bin in the fixed bin storage type, 915. The transfer order has a quantity of 100, which is the maximum bin location and a multiple of the replenishment quantity for this material in storage type 915. This information is shown back in Figure 7.10.

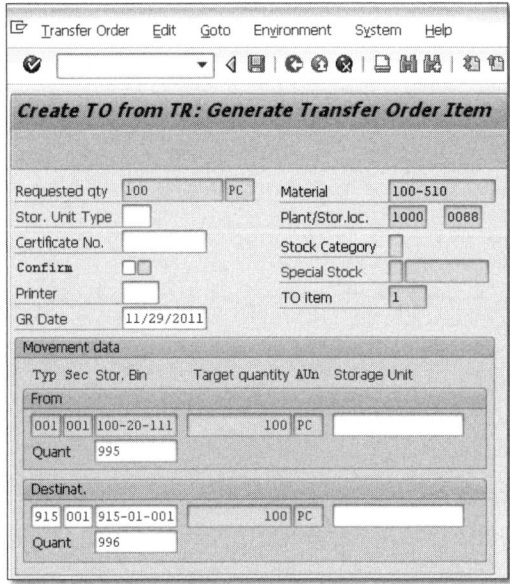

Figure 7.16 Creation of Transfer Order from Transfer Requirement

Once the data in the transfer order has been checked, the transfer order can be completed. The system returns processing to the transfer requirement display, as shown in Figure 7.15, and the transfer order number is shown at the bottom of the screen.

7.2.6 Confirming the Transfer Order

The transfer order is the document that directs the warehouse staff to move the material from the source to the destination storage bins. For replenishing fixed bins, the material is moved from the source bin in the main warehouse to the picking area.

The confirmation of the transfer order is Transaction LT12, which you can find by following the menu path SAP • LOGISTICS • LOGISTICS EXECUTION • INTERNAL WHSE PROCESSES • STOCK TRANSFER • CONFIRM TRANSFER ORDER • SINGLE DOCUMENT • IN ONE STEP.

Figure 7.17 shows the initial screen for confirming the transfer order. The transfer order number and warehouse number are required. You have the option to confirm the transfer order in the foreground or background and to select PICK, TRANSFER, or PICK + TRANSFER.

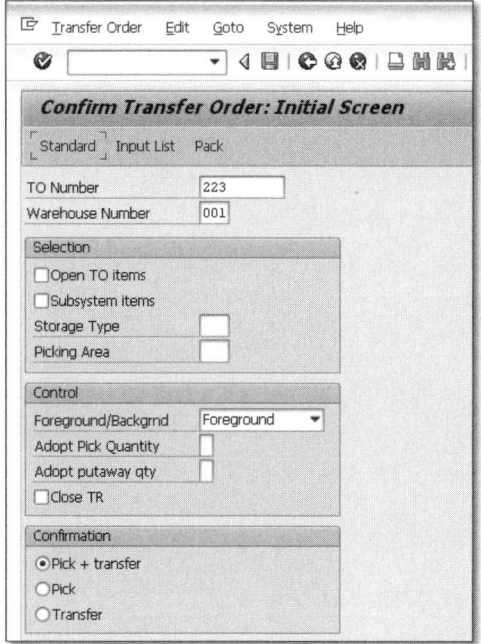

Figure 7.17 Initial Screen for Confirming a Transfer Order: Transaction LT12

Figure 7.18 shows the line item of the transfer order that describes the movement of material 100-510 from source bin 100-20-111 to fixed bin 915 – 01 – 001 in the picking area. You can process the confirmation by clicking the CONFIRM INTERNALLY button on the application toolbar and then saving the transaction.

7 | Stock Replenishment

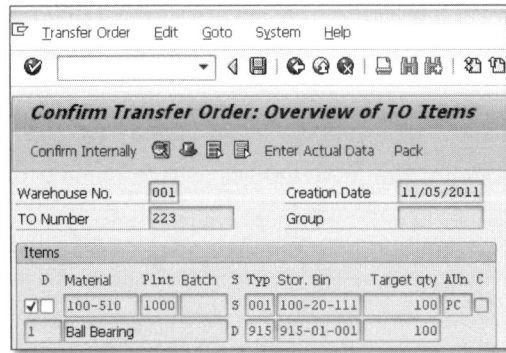

Figure 7.18 Overview of Transfer Order Items for Confirmation

7.2.7 Reviewing the Stock Overview

After confirmation of the transfer order, a review of the stock in the warehouse shows that the material is stored in the fixed storage bin in the picking area.

The transaction used to view the bin stock for a material is LS24. To access this transaction, follow the menu path SAP • LOGISTICS • LOGISTICS EXECUTION • INTERNAL WHSE PROCESSES • BINS AND STOCK • DISPLAY • BIN STOCK PER MATERIAL.

Figure 7.19 shows that the confirmed transfer order moved a quantity of 100 to fixed storage bin 915 – 01 – 001.

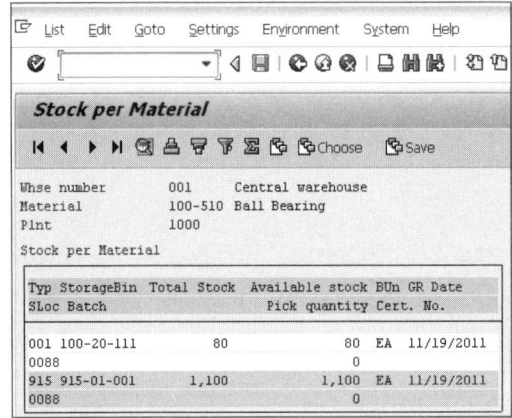

Figure 7.19 Bin Stock Display for Material 70000003: Transaction LS24

266

This section has discussed the replenishment of fixed bins; the next section will examine the process of posting changes.

7.3 Posting Changes

A posting change is a change to the stock level of a material. This can result from a change in the status of a material in a storage bin. The material does not physically move, but the status changes. Several posting changes can be made to material in the warehouse, including:

- Releasing from quality inspection stock
- Posting change from material number to material number
- Dividing batches among other batches

Let's examine these in detail now.

7.3.1 Posting Change for a Release from Quality Inspection Stock

Release of quality inspection stock occurs in both IM and WM, if applicable.

The change in status from quality inspection to unrestricted occurs in SAP IM with a goods movement. In SAP WM, a movement type is also used in conjunction with a posting change notice. The posting change notice is created automatically in WM as a result of the posting of the transaction in IM.

To view the posting change notice for the IM movement, you must know the material document number from the IM posting. The transaction to view the posting change notice is LB12, which you can find by following the menu path SAP • LOGISTICS • LOGISTICS EXECUTION • INTERNAL WHSE PROCESSES • POSTING CHANGE • VIA INVENTORY MANAGEMENT • POSTING CHANGE NOTICE • DISPLAY • FOR MATERIAL DOCUMENT.

Figure 7.20 shows that to view the posting change notice created by the inventory movement, you must enter the material document from that material posting with the relevant year and warehouse number.

The posting change notice shows the information needed to change the status of the material in a storage bin from quality inspection (Q) to unrestricted stock.

7 | Stock Replenishment

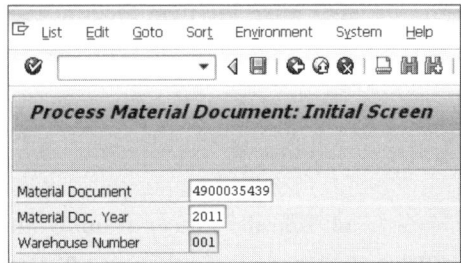

Figure 7.20 Viewing Posting Change Notice for a Specific Material Document

Figure 7.21 shows the details for the posting change notice. The stock details show that the material is being moved from stock category Q to blank, which represents a status change from quality inspection to unrestricted. These item details are used to create the transfer order that will process the status change.

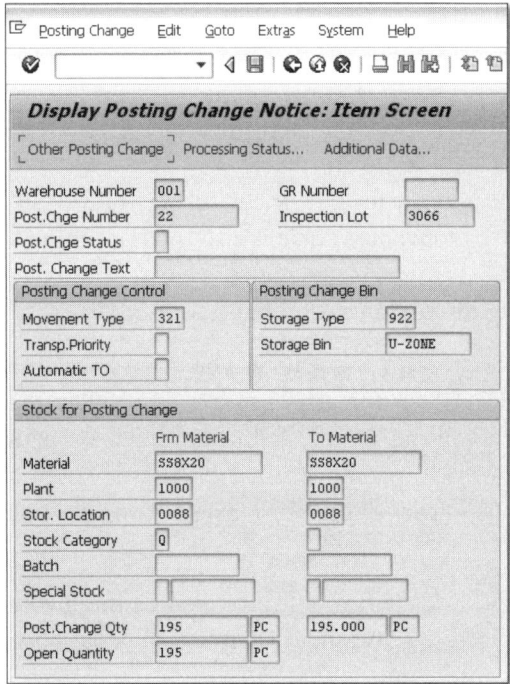

Figure 7.21 Display of Posting Change Notice Details

To create a transfer order from the posting change notice that references a material document, use Transaction LT06. You can find the transaction by following the menu path SAP • LOGISTICS • LOGISTICS EXECUTION • INTERNAL WHSE PROCESSES • POSTING CHANGE • VIA INVENTORY MANAGEMENT • TRANSFER ORDER • CREATE • FOR MATERIAL DOCUMENT. The initial screen requires the material document number, year, and warehouse.

Figure 7.22 shows the stock that is available to have its status changed from quality to unrestricted. The overview shows that there is a quantity of 195 in storage type 002. This quantity is greater than the quantity of the status change. As a result, processing will require manual input to determine the specific material and in what storage bins this material is currently stored. By selecting the line item, posting the transaction, and pressing [Ctrl]+[S], you can stop the processing and require the manual input shown in Figure 7.23.

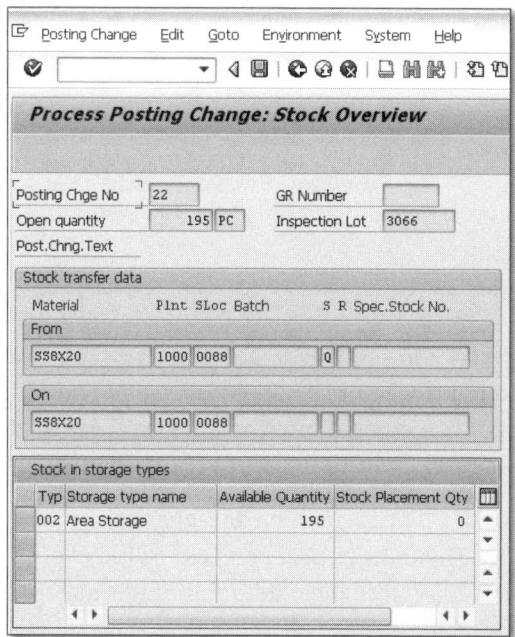

Figure 7.22 Stock Overview for Posting Change Notice Relevant to Material Document

Manual input is required in this example because the quantity to be moved to unrestricted could have been split over two bins or stored in one bin. In the example shown in Figure 7.23, the quantity to be moved to unrestricted is all stored in storage bin 900 – 01 – 01.

7 | Stock Replenishment

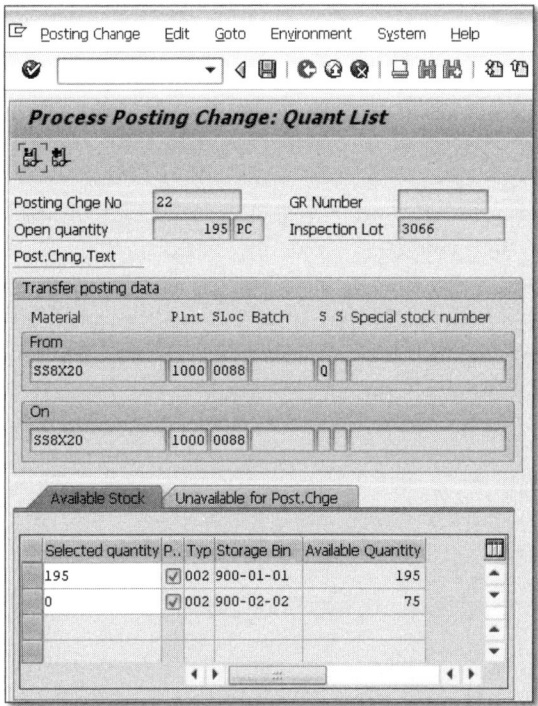

Figure 7.23 Quant List for Posting Change Notice

You can now post the transaction be pressing Ctrl+S, and the transfer order will be created. If you review the material stock in the warehouse, using Transaction LS24, you will see the material that was entered into the transfer order with the posting change notice.

Figure 7.24 shows storage bin 900 – 01 – 01 containing the quantity of 195, which has a status of quality inspection. The transfer order created from the posting change notice, as shown in Figure 7.23, will change the status of this material in storage bin 900 – 01 – 01 to unrestricted.

You can confirm the transfer order with Transaction LT12 or by following the menu path SAP • LOGISTICS • LOGISTICS EXECUTION • INTERNAL WHSE PROCESSES • POSTING CHANGE • VIA INVENTORY MANAGEMENT • TRANSFER ORDER • CONFIRM • IN ONE STEP.

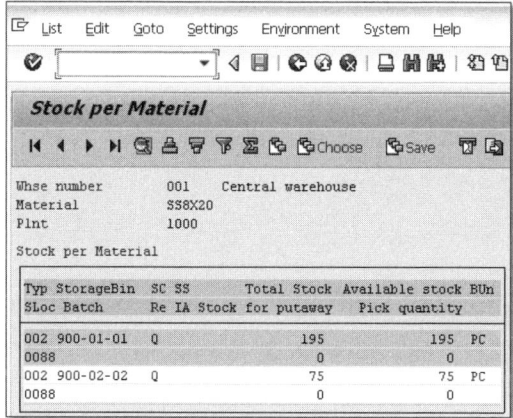

Figure 7.24 Stock Overview of Material in Warehouse: Transaction LS24

Figure 7.25 shows the transfer order item details for the posting change. The material does not physically move from the storage bin but moves in the system using interim storage type 922. The interim storage type is a logical location that allows changes to be made to the material, even though the material does not necessarily move from the bin it is stored in. To check that the material has changed status, use the material overview in the warehouse: Transaction LS24.

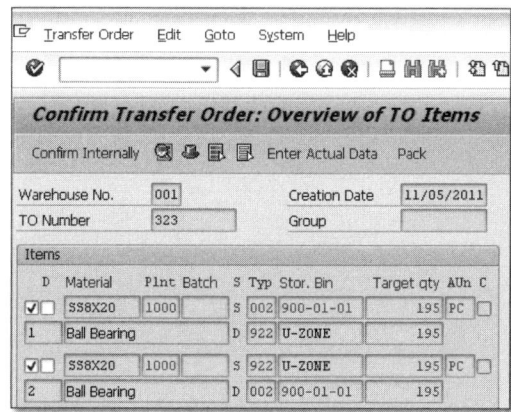

Figure 7.25 Confirmation of Transfer Order for Posting Change Notice

Figure 7.26 shows that the material in storage bin 900 – 01 – 01 does not have a stock category of Q but is blank, showing that it is unrestricted stock.

7 | Stock Replenishment

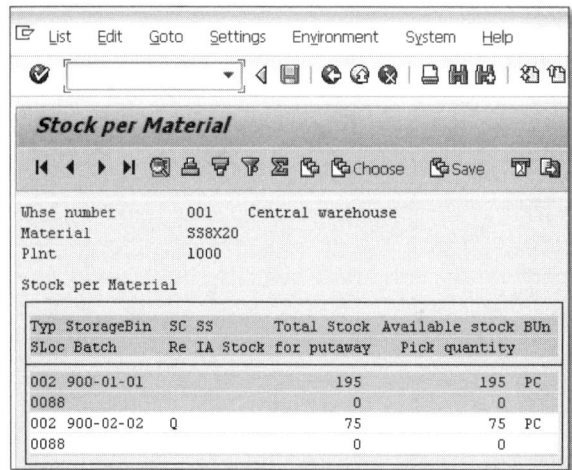

Figure 7.26 Stock Overview of Material in the Warehouse: Transaction LS24

7.3.2 Posting Change from Material Number to Material Number

A material number may be changed while there is still material in stock. This may result from a duplicate part number or a business requirement.

The material number changes when a transfer posting occurs in inventory management that moves the material stock from the old material number to the new material number.

The corresponding movement in WM occurs when a posting change notice has been created via an IM material document, as shown in Figure 7.20 and Figure 7.21 in Section 7.3.1.

To view the posting change notice for the IM movement, you must know the material document number from the IM posting. The transaction to view the posting change notice is LB12 and can be found via the menu path SAP • LOGISTICS • LOGISTICS EXECUTION • INTERNAL WHSE PROCESSES • POSTING CHANGE • VIA INVENTORY MANAGEMENT • POSTING CHANGE NOTICE • DISPLAY • FOR MATERIAL DOCUMENT.

Figure 7.27 shows the two material numbers for the transfer posting. The movement type for this transfer posting is 309, which is used for material to material postings.

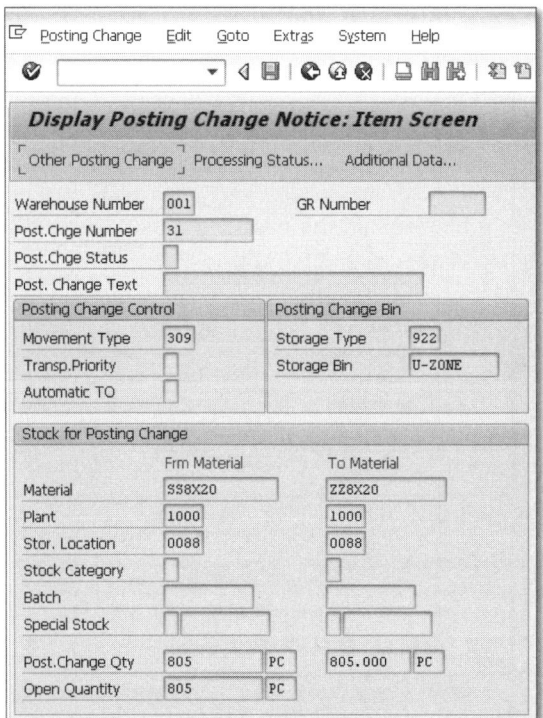

Figure 7.27 Display of Posting Change Notice for Transferring Material Number to Material Number

To create a transfer order from the posting change notice, which references the material document for the material to material transfer, use Transaction LT06, which you can find by following the navigation path SAP • LOGISTICS • LOGISTICS EXECUTION • INTERNAL WHSE PROCESSES • POSTING CHANGE • VIA INVENTORY MANAGEMENT • TRANSFER ORDER • CREATE • FOR MATERIAL DOCUMENT.

Figure 7.28 shows the details of the posting change notice where a quantity of material SS8X20, is transferred to material ZZ8X20. The selection has been made to transfer a quantity from storage bin 900 – 01 – 03.

You can confirm the transfer order for the material posting with Transaction LT12 or by following the menu path SAP • LOGISTICS • LOGISTICS EXECUTION • INTERNAL WHSE PROCESSES • POSTING CHANGE • VIA INVENTORY MANAGEMENT • TRANSFER ORDER • CONFIRM • IN ONE STEP.

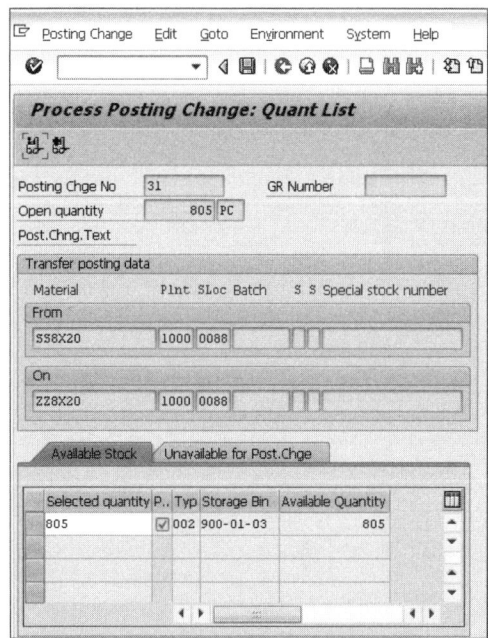

Figure 7.28 Item Detail for a Posting Change Notice for Material to Material Transfer Posting

Figure 7.29 shows the details of the transfer order where the two materials are shown. The new material does not remain in the same storage bin as the old material number, and the transfer order has proposed an empty storage bin in the same storage type in which to place the stock with the new material number.

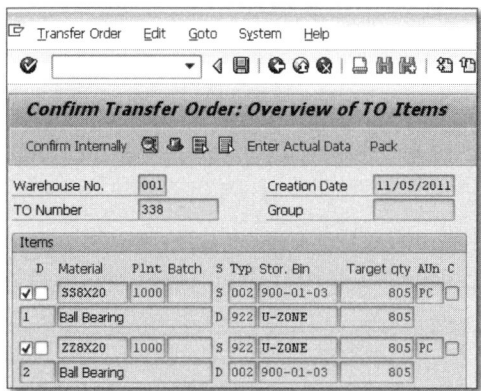

Figure 7.29 Confirmation of a Transfer Order for a Posting Change Notice for Material to Material Posting

To check whether the material has been transferred to the new material number, use the material overview in the warehouse: Transaction LS24.

Figure 7.30 shows the stock with the new material number, ZZ8X20, in storage bin 900 – 01 – 03, transferred from material SS8X20.

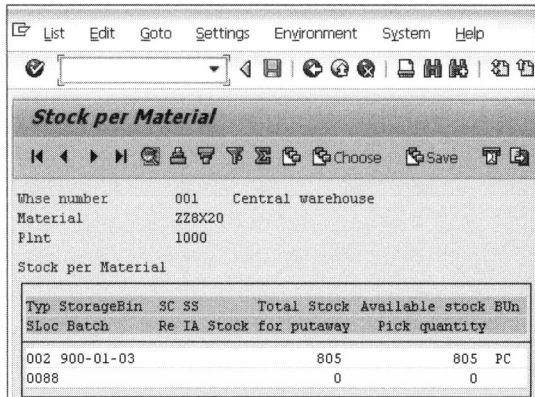

Figure 7.30 Stock Overview of Material in the Warehouse: Transaction LS24

7.3.3 Dividing Batches Among Other Batches

This process is similar to the material to material transfer except that the material batch numbers are changed, and not the material number, which stays the same. The batch number change can occur if material batches are combined or divided. For example, if a quantity of sheet metal is stored as one batch number in a storage location, it may be divided into two storage bins, each with its own batch number.

The transfer posting occurs in IM with movement type 309, the same as a material to material transfer, but the batch number is changed rather than the material number.

The posting change notice created by the material document shows the batch numbers that were entered into the inventory posting, as shown in Figure 7.31.

The posting of the posting change notice produces the transfer order, which when confirmed will move a quantity of the material from one batch number to another.

7 | Stock Replenishment

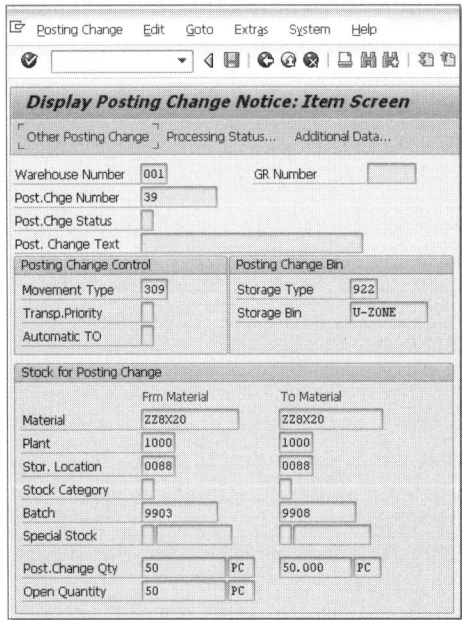

Figure 7.31 Display of Posting Change Notice Details for Batch To Batch Transfer

Figure 7.32 shows details of the transfer order with the two batches for the same material shown. The new batch does not remain in the same storage bin with the old batch. The transfer order has proposed an empty storage bin in the same storage type in which to place the stock with the new batch number.

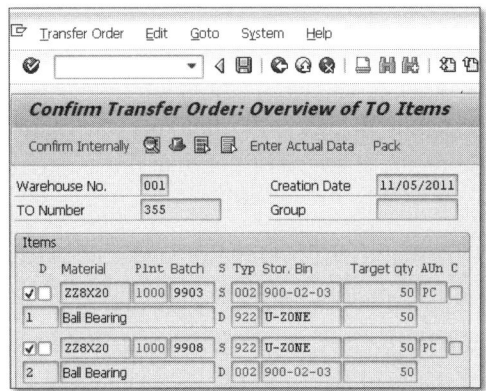

Figure 7.32 Transfer Order Confirmation for a Posting Change Notice for Batch to Batch Posting

This section has examined the aspects of the posting changes process; now we will look at some real-life business examples.

7.4 Business Examples—Stock Replenishment

Replenishment of storage bins in the warehouse requires moving material from one location to another. The material movement can be triggered by a movement in IM or a need within the warehouse to relocate stock; for example, replenishing the areas used for production orders.

7.4.1 Internal Stock Transfers

The internal stock transfer can only be triggered by a requirement to move a material from one part of the warehouse to another, storage bin to storage bin. There are several reasons why material needs to be moved in the warehouse such as moving older stock to racks further away from the loading docks.

Example

Making the warehouse as efficient as possible ensures that deliveries are processed on time and stock is put away so that it is available for customer orders. A British beverage company had been running SAP WM for about four months. Before the WM implementation, the warehouse was run as several storage locations using inventory management. Although the company had reconfigured their warehouse for SAP WM, the warehouse managers had not really changed the processes by which material was moved in and out of the warehouse.

After four months, analysis of the number of picks in the warehouse showed that the throughput had fallen since the second month. The supply chain team looked at the travel of forklift operators for a selection of transfer orders and found that the more recent picks required 30% more travel time. The supply chain team found that the storage bins closest to the loading dock contained material that was in less demand or was close to its expiry date. They proposed that after the next warehouse inventory count, the material that was more frequently picked should be placed in bins close to the loading dock, and less frequently picked items be moved to locations further away.

To achieve this, the warehouse team created a series of transfer orders to move the material to more appropriate storage bins.

7.4.2 Fixed Bin Replenishment

A fixed storage bin is a storage bin where a specific material is always stored. This may be because it has been specifically created for the material. In fixed storage bin replenishment, the storage bin in the picking area needs to be replenished so that the outbound deliveries remain at maximum efficiency.

Example

As in the previous example, a British beverage company had been running SAP WM for about four months and was previously operating the warehouse using SAP MM. After the warehouse had fixed the issues with correct stock being closer to the loading dock, the company began reselling an imported beverage that required oversized crates to store the individual bottles. The pallets of the imported beverage were too tall for the standard racks that had been used for many years. The oversized pallets were stored in an open storage area near the warehouse office where damaged items were usually stored.

The warehouse manager did not want to keep the oversized pallets near the office, as it was a long way from the loading dock and they were taking up room required for damaged goods. The warehouse team modified several storage bins into one large storage bin closer to the loading dock so they could accommodate pallets of the imported beverage.

To ensure that the pallets of the imported beverage were always placed in the same storage bin, the material master record for the imported beverage was amended so that the fixed bin was entered.

7.4.3 Posting Changes

A posting change is an adjustment to the stock level of a material. This can result from a change in the status of a material in a storage bin. The material does not physically move, but the status changes. Several posting changes can be made to material in the warehouse, including release from quality inspection or dividing batches.

Example

A manufacturer of paint additives produced batches of material that usually filled at least two 55-gallon drums. The batches were received into stock and placed into a warehouse storage bin. All movements from the production line were received into quality inspection so the quality control team could test the contents of each drum to ensure the tested values were within the allowed limits.

On occasion, the quality control team would test the contents of each drum from a batch and find that the tested values were different. This could occur if there were any contaminants in the drum or if there was a delay in placing the product into the drums.

If the quality control team found that the inspected values were different from drum to drum, then they would recommend to the warehouse manager that each drum be stored as a separate batch. To do this, the warehouse manager would create a posting change so that the one batch was split into two, but they would remain in the same storage bin.

7.5 Summary

In this chapter, we discussed internal transfers and stock replenishment using internal transfers and posting changes. Material is moved around the warehouse every day. Therefore, it is important that the system transactions are kept up to date to ensure that the warehouse stock is in the right bin with the right quantity and the right status.

In Chapter 8, we will discuss the different picking strategies that can be assigned, how these are configured, and how they are used.

Picking strategies are important to the outbound process of the warehouse. Implementing the correct strategy can vastly improve efficiency in this critical area. Choosing a picking strategy that makes processing more complex can severely increase picking time and hinder deliveries.

8 Picking Strategies

A picking strategy is a method that determines the way a material is chosen to be picked.

> **Example**
>
> A material may be selected because of a strategy to pick materials by their remaining shelf life or by the sequence in which they are added to stock.

When picking strategies are discussed, there is often confusion between the method of picking the material and the strategy for which material is to be removed. The method of picking involves how a company physically removes the stock; for example, batch picking or wave picking.

The strategy of picking involves deciding what material is to be picked. A number of picking strategies can be used, including the following:

- First in, first out (FIFO)
- Last in, first out (LIFO)
- Fixed storage bin
- Shelf life expiration
- Partial quantities
- Quantity relevant

The warehouse operation doesn't need to introduce picking strategies into the material removal process, but how material is removed from the warehouse should be discussed and effective strategies adopted.

Once the picking strategy has been adopted, the warehouse management system uses the picking strategy to assign the appropriate picking location. There is a chance to manually intervene for certain stock movements, where it is possible to change the source and destination storage bins that the system has already proposed.

Accepting the system-generated picking location removes a responsibility from the warehouse staff and effectively reduces picking time. Manual changes should be kept to a minimum and reviewed periodically to ensure that the picking strategies still follow the most effective configuration.

You need to complete several steps to configure the picking strategies before the strategy can be applied to materials. These steps begin with the storage type indicator.

8.1 Storage Type Indicator

The storage type indicator in SAP WM allows only certain materials to be picked from storage types, and the order of picking can be defined by the storage type search for each storage type indicator. It is not necessary to configure the storage type indicator if all materials are picked the same way within the same storage type.

If the storage type indicator is to be used, it needs to be configured using Transaction OMLY or following the menu path IMG • LOGISTICS EXECUTION • WAREHOUSE MANAGEMENT • STRATEGIES • ACTIVATE STORAGE TYPE SEARCH.

Figure 8.1 shows the selection available for the storage type search transaction. To configure the storage type indicator, click the DEFINE button. If you need to configure a storage type indicator to create a separate search for a group of materials, you can make the entry in the screen shown in Figure 8.2.

The entry for a storage type indicator is simply the warehouse number, the storage type indicator that has been chosen, and a relevant description. Figure 8.2 shows some storage type indicators and descriptions.

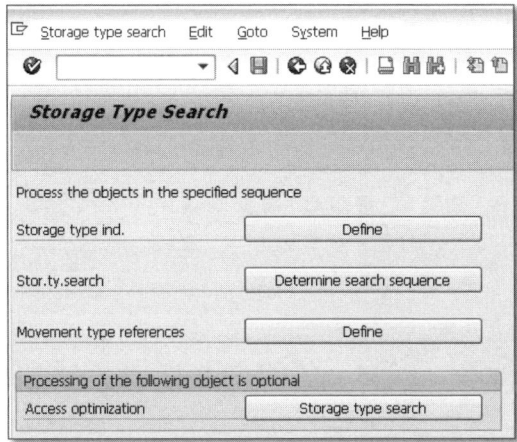

Figure 8.1 Storage Type Search Selection Screen: Transaction OMLY

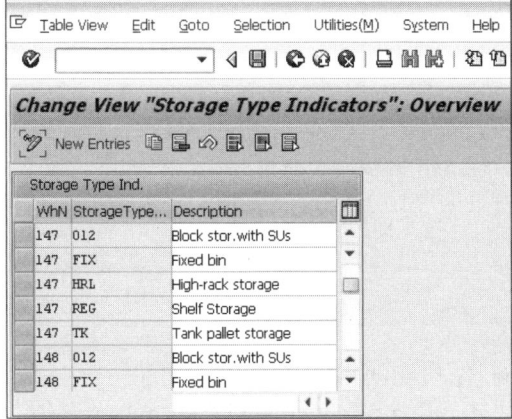

Figure 8.2 Creating a Storage Type Indicator

Figure 8.3 shows the warehouse information entered into the material master record for item 700000031. The material has been configured with the storage type indicator FIX for picking. This means the storage type search that contains the storage type indictor FIX will be the only storage type search applicable for this material.

Now that we have discussed the storage type indicator, we'll examine the storage type search functionality.

8 | Picking Strategies

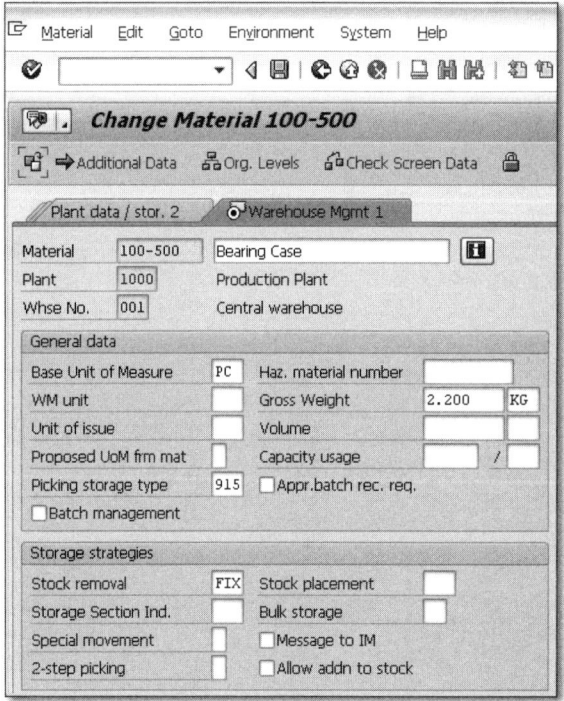

Figure 8.3 Storage Type Indicator Entered into the Material Master Record

8.2 Storage Type Search

Once you have configured the storage type indicator, you can configure the storage type search. You don't have to configure a single storage type indicator, but you can confer with the warehouse staff to decide if the storage type search differs for certain materials or groups of materials.

8.2.1 Configuring the Storage Type Search

The creation of a storage type search begins in the selection menu in Transaction OMLY, as shown in Figure 8.1. The storage type search is the starting point for picking material from the warehouse. The search defines what storage type is to be used for the picking strategy.

Before entering the storage type search, choose the search in consultation with the warehouse management staff that plans the layout of the material in the warehouse. How they have stored certain material and how the storage types are positioned determines the configuration of the sequence of storage types that are searched.

Figure 8.4 shows the information entered for each storage type search. Each line entry is relevant for a particular warehouse. The unique keys for each entry are as follows:

- Warehouse
- Warehouse operation
- Storage type indicator
- Stock category
- Special stock indicator

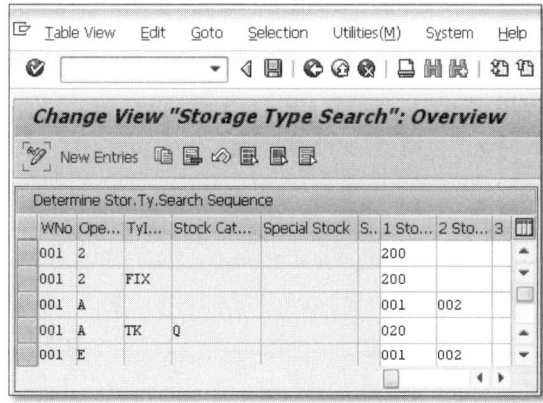

Figure 8.4 Detail Screen for a Storage Type Search

For the warehouse indicator enter "2" for two-step picking, "A" for stock picking, and "E" for stock putaway. The stock category and special stock indicators are used when a different storage type search is required for materials with these special statuses.

Using the example in Figure 8.4 where the warehouse operation is A for picking and the stock category is Q for quality inspection (QI) stock, the picking strategy will search storage type 001, and if no appropriate material is located, then the search will be processed in storage type 002. If no material is found in storage type 002, the process will require manual intervention.

A maximum of 30 storage types can be configured for each search. Depending on the complexity of the warehouse and the location of the material, the number of storage types entered per search will vary.

8.2.2 Configuring Storage Section Search

In addition to the storage type indicator and storage type search, there is similar configuration and functionality for the storage section. In complex warehouses, storage section functionality is frequently used, and searching by storage section is a way to increase warehouse picking efficiency.

You configure the storage section indicator with Transaction OMLZ, or you can find it by following the menu path IMG • LOGISTICS EXECUTION • WAREHOUSE MANAGEMENT • STRATEGIES • ACTIVATE STORAGE SECTION SEARCH.

Figure 8.5 shows the configuration of the storage section indicator. The indicator is configured specifically for each warehouse. It enables the definition of a group of materials that can all be allocated to one storage section search.

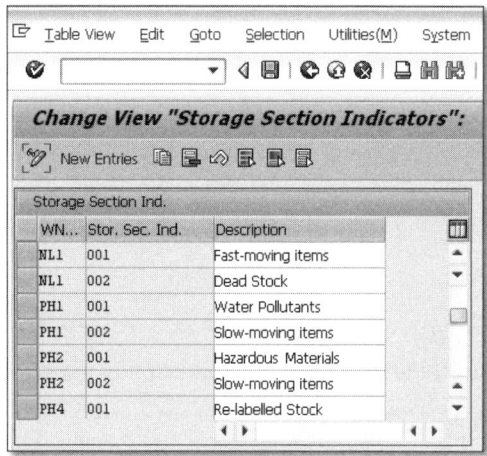

Figure 8.5 Configuration of a Storage Section Indicator

Figure 8.6 shows the configuration for a storage section search if it is required. The storage section indicator is part of the unique key along with the warehouse, storage type, hazardous material storage class, and water pollution class. It is possible to configure up to 10 storage sections for each unique search.

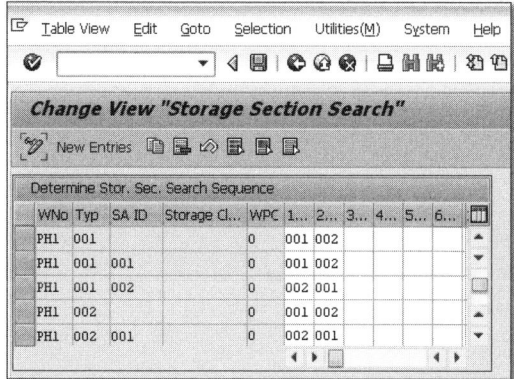

Figure 8.6 Configuration for a Storage Section Search

This section examined the storage type search. We'll now discuss the first in, first out picking strategy.

8.3   FIFO (First In, First Out)

The picking strategy for first in, first out—or FIFO, as it is more commonly known—removes the oldest quant from the storage type defined in the storage type search. This is used in most manufacturing industries where the material companies want to sell first is that which has been stored in the warehouse the longest.

FIFO is a very common picking strategy. It ensures that the oldest material is removed from the warehouse for production or sales orders. In many instances, the warehouse layout is configured to optimize FIFO picking.

Warehouses that have deep racks make it difficult for warehouse staff to get to the correct material. One method of ensuring that the oldest material is picked is to use gravity flow racks for materials that are picked individually and not in boxes. The boxes are placed at the back of the rack, and the flow racks are filled so that the picking at the front moves material forward from the back. This is important in picking areas.

8.3.1 Configuring the FIFO Picking Strategy

You can define the FIFO picking strategy by following the menu path IMG • LOGISTICS EXECUTION • WAREHOUSE MANAGEMENT • STRATEGIES • STOCK REMOVAL STRATEGIES • DEFINE FIFO STRATEGY.

Figure 8.7 shows the configuration of the stock removal strategy for warehouse 001 and storage type DRW. The stock removal strategy is F for FIFO.

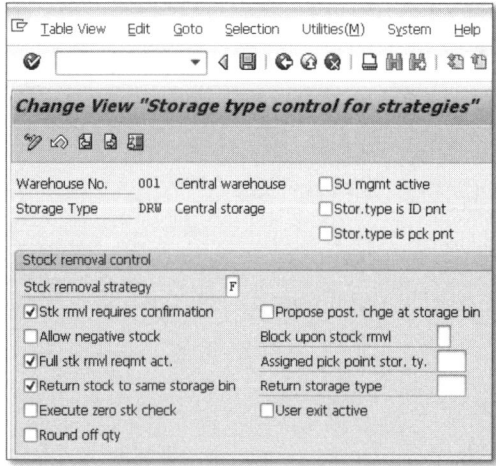

Figure 8.7 Defining a Stock Removal Strategy as FIFO

8.3.2 Stock Removal Control Indicators

Figure 8.7 shows that, apart from the stock removal strategy, several other control indicators can be configured for the strategy:

- **Stk rmvl requires confirmation**
  If this checkbox is selected, the picking of the entire item must be confirmed in the destination storage type or return storage type before the quantity is made available.

- **Allow negative stock**
  Negative stock is allowed for interim storage areas. When this checkbox is selected, the system allows the posting of negative quants in the storage type.

- **Full stk rmvl reqmt act**
  Select this checkbox when the entire quant must be picked, regardless of the quantity required for the pick.

- **Return stock to same storage bin**
  Select this checkbox when the picked stock that was not needed has to be returned to the same bin it was picked from.

- **Execute zero stk check**
  If the warehouse needs a zero stock check when a storage bin is emptied after a stock pick, then select this checkbox. When the zero stock check is made, the storage bin can only be used for putaways when the zero stock check is completed and confirmed.

- **Round off qty**
  This field is for rounding off the requested quantity for picking. When this checkbox is selected, the processing uses the rounding off quantity in the warehouse screen for the storage type in the material master record.

- **Propose post chge at storage bin**
  This checkbox is selected when the warehouse needs to post and leave materials in same storage bin, a key procedure in relabeling. This signals that no transfer is to take place for a posting change.

- **Block upon stock rmvl**
  This field can be filled in when the blocking checkbox has to be set when the material is picked. The values that can be used are 1 for blocking a storage bin and 2 for blocking the quant only.

- **Assigned pick point stor. ty.**
  This field can be entered with the assigned pick point for the storage type.

- **Return storage type**
  This field contains the storage type into which any remaining quantity of the picked material to be stored.

After reviewing this list of indicators, you can move on to an example of a FIFO picking strategy.

8.3.3 Example of FIFO Picking Strategy

The following example will show you how the FIFO configuration for a storage type affects how the material is picked in the warehouse.

You can use Transaction LS24 to show the material stock. Figure 8.8 shows the warehouse stock for material 100-500. The material is stored in two bins in storage type 001, but the material in storage bin 02 – 01 – 03 was received into stock before the material in storage bin 03-01-08. Therefore, in any FIFO picking strategy the material in storage bin 02 – 01 – 03 should be selected first.

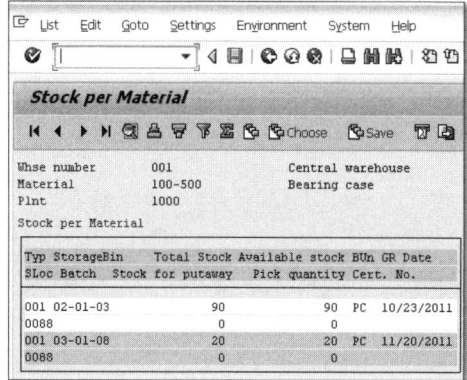

Figure 8.8 Stock Overview for Material in a Warehouse

To display the picking strategy configuration for a storage type, follow the menu path IMG • LOGISTICS EXECUTION • WAREHOUSE MANAGEMENT • STRATEGIES • STOCK REMOVAL STRATEGIES • DEFINE FIFO STRATEGY.

Figure 8.9 shows that for storage type 001, the picking strategy is FIFO, option F, and this will be used when material is withdrawn from any storage bin in the storage type. You can use Transaction LT01 to create a transfer order that will pick material from the storage type 001.

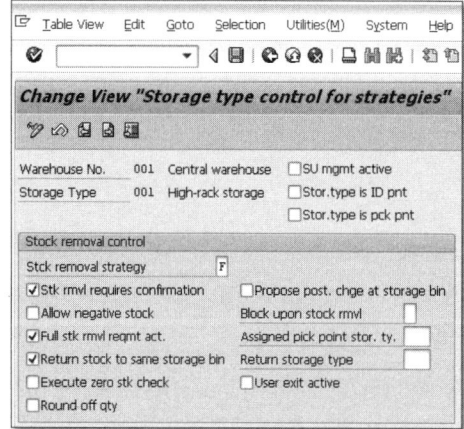

Figure 8.9 FIFO Picking Strategy for Storage Type 001

Figure 8.10 shows the initial screen for the creation of a transfer order to pick material from storage type 001. Movement type 201 is used because it will remove the material and consume it at a cost center.

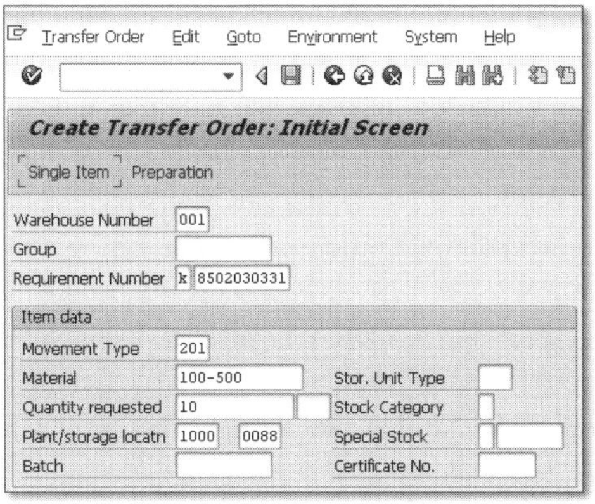

Figure 8.10 Creating a Transfer Order: Transaction LT01

Figure 8.11 shows the system-generated transfer order item information for material 100-500. Based on the configuration for storage type 001, the material that has been selected is from storage bin 02 – 01 – 03, which is the material that was receipted into stock first.

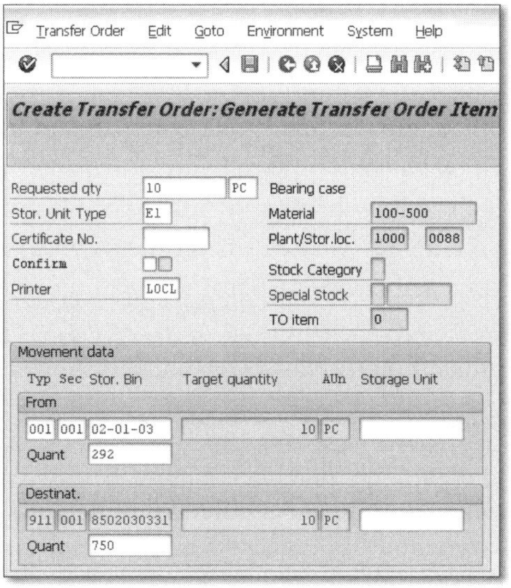

Figure 8.11 System-Generated Source Storage Bin Based on FIFO Picking Strategy

8 | Picking Strategies

Now that we've discussed the FIFO picking strategy, let's consider the opposite picking strategy, which is last in, first out, or LIFO.

8.4 LIFO (Last In, First Out)

Last in, first out—or LIFO—is based on the principle that the last delivery of material to be received is the first to be used. Many companies use LIFO for inventory cost accounting. The value of warehouse stock impacts reported gross profit margins. Investors tend to carefully review gross profit margins, which are often considered a measure of the value provided to consumers. LIFO can give a more accurate valuation of warehouse stock.

Retailers such as Walgreens and Kohl's use LIFO picking. When LIFO picking occurs, no value change occurs for older material when new materials are received. Because the LIFO method is in effect, the older material is not affected by the potentially higher prices of the new deliveries of material. If the older material is not affected, that means it is not valuated at the new material price. If the older material value is not increased, this prevents false valuation of current inventory.

Picking with the LIFO method is not as common as FIFO picking. It may be used if the financial department wants to report inventory using LIFO because it gives a more conservative view of the cost of inventory and therefore is seen in a positive light by some financial analysts. Check with the warehouse staff and accounting department to determine whether any storage types need to be configured for LIFO picking.

8.4.1 Configuring the LIFO Picking Strategy

You can define the LIFO picking strategy by following the menu path IMG • LOGISTICS EXECUTION • WAREHOUSE MANAGEMENT • STRATEGIES • STOCK REMOVAL STRATEGIES • DEFINE LIFO STRATEGY. For this configuration, we are changing the picking strategy of storage type 001 from FIFO to LIFO.

Figure 8.12 shows that for storage type 001, the picking strategy has been changed to LIFO, option L, and this will be used when material is withdrawn from any storage bin in the storage type.

8.4 LIFO (Last In, First Out)

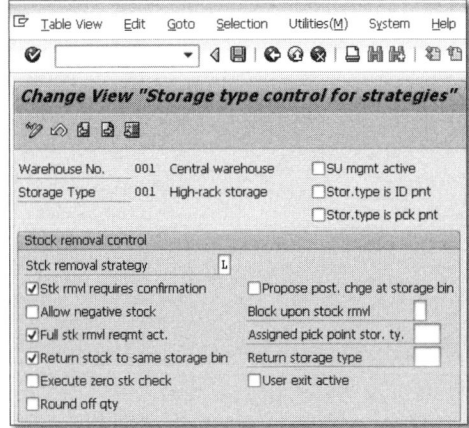

Figure 8.12 LIFO Picking Strategy for Storage Type 001

8.4.2 Example of LIFO Picking Strategy

The following example will show how the LIFO configuration for a storage type affects the way the material is picked in the warehouse. Transaction LS24 displays the warehouse stock for material 100-500.

Figure 8.13 shows the stock position for material 100-500 in storage type 001. When a transfer order for this material is created, the LIFO picking strategy configured for storage type 001 should select the material in storage bin 03 – 01 – 08, because it is the last material to be goods-receipted.

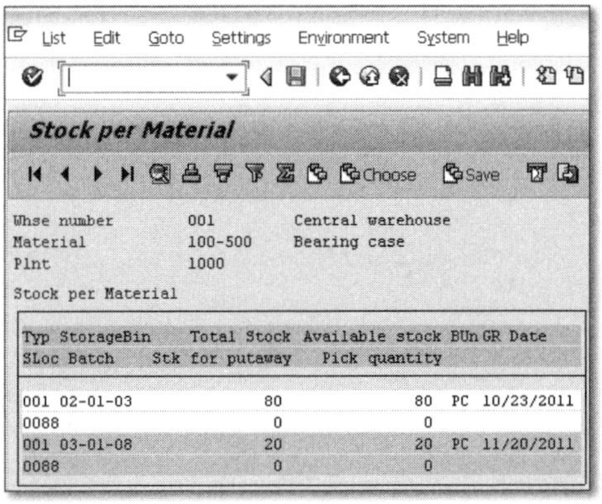

Figure 8.13 Stock Overview for Material in a Warehouse

You can use Transaction LT01 to create a transfer order to pick material from storage type 001. Figure 8.14 shows the initial screen for creating a transfer order to pick material from storage type 001. The movement type, 551, is used for scrapping materials. This will remove the material from the warehouse for disposal. This is similar to consuming the material at a cost center.

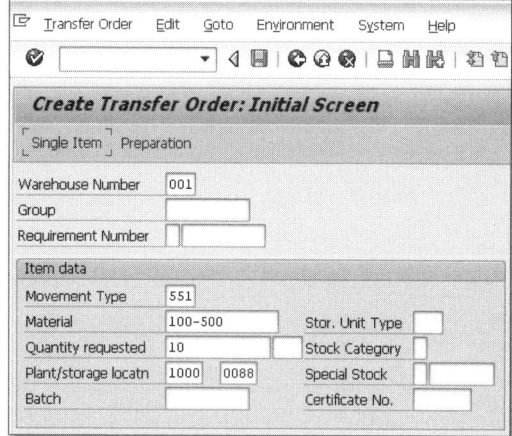

Figure 8.14 Creating a Transfer Order: Transaction LT01

Figure 8.15 shows the system-generated transfer order based on the LIFO picking strategy. In this case, the material has been removed from the storage bin where the material has a goods receipt date later than material in the other storage bins.

Having explored the functionality of the LIFO picking strategy, we will continue by discussing the fixed storage bin picking strategy.

8.5 Fixed Storage Bin

The picking strategy for fixed storage bins relies on the data that has been entered into the material master record for the material to be picked.

8.5.1 Fixed Storage Bin in Material Master

The fixed storage bin is entered into the material master record in the SAP WM screen.

Fixed Storage Bin | **8.5**

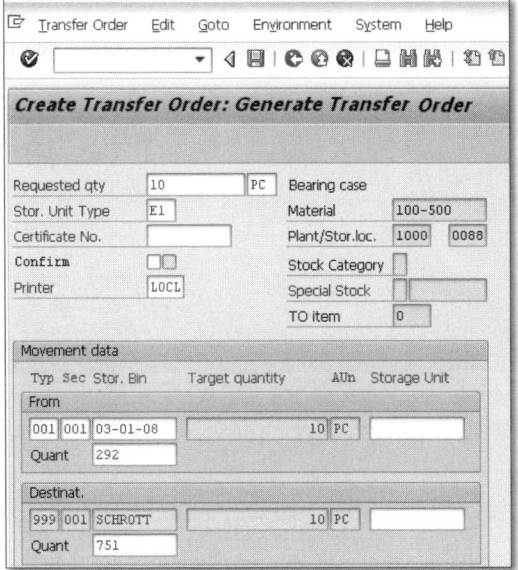

Figure 8.15 System-Generated Source Storage Bin Based on LIFO Picking Strategy

> **Note**
>
> In SAP ECC 6.0, this is the second WM screen, but this may vary depending on the version you are using.

Figure 8.16 shows the WM screen for material 100-500. In the storage bin stock section of the screen, the storage bin has the entry A–01. This is the storage bin fixed for this material in this specific storage type, 005. This information is used for the fixed bin picking strategy.

The material in storage type 005 should be stored in storage bin A –01; however, it may have been manually moved to other bin locations if there was an overflow of material. Transaction LS24 enables you to see the stock situation for the material.

Figure 8.17 shows that material 100-500 is in fact located in three storage bins in storage type 005. The fixed bin picking strategy generates a transfer order that picks material from the fixed storage bin as noted in the material master record.

295

8 | Picking Strategies

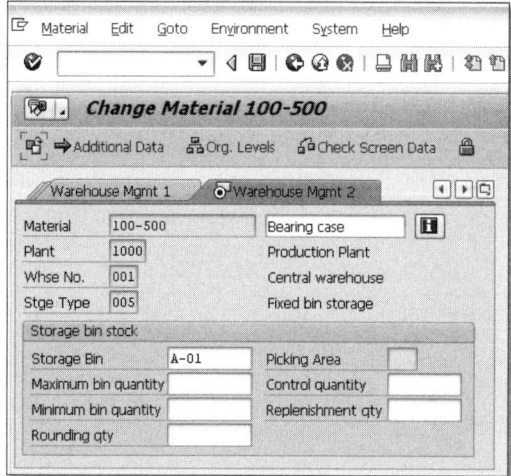

Figure 8.16 Fixed Storage Bin Information in Material Master Record: Transaction MM02

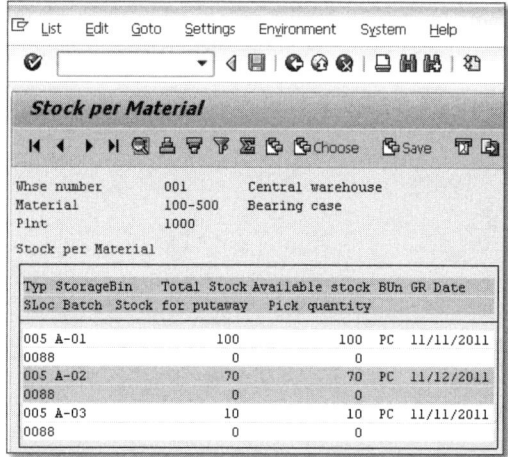

Figure 8.17 Stock Overview for Material in a Warehouse

8.5.2 Configuring the Fixed Bin Picking Strategy

You can define the fixed bin picking strategy by following the menu path IMG • Logistics Execution • Warehouse Management • Strategies • Stock Removal Strategies • Define Fixed Bin Strategy.

Figure 8.18 shows that for the storage type 005, the picking strategy has been configured to option P, which represents fixed bin, and this strategy will be used when material is withdrawn from any storage bin in the selected storage type.

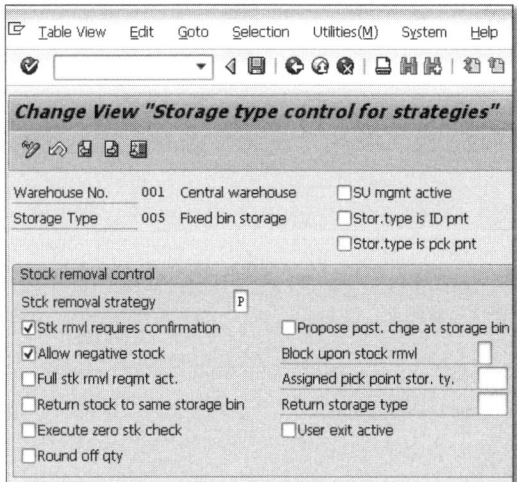

Figure 8.18 Fixed Bin Picking Strategy for Storage Type 005

8.5.3 Example of Fixed Bin Picking Strategy

In this section, we will show you how the fixed bin picking strategy configuration for a storage type affects how the material is picked in the warehouse. You can use Transaction LT01 to create a transfer order to pick material from the fixed bin defined in the material master for storage type 005.

Figure 8.19 shows the initial screen for creating a transfer order to pick material from the fixed bin in storage type 005. The movement type, 551, is used for scrapping materials. This will remove the material from the warehouse for disposal.

Figure 8.20 shows the system-generated transfer order based on the fixed bin picking strategy. In this case, the material has been removed from the storage bin, A-01, that is defined in the material master for storage type 005.

This section has described the fixed bin picking strategy. Let's now focus on the picking strategy that uses shelf life expiration.

8 | Picking Strategies

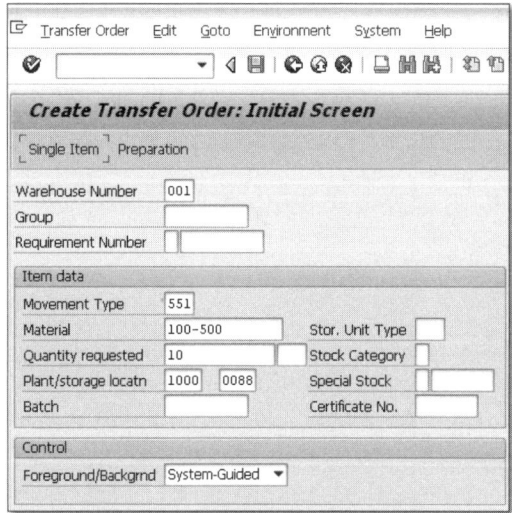

Figure 8.19 Creating a Transfer Order: Transaction LT01

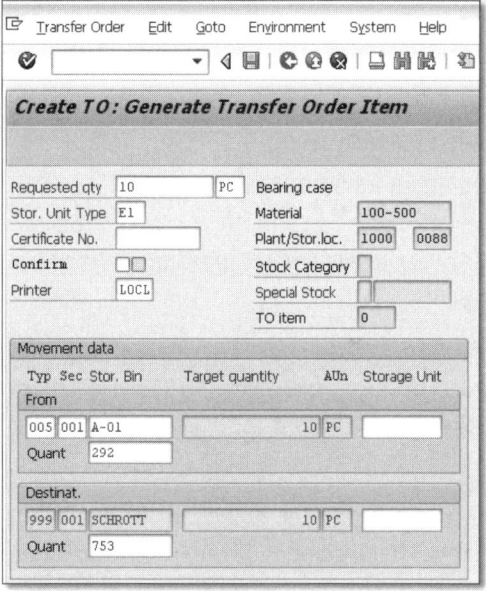

Figure 8.20 System-Generated Source Storage Bin Based on Fixed Bin Picking Strategy

8.6 Shelf Life Expiration

In many industries, especially retail and grocery, the shelf life of materials is a very important characteristic. This can be a sale-focused shelf life, where the material can only sit on a store shelf until its sell by date. Alternatively, it can be production focused, as when chemicals and raw materials can be kept only for so long and still meet tolerance limits for use in the production process. It is important that warehouse managers review shelf life expiration dates (SLEDs) to ensure that out of date material does not have to be scrapped.

Under the shelf life expiration picking strategy, the material is picked based on the shelf life of the quants of material in the warehouse. To ensure that this picking strategy produces the correct results, WM users must perform several configuration steps or check them for accuracy.

8.6.1 SLED Picking and the Material Master

Before using the shelf life picking strategy, check that the material to be picked has the correct information regarding the shelf life characteristics entered on the plant storage view. Use Transaction MM03 to display the material or Transaction MM02 to change the material.

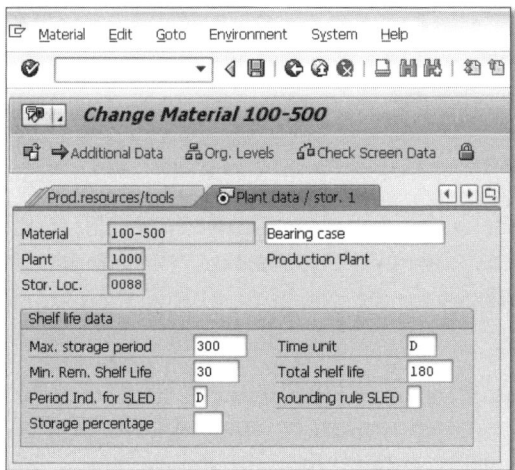

Figure 8.21 Shelf Life Expiration Data Entry on Plant Data Screen of Material Master Record

8 | Picking Strategies

Figure 8.21 shows the shelf life data that has been entered for material 100-500. This data is used in calculating the shelf life expiration date in batch determination and is used in the picking strategy.

8.6.2 Configuring Shelf Life Expiration Picking Strategy

You can define the fixed bin picking strategy by following the menu path IMG • LOGISTICS EXECUTION • WAREHOUSE MANAGEMENT • STRATEGIES • STOCK REMOVAL STRATEGIES • DEFINE STRATEGY FOR EXPIRATION DATE.

Unlike some other picking strategies, this configuration has two parts, as shown in Figure 8.22. The first part of the configuration is to activate the shelf life expiration date management for the warehouse where the picking will take place. The second part is to activate the stock removal strategy for shelf life expiration for the warehouses that require it.

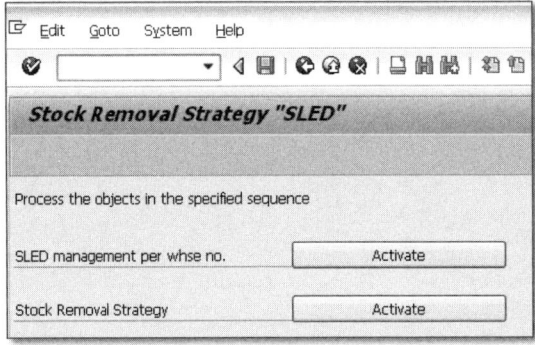

Figure 8.22 Two-Part Configuration for SLED Picking Strategy

Activate the SLED management for the warehouse by selecting the checkbox, as shown in Figure 8.23 (001; CENTRAL WAREHOUSE). After making this configuration, you can configure the picking strategy for the storage type, using the second option shown in Figure 8.22.

Figure 8.24 shows that for storage type 001, the picking strategy has been configured to be shelf life expiration, which is represented by option H. This will be used when material is withdrawn from any storage bin in the storage type.

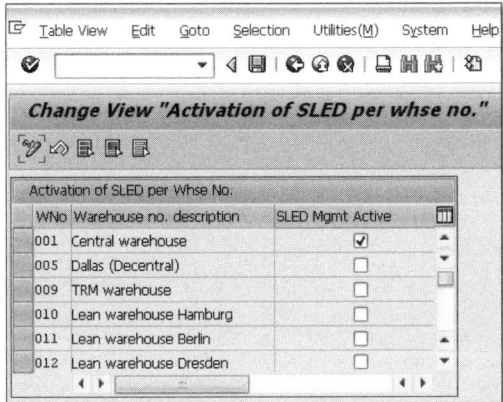

Figure 8.23 Configuration to Activate SLED for a Warehouse

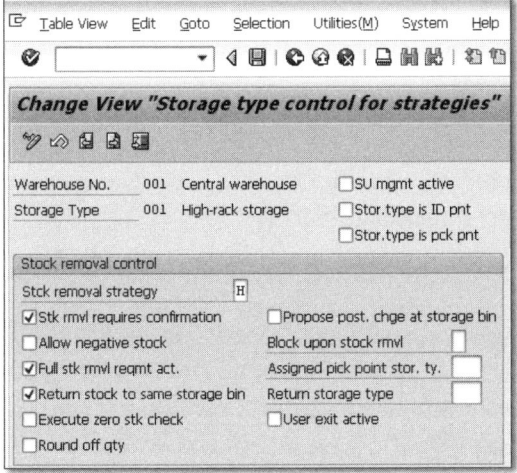

Figure 8.24 Shelf Life Expiration Picking Strategy for Storage Type 001

8.6.3 Displaying SLED Stock

The shelf life expiration date control list shows stock in the warehouse that has an expiration date. You can run the SLED control list with Transaction LX27 or via the menu path SAP • LOGISTICS • LOGISTICS EXECUTION • WAREHOUSE MANAGEMENT • MASTER DATA • MATERIAL • EVALUATIONS • SLED CONTROL LIST.

Figure 8.25 shows the entry of the material, warehouse number, plant, and storage type along with the remaining shelf life in days for the maximum storage time allowed for a material in the warehouse.

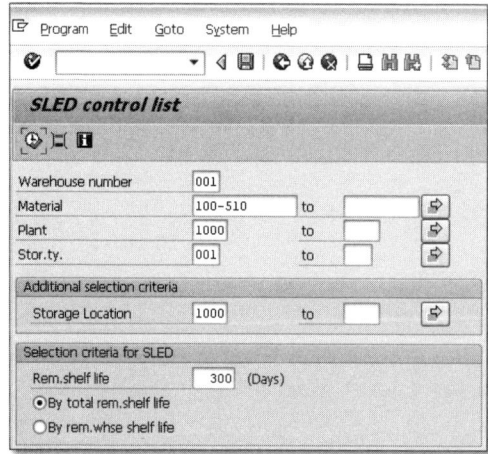

Figure 8.25 Initial Screen for Shelf Life Expiration Date Control List: Transaction LX27

The program reviews the SLED date entered when the transfer order was created against the current date to calculate the remaining shelf life.

Figure 8.26 shows the shelf life expiration date control list. The report shows the quants of material 100-500 in the warehouse that are active for SLED and are within the parameters entered in Figure 8.25.

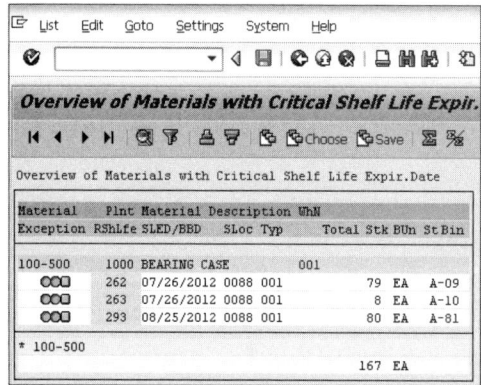

Figure 8.26 Results Screen for Shelf Life Expiration Date Control List: Transaction LX27

8.6.4 Example of Shelf Life Expiration Picking Strategy

In this section, we'll explain how the shelf life expiration picking strategy configuration for a storage type affects the way material is picked in the warehouse.

You can use Transaction LT01 to create a transfer order to pick material with the shortest shelf life defined in the material master for storage type 001.

Figure 8.27 shows the initial screen for creating a transfer order to pick material from storage type 001. The movement type, 201, is used because it will remove the material and consume it at a cost center.

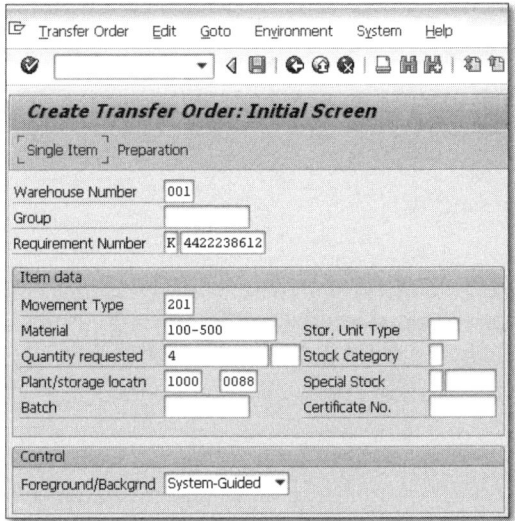

Figure 8.27 Creating a Transfer Order: Transaction LT01

Figure 8.28 shows the system-generated transfer order based on the shelf life expiration picking strategy. In this example, the material has been removed from storage bin A-09 because this is the bin that contains the material with the shortest shelf life, as shown in Figure 8.26.

Now that we have reviewed the picking strategy for shelf life expiration, let's examine the partial quantities picking strategy.

303

8 | Picking Strategies

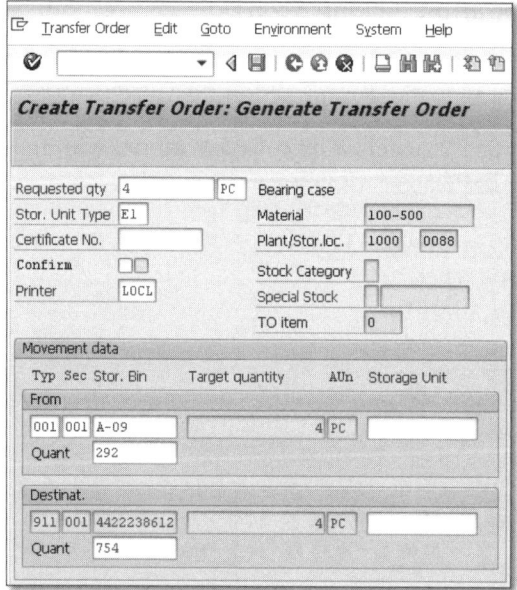

Figure 8.28 System-Generated Source Storage Bin Based on Shelf Life Expiration Picking Strategy

8.7 Partial Quantities

The picking strategy for partial quantities is associated with storage unit management, which we'll discuss in Chapter 11. A warehouse may require the partial pick if the warehouse manager does not want to pick all the contents of a storage unit and then have to return some to the storage bin. A partial quantity allows the staff to remove some of the contents of a storage unit.

Members of the warehouse staff often try to reduce the number of storage units with partial quantities, and the partial quantities picking strategy can be an appropriate way to accomplish this.

8.7.1 Configuring Partial Quantities Picking Strategy

You can define the partial quantities picking strategy by following the menu path IMG • LOGISTICS EXECUTION • WAREHOUSE MANAGEMENT • STRATEGIES • STOCK REMOVAL STRATEGIES • DEFINE STRATEGY FOR PARTIAL PALLET QUANTITY.

304

Figure 8.29 shows that for storage type 001, the picking strategy has been configured for partial pallet quantity, which is represented by option A. This will be used when material is withdrawn from any storage bin in the storage type.

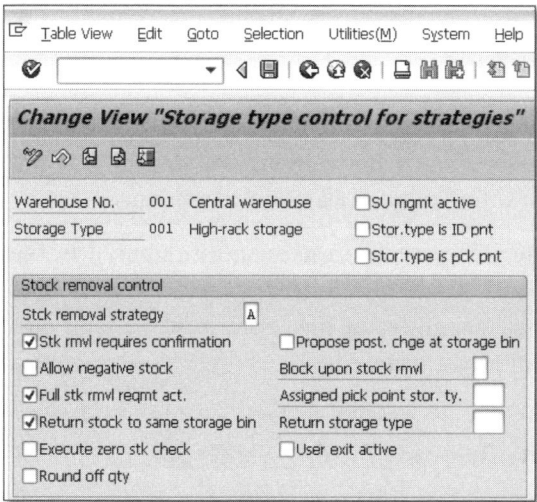

Figure 8.29 Partial Quantity Picking Strategy for Storage Type 001

8.7.2 Using the Partial Quantities Picking Strategy

When a transfer order is created for a material with the storage type configured for partial quantities picking, transaction processing searches for a relevant quant of material. The logic behind the picking strategy is defined as follows:

- Initially the system determines whether the quantity in the transfer order equals or is greater than the quantity of a standard storage unit. If this is the case, then a standard storage unit can be picked from stock. However, if no standard storage units are available, the partial storage unit quantities in the warehouse are used.

- If the system determines that the quantity in the transfer order is less than the quantity of the standard storage unit, then the system initially proceeds to remove partial storage unit quantities from the warehouse. However, if no partial storage unit quantities are available, the system needs to break down full storage units to obtain the correct quantity for the transfer order.

We'll provide further information regarding storage units in Chapter 11. After this discussion of partial quantities picking, we now turn our attention to the quantity-relevant picking strategy.

8.8 Quantity-Relevant Picking

The quantity-relevant picking strategy is less frequently used but is useful for companies whose warehouses store the same material in varying sizes of bins and storage types. We find this scenario often in older warehouse buildings.

The quantity-relevant picking strategy is based on the quantity required in the transfer order and whether that quantity is defined as *large* or *small*. Warehouses may have storage types where small quantities of material are stored and also have storage types where large quantities are stored.

8.8.1 Configuring the Quantity Relevant Picking Strategy

You can define the quantity-relevant picking strategy by following the menu path IMG • Logistics Execution • Warehouse Management • Strategies • Stock Removal Strategies • Define Strategy for Large/Small Quantities.

Unlike some other picking strategies, this configuration has two parts, as shown in Figure 8.30. The first part of the configuration is to activate the quantity-relevant strategy for the warehouse where the picking will take place. The second part of the configuration is to determine the sequence in which the storage types are searched so that the relevant material to be picked is found.

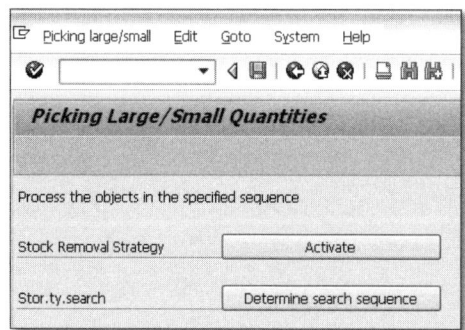

Figure 8.30 Two-Part Configuration for Quantity Relevant Picking Strategy

Figure 8.31 shows that for storage type 001, the picking strategy has been changed to quantity relevant, option M, and this will be used when material is withdrawn from any storage bin in the storage type. The second part of the configuration is to define the search sequence for the storage type.

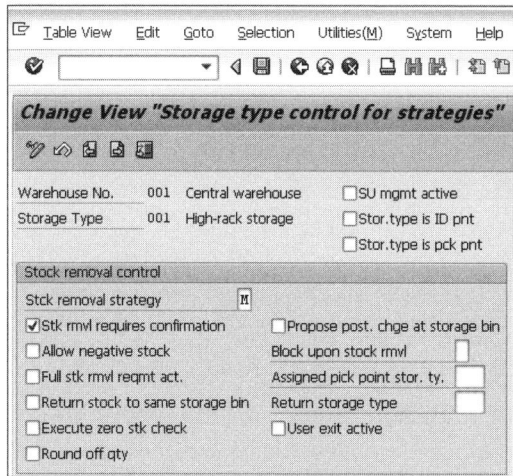

Figure 8.31 Quantity-Relevant Picking Strategy for Storage Type 001

When the entries in the storage type search sequence are made, it is necessary to enter the first storage type for the smallest quantity. The second in the sequence should be larger than the first, and subsequent storage types should get larger in the search sequence, as shown in Figure 8.32.

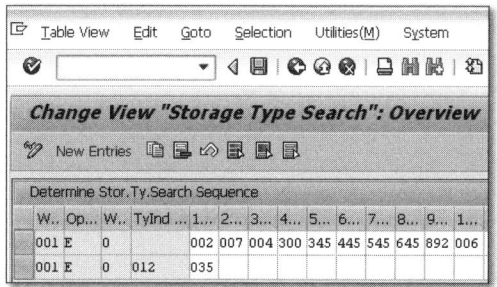

Figure 8.32 Storage Type Search Sequence for Quantity-Relevant Picking

Figure 8.32 shows the storage types that have been entered in the storage type search sequence. The picking functionality will search these storage types in sequence.

In Figure 8.32, two sequences of storage types can be used to find the relevant material for picking. In the first line, this is the sequence used for warehouse 001, and the operation is E, for picking. For a transfer order that uses quantity-relevant picking to pick material in warehouse 001, the function will review the material in the first storage type, 002. If the material cannot be found in this storage type, the system will review the material in the second storage type, 007, and so forth until the material is found.

If the material cannot be found, then warehouse staff has to process the transfer order manually and enter a storage type and storage bin into the transfer order.

8.8.2 Quantity-Relevant Picking and the Material Master Record

When a transfer order is being processed, the transaction determines whether the transfer order line item quantity is *small* or *large*. The source storage bin that is proposed in the transfer order will be from either a small-quantity storage type or a large-quantity storage type.

The check for this definition of *large* versus *small* quantity is performed for this picking strategy based on the control quantity field of the WM screen in the material master record. The control quantity that is entered for this material and storage type combination is the threshold that divides large from small.

In this case, as shown in Figure 8.33, the dividing threshold is a quantity of 20. This means a transfer order line item with a quantity of 18 is deemed a small quantity, and a line item quantity of 21 is deemed large. This threshold will vary from material to material and storage type to storage type.

For the quantity-relevant picking strategy, the system uses movement type 603 to determine which storage type is to be used in the transfer order for picking.

Figure 8.33 Control Quantity Field in the Material Master Record

8.9 Business Examples—Picking Strategies

A picking strategy for the warehouse is a method that determines the way a material is chosen to be picked for a production order or for a customer sales order. The strategy of picking material involves deciding what material is to be picked. Several picking strategies can be used, including first in, first out (FIFO); last in, first out (LIFO); and shelf life expiration date (SLED).

8.9.1 Storage Type Search

Some companies have complex warehouse facilities and invest a lot of time and resources into managing their warehouse for maximum efficiency. One way they can do this is to design specific storage type searches where only certain materials to be picked from storage types and the order of picking can be defined by the storage type search.

Example

Some companies do not implement a storage type search for picking, as they believe they have a simple warehouse operation that does not require any assistance from the system. One company that believed this was a manufacturer of locomotive parts based in Baltimore. The company had been manufacturing parts for a variety of industries since the 1940s. Their process was manufacturer parts on a contract basis from multinational transportation companies. The company manufacturers thousands of the same part each week, and they store less than 50 stock items in their warehouse.

The manufacturer implemented an SAP system in the 1990s and used a basic WM configuration without stock removal strategies. That decision was based on the fact that they stored so few parts that all the warehouse staff knew where each part was located.

The company found that after 2002, the contracts they were receiving required that they indicate which parts were made from a particular batch of raw material, and finished goods needed to be identified using batch management. Once this change was implemented, the picking of parts in the warehouse became significantly more complicated. The warehouse staff knew where the parts were but not the batch. As picks required a certain batch to be pulled, the warehouse foreman spent a lot of time creating transfer orders. Once management noticed that warehouse efficiency was declining, a recommendation to implement storage type search was proposed and then implemented.

8.9.2 First In, First Out (FIFO)

The picking strategy for first in, first out, or FIFO, as it is more commonly known, removes the oldest quant from the storage type defined in the storage type search. This is found in most manufacturing industries where the material companies want to sell first is that which has been stored in the warehouse the longest time.

Example

In the manufacturing industry, most companies want to rotate their stock so that the finished goods that are placed in the warehouse first are taken out of the warehouse first and delivered to the customer. A Michigan-based manufacturer of hand tools was purchased by a German multinational manufacturing company, which led to a simple implementation of an SAP system a year later. The company manufactured thousands of the same items each day, and they were stored in the warehouse before being sold to customers. Finished goods tended to stay in the warehouse for less than a week before being shipped to customers or distributors.

Due to the limited time that product remained in the warehouse, the company did not implement a FIFO or SLED policy. Sales orders began to slow down at the beginning of 2008, and by summer, the warehouse was filling up, as manufacturing was producing product based on plans that needed to be revised. The finance department asked the warehouse to make sure the finished goods that were picked for a sales order were the oldest in the warehouse. The system records the date on which the items are receipted into the warehouse, so the supply chain team made configuration changes to instigate a first in, first out strategy that ensured that the oldest material was picked first.

8.9.3 Fixed Bin

Many companies require that certain materials always be placed in the same location within the warehouse. This may be because of the size of the item or characteristics of the item that require a specific location to be selected. The picking strategy for fixed storage bins relies on the data that has been entered into the material master record for the material to be picked.

Example

A British beverage company had been running SAP WM for about four months and previously operated the warehouse using SAP MM. After the warehouse fixed the issues with correct stock being closer to the loading dock, the company began reselling an imported beverage that used oversized crates to store the individual bottles. The pallets of the imported beverage were too tall for the standard racks that had been used for many years. The oversized pallets were stored in an open storage area near the warehouse office where damaged items were usually stored.

The warehouse team modified several storage bins into one large storage bin closer to the loading dock so that they could accommodate pallets of the imported beverage. The imported beverage was always placed in the same storage bin, which was entered on the material master, and this was the fixed bin from which the material was always picked from.

8.9.4 Shelf Life Expiration Date (SLED)

When you look at an item in a supermarket, you almost always see an expiration date. This is relevant to any item that has a shelf life, not just food items. In an increasing number of industries the shelf life of materials is a very important characteristic. It is important that warehouse managers review the shelf life expiration dates (SLEDs) to ensure that out of date material does not have to be scrapped.

Example

In the food industry, it is important to ship product to customers so that items in the warehouse do not pass their expiry date. For canned goods the urgency to ship product is less than fresh items, which generally have a very short shelf life. A British manufacturer of snack foods produced items that had a shelf life of between six weeks and one year. For items with a short shelf life it was important to ensure that no items in the warehouse had a shelf life that made them unsellable. Generally, no customer would take product with less than three weeks of remaining shelf life. If items in the warehouse did have a shelf life of less than three weeks, then these would either be sold at a loss in the staff shop or donated to charity.

The company had been using a combination of off-the-shelf software and custom systems to assist with warehouse operations and shelf life processes. In the early 2000s, a Swiss multinational food company purchased the firm, and the legacy systems were replaced with an SAP system. The warehouse management implementation was deemed to be of great importance, as ensuring that product was delivered to the customer with the correct shelf life was vital to the company. The implementation team used the picking shelf life strategy in combination with entering the correct shelf life information on the material master records. The warehouse foreman was able to see shelf life across the warehouse for the items stored there and was able to reduce the amount of material could not be shipped to customers.

8.10 Summary

This chapter discussed picking strategies used in the warehouse. All of the strategies we have discussed here may be used at any site. Although FIFO and fixed bin picking strategies are very common, do not discount other picking strategies that may improve the efficiency of a particular warehouse.

Some retail companies, such as Walgreens and Kohl's, use picking strategies that are not FIFO, so be prepared to ask companies' financial departments how they value their stock and whether FIFO is the strategy they want to use. Consult with the warehouse staff to see if the picking strategies in the SAP system reflect the way they need to work. Be prepared to demonstrate how each of the strategies works and how material is assigned to the transfer order. Meeting the needs of warehouse management may require changes to the configuration of the picking strategies.

In Chapter 9, we will discuss the different putaway strategies that can be assigned, how these are configured, and how they are used.

Putaway strategies are important in locating material quickly and logically and thus helping to improve warehouse efficiency. Material for which putaway is performed without a protocol is often difficult to locate and costs extra time and money to move and ship.

9   Putaway Strategies

The putaway, or stock placement, strategies discussed in this chapter will help you to decide where to store material received into the warehouse. Several putaway strategies are possible, including:

- Fixed bin storage
- Open storage section
- Next empty storage bin
- Bulk storage
- Near picking bin

You do not have to define a putaway strategy for placement of material into the warehouse; indeed, many warehouses manually determine the putaway storage bin during the transfer order process. However, in your efforts to produce warehouse efficiency using SAP WM, it is important to discuss the process of material putaway in the warehouse and to adopt putaway strategies if necessary.

Once the putaway strategy has been adopted, the system uses it to assign the appropriate storage bin to store the material. A putaway strategy may not be necessary, but accepting the system-generated putaway location relieves the warehouse staff of one more responsibility and effectively speeds up material putaway.

Having introduced the concept of putaway strategies, let's look at the first of these, the fixed bin storage putaway strategy.

9 | Putaway Strategies

9.1 Fixed Bin Storage

The putaway strategy for fixed bin storage takes into account the data that has been entered into the material master record for the material to be placed in stock. The material is stored in a single bin, that is, a fixed bin. The data regarding this bin and the parameters of the bin are located in the material master record of the material. For example, the storage bin is entered into the material master record and does not change unless the material master record is changed.

9.1.1 Fixed Storage Bin in the Material Master

The fixed storage bin is entered into the material master record in the WM screen.

> **Note**
>
> In SAP ECC 6.0, this is the second WM screen, but it may vary depending on the version you are using. This storage bin is used for fixed bin picking and fixed bin putaway.

Figure 9.1 shows the WM screen for material 100-500. In the STORAGE BIN STOCK section of the screen, the STORAGE BIN field has the entry A-01. This is the storage bin fixed for this material in this fixed bin storage type: 005. This information is used for the fixed bin putaway strategy.

Figure 9.1 Fixed Storage Bin Information in the Material Master Record: Transaction MM02

9.1.2 Configuring the Fixed Bin Storage Putaway Strategy

You can define the fixed bin storage putaway strategy by following the menu path IMG • LOGISTICS EXECUTION • WAREHOUSE MANAGEMENT • STRATEGIES • PUTAWAY STRATEGIES • DEFINE STRATEGY FOR FIXED BINS.

Figure 9.2 shows the putaway strategy for storage type 005. The fixed bin storage strategy is entered as an F for fixed bin storage putaway. You can set a number of other stock placement configuration fields as well.

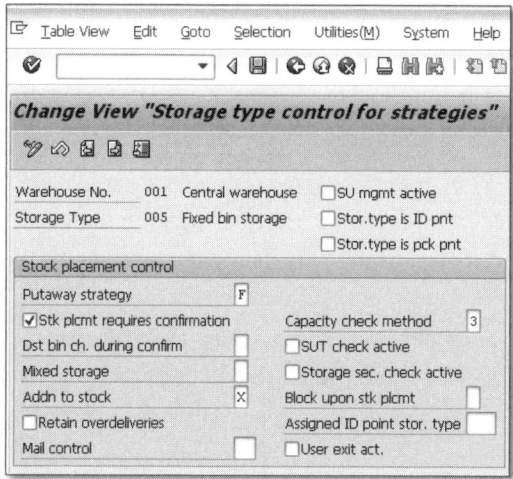

Figure 9.2 Configuring the Fixed Bin Storage Putaway Strategy

9.1.3 Stock Placement Control Indicators

Figure 9.2 shows that, apart from the stock putaway strategy, you can configure several other control indicators. These are described here:

- **Stk plcmt requires confirmation**
  Select this checkbox when putaway must be confirmed, including confirmation of removal from the source storage bin, placement in the destination bin, and placement in the return bin, if relevant.

- **Dst bin ch. during confirm**
  This field controls whether the transaction allows a change to the destination storage bin during confirmation of the transfer order. If this field is selected, it is possible to change the destination storage bin during confirmation of the

transfer order. If the field is not selected, then it is not possible to change the destination storage bin.

- **Mixed storage**
  Set this field to allow different quants to be stored in a storage bin in this storage type. There are several options for this field:
  - **Blank**
    Mixed storage is not allowed.
  - **A**
    Several storage units with the same material can be stored in a single bin.
  - **B**
    This allows one material, but in different batches per bin and storage unit. Each storage unit can contain more than one batch of the same material.
  - **C**
    This option allows several batches in one storage bin but only one material. However, it is not possible to put different batches in a single storage unit.
  - **X**
    This option allows any mixed storage without restrictions. Different material numbers and different batches can coexist in the storage bin and in individual storage units.
- **Addn to stock**
  This field allows a quant of a material and a batch number to be stored in a storage bin with the same material and the same batch as an addition to existing stock.
- **Retain overdeliveries**
  Select this checkbox if the storage type into which the material is being placed can accommodate the overdelivery.
- **Mail control**
  This field is the mail control for the replenishment storage type. If an error occurs during automatic creation of transfer orders in production planning, this field is used to define which user is to be informed.
- **Capacity check method**
  Setting this field means a capacity check will be carried out for the storage bins in this storage type. This field is required if there is a possibility that the capacity can be exceeded. There are several options for the capacity check method:

- **Blank**
  No check of capacity
- **1**
  Check of maximum weight
- **2**
  Check based on palletization of storage unit type
- **3**
  Check of maximum quantity per storage bin in a storage type
- **4**
  Capacity usage check based on material
- **5**
  Capacity usage check based on storage unit type (SUT)
- **6**
  Capacity usage check based on the sum of the material and the storage unit (SU)

- **Act. Capac**
  This is the active capacity check. Selecting this indicator ensures that an active capacity check is executed when goods are placed into stock. This is not needed for strategies B, F, and I.

- **SUT check active**
  Selecting this checkbox activates the storage unit type check for the putaway. The storage unit type must be entered for transfer orders using this putaway strategy. The storage unit type refers to the type of storage unit, such as a pallet or wire container.

- **Storage sec. check active**
  Select this checkbox is set when a storage section check is required for stock putaway. When the indicator is selected, the transfer order will search the storage bins in the storage sections that have been identified in the configuration of the storage section search.

- **Block upon stk plcmt**
  Setting this field will execute a blocking indicator at the time of storage putaway. Two blocks can be activated: one for the storage bin and one for the quant. If the storage bin block is set, the storage bin is blocked from any activity when the material is placed into it. This may be done to make sure the material is not moved or sold until a check or inspection is made on the contents of

the bin. If a block is activated only on the quant, then this block applies only to that quant that has undergone putaway and not to any other quants in the storage bin.

▶ **Assigned ID point stor. Type**
This field is the identification point for a storage type. Any goods movements that do not have a specific storage bin in this storage type as their destination are first directed to the identification point. At that point the material is identified and a transfer order is generated for the transfer of the material into the correct storage type.

Now that you have a good understanding of these indicators we can move on to an example of the putaway strategy for fixed bin storage.

9.1.4 Example of Fixed Bin Storage Putaway Strategy

In this section, we will show you how the fixed bin strategy configuration for a storage type affects material putaway in the warehouse. The putaway strategy has been configured for storage type 005 as a fixed bin, as shown in Figure 9.2.

A stock placement is initiated by the creation of a transfer order that will move the material from a location. Normally, this is a movement from a goods receipt interim storage type to the fixed bin storage bin of the storage type defined in the material master.

You can use Transaction LT01 to create a transfer order that will move the material into fixed bin storage type 005. The material assigned for putaway has been goods-receipted into storage type 902 and the storage bin for receiving, which is WE-ZONE.

Figure 9.3 shows the initial screen for creating a transfer order for putaway of the material from a goods receipt. The transfer uses movement type 501, as it will remove the material from the goods receiving interim storage type 902 and place it in the appropriate storage bin for the fixed bin storage strategy.

Figure 9.4 shows the system-generated transfer order item information for material 100-500. Based on the configuration for the fixed bin putaway strategy, the material has been moved from the interim storage for the goods receipt and selected for transfer to the fixed bin defined in the material master record for material 100-500.

Fixed Bin Storage | **9.1**

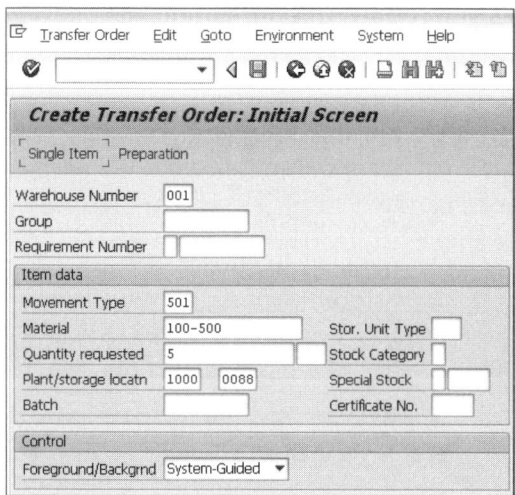

Figure 9.3 Creating a Transfer Order: Transaction LT01

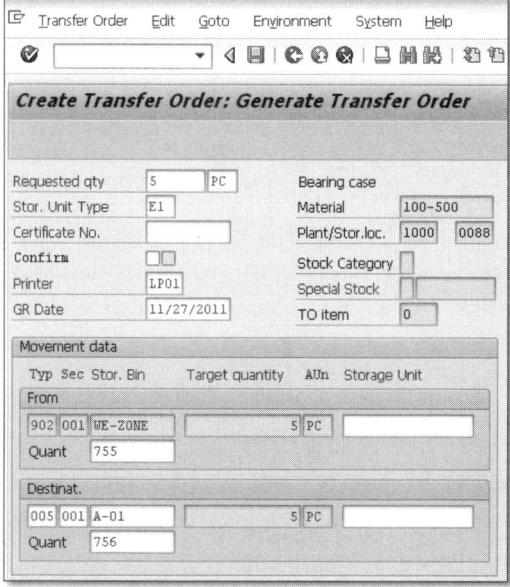

Figure 9.4 System-Generated Destination Storage Bin Based on the Fixed Bin Storage Putaway Strategy

9 | Putaway Strategies

Figure 9.5 shows that quantity of material 100-500 has now been placed in fixed bin location A-01 in storage type 005. This was achieved by using Transaction LS24.

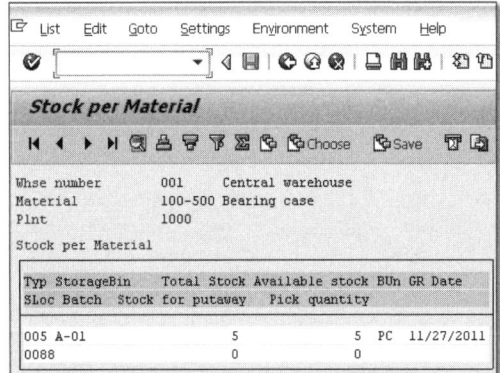

Figure 9.5 Stock Overview for Material 100-500 in Warehouse 001

After reviewing the functionality of putaway strategies for fixed bins, we'll turn our attention to the open storage putaway strategy.

9.2 Open Storage

The concept of open storage applies when materials are stored in areas of open floor, where there are no racks or lines. The storage type is roughly divided into storage sections, and the protocol is that one storage section is represented by one storage bin.

9.2.1 Configuring the Open Storage Putaway Strategy

You can define the open storage putaway strategy by following the menu path IMG • LOGISTICS EXECUTION • WAREHOUSE MANAGEMENT • STRATEGIES • PUTAWAY STRATEGIES • DEFINE STRATEGY FOR OPEN STORAGE.

Figure 9.6 shows the putaway strategy for storage type 003. The open storage strategy is entered as a C for fixed bin storage putaway. Because the storage is open and not as restrictive as rack storage, you must select the MIXED STORAGE and ADDN TO STOCK fields so that multiple materials can be entered into the one storage bin.

9.2 Open Storage

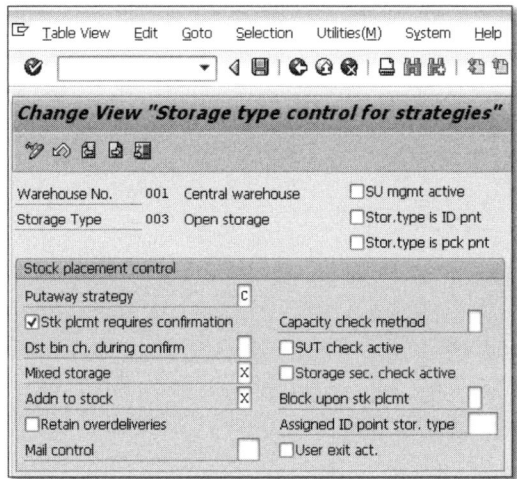

Figure 9.6 Configuration for the Open Storage Putaway Strategy

9.2.2 Example of Open Storage Putaway Strategy

Now let's see how the open strategy configuration for a storage type affects material putaway in the warehouse.

Open storage allows the storage of different materials in the same storage bin. The current stock in one open storage bin shows that two materials are stored in one bin. You can see this by using Transaction LS02N or by following the menu path SAP • LOGISTICS • LOGISTICS EXECUTION • INTERNAL WHSE PROCESSES • BINS AND STOCK • SINGLE DISPLAYS • STORAGE BIN.

Figure 9.7 shows that in one storage bin—C-008—there are two materials. The configuration for the open storage putaway allows for mixed storage and an addition to existing storage. This is how open storage works.

You can use Transaction LT01 to create a transfer order for material putaway into open storage type 002. The material for putaway has been goods-receipted into storage type 902 and the storage bin for receiving, which is WE-ZONE.

Figure 9.8 shows the initial screen for the creation of a transfer order for putaway of the material from a goods receipt. The transfer uses movement type 501 because it will remove the material from the goods receiving interim storage type 902 and place it in the appropriate storage bin for the open storage strategy.

323

9 | Putaway Strategies

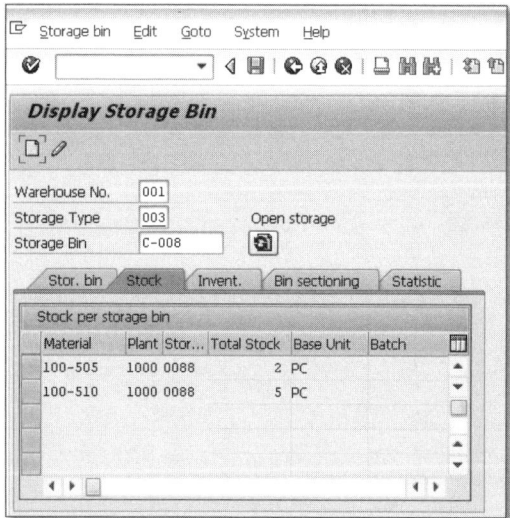

Figure 9.7 Materials Stored in Open Storage Type 003: Transaction LS02N

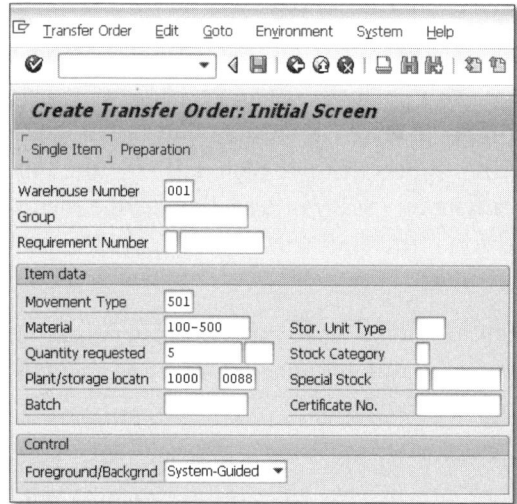

Figure 9.8 Creating a Transfer Order: Transaction LT01

Figure 9.9 shows the system-generated transfer order item information for material 100-500. Based on the configuration for open storage putaway strategy, the material has been moved from the interim storage for the goods receipt and selected to be transferred to the open storage bin—bin C-008.

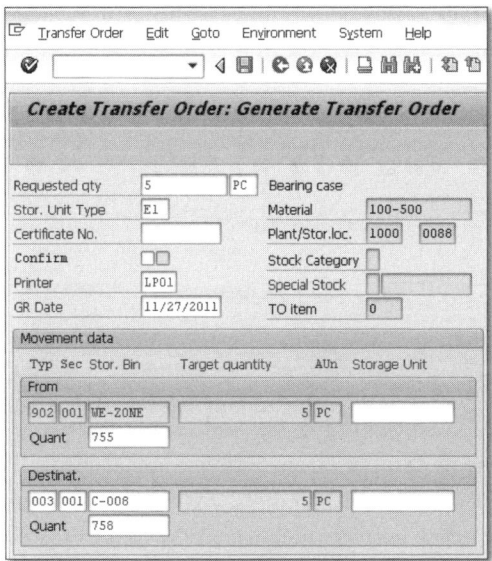

Figure 9.9 System-Generated Destination Storage Bin Based on the Open Storage Putaway Strategy

Figure 9.10 shows information about open storage bin C-008 for open storage. It shows that the bin has three materials stored in it and that this can continue if material needs to be stored in the open storage type of the warehouse.

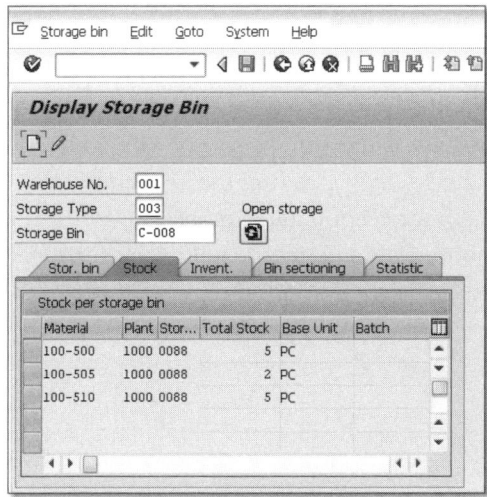

Figure 9.10 Materials Stored in Open Storage Type 003: Transaction LS02N

Now that we've reviewed the open storage putaway strategy, we'll examine the next empty bin putaway strategy.

9.3 Next Empty Bin

Some warehouses are structured so that material can be stored in any bin within the storage type. This structure can result from the nature of the material stored in the warehouse; for example, different materials may all be stored in the same size container. If this is the case, the putaway strategy can be configured so that the system will select the next empty bin.

In manufacturing industries that produce electronic components, the parts are often small, delicate, and prone to damage by static. These components are stored in the warehouse in containers that are safe for all products. Many warehouses that store these products use carousel storage, where the parts are stored in identical containers in a carousel system that places new items in the next empty bin available.

9.3.1 Configuring the Next Empty Bin Putaway Strategy

You can define the next empty bin putaway strategy by following the menu path IMG • LOGISTICS EXECUTION • WAREHOUSE MANAGEMENT • STRATEGIES • PUTAWAY STRATEGIES • DEFINE STRATEGY FOR EMPTY STORAGE BIN.

Figure 9.11 shows the putaway strategy for storage type 001. The next empty bin putaway strategy is entered as L for next empty bin. Note that other indicators are selected for this strategy. The most significant is the storage section check checkbox: STORAGE SEC CHECK ACTIVE. Because the strategy is to find the next empty bin, you can use additional strategies at the storage section and storage bin. Defining a storage section search gives the warehouse staff a better idea of where the next empty bin will be located. This is not necessary but is often used with the next empty bin strategy.

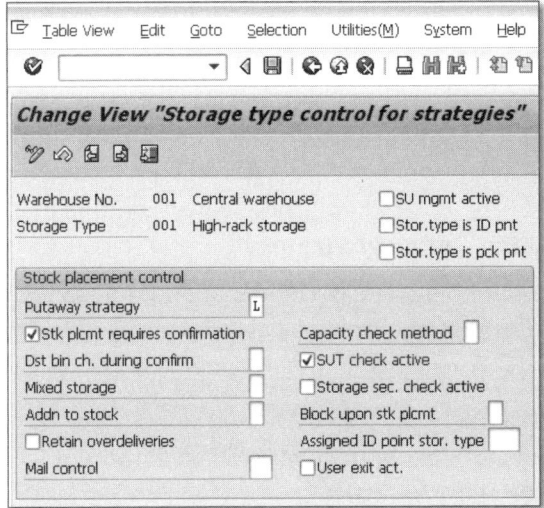

Figure 9.11 Configuration for the Next Empty Bin Putaway Strategy

9.3.2 Displaying Empty Bins

You can view the empty bins for a warehouse and storage type by using Transaction LS04 or following the menu path SAP • LOGISTICS • LOGISTICS EXECUTION • INTERNAL WHSE PROCESSES • BINS AND STOCK • DISPLAY • EMPTY STORAGE BINS.

Sec	StorageBin	Sort C	BT	IA	Maximum Weight	WUn	Total capacity
001	01-09-04	0904	E1		1,000	KG	0.000
001	01-09-05	0905	E1	X	1,000	KG	0.000
001	01-09-06	0906	E1		1,000	KG	0.000
001	01-09-07	0907	E1	X	1,000	KG	0.000
001	01-09-08	0908	E1		1,000	KG	0.000
001	01-09-09	0909	E1	X	1,000	KG	0.000
001	01-09-10	0910	E1	X	1,000	KG	0.000
001	01-10-01	1001	E1	X	1,000	KG	0.000
001	01-10-02	1002	E1	X	1,000	KG	0.000
001	01-10-03	1003	E1	X	1,000	KG	0.000

Figure 9.12 Display of Empty Bins in Storage Type 001: Transaction LS04

Figure 9.12 shows the empty bins that can be used for a stock putaway. However, the bins with an "X" in the IA field are unavailable because of an inventory count. These bins need to be counted and therefore cannot be used in stock putaway. The only bins in storage type 001, storage section 001 that can be used in the next empty bin strategy are 01 – 09 – 04, 01 – 09 – 06, and 01 – 09 – 08.

9.3.3 Example of Next Empty Bin Putaway Strategy

Let's now examine how the next empty bin strategy configuration for a storage type affects the material putaway in the warehouse.

Transaction LT01 is used to create a transfer order for material putaway into storage type 001. In this case the material has been created for only storage type 001 and no other. The material to be put away has been goods-receipted into storage type 902 and the storage bin for receiving (WE-ZONE).

Figure 9.13 shows the initial screen for creating a transfer order to put away the material from a goods receipt. Movement type 501 is used because it will remove the material from the goods receiving interim storage type 902 and place it in the appropriate storage bin for the next empty bin putaway strategy.

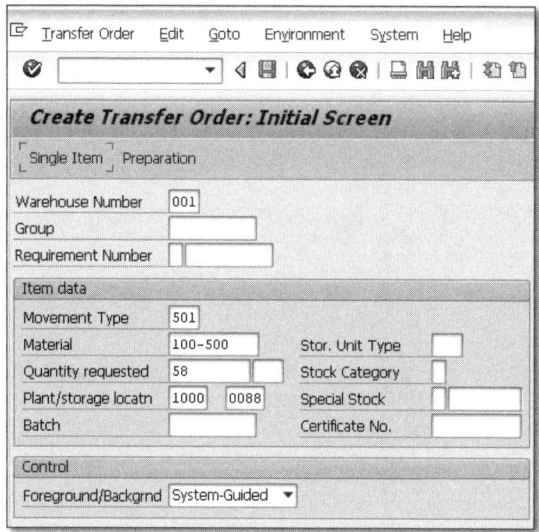

Figure 9.13 Creating a Transfer Order: Transaction LT01

Figure 9.14 shows the system-generated transfer order item information for material 100-500. Based on the configuration for the next empty bin putaway strategy, the material has been moved from the interim storage for the goods receipt and selected to be transferred to the next empty bin in storage type 001, which is 01 – 09 – 04, as we saw previously in Figure 9.12.

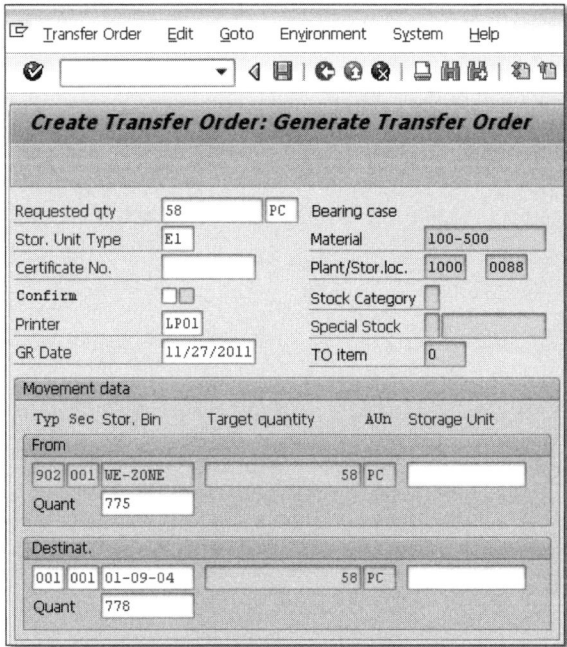

Figure 9.14 System-Generated Destination Storage Bin Based on Next Empty Bin Putaway Strategy

After the material has been stored in empty storage bin 01 – 09 – 04, Transaction LS04 should only show two valid empty storage bins: 01 – 09 – 06 and 01 – 09 – 08. These lack the indicator in the IA column to show that they are blocked for an inventory count, while the other storage bins have an "X" in the IA column to indicate they are blocked for the inventory count, as shown in Figure 9.15.

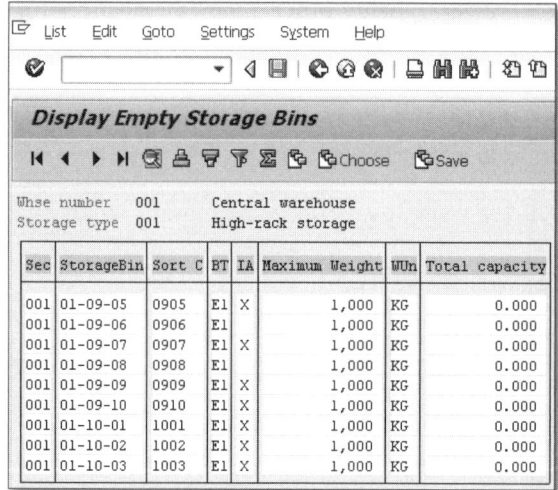

Figure 9.15 Display of Empty Bins in Storage Type 001: Transaction LS04

9.3.4 Cross-Line Stock Putaway

Using the next empty bin putaway strategy can be problematic if the storage bins are selected from only one part or one side of the warehouse. Therefore, it is possible to create a search variable that allows the next empty bin to be selected based on criteria. It is important to remember that before any storage bins can be created for this storage type, the cross-line stock putaway strategy must be configured.

Before you can begin configuring cross-line stock putaway, review the storage bin structure. Without understanding how the bin coordinates have been configured, you cannot design the sort sequence.

Storage Bin Structure

You can configure the storage bin structure with Transaction LS10 or by following the menu path IMG • LOGISTICS EXECUTION • WAREHOUSE MANAGEMENT • MASTER DATA • STORAGE BINS • DEFINE STORAGE BIN STRUCTURE.

Figure 9.16 shows that the structure of the storage bin has the bin definition template configured as two numeric characters (represented by an N), followed by a constant (represented by a C), then two more numeric characters (represented by an N), one more constant, and then two more numeric characters. The configuration includes start and end values as well as the increment of the storage bin when the bins are created automatically.

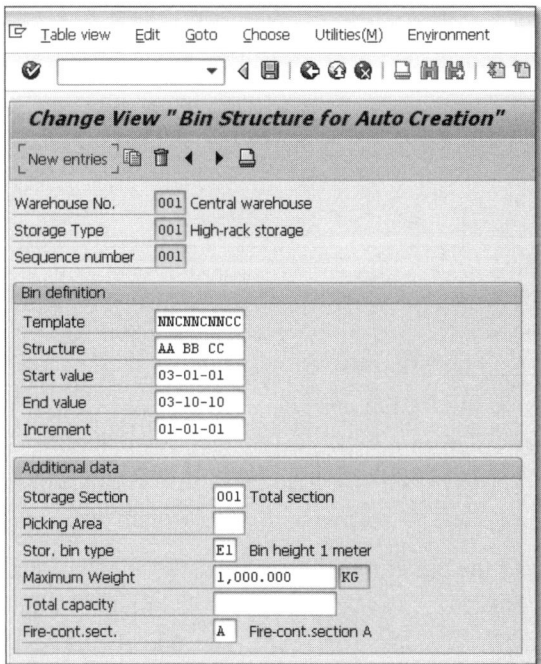

Figure 9.16 Configuration of the Storage Bin Structure for Storage Type 001: Transaction LS10

Once you have reviewed the bin structure for storage type 001, you can configure the cross-line stock putaway using a sort sequence based on the bin structure.

Cross-Line Stock Putaway Configuration

You can configure the cross-line stock putaway with Transaction OMLM or by following the menu path IMG • LOGISTICS EXECUTION • WAREHOUSE MANAGEMENT • STRATEGIES • DEFINE SORT SEQUENCE FOR PUTAWAYS.

Figure 9.17 shows how the sort configuration can select any of the 10 characters that can make up the storage bin. In our example for storage type 001, the storage bin uses only eight characters. Positions 3 and 6 are nonnumeric and therefore cannot be used in the sort sequence.

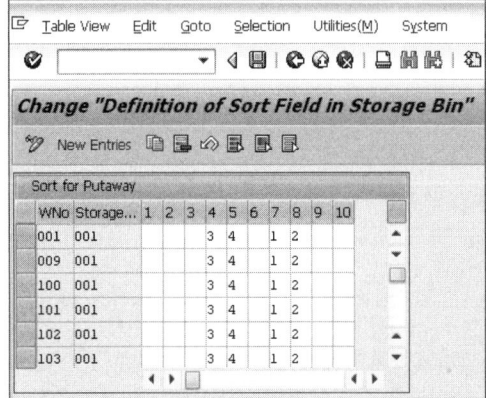

Figure 9.17 Configuration of Cross-Line Stock Putaway Strategy: Transaction OMLM

In this example, the structure of the storage bin is based on a row, stack, level scenario, which is very common. The configuration in Figure 9.17 shows that the numeric characters in positions 7 and 8 are the first part of the sort. Therefore, the level is the primary sort characteristic, and the empty bins on a level will be filled first.

The next part of the sort is configured for the numeric characters in positions 4 and 5, which represent the stack. Therefore, the level will be filled first, and the next empty bin will be found on the next stack. The row is not part of the sort sequence and has no role in the selection of the next empty bin.

That concludes our discussion of the next empty bin putaway strategy. Now we will examine the bulk storage putaway strategy.

9.4 Bulk Storage

Bulk storage is used for material that is stored in large quantities. This is not to be confused with material that can be stored in bulk containers, such as grain, sand, cement, fertilizer, and so on.

> **Example**
> In the beverage industry, a production run of beer may produce several thousand cans of product. Once this is placed in packs and then stored on pallets, it will be stored in the bulk storage type.

You can define the options for the bulk storage putaway strategy with the Transaction OMM4 or via the menu path IMG • LOGISTICS EXECUTION • WAREHOUSE MANAGEMENT • STRATEGIES • PUTAWAY STRATEGIES • DEFINE STRATEGY FOR BULK STORAGE.

Figure 9.18 shows that a number of options that can be configured for bulk storage putaway. The first option is for activating the bulk storage putaway strategy for the storage type. The other three options shown in Figure 9.18 all relate to bulk storage putaway scenarios that involve storage units. Storage unit management will be discussed in Chapter 11.

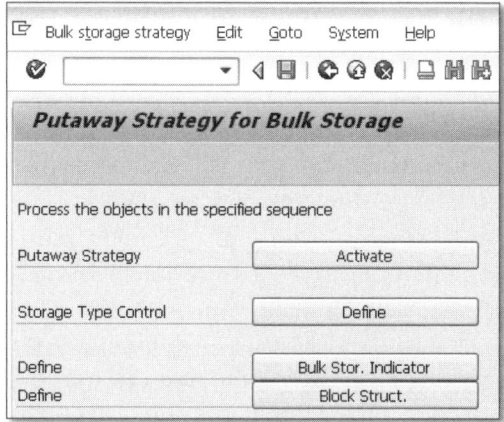

Figure 9.18 Configuration Options for the Bulk Storage Putaway Strategy

Figure 9.19 shows the bulk storage putaway strategy for storage type 004. The strategy is entered as a B for bulk storage. Note that other indicators are selected for this strategy. The storage unit check (SUT CHECK ACTIVE) checkbox is selected because much of bulk storage uses storage units. The other field to be selected is the addition to stock (ADDN TO STOCK). This allows more material to be added to the same kind of material currently in the bulk storage type.

Now that we have reviewed the bulk storage putaway strategy, we can discuss the next putaway strategy. This is called near picking bin.

9 | Putaway Strategies

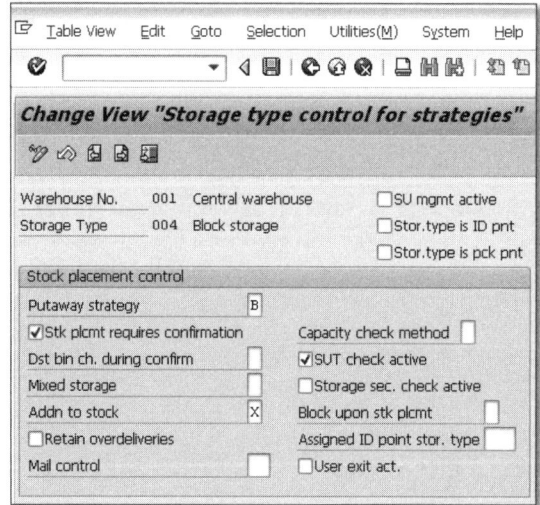

Figure 9.19 Configuration of Bulk Storage Putaway for Storage Type 004

9.5 Near Picking Bin

This strategy is used for material that is frequently picked, because it is appropriate to store the material close to the picking area. The warehouse can use this strategy to see of the material can be placed in a fixed bin. If not, the system will try a reserve area and finally try to find a bin that is closest, using a configured search.

You can define the options for the next picking bin putaway strategy with Transaction OMLA or via the menu path IMG • LOGISTICS EXECUTION • WAREHOUSE MANAGEMENT • STRATEGIES • PUTAWAY STRATEGIES • DEFINE STRATEGY FOR NEAR PICKING BIN.

The options in Figure 9.20 show the configuration that can be carried out to fully define the strategy for the near picking bin. This screen shows six possible configuration selections:

- Putaway strategy activation
- Storage type control definition
- Search per level definition
- Row and shelf assignment

334

- Storage bin generation
- Consistency check

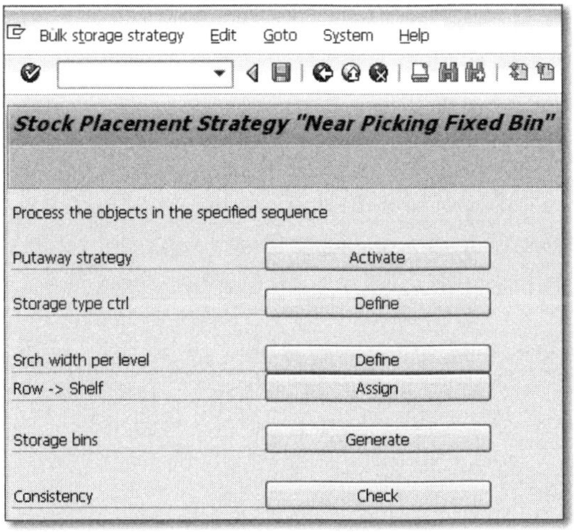

Figure 9.20 Configuration Options for the Near Picking Bin Putaway Strategy

The first option is the activation of the putaway strategy. This may be the only configuration that is required for a simple strategy if that is all the warehouse management recommends.

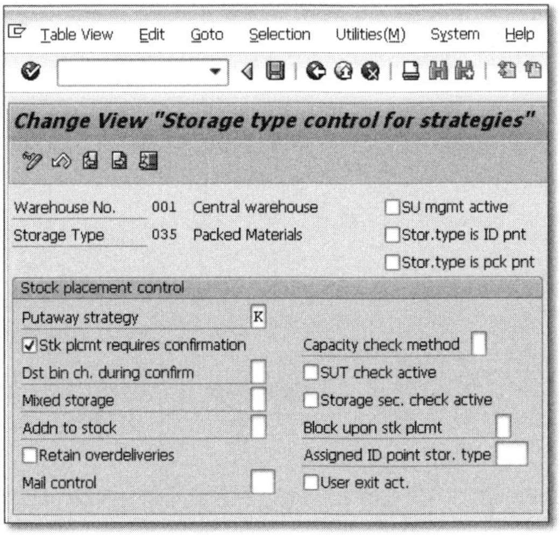

Figure 9.21 Configuration of Near Picking Bin Putaway for Storage Type 035

Figure 9.21 shows the near picking bin putaway strategy for storage type 035. The strategy is entered as a K for the near picking bin. It is correct to leave the configuration with just this one setting. This will perform putaway in the reserve storage bin, without searching for the fixed bin or carrying out a search for a relevant bin.

9.5.1 Storage Type Control Definition

If the storage type control is configured, this can be used when the fixed bin storage is full. The control enables configuration of a reserve storage type for a fixed bin area and specifies how that area is to be filled.

Figure 9.22 shows that storage type 035 has been configured as the reserve area for fixed bin storage type 005. When the fixed bin area is checked for open bins, using putaway strategy F, the system will look at storage type 035, which is used for putaway strategy K, to find an empty storage bin.

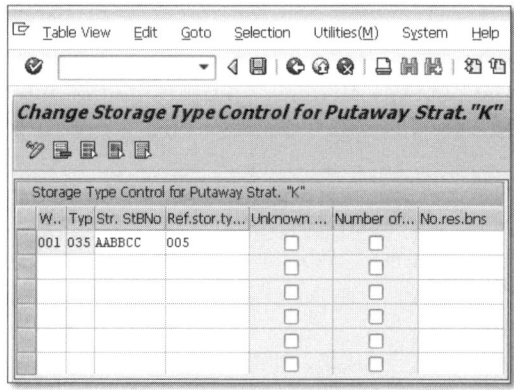

Figure 9.22 Storage Type Control Function Configuration for Storage Type 035

The structure of the storage bin name is configured in the STR.STBNO field. The A coordinate represents the shelf, the B coordinate represents the stack, and C represents the level.

You can select the UNKNOWN MATERIAL checkbox if storage of a material is allowed in the reserve area even if it is not assigned to the reference storage type, in this case 005. This allows warehouse staff to add material to the reserve area even if that reserve area is not meant for the material assigned for putaway.

The NUMBER OF RESERVE BINS LIMITED field allows the number of bins set aside as reserve bins to a set to a limited number. The actual number of reserve bins can be set in the last field, NO. RES BNS.

9.5.2 Search per Level Definition

This configuration allows the search for a bin to be confined, initially, to a limited area. For example, materials of a specific height may be stored on only one level, and the search should only take into account that one level, given that the material would not be stored elsewhere. The first part of the configuration is the search on each level.

Figure 9.23 shows the configuration needed to search for an empty storage bin within the reserve storage type. If a fixed bin is selected but is occupied, this configuration initially determines how many stacks to either side of the fixed bin — in this case a fixed bin on level one — should be checked for an empty bin. The value in the SRCH WIDTH field is the number of stacks that are searched on either side of the fixed bin. If there is no configuration for a level in this transaction, then the search for an empty bin will occur across the whole level.

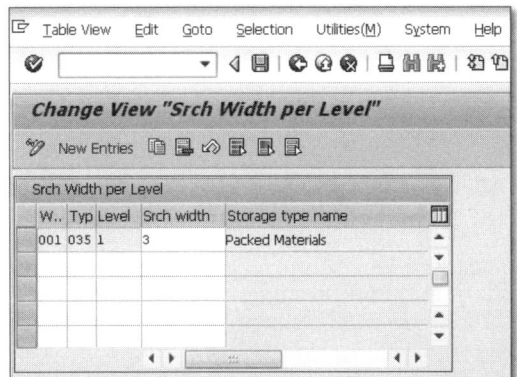

Figure 9.23 Configuration for a Search for a Bin on a Certain Level

Figure 9.24 should be configured only if the storage type is not numbered by aisles. Check with the warehouse staff before setting this configuration. If a storage type is numbered by aisles, then the shelves on either side of the aisle will be numbered the same. If they are not numbered by aisle, then they will be different.

9 | Putaway Strategies

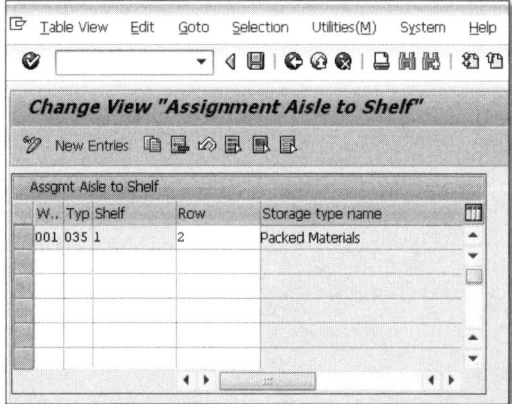

Figure 9.24 Assignment Aisle to Shelf Configuration

> **Example**
>
> If you are standing in an aisle between two racking systems, there are shelves on either side at the same level. If the physical entity of the storage type is made up of the aisle and the shelves on each side of the aisle, then the shelves have the same number. However, some storage types are physically divided by the aisle so the shelves on either side are numbered differently.

9.6 Business Examples—Putaway Strategies

When material arrives in the warehouse, it needs to be stored in the most appropriate location. Putaway strategies help you to decide where to store material in the warehouse. There are several putaway strategies you can use, including fixed bin, open storage, next empty storage bin, and bulk storage.

9.6.1 Fixed Bin Storage

The putaway strategy for fixed bin storage takes into account the data that has been entered into the material master record for the material to be placed in stock. The material is stored in a single bin, and the data regarding this bin and the parameters of the bin are found in the material master record of the material.

Example

A British beverage company had been using SAP WM for about four months and previously operated the warehouse using SAP MM. After the warehouse had fixed the issues with correct stock being closer to the loading dock, the company began reselling an imported beverage that used oversized crates to store the individual bottles. The pallets of the imported beverage were too tall for the standard racks they had used for many years. The oversized pallets were stored in an open storage area near the warehouse office where damaged items were usually stored.

The warehouse team modified several storage bins into one large storage bin closer to the loading dock so they could accommodate pallets of the imported beverage. The imported beverage was always stored in the same storage bin, which was entered on the material master, and this was the fixed bin where the material was always placed when the material was receipted into the warehouse.

9.6.2 Open Storage

The concept of the open storage strategy applies when materials are stored in areas of open floor, where there are no racks or lines. The storage type is roughly divided into storage sections, and the norm is that one storage section is represented by one storage bin.

Example

A manufacturer of chemicals used in paint manufacturing sold over 40 variations of one product. The chemical composition of the material determined which customer would purchase the finished good, and the item had a short shelf life when the characteristics remained within tolerances. The finished goods were stored in drums and pales on racking systems in the warehouse. The company also produced a semifinished product that had a stable composition and a shelf life of over a year. The semifinished product only remained in the warehouse for an average of nine days, and often the company would have several backorders.

Unlike the finished goods, the semifinished item was not required to be identified by shelf life or batch number, so the items were stored close to the end of the production line rather than in the racking. By storing the semifinished material in an open storage area, the warehouse staff did not have to spend time moving the drums to racking and then pulling them from the racking when an order came in.

The open storage placement strategy was perfect for the semifinished material, as it did not have the complexities of the company's finished goods and therefore required less of the warehouse operator's time.

9.6.3 Next Empty Bin

Some warehouses are structured so that material can be stored in any bin within the storage type. This structure can result from the nature of the material stored in the warehouse, for example, if many different materials can be placed in the same-size container. If this is the case, the putaway strategy can be configured so that the system will select the next empty bin.

Example

A California-based distributor of imported electronics parts had used an SAP system for over a decade and was using WM with some degree of success. Material was stored in racking that was segregated into storage types based on the rack size. The warehouse operation was not as efficient as it could be, and the company was considering redesigning the warehouse. Before any redesign was implemented, the company sold its warehouse in Silicon Valley and leased a smaller warehouse to reduce costs.

The company rationalized the material it stored in the warehouse and moved only 75% of the materials to the new warehouse. To accommodate the material in the smaller warehouse, the company decided to use several automated storage and retrieval systems (AS/RS). The benefits of using this type of storage instead of traditional racking were that they gave the company a high-density, automated storage system that took advantage of all the overhead warehouse space. The company installed vertical storage systems, and this required the WM configuration to be altered to allow for the next empty bin placement strategy to be used. When items arrived at the warehouse, the system allocated the next empty bin so that the storage systems were used as efficiently as possible.

9.7 Summary

Putaway strategies are often less well thought out than the picking strategies that define warehousing management decisions. Whereas considerable time and effort are spent tweaking the efficiency of the outbound picking procedures, management often forgets the time and effort involved in locating a material for which putaway was illogical.

If putaway is not performed sensibly, all the effort involved in efficient shipping will not bear fruit, because the material for picking will not be moved to the picking area in a timely manner. The strategies for putaway are important to the efficient flow within the warehouse and should be carefully examined to determine which configuration is best for the warehouse.

In Chapter 10, we will discuss inventory procedures such as cycle counting and physical inventory.

Inventory procedures are important because they ensure that system information about the material in the warehouse is correct. Materials can be counted by annual inventory or by frequent cycle counting, which is more popular and can yield more accurate results.

10   Inventory Procedures

Inventory counts occur in every warehouse, but the method of counting inventory varies among companies and often among locations within the same companies. An annual inventory count often starts with a group of trained and untrained counting staff and ends up with a large number of discrepancies that need to be investigated rather than adjusted immediately.

Other procedures have been adopted, such as continuous and cycle counting, which reduce the emphasis on the annual count. In this chapter, we'll discuss the inventory procedures that clients use and how these are performed within the system.

Now that we have outlined the contents of this chapter, let's examine the first topic: the annual physical inventory.

10.1   Annual Physical Inventory

The annual physical inventory occurs in many places other than the warehouse. At the end of the fiscal year, company finance departments require the counting of assets and stock to start the fiscal year with an accurate financial picture. For an annual count to be as painless as possible, the organization needs formal procedures and documents, as well as fully trained counters.

10.1.1   Before the Count

The count often takes place on a weekend or on a day when vendors have been told that deliveries will not be received while the physical inventory is in progress. Making sure all physical purchase orders have a *nondelivery* notice stamped on them for the day of the inventory effectively reinforces this. Accounting staff should be available for any financial issues that occur or decisions that need to be made. Because stock movement in the warehouse will be impossible, the sales force and customers need to be informed about the nonshipment period.

The organization should use the experience of previous inventory counts to calculate the staff required for a successful count and fully train the employees designated as counters. The counters should be trained just before the count, with an emphasis on accuracy.

If the annual inventory is the first in a location or has not been successful in the past, it may be prudent to perform a test count of a small storage type, noting the number of storage bins counted and the time required. This is a good way to determine how many counters and how much time is needed for the physical inventory.

To make sure the process is as easy as possible for the counters, it is best to send the warehouse a team to make sure materials are contained within their assigned locations and all materials and storage bins are clearly identified. Often, a lot of time is wasted when the material cannot be identified or counters cannot find a specific location. That warehouse team also can count in advance the bulk storage types and dead stock. This reduces the shutdown time caused by the inventory count.

> **Tip**
>
> Counted material and material not to be counted, such as warehouse equipment and packaging, should be clearly labeled to prevent confusion. It's also a good idea to label damaged material and material that has been written off and is awaiting disposal.

10.1.2 Configuring Annual Inventory

You need to address a number of configuration steps before any count can be performed. Let's review these now:

1. Set the default values for each storage type in the warehouse via the menu path IMG • LOGISTICS EXECUTION • WAREHOUSE MANAGEMENT • ACTIVITIES • PHYSICAL INVENTORY • DEFINE DEFAULT VALUES.

2. You need to configure the default values for each storage type, shown in Figure 10.1, before the physical inventory. The following variables need to be addressed:

   - **PrintMat**
   Select this checkbox if you have to have the material information printed on the count document. The material information is quite extensive and includes the material number, material description, plant number, batch number (if defined), special stock indicator, special stock number, stock category, and quant number.

   - **No.Bins**
   Select this checkbox if the storage bin must be displayed during the entry of the inventory. If manual entry is required, do not select this checkbox.

   - **No.Mat**
   Select this checkbox if you need the material number to be displayed during the entry of the inventory. If manual entry of the material is required, then do not select this checkbox.

   - **Entry**
   This field defines the input method for the inventory count. There are three possible entries: P for via a list of items, S for page by page, and A for sequential.

   - **DblLn**
   If selected, this checkbox allows the inventory to be counted on two lines rather than one.

   - **Diff.**
   This field allows configuration of a percentage value for deviation between book and actual stock. If the material counted is entered and is greater than the percentage configured in this field, a warning message will be displayed and a decision made to allow the difference or reject it. For example, if percentage of 5 is entered and the counted material is 10% greater than the book stock, then a warning will be issued. Normally, this deviation value is very low or is zero because most deviations will require investigation.

   - **Next Page**
   This checkbox allows quants in the same bin to be printed on different pages. This need arises when mixed storage occurs, such as in open storage bin locations.

10 | Inventory Procedures

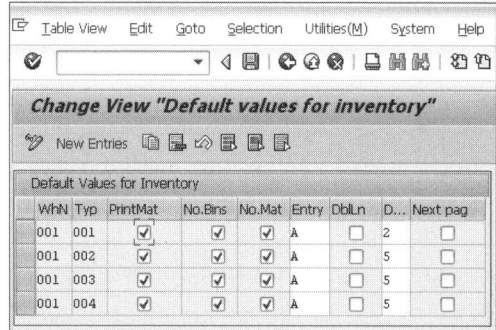

Figure 10.1 Physical Inventory Configuration Values for Storage Types

3. Set the inventory type for each storage type via the menu path IMG • LOGISTICS EXECUTION • WAREHOUSE MANAGEMENT • ACTIVITIES • PHYSICAL INVENTORY • DEFINE TYPES PER STORAGE TYPE.

This transaction, shown in Figure 10.2, allows configuration of the storage type for annual, continuous, or cycle counting. You can configure the following fields:

▶ **Invent.**
This field defines the inventory procedure for the storage type. This can be ST for annual inventory, PZ for continuous inventory, or blank for no specific inventory method.

▶ **Plcmnt Inv**
Select this checkbox when you must make an inventory each time material is moved into an empty bin. The checkbox is often selected when a company uses continuous inventory procedures.

▶ **Zero CkIn**
This checkbox is used for continuous inventory based on zero stock checks. When this checkbox is selected, a count should be taken for all storage bins in this storage type when the remaining material is removed from a bin.

▶ **ZeroCheck**
Select this checkbox to trigger a zero stock check, but not just for continuous inventory. If this checkbox is selected, a zero stock check is required when a storage bin becomes empty.

▶ **Cycle Co**
Selecting this checkbox sets the storage type for the cycle counting procedure that is discussed later in this chapter.

346

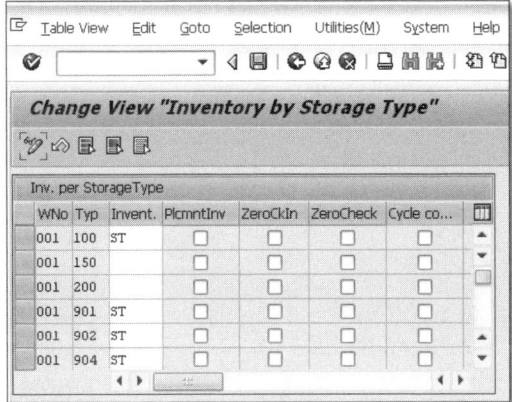

Figure 10.2 Inventory Configuration for Storage Types

4. Set the procedure for inventory differences and the movement types to deal with these. You can find this by following the menu path IMG • LOGISTICS EXECUTION • WAREHOUSE MANAGEMENT • ACTIVITIES • PHYSICAL INVENTORY • DEFINE DIFFERENCES AND DOCUMENT LIMITS.

Figure 10.3 shows the movement types and document limits that have been configured for warehouse 001.

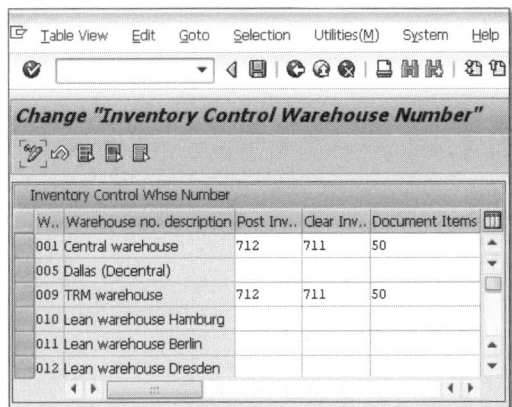

Figure 10.3 Configuration for Differences and Document Limits for Each Warehouse

The movement types are configured for posting of any inventory differences or clearing any differences that may occur when the count document is entered. The document that the counter used may have a quantity different from the book stock, and after investigation and more checks a difference is agreed upon. The difference is posted, and the internal movement type defined in this configuration is used to post the difference to an interim record.

The DOCUMENT ITEMS field refers to the number of items that are allowed for each record. You can change this to a larger or smaller amount as required.

10.1.3 Processing Open Transfer Orders

When the physical inventory count begins, the storage types to be counted must be clear of open transfer orders. Check for open transfer orders by using Transaction LT22 or following the menu path SAP • LOGISTICS • LOGISTICS EXECUTION • INTERNAL WHSE PROCESSES • STOCK TRANSFER • DISPLAY TRANSFER ORDER • FOR STORAGE TYPE.

Figure 10.4 shows the selection screen for Transaction LT22. In this instance, you must view all open transfer orders for the storage type that is ready to be counted. You need to ensure that the open transfer orders are displayed, because it will be necessary to confirm or close these open transfer orders.

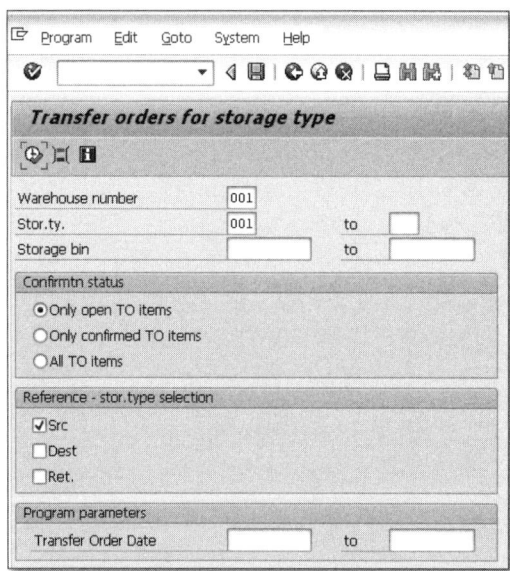

Figure 10.4 Initial Screen for Displaying Transfer Orders per Storage Type

Figure 10.5 shows that there are two open transfer orders for storage type 001. You can see that the transfer orders are still open because the confirmation indicator, Co, is still red, which means not confirmed. The open transfer orders need to be confirmed or closed, depending on whether the material can be transferred, has been transferred, or cannot be transferred before the count starts.

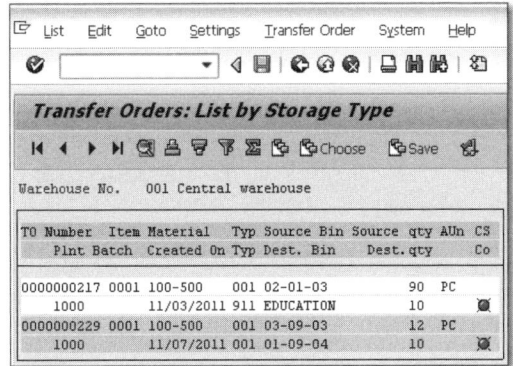

Figure 10.5 Display of Open Transfer Orders for Storage Type 001

You can confirm each transfer order with Transaction LT12 or by following the menu path SAP • LOGISTICS • LOGISTICS EXECUTION • INTERNAL WHSE PROCESSES • STOCK TRANSFER • CONFIRM TRANSFER ORDER • SINGLE DOCUMENT • IN ONE STEP.

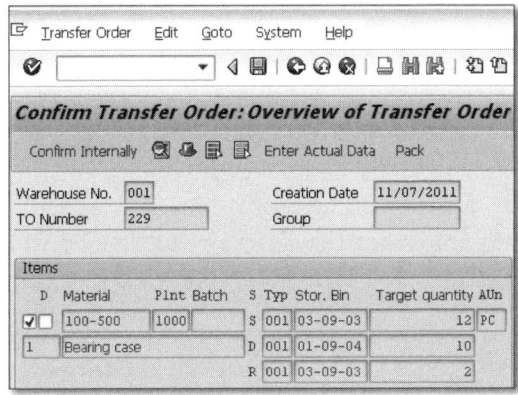

Figure 10.6 Confirmation of Transfer Orders Prior to Inventory Count

Figure 10.6 shows the confirmation of an open transfer order for the storage type to be counted. Once all the transfer orders are closed for the storage type that will be counted, they can be blocked so that no other inbound or outbound movements can take place.

10.1.4 Blocking the Storage Type

To block the storage type for stock placement and stock removal, use Transaction LI06 or follow the menu path SAP • LOGISTICS • LOGISTICS EXECUTION • INTERNAL WHSE PROCESSES • PHYSICAL INVENTORY • IN WAREHOUSE MANAGEMENT • BLOCK STORAGE TYPE.

Figure 10.7 shows the block on storage type 001 for both stock placement and stock removal. The block should remain in place until all the inventory documents have been processed for the storage type.

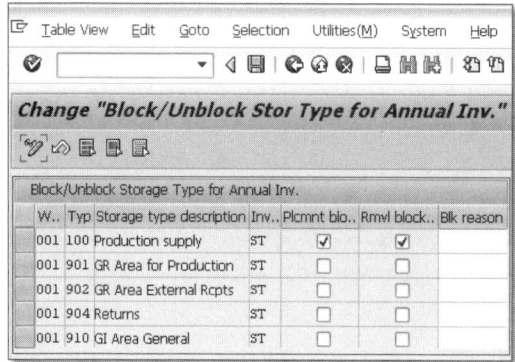

Figure 10.7 Blocking Stock Placement and Removal for Storage Type 001

10.1.5 Creating Annual Inventory Documents

Once the storage types to be counted have been decided upon, checked for activity, and blocked for movements, the count documents can be printed and given to the counters.

The transaction to produce the count documents is Transaction LX15, which you can find by following the menu path SAP • LOGISTICS • LOGISTICS EXECUTION • INTERNAL WHSE PROCESSES • PHYSICAL INVENTORY • IN WAREHOUSE MANAGEMENT • PHYSICAL INVENTORY DOCUMENT • CREATE • ANNUAL INVENTORY.

The initial selection screen, shown in Figure 10.8, allows entry of specific storage bins if not all the bins in the storage type are to be counted.

Annual Physical Inventory | 10.1

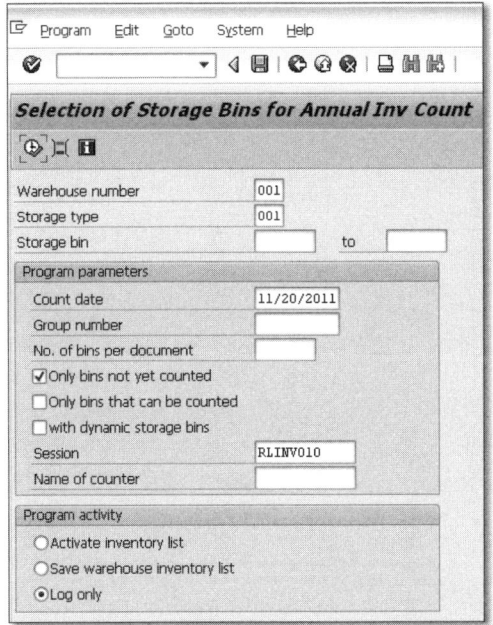

Figure 10.8 Selection of Storage Types for Annual Inventory Count

The session name is used to create the documents in a batch job. This can be run in the background or in the foreground. After you enter the data that may be required, you can execute the transaction, and the process will display a summary of the counting that can begin.

Figure 10.9 shows the bins that can be counted, in this case 53, with 77 quants.

To process the documents, you can activate the transaction by selecting PHYSICAL INVENTORY DOCUMENT • ACTIVATE or by pressing [Shift]+[F4]. The transaction will create a background job so that the documents can be printed.

The background session called RLINV010 has been created, as shown in Figure 10.10. It can be processed to create the two new count documents based on the information that was entered in Figure 10.8. To execute this transaction, click the PROCESS button or select SESSION • PROCESS SESSION.

The dialog box shown in Figure 10.11 is displayed after the session has begun processing. You can enable processing in the background or foreground and choose additional functions such as the ability to cancel if an error log is triggered.

10 | Inventory Procedures

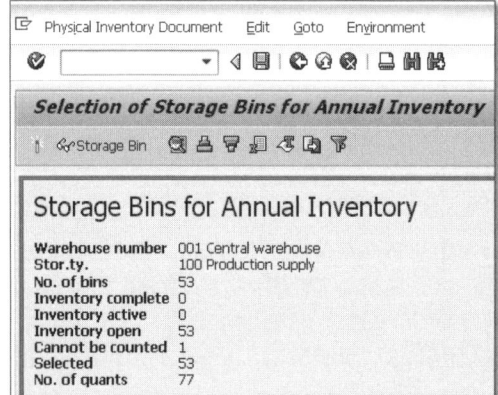

Figure 10.9 Summary of Physical Inventory Count that Can Be Processed

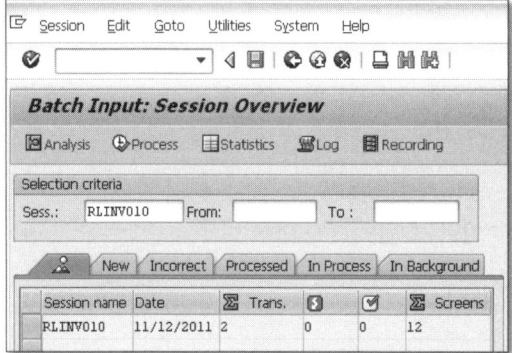

Figure 10.10 Batch Input Session for Processing Inventory Count Documents

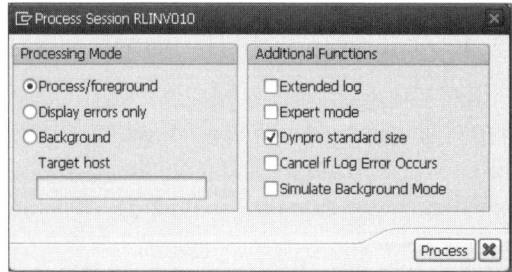

Figure 10.11 Dialog Box During Processing Session for Count Documents

10.1.6 Displaying the Count Documents

After the count documents have been processed you can view by using the Transaction LX22 or following the menu path SAP • LOGISTICS • LOGISTICS EXECUTION • INTERNAL WHSE PROCESSES • PHYSICAL INVENTORY • IN WAREHOUSE MANAGEMENT • PHYSICAL INVENTORY DOCUMENT • OVERVIEW. Figure 10.12 shows the initial data entered to select the count documents created by the batch processing. The warehouse number and storage type have been entered, along with the criteria to show only documents that have not been counted. Once the data has been entered, you can press the [F8] function key or click the EXECUTE button to process the transaction.

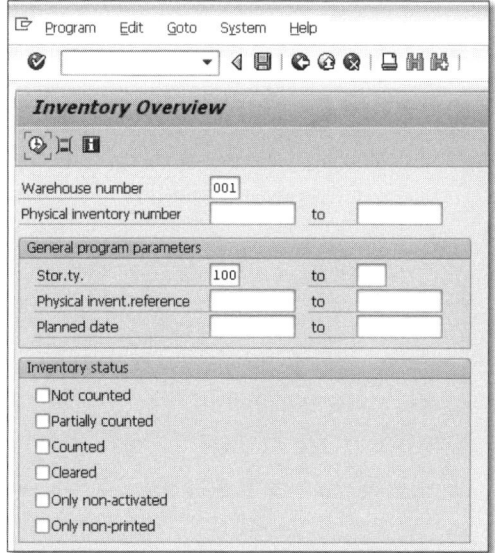

Figure 10.12 Initial Selection Screen for Displaying Count Documents: Transaction LX22

Figure 10.13 shows the six inventory count documents created by Transaction LX15. You can activate these documents by clicking the ACTIVATE button and then print them by clicking the PRINT button on the application toolbar or by selecting LIST • PRINT.

Figure 10.14 shows the first page of the count document that has been printed for storage type 001. The count document is handed to the counter, who then manually enters the count figure into the document. Once finished, the count document is returned for data entry.

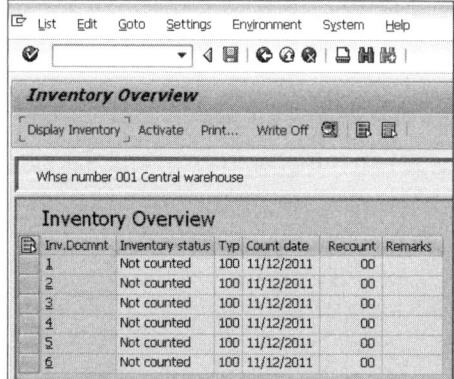

Figure 10.13 Overview of Six New Inventory Count Documents

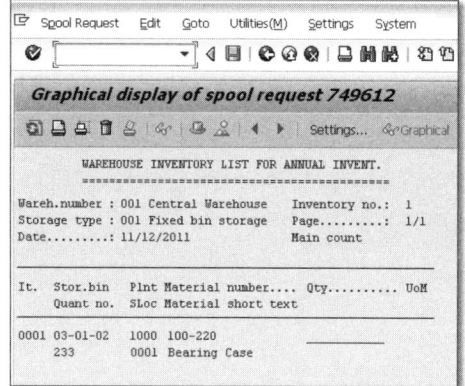

Figure 10.14 First Page of Printed Inventory Count Document for Storage Type 001

10.1.7 Entering the Inventory Count

After the counter has returned the count document to the data entry area, the count document can be entered into the SAP system. The transaction to enter count documents is Transaction LI11N, which can be reached through the menu path SAP • LOGISTICS • LOGISTICS EXECUTION • INTERNAL WHSE PROCESSES • PHYSICAL INVENTORY • IN WAREHOUSE MANAGEMENT • COUNT RESULTS • ENTER.

Figure 10.15 shows the initial screen for entering the count document. You can enter the count document number, the warehouse, and the count date. Enter the name of the counter if there are many counters and recounts may require different counters.

Annual Physical Inventory | **10.1**

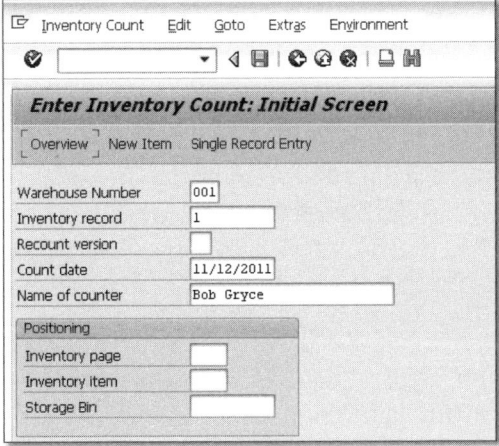

Figure 10.15 Initial Entry Screen to Enter a Count Document: Transaction LI11N

Figure 10.16 shows the detail screen, which reflects the information on the count document. The data entry clerk enters the amount from the count document into the appropriate line in this transaction. If the counter finds additional material, and there is not a line on the count document to reflect this, the data entry clerk can add this by clicking the NEW ITEM button on the application toolbar.

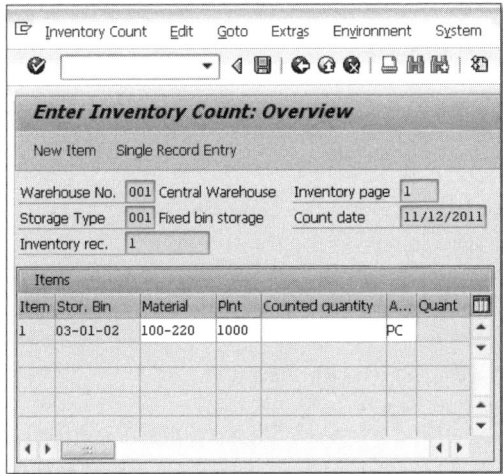

Figure 10.16 Detail Screen for Entering Data from the Inventory Count Document

After the total count for the document has been entered, you can post the document by pressing the [Ctrl]+[S] or selecting INVENTORY COUNT • POSTING.

10.1.8 Count Differences

After the count has been entered, it can be accepted or recounted if the variance is too great. You can see the variance by using Transaction LI14, which you can find following the navigation path SAP • LOGISTICS • LOGISTICS EXECUTION • INTERNAL WHSE PROCESSES • PHYSICAL INVENTORY • IN WAREHOUSE MANAGEMENT • COUNT RESULTS • RECOUNT.

Figure 10.17 shows the initial screen for Transaction LI14, to initiate a recount. You can allow a certain percentage deviation in book inventory against the count or allow a value deviation.

> **Note**
>
> A large deviation in the count may only account for a few dollars in value, which the accounting department will allow. When a small deviation in the count causes a large difference in value, the accounting department may require a special investigation of the deviation.

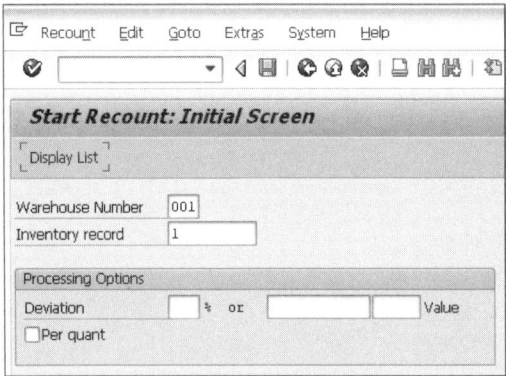

Figure 10.17 Initial Screen for Recounting an Inventory Count Document

Figure 10.18 shows part of the count for the document entered. The count is for storage bin 03 – 01 – 02 that has only a 2.89% count variance but a value variance of $9.00.

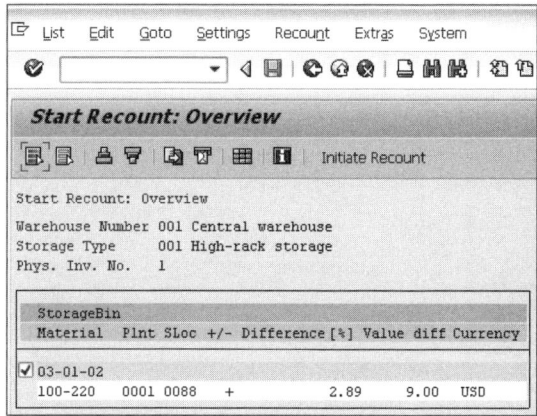

Figure 10.18 Count Document and Deviations in Value and Count

Depending on the accounting department's procedures on variance, a recount may be required for certain storage bins in this count document. To create a recount document, click the INITIATE RECOUNT button or press Shift + F4. The processing returns to the initial screen and a message is displayed that shows the recount number.

10.1.9 Entering a Recount

After the recount has been initiated and you know the recount number, you can enter the recount into the transaction used for the initial count—Transaction LI11N. You can reach this via the menu path SAP • LOGISTICS • LOGISTICS EXECUTION • INTERNAL WHSE PROCESSES • PHYSICAL INVENTORY • IN WAREHOUSE MANAGEMENT • COUNT RESULTS • ENTER.

You enter the recount into Transaction LI11N with the same information as the original count (as shown in Figure 10.19) but with the recount number that was provided. In this case, the recount number is 01.

The recount document, shown in Figure 10.20, can be printed and given to a counter to perform the recount. Once the line items have been recounted, the document can be returned to the data entry clerk for re-entry. If the accounting department wants to ensure the most accurate count, the organization can perform an additional recount using Transaction LI14.

10 | Inventory Procedures

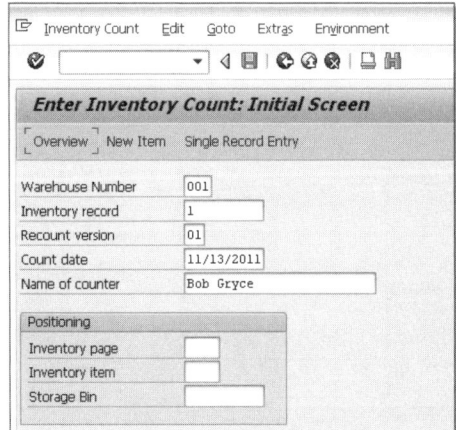

Figure 10.19 Initial Screen for Recount Document Entry

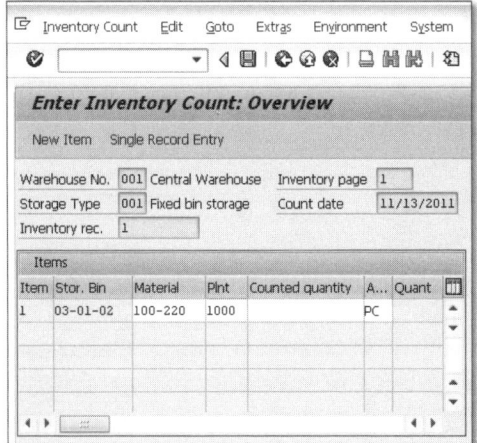

Figure 10.20 Line Items from Count Document that Are Part of Recount

10.1.10 Clearing Differences

If no more recounts have been deemed necessary, the count differences can be cleared and a final posting made to the warehouse inventory.

The differences between the book inventory and the count information can be written *off* or *on* by using Transaction LI20 or following the menu path SAP • LOGISTICS • LOGISTICS EXECUTION • INTERNAL WHSE PROCESSES • PHYSICAL INVENTORY • IN WAREHOUSE MANAGEMENT • CLEAR DIFFERENCES • WAREHOUSE MANAGEMENT.

Figure 10.21 shows the initial screen for allowing differences between the book stock and the count to be made. There is an allowance to enter a variance in percentage or in value to restrict the write-off. In the example shown in Figure 10.21, no variance has been entered.

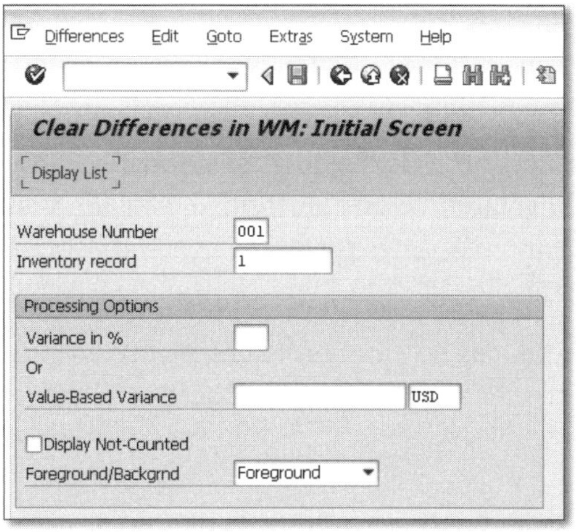

Figure 10.21 Initial Screen for Transaction to Clear Inventory Count Differences

Figure 10.22 shows the storage bin that has a material variance between the inventory count and the book stock. The details show the percentage difference and the difference in value.

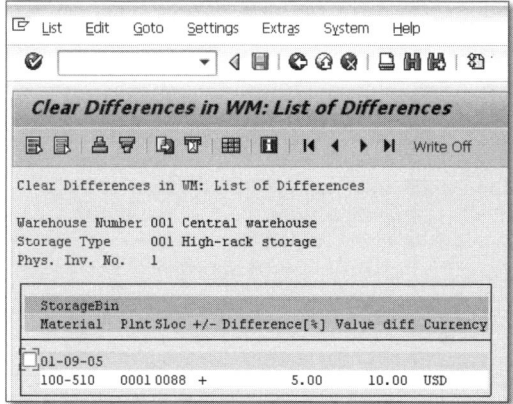

Figure 10.22 Materials with Variance Between Book Stock and Inventory Count

You can write off the difference between the book value and the count value by clicking the WRITE OFF button on the application toolbar or pressing [Shift]+[F5].

Now that we've examined the processes involved in the annual physical inventory, we'll move on to a process called continuous inventory.

10.2 Continuous Inventory

The principle behind continuous inventory is that dividing the annual physical inventory count into several smaller inventory counts performed over the year ensures that all material is counted. Many companies prefer this method because it reduces the effort required and the stress involved in conducting a single count.

The key to performing a successful continuous inventory is to ensure that all storage bins are counted in a systematic manner and the counts are successfully documented.

10.2.1 Configuring Continuous Inventory

The configuration for continuous inventory is to set the inventory type for each storage type. You can find this by following the menu path IMG • LOGISTICS EXECUTION • WAREHOUSE MANAGEMENT • ACTIVITIES • PHYSICAL INVENTORY • DEFINE TYPES PER STORAGE TYPE.

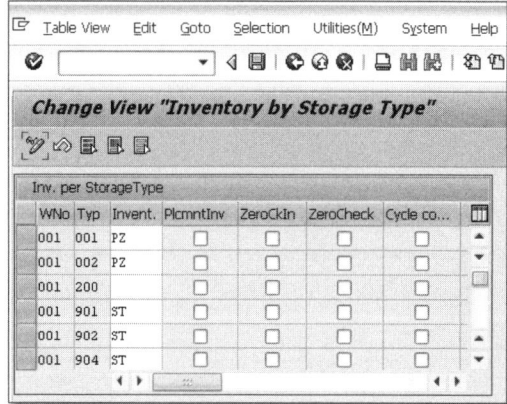

Figure 10.23 Configuration for Continuous Inventory for Storage Types

Figure 10.23 shows the configuration that has been entered for storage types 001 and 002 is PZ, which indicates continuous inventory.

10.2.2 Creating a Continuous Inventory Count Document

The transaction to produce the count documents for continuous inventory is Transaction LX16, which you can find via the menu path SAP • LOGISTICS • LOGISTICS EXECUTION • INTERNAL WHSE PROCESSES • PHYSICAL INVENTORY • IN WAREHOUSE MANAGEMENT • PHYSICAL INVENTORY DOCUMENT • CREATE • CONTINUOUS INVENTORY.

Figure 10.24 shows the initial screen for creating a continuous inventory count document. The warehouse number and storage type are entered, and a range of storage bins can be selected. The following parameters are available:

- **Group number**
  This is a user-assigned number for grouping together certain counts. This can be as simple as the number of the week if you are combining counts that take place the same week.

- **Bins with qty. less than**
  The bins will be selected if they contain a quantity of material that is less than the figure entered in this field.

- **No activity since (no. of days)**
  This bin will be selected if there has been no activity in it for more than the number of days entered in this field.

- **Max. no. of quants per bin**
  The bin will be selected if the number of quants in the bin is less than the number entered into this field.

- **Only empty bins**
  Select this checkbox if only empty bins are to be selected.

After entering all the required parameters, you can execute the transaction by pressing the [F8] function key.

Figure 10.25 shows that there are three storage bins with material that can be counted in warehouse 001, storage type 001. You can highlight these and activate them for counting by pressing [Shift]+[F4] or selecting PHYSICAL INVENTORY DOCUMENT • ACTIVATE.

10 | Inventory Procedures

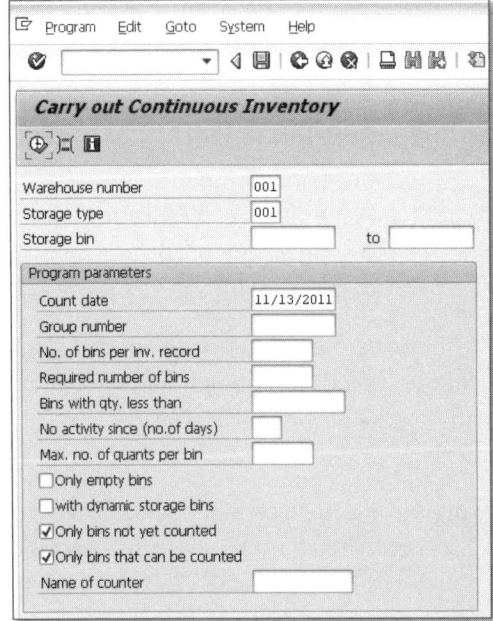

Figure 10.24 Initial Data Entry Screen to Create Continuous Inventory Count Document: Transaction LX16

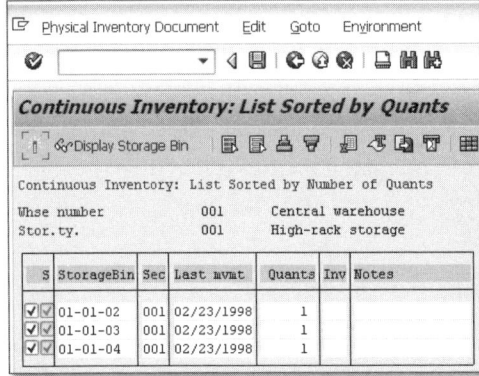

Figure 10.25 List of Quants that Can Be Counted as Continuous Inventory

Figure 10.26 shows that after the three storage bins were activated, Transaction LX16 created continuous count document 7. This document can then be printed.

10.2 Continuous Inventory

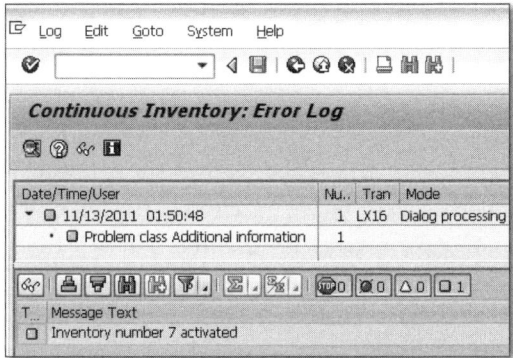

Figure 10.26 Continuous Inventory Document 7

10.2.3 Printing a Continuous Inventory Count Document

You can print the continuous count document can be printed using the Transaction LI04 or by following the menu path SAP • Logistics • Logistics Execution • Internal Whse Processes • Physical Inventory • In Warehouse Management • Physical Inventory Document • Print Warehouse Inventory List.

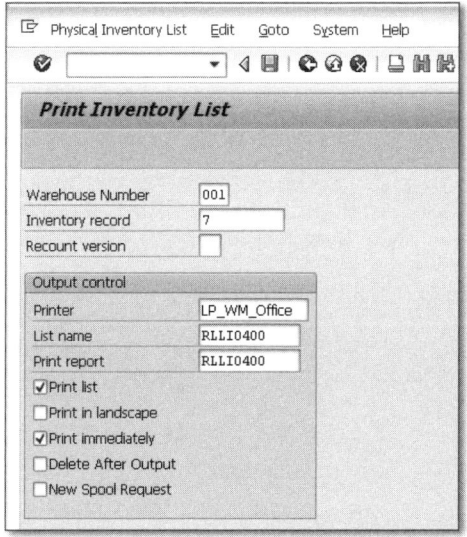

Figure 10.27 Initial Entry Screen for Printing Continuous Count Document 7

Figure 10.27 shows the initial screen for printing the continuous count document. Enter the warehouse and document number as well as the recount number, if appropriate. Select the printer and other options such as print in landscape, print immediately, and so on.

Figure 10.28 shows the count document that is printed via Transaction LI04. The document shows the storage bins to be counted, the material expected in those storage bins, and a space where the counter can write the quantity that he counts in the storage bin.

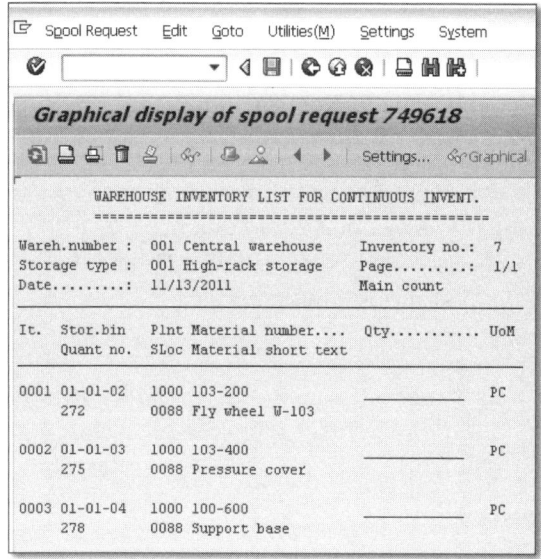

Figure 10.28 Printout of Continuous Inventory Count Document

The completed count document should be returned to the warehouse staff member responsible for entering continuous inventory counts.

10.2.4 Entering the Count Results

Once the items on the continuous count document have been counted, the count figures can be entered into Transaction LI11N. You can find this transaction via the menu path SAP • LOGISTICS • LOGISTICS EXECUTION • INTERNAL WHSE PROCESSES • PHYSICAL INVENTORY • IN WAREHOUSE MANAGEMENT • COUNT RESULTS • ENTER.

Figure 10.29 shows the count that has been entered for the continuous inventory count document. Once all the figures are entered, you can save the count.

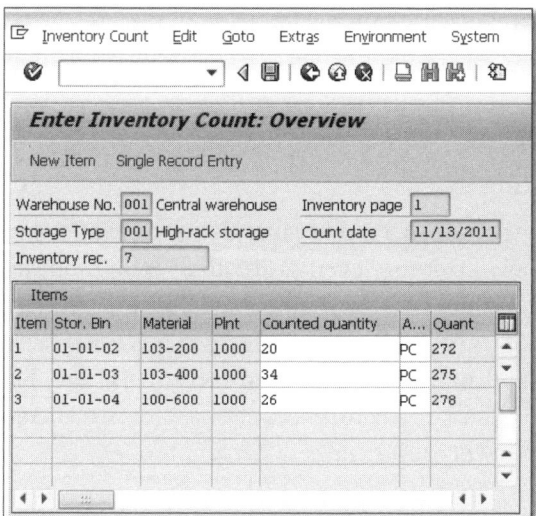

Figure 10.29 Count Entered for Continuous Inventory Count Documents

Now that the three storage bins have been counted, they do not need to be counted again until the next fiscal year. If you try to include these storage bins in a count document, the bins will not appear. A manual check of the materials might be made for some outbound orders, although this would take place outside of normal cycle-counting procedures.

After the fiscal year is complete and all the bins have been counted, the storage bins should become available for counting. To ensure that the storage bin table — LAGP — is clear of the count date and time of the previous fiscal year, report RLRE-OLPQ should be run using Transaction SE38 or included as part of an end-of-year batch job. Make sure the Basis team knows this needs to be performed. We suggest that you ask if this job can be placed in any end-of-year batch runs that may occur for the finance or production department.

Now, after examining the processes of continuous inventory, we can focus on the popular method used in counting inventory known as cycle counting.

10.3 Cycle Counting

Cycle counting is basically the process of continually validating the accuracy of the inventory in the warehouse by regularly counting a portion of the inventory, on a daily or weekly basis. This way, every item in the warehouse is counted at least several times a year.

10.3.1 Benefits of Cycle Counting

Many companies choose the cycle counting method because they cannot afford to pay the costs involved in large annual inventory events. Frequent cycle counting shortens the time between physical counts of any material and, as a result, any discrepancies that turn up during a cycle count have occurred recently. This gives the warehouse management the opportunity to understand the cause of the discrepancy and perform any remedial action. Inventory write-offs, as a percentage of inventory investment, are much lower with regular cycle counting.

10.3.2 Materials Management Configuration Steps with Cycle Counting

You configure the cycle counting indicators, A, B, C, and so on using Transaction OMCO, which is located in the configuration of the Materials Management module (SAP MM). The menu path is IMG • MATERIALS MANAGEMENT • INVENTORY MANAGEMENT AND PHYSICAL INVENTORY • PHYSICAL INVENTORY • CYCLE COUNTING.

Figure 10.30 shows the configuration fields for the four cycle-counting indicators, A, B, C, and D:

- **No. of phys. Inv**
  This field defines the number of times a material must be counted per year. For example, materials that are assigned an "A" indicator will be counted 12 times.
- **Interval**
  The interval is the maximum number of work days, as defined by the factory calendar, that can pass before the material has to be counted again.
- **Float time**
  The float time is defined as the number of days after the planned count date that the material can be still be counted.

▶ **Percentage**

This field is the percentage of materials assigned an indicator. Therefore, in the example shown in Figure 10.30, 56% can be allocated A materials, 28% are B materials, 14% are C materials, and only 2% are D materials. The total must add up to 100 percent. These percentages are used in defining the indicators for the materials in the plant.

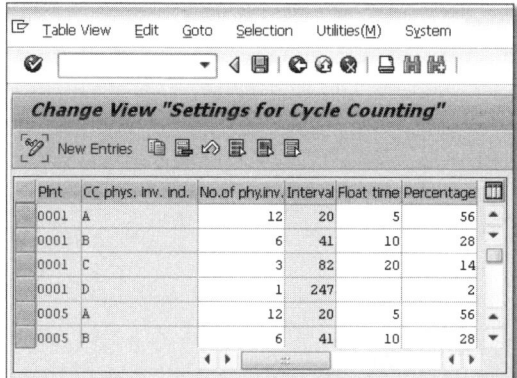

Figure 10.30 Configuration for Cycle Counting: Transaction OMCO

To automatically determine the indicators for materials in a plant, execute the ABC analysis.

10.3.3 Using the ABC Analysis

If the ABC indicators are configured for a plant, you can perform an ABC analysis to assign the correct indicator to each material. You can run the ABC analysis for cycle counting with Transaction MIBC by following the menu path: SAP • LOGISTICS • MATERIALS MANAGEMENT • PHYSICAL INVENTORY • SPECIAL PROCEDURES • CYCLE COUNTING • SET CYCLE COUNTING INDICATOR.

Figure 10.31 shows Transaction MIBC, which allows the entry of the plant and a material type. In this case, the ABC analysis will be performed on material type FERT: finished goods.

The transaction proposes a range of dates for either consumption or requirements. The user then decides whether to use the material consumption data or material requirement data as the basis for defining the ABC indicator. You also have the option of altering the percentages already configured for the plant.

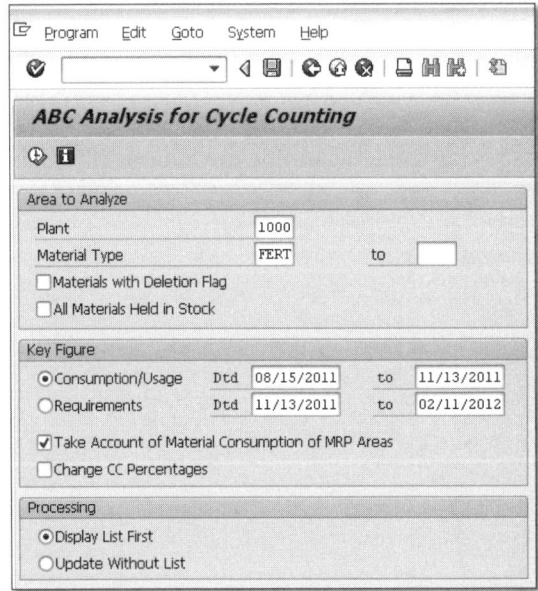

Figure 10.31 Execution of ABC Analysis to Assign ABC Indicators

Figure 10.32 shows the results of the ABC analysis that was performed on the finished goods in plant 1000. The results show that several materials have changed ABC indicators. This will result in a change in the number of cycle counts needing to be performed.

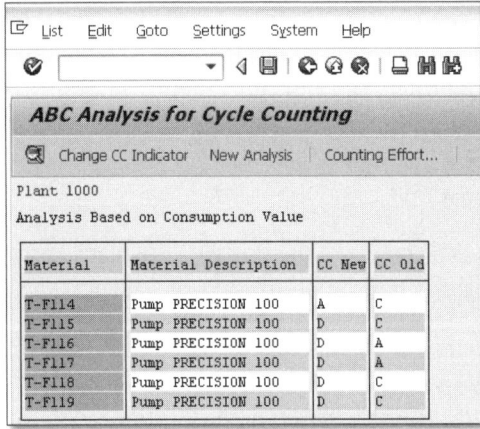

Figure 10.32 Results of ABC Analysis Performed on Finished Goods in Plant 1000

10.3.4 ABC Indicator and Material Master

After the ABC analysis has been performed and the ABC indicator has been assigned to the material, the indicator is written into the material master record. You can see the ABC indicator by viewing the plant data screen in the material master, using Transaction MM03.

Figure 10.33 shows the plant data screen for the material master record of material T-F144. In Figure 10.32, this material is the first material in the list and is assigned an A indicator. In the plant-data screen, this indicator is seen as the cycle count physical inventory field: CC Phys. Inv. Id.

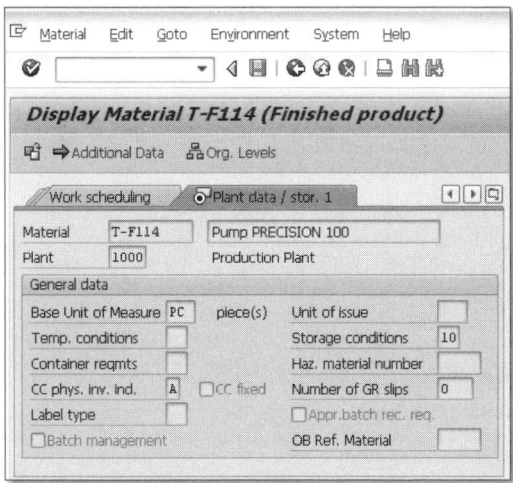

Figure 10.33 ABC Indicator Shown on Material Master Record as Cycle Count Physical Indicator

There is also a field next to that checkbox labeled CC fixed. You can set this checkbox manually on the material master to prevent the ABC analysis process from changing the ABC indicator. This guarantees that no matter how much the consumption or requirements of this material change, the ABC indicator remain the same unless it is manually changed on the material master record. Check with the warehouse staff to ensure that this indicator is set correctly.

10.3.5 Cycle Counting Configuration for Storage Type

You can set the configuration for cycle counting to the inventory type for each storage type. To do this, follow the menu path IMG • Logistics Execution • Ware-

House Management • Activities • Physical Inventory • Define Types per Storage Type.

Figure 10.34 shows the configuration for warehouse 092, storage type 101. No inventory method is defined—neither continuous nor annual—but the cycle counting indicator is set for these four storage types. Therefore, the storage types will use the cycle counting indicators set in the material master records to define how the material is counted.

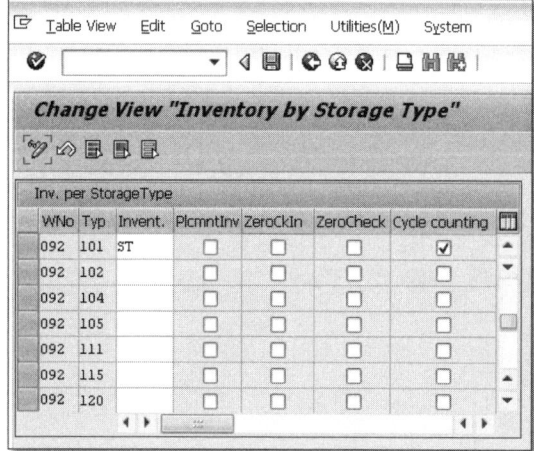

Figure 10.34 Cycle Counting Configuration for Storage Types

10.3.6 Creating a Cycle Count Document

Transaction LX26 produces the count documents for cycle counting. You can find it by following the menu path SAP • Logistics • Logistics Execution • Internal Whse Processes • Physical Inventory • In Warehouse Management • Physical Inventory Document • Create • Cycle Counting.

Figure 10.35 shows the selection entered into Transaction LX26 for warehouse MG1 and storage type 101. When this transaction is executed, the system will review all the material in the storage bins to ascertain whether a cycle count is required, based on the cycle count indicator on the material master and the last time the material was counted.

Cycle Counting | 10.3

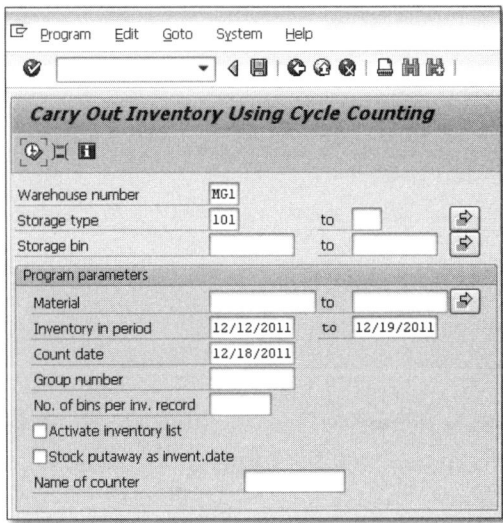

Figure 10.35 Creating a Cycle Count Document: Transaction LX26

Figure 10.36 shows an overview of the count documents that can be created for the warehouse number and storage type entered in the initial selection screen. In this example, two storage bins that have been selected: 01 – 01 – 01, where the cycle count is overdue, and 01 – 01 – 02, where a cycle count is scheduled.

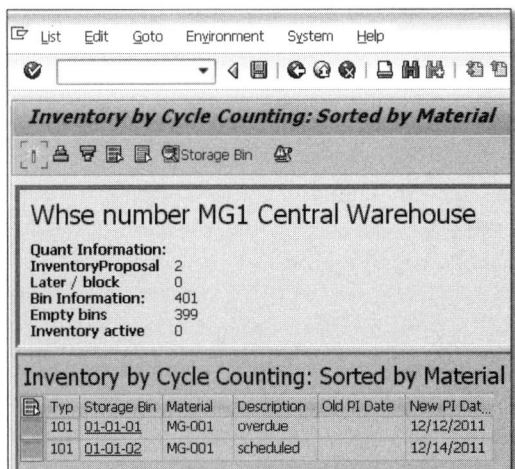

Figure 10.36 Review of Storage Bins that Require Cycle Counting

To activate a count document, highlight the line item and select the activate icon. The transaction returns the inventory count document number for the cycle count selected.

10.3.7 Printing the Cycle Count Document

After the cycle count document has been created, you can print it for warehouse staff to perform the count. Use Transaction LI04 or follow the navigation path SAP • LOGISTICS • LOGISTICS EXECUTION • INTERNAL WHSE PROCESSES • PHYSICAL INVENTORY • IN WAREHOUSE MANAGEMENT • PHYSICAL INVENTORY DOCUMENT • PRINT WAREHOUSE INVENTORY LIST.

You can give the cycle count document to a member of the warehouse staff to perform the count as part of his daily warehouse routine. Figure 10.37 shows the printout of the count document that the warehouse operator will use to record the count of the storage bin.

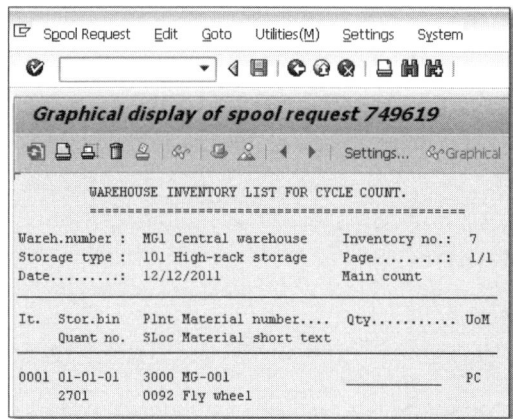

Figure 10.37 Printout of Cycle Count Document Created by Transaction LI04

10.3.8 Entering the Cycle Count

After the item on the cycle count document has been counted, the result can be entered into Transaction LI11N. You can find this transaction by following the menu path SAP • LOGISTICS • LOGISTICS EXECUTION • INTERNAL WHSE PROCESSES • PHYSICAL INVENTORY • IN WAREHOUSE MANAGEMENT • COUNT RESULTS • ENTER.

Figure 10.38 shows the information for the storage bin that has been counted. Once all the figures are entered, you can save the count.

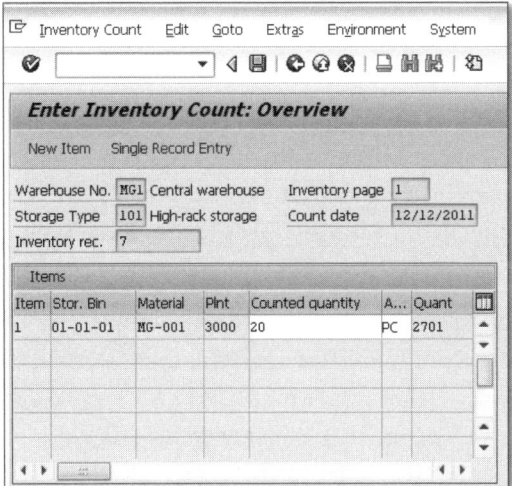

Figure 10.38 Entering the Count from the Cycle Count Document

Now that the count has been entered for this storage bin, the material does not need to be counted again until the date that is determined by the configuration of the ABC indicators for this plant. In this case, the material has an A indicator, and the configuration for the plant is set for the material to be counted six times a year.

Now that we have examined the functionality of cycle counting, we will examine the zero stock check.

10.4 Zero Stock Check

A zero stock check is the process of performing a stock check on a storage bin after the material has been removed, in order to ensure that the storage bin is empty. You cannot do this in storage types such as open storage where there is mixed storage or for storage-unit-managed bulk storage.

However, in warehouses with very few open storage bins, the zero stock check is a valuable tool to ensure that the next transfer order to use the storage bin will not fail. The zero stock check is a good step to take when the warehouse has not been good at maintaining inventory accuracy. If the warehouse is new to SAP and in the past has not been accurate regarding bin contents, a zero stock check can provide a level of comfort to ensure that the inventory accuracy is improving.

10.4.1 Configuring Zero Stock Check

You can set the ZERO STOCK CHECK checkbox for each storage type. The configuration can be set in the inventory type configuration for each storage type, which you can find by following the menu path IMG • LOGISTICS EXECUTION • WAREHOUSE MANAGEMENT • ACTIVITIES • PHYSICAL INVENTORY • DEFINE TYPES PER STORAGE TYPE.

This transaction, shown in Figure 10.39, enables configuration of the storage type for annual, continuous, or cycle counting. The other fields allow configuration of the zero stock check with and without continuous inventory and are described here:

- **ZeroCkIn**
  This checkbox is used for continuous inventory based on zero stock checks. When this checkbox is set, a count should be taken for all storage bins in this storage type when the remaining material is removed from a bin.

- **ZeroCheck**
  Set this checkbox to trigger a zero stock check, but not just for continuous inventory. If this checkbox is set, a zero stock check is required when a storage bin becomes empty.

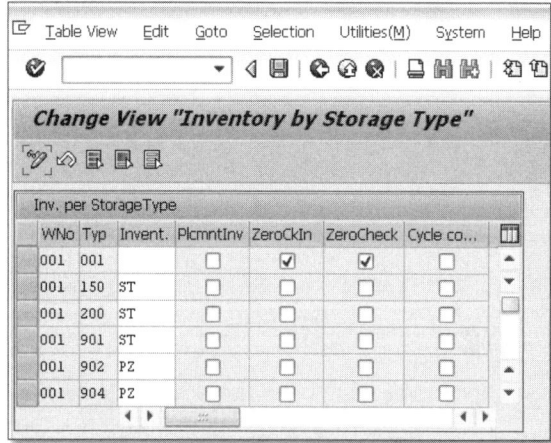

Figure 10.39 Zero Stock Check Configuration for Storage Type 001

10.4.2 Performing an Automatic Zero Stock Check

If the configuration for a storage type is set to require a zero stock check on the removal of all materials from a storage bin, the check will be triggered from the transfer order.

Using transaction LS24, you can review the stock overview for material 100-500, seen in Figure 10.40. It shows that there is a quant of 10 pieces in storage bin 01 – 09 – 04 located in storage type 001. From the configuration shown in Figure 10.39, we know that the zero stock check is required when a storage bin has been emptied. Therefore, a transfer order from this bin to the KANBAN area in the warehouse will empty the bin in and create the requirement for a zero stock check.

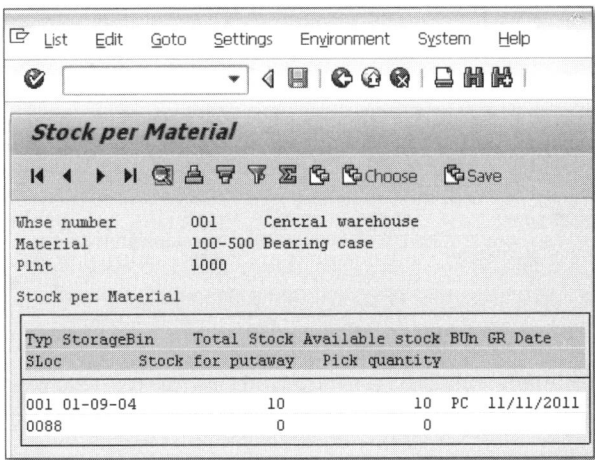

Figure 10.40 Warehouse Stock Overview for Material 100-500

Figure 10.41 shows a transfer order created by Transaction LT10 to move the total material from storage bin 01 – 09 – 04 to the KANBAN storage bin in the production supply area, storage type 150. The zero stock check checkbox is set for this storage type, so it is possible to view this inside the transfer order. You can do this by selecting EXTRAS • OTHER DATA or by press the [F7] function key.

10 | Inventory Procedures

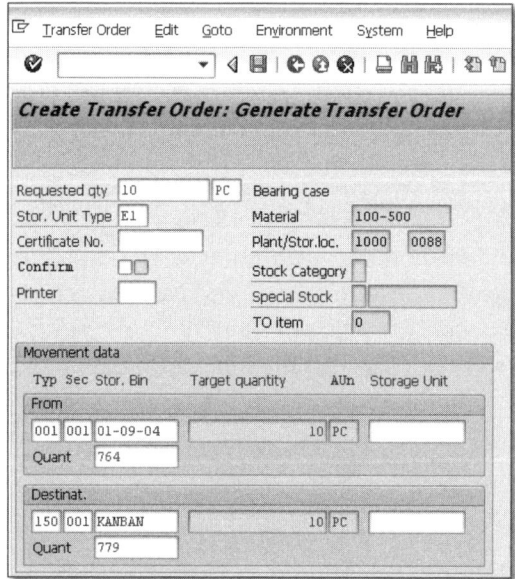

Figure 10.41 Transfer Order to Trigger a Zero Stock Check

Figure 10.42 shows the physical inventory information based on the item in the transfer order. In this case there are three fields, which are relevant for the zero stock check:

- **Invent. method**
  This inventory method is designated via the configuration. In this case, PN represents continuous inventory based on zero stock check. Other options are PZ for continuous inventory, ST for annual inventory, MA for manual inventory, and CC for cycle counting.

- **Inventory rec.**
  This is a system-defined inventory record number based on the zero stock count that needs to be carried out.

- **Zero stock chck**
  This field is the status for the zero stock check. The options are:
  - **1**
    System requires a zero stock check to be carried out
  - **2**
    Manual requirement for a zero stock check to be carried out

- 3

    Bin is empty, after system check

- 4

    Bin is empty, after manual check

- 5

    Bin is not empty, after system check

- 6

    Bin is not empty, after manual check

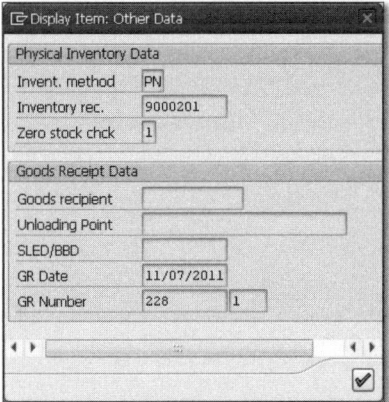

Figure 10.42 Physical Inventory Data of Transfer Order

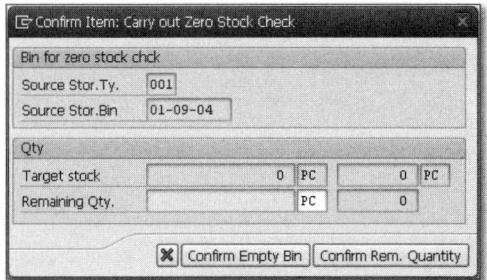

Figure 10.43 Zero Stock Transfer Order Confirmation Check

Figure 10.43 shows the zero stock check dialog box that appears during the confirmation of the transfer order. If the transfer order has removed all the material from the storage bin, then the check is required to ensure that this is correct. If it is not, then an amount can be entered into this screen, and the information needs to be investigated before posting.

10.4.3 Performing a Manual Zero Stock Check

If there is no continuous inventory configuration for a zero stock check for a storage type, then a manual zero stock check can be carried out if the storage bin is noted as empty after a transfer order has removed stock from the bin.

Figure 10.44 shows that the configuration for a continuous inventory zero stock check has been removed, but the configuration for a zero stock check remains on stock removal triggered manually from a transfer order.

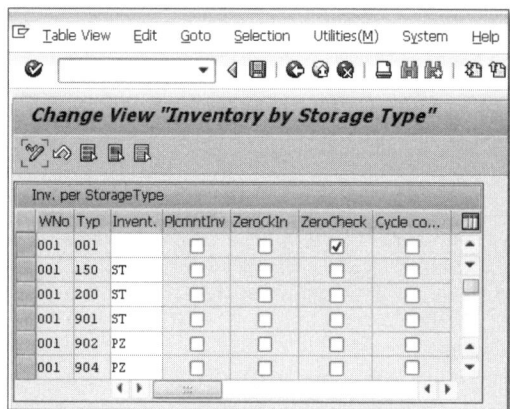

Figure 10.44 Zero Stock Check for Storage Removal Without Continuous Inventory

Figure 10.45 shows the stock overview for material 100-500. You can see that there is a quant of 90 pieces in storage bin 01 – 09 – 04 in storage type 001. The configuration has now been changed for storage type 001, and the system does not require a zero stock check when a bin is empty. Therefore, the only way a zero stock check can be triggered is manually.

Confirming a transfer order by each item, as performed in Transaction LT11, enables manual creation of a zero stock check. You can find the transaction by following the menu path SAP • LOGISTICS • LOGISTICS EXECUTION • INTERNAL WHSE PROCESSES • STOCK TRANSFER • CONFIRM STOCK TRANSFER • SINGLE ITEM • IN ONE STEP.

Zero Stock Check | **10.4**

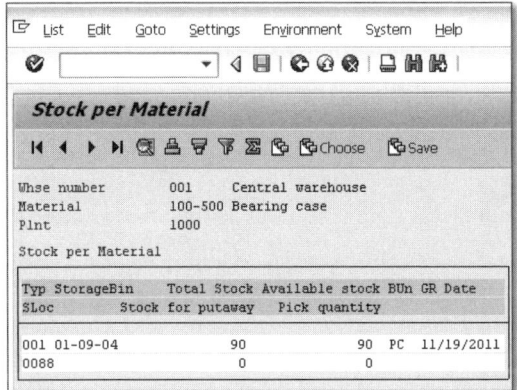

Figure 10.45 Warehouse Stock Overview for Material 100-500

Figure 10.46 shows confirmation of line item 1 in transfer order 398. The line item shows that the all the material from the storage bin is going to be transferred to the KANBAN storage bin. In this instance, you can manually trigger a zero stock check by clicking the ZERO STOCK CHECK button on the application toolbar or by selecting GOTO • ZERO STOCK CHECK.

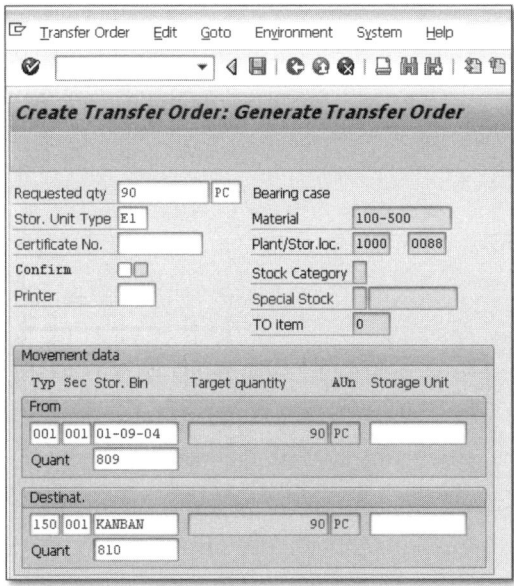

Figure 10.46 Confirmation of a Transfer Order with Zero Stock Check

379

The screen shown in Figure 10.47 allows the warehouse staff to enter a value in the remaining quantity box if there is any material in the storage bin even though the system indicates that the bin should be empty. If a value is entered that is not zero, an investigation may be required before the value is posted to the system.

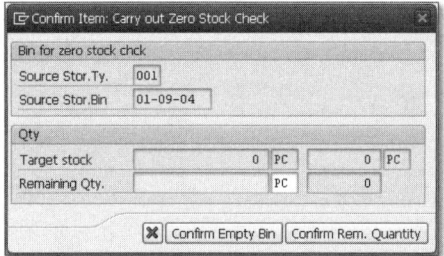

Figure 10.47 Dialog Box Allowing Zero Stock Check in Transfer Order Confirmation

Now that we have examined the zero stock check function, let's look at some business examples of inventory procedures.

10.5 Business Examples — Inventory Procedures

At some time every warehouse counts the inventory it holds. The method of counting inventory varies among companies and sometimes among locations within companies. The count can take place once a year, as with an annual inventory count, or on a regular basis such as continuous inventory or cycle counting.

10.5.1 Annual Physical Inventory

At the end of the fiscal year, a company performs a count of assets and stock to provide an accurate financial picture. For an annual count to be successful, an organization should implement formal procedures and documents, as well as use fully trained counters.

Example

A U.S. manufacturer of industrial tools implemented an SAP system after using a number of disparate PC systems for many years. In their legacy system, the physical inventory was taken each weekend for the company's main warehouse and once a month for material stored in offsite third-party warehouses.

With the advent of their SAP implementation, the company initially continued weekly physical inventories and found that inventory accuracy was significantly higher than previously. With more accurate data the company decided to perform counts on the weekend for items that had inaccuracies during the week. The weekend count now only represented 10 to 20 items having to be counted. The count was performed for these items, but it produced conflicting results. Some of the counted materials showed a count total equal to the book total, whereas others were significantly different, with some variations greater than the issues during the week.

The supply chain management team decided to postpone any more weekend counts until the issue was resolved. The ensuing investigation of the count process found that the preparation work before the count was causing the inaccuracies. The team had asked the warehouse second shift to print the count documents so that the counters could start early on Saturday morning. What was happening was that the count documents were printed before all movements in the warehouse were completed. Some material was moved in the warehouse late Friday night, but the confirmation of the warehouse transfer orders were not processed until Monday morning. This caused material to physically be in the correct bin, but the system did not reflect this. The count documents therefore did not show the correct physical total in the bin, and the count could never be accurate. Once this was identified, the management asked that all transfer orders be processed before the count documents were printed. This change in the preparation allowed a more successful count to take place.

10.5.2 Continuous Inventory

The principle behind continuous inventory is that dividing the annual physical inventory count into several smaller inventory counts performed over the year ensures that all material is counted. Many companies prefer this method because it reduces the effort required and the stress involved in conducting a single count.

Example

An Austrian beverage company produced small batches of alcoholic beverages for the European market. The firm produced small amounts of its finished goods and in its warehouse stored items that were not already allocated for customer sales orders. The warehouse was never more than 20% full, so the company counted the warehouse stock each week. As the demand for their products grew, the company doubled the number of its finished goods and decided to sell products for smaller beverage manufacturers in Austria and Germany. This increase in sales led to the company having to store a significantly larger number of products, and soon it had to lease a new warehouse to contain the ever growing inventory.

The weekly count was no longer an option, and the supply chain team considered a cycle count approach to inventory counting, but instead opted for the continuous inventory process. The supply chain team divided the two warehouses into 12 sections, based on the storage types, and then instigated a monthly count where each month they counted a different section. This approach allowed the whole warehouses to be counted at least once each year.

10.5.3 Cycle Counting

Cycle counting is the process of continually validating the accuracy of the inventory in the warehouse by regularly counting a portion of the inventory, on a daily or weekly basis. This way, every item in the warehouse is counted at least several times a year.

Example

A California electronics company packed components they purchased from manufacturers in the United States, Taiwan, and China and sold them to businesses and consumers in North America. Originally the company suffered from poor inventory control, and customer orders were often delayed due to the inability to find items in the warehouse and the lack of faith in the inventory figures that were calculated by aging PC systems. When the company wanted to expand, by purchasing a local competitor, the investment group they approached for funding required that they replace their computer systems and improve record taking as part of the deal. The company implemented an SAP system and installed two vertical carousels in the warehouse for high-density, automated storage.

As the company's inventory accuracy was poor, below 80%, they decided to implement a cycle counting policy where fast-moving stock was counted frequently. The company used ABC analysis to identify which materials needed to be counted at the different frequencies. The accuracy of inventory of the fast-moving goods improved initially after the implementation of cycle counting, reducing the number of customer orders that had to be delayed due to inventory inaccuracies. The company still found inventory accuracy issues with slow-moving stock, but after a year of cycle counting, the company's inventory accuracy was above 96%.

10.6 Summary

In this chapter, we discussed the ways a company can accurately keep track of its physical inventory and ensure that it is reflected in the warehouse management system. However, counting material is a process that is subject to human error.

The traditional annual inventory is a once a year attempt to count the stock in a warehouse, and if the count is wrong it remains wrong until the next year. In today's warehouses, the traditional annual inventory is being superseded by frequent cycle counting. Cycle counting is thought to be a more accurate method of counting but still is subject to the same level of human error. The benefit of cycle counting is that the more you count, the more likely it is that the count will be correct.

More frequent counting produces a more accurate picture of the stock in the warehouse and eliminates the stress on the warehouse caused by an annual inventory. Cycle counting should be considered a quality assurance procedure whereby the counting ensures the quality of the count.

The other aspect of quality assurance is to correct the count errors when they are found and to investigate why the errors occurred. Other methods that support the accuracy of the warehouse stock include the zero stock check. This can improve warehouse stock accuracy, as it provides extra counting events when a bin is expected to be empty and thus is an easy addition to frequent cycle counting.

In Chapter 11, we will examine storage unit management and discover how storage units affect standard stock placement and removal.

Storage unit management was developed to enable warehouse management to identify the container that holds a material as it moves around the warehouse. It is often important to manage the movement of the container as well as the material or materials it contains.

11 Storage Unit Management

Storage Unit Management is the warehouse management equivalent of handling unit management, the functionality found in SAP IM. Storage unit management was developed exclusively for WM, and from it SAP developed handling unit management for SAP Materials Management (MM). There are slight differences between the two, as seen here:

- Handling unit management allows for the nesting of handling units, that is, a handling unit containing several other handling units, whereas storage unit management does not allow the nesting of storage units.
- Handling unit management requires that an item be unpacked and packed, whereas this is not required for storage unit management. The storage unit is used to contain a quantity of material for its movement around the warehouse.

The storage unit comprises one or more materials and a container such as a pallet or a packing box. These items together make up the uniquely identifiable storage unit that can be moved and stored within the warehouse.

This chapter will introduce some of the key elements of storage unit management. You'll learn how a storage unit is created and how the storage unit can be planned before the material arrives at the receiving dock. The chapter will thoroughly explain other key functionalities, including the use of storage unit management in putaway and picking within the warehouse.

Now that we have highlighted some of the key topics in this chapter, we will introduce the storage unit management functionality.

11 Storage Unit Management

11.1 Introduction to Storage Unit Management

In modern warehouses, deliveries from a vendor may not arrive separated into quants of specific materials. In many retail operations, vendors send different materials on one pallet, and these arrive at the warehouse and are unloaded on the pallet. At this point, the warehouse staff can break down the pallet into distinct material quants. They then store the quants separately or store the pallet of material as a whole.

The pallet and the material on the pallet can be described as a single unit—a storage unit—made up from the container and the material stored with the container.

If the warehouse staff decides to store material in the container, then storage unit management will need to be configured for the warehouse. Although the entire warehouse need not be designated for storage units, certain storage types need to be identified to accept storage units.

To allow storage unit management to be used in the warehouse, you must carry out several configuration steps.

> **Note**
> Using storage unit management when handling unit management is already used in SAP IM can cause some confusion. Before configuring any storage unit management steps, confer with the supply chain team to avoid miscommunication.

11.1.1 Activating Storage Unit Management

For each warehouse where storage unit management is to be used, it must be configured to be active. You can find the configuration step by following the menu path IMG • LOGISTICS EXECUTION • WAREHOUSE MANAGEMENT • STORAGE UNITS • MASTER DATA • ACTIVATE STORAGE UNIT MANAGEMENT PER WAREHOUSE.

Figure 11.1 shows the checkbox for activating storage unit management for warehouse 009. No storage unit management can take place until this checkbox is set for the relevant warehouse.

Introduction to Storage Unit Management | 11.1

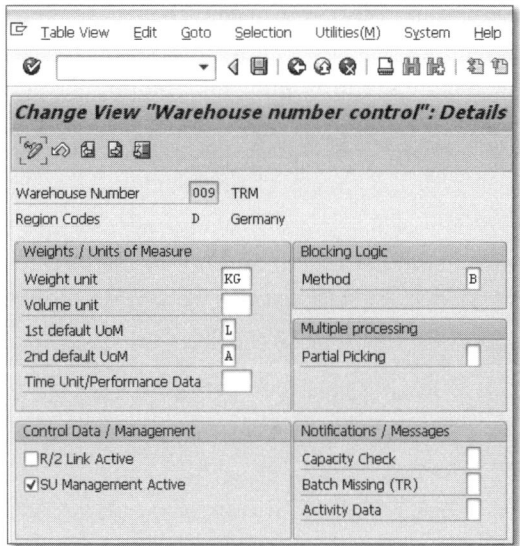

Figure 11.1 Activating Storage Unit Management for Warehouse 009

11.1.2 Defining Storage Unit Number Ranges

For each of the warehouses activated for storage unit management, you need to define the number range for the storage unit. To find this configuration, follow the menu path IMG • LOGISTICS EXECUTION • WAREHOUSE MANAGEMENT • STORAGE UNITS • MASTER DATA • DEFINE NUMBER RANGES.

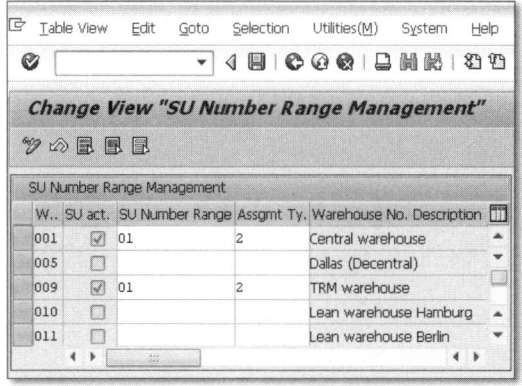

Figure 11.2 Defining a Number Range for Warehouses with Storage Unit Management

Figure 11.2 shows the configuration for warehouse 009, where the storage unit number range is set as 01 and the assignment type as 2. These settings mean that the storage unit number is internally assigned, and it allows for numbers to be used more than once.

11.1.3 Defining Storage Type Control

The storage type control is configured for the placement and removal strategies explained in earlier chapters. In this instance, the storage type control is configured for the storage unit management controls of those strategies.

You can find the configuration steps by following the menu path IMG • LOGISTICS EXECUTION • WAREHOUSE MANAGEMENT • STORAGE UNITS • MASTER DATA • DEFINE STORAGE TYPE CONTROL.

Figure 11.3 shows the configuration for storage type control for storage type 001 in warehouse 009. To ensure that the configuration is correct for a storage type when storage unit management is active, you should consider the settings described here:

- **SU mgmt active**
  Select this checkbox to show that this storage type is storage unit managed.
- **Putaway strategy**
  This is set to P, which means the storage unit type putaway has been selected.
- **Mixed storage**
  Because different materials can be moved on the same pallet as a defined storage unit, the mixed storage field must be marked with an "X."
- **Full stk rmvl reqmt**
  If this checkbox is selected, it affects the storage unit, not just the materials. A complete removal involves the complete storage unit.

Discuss these configuration settings with warehouse staff to ensure that you have correctly identified the way the warehouse needs storage unit management to operate.

Introduction to Storage Unit Management | **11.1**

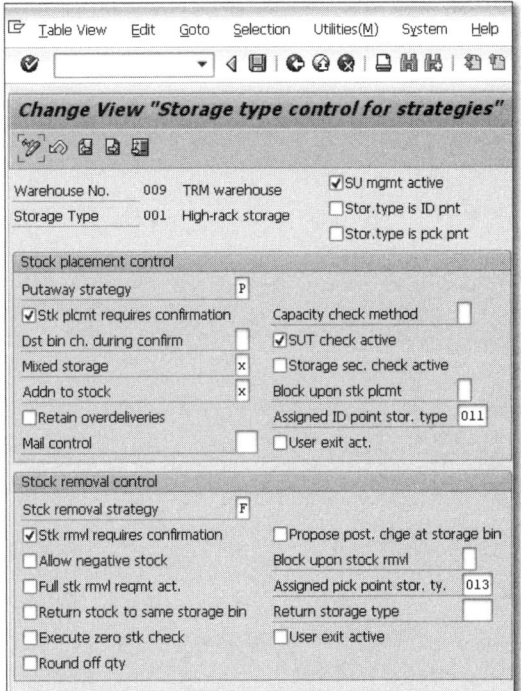

Figure 11.3 Storage Unit Management Configuration for Storage Type Control

11.1.4 Defining the Storage Unit Type

The storage unit type distinguishes the containers used in conjunction with the materials to comprise the storage unit. A storage unit type is configured as a three-character field, and you can also enter a 20-character description.

You can find the configuration steps by following the menu path IMG • LOGISTICS EXECUTION • WAREHOUSE MANAGEMENT • MASTER DATA • MATERIAL • DEFINE STORAGE UNIT TYPES.

Figure 11.4 shows the storage unit type configured for each warehouse. Each container used in the warehouse should be configured. We identify the different storage unit types because the sizes of these containers depend on the type of racking they are designed for or the storage facilities they are part of, such as storage carousels. The storage unit type identifies the physical aspects of the container, which is important during storage bin searches.

389

11 | Storage Unit Management

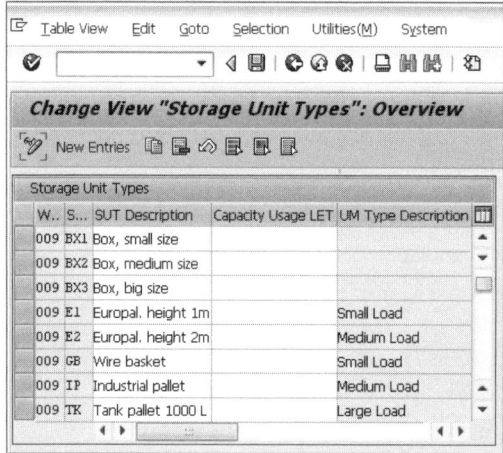

Figure 11.4 Configuration of Storage Unit Types

That concludes the introduction to storage unit management. We'll continue by explaining the storage unit record.

11.2 Storage Unit Record

The storage unit does not come into use outside of warehouse management and can only exist when material needs to be moved within the warehouse. Therefore, the storage unit is created when the material making up the storage unit is first proposed. This can happen in response to a receipt from a purchase order or be created later for movement within the warehouse.

11.2.1 Creating a Storage Unit Record by Transfer Order

The storage unit can be created when the movement is triggered. The transfer order, which is the procedure for moving material around the warehouse, is the catalyst for creating a storage unit record.

Use Transaction LT07 to create a transfer order for a new storage unit. You can find the configuration steps by following the menu path SAP • LOGISTICS • LOGISTICS EXECUTION • INTERNAL WHSE PROCESSES • STOCK TRANSFER • CREATE TRANSFER ORDER • CREATE STORAGE UNIT.

Figure 11.5 shows the initial screen of Transaction LT07. The storage unit does not exist until this transfer order is created. The actual movement of the material with its container requires that the transfer order create the storage unit as part of the process. If the storage unit is numbered externally, you can add the relevant number on this screen. Systems often need to have the number of the storage unit created internally.

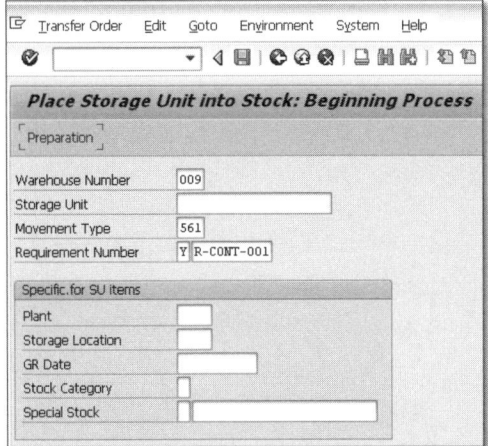

Figure 11.5 Initial Screen for Creating a Storage Unit: Transaction LT07

The initial screen must contain the warehouse number and the movement type. In this instance, entering the movement type requires that a requirement number be entered.

Figure 11.6 shows the entry of an item into a transfer order that will create the storage unit. This screen shows the details required for creating a transfer order: warehouse number, movement type, plant, material, and material quantity. In addition, the data required to create the storage unit has been entered, such as the storage unit type. The configuration of storage unit types is shown in Figure 11.4.

Once the data is entered correctly into the screen, click CREATE TRANS. ORDER to create the transfer order and the storage unit.

Figure 11.7 shows the transfer order with the source and destination storage types. The destination storage type shows that there is a new storage type to be entered. This has been created from the data entered into the screen shown in Figure 11.6.

11 | Storage Unit Management

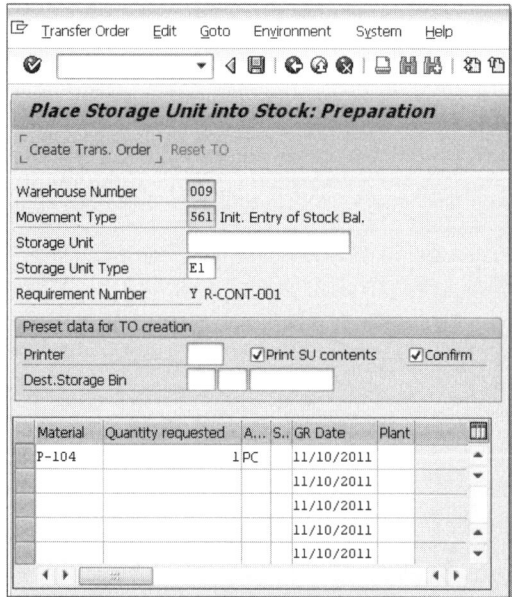

Figure 11.6 Entering Items to Create a Storage Unit: Transaction LT07

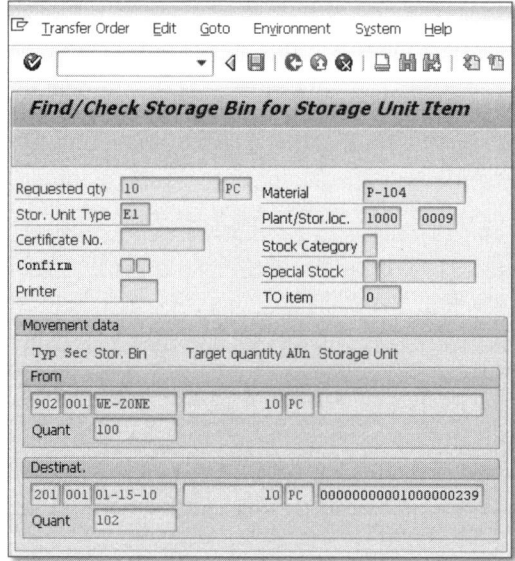

Figure 11.7 Transfer Order Created with Storage Unit Placed into Stock

11.2.2 Displaying a Storage Unit

After the transfer order is confirmed, you can display the details of the storage unit. The transaction for this is Transaction LS33, which you can find by following the menu path SAP • LOGISTICS • LOGISTICS EXECUTION • INTERNAL WHSE PROCESSES • BINS AND STOCK • DISPLAY • SINGLE DISPLAYS • STORAGE UNIT.

Figure 11.8 shows the details of the storage unit that has been entered. The information displayed is from the entry of the transfer order. The movement data reflects the last time the storage unit was moved and the transfer order that performed the movement.

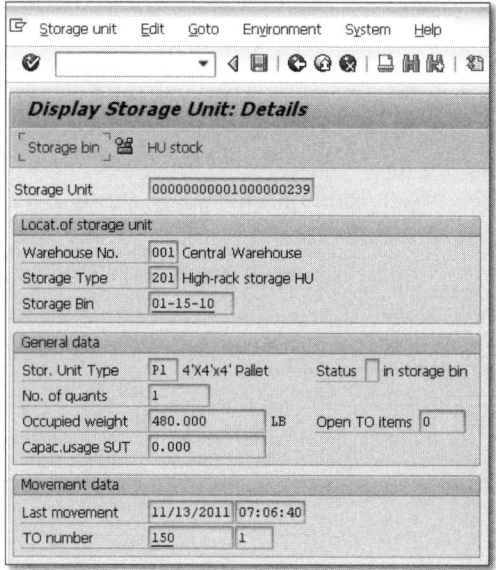

Figure 11.8 Details of a Storage Unit: Transaction LS33

Now that we have explained the creation and layout of the storage unit record, we will go on to describe how to plan storage units.

11.3 Planning Storage Units

The storage unit can be planned before the material arrives in the warehouse. The warehouse manager can prepare the containers for the arriving material so the material can be scanned on the receiving bay and placed in the container with which it is combined to make up the storage unit.

Planning storage units is the process of creating the transfer orders but not confirming them. Creating the transfer order creates the storage unit, so that it will exist when the material arrives at the receiving dock.

11.3.1 Planning Storage Units by Transfer Order

Warehouse management can plan storage units for incoming materials by using Transaction LT0A, which can be found via the menu path SAP • LOGISTICS • LOGISTICS EXECUTION • INBOUND PROCESSES • GOODS RECEIPT FOR PURCHASE ORDER, ORDER, OTHER TRANSACTIONS • PUTAWAY • CREATE TRANSFER ORDER • PREPLAN STORAGE UNITS.

Figure 11.9 shows the initial screen for Transaction LT0A, creating storage units for planning purposes. The quantity of the material entered on the transfer order is the amount that is expected to arrive on the inbound delivery. Because the movement type is for the planning of storage units, it requires entry of the storage unit number and the code Y for storage units. To continue with the planning, click the PREPARATION button.

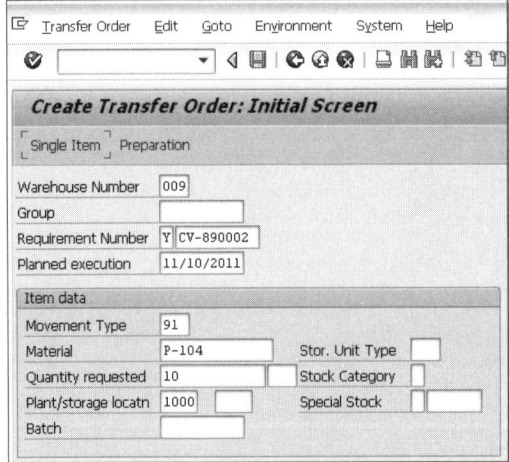

Figure 11.9 Creating Storage Units for Planning: Transaction LT0A

Figure 11.10 shows the next screen for planning storage units. The transfer order creation program defaults the storage type and a source bin for the container. At this point in the transaction, you can create the transfer order in the foreground by pressing the F5 function key or in the background by pressing F6.

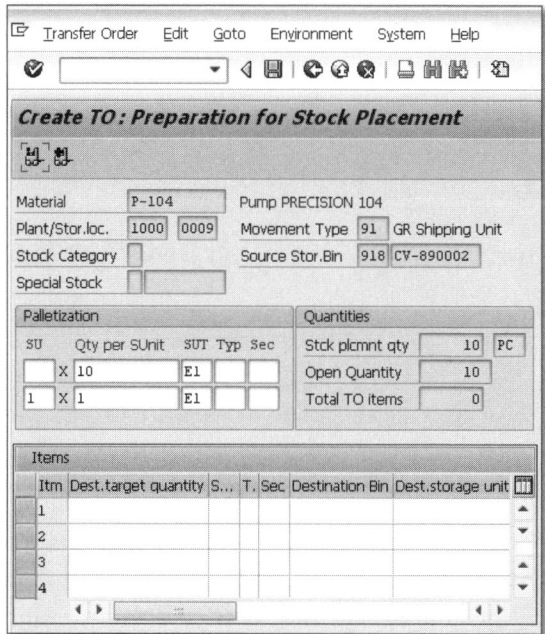

Figure 11.10 Planning for Storage Units: Transaction LT0A

Figure 11.11 shows the transfer order that has been created for the inbound material. The material will be moved from the goods-receipt area using the container, and this will be storage unit CV-8990002. The storage unit will be moved to storage type 005, bin location 01-15-10.

The transfer order is not confirmed at this point; this process is for planning the movement. Storage unit documents are printed that are stored until the material arrives. The confirmation takes place when the material arrives at the receiving dock and is moved to the storage bin.

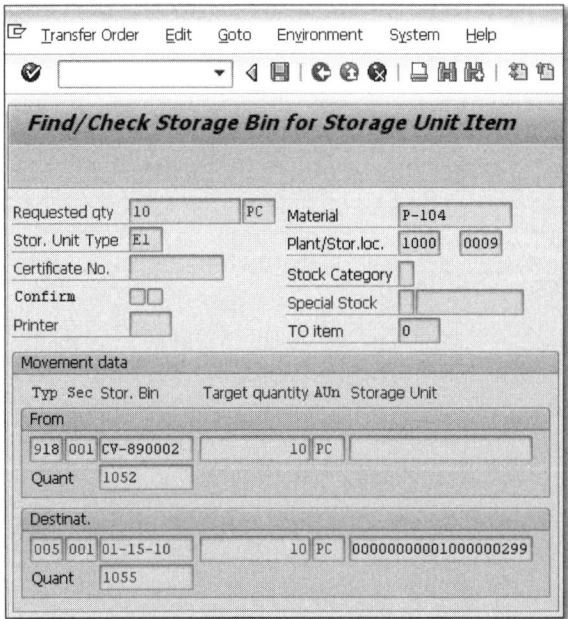

Figure 11.11 Completing the Transfer Order: Transaction LT0A

11.3.2 Receiving Planned Storage Units

Once the planned storage unit has been assigned, the transfer order remains unconfirmed until the material arrives. When the material arrives and is checked, it can be moved into stock using Transaction LT09, which you can find by following the menu path SAP • Logistics • Logistics Execution • Internal Whse Processes • Stock Transfer • Create Transfer Order • Move Storage Unit.

Figure 11.12 shows the storage unit that was created in Figure 11.11, entered along with the movement type. The transfer order is for the planned storage unit and the material arriving at the receiving dock.

The transfer order can be confirmed internally, or—if there is a difference in the actual amounts—a change can be made, identifying the difference.

11.3 Planning Storage Units

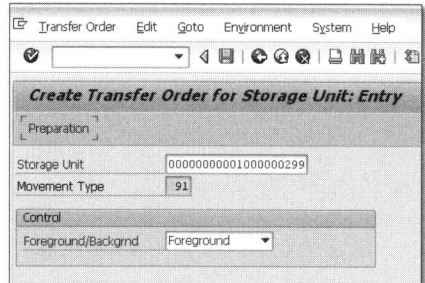

Figure 11.12 Placing Material into Stock from a Planned Storage Unit

11.3.3 Recording Differences in Planned Storage Units

In Figure 11.11 there was no difference between the actual amount received and the amount planned. If there was a difference, then that difference could have been recorded in Transaction LT09.

After entering the storage unit and movement type, you can select the transfer for confirmation, as shown in Figure 11.12. Instead of confirming internally, you can use a worklist to record the material differences.

Figure 11.13 shows a quantity variance in the incoming material. The transfer order was created with a quantity of ten, and the quantity that arrived at the receiving dock was a quantity of eleven. The material quantity variance is entered, and the transfer order is confirmed.

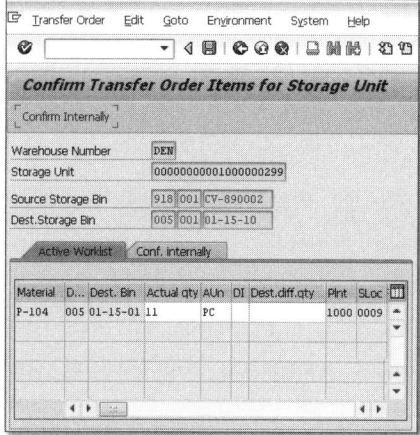

Figure 11.13 Confirming a Transfer Order with a Quantity Variance

From the planning of storage units, we'll now move on to discuss the documents related to storage units.

11.4　Storage Unit Documentation

You can print the following four documents to aid the storage unit process:

- Transfer order document
- Storage unit contents document
- Storage unit document
- Storage unit—transfer order document

We'll describe these documents more fully in the subsections that follow.

11.4.1　Transfer Order Document

The transfer order document is simply the transfer order that can be printed with or without storage unit management. The transfer order printout shows the detailed information about the movement of a single item in a storage unit. A separate transfer order document is printed for each item on the transfer order. The format of the document can be determined by the warehouse staff and can be modified by ABAP code. The document can display any information from the transfer order and can be configured to print bar codes so that data can be entered using a radio frequency (RF) scanning device.

The transfer order document can be printed manually via Transaction LT32 by following the menu path SAP • LOGISTICS • LOGISTICS EXECUTION • INBOUND PROCESSES • GOODS RECEIPT FOR PURCHASE ORDER, ORDER, OTHER TRANSACTIONS • PRINT AND COMMUNICATION • TRANSFER ORDER FOR STORAGE UNIT.

Figure 11.14 shows the selection screen that prints several documents relating to a storage unit. Enter the storage unit, and select printing of just the transfer order or of the other three storage unit documents. You can enter the print code, printer, and spool control data if the system is configured for this.

Figure 11.15 shows the transfer order printout for storage unit 1000001581. The transfer order and the transfer order item number are printed as bar codes for scanning by an RF device.

Storage Unit Documentation | 11.4

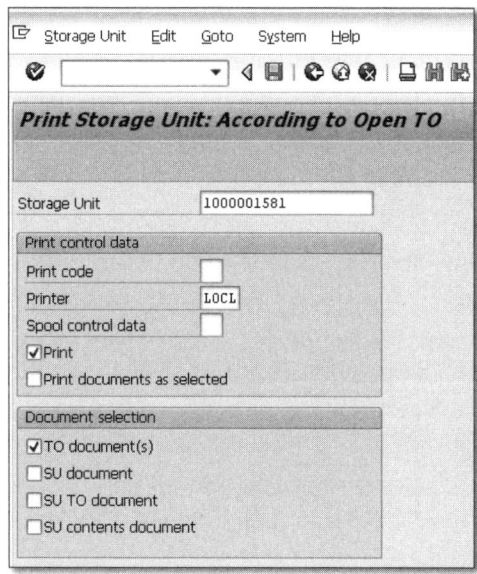

Figure 11.14 Print Transfer Order for Storage Unit Entered: Transaction LT32

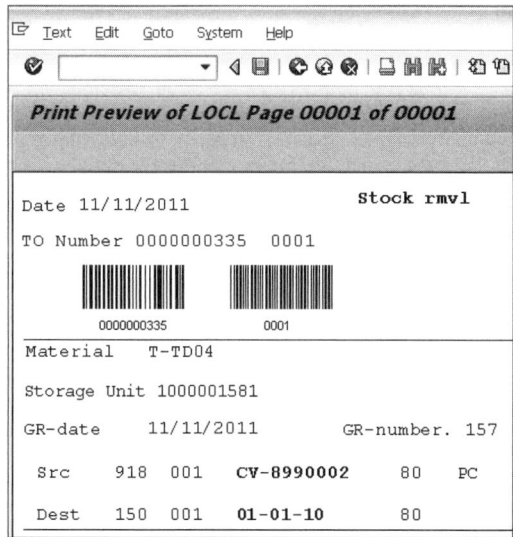

Figure 11.15 Printout of Transfer Order from Transaction LT32

11.4.2 Storage Unit Contents Document

The storage unit contents document displays a list of the contents and quantities of all the materials in a storage unit. The storage unit number is usually printed in both numerical and bar code formats. You can select this document by choosing the SU CONTENTS DOCUMENT checkbox in Figure 11.14.

The print preview screen shown in Figure 11.16 displays the contents of the storage unit. Two materials combine to make up the storage unit. In this example, the storage unit number has been bar-coded for easy scanning on the warehouse floor. This can be printed and kept with the storage unit as it is moved in the warehouse. This gives warehouse staff an easy way of identifying what is in the storage unit without examining the actual material.

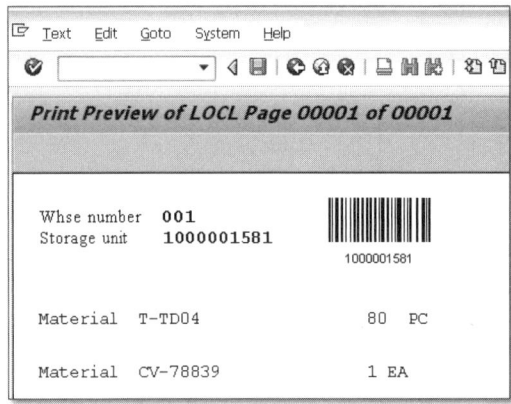

Figure 11.16 Storage Unit Contents Document

11.4.3 Storage Unit Document

The storage unit document displays multiple prints of storage unit numbers in numerical and bar code formats. This document is often printed on paper that can be used for labels.

To print this document, select the checkbox for SU DOCUMENT in Transaction LT32 as shown in Figure 11.14.

Figure 11.17 shows the storage unit number and bar code printed for administration.

Storage Unit Documentation | 11.4

Figure 11.17 Sample Storage Unit Document

11.4.4 Storage Unit Transfer Order Document

The storage unit transfer order document describes the movement of the storage unit. It resembles the printout of the transfer order but can be modified by ABAP code if your organization needs details added or additional bar codes printed because many RF devices are used on the warehouse floor.

To print this document, select the checkbox SU TO DOCUMENT, in Transaction LT32 as shown in Figure 11.14. Figure 11.18 shows the details of the storage unit and the movement of the storage unit in the warehouse.

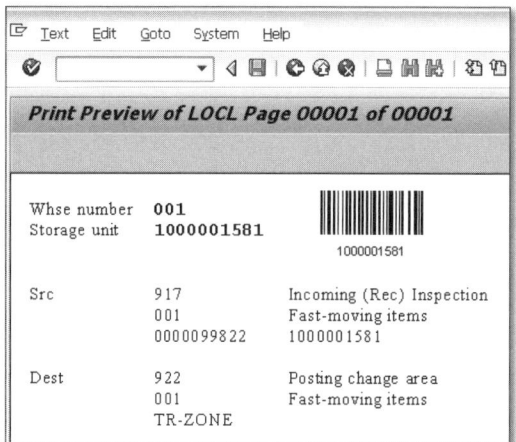

Figure 11.18 Storage Unit Transfer Order Document

Now that we have discussed the storage unit documents, the next topic is the role of storage unit management in stock putaway.

11.5 Putaway with Storage Unit Management

Storage units are often created when material arrives at the receiving dock and needs to be placed into storage using a container. Storage units can be created with one material or with many different materials combined. It is also possible to move material from the receiving dock into a storage unit that already exists in the warehouse.

11.5.1 Creating a Storage Unit

In this chapter, we have already seen how to create a storage unit using a transfer order, as shown in Figures 11.5, 11.6, and 11.7. We'll now describe three methods of material putaway in the warehouse:

- Storage unit—single material
- Storage unit—multiple materials
- Storage unit—add to existing stock

These are described more fully in the subsections that follow. Let's first examine a situation where the storage unit is created for one material that will not be stored with other material.

11.5.2 Storage Unit—Single Material

You can create the storage unit for a single material with Transaction LT01, which you can find by following the menu path SAP • LOGISTICS • LOGISTICS EXECUTION • INTERNAL WHSE PROCESSES • STOCK TRANSFER • CREATE TRANSFER ORDER • NO SOURCE OBJECT.

Figure 11.19 shows the initial screen in Transaction LT01, where the transfer order is created with no reference. The movement type used in this Transaction is 501: goods receipt without a purchase order. The material is entered along with the warehouse number, quantity of material, plant, storage location, and storage unit type. Click the PREPARATION button to process the transfer order.

11.5 Putaway with Storage Unit Management

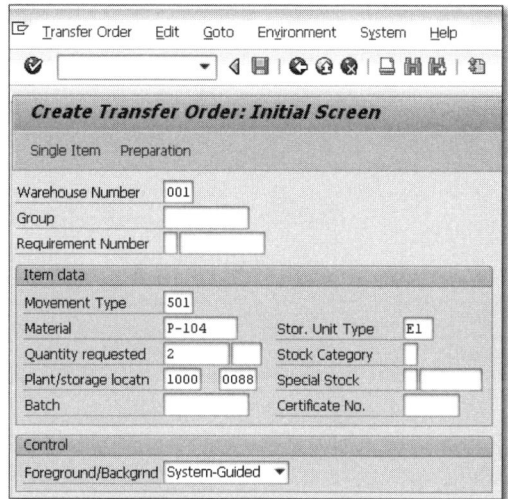

Figure 11.19 Initial Screen to Create a Storage Unit with One Material

Figure 11.20 shows the material and the source storage bin where the material is located now. You can add the destination storage bin and then create the transfer order in the background by pressing the [F6] function key.

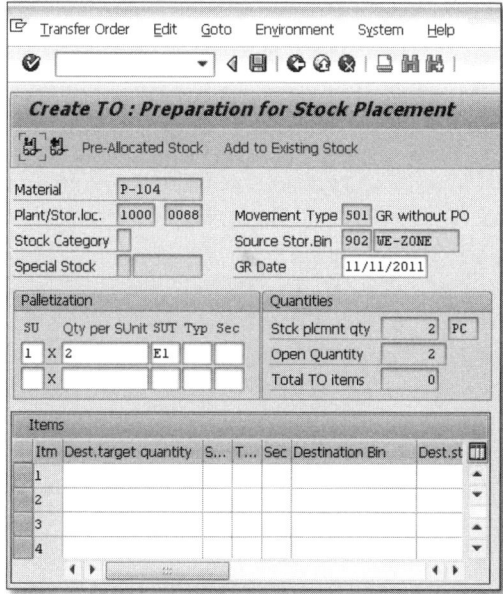

Figure 11.20 Preparation for Stock Placement Screen

11.5.3 Storage Unit—Multiple Materials

You can create a storage unit that contains multiple materials with Transaction LT07, which you can find by following the menu path SAP • LOGISTICS • LOGISTICS EXECUTION • INTERNAL WHSE PROCESSES • STOCK TRANSFER • CREATE TRANSFER ORDER • CREATE STORAGE UNIT.

Figure 11.21 shows the initial screen for Transaction LT07. Enter the warehouse number, movement type, plant, and storage location. Click the PREPARATION button to process the transfer order.

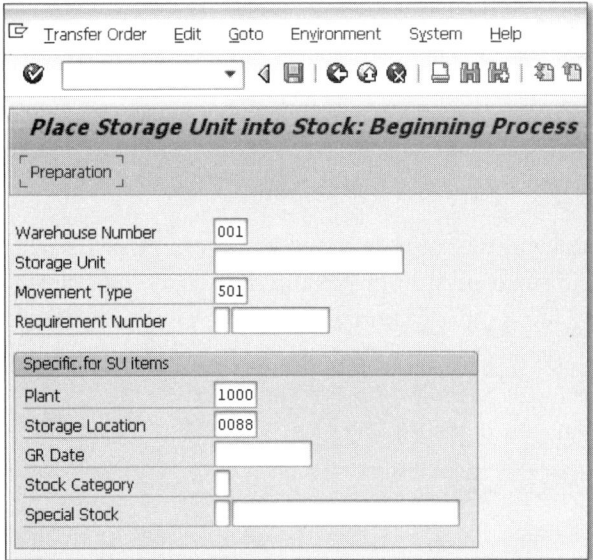

Figure 11.21 Initial Screen for Creating a Storage Unit with Multiple Materials

Figure 11.22 allows the entry of the materials that will be associated with the one storage unit. You can add several materials and their quantity to the storage unit. Once you have added all the materials, click the CREATE TRANS. ORDER button to create the storage unit and the transfer order.

Putaway with Storage Unit Management | 11.5

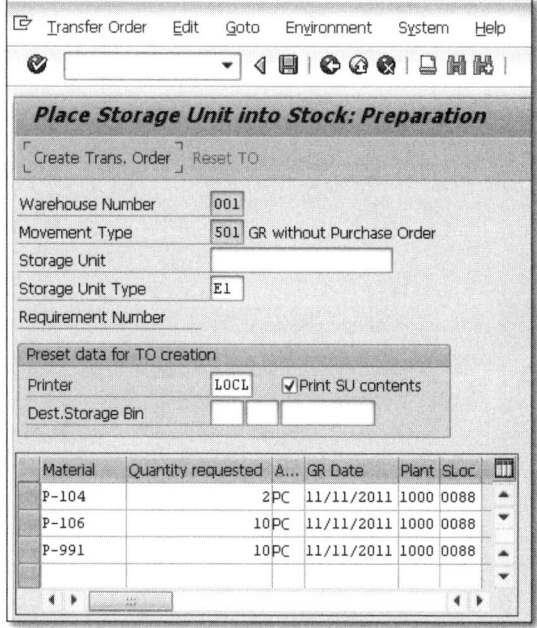

Figure 11.22 Entering Multiple Materials When Creating a Storage Unit

11.5.4 Storage Unit—Add to Existing Stock

To create a storage unit that contains multiple materials, you can use Transaction LT08 by following the menu path SAP • LOGISTICS • LOGISTICS EXECUTION • INTERNAL WHSE PROCESSES • STOCK TRANSFER • CREATE TRANSFER ORDER • EXPAND STORAGE UNIT.

Figure 11.23 shows the initial screen for adding material to an existing storage unit that already contains stock. This is needed when material arrives in the receiving area later than it should have and the storage unit it was to be in has already been created using other materials that were scheduled to be part of that storage unit.

Completing the initial screen of Transaction LT08 requires that the storage unit be entered along with the movement type and plant number. Once the data is entered, click the PREPARATION button to process the transfer order.

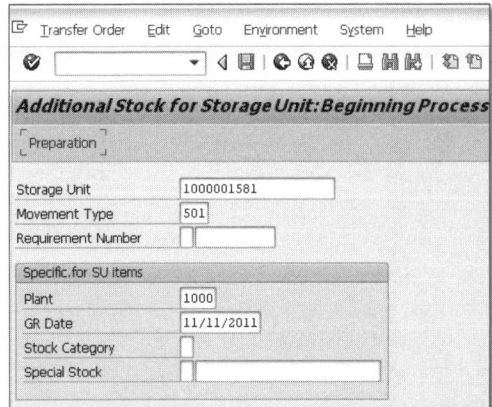

Figure 11.23 Initial Screen for Adding Stock to an Existing Storage Unit

Figure 11.24 shows the entry of the material and the quantity to be added to storage unit 1000001581. After the materials have been added to this screen, click the CREATE TRANS. ORDER button to add the materials to the storage unit via creation of the transfer order.

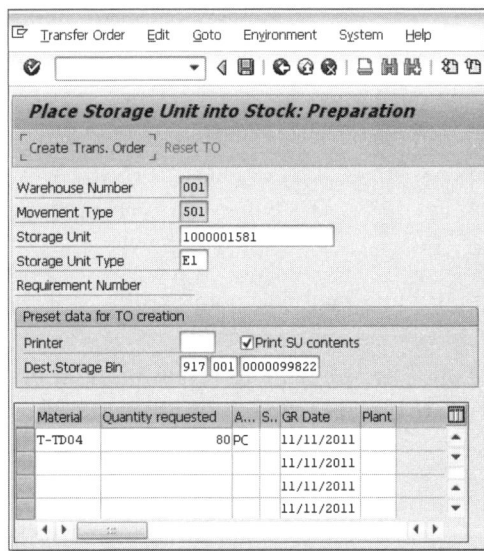

Figure 11.24 Entering Material to Add to an Existing Storage Unit

Now that we know how storage unit management is used with stock putaway, we'll examine how it integrates with stock picking.

11.6 Picking with Storage Unit Management

Material to be removed from the warehouse can be picked from storage units. The material can be removed in such a way that the whole storage unit is consumed by the pick or so that a partial pick is made from the storage type. For example, if a customer order requires a quantity of 40 and the storage unit is a full pallet with a quantity of 160, the pick from this storage unit will be a partial pick.

11.6.1 Complete Stock Pick

The entire storage unit can be picked for a goods issue even if the requirement is for less than the quantity in the storage unit. To do this, you must set the configuration at the storage type level. You can find this by following the menu path IMG • LOGISTICS EXECUTION • WAREHOUSE MANAGEMENT • MASTER DATA • DEFINE STORAGE TYPE.

Figure 11.25 shows the configuration for a storage type that allows an entire storage unit to be picked even when the requirement is only for a partial amount. Select the FULL STK RMVL REQMT ACT checkbox to force the whole storage unit to be removed.

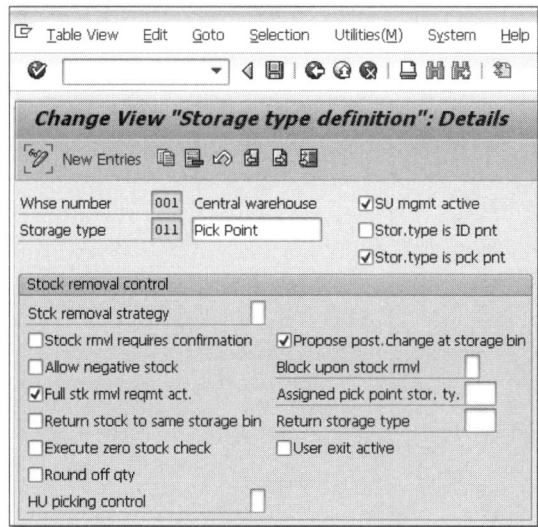

Figure 11.25 Configuration for a Storage Type to Allow Full Stock Removal

11.6.2 Partial Stock Pick

If the FULL STK RMVL REQMT ACT checkbox is not selected in the storage type configuration to force a full stock removal, as it is in Figure 11.25, it is possible to perform a partial pick from a storage unit. This would allow the partial pick for a customer order of 40 units of material from a storage unit with a full 160 units on the pallet.

11.6.3 Complete Stock Pick with Return to Same Bin

A partial pick can be performed when the full stock removal checkbox is selected, but this requires that the RETURN STOCK TO SAME STORAGE BIN checkbox be selected in the configuration for the storage type. You can find this configuration step by following the menu path IMG • LOGISTICS EXECUTION • WAREHOUSE MANAGEMENT • MASTER DATA • DEFINE STORAGE TYPE.

Figure 11.26 shows the storage type configuration for storage type 001, where both the checkbox for full stock removal requirement and the checkbox for returning stock to the same storage bin are selected. This allows the full storage unit to be removed from stock for a pick, but if the goods issue does not require the full amount, the remaining stock will be returned to the same storage bin.

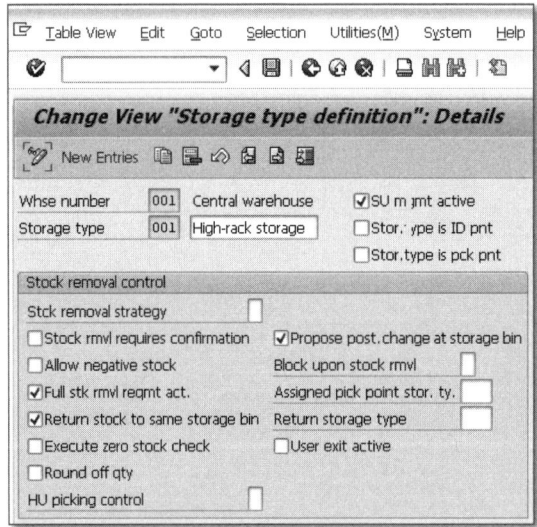

Figure 11.26 Configuration to Select the Checkbox for Returning Stock to the Same Storage Bin

11.6.4 Partial Stock Removal Using a Pick Point

A partial pick can be performed on a storage unit with the use of a pick point. A pick point is a location in the warehouse where materials are removed for a partial stock pick from a storage unit. The pick point is defined in storage type configuration, which you can find via the menu path IMG • LOGISTICS EXECUTION • WAREHOUSE MANAGEMENT • MASTER DATA • DEFINE STORAGE TYPE.

Figure 12.27 shows that the STOR. TYPE IS PCK PNT field is set for storage type 011. This allows partial removal of storage units using the functionality of the pick point.

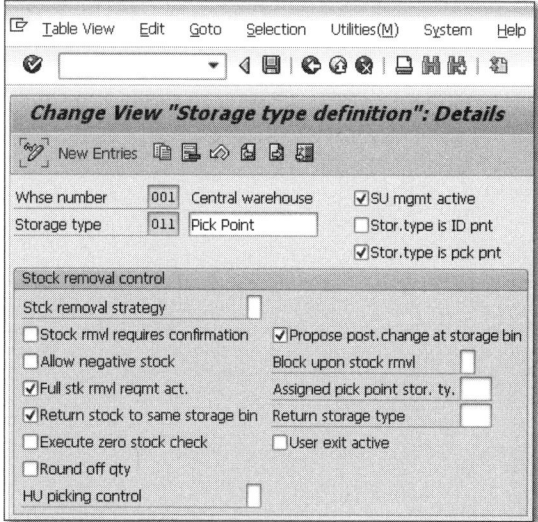

Figure 11.27 Configuration to Set the Storage Type as the Pick Point

When you remove storage units from a pick point, the storage unit information is not lost, as it would be if the material was removed to an interim goods issue and then a partial amount was returned to stock.

When a transfer order confirms a quantity of material to be moved from the pick point to the goods issue area for the outbound transfer order, the system posts the remaining material quantity from the storage unit to the pick point. The remaining material from the storage unit can be moved back to the original storage bin or to a new storage bin, depending on how the warehouse management uses storage unit functionality.

This concludes the examination of picking with storage unit management. Now let's look at some business examples.

11.7 Business Examples—Storage Unit Management

Storage unit management is the WM equivalent of handling unit management, the functionality found in SAP IM. Storage unit management was developed exclusively for WM, and from it SAP developed handling unit management for SAP Materials Management (MM).

11.7.1 Planning Storage Units

The storage unit can be planned before the material arrives in the warehouse. The warehouse staff can prepare the containers for the material so it can be scanned on the receiving dock and placed in the container with which it is combined to make up the storage unit.

Example

A California electronics component company implemented SAP WM when they merged with a competitor. The combined warehouse used small bins to store items, and this caused the issue of having dozens of bins all containing the same material. As the company grew, the use of the small bins became more problematic so they reconfigured their tracking system so that the size of the bin location was larger and was based on a standard-size tote. The warehouse was redesigned so that the items were stored in a larger container, or storage unit, than could be moved from the goods receiving dock to the warehouse and back to the shipping door.

The warehouse racking was divided into bin locations that would accept a single container. If the bin location was empty, then no container would be stored there.

To make sure material was stored efficiently in the warehouse, the warehouse manager reviewed the inbound deliveries. They then preplanned the containers so that each material received could be placed immediately in a container so it could be easily moved around the warehouse.

11.7.2 Putaway with Storage Units

Storage units can be created when material arrives at the receiving dock and is then placed into storage inside a container. Storage units can be created with one material or with many materials combined. It is also possible to move material from the receiving dock into a storage unit that already exists in the warehouse.

Example

A manufacturer of consumer hand tools had implemented an SAP system, including WM, when the company was purchased by a private investment firm. The company did not implement storage unit management, and the process for receiving goods into the warehouse involved the warehouse staff removing the raw materials from shipping pallets and placing the items into storage bins.

The receiving process would sometimes take considerable time, as the shipping pallet sometimes held several different items that needed to be removed and stored. This led to a bottleneck at the receiving dock while the pallets were unloaded. The company hired a consulting firm to review warehouse operations, and one of the recommendations was to stop unloading the mixed pallets but store the materials together in one storage bin. The company implemented storage unit management and allowed the contents of the incoming pallets to be stored together as quants in the same storage bin.

11.7.3 Picking with Storage Units

Material removed from the warehouse can be picked from storage units. The material can be removed in such a way that the whole storage unit is consumed by the pick or so that a partial pick is made from the storage type.

Example

A manufacturer of metal fasteners stored their finished goods in a warehouse that had implemented SAP WM. The finished goods warehouse layout was primarily a series of racking that contained pallets of the same item. The pallets were made up boxes of fasteners, and items were sold to customers by the box.

Because the boxes were stored on a storage unit, that is, a pallet, the warehouse operators would pull the pallet for the transfer order and deliver the pallet to the shipping dock. The shipping team would then remove the number of boxes required by the sales order. If there were boxes remaining on the pallet those boxes and the pallet were returned to the original storage bin.

11.8 Summary

The storage unit management functionality was designed for the warehouse and is a useful tool for materials that need to be moved around the warehouse in a container. It is simpler than handling unit management, a method used in SAP MM, because it does not require packing or unpacking. Once a storage unit is created in a transfer order, assignment of materials is all that is required. Storage units can contain one material or several materials.

Many warehouses use containers, pallets, and transportation materials to move material from one storage type to another. In many cases, warehouses do not frequently use storage unit management because they have been told it is too complicated or cumbersome for efficient warehouse operations. This is not the case, and it is the responsibility of the consultant or employee to discuss and propose this and other SAP WM functionalities that may improve warehouse efficiency.

In Chapter 12, we will discuss the functionality available to the warehouse manager to manage hazardous materials in the warehouse.

Hazardous materials are used in many production processes and have to be stored in the warehouse. Many regulations govern the storage and transportation of these materials. The hazardous materials functionality in SAP WM provides a structure for correctly managing this process.

12   Hazardous Materials Management

Hazardous materials are often found in warehouses. These materials are either raw materials or finished goods, depending on the nature of the company's products. A hazardous material is one that can produce harmful immediate physical effects such as a fire, sudden release of pressure and explosion, acute health problems such as burns and convulsions, and chronic illness such as organ damage and cancer.

Having hazardous materials in a warehouse is a great responsibility for warehouse owners. They operate, in the United States, within limits set by federal, state, and local agencies that regulate hazardous materials to protect human health and the environment.

These agencies have regulations that pertain to the handling, storage, and distribution of hazardous materials. In the United States, these include the federal Clean Air Act, Clean Water Act, Comprehensive Environmental Response, Compensation, and Liability Act (CERCLA, also known as the Superfund), Resource Conservation and Recovery Act (RCRA), Safe Drinking Water Act (SDWA), Hazardous Materials Transportation Act (HMTA), Toxic Substances Control Act (TSCA), and many others.

Apart from the federal laws in the United States, states have their own strict regulations that must be observed. Some of the state laws are the California Safe Drinking Water & Toxic Enforcement Act, Connecticut Manufacturing Employer Hazardous Materials Notification Act, and Louisiana Hazardous Materials Information, Development, Preparedness, and Response Act.

In other countries, organizations exist to work in the same manner as the federal Environmental Protection Agency (EPA) in the United States. These include the Canadian Environmental Assessment Agency (CEAA), the Department of the Environment and Water Resources in Australia, and the Department for Environment, Food, and Rural Affairs (DEFRA) in the UK.

12.1 Introduction to Hazardous Materials

To safely and properly handle and store hazardous materials, it is important to know the hazards of those materials. Many companies, laboratories, and educational establishments have hazard communication programs that help their personnel working with hazardous materials be aware of the materials stored in the facility.

12.1.1 Classification of Hazardous Materials

Any number of hazardous materials may be stored in a warehouse. They are generally be assigned to one or more of the following classifications:

- **Flammable liquid**
  This includes any liquid with a flash point below 100° Fahrenheit, such as gasoline or paint lacquers.
- **Combustible liquid**
  This includes any liquid with a flash point between 100 and 200° Fahrenheit that produces enough vapor to ignite if exposed to an ignition source. Examples are diesel fuel and home heating oil.
- **Flammable solid**
  This is any substance that can cause a fire through friction, absorption of moisture, or spontaneous chemical changes and that, when ignited, will burn so vigorously that it creates a hazard. Flour and white phosphorous, for example, are both flammable materials.
- **Oxidizer**
  This is a substance that readily yields oxygen to stimulate the combustion of organic matter. Common household bleach is an example of an oxidizer.
- **Corrosive**
  This is any liquid that corrodes steel (SAE 1020) at a rate greater than 0.250

inches at a test temperature of 130° Fahrenheit or has a pH of less than 2 or greater than 12.5. Common acids, including hydrochloric acid, sulfuric acid, and nitric acid, are all corrosive materials.

- **Organic peroxide**
  This is an organic compound containing the chemical bond of oxygen joined to oxygen. Organic peroxides are used in many industries. For example, benzoyl peroxide is an organic peroxide that is used in acne medication.

- **Poison**
  This is a substance so toxic that it presents a risk to life or health. Examples are potassium cyanide and mercuric chloride.

- **Compressed gas**
  This is a substance in gas or liquid form contained in a vessel under pressure. This includes cylinders, lecture bottles, and aerosol cans. These substances may be flammable, nonflammable, or poisonous. Examples include propane and hydrogen.

- **Cryogenics**
  This includes substances that are extremely cold, such as liquid nitrogen, liquid helium, and dry ice. These substances may also become asphyxiation hazards if spilled in nonventilated areas.

- **Radioactive**
  This includes any material with a specific activity greater than 0.002 micro curies per gram (uCi/g), such as uranium and plutonium.

- **Biomedical**
  This includes tissues, organs, and blood from humans and primates.

12.1.2 Master Data Configuration for Hazardous Materials

If a warehouse contains hazardous material, then certain master data configuration steps must be made to define the sections, warnings, and hazardous material management strategy.

Fire-Containment Sections

Fire-containment sections must be configured if there are areas in the warehouse with different fire-containment properties. For example, some areas in the warehouse that may contain hazardous material may have two-hour minimum fire

12 | Hazardous Materials Management

resistance, whereas other areas may have four-hour minimum resistance. Once configured, these sections can be assigned to storage bins.

To find this configuration, follow the menu path IMG • LOGISTICS EXECUTION • WAREHOUSE MANAGEMENT • HAZARDOUS MATERIALS • MASTER DATA • DEFINE FIRE-CONTAINMENT SECTIONS.

Figure 12.1 shows the configuration for the fire-containment sections that can be set up for each warehouse. In this example, the sections are identified by their fire resistance. Some warehouses may have a series of fire-containment storage cabinets or areas that can be identified as configurable sections.

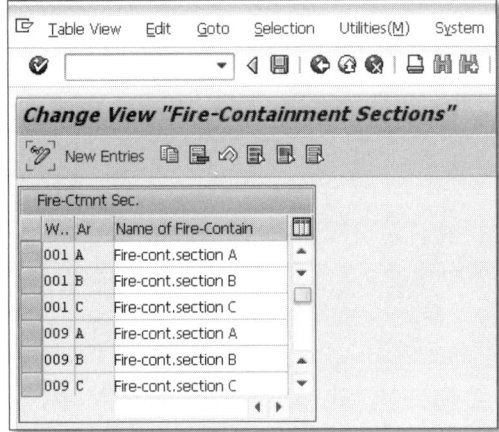

Figure 12.1 Configuration for Fire-Containment Sections for Each Warehouse

Hazardous Material Warnings

You can configure warnings to be used with hazardous materials. The configuration allows the creation and assignment of many material warnings when dealing with hazardous materials.

For this configuration, follow the menu path IMG • LOGISTICS EXECUTION • WAREHOUSE MANAGEMENT • HAZARDOUS MATERIALS • MASTER DATA • DEFINE HAZARDOUS MATERIAL WARNING. These hazardous material warnings, as shown in Figure 12.2, can be configured for the whole system. The warnings may be different for different warehouses that may be situated in different countries. The environmental agency for the country where each warehouse is situated may be able to advise you on hazardous material warnings.

Introduction to Hazardous Materials | 12.1

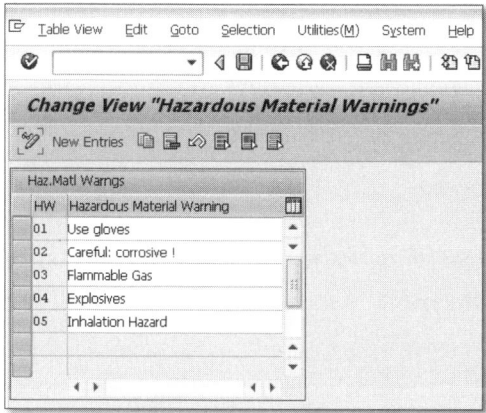

Figure 12.2 Configuration for Hazardous Material Warnings

Hazardous Material Storage Warnings

Certain warnings are required when hazardous materials are being transported or when they are placed in storage. Configuring this in the system allows the assignment of many storage warnings when dealing with hazardous materials.

To find this configuration, follow the menu path IMG • LOGISTICS EXECUTION • WAREHOUSE MANAGEMENT • HAZARDOUS MATERIALS • MASTER DATA • DEFINE HAZARDOUS MATERIAL STORAGE WARNING.

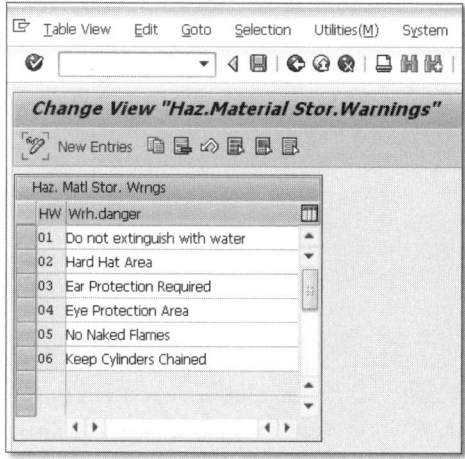

Figure 12.3 Configuration for Hazardous Material Storage Warnings

417

12 | Hazardous Materials Management

Figure 12.3 shows the configured hazardous material storage warnings. These are not specific to a particular warehouse, so each warehouse management team has to ensure that the storage warnings can be adopted for their warehouse, or further configuration will be required.

Aggregate States

You configure the aggregate state by following the menu path IMG • LOGISTICS EXECUTION • WAREHOUSE MANAGEMENT • HAZARDOUS MATERIALS • MASTER DATA • DEFINE AGGREGATE STATES.

The aggregate state is given a material in its normal conditions, that is, a temperature of 20°C and a pressure of 1 atmosphere. The aggregate state of the material is solid, liquid, or gas. Radioactive elements can be denoted as a different aggregate state, but all radioactive materials are solid. Because there can be a maximum of only four aggregate states, as shown in Figure 12.4, no further configuration is required.

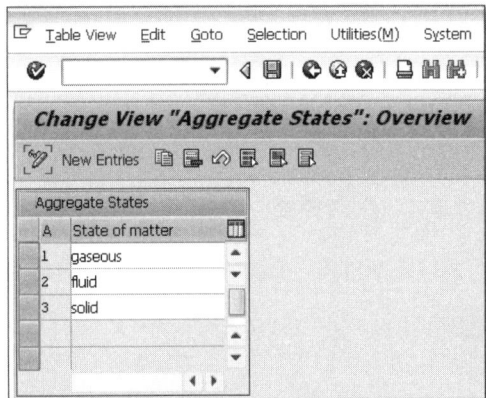

Figure 12.4 Configuration of Aggregate States for Hazardous Materials

Region Codes

Because a company's warehouses can be in different countries, it is possible to configure different regions for hazardous material management. You can configure the region codes via the menu path IMG • LOGISTICS EXECUTION • WAREHOUSE MANAGEMENT • HAZARDOUS MATERIALS • MASTER DATA • DEFINE REGION CODES.

Figure 12.5 shows a number of region codes that have been configured for hazardous materials. These region codes are not the same as SAP country codes; the region codes can incorporate different countries, such as European Community (EC) countries or former Soviet republics. You could configure a region code that incorporates more than one country; for example, a region code may include the countries of Belgium, The Netherlands, and Luxemburg.

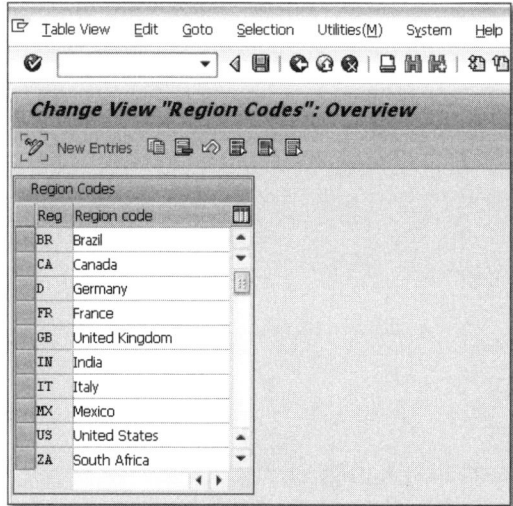

Figure 12.5 Configuration of Region Codes for Hazardous Materials Management

Storage Classes

You can configure storage classes to classify hazardous materials based on their features. A storage class can be used by stock putaway strategies. The definition of the storage classes used in SAP is based on the guidelines issued by the U.S. Department of Transportation, which administers the HMTA.

You can configure storage classes by following the menu path IMG • LOGISTICS EXECUTION • WAREHOUSE MANAGEMENT • HAZARDOUS MATERIALS • MASTER DATA • DEFINE STORAGE CLASSES.

Figure 12.6 shows the defined storage classes as defined by the U.S. Department of Transportation. If there are more appropriate storage classes for the company's warehouse, they can be configured here.

12 Hazardous Materials Management

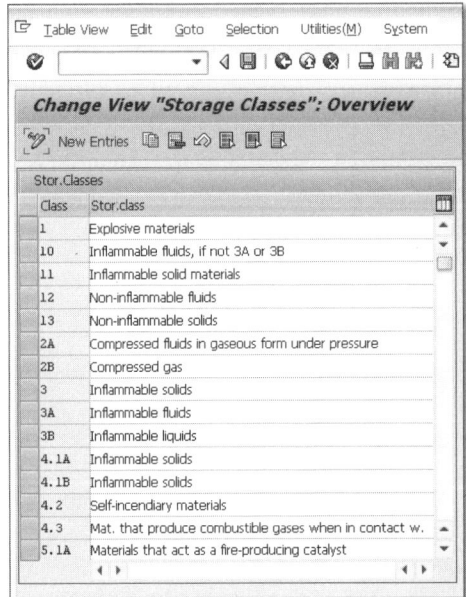

Figure 12.6 Configuration of Storage Classes for Hazardous Material Management

12.1.3 Configuring Hazardous Material Management

This next phase of configuration is for activating the hazardous material management. You can find this configuration by using Transaction OMM2 or via the menu path IMG • LOGISTICS EXECUTION • WAREHOUSE MANAGEMENT • HAZARDOUS MATERIALS • STRATEGIES • ACTIVATE HAZARDOUS MATERIAL MANAGEMENT.

Figure 12.7 shows the configuration required for hazardous material management. The first configuration step is to activate the hazardous material check.

Activating the Hazardous Material Check

This configuration step activates the section check, the hazardous material management, and the water-pollution class for a designated storage type in a warehouse.

In Figure 12.8, the configuration has been set for storage type 006 in warehouse 001. Storage type 006 has the section check activated. The X in the field shows that the storage section is determined and a check was made. Entering Y means a storage section determination is made, but no check.

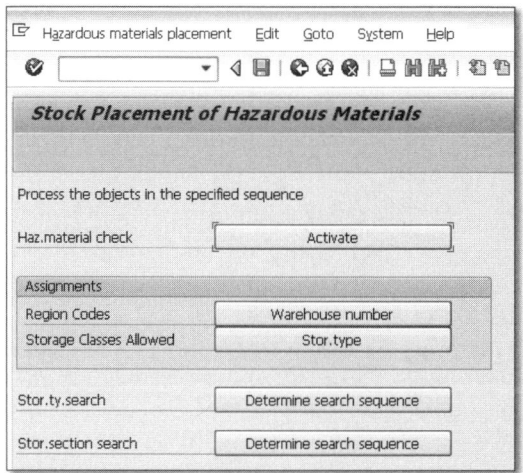

Figure 12.7 Configuration for Hazardous Material Management

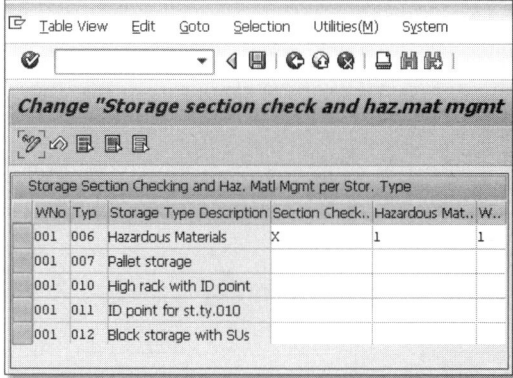

Figure 12.8 Activate Storage Section Checking and Hazardous Material Management

The hazardous material management field has been configured with the value 1. This means the hazardous material check is made at the storage-type level only. Entering "2" in this field requires a check at the storage-type and the storage section level.

The water pollution class (WPC) classifies a material in terms of its capability of polluting water. The values are defined as:

- 0

  Not a water pollutant

- 1

  Minimal water pollutant

- 2

  Water pollutant

- 3

  Extreme water pollutant

Entering "1" in the WPC field allows materials with WPCs of 0 and 1 to be stored in the storage type.

Assigning a Region Code

Once the region codes have been configured, as shown in Figure 12.5, they can be assigned to the active warehouses.

Figure 12.9 shows the assignment of the configured region codes to the active warehouses.

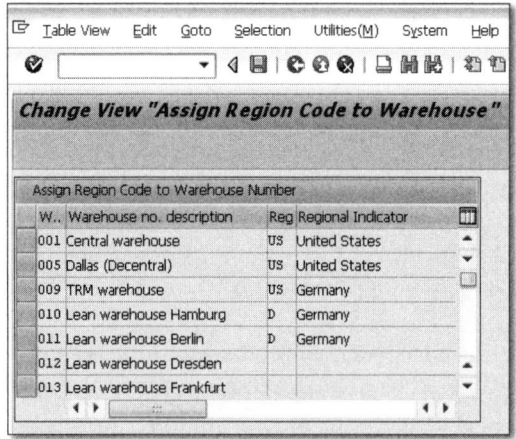

Figure 12.9 Assignment of Region Code to a Warehouse

Storage Classes per Storage Type

In this configuration step, you can assign all the storage classes, defined as shown in Figure 12.6, to a certain storage type in the warehouse. For example, some storage types are suitable for containing compressed gas but not organic peroxides. This depends on the physical attributes of the storage type and whether those attributes are suitable to store materials of specific storage classes.

Figure 12.10 shows the assignment of storage class 5.2, organic peroxides, to storage type 006 in warehouse 001. This means storage type 006 allows the storage of organic peroxides. The other fields in this configuration relate to the priority of the storage class in the storage type.

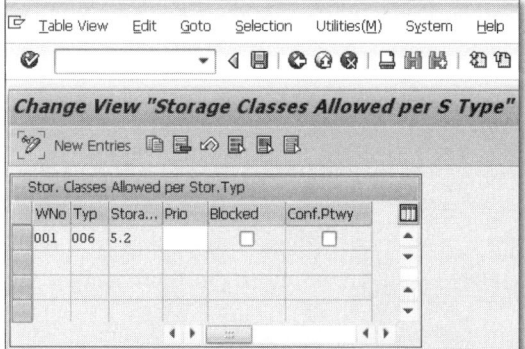

Figure 12.10 Assignment of Storage Classes to Storage Types

> **Example**
> A storage type may allow several storage classes to be stored in it, but the priority determines which storage class is given priority over the others.

The BLOCKED checkbox temporarily blocks the storage type for a particular storage class. This may occur if certain materials have been stored in the storage type, rendering it unavailable for hazardous materials of other storage classes.

Selecting the CONF.PTWY checkbox requires that any stock placement for this storage class be performed in the foreground, overriding any other requirement for that storage type.

Storage Type Search

This allows the additions to the storage type search to allow for any storage class configuration that has been made.

Figure 12.11 shows that a new storage type search has been added to include reference to a hazardous material storage class. The storage type search now includes a search where the storage class is 5.2. This search will try to find an empty storage bin in storage type 006 if the material has a storage class of 5.2.

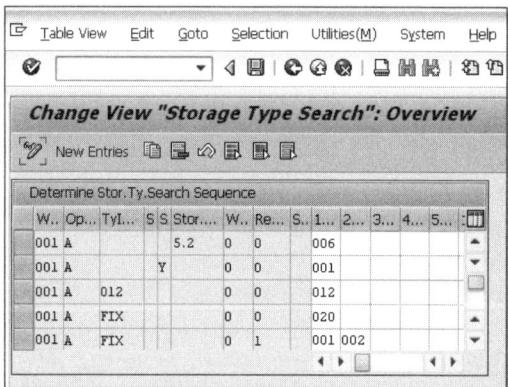

Figure 12.11 Additions to Storage Type Search Configuration

Storage Section Search

If the warehouse is using a storage section search as well as a storage type search, then you can configure the storage section search to include the storage class.

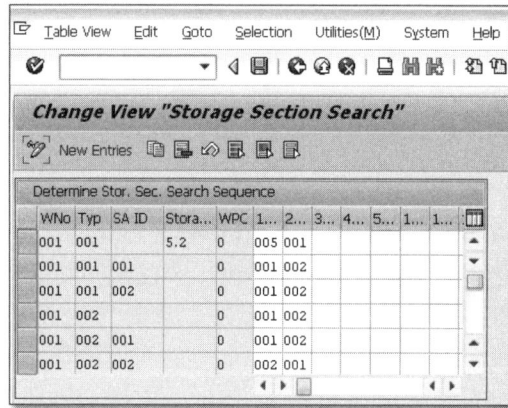

Figure 12.12 Storage Section Search Including the Storage Class

Figure 12.12 shows the configuration for warehouse 001 and storage type 006. The new configuration line shows that if the material has a storage class of 5.2, the system will search for an empty bin in storage section 005 first and then storage section 001.

Now that we have examined the basics of hazardous materials, we'll focus on the hazardous material record.

12.2 Hazardous Material Record

The warehouse needs to create hazardous material records for materials that require special handling or storage due to their hazardous nature. The hazardous material record contains many fields that describe the hazardous nature of a material, such as the water-pollution class if the material is a water pollutant. In addition, it contains the various hazardous material warnings that may have to be displayed if the material is transported and a breakdown of any other hazardous material that is a component of the transported material.

12.2.1 Creating a Hazardous Material Record

You can create a hazardous material record with Transaction VM01, which you can find by following the menu path SAP • LOGISTICS • LOGISTICS EXECUTION • MASTER DATA • MATERIAL • HAZARDOUS MATERIAL • CREATE.

Figure 12.13 shows the data entered for the hazardous material record. SAP does not assign the hazardous material number, so you must decide on an external number.

The general data lets you include more detailed information for the material, including the storage class, water pollution class, aggregate state, and flash point. Also, you can describe the material in terms of its components, which themselves can be hazardous. The percentages can be given for each of the components.

Once you save the hazardous material record, you can assign it to a material master record.

12   Hazardous Materials Management

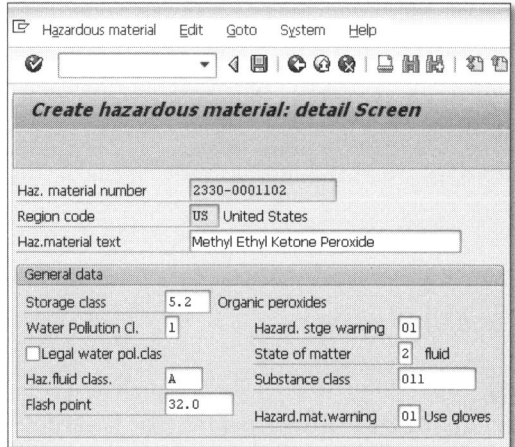

Figure 12.13 Entry of Hazardous Material Record

12.2.2   Assigning the Hazardous Material to a Material Master Record

You can assign the hazardous material record to an existing material master record. Because the hazardous material information is held within SAP WM, the hazardous material number is assigned to the material master record in the WM screen of the material master.

Figure 12.14 Hazardous Material Assigned to a Material Master Record

Figure 12.14 shows the WM screen for material 1829. The material is a 55-gallon drum of methyl ethyl ketone peroxide, which is hazardous material number 2330 – 0001102, as shown in Figure 12.13. The hazardous material number is assigned to the material master record. Therefore, any warehouse movements of the material will show that it is a hazardous material and special circumstances may apply.

12.3 Hazardous Material Functionality

To ensure that a hazardous material is tracked, the warehouse staff can use several reports. For emergencies, there are reports for the fire service or hazmat teams, detailing where the hazardous materials are.

12.3.1 List of Hazardous Materials

The list of hazardous materials can be selected by region, and it shows all of the hazardous materials with records on the system. This does not imply that all the materials are stored in any particular warehouse, but it does show all hazardous materials that potentially could be in stock within the region.

The transaction for this is LX24, which you can find by following the menu path SAP • LOGISTICS • LOGISTICS EXECUTION • INFORMATION SYSTEM • WAREHOUSE • STOCK • HAZARDOUS MATERIAL • LIST.

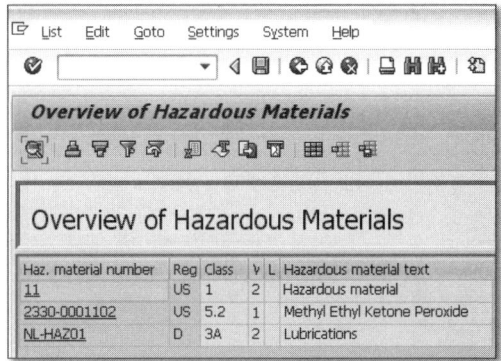

Figure 12.15 List of Hazardous Materials for a Specific Region

Figure 12.15 shows a list of all the hazardous materials that have been entered for the region of the United States. The list should be reviewed periodically, as local laws and regulations can and do change. The warehouse management and the environmental health and safety manager for the plant should carry out the review.

12.3.2 Fire Department Inventory List

Periodically, the warehouse facility may be inspected by regulatory authorities or by the local fire department. At any of these inspections, the reports identifying the hazardous material stored within the warehouse may be required. The fire department inventory list is a report on the quantity of material in each fire containment area, by storage class. The fire department can review the potential hazards and offer advice about storage changes.

You can use Transaction LX06 to produce the fire department inventory list, or follow the menu path SAP • LOGISTICS • LOGISTICS EXECUTION • INFORMATION SYSTEM • WAREHOUSE • STOCK • HAZARDOUS MATERIAL • FIRE DEPARTMENT INVENTORY LIST.

The fire department inventory list, shown in Figure 12.16, identifies each fire containment area and the hazardous storage classes currently stored inside. The weight and quantity of the material shows the fire department the level of potential hazard within each containment area. If the fire department decides that there is too much stock of a certain hazardous storage class in a containment area, the warehouse would have to move some quants to other suitable storage bins.

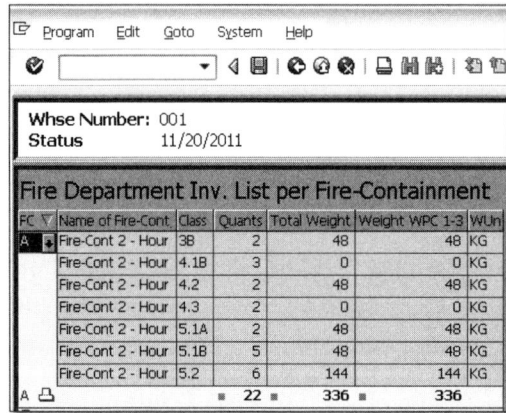

Figure 12.16 Display of Fire Department Inventory List

12.3.3 Check Goods Storage

The check-goods storage report is used to ensure that all hazardous material has been stored correctly. The report reviews all of the quants of material to see where they are stored and checks against the configuration entered for hazardous materials. It checks that:

- Hazardous materials are not stored in storage types managed specifically for nonhazardous materials
- Material are stored in the correct storage type based on water-pollution class
- Materials are stored in the correct storage type based on storage class

If any of these checks produce an error, the report produces an error log showing how many errors have occurred for each storage type. Figure 12.17 shows an example.

You can product the check-goods storage list can be produced using Transaction LX07 or via the menu path SAP • LOGISTICS • LOGISTICS EXECUTION • INFORMATION SYSTEM • WAREHOUSE • STOCK • HAZARDOUS MATERIAL • CHECK GOODS STORAGE.

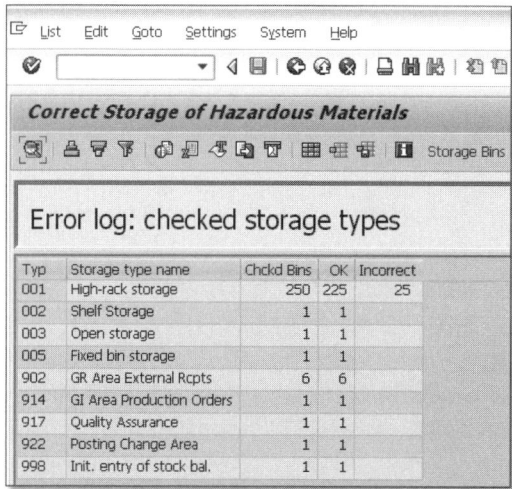

Figure 12.17 Error Log Produced by the Check Goods Storage Report

Figure 12.17 shows that for storage type 001 there are 25 instances where hazardous material is incorrectly stored. More detailed information is required to find out why each quant has been stored incorrectly. You can display the information at the storage-bin level for each storage type by highlighting the storage type and pressing ⌈Shift⌉+⌈F4⌉ or clicking the STORAGE BINS button on the application toolbar.

Figure 12.18 shows the error log at the storage-bin level. The incorrect storage column indicates the error code. The codes are as follows:

▶ 0

Hazardous material in a storage type not managed for hazardous materials

▶ 1

Water pollution class not maintained for storage type

▶ 2

Storage class not maintained for storage type

▶ 3

Hazardous material not maintained for storage section

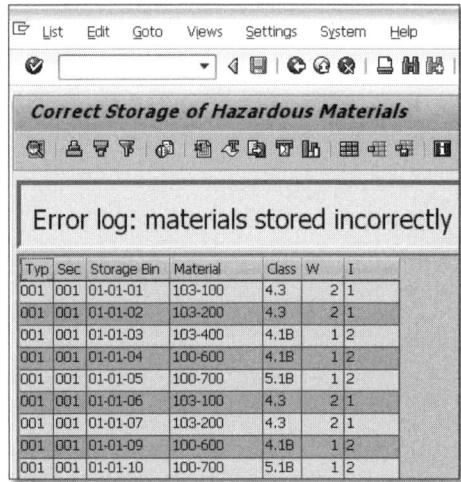

Figure 12.18 Error Log at the Storage Bin Level

The report should be used to ensure that hazardous materials are correctly stored in the warehouse. If materials are not stored correctly, they should be moved to a correct location to ensure warehouse safety.

12.3.4 Hazardous Substance List

The hazardous substance list produces a report of all the hazardous material that is stored in a particular warehouse or storage type or fire-containment area.

You can produce the hazardous substance list using Transaction LX08 or by following the menu path SAP • LOGISTICS • LOGISTICS EXECUTION • INFORMATION SYSTEM • WAREHOUSE • STOCK • HAZARDOUS MATERIAL • HAZARDOUS SUBSTANCE LIST.

Figure 12.19 shows the hazardous material stored in the warehouse. The report shows the fire-containment area where the material is stored, as well as the hazardous storage class and water pollution class.

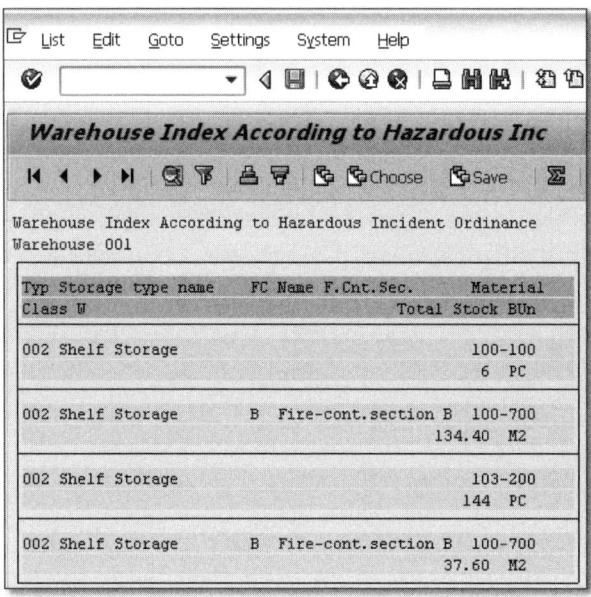

Figure 12.19 Hazardous Substance List: Transaction LX08

12.4 Business Examples—Hazardous Materials Management

In warehouses there is a possibility that some of the materials stored are hazardous in nature. It is important to safely and properly handle hazardous materials as they are received, stored, and shipped from the warehouse. Your company or client may have hazard communication programs that help their personnel working with hazardous materials to be aware of the materials stored in the facility.

12.4.1 Storing Hazardous Material

Material that has been identified as hazardous is required to be identified as such and stored in the designated area. A hazardous material is an item that is capable of producing harmful physical or health effects. Some materials need to be stored in areas with materials that have the same hazard, for example, storing flammable materials with other flammable materials.

Example

Many warehouses contain hazardous materials that are used in the manufacture of finished goods or for cleaning equipment on the production line. A manufacturer of consumer hand tools did not use any hazardous materials, as the operations that required the use of hazardous materials were performed by subcontractors.

After a subcontractor declared bankruptcy, the company brought the painting operation for some of their products back in-house. This meant the company needed to purchase and store a selection of paints, paint additives, and lacquers. Some of these items were classified as hazardous, and the company realized they should be stored separately from other materials. The material safety data sheet (MSDS) contained the information that the company needed to help it store the material in the warehouse. Because some of the materials were flammable, the company had to store the material in the warehouse in a separate room that was fire resistant and had suitable ventilation.

12.4.2 Hazardous Material Functionality

To ensure that hazardous material is tracked, several reports are used in the warehouse. If there is an emergency in the warehouse or within the plant, the warehouse staff can print reports for the fire service or hazmat teams, detailing where the hazardous materials are stored.

Example

A Canadian electrical components company opened it first American manufacturing plant in Nevada. The company used several hazardous materials in the manufacturing process, and the materials were stored according to the information in the material safety data sheet (MSDS). They applied for a hazardous materials permit from the Nevada Department of Public Safety, they were informed that they needed to report details about hazardous materials if they stored, transported on-site, dispensed, or handled hazardous materials. The company was required to report extremely hazardous substances (EHSs), hazardous materials, gasoline, and diesel fuel.

The company had implemented an SAP system when the manufacturing facility was opened, and they were using the hazardous material functionality, which allowed reports to be generated. The state of Nevada allowed companies to enter their hazardous material information online using the state's online hazardous materials reporting system. The company had the ability to print reports for emergency services in the case of a problem, and the data entered online was immediately available for use by emergency planning and response agencies, avoiding delays that might occur with processing of hard copies.

12.5 Summary

Hazardous materials are used to produce finished goods in thousands of companies every day. Laws and regulations at different levels of government in every country govern the storage of hazardous materials. In the United States, federal and state laws determine what materials are treated as hazardous and how they should be stored.

The SAP WM configuration for hazardous materials allows such material to be stored in the correct storage bin in the correct storage type. Any error in the storage of hazardous material is not only potentially dangerous, but can result in penalties levied against the warehouse owner.

In Chapter 13, we will examine the functionality of electronic data interchange, better known as EDI.

Electronic data interchange (EDI) is a standard for passing data between trading partners. SAP supports this functionality by the use of intermediate documents (IDocs).

13   Electronic Data Interchange (EDI)

Electronic data interchange, commonly known as EDI, is a standard format for exchanging data. The standard is ANSI X12, and it was developed by the Data Interchange Standards Association. EDI is used throughout the business world to move data from one company to another, known as trading partners.

The EDI message contains a string of data elements, each of which represents a singular fact, such as a material number, quantity, price, and so on, that are separated by delimiters. The EDI message consists of what would usually be contained in a typical business document or form, such as a purchase order or an advance shipping notice.

SAP supports EDI through the use of intermediate documents, more commonly known as IDocs.

13.1   Introduction to EDI

EDI has been used since the 1960s and is a way in which standard business documents are exchanged between companies using a computer system. The standard documents that can be exchanged include purchase orders, shipping notices, and invoices.

13.1.1   Advantages of Using EDI

The advantages of using EDI over paper-based documents or telephone instructions are that it offers greatly reduced data entry errors, reduced processing time, the availabilty of data in electonic form, reduced cost, a standard means of communications, and an efficient business processes.

Data Accuracy

One of benefits of EDI is that is gives better data accuracy. EDI eliminates the need to copy data from one paper document to another or to key the data into an SAP transaction. Data accuracy is lower when data is manually transferred. EDI transactions also verify the data prior to transfer, so data does not need be verified a second time when the SAP system receives it.

Processing Time

It takes only seconds or minutes to transmit EDI data around the world. Data processed by sending a physical document can take days, and data sent by fax takes time to print, fax, and re-enter into the SAP system. The data sent by EDI is available in the SAP system far quicker than any other means.

Reduced Costs

The obvious reduction in cost is that it reduces the amount of data processing by employees. The hourly cost of a data processing clerk is immediately saved when EDI is implemented. There are cost savings of the mail sorting, envelopes, telephone, postage, and courier services. Nonphysical cost savings include the labor costs of finding and dealing with errors that are introduced during data entry.

One other cost benefit that companies may take advantage of, based on the speed with which documents arrive via EDI, is any discounts vendors offer for prompt payment.

Competitive Advantage

Using EDI may give your company a competitive advantage if your competitors are not taking advantage of EDI. However, if your company's competitors have implemented EDI and your company has not, then it will be at a disadvantage despite any other efficient processes it has in place.

13.1.2 Types of EDI

EDI transactions are used between millions of companies each day. There are many EDI transactions and different types of EDI implementations. This section will look at the different types of EDI environments.

Web-Based EDI

The types of EDI that are available for companies to implement offer a wide array of products that suit companies that have no technology department through to companies that have hundreds of IT consultants.

If your company has no technology staff or does not have the capability to implement EDI, then a web-based EDI service may be most appropriate. This type of EDI replicates the contents of a paper-based document on a website. The form on the website contains several boxes where users can enter information. After the necessary information has been entered to the form, the information is automatically converted into an EDI message and then securely sent to the trading partner.

EDI via a Value-Added Network (VAN)

Companies can use a value-added network (VAN) for their EDI needs. A VAN is a private network that provides a secure environment for EDI information to be exchanged between trading partners. A company can have an account with a VAN, which acts as an electronic mail box where companies can send and receive EDI documents.

EDI via a Virtual Private Network (VPN)

A virtual private network (VPN) is a facility that uses the public communication infrastructure to conduct private communications. Millions of companies use this type of communication. A VPN authenticates users, encrypts data, and manages private communications. EDI messages can be passed securely across the VPN.

EDI and AS2

AS2 is not a type of EDI but is a communication protocol used to exchange EDI documents. The growth in the use of AS2 has been due to the requirement of the retail giant Wal-Mart, which maintains that suppliers must communicate with them using the AS2 protocol. AS2 communication creates an envelope for a message, which is then sent securely over the Internet using digital certificates and encryption.

13.1.3 EDI and IDOCS

An IDoc is a uniquely numbered intermediate document that can be used to exchange data between any two processes. An IDOC consists of several segments, each of which contains several fields. The IDoc is made up of three types of records: a control record, one or more data records, and one or more status records. It is a perfect vehicle for EDI transmissions, as it allows data to be exchanged without conversion from one format to another.

You can use Transaction WE05 to view IDocs that have been transmitted, as shown in Figure 13.1. The selection screen offers the user a choice of fields to restrict the output.

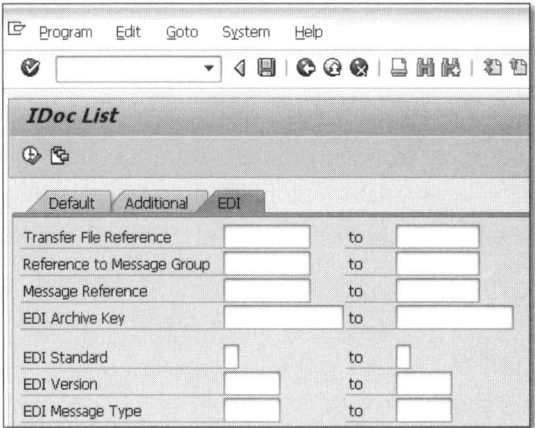

Figure 13.1 Selection Screen to View IDocs

The system returns a list of IDocs that have been transmitted or received. Figure 13.2 shows an example.

From the list of IDocs it is possible to select one and click the detail icon to see the data elements that comprise the IDoc. Figure 13.3 shows an example of the data contained in an IDoc.

Now that we have examined the basics of the EDI functionality we will look at the EDI processes that affect the warehouse.

Introduction to EDI | 13.1

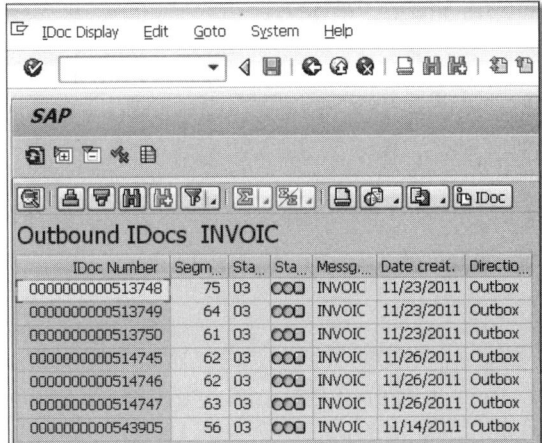

Figure 13.2 Outbound IDocs for EDI

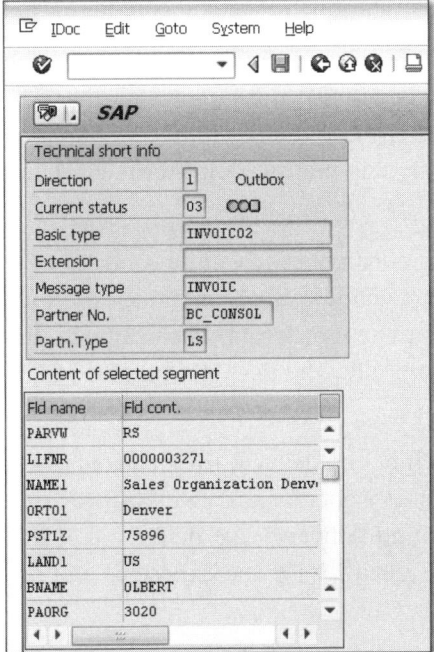

Figure 13.3 Data Segment from an IDOC

13.2 Using EDI in Warehouse Management

When your company has implemented EDI, it can communicate with trading partners such as vendors and customers. The SAP system uses IDocs to support the EDI function. When you process a transaction in the SAP system, it can produce an IDoc that can be used to send the EDI message to your trading partner. Several EDI transactions are used in the warehouse, and these revolve around the inbound and outbound functions of the warehouse processes.

13.2.1 Inbound Processing

The inbound logistics functionality offers visibility for incoming deliveries to the warehouse, allowing for detailed planning and therefore greater warehouse efficiency. The inbound logistics process in the SAP system starts when your company's purchase orders are processed at the vendor. The purchase order can be sent to the vendor using EDI document 850, and this informs the vendor what items you need and where you need the items to be shipped.

Once the vendor receives the purchase order via EDI document 850, they can send back an EDI 997 acknowledgement confirming the receipt of the purchase order. Your vendors can then send a shipping notification from which an inbound delivery can be created.

The advance shipping notification (ASN) is a document the vendor sends to your company via the EDI interface. Instead of the vendor calling or faxing your purchasing department to tell them a certain purchase order has been shipped, the vendor sends a shipping notification electronically. The document that is sent is called an EDI 856 advance ship notice.

The receipt of an ASN via EDI can trigger an inbound delivery to be created in the SAP system. The information from the ASN EDI document creates an IDoc that contains the information to create an inbound delivery. The delivery contains information on the vendor, the items, the quantities to be expected, and the delivery details.

Once the vendor fulfills the order, they send an EDI 810 invoice informing you that the items were shipped and providing the cost of the items and the delivery information.

13.2.2 Outbound Processing

The outbound logistics functionality is equally as important to your company's supply chain because it offers visibility to the outgoing deliveries, allowing detailed planning for packing and shipping, leading to greater warehouse efficiency.

When a customer places an order to your company, the SAP system creates a sales order, and the outbound delivery document is created to facilitate the picking, packing in the warehouse, and ultimate goods issue of the items as they are delivered to your customer.

If you have a remote warehouse, then the warehouse could be sent an EDI document 940. The manufacturing facility sends the EDI 940 to the warehouse. It is a request to ship document that directs the warehouse to ship an order with all of the associated shipment details including items and customer ship-to information.

When the warehouse has completed the shipment, it can send a return document back to the manufacturer. The remote warehouse sends the EDI 945 shipment advice, which contains the information required to invoice the customer.

Two other EDI transactions are used at remote warehouses. The first is an EDI 943 document, which a manufacturer uses to notify a warehouse that it is sending material to the warehouse. Once the material arrives at the warehouse, an EDI 944 document is sent to the manufacturer informing them that the material has been received.

If a change to the warehouse inventory has to be made, a manufacturer can send an EDI 947 document called a warehouse inventory adjustment advice. The transaction is used to change the quantity or status of material in the warehouse.

This section has examined the use of EDI in WM. Now we'll look at some business examples of EDI processes.

13.3 Business Examples—EDI

EDI is a process that is used daily in companies worldwide. It offers great benefits for businesses, not only in direct cost savings, but also in data accuracy and reduced processing time.

EDI in the Warehouse

Warehouses process inbound and outbound transactions that can be triggered by EDI transactions; for example, an advance ship notice EDI transaction sent by a vendor can trigger an inbound delivery document. The implementation of EDI can significantly improve the efficiency of warehouse processes.

Example

A distributor of automotive parts operated three West Coast distribution warehouses that satisfied orders from auto parts stores on the West Coast and Southwest of the United States. The company ordered parts from spares manufacturers and automotive manufacturers using faxes or verbal purchase orders. The purchasing department would give a blanket order for a large quantity of parts, and the deliveries would arrive at the facilities unexpectedly despite an agreed upon delivery schedule.

The warehouses would find themselves in a situation where there were trailers parked in the yard that could not be unloaded for several days. Other times the warehouse would only unload one trailer in a day.

The company decided to implement an enterprise-wide EDI solution that would require the purchasing department to continue to create purchase orders in the SAP system, but the transaction would send an EDI 850 document to each vendor. The company required that all vendors send an EDI 856 advance shipping notification in response so that the company knew when the items would arrive at the warehouses. The EDI implementation and the introduction of the advance ship notice reduced the backlog of trailers at the warehouses. It also allowed the warehouse manager to more accurately manage his staffing level due to his greater visibility of incoming deliveries.

13.4 Summary

Electronic data interchange (EDI) is used by millions of companies and can be used seamlessly with SAP systems. Once EDI is implemented at your company it offers cost saving benefits as well as greater efficiencies across the enterprise. Several EDI transactions that assist in creating a more efficient warehouse are used in WM for both inbound and outbound processes.

In Chapter 14, we will look at the processes of mobile data entry in the warehouse.

Mobile data entry allows the remote entry of data by the use of bar codes and radio frequency (RF) technology. SAP has incorporated mobile data entry into warehouse management transactions, reducing the level of data entry error and shortening the time needed to complete transfer orders.

14 Mobile Data Entry

Mobile data entry in the warehouse today involves the use of wireless radio frequency (RF) terminals or devices carried by the warehouse staff to record data. The data that the staff records is usually in bar code form, either printed on the paperwork for transfer orders or as bar code labels that identify products, storage bins, or other objects.

The display on a RF device can use a graphical user interface (GUI). The information is transmitted from the SAP system, and individual transactions can be executed using a touch screen or keys. A device either has a GUI or is character-based with a special, nongraphical user interface.

Standard SAP systems support RF devices, and several functions within the warehouse can be executed via RF.

> **Note**
>
> The standard SAP system has incorporated RF technology since the release of SAP ERP 4.6B.

The following list shows the timeline of RF technology in SAP systems:

- **Release 4.6B**
  Introduction of RF transactions and SAPConsole
- **Release 4.6C**
  Standard transactions delivered for handling unit management

- **Release 4.7 Enterprise**
  RF for Task and Resource Management, Yard Management, and Value-Added Services
- **Release ECC 5.0**
  The first RFID scenarios

This chapter will examine the use of mobile data entry in the current system, SAP ECC 6.0, and how technologies such as bar codes and RF are used in warehouse functionality.

The next section discusses RF devices and SAPConsole.

14.1 Introduction to RF Devices

SAP transactions can be executed on RF devices that are handheld or forklift-mounted. No middleware software is required to connect the devices to the SAP system.

The SAP system's functionality enables real-time handling of material flow through RF scanning devices. Having the screens and the business logic within the SAP system makes it easy to distribute new processes to each device. Two standard RF devices can be used with SAP systems:

- GUI devices
- Character-based devices

The main difference is that the character-based device uses terminal emulation, and the GUI devices use a Microsoft Windows–based operating system. Let's take a more detailed look at each of these now.

14.1.1 Graphical User Interface Devices

The graphical user interface (GUI) RF device uses a small keypad, touch screen, or some other interface, but the data is always displayed in a graphical manner, as you would expect to see with a device such as a PDA or cell phone. The device is connected to the SAP system, as any other standalone computer would be.

14.1.2 Character-Based Devices

The character-based device is not connected directly to the SAP system but communicates via an interface called SAPConsole that was introduced in SAP ERP Release 4.6B. Communication between SAPConsole and the RF device can be achieved by using a Telnet server. SAP supports two industry standards for screen sizes:

- RF devices for forklifts: 8 lines by 40 characters
- Portable RF devices: 16 lines by 20 characters

14.1.3 SAPConsole

SAPConsole is a tool that enables RF devices to be run within SAP applications. Introduced in 1999, SAPConsole was shipped with SAP ERP Release 4.6B and was used for bar code and handheld RF applications in the Logistics Execution System (LES), which included WM.

SAPConsole can be described as a framework for automatic data collection (AIDC) in a warehouse environment. It translates GUI screens to character-based screens that are used on a variety of data collection devices.

SAPConsole does not contain business logic, databases, or external functionality. Its sole function is to translate SAP GUI screens in the SAP environment to the character-based equivalent. SAPConsole consists of four components:

- RF Terminal, which is the Telnet client
- RF Access Point, which allows for Wireless Ethernet
- Telnet Server/SAPConsole Administrator, which allows each RF terminal to connect to the Windows machine in character-based mode and supports VT220 terminal emulation
- SAP R/3 System that receives the data from the mobile terminals

An SAPConsole session allows a connection to the SAP system in real time, exactly like an SAP GUI session. All the functionality and business logic resides within the SAP application. SAPConsole connects the user to that business logic.

14.1.4 Functionality Available with SAPConsole

In SAP ECC 6.0, many transactions are defined as mobile data entry and are available for use with RF devices. These include:

- Goods receipt
- Goods issue
- Material putaway
- Material picking
- Packing and unpacking
- Physical inventory
- Loading and unloading
- Serial number capture
- Stock overview

This section has examined the use of RF devices and the warehouse functions that are available with SAPConsole. The next section will discuss bar code functionality.

14.2 Bar Code Functionality

The first bar code patent was issued in 1952 to Joseph Woodland and Bernard Silver. Their invention was described as a "bull's eye" symbol made up of concentric circles of varying thicknesses. The initial push for the bar code came from a grocery retailer, and as the bar code was developed—first by RCA and then IBM—the grocery industry was the leading force behind its adoption. In the late 1960s, Joseph Woodland, then working for IBM, helped develop the most popular version of the bar code technology: the Universal Product Code (UPC).

On April 3, 1973, the UPC was adopted as the industry standard. From then on, any bar code on any product could be read and understood by any bar code reader. Standardization made it cost effective for manufacturers to put bar codes on their packages and for printer manufacturers to develop new technology to reproduce the bar code with the exact tolerances it required.

14.2.1 UPC Bar Code Format

The UPC bar code is split into two halves of six digits each. The first character is always zero, except for some materials that have variable weight or special materials. The next five characters are the manufacturer's code, followed by a five-digit product code and a check digit. In addition, there are hidden cues in the structure of the bar code to inform the scanner which end of the bar code is the start and which is the end. This allows the bar code to be scanned in either direction.

Manufacturers register with the Uniform Code Council (UCC) to obtain a unique manufacturers code for their company.

Manufacturers Code

All materials produced by a given company use the same manufacturer code. Some codes are called variable-length manufacturer codes. Assigning fixed-length five-digit manufacturer codes means that each manufacturer can have up to 99,999 product codes. Most manufacturers do not have that many products, which indicates that thousands of potential product codes are wasted on manufacturers with only a few products. Therefore, if a manufacturer knows it will produce a small number of products for bar coding, the UCC may issue it a longer manufacturer code, leaving less space for the product code. This results in more efficient use of the available manufacturer and product codes.

Product Code

The product code is a unique code assigned by the manufacturer. Unlike the manufacturer code, which the UCC assigns, the manufacturer is free to assign product codes to each of its materials that require bar coding. Because the UCC guarantees that the manufacturer code is unique, the manufacturer needs to ensure that it does not duplicate product codes.

Check Digit

The check digit is an additional digit used to verify that a bar code has been scanned correctly. A scan can produce incorrect data because of inconsistent scanning speed, print imperfections, or environmental issues, so it is important to verify that the preceding digits in the bar code have been correctly interpreted.

The check digit is calculated based on the other digits of the bar code. Normally, if the check digit matches the value that could be calculated based on the data that has been scanned, then there is a high level of confidence that the bar code was scanned correctly.

14.2.2 UPC and EAN

After the UPC was adopted in 1973, the global interest in bar coding, especially in retailing, led to the adoption of the International Article Numbering Association's European Article Numbering (EAN) code in December 1976.

The EAN code has 13 characters but is identical to the UPC code in that the actual unique code is 10 digits long. In the UPC, the first digit is for the product, and the last is a check digit. EAN has three characters that are not used for the unique code. The three flag digits are used for the check digit and the country that issued the bar code, not the product's country of origin. Each country has a numbering authority that assigns manufacturer codes to companies within its jurisdiction. The manufacturer code is still five digits long, as is the product code, and the check digit is calculated in exactly the same way as for the UPC code.

For the UPC and EAN to be compatible, the United States was issued the country flags 00, 01, 03, 04, and 06 through 13. Because the EAN, sometimes called the EAN-13, is a superset of the UPC, any software or hardware capable of reading an EAN-13 symbol can also read a UPC code.

The Japanese Numbering Authority (JAN) codes are exactly the same as EAN codes but are strictly for Japan and carry the country code 49.

14.2.3 Bar Code Structure

A physical bar code is a series of vertical lines of varying width that are called bars, and spaces. The bars and spaces are called elements. Different combinations of the bars and spaces represent different characters.

When a bar code scanner is passed over the bar code, the light source from the scanner is absorbed by the dark bars and is not reflected, but it is reflected by the light spaces. A photocell detector in the scanner receives the reflected light and converts the light into an electrical signal.

As the laser is passed over the bar code, the scanner creates a low electrical signal for the spaces, which is the reflected light, and a high electrical signal for the bars, where nothing is reflected. The duration of the electrical signal determines whether the scanner has detected a wide or a narrow element. The bar code reader's decoder then interprets the signal. The decoder converts this into the characters that the bar code represents. The decoded data is then passed to the system in a traditional data format.

14.2.4 Bar Code Readers

Three types of bar code readers are available: fixed bar code readers, portable readers with batch uploading, and portable RF readers. Let's examine these in detail now.

Fixed Bar Code Reader

This is the type of bar code reader you find at a retail store, where the reader is tethered to the cash register and is used to scan items that are purchased.

Portable Batch Readers

These readers are battery powered and are used away from their host to collect information and store it for a later batch upload to the host. These are used frequently in retail stores for taking inventory on store shelves and then uploading that information to the host system at the end of inventory taking. Some newer batch readers, from companies such as Symbol Technologies, Hand Held Products, and PSC, Inc., enable collection of more than 50,000 bar codes and can run for more than 12 hours on a single charge.

Portable RF Reader

This reader is the most sophisticated because it allows the operator to record data and transmit in real time. The communication is two-way and allows the operator to receive updated instructions based on the data he collects. United Parcel Service (UPS) uses this type of reader to record tracking data and the receiver's signature. The Delivery Information Acquisition Device (DIAD) sends delivery information to the UPS data center as soon as the delivery information is entered. Drivers scan the package bar code, collect the receiver's signature electronically, type in the receiver's last name, and press a single key to complete the transaction and send the data without returning to the vehicle.

14.2.5 Bar Code Reader Technologies

Three technologies are in use for reading bar codes:

- Photodiode
- Charge-coupled device (CCD)
- Laser

Let's examine these further now.

Photodiode

Photodiode technology can be found in pen-style bar code readers. The photodiode and a light source are contained in the pen reader. As the reader is dragged across the bar code, the photodiode measures the intensity of the light reflected back from the light source and generates a waveform. This is used to measure the widths of the bars and the spaces in the bar code.

Dark bars in the bar code absorb light and white spaces reflect light. As a result, the voltage waveform generated by the photodiode is an exact duplicate of the bars and spaces in the bar code. The scanner decodes this waveform. This type of scanner was very popular in public libraries in the 1980s and 1990s. These wand bar code readers are still widely available and plug directly into the USB sockets of computers. Companies such as Unitech, ZBA, Inc., and Wasp Barcode Technologies still manufacture these wand-style bar code readers.

Charge-Coupled Device

A charge-coupled device (CCD) is an image sensor consisting of an integrated circuit containing an array of linked or coupled light-sensitive capacitors. The CCD reader uses an array of hundreds of sensors lined up in a row in the head of the reader. Each sensor acts like a single photodiode that measures the intensity of the light immediately in front of it. The voltage pattern read by the reader is identical to the pattern in a bar code.

CCD readers do not have moving parts, are considered extremely durable, and require less maintenance than laser readers. CCD scanners consume very little power and work under most lighting conditions. They are often cheaper than laser scanners because they do not have as great a range and have to be closer to the bar code to be read. In brief, these scanners are a low-cost option compared with laser scanners but are robust and low maintenance.

Because they do not offer as great a scanning distance as laser readers, some warehouse operations do not use CCD readers, but they can be found alongside laser scanners in most warehouse operations. The large companies involved in RF technology, such as Intermec Technologies Corporation and Hand Held Products, manufacture these scanners.

Laser

Laser scanners work the same way as pen-type readers except that they use a laser beam as the light source and typically employ either a reciprocating mirror or a rotating prism to scan the laser beam back and forth across the bar code. Like the pen type reader, they use a photodiode to measure the intensity of the light reflected back from the bar code.

Laser scanners can read bar codes at a greater distance from the head of the device than can a CCD scanner, enabling supermarkets to read codes on round cans and flexible packages more easily. Laser scanners are often more expensive than CCD scanners but have the advantage of reading longer and smaller-density bar codes as well as working at greater scanning distances. Because of the ability to read slightly curved bar codes, the laser scanner is the choice of supermarkets and retailers. There are many manufacturers of laser bar code readers including Symbol, Metrologic Instruments, Inc., Intermec, and Hand Held Products.

14.2.6 Bar Code Support in SAP Systems

SAP systems read bar codes for identification and verification. The items that can be identified include:

- Storage bin
- Material
- Storage unit

- Handling unit
- Quantity
- Delivery
- Staging area
- Shipment
- Pick wave

It is possible to scan items for verification purposes, and these scanable fields include:

- Storage unit
- Storage bin
- Material
- Quantity

This list of fields that can be used for bar codes will probably increase with future releases of SAP systems.

14.2.7 Configuration for Bar Codes

Before bar codes can be used for mobile data entry, configuration needs to be entered and reviewed to ensure that the correct format is being used.

Defining Verification Profiles

The verification profile is a set of fields that the user can verify. Several profiles can be created for each warehouse, and each profile can contain several fields to be verified.

You can find the configuration by following the menu path IMG • LOGISTICS EXECUTION • MOBILE DATA ENTRY • VERIFICATION CONTROL • DEFINE PROFILES.

Figure 14.1 shows the profiles created for warehouses 001, 009, and 039. Each profile verifies a different number of fields. The fields that can be attached to a profile include:

- Source bin
- Destination bin

- Storage unit identification at the source storage bin
- Storage unit identification at the destination storage bin
- Quantity of the material to be picked at the source storage bin
- Quantity of the material to be put away at the destination storage bin
- Material identification at the source storage bin
- Material identification at the destination storage bin

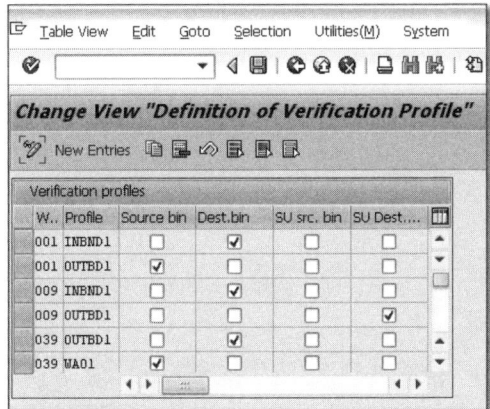

Figure 14.1 Configuration for Defining Verification Profiles

The system uses this configuration if scanning devices communicate directly with the SAP system. For a given warehouse movement, this configuration specifies a unique verification profile that determines what data the user must scan or key in manually.

> **Example**
>
> If material is put away by storage unit number, the scanner operators have to verify that they have completed putaway of the storage unit in the storage bin proposed by the system.

Assigning Verification Profiles

After the verification profile has been configured, it can be assigned to movement types used in the warehouse that will be subject to bar code scanning. You can find the configuration by following the menu path IMG • LOGISTICS EXECUTION •

MOBILE DATA ENTRY • VERIFICATION CONTROL • ASSIGN VERIFICATION PROFILES TO GOODS MOVEMENTS.

Figure 14.2 shows the assignment of the verification profiles. The profile is assigned to a movement type used between a source and destination storage type. Therefore, in warehouse 001, the verification profile OUTBD1 is assigned to movement type 601 when the movement is between any source storage type, 005 and the destination storage type 916.

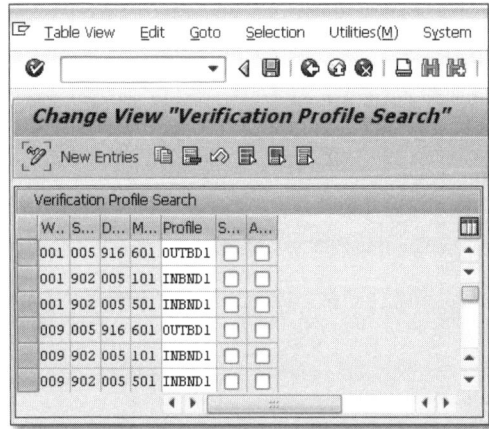

Figure 14.2 Assigning Verification Profiles to Movement Types

Defining Bar Codes for Warehouses

The configuration for bar codes allows certain bar code types to be used in certain warehouses. If the company uses one bar code throughout, then this is a simple configuration task. Check with the company to configure the correct bar code type used for each warehouse.

You can find the configuration by following the menu path IMG • LOGISTICS EXECUTION • MOBILE DATA ENTRY • BAR CODE • ASSIGN BAR CODE TYPES TO WAREHOUSES.

Figure 14.3 shows bar code types assigned to each warehouse. The configuration needs to be in place so that the system can interpret the correct bar code format.

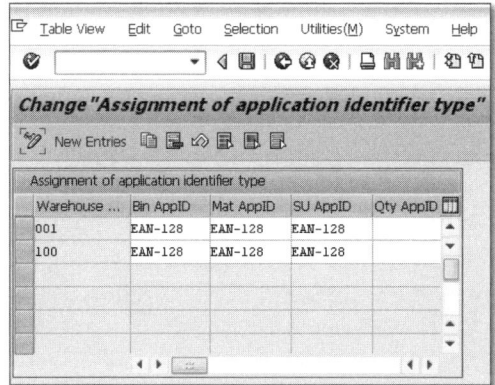

Figure 14.3 Assigning Application Identifier Types for Warehouses

Maintaining Bar Code Specifications

This configuration step defines the parameters for the bar code type. The minimum and maximum lengths determine the length of the bar code type. The prefix identifies first part of the bar code string with an introductory character string. If the specific data field that is attached to the bar code type has a variable length, then a delimiter must close it.

You can find the configuration by following the menu path IMG • LOGISTICS EXECUTION • MOBILE DATA ENTRY • BAR CODE • MAINTAIN BAR CODE SPECIFICATION.

Figure 14.4 shows that the bar code type EAN-128 has defined minimum and maximum lengths. Different bar code types have different configurations that are specified in this configuration step.

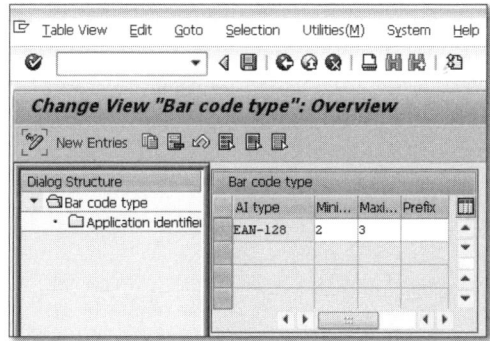

Figure 14.4 Configuration to Maintain Bar Code Type

This section has discussed the functionality of bar codes. Now we'll examine the processes in WM that support RF.

14.3 Radio Frequency—Supported Processes in SAP WM

The use of RF transactions is important in the warehouse because of the physical size of warehouses and the time needed to perform tasks. Collecting data using RF devices saves labor and time and improves the accuracy of data collection in the warehouse.

Each user who operates an RF device must be entered into the system with the information regarding his device. In addition, the user has to be assigned to a queue that shows all transfer orders that require materials movement from a certain storage type. The queues are configured in the IMG.

14.3.1 Defining the Radio Frequency Queue

To assign a range of warehouse activities to certain users, you define functionality called the RF queue management in the SAP Implementation Guide (IMG). This is a two-part configuration where the queue is defined and then activities are assigned.

You can find the configuration by following the navigation path IMG • LOGISTICS EXECUTION • MOBILE DATA ENTRY • RF QUEUE MANAGEMENT.

Figure 14.5 shows several queues created for several warehouses. The queues are easily identifiable for picking, putaway, and goods receipt. The queues can be assigned the relevant areas.

Figure 14.6 shows the unique queues for each warehouse with assigned areas. For example, queue PUTAWAY01 for warehouse 001 has been assigned transaction type E, stock placement, between source storage type 902 and any destination storage type, denoted by ***.

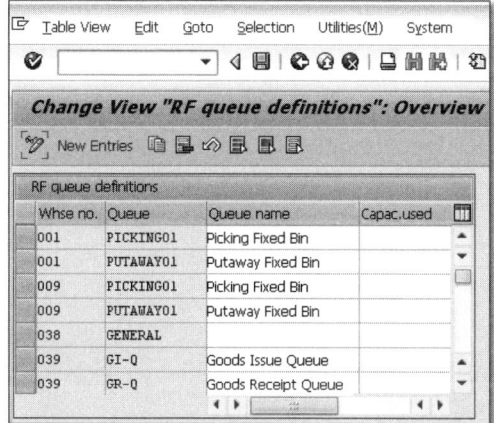

Figure 14.5 Creation of Queues for RF Transaction

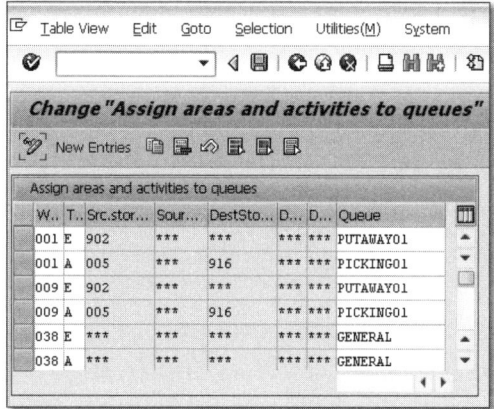

Figure 14.6 Assignment of Areas to RF Queues

14.3.2 Adding a User for Mobile Data Entry

Each user who is assigned an RF device has to be assigned a particular area to work in. If the warehouse is small, then users may work with several queues. In larger warehouses, users may be specifically assigned to only work with certain storage types.

Use Transaction LRFMD to add users for mobile data entry. You can find it via the menu path SAP • LOGISTICS • LOGISTICS EXECUTION • INTERNAL WHSE PROCESSES • MOBILE DATA ENTRY • USER MASTER DATA FOR MOBILE DATA ENTRY.

The users are entered and assigned to a queue. In addition, you can define the screen format and the user's main menu, as shown in Figure 14.7. Once the user has been added, he can use the RF device to access the queue to which he has been assigned.

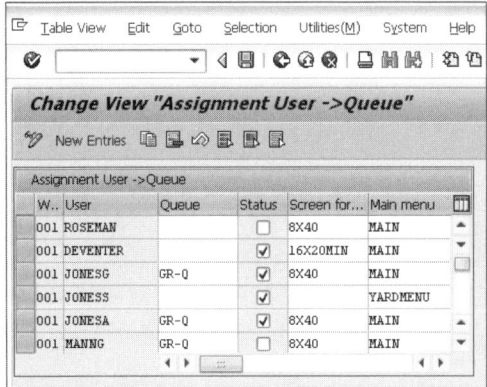

Figure 14.7 Adding a User for Mobile Data Entry

14.3.3 Logging on for Mobile Data Entry

The user can log on for mobile data entry using Transaction LM00, via the menu path SAP • LOGISTICS • LOGISTICS EXECUTION • INTERNAL WHSE PROCESSES • MOBILE DATA ENTRY • MOBILE DATA ENTRY.

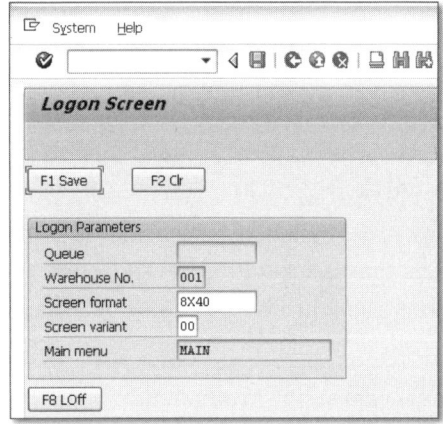

Figure 14.8 Logon Screen for Mobile Data Entry

Figure 14.8 shows the screen that is displayed when a user logs on using Transaction LM00. The user can then use the RF device to perform the transactions he is assigned.

14.3.4 RF Menus and WM Processes

You can view the menus displayed on the RF devices using Transaction LM00 and program the displayed items using ABAP code. The menu structure that has been defined for this example is shown in the following figures.

Figure 14.9 shows the initial menu selection for the RF devices. The supported transactions are divided into five selections: inbound processes, outbound processes, stock transfer, internal warehouse processes, and inquiries.

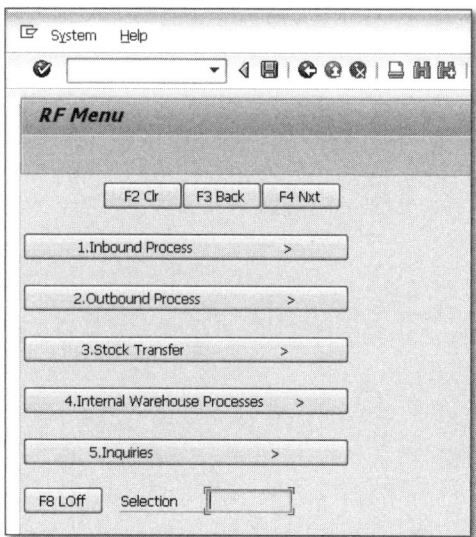

Figure 14.9 Initial RF Menu Screen

To illustrate the menu paths that have been designed for the RF menu, Figure 14.10 shows the selections for the inbound processes.

If the GOODS RECEIPT option is selected, the system displays the menu shown in Figure 14.11.

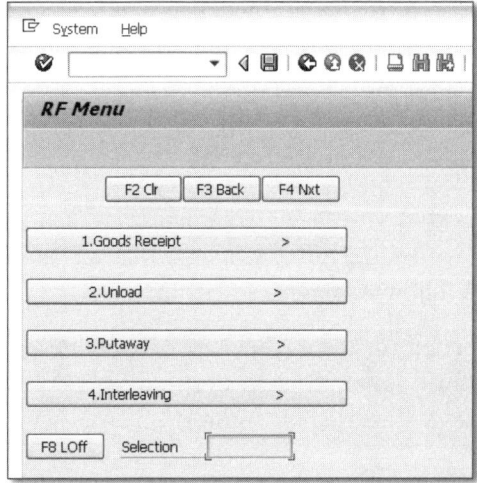

Figure 14.10 Menu Selections for Inbound Processes

Figure 14.11 shows the menu selections for the goods-receipt menu option. These five transactions are available for the RF device user. If the user wants to select a delivery, he selects option 1 and scans in or enters the delivery number.

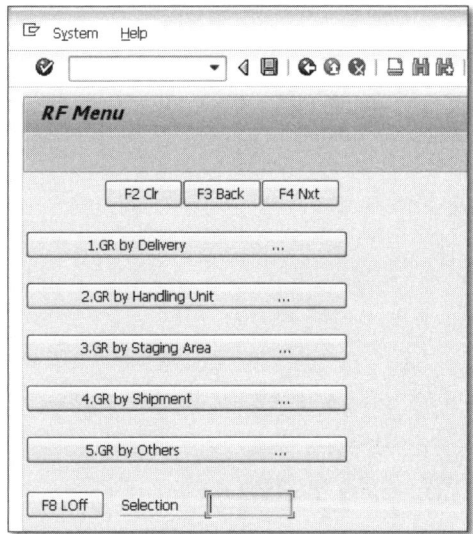

Figure 14.11 Menu Selections for Goods Receipts

Figure 14.12 shows the delivery details displayed on the RF device after the user had scanned in the inbound delivery number. The user can select from several function key options to perform a process.

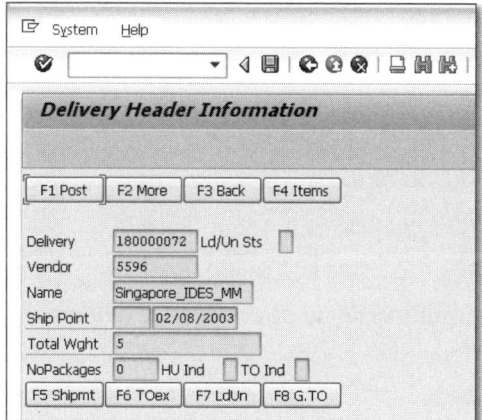

Figure 14.12 Display of Inbound Delivery Details

This is one example of how transactions appear on the RF devices. Among the supported transactions for RF are:

- Goods receipt
- Goods issue
- Material putaway
- Material picking
- Packing and unpacking
- Physical inventory
- Loading and unloading
- Serial number capture
- Stock overview

You can see that many processes are RF-supported. The next section will describe the RF monitor.

14.4 Radio Frequency Monitor

The RF monitor is a tool warehouse managers can use to view the queues that are being worked on in the warehouse. Users with RF devices can only see the items in their queue; only the users of the RF monitor have the overall picture of the RF operations in the warehouse. Using the RF monitor benefits the warehouse by enabling staff to:

- Monitor the queues and review the number of assigned transfer orders, the number of users, and the ratio of workload to users
- Assign transfer orders and users to other queues
- Change the processing priorities of the transfer orders in the queues
- Give the warehouse manager a significant overview of the devices being used and the work being performed

Let's see how to access and use this monitor.

14.4.1 Accessing the RF Monitor

You can find the RF monitor in the SAP menu. The transaction to use is Transaction LRF1, which you can access via the menu path SAP • LOGISTICS • LOGISTICS EXECUTION • INTERNAL WHSE PROCESSES • MOBILE DATA ENTRY • MONITOR MOBILE DATA ENTRY.

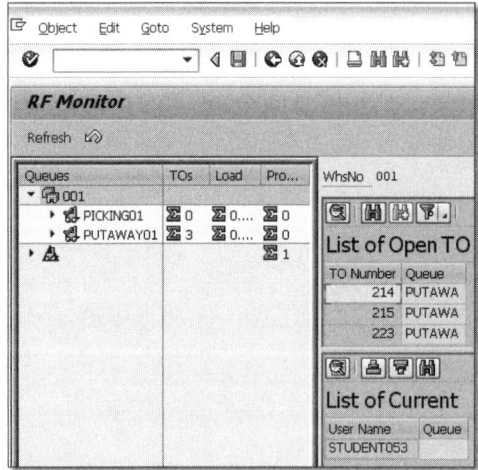

Figure 14.13 RF Monitor Display

Figure 14.13 shows the elements of the RF monitor. The navigation area is the section on the left side of the screen that shows the number of users and the number of transfer orders. In this case, there is only one user and one transfer order in the queue. The right side of the screen is the ALV (SAP List Viewer). It shows the details from the transfer order; the section below shows details on the user and the queue to which he is assigned.

14.4.2 Using the Radio Frequency Monitor

The RF monitor allows the warehouse manager to move transfer orders to other queues by simply identifying the transfer order in the navigation area and dragging it to another queue folder.

Assigning users to other queues follows a similar process, where the user is highlighted in the navigation area and dragged and dropped into the queue required. The RF monitor is kept updated by refreshing the transaction by pressing the F5 function key.

This section has examined the use of the RF monitor and the benefits that can be gained by moving transfer orders to different queues to maximize efficiencies. Next, we will summarize the contents of this chapter on mobile data entry.

14.5 Business Examples—Mobile Data Entry

Mobile data entry in the warehouse involves the use of wireless radio frequency (RF) terminals or devices operated by warehouse personnel to record data. The data they record is usually in bar code form, either printed on the paperwork for transfer orders or as bar code labels that identify products, storage bins, or other objects.

14.5.1 Bar Code Functionality

Bar codes are found on every product we purchase from the supermarket, and scanners are used in our everyday lives. In the warehouse the bar code is an important tool that not only reduces manual entry of data into the SAP system, but improves warehouse efficiency.

Example

A distributor of automotive parts implemented SAP WM and was using transfer orders to place and remove stock in the warehouse. The layout was made up of racking with storage bins large enough for a pallet of parts. Each of the storage bins was identified with a numeric number, and a label with this number was affixed to the top of the bin.

The company did not implement any RF solution and was operating with non–bar coded documents. The printed transfer order documents identified the material and storage bins in numeric form, so that the warehouse operator had to write on the transfer order document if any changes were made, such as differences in storage bin or quantity. The document was then given back to the warehouse shift manager so he could made an amendments in the SAP system.

Although changes to the picking and placement documents were relatively infrequent, the amendments in the system were sometimes incorrect due to mistyping or errors in identifying the correct storage bin. These errors led to inventory inaccuracies that were found during cycle counting.

The supply chain team identified that not only were there issues with the accuracy of warehouse operator notations and data entry, but the efficiency of the warehouse operators was hindered by having to stop and write information on a physical document. The recommendation was that the company implements a pilot bar code program and handheld devices so that the operators could scan the information from the picking document as well as the pallet and storage bin.

The company developed a pilot project for raw material stock placements with three forklift trucks fitted with handheld devices to read bar codes on the transfer order document, pallet labels, and storage bins. The supply chain team reviewed the data after a month of the trial and found that no errors were generated by the use of bar codes. The company then decided to extend the project to include bar codes for both stock placement and stock removal.

14.5.2 RF Functionality

The use of RF transactions is important in the warehouse because of the physical size of warehouses and the time needed to perform tasks. Collecting data using RF devices saves labor and time and improves the accuracy of data collection in the warehouse.

Example

Bar codes and limited use of handheld devices were implemented at an electronics distributor. The company imported electronic components from abroad and then resold them to retail customers through the Internet or large customers via consignment.

The components were either stored in their own packaging, or if they arrived without packaging, the components were stored in plastic bags and then a bar code label was applied with the material number. The company used handheld RF devices for picking and putaway using transfer orders, but other transactions were manually completed.

The company operated with a warehouse that had very little free space. On occasion the warehouse staff could not place material in the warehouse, as there were no available empty bins. The company decided to hire a consulting firm to assess the warehouse layout and offer recommendations on how to make the warehouse more efficient.

The consultants came with some changes to the racking and the use of narrower aisles to create 15% more space in the warehouse. Other recommendations included extending the use of handheld devices to other SAP transactions such as physical inventory. The company assessed the cost of purchasing more handheld devices and the resources needed to develop the use of other transactions.

After some cost analysis the company decided to implement one new transaction using the RF devices and then another transaction every six months. They decided to implement the physical inventory process first followed by stock overview.

14.6 Summary

The use of bar codes and RF devices has made warehouse operation more efficient. Data entry errors are fewer, and the time needed to perform operations in the warehouse has been reduced because RF devices can collect data without requiring manual collection and manual entry of data after the user has returned to the warehouse office.

The use of RF devices for data collection and transaction processing in WM has been increasing over a number of SAP releases. The modern efficient warehouse uses RF technology and constantly reviews procedures to further adopt the technology to improve operations. As the support for mobile data entry increases in WM, the use of the RF monitor will become more important to efficient mobile data collection.

In Chapter 15, we will discuss the next logical step from RF technology — the adoption of radio frequency identification (RFID).

Radio frequency identification (RFID) technology has been available for decades, but recently we have seen the push to use it as the ultimate tool for tracking inventory. Large companies such as Wal-Mart and Target expect RFID to reduce warehouse costs and improve supply chain efficiencies.

15 Radio Frequency Identification Technology

Every industry publication has articles and commentary on radio frequency identification (RFID); however, it is not a new technology. The first use of RFID was documented in the 1940s by the British Royal Air Force to identify aircraft in World War II and was part of the refinement of radar. It was during the 1960s that RFID was first considered as a solution for the commercial world. The first commercial applications involving RFID were developed throughout the 1970s and 1980s. These commercial applications were concerned with identifying material inside a single location.

The latest attempt to commercialize the use of RFID started in 1998, when researchers at the Massachusetts Institute of Technology (MIT) Auto-ID Center began to research new ways to track and identify objects as they moved between physical locations. This research centered on radio frequency technology and how information that is held on tags can be effectively scanned and shared in real time.

RFID is known today as the reading of physical tags on single products, cases, pallets, and reusable containers that emit radio signals to be picked up by RFID reader devices. Industries see this technology as a way of identifying material more accurately than with traditional means.

This chapter will give you an understanding of the technology behind RFID, the history of that technology, the development of the technology into a commercial application, and where that applied technology is used within the framework of SAP and WM.

15.1 Introduction to Radio Frequency Identification

Simply stated, RFID is a means of identifying an object using a radio frequency transmission. The technology can be used to identify, track, sort, or detect a wide variety of objects. Communication takes place between a reader or interrogator and a transponder or tag.

Tags can either be active, powered by battery, or passive, powered by the reader field. A reader field is an RF field that is transmitted by the reader to interrogate the RFID tag. The communication frequencies used depend to a large extent on the application; they range from 125 KHz to 2.45 GHz. Most countries impose regulations to control RF emissions and prevent interference with other industrial, scientific, or medical equipment.

15.1.1 Mechanism of RFID

In a typical system, tags are attached to objects. Each tag has a certain amount of internal memory that it uses to store information about the object, such as its unique ID number or details including manufacture date and material information. When a tag passes through a field generated by a reader, it transmits this information back to the reader, which identifies the object.

Until recently, RFID technology focused mainly on tags and readers, which were used in systems handling where relatively low volumes of data. This is now changing. RFID in the supply chain is expected to generate huge volumes of data, which have to be filtered and routed to ERP systems. To solve this problem, companies have developed special software packages called savants, which act as buffers between the RFID frontend and the ERP backend.

15.1.2 Electronic Product Code

The Electronic Product Code (EPC) is the emerging RFID standard developed by the MIT AutoID Center. It is the RFID version of the Universal Product Code (UPC) bar code standard. Like the UPC, the EPC is intended to be used for specific product identification as well as case and pallet identification. However, the EPC goes beyond the UPC: It not only identifies the material, but also provides access to additional data about the origin and history of the specific batches or serial numbers.

The EPC tag identifies the manufacturer, product, version, and serial number. It's the serial number that takes the EPC to the next level by providing access to data related to a specific unit. This allows the tracking of the specific serialized unit history as it moves through the supply chain. This data may be stored elsewhere, but a standardized architecture allows more ease of access. This architecture is known as the EPC Network.

The EPC has become increasingly important because it is the standard being utilized by Wal-Mart, Target, Best Buy, and the U.S. Department of Defense in their RFID mandates.

15.1.3 The Wal-Mart RFID Mandate

In June 2004, Wal-Mart announced that it would require its top 100 suppliers to put RFID tags on all shipping crates and pallets by January 1, 2005. This would then expand to its next largest 200 largest suppliers by January 1, 2006. Wal-Mart requires that each tag store an EPC that can be used to track products as they enter Wal-Mart's distribution centers and then in turn are shipped to individual stores. As the world's largest company in terms of revenue, Wal-Mart's mandate had a profound affect on the RFID strategy of many large companies that sought to remain direct suppliers.

By 2007, Wal-Mart had found that RFID's ability to improve the supply chain was limited by business partners' willingness to participate. Wal-Mart's targeted suppliers for the RFID program had some of the most efficient supply chains in the industry, and these companies did not initially realize the benefit of RFID. Forrester Research calculated that the large Wal-Mart suppliers would have to invest more than $9 million to cover costs associated with RFID to achieve the results that Wal-Mart was expecting.

Despite the large investment required, many companies have accepted that the increase in the use of RFID will occur in the coming years and that early adoption of the technology is good business. Some Wal-Mart suppliers were quick to comply with the mandate. Proctor & Gamble, itself a giant company, introduced an RFID policy in its organization, with the Wal-Mart mandate as a driver for its own development of RFID. Other suppliers to Wal-Mart, such as Gillette, Kimberly-Clark, and Kraft all started RFID projects at that time.

15.1.4 RFID Benefits

Supply chain management at large companies such as Wal-Mart is interested in RFID advances that can achieve visibility of material through the supply chain. These kinds of benefits are improving with other methods, such as electronic data interchange (EDI), bar coding, and advance ship notifications (ASN).

Other benefits to companies lie outside of the supply chain, such as a reduction in theft from the store and during transport and storage and a deterrent to the growing problem of product counterfeiting. Both of these issues cost companies billions of dollars each year. Pharmaceutical companies are increasingly worried about counterfeiting, and RFID tags on products may help. However, the level of security needed to combat theft and counterfeiting would require an RFID tag on each product sold. The cost of the tag and placement of the tag on the product will have to drop significantly for this to be viable.

> **Note**
> Today, in 2012, most companies that sell RFID tags do not quote prices because pricing is based on volume, the amount of memory on the tag, and the packaging of the tag. The cost of a 96-bit EPC tag is approximately 20 to 40 U.S. cents. However, if the tag is embedded in a thermal transfer label on which companies can print a bar code, the price will rise beyond 40 cents. A transponder in a plastic card or key fob can cost more than $4.

15.1.5 RFID vs. Bar Codes

RFID has advantages over bar codes but has some disadvantages that still have to be overcome. Until the disadvantages become insignificant, bar codes will still play a part in supply chains and in warehousing.

Advantages of RFID

RFID technology does not require line-of-sight reading. The RFID tag can be read through other materials, whereas bar codes require line of sight. This implies that an RFID reader could read a pallet of mixed products, all of which contain individual RFID tags, without the need to physically move any of the materials or open any cases.

If the pallet was full of mixed products, the large number of RFID tags could be read almost instantaneously. The tags would be read sequentially, not simultaneously, but the reading still could be completed in microseconds.

The data on RFID tags can be changed or added to as a tag passes through specific operations. Read-only tags are less expensive than read/write tags. RFID tags are less susceptible to poor environmental conditions in which bar code labels become unreadable. RFID tags can be sealed within a plastic enclosure, eliminating many of the problems that plague bar codes in harsh environments, where they are exposed to chemicals, heat, and other damaging effects.

Disadvantages of RFID

Currently, cost is the biggest roadblock to the widespread use of RFID tags and the replacement of bar codes for item-level tracking. Bar codes can be produced for less than one cent. Currently RFID tags cost between 20 and 40 cents for the most basic of tags. Even if the cost falls to several cents per tag, the cost is still a significant addition to the cost of an item that is a low-cost piece of consumer goods.

RFID signals can encounter problems when being read through some materials, such as metals and liquids. Tag placement is found to be of great importance for some materials that are in particular kinds of containers, crates, or shrink-wrapped pallets. Some case-level RFID tags have to be placed in a specific location on the case and cases must be stacked in a specific orientation or configuration to obtain a consistent read from the RFID tag.

The ability of RFID not to require line of sight is also a disadvantage. A RFID reader reads tags within its range, and this may be problematic if the wrong tag is selected. Therefore line-of-sight reading is preferred for some RFID applications. If an RFID tags fails, it is not as obvious as the failure of a bar code. If the RFID tag is not seen, then there is no check to know that a tag failed.

Now that we have discussed the basics of RFID, the next section will describe in more detail the types of RFID tags that are available.

15.2 Types of RFID Tags

Every object to be identified in an RFID system needs to have a tag attached to it. Tags are manufactured in a wide variety of packaging formats designed for different applications and environments. The basic assembly process involves a substrate material, such as paper, PVC, and so on, upon which an antenna is deposited.

The antenna is made from one of many conductive materials including silver ink, aluminum, and copper. Next, the tag chip is connected to the antenna, using techniques such as wire bonding or flip chip. Finally, a protective overlay made from materials such as PVC lamination, epoxy resin, or adhesive paper may be added to allow the tag to support some of the physical conditions found in many applications, such as abrasion, impact, and corrosion.

15.2.1 Tag Classes

One of the main ways of categorizing RFID tags is by their ability to read and write data. This leads to the following four classes:

- **Class 0—read only: factory programmed**
  These are the simplest type of tags, where the data—usually a simple ID number (EPC)—is written only once into the tag during manufacture. The memory is then disabled from any further updates. Class 0 is also used to define a category of tags called electronic article surveillance (EAS) or antitheft devices, which have no ID and only announce their presence when passing through an antenna field.

- **CLASS 1—write once read only (WORM): factory or user programmed**
  In this case, the tag is manufactured with no data written into the memory. Data can either be written by the tag manufacturer or by the user, but only once. No further writes are allowed, and the tag can only be read. Tags of this type usually act as simple identifiers

- **CLASS 2—read write**
  This is the most flexible type of tag, where users have access to read and write data into the tags memory. They are typically used as data loggers and therefore contain more memory space than is needed for a simple ID number

- **CLASS 3—read write with onboard sessions**
  These tags contain on-board sensors for recording parameters such as temperature, pressure, and motion, which can be recorded by writing into the tags'

memory. Because sensor readings must be taken in the absence of a reader, the tags are either semipassive or active.

▶ **CLASS 4—read write with integrated transmitters**
These are like miniature radio devices, which can communicate with other tags and devices without the presence of a reader. This means they are completely active with their own battery power source.

15.2.2 Active and Passive Tags

The first decision when considering a tag is between passive, semipassive, and active. Passive tags can be read at a distance of up to 4 to 5 meters using the UHF frequency band, whereas the other types of tags (semipassive and active) can achieve much greater distances of up to 100 meters for semipassive and several kilometers for active. This large difference in communication performance can be explained by the following:

▶ Passive tags use the reader field as a source of energy for the chip and for communication from and to the reader. The available power from the reader field not only declines very rapidly with distance but is controlled by strict regulations, resulting in a limited communication distance of 4to 5 meters when using the UHF frequency band (860 to 930 MHz).

▶ Semipassive or battery-assisted tags have built-in batteries and therefore do not require energy from the reader field to power the chip. This allows them to function with much lower signal power levels, resulting in greater communication distances of up to 100 meters. Distance is limited mainly because the tag does not have an integrated transmitter and till must use the reader field to communicate back to the reader.

▶ Active tags are battery-powered devices that have active transmitters on board. Unlike passive tags, active tags generate RF energy and apply it to the antenna. This autonomy from the reader means they can communicate at distances of several kilometers or more.

The experience gained by different companies running various trials and evaluations has so far shown that of the different RFID frequencies (LF, HF, UHF, and microwave), HF and UHF are the best suited to the supply chain. In addition, it is expected that UHF, because of its superior read range, will become the dominant frequency. This does not mean, however, that LF and microwave will not be used in certain cases.

This section has looked at the types of RFID tags. Now we will examine some current uses of RFID.

15.3 Current Uses of RFID

RFID technology is already well established in several areas such as electronic payment, supply chain management, and livestock tracking, as well as previously unforeseen areas such as data conveying.

15.3.1 Electronic Payments

In many countries, smart cards based on RFID technology are becoming more common in transport situations. Hong Kong introduced the *Octopus* system in 1997, and it is now used by more than 95% of the population.

The *Oyster card*, a Transport for London (TfL) contactless ticketing scheme, is a smart card. TfL estimates that 1 million fewer transactions per week are made at ticket offices and that there is a 30% improvement in the speed of passengers passing through the ticket gates. It is more difficult to copy Oyster cards than it is to copy the magnetic stripe cards, and because each card contains a unique ID number, it can be immediately cancelled if the card is reported lost or stolen.

15.3.2 Retail Stores

Large retail companies are pushing the adoption of RFID tags as a way of achieving supply chain visibility and reducing theft and product counterfeiting. These companies see RFID technology as a way of preventing *out-of-stock* occurrences, the overstocking of products in warehouses, and the theft or loss of goods.

For instance, the total cost of crime, including crime prevention, for UK retailers was £2.25 billion in 2002. Marks & Spencer tagged 3.5 million returnable food produce delivery trays in 2002. This is among the largest supply chain operations involving RFID in the world. The tagged trays are filled with individual food items at the supplier, carried by the distributor to the shop, emptied, and then returned. The information on the tagged trays is read at each distribution point, resulting in improved food delivery logistics and fresher food in stores.

U.S. fashion retailer American Apparel launched a 50-store pilot program in 2011 using RFID-embedded hangtags in all items sent to RFID-enabled stores. The main purpose of the pilot was to investigate the use of RFID for inventory management.

Executives at American Apparel reported that the pilot RFID-enabled stores have reduced the level of inventory shrinkage, improved overall stock levels, and reduced employee turnover. All of the stores in the pilot program outperformed non-RFID enabled stores.

15.3.3 Individual Product Tagging

Retailers are already looking at the tagging of individual products to allow for better control of product recalls and better-targeted marketing campaigns. In the United Kingdom, the retail store Tesco undertook an RFID trial at one store in 2003, which involved tagging individual DVDs. RFID readers were built into the store shelves to monitor each item. Not only was the stockroom alerted when a shelf needed restocking, but staff were alerted when browsing customers replaced DVDs in the wrong section.

15.3.4 Parts Tracking

Virgin Atlantic Airways has introduced RFID as a project to track critical, high-value aviation assets moving through its logistics supply chain at England's Heathrow Airport. The aim is to track and trace high-value repairable aircraft parts often at short notice.

Virgin tags serviceable airplane parts that pass through its Heathrow warehouse. When an item enters the warehouse, employees use a desktop computer to enter the item into the aviation maintenance and parts-inventory tracking system the airline already uses.

The next stage is a full inspection of the part. If it passes inspection, the part is given a goods-receipt number, which triggers the generation of an RFID label. Virgin Atlantic employees then attach the label to the container holding the part. They also attach a tag to a storage bin. Once the containers and storage bins are tagged at the warehouse entrance and inspection area, the items and bins are either placed on storage racks or sent out of the warehouse for immediate use on an airplane.

This section has examined current commercial uses of RFID technology. Now we will review the use of RFID in SAP systems.

15.4 RFID and SAP

SAP currently offers an RFID solution called SAP Auto-ID Infrastructure (SAP AII). This is part of the SAP Business Suite, similar to SAP Supply Chain Management (SCM), and it integrates RFID with current SAP functionality.

SAP AII can be implemented either as a standalone system or in the supply chain function. The latest release of SAP AII is 4.0 SP03, and we'll describe that version in detail in this section.

15.4.1 Supported Functions in SAP AII

Several processes are supported by SAP Auto-ID Infrastructure (AII). In addition to desktop user interfaces, mobile and fixed RFID devices support:

- Outbound processing (slap-and-ship)
- Flexible delivery processing
- Generation of pedigree notifications
- Returnable transport items processing

These processes will be discussed in more detail in the next four sections.

15.4.2 Outbound Processing (Slap and Ship)

Slap-and-ship is an approach to complying with customer requirements for physical identification of materials shipped through the outbound processes. The main goal of the slap-and-ship strategy is to invest the minimum amount of capital into an RFID implementation needed to comply with the mandates set forth by both Wal-Mart and the Department of Defense.

15.4.3 Flexible Delivery Processing

The flexible delivery process allows the automation of outbound and inbound processing. The process allows organizations to:

- Create outbound deliveries in the ERP system
- Pack and load outbound deliveries in SAP AII
- Post goods issue in the ERP system
- Send advance shipping notifications
- Create inbound deliveries in the ERP system
- Unload inbound deliveries in SAP AII
- Post goods receipts in the ERP system

These processes are particularly suitable for current RFID technology and for the goals of a great many retail customers.

15.4.4 Generation of Pedigree Notifications

Drug counterfeiting has become a major problem for the pharmaceutical industry and it is estimated to cost $46 billion a year in lost profits. Although drug counterfeiting is relatively rare in the United States, the amount of counterfeit pharmaceuticals from overseas has increased in recent years.

The U.S. Food and Drug Administration (FDA) believe RFID will work effectively to fight drug counterfeiting. The FDA's Counterfeit Drug Task Force has been investigating RFID technology and the concept of an electronic pedigree, called e-pedigree, a procedure that records where a drug is manufactured and how it is distributed.

The adoption of RFID at the case and pallet level would help secure the integrity of the drug supply chain so that pharmaceutical companies can reliably provide greater assurances that a product was manufactured and distributed safely. Many drug manufacturers, such as Pfizer, Purdue Pharma, and GlaxoSmithKline, have introduced RFID drug-pedigree projects.

The drug-pedigree system will authenticate pharmaceuticals as legitimate throughout the supply chain. The system uses RFID to match each container with its corresponding pedigree. During manufacture, or at any time prior to distribution, RFID tags can have a randomly generated code written to a chip or an already embedded code used to identify products. This code is unique to a product at one or more levels of packaging. It is stored along with related data and is thereby available for authentication.

At various stages in the movement of the product, the tag is scanned to create a digital record of the many transactions. When the material reaches stores, ready for sale to consumers, a complete record of its distribution has been created and stored.

SAP AII enables the generation of pedigree notifications. These XML messages contain information that third-party vendors can use to create pedigrees that satisfy state requirements. Pedigree notifications provide data regarding:

- Manufacturer (e.g., name, address, state license number)
- Drug (e.g., name, dosage form, dosage strength, container size, expiration date, lot number, ID)
- Trading partner (e.g., name, address)
- Person who should certify the delivery or the receipt of a drug (e.g., name, address, phone, email)
- Date of transaction

More data may be available for pedigree notifications in future SAP AII releases.

15.4.5 Returnable Transport Item Processing

Returnable transport items (RTIs) are assets that can be identified if they are allocated with a tag encoded with Global Returnable Asset Identifiers (GRAIs). A returnable transport item or asset is one the owner delivers to the custody of another business entity, usually for a fee. RTI processing includes functions to:

- Manage, load, and unload RTIs filled with products or with other RTIs
- Track the current location of RTIs and evaluate stocks and cycle times
- Achieve transparency across stocks of RTIs
- Automate processes, reduce stocks, shorten cycle times, and recognize bottlenecks

The GRAI provides a unique identification of an asset. It uses the prefix assigned to companies by the Uniform Code Council (UCC) to develop, assign, and maintain a unique asset number for equipment, resources, supplies, and so on to track location. Therefore, the GRAI is a unique code that is specific to the asset. The EAN identification number of a returnable asset, GRAI, is defined as a physical item with no reference to the contents. The EAN ID of a returnable asset enables tracking as well as recording of all relevant data.

Returnable assets such as pallets, barrels, rail cars, and trailers for further use in transport and trade processes are becoming increasingly important. The main focus is to manage returnable assets within harmonized business processes and leverage the EAN system in the unique identification of assets.

Now that we have reviewed the RFID applications available in SAP AII, we will summarize what we have discussed in this chapter.

15.5 Business Examples—RFID

RFID is a means of identifying an object using a radio frequency transmission. The technology can be used to identify, track, sort, or detect a wide variety of objects. Communication takes place between a reader or interrogator and a transponder or tag. The use of RFID has increased recently and is widely used in the retail industry.

Current Uses of RFID

RFID tags are found in many areas of the supply chain and are becoming increasingly common in warehouse situations. As the price of the technology decreases, the use of RFID will increase further.

Example

A manufacturer of sports footwear supplied the major discount stores in North America. Several of their larger customers used RFID so they could uniquely identify pallets as they entered their warehouse. This allowed the customer to perform a goods receipt of each pallet as it arrived.

The footwear company identified their pallets on four sides with labels that displayed barcodes for the material and batch. The labels were used by retailers that used scanners when pallets arrived at their receiving docks. The retailer's requirement for RFID tags allowed them to identify pallets as they entered the facility without having to move the pallet through a particular conveyor. The system received the information generated by the RFID tag on each pallet.

For the footwear manufacturer to comply with the new RFID requirements, they worked with an RFID tag manufacturer to develop a "slap and ship" label. The information on the tag included the material number, pallet number, and batch number. The company decided to operate a standalone SAP AII system for the RFID project that allowed tag picking, tag attachment, and the creation of delivery notes.

15.6 Summary

Radio frequency identification (RFID) technology has recently become commercially and technologically viable. RFID tags are essentially microchips that act as transponders, always listening for a radio signal sent by RFID readers. When a transponder receives a certain radio query, it responds by transmitting its unique ID code back to the transceiver. Most RFID tags do not have batteries; instead, they are powered by the radio signal requesting a reply.

RFID can be used in the warehouse. Since large corporations such as Wal-Mart first mandated the use of RFID, many companies have been investigating RFID for tracking the movement of materials. Although they may not reach the level of the pedigree system proposed by the FDA, they can expect to improve the visibility of material through the supply chain.

The SAP Auto-ID Infrastructure (SAP AII) solution is available for companies that want to use RFID with their ERP system. SAP AII requires configuration for the interaction of the RFID processes with the ERP functions. As the cost of RFID tags and readers falls, we can look forward to the proliferation of RFID and the need for a more integrated RFID system.

In Chapter 16, we will examine the use of cross-docking in the warehouse and how it can improve customer delivery times, reduce the need for warehouse space, and cut labor costs.

Cross-docking matches inbound and outbound deliveries to avoid having to store material in the warehouse. Not all material is suitable for cross-docking, but when it can be used it reduces labor costs, delivery time to the customer, and the amount of warehouse space used.

16 Cross-Docking

Cross-docking means taking an item of finished goods from the production plant and delivering it directly to the customer with virtually no material handling in between. Cross-docking reduces material handling and storage of the material in the warehouse. In most cases, the material sent from production to the loading dock has been allocated for outbound deliveries. The many benefits to a company that uses cross-docking include:

- Lower labor costs because the material no longer requires picking and putaway in the warehouse
- Less time moving material from production to the customer, improving customer satisfaction
- Less need for warehouse space, because the material is not stored

The finished goods are delivered from the production area directly to a location near the loading dock and from there are packed and shipped. In some instances, the material does not arrive at the loading dock from the production area, but may arrive for shipment from the warehouse as a purchased product to be resold or delivered from another company's manufacturing plants.

This chapter will review the cross-docking functionality in SAP ECC 6. We'll discuss planning for cross-docking, how the cross-docking actually takes place, and how to use the cross-docking monitor. Let's start with the first of those topics: planning cross-docking.

16 Cross-Docking

16.1 Planned Cross-Docking

Cross-docking has been used in warehouses for more than 50 years, but with the current drive to reduce costs and increase customer satisfaction, practitioners of supply chain management are using cross-docking as an important tool for warehouse efficiency.

16.1.1 Types of Cross-Docking

Several cross-docking scenarios are available to the warehouse management. In her paper *Making the Move to Cross Docking* (WREC, 2000), Maida Napolitano concluded that many warehouse operations involve a rapid turnaround of stock from receiving to outbound delivery. Napolitano defined these types of cross-docking:

- **Manufacturing cross-docking**
  This operation involves receiving purchased and inbound material required by manufacturing. The warehouse may receive the material and prepare subassemblies for the production orders.

- **Distributor cross-docking**
  This process can consolidate inbound materials from different vendors into a mixed material pallet, which is delivered to the customer when the final material is received. For example, computer parts distributors often source their components from various vendors and manufacturers and combine them into one shipment for the customer.

- **Transportation cross-docking**
  This operation combines shipments from different shippers in the less-than-truckload (LTL) and small-package industries to gain economies of scale.

- **Retail cross-docking**
  This process involves receipt of material from multiple vendors and sorting onto outbound trucks for several retail stores. This method was a key cost-saving measure for Wal-Mart stores in the 1980s. Wal-Mart procures two types of products: material it sells each day of the year and large quantities of material purchased once and sold by the stores and not usually stocked again. The first product type is called staple stock, and the second is called direct freight. Wal-Mart minimizes any warehouse costs with direct freight by using cross-docking and keeping material in the warehouse as briefly as possible.

- **Opportunistic cross-docking**
  Opportunistic cross-docking is the opposite of planned cross-docking because it occurs without creating a known link between the inbound delivery and the outbound requirement. The link is manually created. Opportunistic cross-docking can be used in any warehouse, transferring a material directly from the goods-receiving dock to the outbound shipping dock to meet a known demand, that is, a customer sales order.

Not all these types of cross-docking will be used at a warehouse. The amount of cross-docking at the warehouse depends on the types of material entering the warehouse and whether those materials are suitable for immediate shipment to a customer. The next section describes the types of material that are suitable for cross-docking.

16.1.2 Types of Material Suitable for Cross-Docking

Some warehouses do not use cross-docking because the materials stored in the warehouse may not be suitable. Some materials are better suited to cross-docking than others, including:

- Perishable materials that require immediate shipment
- High-quality items that do not require quality inspections during goods receipt
- Materials that are pretagged (bar coded, RFID), preticketed, and ready for sale to the customer
- Promotional materials and materials that are being launched
- Staple retail materials with a constant demand or low demand variance
- Prepicked, prepackaged customer orders from another production plant or warehouse

16.1.3 Planned Cross-Docking in SAP

SAP WM enables warehouse managers to plan the cross-docking process or to allow opportunistic cross-docking. The main difference between the two is that planned cross-docking allows decisions to be made before the material arrives at the warehouse, whereas opportunistic cross-docking decisions are made after the material has arrived.

Both types of cross-docking may occur in the warehouse, but planned cross-docking reduces the need to deal with material once it has arrived at the warehouse.

This is an important benefit for retail warehouses that need to move produce with short shelf lives, such as fruit and vegetables, to the retailer as quickly as possible.

16.1.4 Configuration for Cross-Docking

The initial configuration to complete is for planned and opportunistic cross-docking for the warehouse and the storage type. You can find the transaction by following the menu path IMG • LOGISTICS EXECUTION • WAREHOUSE MANAGEMENT • CROSS DOCKING • GENERAL SETTINGS • MAINTAIN WAREHOUSE LEVEL SETTINGS.

Figure 16.1 shows the configuration entered for the warehouse. The storage type is the location where the two-step cross-docked material will be located. In this example, the storage type is called XCD, shorthand for cross-docking. Only select the two-step checkbox when planned cross-docking is required.

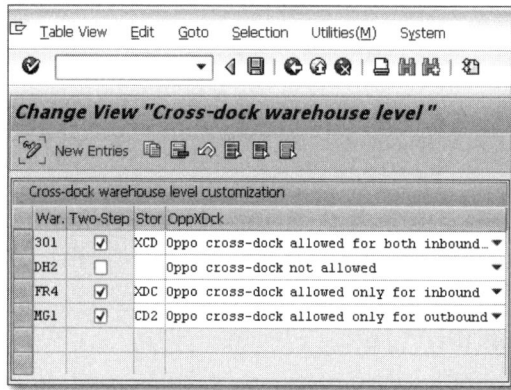

Figure 16.1 Warehouse Configuration for Planned Cross-Docking

This transaction allows the configuration for opportunistic cross-docking in the warehouse for inbound, outbound, both, or not at all. There are other configurations not shown in Figure 16.1 that can be determined in this transaction. These are:

- **Consider FIFO**

    Select this indicator to allow the system to consider first in, first out (FIFO) before implementing a cross-docking decision. In normal cross-docking the FIFO rules are overridden because the material arrives and is shipped before the material already in the warehouse.

▶ **FIFO Tolerance**
This field allows the entry of a FIFO tolerance between the material in stock and the material arriving so that material within the entered tolerance can be cross-docked even though it contradicts FIFO rules. If the inbound material is older than the tolerance allowed, then the cross-docking decision cannot be made.

▶ **Time Ref**
This field enables you to choose a date and time reference from which you can calculate the default release date and time. The choices include delivery loading date and time, delivery picking date and time, and delivery planned goods movement date and time. The release time for an outbound document is the planned time for creating a transfer order for the document so it can be released.

The next configuration step is to confirm that a movement type that is to be used for cross-docking is set to allow cross-docking. You can find the transaction by following the menu path IMG • LOGISTICS EXECUTION • WAREHOUSE MANAGEMENT • CROSS DOCKING • GENERAL SETTINGS • DEFINE CROSS-DOCKING RELEVANCY FOR MOVEMENT TYPES.

Figure 16.2 shows the configuration for the movement type applicable in each warehouse. The CD RELEVANT checkbox should be selected for movement types to be used for cross-docking.

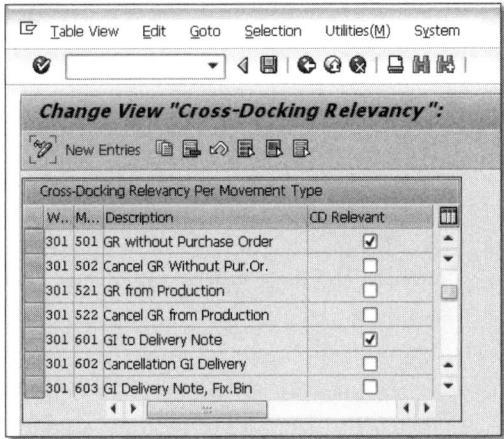

Figure 16.2 Configuration of Movement Types for Cross-Docking

16.1.5 Cross-Docking Decisions

A cross-docking decision is a link that can be made between a planning document, which can be an inbound or outbound delivery, and a candidate document, which is another inbound or outbound delivery.

> **Example**
> If an inbound delivery is expected for 20 units of material XYZ, and there is a planned outbound delivery of 20 units of XYZ to a customer, then these two documents, the planning and the candidate, can be linked by a cross-docking decision.

The cross-docking decision can be made by two methods:

- **Manual creation**
  The warehouse staff can decide to link a planning and a candidate document. The decision can be made with the aid of the cross-docking monitor, which we will discuss later in this chapter.

- **Automatic creation**
  The system can automatically make the decision. When a transfer order is created for an inbound or outbound delivery, the system reviews all potential candidate documents to ascertain whether a link can be made and a cross-docking decision created.

Now that we have examined the planned cross-docking functionality, we will go on to review the cross-docking movements that occur in the warehouse.

16.2 Cross-Docking Movements

When a cross-docking decision is made before the material arrives, the movement can be processed as a one-step or two-step cross-docking process. Both of these movements are described next.

16.2.1 One-Step Cross-Docking

As the name suggests, this movement processes the cross-docking movement in one step, directly from the inbound goods receiving area to the outbound goods issuing area.

For one-step cross-docking to be active, check the configuration for the warehouse to ensure that the two-step cross-docking checkbox is not selected. In Figure 16.1, the cross-docking configuration for the warehouse shows the checkbox that can be selected to force two-step cross-docking.

In planned cross-docking, the inbound delivery is linked to the outbound delivery, and a transfer order is created to move the material from the goods receiving area to the outbound delivery area.

Figure 16.3 shows the shipping notification for the inbound delivery. The material to be received from this inbound delivery is linked to the outbound delivery of the same material.

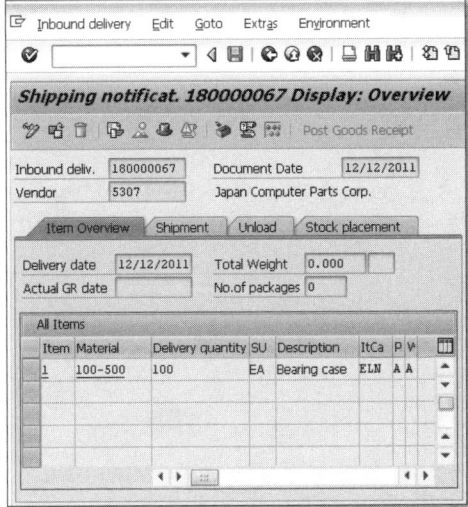

Figure 16.3 Inbound Delivery Linked to Outbound Delivery via Cross-Docking

When the material arrives in the goods receipt area, it is unloaded, and a goods receipt is posted in SAP IM. Figure 16.4 shows an outbound delivery with a planned goods issue of a quantity of 100 for material 100-500. This is the same quantity of material that is expected from the inbound delivery.

When the goods-receipted material is put away, a transfer order is created for the material. If this cross-docking is planned, transfer order processing retrieves that cross-docking decision. The system then creates a transfer order that proposes the goods issue area, storage type 916, as the destination storage type on the transfer order.

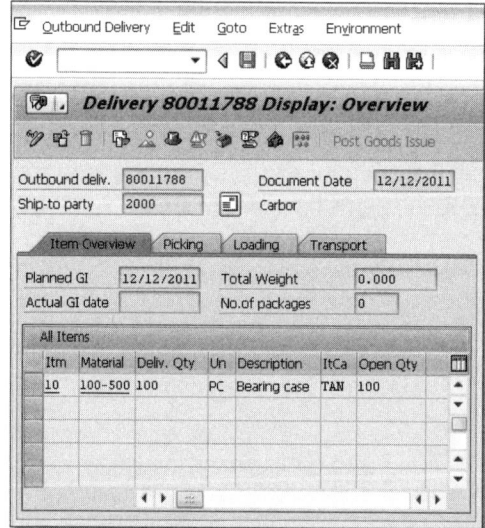

Figure 16.4 Outbound Delivery Linked to Inbound Delivery via Cross-Docking

Figure 16.5 shows the transfer order for the cross-docking decision linking the inbound goods receipt with the outbound delivery.

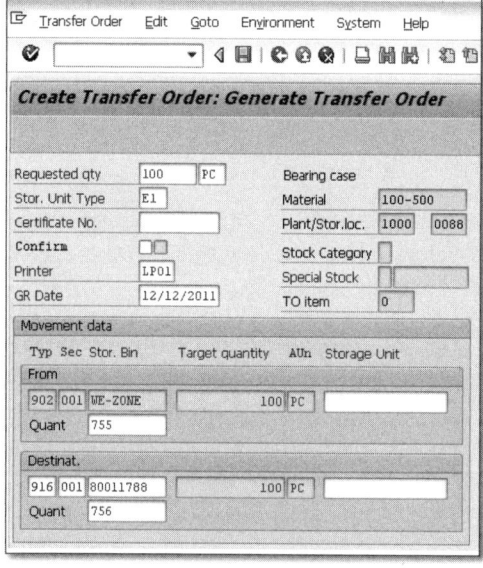

Figure 16.5 Transfer Order for One-Step Cross-Docking Process

Goods receipt area 902 is defined as the source storage type, and goods issue area 916 is defined as the destination storage type. After the transfer order is confirmed, the inbound delivery and outbound delivery documents are updated with the actual recorded pick and putaway quantities.

16.2.2 Two-Step Cross-Docking

In cross-docking where the two-step procedure has been configured, as seen for some warehouses in Figure 16.1, materials to be cross-docked are initially moved from the goods receipts area to a cross-docking storage type. In the second step, the material is moved to the goods issue area from the cross-docking storage type when the outbound delivery is released.

The cross-docking storage type is defined in the same transaction as shown in Figure 16.1, which you can find by following the menu path IMG • LOGISTICS EXECUTION • WAREHOUSE MANAGEMENT • CROSS DOCKING • GENERAL SETTINGS • MAINTAIN WAREHOUSE LEVEL SETTINGS.

Figure 16.6 shows the warehouse and the cross-docking storage type that have been defined. For warehouse 001, the two-step cross-docking checkbox has been selected, and the cross-docking storage type is defined as XDC.

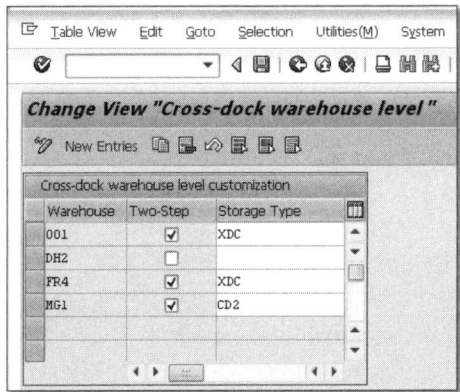

Figure 16.6 Defining Cross-Docking Storage Type for Each Warehouse

When a link is created between an inbound and outbound delivery as part of a cross-docking decision, the system reviews the decision to perform either a one-step or two-step process. In a two-step process, the system creates two transfer orders:

16 | Cross-Docking

- A transfer order for the inbound delivery materials from the goods receipt storage type to the cross-docking storage type
- A transfer order from the cross-docking storage type to the goods issue storage type

Figure 16.7 shows the shipping notification for the inbound delivery. The material to be received from this inbound delivery is linked to the outbound delivery for the same material: 100-500. When the material arrives in the goods receipt area, it is unloaded, and a goods receipt is posted in SAP IM.

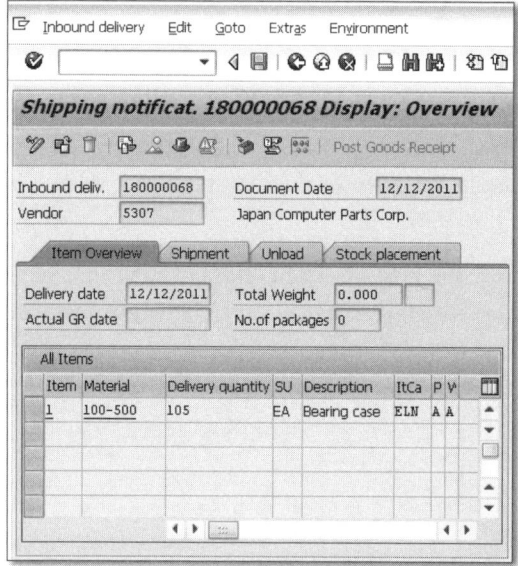

Figure 16.7 Inbound Delivery Linked to Outbound Delivery via Cross-Docking

Figure 16.8 shows the transfer order created for the first step of two-step cross-docking. The material is received, a goods receipt posted, and a transfer order created to move the material from the goods issue storage type to the cross-docking storage type XDC, where it will remain until the outbound delivery is ready to be goods-issued.

Figure 16.9 shows the outbound delivery with a planned goods issue of a quantity of 105 for material 100-500. This is the same quantity expected from the inbound delivery.

Cross-Docking Movements | 16.2

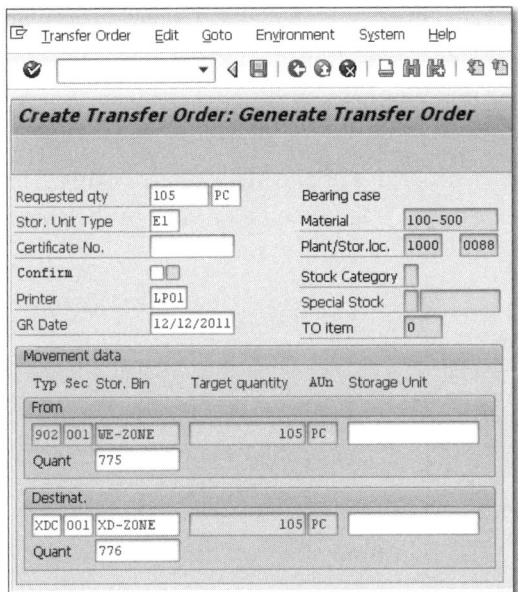

Figure 16.8 Transfer Order for First Step of Two-Step Cross-Docking

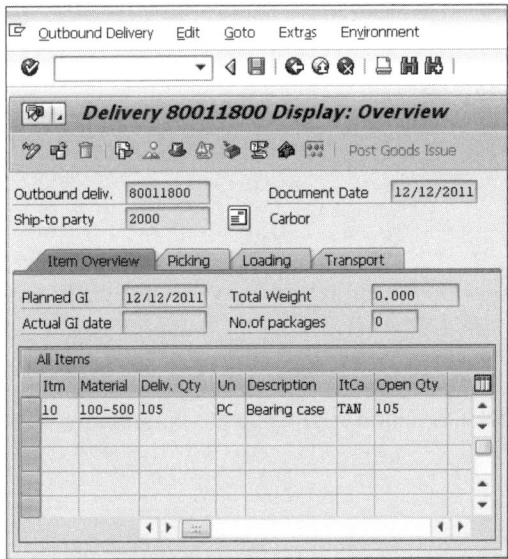

Figure 16.9 Outbound Delivery Linked to Inbound Delivery via Two-Step Cross-Docking

When the outbound delivery is released, the system creates a transfer order that moves the cross-docked material from the cross-docking storage type and proposes the goods issue area, storage type 916, as the destination storage type on the transfer order.

Figure 16.10 shows the second transfer order in the two-step cross-docking. The material is removed from the cross-docking storage type and placed in the goods issue storage type for the outbound delivery.

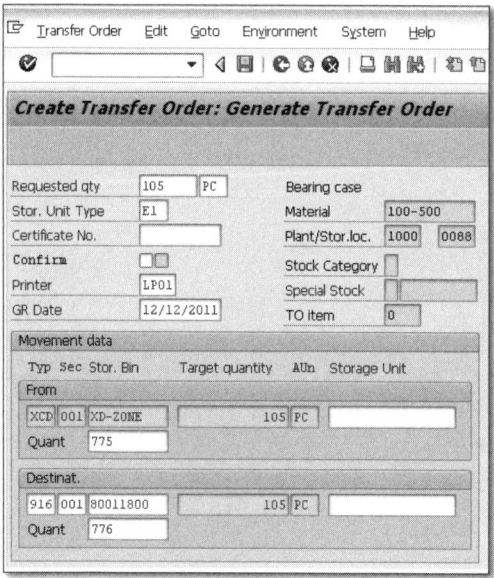

Figure 16.10 Transfer Order for Second Step of Two-Step Cross-Docking

After both transfer orders are confirmed, the inbound delivery and outbound delivery documents are updated with the actual recorded pick and putaway quantities.

This section examined the movements associated with cross-docking. Now we'll turn our attention to the SAP cross-docking monitor.

16.3 Cross-Docking Monitor

Warehouse managers use the cross-docking monitor to review the cross-docking situation in the warehouse and make any necessary changes. The monitor displays all inbound and outbound deliveries as well as transfer requirements, shipments, groups, and cross-docking decisions.

16.3.1 Accessing the Cross-Docking Monitor

You can display the cross-docking monitor with Transaction LXDCK or via the menu path SAP • LOGISTICS • LOGISTICS EXECUTION • CROSS DOCKING • CROSS DOCKING MONITOR.

Figure 16.11 shows the selection screen for the cross-docking monitor. The warehouse manager can select the warehouse and the planning direction, which is either inbound to outbound or outbound to inbound.

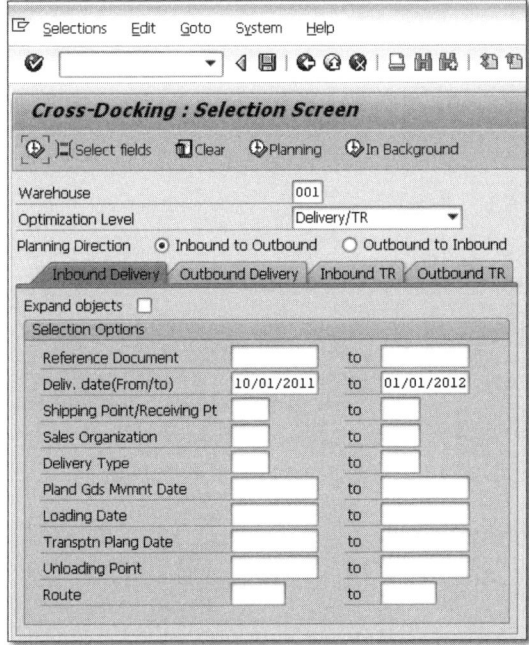

Figure 16.11 Initial Selection Screen for Cross-Docking Monitor

The other selection parameters include a date range, shipping point, sales organization, delivery type, unloading point, and route.

It is important to enter the date range. If cross-docking in the warehouse is operated with small delays between inbound and outbound delivery—possibly because of a lack of floor space—a narrow range of dates should be entered.

You can click the IN BACKGROUND button to create cross-docking decisions using the system optimization. If the warehouse manager wants to go directly to create cross-docking decisions based on the inbound and outbound documents in the system, you can click the PLANNING button.

Figure 16.12 shows the inbound and outbound transfer requirements for the date entered into the selection screen. The warehouse manager can opt to use the planning tool by clicking the PLAN button or to select documents for creating manual decisions.

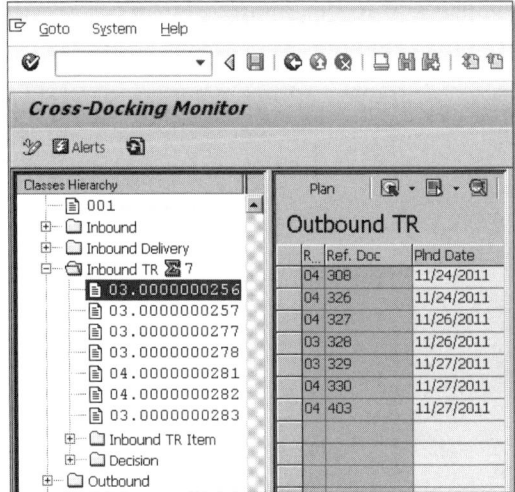

Figure 16.12 Cross-Docking Monitor Detail Showing Inbound and Outbound Transfer Requirements

16.3.2 Cross-Docking Alert Monitor

The warehouse manager uses the cross-docking alert monitor to identify potential issues with cross-docking. You can access the alert monitor while working in the cross-docking monitor by clicking the alert icon. You can also access it via Transaction LXDCA or the menu path SAP • LOGISTICS • LOGISTICS EXECUTION • CROSS DOCKING • ALERT MONITOR.

Figure 16.13 shows one of the three alert screens that are available in the alert monitor. The figure shows the deliveries for warehouse 001 that have been released and that are now outside of the tolerance. The other two alert screens are for transfer requirements that are outside of their tolerances and for cancelled transfer orders without replacements. The three alert screens are described in more detail as follows:

- **Deliveries with Release Time in the Past**
  This alert shows cross-docking-relevant outbound deliveries whose release times and latest release times have passed. The yellow alert is displayed when the release time is passed. The red alert is displayed when the latest release time has passed.

- **Transfer Requirements with Release Time in the Past**
  This alert shows cross-docking-relevant transfer requirements whose release times and latest release times have passed. The yellow alert is displayed when the release time is passed. The red alert is displayed when the latest release time has passed.

- **Cancelled Transfer Orders Without Replacement TOs**
  This alert shows transfer orders that have been cancelled without replacement transfer orders being created.

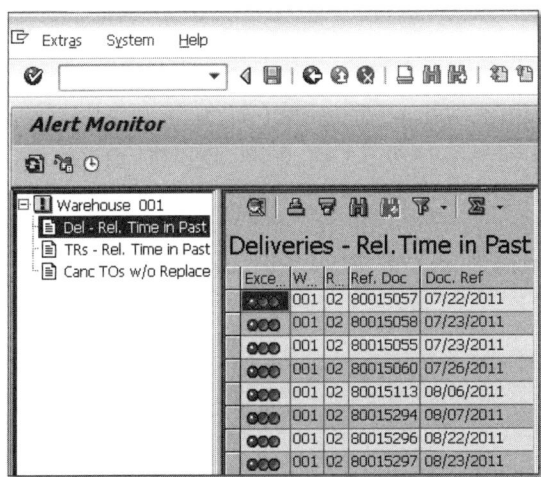

Figure 16.13 Cross-Docking Alert Monitor Showing Past Delivery Dates

You can access three of the alert screens from Transaction LXDCA and display the different screens within one transaction.

This section has reviewed the functionality and usability of the SAP cross-docking monitor. In the next section we'll look at some business examples of cross-docking.

16.4 Business Examples—Cross-Docking

Cross-docking allows finished goods from production to be delivered directly to the customer with virtually no material handling in between. Cross-docking reduces material handling and storage of the material in the warehouse. Usually the material moved from production to the loading dock has been allocated for outbound deliveries.

16.4.1 Planned Cross-Docking

Warehouse managers can plan the cross-docking process or allow opportunistic cross-docking. The main difference between the two is that planned cross-docking allows decisions to be made before the material arrives at the warehouse, whereas opportunistic cross-docking decisions occur after the material has arrived.

Example

A small manufacturer of consumer electronic goods operated three distribution centers in the United States. The finished goods were taken directly from the production line and transported to one of the three distribution centers, as there was very limited warehouse space at the production facility. Once the finished goods arrived at the distribution centers they were received into a warehouse, where they remained until they were shipped to a customer. The company used several off-the-shelf distribution software packages as well as custom-built warehouse and sales systems.

The company replaced their systems with an SAP system as part of a Y2K project but kept their warehouse system, as it was a new development. The SAP and warehouse systems were successfully integrated so that the three distribution centers operated with adequate efficiency.

The company extended its product line, and several of their kitchen appliances were very popular. A new production line was installed to cope with the added demand for the new items. The distribution centers found that they could not always keep up with customer deliveries, and often trucks waited for product to arrive from the manufacturing facility. Unfortunately the warehouse staff had to receive the items into the warehouse before they could be picked and delivered to the customer.

The logistics team recommended to management that they implement SAP WM to obtain the benefits they did not have with their custom system. This included the ability to perform cross-docking so that customer deliveries could be expedited.

A pilot SAP WM implementation was proposed for one of the distribution centers, which was used to evaluate not only cross-docking but other warehouse functionality. The warehouse manager was able to plan the cross-docking before items arrived from the production facility and give customers better service.

The pilot program showed management they could benefit from SAP WM functionality and especially cross-docking, so a decision was made to roll out the pilot program to the other distribution centers.

16.4.2 Cross-Docking Movements

When a cross-docking decision is made before the material arrives, the movement can be processed as a one-step or two-step cross-docking process. A one-step movement processes the cross-docking movement in a single step, directly from the inbound goods receiving area to the outbound goods issuing area.

A two-step cross-docking movement requires materials to be initially moved from the goods receipts area to a cross-docking storage type. In the second step, the material is moved to the goods issue area from the cross-docking storage type when the outbound delivery is released.

Example

A manufacturer of fresh-baked goods and snack items operated 8 manufacturing facilities and 30 distribution centers across the United States and Canada. The manufacturing sites produced items 24 hours a day and shipped to the distribution sites when the items were ready; this depended on the finished good. The distribution facilities either shipped to customer warehouses using their own transport, or the customer provided their own trailers, especially for deliveries of fresh-baked goods. The company had used an SAP system for many years, and the use of cross-docking had been implemented at most of the distribution centers. Initially the company had decided to operate with a one-step cross-docking process where all items, whether or not they were fresh-baked goods, were moved directly to the outbound loading docks.

The company had received some negative feedback from customers indicating that their trailers were not being loaded for several hours after their expected loading time. The distribution center management performed some analysis of the movements of items and found that on occasion the warehouse could get behind in loading, leading to delays of several hours for some deliveries.

To address the needs of the customers with fresh-baked goods deliveries, the company decided to change the way cross-docking operated in some distribution centers. Because some deliveries of snack items were not as time critical as fresh-baked goods, the company decided to prioritize the deliveries that contained fresh-baked goods.

To change the process, they decided to divide the distribution center into two warehouses: one for fresh-baked goods operating one-step cross-docking and one for all other items, which could operate with two-step cross-docking. The two-step process allowed the incoming items to be moved from the receiving dock to a staging area close to the shipping docks and then moved to the goods issue area when required.

16.5 Summary

Supply chain management involves a constant search for ways to make warehousing more efficient, improve customer satisfaction, and cut costs. If possible, material should be shipped directly from the manufacturer to the customer, avoiding any warehouse costs. The next best thing is to implement cross-docking, which removes the need for inspection on goods receipt, goods receipt staging, putaway, storage, picking, and goods issue staging.

Not all material is suitable for cross-docking, but using SAP cross-docking functionality makes it possible for some items. Many large organizations use cross-docking. It is most effective in the movement of items in the grocery industry, where food is stored as little as possible and the speed of delivery to the retail store is of the utmost importance.

In Chapter 17, we will discuss the processes that are included in the yard management functionality.

The yard management functionality extends the visibility of stock beyond the warehouse and expands the opportunity to increase efficiencies in the warehouse.

17 Yard Management

The yard management functionality of SAP ERP tracks materials that are not in the warehouse but are located in trailers and vehicles that are waiting to be unloaded. The area outside the warehouse is described as the "yard" and is a physical location where vehicles from vendors or third-party companies wait to be unloaded or to be picked up for delivery. In some instances the vendor may drop off the trailer so that the vehicle can pick up another trailer for an outbound delivery. The trailers that are full of materials are located in the yard and can be tracked using the yard management functionality. Some companies operate in this manner and can have dozens of trailers waiting outside the warehouse to be unloaded or delivered. In that instance the company uses yard management to give greater visibility to material in their supply chain.

17.1 Introduction to YM

Yard management functionality is available in standard SAP ECC6 and is available to be configured in Extended Warehouse Management (EWM). Some companies have significant amounts of material not in the warehouse, but in trailers and vehicles outside the warehouse. The YM functionality allows those companies to have greater visibility but requires some configuration to set up the yard in the system.

17.1.1 Yard Management Configuration

The yard management function is an extension of the warehouse and therefore uses warehouse processes. To use yard management functionality, you need to do some configuration, including defining the yard, doors, and staging areas.

Defining the Yard

You have to define the yard in configuration by following the menu path IMG • LOGISTICS EXECUTION • YARD MANAGEMENT • GENERAL SETTINGS • DEFINE YARD. The yard is defined as a three-character field that can be the same as the warehouse number. Several characteristics are required in the definition of a yard, such as the warehouse number the yard is associated with, the vehicle type, which is the vehicle used to transport material around the yard, and the default packaging material of the handling unit. The handling unit is created when a delivery is assigned to a vehicle in the yard. The vehicle cannot contain any deliveries, so a logical handling unit is defined for the delivery that is contained in the vehicle.

The other information you can assign when configuring a yard includes a scheduling time horizon, a yard scheduling profile, a time unit of measure, a default weight unit of measure, an indicator to flag if vehicle sealing is required, a vehicle waiting time, and the activity number range. Figure 17.1 shows the configuration for defining a yard.

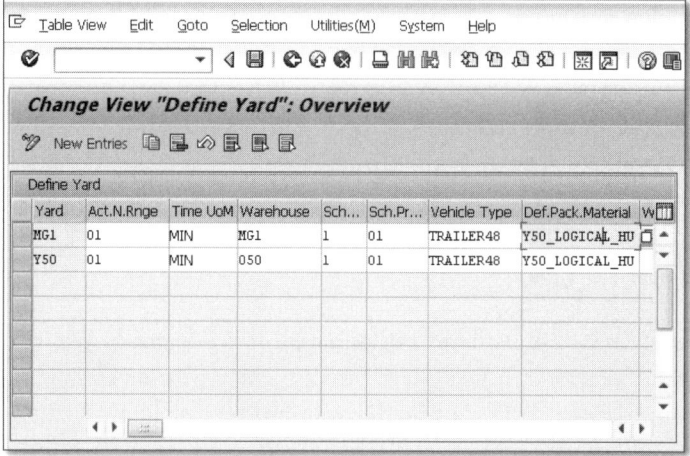

Figure 17.1 Defining the Yard

Yard Activities

When an activity takes place in the yard, a document is created and a number range has to be created. In configuration, you can find this transaction by following the menu path IMG • LOGISTICS EXECUTION • YARD MANAGEMENT • GENERAL SETTINGS • DEFINE YARD ACTIVITY NUMBER RANGES. The number range for yard activities is assigned to the yard, and the number range is identified using a two-character field, as shown in Figure 17.2.

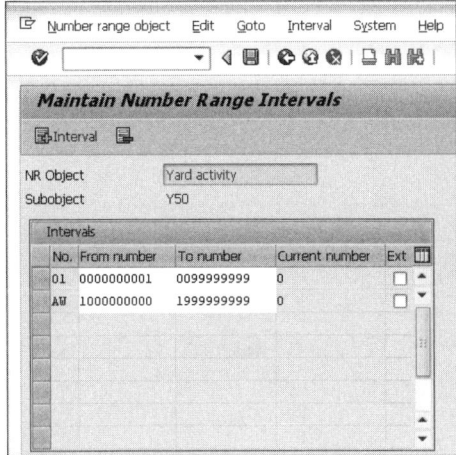

Figure 17.2 Maintaining the Number Ranges for Yard Activities

Reason Codes

When a user is using the yard activity monitor, he may want to block a vehicle, and this may require a reason code to be entered. To define the reason codes in configuration, follow the menu path IMG • LOGISTICS EXECUTION • YARD MANAGEMENT • GENERAL SETTINGS • DEFINE REASON CODES. Each reason code is a two-character code assigned to a yard number or to all yards if the default is used, as shown in Figure 17.3. Each reason code is triggered by an execution object, such as a changed destination, failed scheduling, or a blocked vehicle. The reason code has a 40-character text associated with it, as well as a 20-character short text. Figure 17.3 shows the configuration for reason codes.

Defining Vehicle Number Ranges

The vehicles used in yard management are implemented as handling units. The vehicle types are assigned to the yard, and the vehicle number ranges are assigned to the vehicle types. You define the vehicle number ranges in configuration by following the menu path IMG • LOGISTICS EXECUTION • YARD MANAGEMENT • VEHICLES • DEFINE VEHICLE NUMBER RANGES. The number range for the vehicles can be external or internal as shown in Figure 17.4.

17 | Yard Management

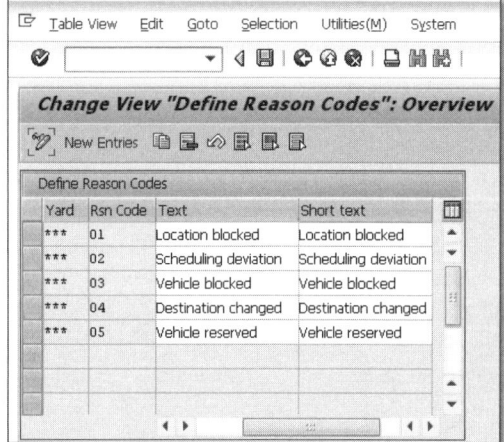

Figure 17.3 Defining the Reason Codes

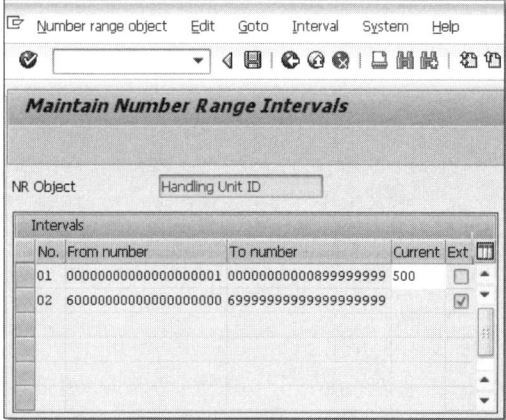

Figure 17.4 Defining the Number Ranges for Vehicles

Defining Vehicle Type Groups

The vehicle type groups are defined in the system as packaging material types. These are used to represent the different types of vehicles that can be used in the yard. You define the vehicle type group in configuration by following the menu path IMG • LOGISTICS EXECUTION • YARD MANAGEMENT • VEHICLES • DEFINE VEHICLE TYPE GROUPS. Figure 17.5 shows the existing vehicle type groups. You can enter a new vehicle type group from this screen by pressing the [F5] function key.

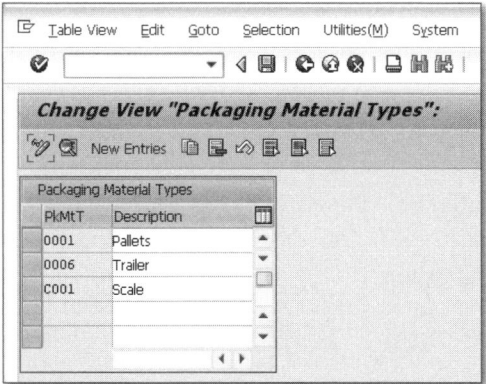

Figure 17.5 Defining Vehicle Type Groups

The vehicle type group or packaging material type is a mandatory four-character field. The user can enter a 20-character description for the vehicle type group and define properties, such as the type of number assignment and applicable vehicle number range intervals, for each group. Subsequently, it is possible to assign a vehicle type to the group in the packaging material's master record. When a vehicle is created, it is assigned to the vehicle type group to which its vehicle type is assigned. Figure 17.6 shows the detailed information for a vehicle type group.

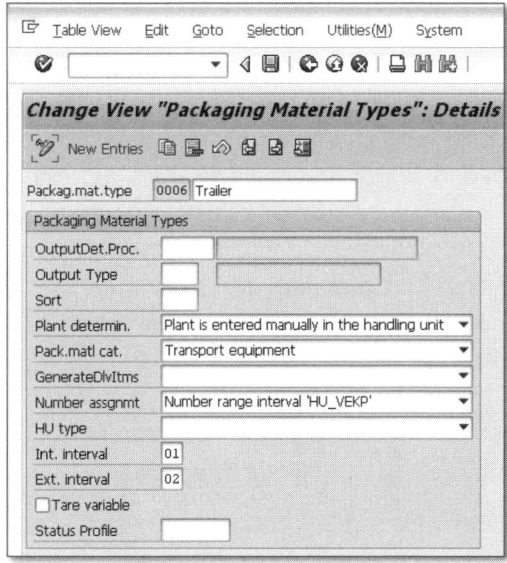

Figure 17.6 Changing Vehicle Type Groups

Material Group for Vehicle Type

For each vehicle type it is possible to create a material group that allows materials of similar characteristics to be stored in the same packaging. For example, materials that are affected by temperature need to be placed in certain packaging that is then assigned to the same material group. You define the vehicle type group in configuration by following the menu path IMG • LOGISTICS EXECUTION • YARD MANAGEMENT • VEHICLES • DEFINE MATERIAL GROUP FOR VEHICLE TYPES. Figure 17.7 shows the configuration for the material groups.

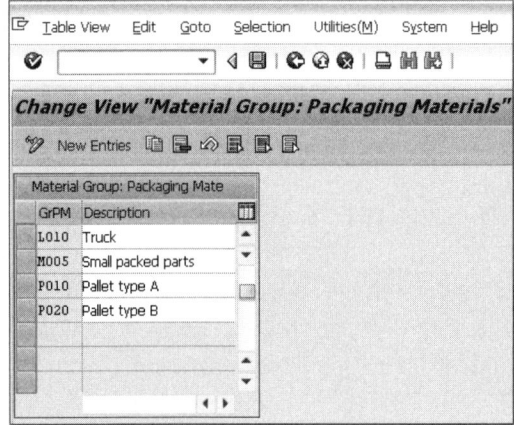

Figure 17.7 Defining Material Groups for Vehicle Types

Allowed Vehicle Types

The vehicle type groups can be assigned to one or more vehicle types. For example, a vehicle type like a trailer can be assigned several vehicle type group or packaging material types, such as certain pallets or containers. You define this assignment in configuration by following the menu path IMG • LOGISTICS EXECUTION • YARD MANAGEMENT • VEHICLES • DEFINE ALLOWED VEHICLE TYPES. Figure 17.8 shows the configuration for the assignment.

Defining Scheduling Profile

The yard scheduling profile contains the defaults the system uses when it performs any automatic scheduling. You can assign the scheduling profile to a yard in configuration.

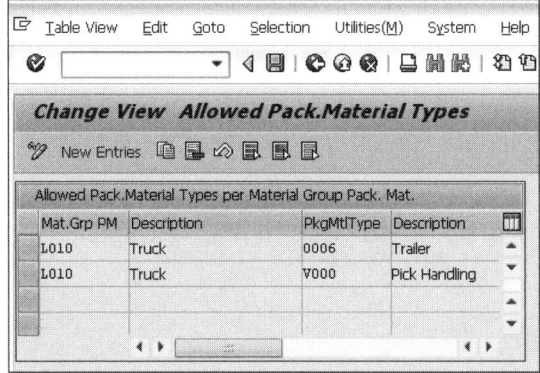

Figure 17.8 Defining Allowed Vehicle Types

The identifier for the scheduling profile is a two-character field and is defined for a specific yard. The components you can define for the scheduling profile include the type of document such as inbound delivery, outbound delivery, shipment, or return, or can be for all documents. The profile can also allow the user to create defaults for start and end times and a specific calendar. You define the scheduling profile in configuration by following the menu path IMG • LOGISTICS EXECUTION • YARD MANAGEMENT • LOCATION DETERMINATION AND SCHEDULING • DEFINE SCHEDULING PROFILES. Figure 17.9 shows the configuration for the scheduling profiles.

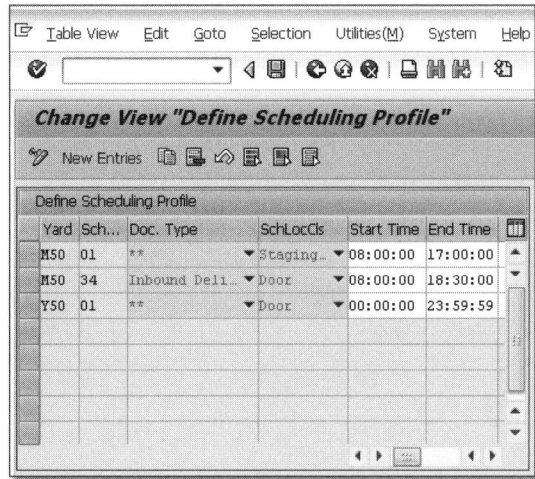

Figure 17.9 Defining Scheduling Profiles

17 | Yard Management

Defining Location Types

In the yard, it is possible to define a physical location type and assign the vehicle type groups for each location type. A location type is defined as a two-character field that can represent a location class such as a door, a parking space, or any location in the yard. You define the location type in configuration via the menu path IMG • LOGISTICS EXECUTION • YARD MANAGEMENT • LOCATION DETERMINATION AND SCHEDULING • DEFINE LOCATION TYPE. Figure 17.10 shows the configuration for the location type.

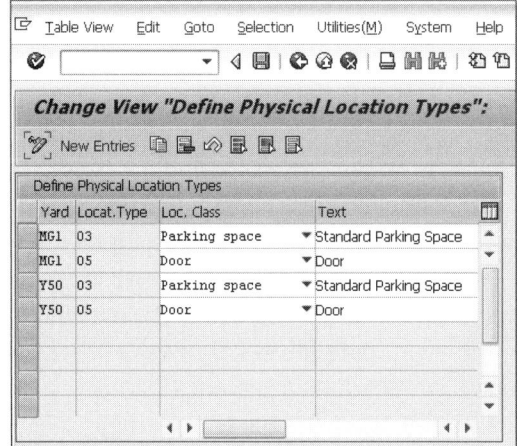

Figure 17.10 Defining Location Types

Defining Location Groups

A location group can contain several physical locations. For example, a location group can represent the parking spaces on the east side of the yard. The configuration requires that the location group be assigned to a specific yard. You define the location group in configuration by following the menu path IMG • LOGISTICS EXECUTION • YARD MANAGEMENT • LOCATION DETERMINATION AND SCHEDULING • DEFINE YARD LOCATION GROUP. Figure 17.11 shows the configuration for the location type.

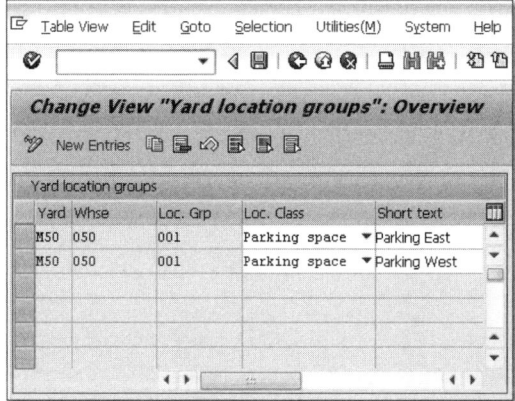

Figure 17.11 Defining Location Groups

17.1.2 Yard Management Structure

A yard is defined as the area outside of the warehouse that can contain trailers and vehicles that are either inbound to the facility or outbound from the facility. In the previous section we discussed how a yard is defined in the system. The yard is associated with a warehouse. Between the yard and the warehouse are areas where the material moves, which are defined as the doors.

Defining Doors

The door is defined as an area that exists between the warehouse and the yard. It is the location where materials leave the warehouse or are moved into the warehouse. You can define a door in configuration via the menu path IMG • LOGISTICS EXECUTION • YARD MANAGEMENT • YARD MAP • DEFINE DOORS. The door is defined with a three-character field and is assigned to a warehouse. You can take several optional configuration steps when defining a door. The door can be allocated a staging area, as well as being defined as a location that accepts goods receipt and performs good issues. Some doors at a warehouse can be dedicated only for receiving inbound delivery or processing outbound deliveries. A door can also be assigned to a physical location type or a location group. Figure 17.12 shows the configuration for a door.

17 Yard Management

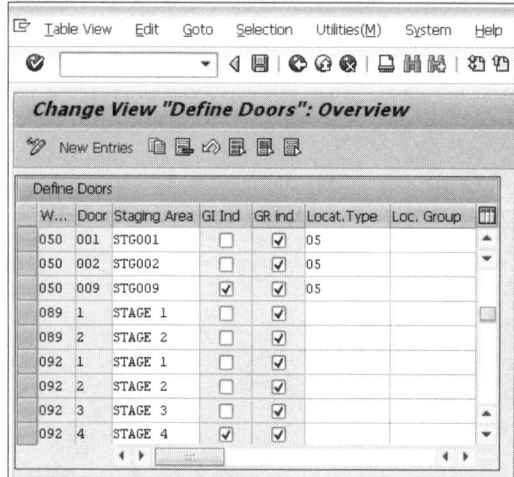

Figure 17.12 Defining Doors

Defining Staging Areas

A staging area is defined as a temporary storage area for items that either are leaving the facility as part of an outbound or have arrived as part of an inbound delivery. Physically, a staging area is close to a door to minimize travel time for the warehouse operators. Staff may prepare an outbound delivery by moving materials from a storage bin to the staging area prior to the time the outbound delivery is due to leave. You can define a staging area in configuration by following the menu path IMG • LOGISTICS EXECUTION • YARD MANAGEMENT • YARD MAP • DEFINE STAGING AREA.

You can define the staging area as a 10-character field that is assigned to a warehouse. You can also assign it to a door at the time of configuration, but this is optional, and defined it as being relevant for goods issue or goods receipt only or for both. Figure 17.13 shows the configuration for defining a staging area.

Defining Yard Locations

A yard location is a physical location in the yard. This can be a packing space for a trailer, a weighing point, a security checkpoint, or a location specific to your company's yard. When trailers arrive at the facility and are directed into the yard, they may be required to park at a security checkpoint where the seals are checked and then may have to be weighed before being moved to a parking space. You can configure these physical locations in the system.

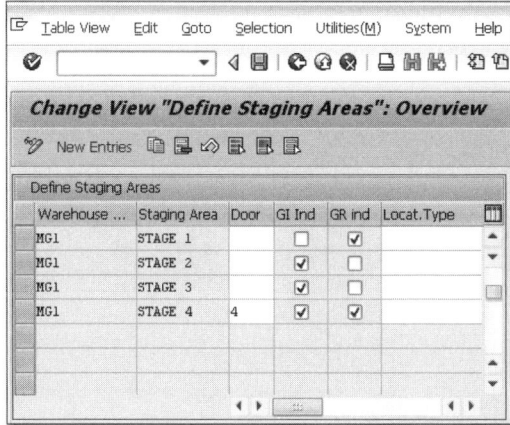

Figure 17.13 Defining Staging Areas

You can define a yard location in configuration by following the menu path IMG • LOGISTICS EXECUTION • YARD MANAGEMENT • YARD MAP • DEFINE YARD LOCATION. Each yard location has to be assigned to a location class, such as parking space, checkpoint, staging area, and so on. Figure 17.14 shows the configuration for defining a yard location.

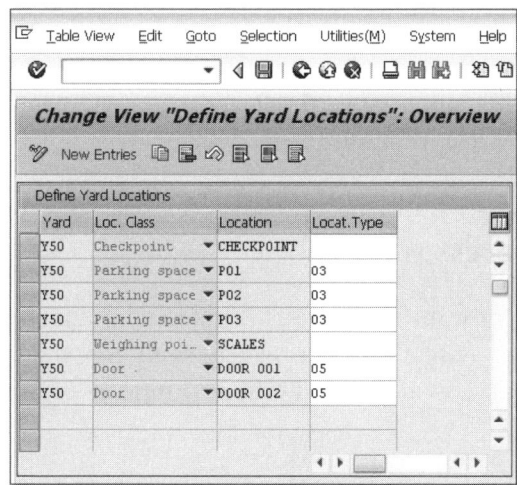

Figure 17.14 Defining Yard Locations

Assign Location Groups to Storage Types

In yard management it is possible to assign a location group, defined in the previous section, to a storage type or types in the warehouse. For example, a location group may be defined as the parking areas in the west side of the yard; this could be defined in the warehouse as a specific storage type or types. You can define a yard location in configuration via the menu path IMG • LOGISTICS EXECUTION • YARD MANAGEMENT • YARD MAP • ASSIGN STORAGE TYPES TO YARD LOCATION GROUPS. Each yard location has to be assigned to a location class, such as a parking space, checkpoint, staging area, and so on. Figure 17.15 shows the configuration for assigning a location group to a storage type.

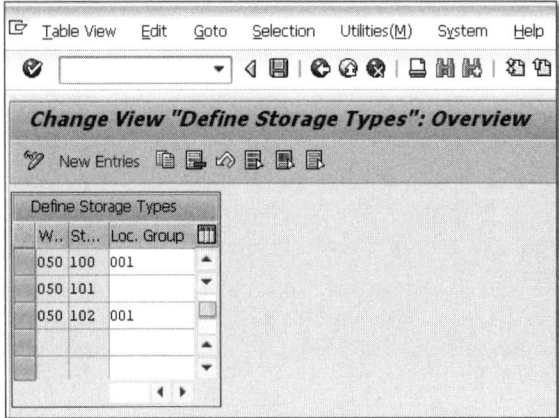

Figure 17.15 Assigning Location Groups to Storage Types

This section has described the configuration of yard management. Now we'll examine the processes you will find when using yard management.

17.2 Yard Management Processes

Companies that use yard management want to manage inbound and outbound movements in the yard. To do this the system provides several monitoring transactions that give management a total view of the yard. The first transaction we will look at is the yard monitor.

Yard Monitor

The yard monitor allows management to review all the movements occurring in a particular yard. The monitor gives the user an opportunity to review inbound shipments, outbound shipments, inbound deliveries, outbound deliveries, vehicles, departed vehicles, activities, and return deliveries. You can access the yard monitor using Transaction LYRDM or by following the menu path SAP • LOGISTICS • LOGISTICS EXECUTION • YARD MANAGEMENT • YARD MONITOR. The initial screen provides a tab for each of the documents, and selection criteria are available for each tab. Figure 17.16 shows the selection criteria for the INBOUND SHIPMENTS tab.

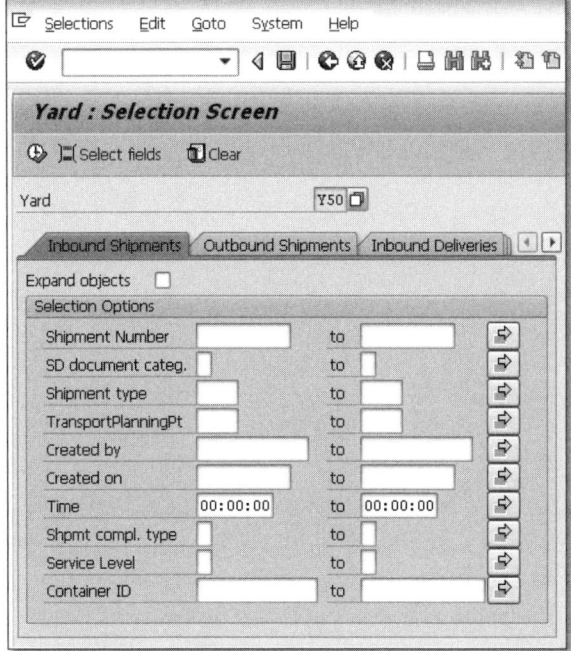

Figure 17.16 Yard Monitor Selection Screen

Once the user has entered the required selection criteria, the yard monitor displays a hierarchy that shows a total for the different classes. The user can select a class in the hierarchy, and the relevant documents will be displayed. Figure 17.17 shows the class hierarchy and the inbound deliveries for yard Y50.

17 Yard Management

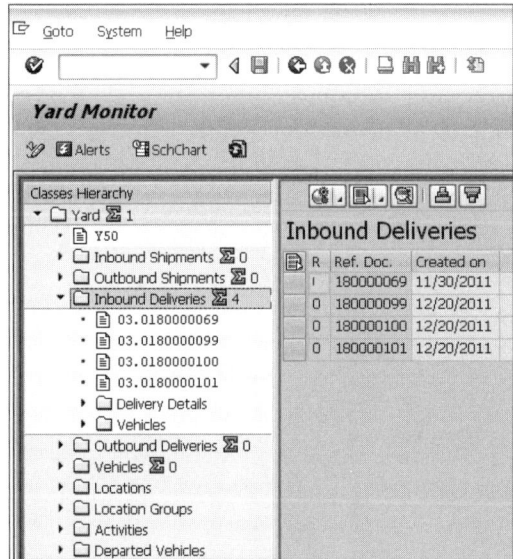

Figure 17.17 Yard Monitor Output

Alert Monitor

Management uses the alert monitor to view objects that are of concern. The transaction code for the alert monitor is LYRDA, and you can also find it by following the menu path SAP • LOGISTICS • LOGISTICS EXECUTION • YARD MANAGEMENT • ALERT MONITOR. The transaction requires that the user enter a yard number, and then the monitoring screen is displayed as shown in Figure 17.18. The alert monitor shows a hierarchy for the chosen yard. Selecting an object in the hierarchy shows the relevant documents. For example, in Figure 17.18, one document is shown for vehicles without scheduling locations.

To ensure that the alerts show the events required by management, you can maintain the alert thresholds and warnings while in transaction LYRDA. Either press [Ctrl]+[F1] or click the UPPER/LOWER LIMIT ALERT CONFIGURATION icon. This displays a screen, as shown in Figure 17.19, where the users can amend the lower and upper thresholds and the upper and lower warning levels for each object at all yards or a specific yard.

Figure 17.18 Alert Monitor Output

Site	Alert	Low. Thre.	Low Warn.	Up Warn	Up. Thre	Unit	U..
****	Vehicles W/O Sched.	1	3	10	12	TIME	HR
****	Vehicles Not Assigned	1	2	8	9	TIME	HR
****	Arrival Time					TIME	
****	Departure Time					TIME	
****	Scheduling Start Time					TIME	
****	Scheduling End Time					TIME	

Figure 17.19 Alert Monitor Maintenance

Checkpoint

The checkpoint transaction allows users to perform activities on vehicles when they are in the yard. For example, if a user wants to check a vehicle into the yard or check a vehicle out of the yard, he uses this transaction. To access the checkpoint, use Transaction LYCHP or follow the menu path SAP • LOGISTICS • LOGISTICS EXECUTION • YARD MANAGEMENT • CHECKPOINT.

Figure 17.20 shows the main screen for the check-in part of the checkpoint tool. The user can enter any selection criteria to display information on vehicles and activities. If the user wants to enter an activity, he can click the INSERT icon and enter information such as the reference document type, that is, inbound delivery, outbound delivery, return shipment, transfer order, or non-SAP document. He can then enter details such as the vehicle license plate, driver information, container information, and vehicle type. If a check-in, move, schedule, weighing, or rejection is to take place, the user can click the appropriate icon.

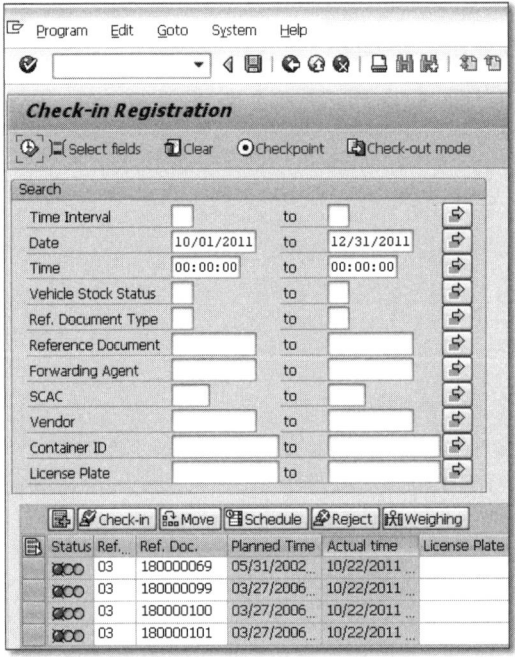

Figure 17.20 Check-in Screen

Loading and Unloading

You perform the loading and unloading of vehicles is performed using Transaction LYLDP, or you can follow the menu path SAP • LOGISTICS • LOGISTICS EXECUTION • YARD MANAGEMENT • LOADING/UNLOADING POINT. The transaction requires the user to enter a yard, and then it displays a set of selection criteria as shown in Figure 17.21.

When the relevant vehicles are displayed, the user can perform several activities such as loading, weighing, and sealing by clicking the icons on the screen.

Figure 17.21 Load Registration Overview

Scheduling Chart

The yard personnel can use Transaction LYSCH to print a scheduling chart of events to take place over a specified period using the transaction LYSCH or do so by following the menu path SAP • LOGISTICS • LOGISTICS EXECUTION • YARD MANAGEMENT • SCHEDULING CHART. The transaction allows the entry of times that the scheduling chart should be printed for. Figure 17.22 shows that the user can enter specific times from the present time to a previous time period. The user can also specify if he requires inbound, outbound, or both types of movements as well as show cancelled events. This scheduling chart is useful for yard managers as they plan the events that need to occur for the yard to operate efficiently.

Yard Inventory

The yard personnel can see at any time what the vehicle inventory of the yard is. They can perform this task using Transaction LYVHC or find it by following the menu path SAP • LOGISTICS • LOGISTICS EXECUTION • YARD MANAGEMENT • YARD INVENTORY. The transaction shows the vehicle inventory for a specific yard. The user has the option of entering selection criteria such as the vehicle stock status, which can be empty, full, or partially full vehicles. Figure 17.23 shows an example of the yard inventory display.

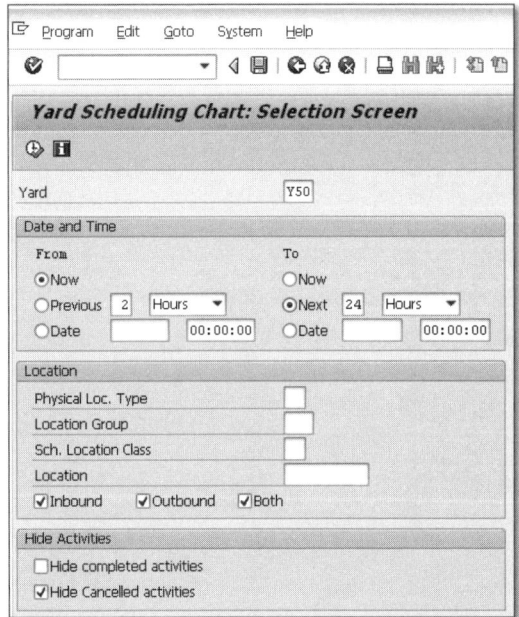

Figure 17.22 Yard Scheduling Chart Selection Screen

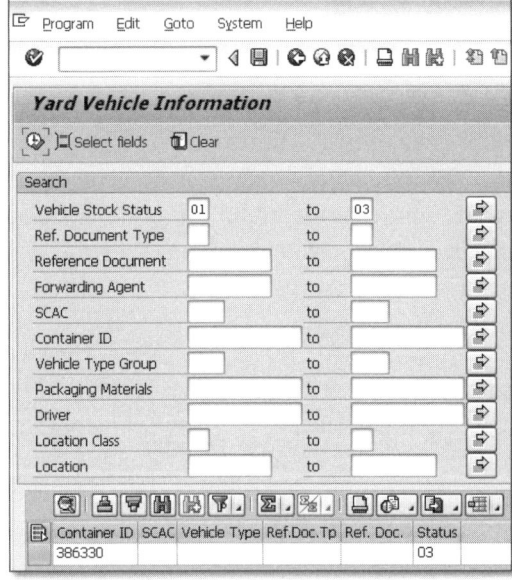

Figure 17.23 Yard Inventory Screen

Now that we have looked at the processes of the yard management function, we will now look at some relevant business examples.

17.3 Business Examples — Yard Management

Yard management is used to track materials that are not in the warehouse but are located in trailers and vehicles that are waiting to be unloaded. The functionality gives management at busy warehouses the ability to view the incoming movements and to manage those movements so that the yard and the warehouse operate efficiently.

Yard Management Processes

The yard management function offers a range of processes that give the user the ability to successfully monitor and schedule movements that are inbound or outbound from the warehouse, increasing efficiency inside and outside of the warehouse.

Example

A distributor of automotive spare parts operated a major distribution facility in Nevada that fulfilled orders for auto parts stores in the Western United States. The facility received parts from automotive manufacturers as well as parts manufacturers across the United States and abroad. The facility was a 24-hour operation and received container-sized loads as well as packages and smaller deliveries. The inbound delivery area was designed to have eight receiving docks that could accommodate a single trailer. The outbound area was similarly designed but with nine docks.

The facility was originally one of three distribution centers in the Western United States, with others being in Portland, Oregon, and Phoenix, Arizona. To reduce costs, the other warehouses were closed and all items were now sourced out of the Nevada warehouse. The results of the other warehouses closing was that the number of deliveries, both inbound and outbound, was more than the facility could deal with in a normal two-shift operation, so a third shift was introduced to deal with the number of trailers.

The company used SAP WM, but the issues were outside of the warehouse, as trailers were often parked at the facility for days waiting to be unloaded. This was due to a lack of visibility on the part of the warehouse staff. The trailers were parked wherever spaces appeared, and this did not give warehouse personnel any idea of what trailers needed to be unloaded first. The same became true of the outbound operation also. The warehouse would expect to be loading certain trailers for an outbound delivery, but they would still be stuck in the inbound parking area waiting to be unloaded.

The company looked at several options to assist with the issues but decided to use the yard management functionality in SAP ERP to provide greater visibility of the vehicles in the yard. Because the issues were immediate, the company did not perform a pilot project. The implementation immediately gave warehouse staff the visibility they required to see which vehicles needed to be unloaded, and using the scheduling function, they were able to produce a document for the day that gave the staff the information they needed to deal with the incoming trailers.

17.4 Summary

Yard management is a tool that some companies need to efficiently deal with the number of vehicles coming into and out of the yard before they reach the warehouse. The visibility the functionality provides is key to increasing the efficiency of the warehouse when dealing with a large number of incoming and outbound vehicles.

In Chapter 18, we will discuss some new developments in warehouse management.

The warehouse management functionality of SAP ERP has evolved from a simple locator system to a full suite of warehouse software that covers the entire warehouse operation. New developments are helping to optimize the use of labor and warehouse operation monitoring.

18   Developments in Warehouse Management

Standard WM has evolved from the earliest functionality in SAP R/2, where it was a good locator system, through the R/3 releases that incorporated putaway and picking strategies, storage-unit management, wave picking, the warehouse activity monitor, SAPConsole, and RF transactions. SAP ECC 6.0 brings additional functionality such as the Warehouse Control Unit.

Because more warehouse functionality is expected in later releases of SAP ERP and SAP Supply Chain Management (SAP SCM), this chapter describes some of the latest SAP developments available in warehouse management. Some warehouse operations use task and resource management (TRM), value-added services (VAS), or Extended Warehouse Management (EWM).

Although these three areas are new compared with the standard WM, they are integrated into common warehouse processes. Your company may already be using manual functions that are similar to VAS or TRM. This chapter will help you understand these developments and know how to help your company take advantage of the functionality.

The next section examines the functionality of TRM and its integration with standard warehouse management.

18   Developments in Warehouse Management

18.1   Task and Resource Management

TRM functionality allows warehouse staff to further maximize their efficiencies by providing processes to help execute planned warehouse tasks. The TRM functions do not plan the warehouse work but help manage the work defined by the planning function and manage the resources to perform the tasks. The functionality in TRM falls into five core areas:

- Resource management
- Request management
- Task management
- Route management
- Bin management

Let's examine these in more detail now.

18.1.1   Definitions in Task and Resource Management

Although TRM functionality relates to tasks and resources that occur in the warehouse, the terms in TRM do not always relate directly to standard warehouse terminology. The terms included in this section are specific to TRM.

Site

The primary physical area defined in TRM is the site. This is not always directly equivalent to a warehouse. A site can be a warehouse, part of a warehouse, or many warehouses. It can also define an area that is not part of the traditional warehouse, such as a parked trailer area or even warehouse offices.

You can define a site in TRM configuration by following the menu path IMG • LOGISTICS EXECUTION • TASK AND RESOURCE MANAGEMENT • MASTER DATA • GENERAL SETTINGS FOR TRM.

Figure 18.1 displays the configuration elements required to create a site. The site number is a four-character field and can represent an area that may be a warehouse, part of a warehouse, or multiple warehouses. The site is a uniquely defined physical area. The other fields to be filled in include the time zone, unit of measure for time and distance, short text, and the number ranges for tasks, resources, requests, and messages.

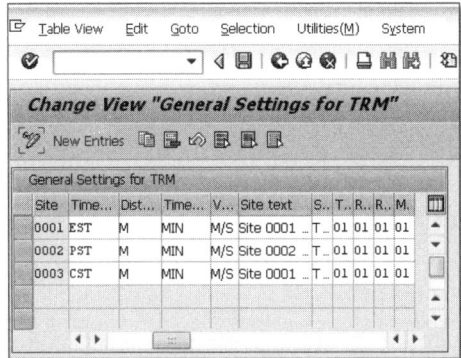

Figure 18.1 Site Configuration for TRM

Site Map

After creating the site, you can define it via different physical properties. These physical properties are defined as part of a site map. The site map allows the planning of efficient routes in the warehouse based on the physical definition. These physical properties are not found in standard WM and require some explanation. They are:

- **Zones**
  This is a physical location within a site that is used for a specific function, for example, a work center or pallet storage area.

- **Nodes**
  A node can be used in two ways: as a physical node where material is placed and as a logical node where resources pass. The logical node may be an entry point or exit point. All physical nodes can be assumed to be logical nodes, but logical nodes are never physical nodes.

- **Obstacles**
  This is simply a physical object or barrier defined in the site as an area through which resources cannot pass. This may be a wall or a rack of fixed equipment. When the system determines a route for a resource to take, it plans around the defined obstacle.

- **Working areas**
  These are physical areas between two zones that are defined as areas where resource planning occurs. For example, a working area may be the physical area between the goods receiving dock and the picking area.

Defining a Zone

You can configure a zone in the TRM function area of the IMG by following the menu path IMG • LOGISTICS EXECUTION • TASK AND RESOURCE MANAGEMENT • MASTER DATA • SITE MAP MANAGEMENT • DEFINE ZONES, OPERATIONS AND SERVING ZONES.

Figure 18.2 shows the zones that are defined for site 0001. The zone can be given a 10-character identifier, and a zone function must be defined as well. The function can be set as a pick-up and drop-off point, work center, storage area, or empty pallet zone.

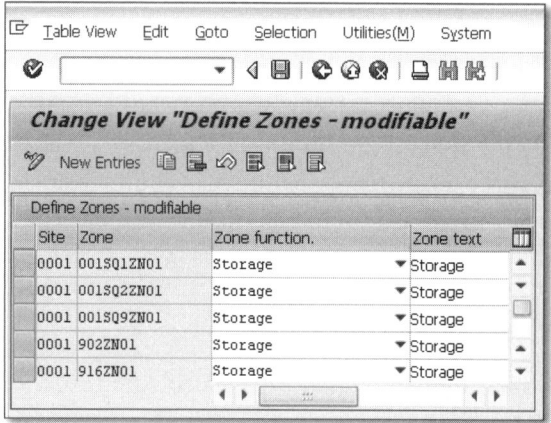

Figure 18.2 Zone Definition for a Site

Defining a Node

You can configure a node in the TRM area of the IMG. The node cannot be defined prior to the zone creation. You can find the transaction by following the menu path IMG • LOGISTICS EXECUTION • TASK AND RESOURCE MANAGEMENT • MASTER DATA • SITE MAP MANAGEMENT • DEFINE NODES AND ENTRIES/EXITS TO/FROM ZONES.

Figure 18.3 shows the definition of each node for the site. The node can be given a 14-character identifier. Use X, Y, and Z coordinates identify the node within the site and allow you to locate the node in a three- dimensional context.

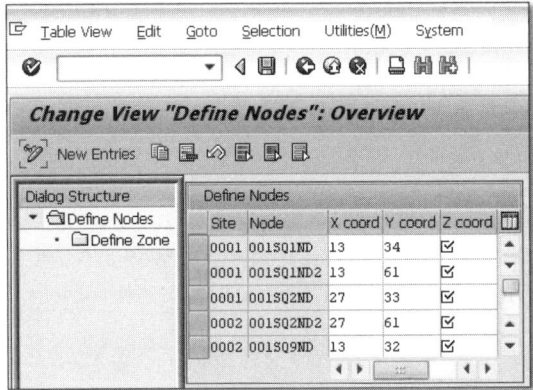

Figure 18.3 Definition of Nodes for a Site

Defining a Zone Entry/Exit

A node can be defined as an exit, entry, or both for a zone. The menu path is the same as for defining a node: IMG • LOGISTICS EXECUTION • TASK AND RESOURCE MANAGEMENT • MASTER DATA • SITE MAP MANAGEMENT • DEFINE NODES AND ENTRIES/EXITS TO/FROM ZONES.

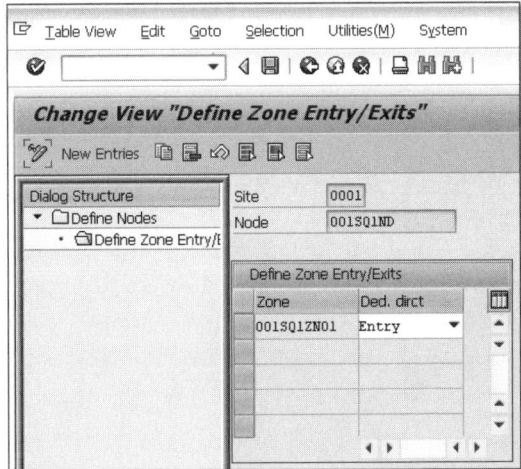

Figure 18.4 Definition of Zone Entry and Exit Points

Figure 18.4 shows the node for the zone. The dedicated direction for the node is defined as an entry, but this can be changed to exit or to both entry and exit. This allows the system to choose a node with the correct direction. For example, if a route from a storage bin to the loading dock requires a path through a node, that node has to be an entry or both an exit and an entry.

Defining an Obstacle

An obstacle is an area that a resource cannot pass through, such as a wall. The planned route must take an obstacle into account and find a pathway around it. The obstacle should be defined to identify the physical definition of the object.

> **Example**
> If the obstacle is a wall, then nodes in each corner should define the wall.

You can configure the obstacle with a transaction found via the menu path IMG • LOGISTICS EXECUTION • TASK AND RESOURCE MANAGEMENT • MASTER DATA • SITE MAP MANAGEMENT • DEFINE OBSTACLES.

Figure 18.5 shows that each obstacle defined for the site is given an obstacle type—WALL or RECTANGLE in this case—and is defined by a series of nodes that have specific coordinates. Therefore, the route planning will avoid the obstacle in determining the route for the resource.

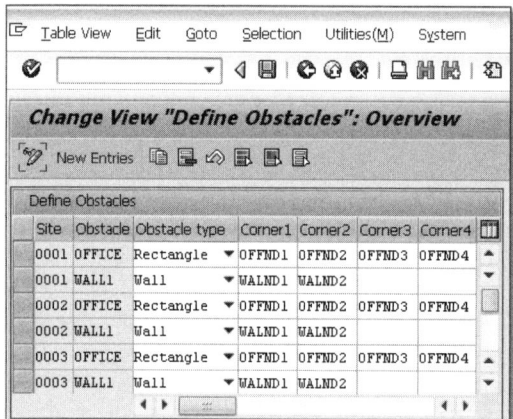

Figure 18.5 Definition of Obstacles in a Site

Defining a Zone Group

A zone group is simply a grouping of zones. You create zones to more easily define the working areas between zones. You can only assign zones to the zone group after the zones have been defined.

To configure the zone group, you can use the transaction found via the menu path IMG • LOGISTICS EXECUTION • TASK AND RESOURCE MANAGEMENT • MASTER DATA • SITE MAP MANAGEMENT • DEFINE ZONE GROUPS AND ASSIGN ZONES.

Figure 18.6 shows the defined zone group and the zones that are assigned. The zone group can be entered with up to 10 alphanumeric characters.

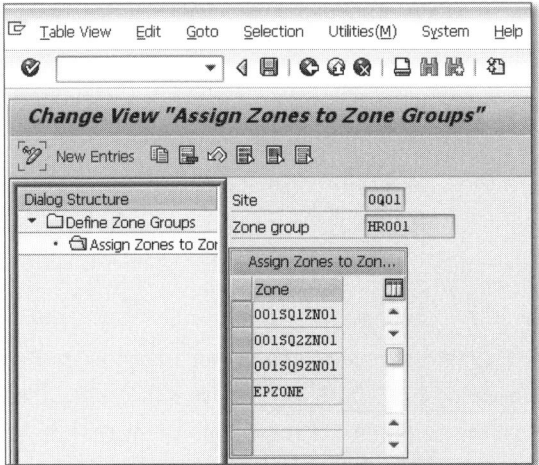

Figure 18.6 Assignment of Zones to a Zone Group

Defining a Working Area

The working area is the physical area between two zones or zone groups that is defined as an area where resource planning occurs. You can configure a working area with the aid of the zones and zone groups that define the working area.

To configure the working area, you can use the transaction found via the menu path IMG • LOGISTICS EXECUTION • TASK AND RESOURCE MANAGEMENT • MASTER DATA • SITE MAP MANAGEMENT • DEFINE WORKING AREAS.

Figure 18.7 shows the working areas that have been defined for a site. A working area can be defined as the area between a source zone or a source zone group and a destination zone or zone group. When defining a working area, you have the option to allow a single path from source to destination; that is, the resource can pass from the source to the destination only or be allowed in both directions.

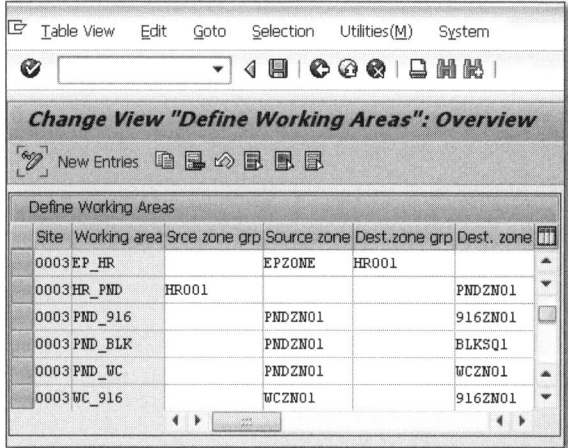

Figure 18.7 Definition of Working Areas Within a Site

Defining a Resource

TRM defines a resource as an object capable of receiving and executing tasks. This resource can be a warehouse employee or a piece of warehouse equipment. You can create the resource using the resource element maintenance wizard, Transaction LRSW, which you can find by following the menu path SAP • LOGISTICS • LOGISTICS EXECUTION • TASK AND RESOURCE MANAGEMENT • RESOURCE ELEMENT MAINTENANCE WIZARD.

Figure 18.8 shows the first screen of resource creation, requiring that you enter the site and activity. The resource is only viable in one site. If the resource works in two sites, then it must be duplicated.

Figure 18.9 shows the entry of the resource. The resource element can have an identifier up to 20 characters long. The element or worker's name can also be up to 20 characters long. On this screen, you select whether the resource is a worker or a device.

18.1 Task and Resource Management

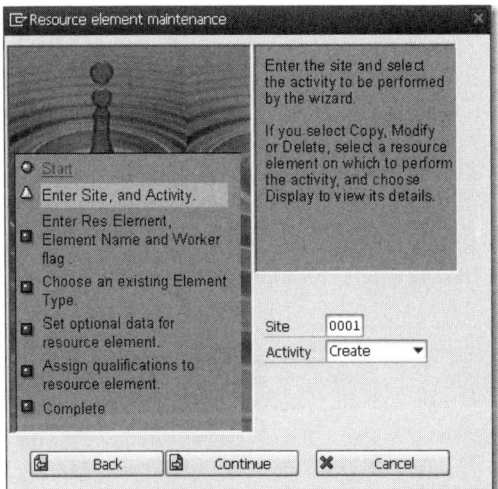

Figure 18.8 Using the Resource Element Maintenance Wizard to Create a Resource

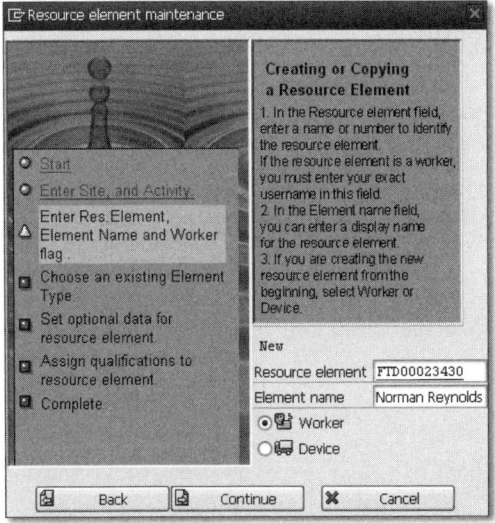

Figure 18.9 Entry of Resource Element and Element Name

Figure 18.10 shows the element type that has been chosen for the resource. In this example, the resource allocated is a forklift truck driver, but it could have been a picker, driver, packer, and so on.

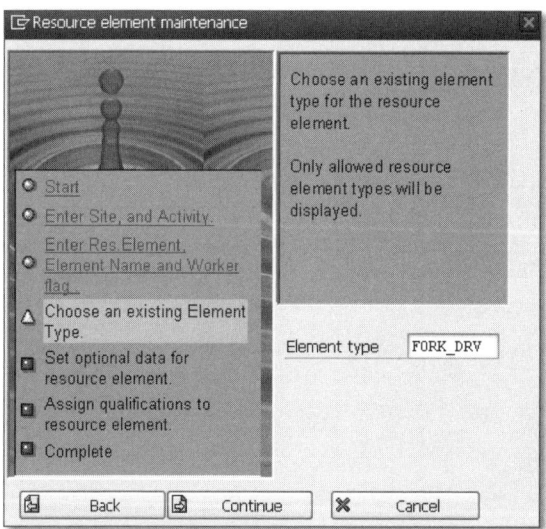

Figure 18.10 Element Type Entry for Creation of Resource

On the next screen for creating the resource, you can add optional attributes. The one field in this screen that should be filled is the ROLE CHECK field. There is an option to allow no role checks, which means the resource can be used in any working area. If you choose to allow no role check, then allocating the resource to working areas is not necessary.

If the role check is selected, the next screen allows the resource to be added to working areas and for those areas to be prioritized for the allocation of tasks.

Figure 18.11 shows that this resource has been added to three working areas and that those working areas are prioritized. Priorities are manually entered. The other tabs on this screen relate to the types of handling units (HUs) that the resource can work with and the priority given to working with the various HU types. The last tab is for element types this resource can work with. For example, a resource can be allocated as a forklift driver and a material picker.

After the entries for this screen are made, the resource details are completed, and the resource has been created.

Task and Resource Management | **18.1**

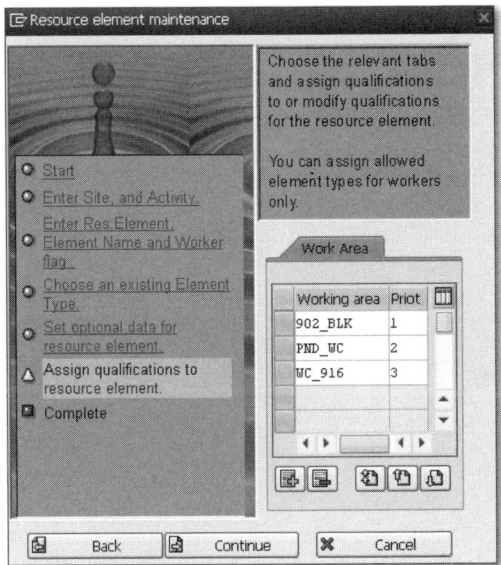

Figure 18.11 Entry of Allocated Working Areas for a Resource

18.1.2 Resource Management

TRM's resource management functionality is one of its core areas. The resource management function manages the resources, whether they are devices or personnel, and can allocate and reallocate the orders that are assigned to the resource. The resource management configuration allows the definition of resource types and resource elements that can be used to create resources.

In configuration, the resource management transaction defines all of the functionality used in creating resources. You can find the transaction by following the menu path IMG • LOGISTICS EXECUTION • TASK AND RESOURCE MANAGEMENT • MASTER DATA • RESOURCE MANAGEMENT.

Defining Resource Element Types

The element type is used to create a resource, with options for a device, such as a forklift or crane or a worker.

Figure 18.12 shows the resource elements that have been configured for site 0001. The elements are in two categories: element types for the device category and element types that can be assigned for workers.

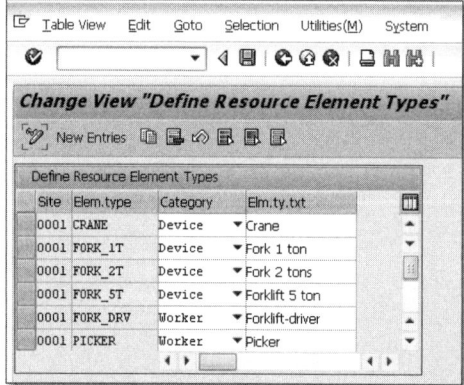

Figure 18.12 Defining Resource Element Types for a Site

Defining Resource Types

A resource type is used for devices such as cranes and forklifts. In this configuration, you can enter the speed of the device so that the route can be timed and scheduled.

Figure 18.13 shows the resource types with their respective velocities in meters per second (M/S). This velocity unit of measure can be changed. The node entered for the resource type is the default node from which the resource receives its first task after logging on to the system.

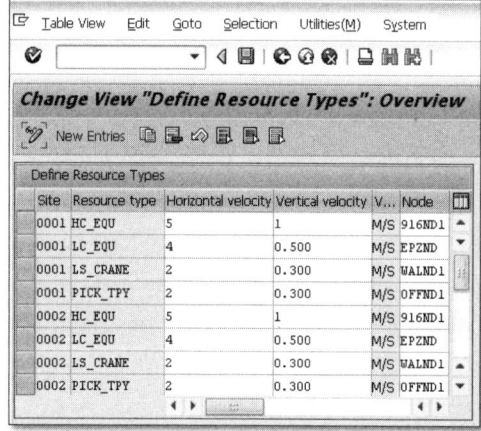

Figure 18.13 Definition of Resource Types for Site

Each resource type has components that when combined make up the resource type. The resource type HC_EQU shown in Figure 18.13 can be defined as a worker and a forklift truck. Therefore, the resource type must be defined in configuration to have components, in this case a driver and a forklift truck.

Figure 18.14 shows the two components: the forklift truck and the forklift truck driver assigned to the resource type. Therefore, when the resource type is used to define a resource, these two components must be defined as well.

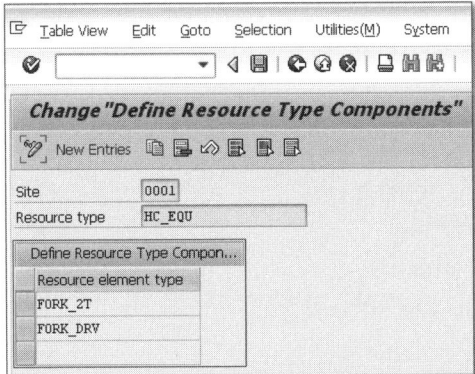

Figure 18.14 Two Components Defined for a Resource Type

Each resource type can be allocated to certain working areas. For example, a forklift truck may be a certain size and only be allowed in certain areas of the warehouse. Therefore, the resource type for this forklift may be restricted to certain working areas.

Figure 18.15 shows the working areas that have been assigned to resource type HC_EQU. The resource type cannot be allocated to working areas not defined in this configuration.

One more definition of the resource type that you can configure is capacities. The resource type cannot hold or move an infinite amount of material in each task, so the capacity of the resource type is configured for each handling unit that it can accommodate.

Figure 18.16 shows the number of HUs the resource type can move or carry. In this example, the resource type has a capacity of 40 small boxes or 1 wire basket.

18 | Developments in Warehouse Management

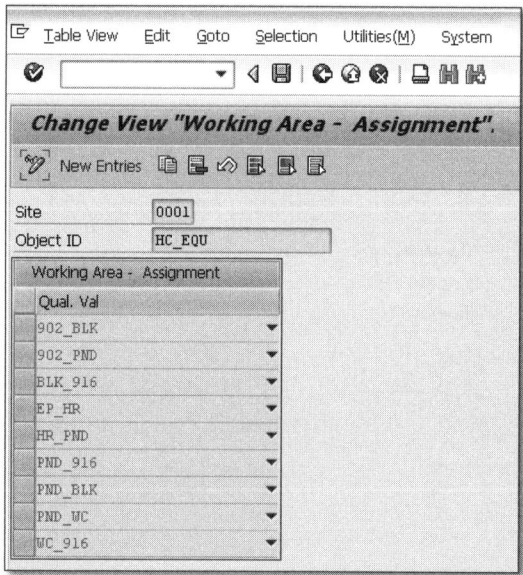

Figure 18.15 Allocation of Working Areas to a Resource Type

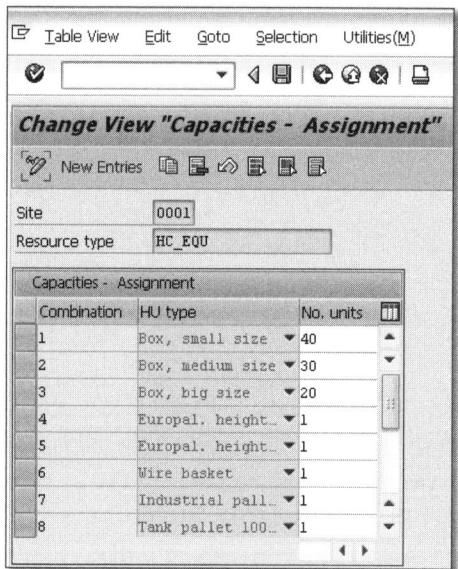

Figure 18.16 Capacities Configuration for a Resource Type

18.1.3 Request Management

The request management function controls the requests that arrive in TRM for the movement of material. The request is derived from the transfer orders created in WM. The transfer order requests that material be moved from one storage bin to another.

The scheduler function within the request management function moves the request to task management when required. When the request is then transferred to the task management function, the program breaks down the request into its individual elements.

After the resources have completed the task, the request management function collects the confirmation, and final confirmation of the move of the material is recorded in the transfer order. The request is removed from the request management function.

18.1.4 Task Management

When the request is moved from request management to task management, it is broken down into individual tasks. The request may contain several individual tasks. You can create a number of scenarios when converting the requests to tasks. Let's take a look at these now.

One Request—One Task

This is a very simple request, for example, one that requires the movement of one pallet from storage bin YXZ to storage bin 123. This simple request may involve moving a pallet of material from high-rack storage to the open storage type.

One Request—Several Tasks

This also may be viewed as a simple request, for example, moving a pallet to a high rack. However, this request may comprise two tasks in TRM: the first task to remove the pallet on a forklift to the rack and a second task to use a larger forklift to stack the pallet in a high rack.

Several Requests—One Task

If there are several transfer orders to move material to an open storage type, this may be performed with one task because the material can be moved on one pallet.

Several Requests—Several Tasks

With this scenario, several transfer order items, or requests, may require picking, packing, and then moving to the loading dock. This requires several tasks, such as picking, placing the material in packing material, and using a forklift to move the packed material to the loading dock.

Creating a Task

Tasks are created from the requests that are forwarded from standard warehouse management. The request management function sorts, schedules, and releases the requests to task management. Task management then identifies and creates the tasks based on the routes necessary to fulfill the request. The tasks are placed in the task pool and resources are assigned to complete the task and fulfill the request.

Task Selection by Resource

The resource is assigned several tasks. The resource uses a presentation device to communicate with the TRM function in the warehouse. This may be a radio frequency (RF device) that the worker resource is using on the warehouse floor. Three modes can be used to select tasks: user selected, system guided, or semi-system guided. In the system-guided option, the task-management function assigns the highest-priority task.

18.1.5 Route Management

Route management contains the functions that determine the route information and calculates route duration and route priority. The basis of route management is the entries already described in this chapter, for example, zones, nodes, working areas, and obstacles.

The route is simply the course that a resource travels between the start and end points. When tasks are being created, the route management function creates the route for a particular resource type to take. This may be a mandatory route because of height or safety restrictions.

Mandatory Routes

You create mandatory routes in configuration. You can find the transaction by following the menu path IMG • LOGISTICS EXECUTION • TASK AND RESOURCE MANAGEMENT • CONTROL DATA • DEFINE MANDATORY ROUTES.

Figure 18.17 shows that for all HUs, the route in site 0001 between zones 001SQ1ZN01 and 902ZN01 must pass via zone PNDN02. The mandatory route between the same two zones may be different for varying HUs if these are required.

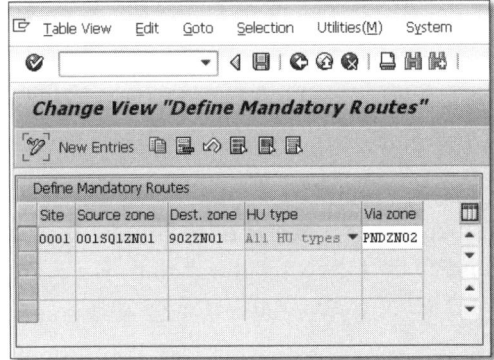

Figure 18.17 Definition of Mandatory Route in Route Management

Route Exceptions

Route exceptions are used when a route between two nodes has been calculated, but due to the nature of the resource type, the route is either not valid or the distance of the route is not as calculated.

You can enter this configuration via the menu path IMG • LOGISTICS EXECUTION • TASK AND RESOURCE MANAGEMENT • CONTROL DATA • DEFINE ROUTE EXCEPTIONS.

In Figure 18.18, the route between nodes WCND1 and EPZND has been configured for an exception for resource type PICK_TPY, which is a warehouse picker.

This may be needed because a picker cannot pass down a particular aisle because of safety concerns and must take a longer route. If the picker could not take that route, it would be flagged as invalid in this transaction and not selected by the route management function.

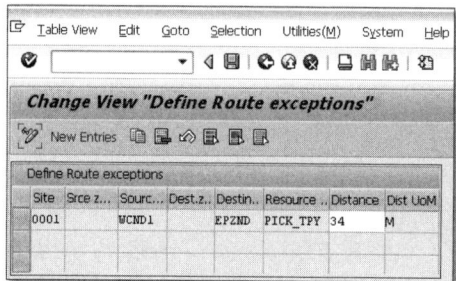

Figure 18.18 Defining Route Exceptions

18.1.6 Bin Management

The storage bins in standard warehouse management are allocated to storage types and storage sections. However, within the TRM function, the site map is created based on X and Y coordinates. Therefore, you need to assign these types of coordinates to the storage bins.

The transaction to set the X and Y coordinates for warehouse storage bins is LSET_BIN_COORDINATES. You can find it by following the menu path SAP • LOGISTICS • LOGISTICS EXECUTION • TASK AND RESOURCE MANAGEMENT • STORAGE BIN • MAINTAIN STORAGE BINS BY SELECTION.

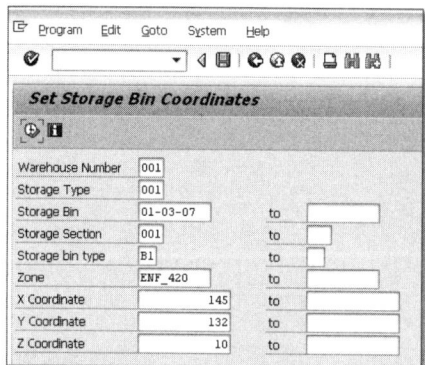

Figure 18.19 Entering Coordinates for Warehouse Storage Bins

Figure 18.19 shows the entry of X and Y coordinates for a warehouse storage bin. The storage bin is allocated to a zone, and the coordinates identify the storage bin as an item into the site map.

18.1.7 TRM Monitor

The TRM monitor is the transaction that keeps SAP WM aware of the situation within the TRM function with respect to transfer orders, inbound and outbound deliveries, tasks, and resources. The transaction for the monitor is LTRMS and you can find it by following the menu path SAP • LOGISTICS • LOGISTICS EXECUTION • TASK AND RESOURCE MANAGEMENT • MONITOR.

Figure 18.20 shows the initial selection screen for the TRM monitor. The monitor has screens for groups, outbound deliveries, inbound deliveries, transfer orders, transfer order items, tasks, and resources.

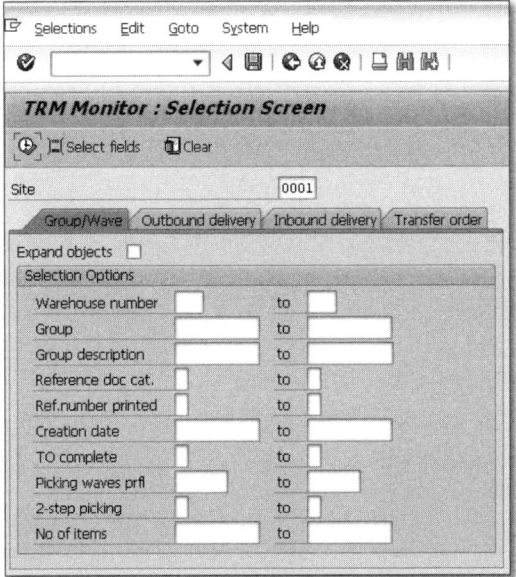

Figure 18.20 TRM Monitor Initial Selection Screen

In this section, we examined the functionality available in task and resource management. The next section discusses the processes available in value-added services.

18.2 Value-Added Services

Value-added services (VAS) are operations performed on materials that improve their value, functionality, or usefulness. These services include repacking, tagging, price marking, labeling, and shrink-wrapping. This generally occurs in the warehouse prior to an outbound delivery to a customer.

You can create VAS orders that instruct warehouse staff to perform certain tasks. These tasks may be part of a VAS template that is used for some materials.

18.2.1 Configuring VAS

You need to complete several configuration steps before using VAS. These include defining a VAS work center and defining VAS for the warehouse. Let's explore configuration in detail now.

Defining a VAS Work Center Profile

A VAS work center is a location where VAS activities, such as packing or labeling, are performed. You should set up these work centers in configuration via the menu path IMG • LOGISTICS EXECUTION • WAREHOUSE MANAGEMENT • VALUE ADDED SERVICES • GENERAL VAS SETTINGS • DEFINE VAS WORK CENTERS.

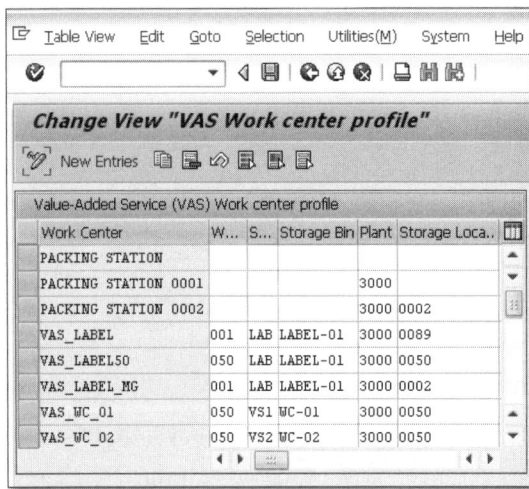

Figure 18.21 Defining VAS Work Centers

Figure 18.21 shows the definition of a VAS work center in relation to a warehouse, storage type, storage bin, plant, and storage location. You can enter additional information for the work center, but the functionality for the additional information will not be available until after release ECC 6.0.

Defining VAS Settings for the Warehouse

For VAS to operate in a warehouse, you need to make some settings for the VAS functionality. You make these settings configuration by following the menu path IMG • LOGISTICS EXECUTION • WAREHOUSE MANAGEMENT • VALUE ADDED SERVICES • GENERAL VAS SETTINGS • DEFINE VAS FOR WAREHOUSE.

Figure 18.22 shows the basic settings for the warehouse in which VAS operations will occur. These settings are:

- **Time unit of measure**
  Seen in Figure 18.22 as TIME UoM, this is the basic unit of measure used for the VAS orders in this warehouse.

- **Procedure**
  This is the procedure that determines which VAS template to use. The procedure is configured in the IMG.

- **Automatic exit from VAS after VAS order confirmation**
  If this checkbox (AUTVASEXIT) is selected, a transfer order from the work center to the next destination is automatically created when the last of the VAS orders in the work center has been confirmed.

- **Internal movement type**
  This field (INT.MVTYPE) is the transfer order movement type to be used in this warehouse for material when it is transferred between work centers. For example, an order may have to be moved from a work center that labels to a work center that shrink-wraps the material on the pallet.

- **Movement type for work center to final outbound destination**
  This field (FEX.MVTYPE) is the transfer order movement type used in this warehouse for material sent from the work center to the final outbound destination.

- **Final putaway movement type**
  This field (FPT.MVTYPE) is the transfer order movement type to be used in this warehouse for material sent from the work center to the final putaway location.

18 | Developments in Warehouse Management

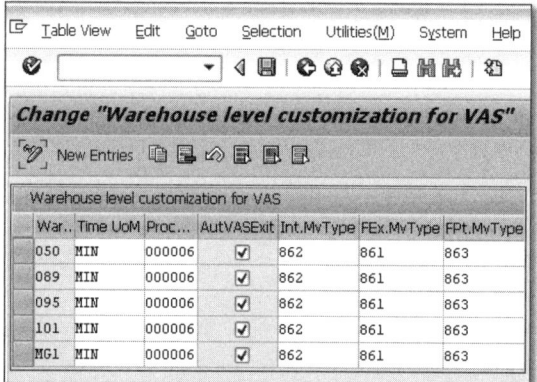

Figure 18.22 Defining VAS Settings for a Warehouse

Defining these movement types for each warehouse ensures that the correct movements will be made when material is moved with VAS orders.

Defining the Procedure for VAS Template Determination

This procedure determines the VAS template to be used. A VAS template enables instructions to be reused for different documents with the same conditions. Therefore, you can create several templates to create orders for different situations without having to enter the conditions each time. The procedure is based on the access sequence and determination type used in areas such as price determination in SD or batch determination in MM.

Condition types, based on access sequences using fields in condition tables, define the procedure.

Figure 18.23 shows that six procedures have been created for the VAS template determination. Each of these procedures is based on a set of sequenced condition types. You make these configuration settings by following the menu path IMG • LOGISTICS EXECUTION • WAREHOUSE MANAGEMENT • VALUE ADDED SERVICES • VAS TEMPLATE DETERMINATION • DEFINE PROCEDURE FOR VAS TEMPLATE DETERMINATION.

The usage field P defines the procedure for packing object determination. The application PO represents the packing object. To review the condition types that make up the procedure, select the procedure and select the CONTROL option in the dialog structure as shown in Figure 18.24.

540

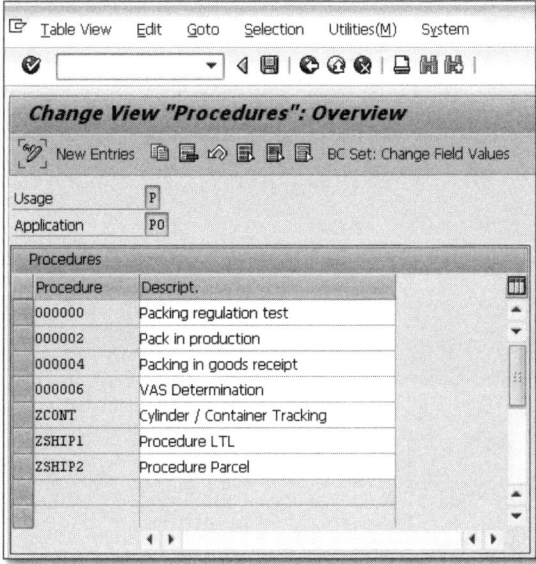

Figure 18.23 Procedures for Determining VAS Templates

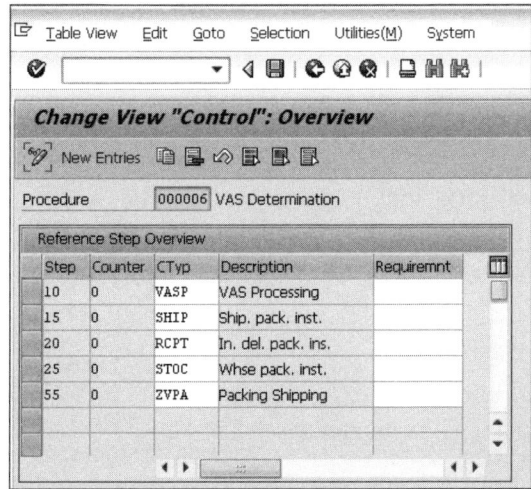

Figure 18.24 Condition Types Defined for VAS Determination Procedure

Figure 18.24 also shows the condition types used in sequence in the procedure to determine the VAS template.

18.2.2 Creating the VAS Template

To define the VAS template, use Transaction LVAST01 or follow the menu path SAP • LOGISTICS • LOGISTICS EXECUTION • INTERNAL WHSE PROCESSES • VALUE ADDED SERVICES • MASTER DATA • VAS TEMPLATE • CREATE.

Figure 18.25 shows the details entered when creating a VAS template. The attributes include:

- **Execution Method**
  This refers to the execution of a VAS order. There are three options: WCNTR while in the work center, TOEXGP during the execution of a transfer order for a group of items, and TOEXIT during the execution of a transfer order for a single item.

- **Template Sequence**
  This entry allows the orders to be sequenced in order when they are displayed at the work center, depending on the template from which they are created. The template sequence is 1 for VAS template 76, and 2 for VAS template 77. Orders created with template 76 are sequenced before orders created with template 77.

- **Instruction Control**
  This field determines what is displayed in the work instructions of any VAS order based on this template. There are three options: A to display all components in the packing instructions, B to not display the packaging items, and C where the instructions are to be displayed on the text.

- **Standard Duration**
  This value represents the time it should take to complete a VAS order based on this VAS template.

- **Total Weight**
  This field specifies the total weight of the handling unit, including the weight of both the packed materials and the packaging materials.

Work center information is entered to allow the use of work centers where the VAS template will be valid and with the priorities given to those work centers.

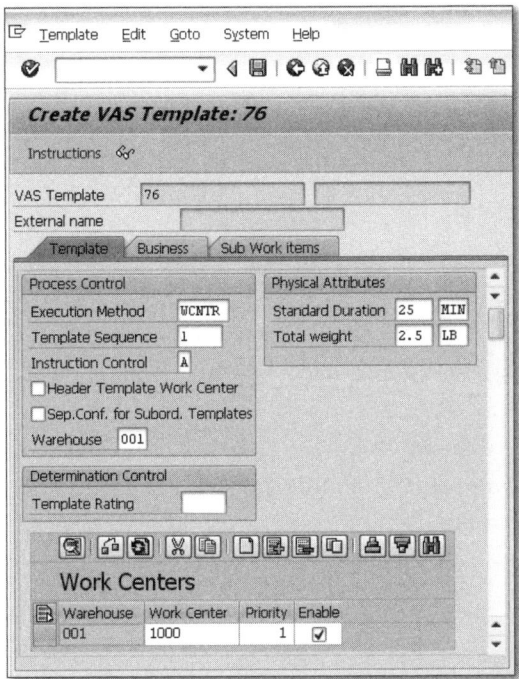

Figure 18.25 Creation of VAS Template: Transaction LVAST01

18.2.3 Creating a VAS Order

You create a VAS template to create VAS orders easily and efficiently. You can create the VAS order with reference to a work center or without reference. To create a VAS order for a work center, use Transaction LVASWC02; to create a VAS order with no reference, use Transaction LVASWOR.

Using Transaction LVASWOR, you can create a VAS order if you know the VAS template. You can find Transaction LVASWOR by following the menu path SAP • LOGISTICS • LOGISTICS EXECUTION • INTERNAL WHSE PROCESSES • VALUE ADDED SERVICES • PROCESSING VAS ORDERS • CREATE WITHOUT REFERENCE.

Figure 18.26 shows the initial screen for creating a VAS order without using a reference. Data required to create an order with Transaction LVASWOR includes the warehouse number, work center number, and a valid VAS template number. Once these are entered, click the EXECUTE VAS button to create the VAS order.

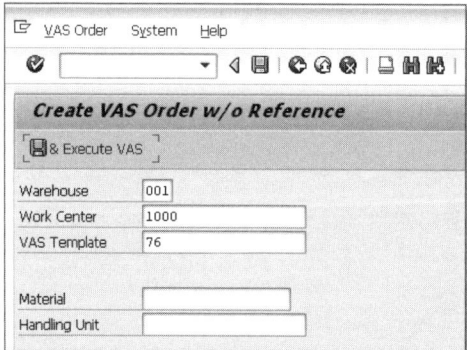

Figure 18.26 Initial Screen for Creating a VAS Order Without Reference

Figure 18.27 shows the details of the created VAS order 10201. The main part of this order shows the work instructions the warehouse staff uses to execute the VAS order. The order shows three steps for the staff to follow, with special instructions on packing and labeling for this material.

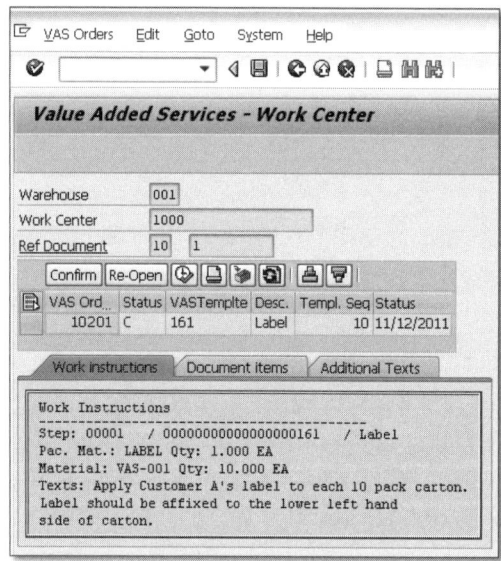

Figure 18.27 Details of a VAS Order

18.2.4 VAS Monitor

Warehouse managers can get an overview of the status of VAS orders at any time with the VAS monitor, accessed via Transaction LVASM. You can find this by following the menu path SAP • LOGISTICS • LOGISTICS EXECUTION • INTERNAL WHSE PROCESSES • VALUE ADDED SERVICES • VAS MONITOR.

Figure 18.28 shows the complete picture of the VAS orders for warehouse 001. Currently, according to the VAS monitor, there is only one VAS order 10201 which was created without reference. The monitor allows the details of any of the orders to be displayed.

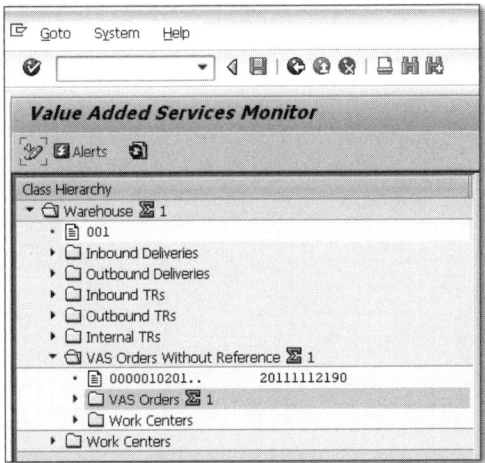

Figure 18.28 Detail Screen of the VAS Monitor: Transaction LVASM

18.2.5 VAS Alert Monitor

You can access the VAS alert monitor from the VAS monitor or via Transaction LVASA. The alert monitor can bring to light any actual and potential problems regarding VAS orders. The alert monitor shows unprocessed VAS orders, issues with regards to expected versus actual bin stock, and VAS orders that are missing transfer orders. VAS alerts can be configured in the IMG.

18.2.6 VAS and TRM

TRM supports the VAS function. For the interaction to be complete, it is important to configure the VAS work centers as work center zones in TRM. The movements to and from a VAS work center are routes in the TRM function.

This section described the functionality within the VAS process. In the next chapter we'll examine the Extended Warehouse Management (EWM) functionality.

18.3 Summary

As warehouse operations become more complex and technology provides more functionality to control and monitor warehouse operations, the software running the warehouse has to be more than a simple locator system. Warehouse management functionality now incorporates such elements as task and resource management, value-added services, and all the Extended Warehouse Management functions such as slotting and rearrangement.

The next chapter examines the processes and functionality that can be found in Extended Warehouse Management (EWM).

Extended Warehouse Management (EWM) provides functionality for efficiently managing complex high-volume and high-velocity warehouses.

19 SAP Extended Warehouse Management

SAP Extended Warehouse Management (SAP EWM) is part of SAP SCM and can be integrated with SAP WM to provide a seamless warehouse system. The basic warehouse operation can be efficiently operated using SAP WM, but in warehouses that have high volume or a complex process, the EWM functionality offers a greater degree of visibility and efficiency.

19.1 Introduction to SAP Extended Warehouse Management

Extended Warehouse Management is part of SAP SCM and extends the functionality of basic SAP WM. EWM can use the organizational structure from SAP WM and goes into greater depth to give additional functionality. EWM can integrate with SAP WM so that documents created in the SAP ERP system trigger events in the EWM system.

19.1.1 History of EWM

Extended Warehouse Management started as part of the SAP R/3 Enterprise Release in 2004. The functionality included yard management, cross-docking, and value-added services. EWM was introduced as a separate standalone product as part of SAP 5.0 in 2005. Since then, EWM has been extended to include labor management and RFID functionality released as SAP EWM 5.1 in 2007. The latest release is called SAP EWM 7.0, and it includes production supply and graphical warehouse layout.

19.1.2 Integrating SAP EWM and WM

Extended Warehouse Management is a separate component as part of the SAP SCM product. It does not replace SAP WM but can be used to manage large and complex warehouses with high volume and velocity. EWM can be used in the same environment as SAP WM, and many SAP customers have decided to operate in this fashion.

19.2 Organizational Structure

The organizational structure of the warehouse can be set up the SAP WM system and then linked to the EWM system. The warehouse number in EWM is a four-character field, whereas it is only a three-character field in SAP ERP. However the EWM system has additional structures in the warehouse such as activity areas.

19.2.1 Activity Areas

The activity area is a structure in EWM that is a group of storage bins. The bins are grouped together for a reason such as stock removal or stock placement. A storage bin can be assigned to more than one activity area.

19.2.2 Product Master

The product master is the EWM version of the material master from SAP ERP. The product master is derived from the material master but has additional information relevant to EWM. The product master has an additional view called Warehouse Management Execution. Some of the additional fields include the handling indicator (which is used describe how a material is moved from one location to another), the warehouse material group, warehouse storage condition, an indicator indicating whether an item is likely to be pilfered, quarantine period, and catch weight (which identifies whether a material is managed using catch weight).

19.2.3 Transportation Data

Extended Warehouse Management data is used in route determination, and the transportation data in EWM reflects this. Transportation lanes are created as a link between two locations, which can be plants, customers, or vendors. The transportation lane defines which products can be shipped between two locations and which method of transport can be used.

Transportation Zones

A transportation zone is created when a transportation route is created. The zone can determine which locations are included, and once data is assigned to the transportation zone it is transferred to all of the locations in the zone. This reduces the amount of data that needs to be entered for each zone.

Transportation Route

The transportation route is used to describe the characteristics of a physical route between two locations. The transportation route is used in determining the most relevant route during route determination. A transportation route has several characteristics such as legs, lead times, and shipping conditions.

19.2.4 Resources

In EWM a resource is an object that performs tasks in the warehouse. A resource can be a piece of equipment, such as a forklift, or a warehouse employee.

Resource Types

You can group similar resources together as resource types in EWM. These resource types can be assigned to bin types, so that a resource type, such as a certain type of forklift, can only have access to certain types of bin, based on aisle width.

Queues

The queue is used in the assignment of warehouse orders. A warehouse order is assigned to a queue, and the resource group is assigned to a sequence of queues. A warehouse order can then be assigned to a particular resource.

19.3 Documents in SAP EWM

Extended Warehouse Management has several documents that are used in the warehouse. EWM documents are found in the outbound delivery process, inbound delivery process, and internal warehouse tasks.

19.3.1 Warehouse Tasks

There are two types of tasks in the warehouse: product warehouse tasks and handling unit warehouse tasks. A product warehouse task performs a movement of stock in the warehouse. These tasks are used for picking, putaway, and internal warehouse movements. A handling unit warehouse task is used to move an entire handling unit within the warehouse.

19.3.2 Warehouse Orders

A warehouse order is a combination of several warehouse tasks that are given to a warehouse resource to perform in a specific period of time. A warehouse task is assigned to a warehouse order based on a set of rules.

19.3.3 Inbound Delivery Notification

When an inbound delivery is processed in the SAP ERP system, the delivery is checked to see if it is relevant for an EWM warehouse. If it is, then an inbound delivery notification (IDN) is created. The IDN is usually activated in the background, and this creates an inbound delivery document in EWM.

19.3.4 Outbound Delivery Request

When an EWM-relevant outbound delivery document is processed in SAP ERP, a document is created in EWM called an outbound delivery request (ODR). Once activated, the ODR creates an outbound delivery order in EWM. A goods issue can be performed on the outbound delivery order, and this creates another document in EWM called the EWM outbound delivery, which can be called the final delivery.

19.4 Processes in SAP EWM

Several processes in EWM create efficiencies in the warehouse. The EWM system provides functionality for inbound and outbound deliveries that help reduce the complex warehouse processes in high-volume and high-velocity warehouses.

19.4.1 Inbound Processing

The inbound process in a warehouse commences when the SAP ERP system receives an advance ship notice (ASN). It can be transferred to EWM, and an inbound delivery notification (IDN) is created. It is possible to activate the IDN, as well as reject the IDN if required by the vendor. An inbound delivery in EWM can be created once the IDN is activated. The inbound delivery includes data such as the product data, quantity to be delivered, movement data, and status. When the vehicle that contains the product arrives at the warehouse for the inbound delivery, the transportation unit (TU) is registered in the yard management function. If the information about the TU was sent in the original ASN, then the TU can be produced automatically when the inbound delivery is transferred from SAP ERP to EWM.

When scheduled, the vehicle can be unloaded, and the status of the TU can be changed manually when the unloading is complete. The physical condition of the product can be inspected, adjustments made if necessary, or the delivery can be rejected. The inbound delivery can be goods-receipted manually or automatically when the putaway warehouse task has been completed. The goods receipt in EWM is then transferred to the SAP ERP system.

19.4.2 Outbound Processing

The outbound process can begin with a sales order creation in SAP ERP or the SAP CRM system. An outbound delivery is generated, and the process begins in the warehouse. The outbound delivery is forwarded to the EWM system, and an outbound delivery request (ODR) is generated. The ODR can be activated, and an outbound delivery order (ODO) is created. After the creation of the ODO, you can manually create warehouse tasks (WTs), and the warehouse order (WO) can also be created. The physical tasks of picking the product, packing, kitting, staging, and loading can also start.

After the products have been loaded onto a vehicle, the ODO can be goods-issued. The final outbound delivery document is generated and transferred to the SAP ERP system.

19.4.3 Internal Warehouse Movements

Several internal movements can be performed in EWM, such as replenishment, rearrangements, ad hoc movements, and posting changes.

Replenishment

The replenishment process in EWM takes product from a reserve area and moves it to a forward picking position in the warehouse. There are five types of replenishment: planned replenishment, order-related replenishment, crate part replenishment, direct replenishment, and automatic replenishment.

Rearrangements

During the rearrangement process the system compares how the product should be placed in the warehouse, based on information entered, with how the product is actually stored in the warehouse. For example, if a product was identified as a slow-moving item but now is in demand, the system will rearrange the product so that the bin locations are located in an area with fast moving stock.

Ad Hoc Movements

Sometimes product is in a bin location that is not close to other bin locations where the product is usually stored. In this instance an ad hoc movement may be instigated so that the warehouse staff can move the product to a different bin location

Posting Changes

A posting change can be driven from the SAP ERP system or in the EWM system. A posting change notice can be created in SAP ERP and transferred to the EWM system as a posting change request.

This section has described some of the processes available in the EWM system.

19.5 Summary

SAP EWM extends the functionality of SAP WM so that companies with complex high-volume warehouses can operate more efficiently. The EWM processes can be triggered by events in the SAP ERP system, and many companies have implemented EWM as an add-on to their current SAP ERP implementation.

After learning about WM, its functionality and configuration issues, it's now time to put it in action and move forward.

20 Conclusion

In the preceding chapters we discussed each element of the major functionality of SAP WM. In this conclusion, we'll examine the lessons learned and make suggestions for further skill development.

20.1 Lessons Learned

In the preface, we noted that this book should be of interest to people other than those who work directly with SAP WM, including those who work in related application areas such as Materials Management (SAP MM), Production Planning (SAP PP), and Sales and Distribution (SAP SD). We are confident that the integration between SAP MM, SAP WM, and SAP SD should now be clear to you.

Warehouse management does not exist in isolation. The material master is the repository of the warehouse data for each material. The SAP MM functionality creates the goods receipts and the movement of material into a storage location that triggers a movement into the warehouse, as does a goods receipt from production.

The outbound deliveries created via SAP SD sales orders trigger the material picking and movement of the material to the goods issue in the warehouse. It is important for those of you working with SAP WM to have a solid understanding of the way it is fully integrated with the other supply chain modules.

Chapter 2 explained the key warehouse structures, and this is basic knowledge that should be learned thoroughly. Understanding the structure and components of the warehouse is vital to understanding how material is stored and moved.

One important lesson to take away from this book is the role of the transfer requirement and the transfer order, as described in Chapter 5. The transfer order moves material in the warehouse—whether it is putaway to a rack or a stock pick for an outbound delivery. Understanding how the transfer order processes the movement is critical.

The picking and placement strategies may not always seem logical. However, the different strategies are key to efficient warehouse operation. Chapters 9 and 10 explained the various picking and putaway strategies. We suggest talking to your warehouse managers about how they use these strategies to optimize warehouse efficiency.

Chapter 13 described electronic data interchange (EDI), which although not specifically part of SAP WM is a subject that users and consultants alike should understand. The use of EDI documents, especially advance shipping notifications (ASNs), is particularly important to the warehouse.

The final chapters in the book reviewed the new technologies being adopted in warehouses. Everyone has seen bar codes and bar code readers, but the recent commercial use of radio frequency identification (RFID) technology has the warehousing community wondering how this will make the warehouse more efficient and how much it is going to cost. We have tried to demystify and clarify these new technologies to help you make your own decisions regarding their adoption and use.

Chapter 15 described SAP Auto-ID Infrastructure (SAP AII), developed for use with RFID and warehouse transactions. Although use of this technology is not widespread, any knowledge about it and about the SAP solution will be helpful as the commercial adoption of RFID becomes more rapid.

Chapter 17 examined the functionality of yard management, and although it is not used by every company that has implemented warehouse management, it is useful for businesses that need visibility of large numbers of trailers in the yard.

Chapter 18 examined three areas that are not standard in SAP WM but are becoming more appealing to traditional SAP WM users. These are task and resource management (TRM) and value-added services (VAS), and Extended Warehouse Management. These topics will become more important in the future, and we advise you to keep tracking their development.

20.2 Future Directions

As you come to the end of this book, we hope you have learned many new aspects of warehouse management that you may not have seen or heard of before. No one can predict what will be released in SAP ECC 7.0 and beyond or in future releases of SAP SCM with even more extended warehouse management. What is clear is that a solid foundation of knowledge of the current standard SAP WM system is a crucial key to success in the future. The advancements in warehouse management will build on the standard functionality. Improvements to transactions may be part of future releases, but the standard functionality is sure to remain.

The new functions of value-added services (VAS) and task and resource management are likely to become more mainstream in warehouse management, so understanding the key elements of these modules now will be useful in your future implementations. Although some of you may not have access to an SAP Supply Chain Management (SCM) system, it is worth rereading Chapter 19 to truly understand the functionality that exists in Extended Warehouse Management (EWM). We encourage you to educate yourself further about this as later releases become available.

And with that thought we would like to conclude this book. We hope you found it useful and valuable for your work and that you will continue using it as a reference guide as and when needed.

Appendices

A	**Bibliography**	561
B	**Glossary**	563
C	**The Author**	569

A   Bibliography

Bacheldor, Beth. "SAP Introduces Software for Product Tracking." *RFID Journal*, March 2007.

Carter, M. Brian et al. *SAP Extended Warehouse Management: Processes, Functionality and Configuration*. Boston: SAP Press, 2010.

Emmett, Stuart. *Excellence in Warehouse Management: How to Minimize Costs and Maximize Value*. John Wiley & Sons, 2005.

Florida State University. "Hazardous Materials Handling and Storage OP-G-1.4.2." *Environmental Health and Safety Policies*, 2007.

Frazelle, Edward. *World-Class Warehousing and Material Handling*, McGraw-Hill, 2001.

Gue, Kevin R. "Crossdocking: Just in Time for Distribution." Graduate School of Business & Public Policy, Naval Postgraduate School, May 2001.

Harrington, Lisa. "Managing Inside and Outside the Box." *Inbound Logistics*, Thomas Publishing Group, April 2005.

Intermec Technologies Corporation. *Practical Uses for RFID Technology in Manufacturing and Distribution Applications*. Intermec Technologies Corporation, 2007.

Jenkins, Creed H. *Modern Warehouse Management*. McGraw-Hill, 1968.

Landt, Jeremy. "Shrouds of Time: The History of RFID." *Association for Automatic Identification and Mobility*, October 2001.

Moose, Chris. "Make Your Picking Moves in SAP WM Strategically." *SCM Expert*, Wellesley Information Services, March 2006.

Mulcahy, David E. *Warehouse Distribution and Operations Handbook*. McGraw-Hill, 1993.

Napolitano, Maida. "Warehouse Management: How to be a Lean, Mean Cross-Docking Machine." *Logistics Management Magazine*, January 2007.

Napolitano, Maida. "Making the Move to Cross Docking." Warehousing Education and Research Council (WERC), 2000.

Navas, Deb. "ERP WMS Solves Integration and Improves Performance." *Supply Chain Manufacturing and Logistics Magazine*, September 2004.

Port of Los Angeles. "Warehouse No 1." Board of Harbor Commissioners of the City of Los Angeles, December 2001.

Swedberg, Claire. "Virgin Uses RFID for Plane Parts." *RFID Journal*, August 2005.

Tompkins, James A. *Warehouse Management Handbook*. 2nd ed. Tompkins Press, 1998.

Trebilcock, Bob. "The ROI from RFID." *Modern Materials Handling Magazine*, February 2007.

UK Parliamentary Office of Science and Technology. "Radio Frequency Identification," Postnote. *The Parliamentary Office of Science and Technology* 225 (2004).

Wal-Mart Corporation. "Corporate Facts: Wal-Mart by the Numbers." Wal-Mart Corporation, November 2006.

Wal-Mart Corporation. "Continued Expansion of Radio Frequency Identification (RFID)." Wal-Mart Corporation, November 2006.

Williams, David H. "The Strategic Implications of Wal-Mart's RFID Mandate." *Directions Magazine*, July 2004.

B Glossary

ABC analysis This analysis is assigned to a material, based on configuration, to indicate how often the material must be counted each year.

active RFID tag This battery-powered tag has an active transmitter onboard.

annual physical inventory A company performs this counting of assets and stock to start the fiscal year with an accurate financial picture.

available stock This is the same as unrestricted stock, that is, material that is free to be sold.

batch A batch is a quantity of material grouped together for various reasons, often because the materials have the same characteristics and values.

batch picking Batch picking is similar to picking a single order, except that the picker picks a batch of orders at one time.

blocked stock This term refers to material that has arrived at the receiving dock damaged and is not available for sale.

bulk storage putaway strategy This strategy is used to place incoming material into bulk storage.

consignment stock Consignment stock comprises material owned by a vendor but stored at the customer's premises.

continuous inventory This process consists of dividing the annual physical inventory count into several smaller inventory counts that are performed over the year. The goal is to ensure that all material is counted.

cross-docking A company performs cross-docking when it takes a finished good from the production plant and delivers it directly to the customer, with little or no material handling in between.

cross-docking monitor Warehouse managers use this tool to review the cross-docking situation in the warehouse and make any necessary changes.

cross-line stock putaway strategy This enhancement to the next empty bin putaway strategy uses search variables that allow the next empty bin to be selected based on various criteria.

cycle counting This is a process whereby a company continually checks the accuracy of the inventory in the warehouse by regularly counting a portion, so that every item in the warehouse is counted several times a year.

distributor cross-docking This process can include consolidation of inbound materials from different vendors into a mixed-material pallet.

downstream sortation picking In this scenario, the picker can deposit all the materials listed on all transfer orders of the wave into the tote on the conveyor.

Electronic Product Code (EPC) The MIT AutoID center developed this RFID standard.

Extended Warehouse Management (EWM) EWM combines an entire physical warehouse under one warehouse number.

fire containment section This area in the warehouse has a specific fire-containment specification.

fire department inventory list This report specifies the quantity of material in each fire containment area, by storage class. The fire department can review the potential hazards and offer advice regarding storage changes.

first in, first out (FIFO) The FIFO picking strategy removes the oldest quant from the storage type defined in the storage-type search.

fixed bin replenishment This strategy specifies when the storage bin in the picking area needs to be replenished so that outbound deliveries remain at maximum efficiency.

fixed bin storage putaway strategy This strategy for fixed-bin storage takes into account the data that has been entered into the material master record for the material to be placed in stock.

fixed storage bin picking strategy This is a strategy for using fixed storage bins that relies on the data entered into the material master record for the material to be picked.

goods issue Goods issue is the movement of material from the warehouse to an external source. This source can be a production order or a customer.

hazardous material A hazardous material is capable of producing harmful physical effects such as a fire, sudden release of pressure and explosion, or acute health effects, such as burns, convulsions, and chronic injuries such as organ damage and cancers.

hazardous material warning This warning is applied to materials to indicate the type and level of hazard.

hazardous substance list This report lists all hazardous material stored in a particular warehouse, storage type, or fire-containment area.

inbound delivery An inbound delivery is the process whereby goods are delivered to a receiving area.

inbound delivery monitor This tool is used to display open and completed deliveries, both inbound and outbound.

inspection stock Inspection stock is material that has been set aside for a quality inspection or another type of review. This material has been valuated but does not count as available stock.

internal stock transfer This process is triggered by the requirement to move a material from one part of the warehouse to another, from storage bin to storage bin.

last in, first out (LIFO) The LIFO picking strategy removes the last delivery of material to be received.

manufacturing cross-docking This operation involves the receiving of purchased and inbound material required by manufacturing.

near picking bin putaway strategy This strategy is used to place incoming material in an area near the picking bin.

next empty bin putaway strategy This strategy determines that the material to be placed in stock is placed in the next empty bin.

node This term can refer both to a physical node where material is placed and to a logical node where resources pass through.

obstacle An obstacle in warehouse management is a physical object or barrier, defined in the site as an area where resources cannot pass through.

one-step cross-docking This movement processes the cross-docking movement in one step, directly from the inbound goods receiving area to the outbound goods issuing area.

open-storage putaway strategy This strategy allows the storage of different materials in the same storage bin.

opportunistic cross-docking Applicable in any warehouse, this strategy involves transferring a material directly from the goods receiving dock to the outbound shipping dock to meet a known demand.

outbound delivery The outbound-deliver process involves picking goods, reducing the storage quantity, and shipping the goods. The process begins with goods picking and ends when the goods are delivered to the recipient.

outbound delivery monitor This tool allows the shipping department of the warehouse to view the deliveries that need to be picked for a variety of criteria entered for the transaction.

partial quantities picking strategy Warehouse staff use this picking strategy to reduce the number of storage units with partial quantities.

passive RFID tag This tag uses the reader field as a source of energy for the chip and for communication from and to the reader.

pedigree notification To authenticate pharmaceuticals as legitimate throughout the supply chain, the system uses RFID to match each container with its corresponding pedigree.

pick point (SUT) The SUT is the location in the warehouse where materials are removed for a partial stock pick from a storage unit.

picking area This term refers to a group of warehouse management storage bins that are used for picking.

picking wave profile Warehouses can us this profile to impose limits on certain criteria when reacting to waves during wave picking.

posting changes This warehouse movement changes the stock level of a material because of a change in the status of a material in a storage bin.

print code This code defines the print format of the transfer order, the sort sequence, and the printer to be used.

progressive assembly picking In this picking method, the content of the transfer order to be picked is moved from one zone to the next.

project stock Project stock is material being stored in the warehouse for a project or a work breakdown structure (WBS) element.

putaway strategy This strategy determines the process of deciding where material received into the warehouse should be stored.

quant This term refers to the stock of material stored in a storage bin.

quantity-relevant picking strategy Warehouses that have varying sizes of bins and storage types where the same material is stored use this strategy.

radio frequency (RF) monitor Warehouse managers use this tool to view the queues that are being worked on in the warehouse.

radio frequency identification (RFID) RFID is a method of using a radio-frequency transmission to identify an object.

rearrangement Part of EWM, this is used to optimize the storage of materials in the warehouse.

requirement type This classifies the origin type, for example, asset, purchase order, cost center, or sales order.

resource (TRM) A TRM is an object that is capable of receiving and executing tasks.

resource element type Warehouse managers configure this object to create a resource. Options can be determined for either a device, such as a forklift or crane, or a worker.

resource type This object is used for devices such as cranes and forklifts. In their configuration, it is possible to enter the speed of the device so that the route can be timed and scheduled.

retail cross-docking This form of cross-docking involves receipt of material from multiple vendors and sorting onto outbound trucks for several retail stores.

returnable transport packaging (RTP) These materials arrive on pallets or containers and may need to be returned to the vendor.

route A route is the path a resource travels between the start and end points in a site.

sales order stock This is individual customer stock that is managed in a warehouse.

SAP auto-id infrastructure (AII) AII is the current SAP solution for RFID functionality.

SAPConsole This SAP tool enables RF devices to be run within SAP applications.

semipassive RFID tag This tag uses built-in batteries and therefore does not require energy from the reader field to power the chip.

shelf life control list This list shows batches in the warehouse that are actively monitored for shelf-life.

shelf life expiration date (SLED) This is the date on which the material is no longer valid for sale.

shelf life expiration picking strategy With this strategy, material is picked based on the shelf life of the quants of material in the warehouse.

shipment type The shipment type classifies the movement types in the warehouse, be they stock removal, stock placement, or posting change.

site A site can be part of a warehouse, many warehouses, or one warehouse.

site map A site map allows warehouse managers to plan efficient routes in the warehouse based on the physical definition.

slap and ship This is a method of complying with customer RFID requirements for physical identification of materials shipped through the outbound processes.

slotting Part of EWM, slotting assesses storage parameters required by the material and proposes the storage section where the material should be stored.

special stock This term refers to material that is managed separately from regular stock.

split picking This process involves the splitting of a transfer order, whereby a new transfer order is created when the picking area is changed.

storage bin The storage bin is the lowest level of storage defined in the warehouse.

storage section A storage section is the part of a storage type that contains storage bins where the material is kept.

storage type A storage type is a defined area of the warehouse.

storage type indicator This tool allows only certain materials to be picked from storage types. The order can be defined by the storage type search for each storage type indicator.

storage type search In this configuration, a sequence of storage types is defined and followed in searching for material that is required for picking.

storage unit A storage unit is an identifiable unit in the warehouse, containing materials and a container or pallet.

storage unit management (SUT) SUT covers the functionality and management of storage units in the warehouse.

transfer order A transfer order is the instruction to move materials from a source storage bin to a destination storage bin in a warehouse.

transfer order print document This is a printed form of a transfer order, with or without storage unit management.

transfer requirement This request covers the transfer of materials from a source storage bin to a destination storage bin in a warehouse.

transportation cross-docking This cross-docking operation combines shipments from different shippers in the less-than-truckload (LTL) and small-package industries to gain economies of scale.

TRM monitor This tool keeps warehouse management aware of the status of the TRM function with respect to transfer orders, inbound and outbound deliveries, tasks, and resources

two-step cross-docking This method first moves materials that are to be cross-docked from the goods receipts area to a cross-docking storage type. In a second step, it creates a transfer order from the interim storage type.

Uniform Code Council (UCC) Manufacturers register with the UCC to obtain an identifier code for their company.

UPC bar code format This format was adopted in 1973 as the industry standard so that any bar code on any product could be read and understood by any bar code reader.

value-added services (VAS) VAS operations enhance materials to improve their value, functionality, or usefulness.

VAS alert monitor This monitor shows unprocessed VAS orders, issues with regard to expected versus actual bin stock, and VAS orders that are missing transfer orders.

VAS template This tool is used for creating VAS orders, based on condition functionality.

VAS work center In this location, value-added services, such as packing or labeling, are performed

wave monitor This tool enables selection of waves for certain outbound deliveries.

wave pick This is a work package that contains several outbound deliveries.

working area Within EWM, a working area is a physical location between two zones that is defined as an area where resource planning occurs.

zero stock check This process consists of a stock check on a storage bin after the material has been removed, to ensure that the storage bin is empty.

zone Within EWM, a zone is a physical location at a site that is used for a specific function.

zone picking This occurs when a picking operator performs picks for storage bins in their area, to reduce travel time between picks.

C   The Author

A native of London, England, **Martin Murray** joined the computer industry upon his graduation from Middlesex University in 1986. In 1991, he began working with SAP R/2 in the materials management area for a London-based multinational beverage concern, and in 1994, he immigrated to the United States to work as an SAP R/3 consultant. Since then, he has been implementing Materials Management (SAP MM) and Warehouse Management (SAP WM) in projects throughout the world. He is employed by IBM Global Business Services.

Martin is the author of the best-selling SAP PRESS titles *Materials Management with SAP: Functionality and Technical Configuration* (3rd Edition), *Discover Logistics with SAP ERP,* and *SAP Transaction Codes: Your Quick Reference to T-Codes in SAP ERP*. He lives with his wife in Orange County, California.

Acknowledgments

The author would like to specially thank Meg Dunkerley of SAP PRESS for her faith in the author and her tireless efforts in getting the second edition of this book completed.

Index

A

ABAP code, 398
   To modify transfer order document, 401
ABC analysis, 367
   Indicator, 369
   Perform, 367
   Process, 369
ABC indicator
   Viewing, 369
Accounting department, 33
Accuracy of warehouse inventory, 366, 382
Active capacity check, 52
Active tag, 473
Activity area, 548
Activity data, 45
Ad hoc movement, 552
Advance shipping notification, 440
Aggregate state, 418
Alert monitor, 512
   Maintenance, 513
   Output, 513
Allowed vehicle type, 504
Annual inventory
   Configuration, 344
Assignment of warehouse, 40
Automatic data collection, 445
Automatic transfer order, 144

B

Bar code, 446
   Configuration, 452
   Defining for warehouse, 454
   For identification and verification, 451
   Reader, 449
   Reader technology, 450
   Scanner, 448
   Structure, 448
   Type, 455
Batch
   Definition, 105, 122
   Determination, 109, 300

Batch (Cont.)
   Management, 88, 104, 122, 123
   Number, 105
   Number assignment, 106
   Recording, 105
   Search procedure, 113
   Strategy type, 112
Batch management, 22
Batch missing, 45
Batch search procedure, 113, 114
Batch status, 108
Batch strategy type, 111
Best Buy, 469
Bin management, 536
Bin status report, 71
Blocked bin, 250
Blocking logic, 44
Book stock, 348, 359
Book value, 360
Break-bulk cargo, 30
Bulk pallet storage, 47
Bulk storage, 90, 315, 332

C

Canadian Environmental Assessment Agency, 414
Capacity check, 45
   Method, 52
Carousel storage, 326
Catalyst International, 34
cGMP, 105
Change notice, 267
Charge-coupled device, 450
Check digit, 447
Check-in, 514
Checkpoint, 513
Clean Air Act, 413
Clean Water Act, 413
Clear difference, 358
Client level, 105
Complete stock pick, 407
   Return to same bin, 408

Comprehensive Environmental Response, Compensation, and Liability, 413
Condition table, 109
Confirmation transaction, 257
Consignment material, 102
Consistency check, 335
Consumer purchasing, 31
Continuous inventory
  Configuration, 360, 378
  Document, 361
  Document printing, 363
Control parameter, 41
Control quantity, 94
Corporation, 31
Count deviation, 356
Count document, 353
  View, 353
Count result, 364
Count value, 360
Counting of assets, 343, 380
Counting of stock, 343, 380
Counts, 23
Creating new warehouse, 41
Crime prevention cost, 474
Cross-docking, 24, 480, 481, 547
  Alert monitor, 494, 495
  Automatic creation, 486
  Benefit, 481
  Configuration, 484
  Decision, 486
  Definition, 481
  Manual creation, 486
  Movement, 486, 497
  One-step, 486
  Planned, 482, 496
  Planned in SAP, 483
  Suitable material, 483
  Two-step, 489
  Type, 482
Cross-docking monitor, 492
  Accessing, 493
Cross-line stock
  Putaway, 331
  Putaway strategy, 330
Cycle count document, 370
  Printing, 372

Cycle counting, 341, 365, 369
  Benefit, 366

D

Data collection, 33, 464, 466
Data element
  String, 435
Data governance group, 39
Data processing, 33
Date, 108
  Available from, 108
  Next inspection, 108
  Production, 107
  Shelf life expiration, 108
Default unit of measure, 43
Defining door, 507
Delivery date, 180
Delivery item status, 212
  Message, 212
  Packing, 212
Department for Environment, Food and Rural Affairs, 414
Department of Defense, 469, 476
Department of the Environment and Water Resources, 414
Destination dynamic storage bin, 132
Destination fixed bin, 131
Destination storage bin, 131
Destination storage type, 131
Destination view, 133
Difference indicator
  Configure, 256
Distribution center, 31
Distribution warehouse, 229
Dock, 27
Document flow, 186
Document limit, 347
Downstream sortation, 242
Drug pedigree system, 477

E

Electronic data interchange, 24, 435
  Advantages, 435

Electronic data interchange, 24, 435 (Cont.)
    Types, 436
    Warehouse, 442
Electronic payment, 474
    Oyster card, 474
    Oyster system, 474
Electronic Product Code (EPC), 468
Empty bin, 327
    Checking, 250
    Display, 327
    Putaway strategy, 330
End value, 61
Environmental Health and Safety, 24
Environmental Protection Agency, 414
e-pedigree, 477
EXE Technologies, 34
Extended Warehouse Management, 25, 91, 442, 498, 518, 519
External ID, 180

F

Finished goods, 367
Fire department inventory list, 428
Fire resistance, 416
Fire-containment section, 415
First in, first out strategy, 287
Fixed bin picking, 316
Fixed bin putaway, 316
Fixed bin replenishment, 23
Fixed bin storage, 316, 338
Flexible delivery process, 476, 477
Full stock removal, 54

G

General view, 133
Generation of pedigree notification, 476, 477
GlaxoSmithKline, 477
Goods issue, 23, 205, 244, 446
    Functionality, 205
    Negative balance, 224
Goods movement data, 220
Goods movement status, 212
Goods receipt, 179, 201, 446
    Area, 487

Goods receipt, 179, 201, 446 (Cont.)
    Process, 22, 178
    Transaction, 188
    With inbound delivery, 179, 201
    Without inbound delivery, 187, 202
    Without inventory management, 196, 203
Goods receiving, 32
Goods storage
    Check, 429
Group, 228
    Creation, 229
    Definition, 228

H

Hand-held product, 451
Handling unit, 24, 55, 186
Hazardous material, 48, 413
    Acute health effects, 413
    Classification, 414
    Correct storage, 430
    List, 427
    Master data configuration, 415
    Number, 89, 426
    Record, 425
    Record creation, 425
    Storage class, 424
    Storage warning, 417
    Warning, 416, 425
Hazardous Materials Transportation Act, 413
Hazardous substance list, 431
Hazmat team, 427, 432
Header status, 153

I

ID point, 50, 53
Inbound delivery, 179, 487
    Creation, 180
    Monitor, 183
    Search criteria, 184
    Transfer order, 182
Inbound delivery notification, 550
Inbound process, 459
Inbound processing, 440, 551
Inbound shipment, 33

Individual product tagging, 475
Industry sector, 82
  Defining, 83
Integration with material master, 80
Inter-company billing, 211
Intermec, 451
Internal warehouse movement, 552
International Article Numbering Association, 448
Inventory, 223
  Annual physical, 343, 360
  Continuous, 360, 381
Inventory count, 343, 354, 380
  Document number, 372
  Documents, 353
  Previous, 344
Inventory Management, 96, 187, 191, 385, 410, 487
  Goods movement, 127
  Movement type, 127
Inventory method, 71
Inventory movement, 101
Inventory procedures, 341, 343
Inventory write-offs, 366
Items, 145

J

Japanese Numbering Authority, 448

L

Laser, 450
Laser scanner, 451
Last in, first out strategy, 292
Legacy system, 34
Loading, 514
Loading equipment quantity, 92
Location group, 506, 507, 510
Location type, 506
Logical movement, 156
Logistics, 30

M

Mail control, 51
Mandatory route, 535
Manhattan Associates, 34
Manufacturer code, 447
  Variable-length, 447
Manufacturing plant, 31
Master material
  Create, 82
Material
  Creation, 123
  Fast-moving, 46
  Level, 106
  Movement between storage bins, 252
  Overview, 271, 275
  Putaway, 315
  Quantity, 391
  Rack storage type, 47
  Slow-moving, 47
  Stock overview, 375
  Type, 367
Material batch number, 275
Material document, 188, 221, 225, 272
  For outbound delivery, 221
  Number, 272
Material group, 504
Material Master, 299
  Record, 294, 295, 311
Material master, 22, 258, 426
  Field, 83
  Proposed unit of measure, 88
  Record, 146, 259
  Replenishment data, 146
Material movement
  Inbound or outbound, 221
Material number
  Change, 272
Material picking, 132, 133
Material putaway, 132, 133
Material type
  Competitive product, 86
  Configurable material, 85
  Empties, 85
  Finished goods, 84
  Kanban container, 83

Material type (Cont.)
  Maintenance assembly, 85
  Manufacturer part, 84
  Nonstock material, 85
  Non-valuated material, 86
  Operating supplies, 84
  Packaging material, 86
  Pipeline material, 85
  Production resources/tool, 84
  Raw material, 86
  Returnable packaging, 85
  Semi-finished goods, 84
  Service, 83
  Spare part, 84
  Trading goods, 84
Material variance, 359
Materials Management, 33, 366, 385, 410
Material-to-material transfer, 273
Maximum bin quantity, 93
Maximum storage period, 117
Means of transport, 180
Means of transport ID, 181
Minimum bin quantity, 148
MIT AutoID Center, 468
Mixed storage, 51
Mobile data collection, 464, 466
Mobile data entry, 24, 443, 457
  Add user, 457
  Logging on, 458
Movement, 139
Movement type, 126, 127, 347, 391, 485
  Creation, 128
  Inventory Management, 138
  Reference, 138
  Warehouse Management, 138
Movement types
  Configuration, 260
Multiple processing, 44, 228

N

National distribution center, 31
Near picking bin, 315, 334
Negative stock, 54

Next empty bin, 326
  Putaway strategy, 326, 340
  Storage, 315

O

Open storage, 322, 339
  Putaway strategy, 322
  Section, 315
Organizational level data, 86
Organizational structure, 547, 548
Outbound delivery, 23, 207, 209, 222, 228, 245, 555
  Document, 220
  Elements of, 209
  Monitor, 215
  Number, 217
Outbound delivery request, 550
Outbound processing, 441, 476, 551
Outbound shipping, 33, 247
Overdelivery, 135

P

Packing, 243
  Area, 243
  Materials and processes, 243
Palletization, 91
Passive tag, 473
Photodiode technology, 450
Physical inventory, 341, 446
  Information, 376
Pick, 169
Pick and transfer, 168
Pick quantity, 100
  Adopt, 167
Picking, 23
  Area, 63, 94, 258, 278
  Operations, 228
  Operator, 242
  Placement strategy, 556
  Point, 50
  Process, 241
Picking and packing, 240

Picking schemes, 241
    Batch picking, 242
    Progressive assembly, 242
Picking schemes, 241 (Cont.)
    Single-order picking, 242
    Zone picking, 242
Picking strategy, 281, 287, 309
    Configuration, 290
    Definition, 281
    For partial quantities, 304
    Quantity relevant, 306, 308
    Type, 281, 309
Planned goods issue date, 208
Planned storage unit
    Receiving, 396
    Recording differences, 397
Plant, 391
Plant level, 106
Plant-maintenance cost center, 223
Port warehousing, 29
Posting change, 96, 267, 552
    Definition, 267, 278
    Notice, 156, 177, 267, 275
Preallocation stock, 135
Print code, 171
Printer designation, 173
Proctor & Gamble, 469
Product code, 447
Product master, 548
Production process, 299, 312
Production supply area, 375
Public warehouse, 32
Purchase order data, 184
Putaway, 23, 385
    Block, 68
    Material for, 323
    Open storage, 323
    With storage unit management, 402
Putaway data, 184
Putaway quantity
    Adopt, 168
Putaway strategy, 313, 315
    Activation, 334, 335
    Configuration, 320
    Type, 315, 338

Q

Quality inspection, 267
Quality management, 96
Quant, 51, 58, 79, 99, 378
    Definition, 51
    Display, 74
    Incorrect storage, 429
    Moved, 249
    Negative, 228
    Number, 74
    Record, 74
Quantity
    Correct, 256
Queue, 549

R

R/2 link, 45
Rack storage, 47
Radio frequency, 33
    Queue, 456
    Terminal or device, 443, 463
Radio frequency device, 443
    Character-based, 444
    For forklift, 445
    GUI device, 444
    Portable, 445
    Type, 444
Radio frequency identification (RFID), 24, 33, 464, 466, 467
    Advantage, 470
    Benefit, 470
    Commercial use, 467
    Current use, 474
    Definition, 467
    Disadvantage, 471
    Frequency, 473
    Mandate, 469
    Reader, 468
    Reader field, 468
    Regulations for use, 468
    Signal, 471
    Tag, 470, 471, 472, 473, 474
Rearrangement, 552
Reason code, 501

Index

Reduction in theft, 470
Reference movement type, 138
Region code assignment, 422
Remaining shelf life, 119
Replenishment, 552
Replenishment control, 260
Replenishment quantity, 94, 148
Report inventory, 292
Request management, 533
Requirement type, 134, 154
   Asset, 134
   Cost center, 134
   Purchase order, 134
   Sales document, 134
   Sales order, 134
   Storage bin, 134
Resource Conservation and Recovery Act, 413
Resource element, 529
Resource element maintenance wizard, 526
Resource management in TRM, 529
Resource type, 530, 549
   Allocation, 531
   Component, 531
   Definition, 530
   Forklift truck, 531
   Forklift truck driver, 531
Retail warehouse, 484
Return storage bin, 132
Return storage type, 132
Returnable transport item, 478
   Processing, 476
Returnable transport packaging, 103
RF Monitor, 24, 462
   Accessing, 462
   Use, 463
RF scanning device, 398
Rounding quantity, 93
Route exception, 535
Route management, 534
Row and shelf assignment, 334

S

Safe Drinking Water Act, 413
Sales data, 208
Sales order, 206
   Creation, 206
   Number, 206
SAP Auto-ID Infrastructure (SAP AII), 476, 556
SAP ECC 6.0, 21, 81, 446
   functionality, 519
   Predefined industry sectors, 83
   WM data entry screens, 87
SAP ERP, 519, 548
SAP EWM, 547
   Document, 550
   Process, 551
SAP MM, 21
SAP PP, 21
SAP SCM, 21, 548
SAP SD, 21
   Sales order, 555
SAPConsole, 444, 519
   Component, 445
   Description, 445
   Session, 445
Scheduler function, 533
Scheduling, 506
Scheduling chart, 515
Scheduling profile, 504
Search per level definition, 334
Sectioned bin, 250
Semipassive tag, 473
Serial number capture, 446
Shelf life
   Minimum remaining, 117
   Time unit, 117
   Total, 118
Shelf life expiration, 22, 297, 303
   Control list, 301
   Date, 299, 312
   Date calculation, 300
   Picking strategy, 300, 303
Shelf life expiration date
   Control list, 119
   Rounding rule, 118
Shelf life functionality, 116, 122
Shipment type, 133, 149, 154, 191
   Posting change, 134
   Stock placement, 134
   Stock removal, 134

Shipping, 32
Shipping point, 207, 233
   Definition, 207
   Details, 208
Ship-to point, 145
Site map, 521
Slap-and-ship strategy, 476
Sort configuration, 331
Source data view, 133
Source dynamic storage bin, 131
Source fixed bin, 131
Source storage bin, 130, 308
Source storage type, 130
Special movement, 90, 139
Special stock, 138, 144
   Indicator, 101, 285
   Number, 101
   Type, 139
Special storage, 48
Spool code, 173
Staging area, 508
Staging material for delivery, 208
Standard movement type, 126
Standard SAP system, 443
Standard stock placement, 383
Standard warehouse terminology, 520
Standard WM, 521
Start value, 61
State regulations for hazardous material, 413
Status of movement, 153
Stock, 94
   Available, 99
   Balance, 227
   Blocked, 97
   Category, 72, 94, 285
   Consignment, 102
   For putaway, 99
   Inspection, 95
   Management, 80, 81
   Movement, 344
   Overview, 446
   Placement, 50, 90
   Position, 293
   Project, 102
   Putaway, 285, 402
   Putaway strategy, 50

Stock, 94 (Cont.)
   Sales order, 101
   Special, 100
   Status, 98
   Unrestricted, 95
Stock category, 145
Stock level, 190
   Review, 198
Stock overview screen, 190
Stock placement control indicator, 317
Stock placement transaction, 68
Stock removal, 23
   Manually triggered, 378
   Strategy, 53, 288, 300
Stock replenishment, 247, 249, 258, 261
Stock transfer, 252
   Confirm, 255
   Internal, 249, 277
Storage bin, 22, 58, 78, 93, 350
   Automatic creation, 60, 66
   Block, 67
   Blocking reasons, 69
   Error log, 430
   Fire-containment section, 64
   Fixed, 258, 278
   Generation, 335
   KANBAN, 375, 379
   Manual creation, 65
   Maximum weight, 64
   New structure, 62
   Structure, 330
   Structure definition, 59
   Total capacity, 64
   Type, 58, 64
Storage class, 419
   Per storage type, 422
Storage location, 33
Storage location reference, 139
Storage section, 22, 56, 63, 89
   Configuration, 56
   Search, 424
Storage type, 22, 46, 76, 252, 510
   Block, 350
   Configuration, 289, 292
   Control, 336, 388
   Control definition, 334

Storage type, 22, 46, 76, 252, 510 (Cont.)
  Count, 350
  Data entry screen, 49
  Indicator, 282, 285
  Search, 284, 286, 423
  Search sequence, 307
  Table, 91
Storage unit
  Add to existing stock, 402
  Contents document, 398, 400
  Creating a record, 390
  Creation, 402
  Display, 393
  Document, 398
  Multiple materials, 402
  Number range, 387
  Picking, 55, 411
  Planning, 393, 410
  Planning by transfer order, 394
  Putaway, 411
  Record, 390
  Single material, 402
  Transfer order document, 398
  Type, 92, 389
Storage unit management, 24, 52, 383, 385, 386, 410
  Configuration steps, 386
  Integrating with stock picking, 406
  Key element, 385
Storing, 32
Supply chain, 27, 470
Supply chain management, 498

T

Target, 469
Task and Resource Management, 25, 519, 556
  Five core areas, 520
Task management, 533
  Scenarios, 533
Time data, 184
Time slot, 235
Toxic Substances Control Act, 413
Traditional warehouse, 520
Transaction
  Post, 270

Transaction processing, 464, 466
Transfer, 169
Transfer order, 23, 137, 156, 225, 239, 254, 308, 556
  Cancellation, 164
  Confirmation, 166, 170, 264, 349, 409
  Confirmation by each item, 378
  Conversion, 229, 263
  Creation, 156, 157, 176, 193, 213, 217, 268, 320, 328, 375, 394
  Definition, 156
  Detail, 271, 276
  Display, 194
  Document, 398
  For goods receipt, 196
  Item information, 324
  Manual creation, 162
  Multiple, 213
  Open, 348, 349
  Posted, 193
  Printing, 171
  Split, 214
Transfer order confirmation, 133
Transfer order creation, 132
Transfer orders
  Creation, 490
  Processing, 487
Transfer posting, 275
Transfer priority, 153
Transfer requirement, 22, 23, 134, 141, 145, 146, 153, 157, 158, 175, 179, 193, 228, 262
  Automatic, 142
  Confirmation, 230
  Deletion, 154
  Display, 191
  Group, 231
  Manual, 143, 145
  Open, 230
Transportation data, 548
Transportation planning status, 211
Transportation route, 549
Transportation zone, 549
Trash tobacco, 28
TRM monitor, 537
Two-step picking, 90
Type of warehouse stock, 94

Index

U

U.S. Food and Drug Administration, 477
Uniform Code Council, 447
Unit gross weight, 89
Unit of measure, 33, 92
Unit volume, 89
Universal Product Code, 446
Unloading, 514
Unloading point, 144

V

Value-added service, 519, 538, 547, 556
    Configuration, 538
    Orders, 538
    Work center profile, 538
Variance procedure, 357
VAS
    Alert monitor, 545
    Monitor, 545
    Order, 542, 544
    Template creation, 542, 543
    Template determination, 540
Vehicle number range, 501
Vehicle type, 504
    Group, 502, 503
Vendor batch, 109
Verification profile, 453
Volume unit, 43

W

Wal-Mart, 31, 469, 476
Warehouse, 29
    Basic functionality, 35
    Basic settings for VAS operations, 539
    Bonded, 28
    Configuration, 38
    Efficiency, 412
    Grid-lock, 249
    Introduction, 27
    Inventory, 358
    Layout, 46
    Management system, 32
    Management system history, 33

Warehouse, 29 (Cont.)
    Movement, 124
    Number, 252, 391
    Operation, 285, 546
    Operation, increasing productivity of operation, 228
    Parameter, 42
    Stock, 121, 293
    Structure, 75
    Tobacco, 28
Warehouse management activities, 210
Warehouse management system, 22
Warehouse movement, 125, 174
Warehouse number, 138
    Criteria, 185
Warehouse order, 550
Warehouse task, 550
Warehouse-to-warehouse transfer, 125, 174
Warehousing, 27
    Cost, 32
    Early example, 27
    Overflow, 32
    Seasonal requirement, 32
Water pollution class, 421, 425, 429
Wave creation, 233
Wave group release and print, 238
Wave Monitor, 233, 234, 238
Wave pick, 233, 236, 238
    Creation, 233
    Group, 233
Wave profile, 236
Weight unit, 43
Work breakdown structure, 102
Working area, 525
    Definition, 525

Y

Yard activity, 500
Yard inventory, 515
Yard location, 508
Yard Management, 25, 499, 517, 547
    Define, 500
    Process, 510, 517
    Structure, 507

Yard monitor, 511
   Output, 512
   Selection, 511

Z

Zero stock check, 54, 373, 379
   Automatic, 375
   Configuration, 374

Zero stock check, 54, 373, 379 (Cont.)
   Definition, 373
   Dialog box, 377
   Indicator, 374
Zone group, 525
   Configuring, 525

www.sap-press.com

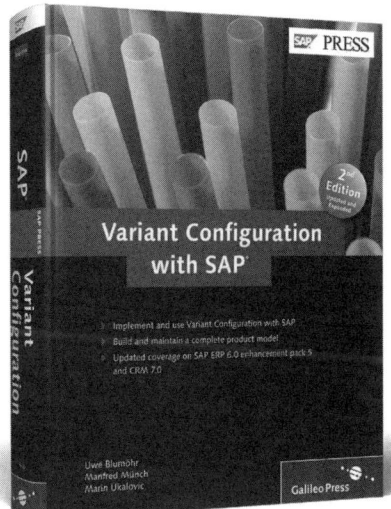

Implement and use Variant Configuration with SAP

Build and maintain a complete product model

Updated coverage on SAP ERP 6.0 enhancement pack 5 and CRM 7.0

Uwe Blumöhr, Manfred Münch, Marin Ukalovic

Variant Configuration with SAP

This is your complete resource to implementing, setting up, and using variant configuration with SAP ERP 6.0 and CRM 2007. You'll learn about the business processes and integration issues, details of configuration in SAP CRM, special features of industry solutions, and the selected challenges of using variant configuration. You'll find real-world case studies and customer examples, so you can learn about the "do's and don'ts" of variant configuration projects in a business environment.

694 pp., 2. edition 2012, 79,95 Euro / US$ 79.95
ISBN 978-1-59229-400-8

>> www.sap-press.com

www.sap-press.com

Learn to easily navigate the SAP system

Work with SAP modules step-by-step

Includes many examples and detailed SAP illustrations

Olaf Schulz

Using SAP:
A Guide for Beginners and End Users

This book helps end users and beginners get started in SAP ERP and provides readers with the basic knowledge they need for their daily work. Readers will get to know the essentials of working with the SAP system, learn about the SAP systems' structures and functions, and discover how SAP connects to critical business processes. Whether this book is used as an exercise book or as a reference book, readers will find what they need to help them become more comfortable with SAP ERP.

388 pp., 39,95 Euro / US$ 39.95
ISBN 978-1-59229-408-4

>> www.sap-press.com

Interested in reading more?

Please visit our website for all
new book releases from SAP PRESS.

www.sap-press.com